NAKAMA 2

NAKAMA 2

INTERMEDIATE JAPANESE: *COMMUNICATION, CULTURE, CONTEXT*

Enhanced Second Edition

Yukiko Abe Hatasa
Hiroshima University

Kazumi Hatasa
Purdue University
The Japanese School, Middlebury College

Seiichi Makino
Princeton University

Australia • Brazil • Mexico • Singapore • United Kingdom • United States

Nakama 2: Introductory Japanese: Communication, Culture, Context
Enhanced Second Edition
Yukiko Abe Hatasa, Kazumi Hatasa, Seiichi Makino

Product Director: Beth Kramer
Senior Product Manager: Martine Edwards
Managing Content Developer: Katie Wade
Associate Content Developer: Gregory Madan
Managing Media Developer: Patrick Brand
Senior Content Project Manager: Lianne Ames
Senior Art Director: Linda Jurras
Manufacturing Planner: Betsy Donaghey
Intellectual Property Analyst: Jessica Elias
Production Service: Inari Information Services
Cover Designer: Tony Saizon
Cover Image: Harold Burch, New York City
Compositor: Inari Information Services

© 2015, 2011, 1998 Cengage Learning.

ALL RIGHTS RESERVED. No part of this work covered by the copyright herein may be reproduced, transmitted, stored, or used in any form or by any means graphic, electronic, or mechanical, including but not limited to photocopying, recording, scanning, digitizing, taping, Web distribution, information networks, or information storage and retrieval systems, except as permitted under Section 107 or 108 of the 1976 United States Copyright Act, without the prior written permission of the publisher.

For product information and technology assistance, contact us at
Cengage Learning Customer & Sales Support, 1-800-354-9706
For permission to use material from this text or product,
submit all requests online at **cengage.com/permissions**
Further permissions questions can be emailed to
permissionrequest@cengage.com

Library of Congress Control Number: 2007926500

ISBN-13: 978-1-285-45374-3

ISBN-10: 1-285-45374-3

Annotated Instructor's Edition:

ISBN-13: 978-1-285-45394-1

ISBN-10: 1-285-45394-8

Cengage Learning
200 First Stamford Place, 4th Floor
Stamford, CT 06902
USA

Cengage Learning is a leading provider of customized learning solutions with office locations around the globe, including Singapore, the United Kingdom, Australia, Mexico, Brazil and Japan. Locate your local office at **international.cengage.com/region**

Cengage Learning products are represented in Canada by Nelson Education, Ltd.

For your course and learning solutions, visit **www.cengage.com**

Purchase any of our products at your local college store or at our preferred online store **www.cengagebrain.com**.

Instructors: Please visit **login.cengage.com** and log in to access instructor-specific resources.

Printed in the United States of America
1 2 3 4 5 6 7 18 17 16 15 14

ABOUT THE AUTHORS

Professor Yukiko Abe Hatasa received her Ph.D. in linguistics in 1992 from the University of Illinois at Urbana-Champaign. She is known nationwide as one of the premier Japanese methodologists in the United States and as an experienced coordinator of large teacher-training programs. She has served as the coordinator of the Japanese language program at the University of Iowa and is currently a professor at Hiroshima University, where her primary responsibilities are teacher training and SLA research.

Professor Kazumi Hatasa received his Ph.D. in education in 1989 from the University of Illinois at Urbana-Champaign. He is currently a professor at Purdue University and Director of the Japanese School at Middlebury College. He is recognized internationally for his work in software development for the Japanese language and distributes most of his work online as freeware.

Professor Seiichi Makino received his Ph.D. in linguistics in 1968 from the University of Illinois at Urbana-Champaign. He is an internationally prominent Japanese linguist and scholar, recognized throughout the world for his scholarship and for his many publications. Before beginning his tenure at Princeton University in 1991, he taught Japanese language, linguistics and culture at the University of Illinois while training lower-division language coordinators. He is an experienced ACTFL oral proficiency trainer in Japanese and frequently trains Japanese instructors internationally in proficiency-oriented instruction and in the administration of the Oral Proficiency Interview. Professor Makino has been the Academic Director of the Japanese Pedagogy M.A. Summer Program at Columbia University since 1996. He also directs the Princeton-in-Ishikawa Summer Program.

CONTENTS

Chapter 2: Travel Plans

Chapter 3: Preparing for the Future

Chapter 4: Asking for Favors

Chapter 5: Asking for and Giving Directions

Chapter 6: Gifts

Chapter 7: Cooking

Chapter 8: Rumors

Chapter 9: Culture and Customs

Chapter 10: Complaints and Apologies

Chapter 11: Talking about Employment

Reference Section

TO THE STUDENT

Nakama 2 is based on the principle that learning another language means acquiring new skills, not just facts and information—that we learn by doing. To further this goal, the chapter materials continue the approach established in *Nakama 1*, and systematically involve you in many activities that incorporate the language skills of listening, speaking, reading, and writing. We believe that culture is an integral component of language. To help you become familiar with Japanese culture, your text includes high-interest culture notes and relevant communication strategies. Chapter dialogues, each featuring the Japanese-American exchange student and her friends introduced in *Nakama 1*, cover a range of real-world situations that you are likely to encounter in Japan.

ORGANIZATION OF THE TEXTBOOK

Nakama 2 consists of a preliminary review chapter and eleven regular chapters. The preliminary chapter reviews the vocabulary and grammar presented in *Nakama 1*. Each of chapters 1–11 focuses on a common communicative situation and contains the following features.

- **Chapter Opener:** Each chapter opens with a theme-setting photograph and chapter contents by section. Keeping in mind the objectives listed at the top of the opener will help you focus on achieving your learning goals.
- **Vocabulary:** The vocabulary is presented in thematic groups, each followed by a variety of communicative activities and activities in context. Supplemental vocabulary is also provided throughout the chapter without demanding that you retain it. All active vocabulary is listed by function at the beginning of each chapter.
- **Dialogue:** The lively dialogues center on Alice Ueda, a Japanese-American college student, who is spending two years studying in Japan. Through the dialogue and accompanying audio, you will get to know a series of characters and follow them through typical events in their lives. Related activities will reinforce your understanding of the content, discourse organization, and use of formal and casual Japanese speech styles.
- **Japanese Culture:** Up-to-date culture notes in English explore social, economic, and historical aspects of Japanese life that are essential to effective communication.
- **Grammar:** Clear, easy-to-understand grammar explanations are accompanied by sample sentences and notes that help you understand how to use the grammar appropriately. In-class pair and group activities let you practice immediately what you've learned. As there is a high correlation between successful communication and grammar accuracy, this section is especially important.
- **Listening:** Useful strategies and pre-listening activities for general comprehension precede the section's main listening practice. Post-listening activities concentrate on more detailed comprehension and apply what you have learned to other communicative purposes.

- **Communication:** This section will provide you with knowledge and practice of basic strategies to accelerate your ability to communicate in Japanese.
- **Kanji:** Chapters 1 through 11 introduce a total of 241 **kanji**. The section begins with useful information such as the composition of individual characters, word formation, and how to use Japanese dictionaries. The presentation of each character includes stroke order to help you master correct penmanship when writing in Japanese and to prepare you for the reading section.
- **Reading:** Each reading passage begins with a reading strategy, and includes pre- and post-reading activities designed to help you become a successful reader of Japanese. **Hiragana** subscripts (**furigana**) are provided for unfamiliar **kanji** throughout the textbook. The readings include a small number of unknown words to help you develop strategies for understanding authentic texts.
- **Integration:** Integrated practice wraps up every chapter using discussion, interviewing, and role-play activities that interweave all the skills you've learned in the current and previous chapters.

STUDENT COMPONENTS

- **Student Text:** Your Student Text contains all the information and activities you need for in-class use. Each regular chapter contains vocabulary presentations and activities, a thematic dialogue and practice, grammar presentations and activities, cultural information, reading selections, writing practice, and ample communicative practice. Valuable reference sections at the back of the book include a list of particles, a **kanji** list, and Japanese-English and English-Japanese glossaries.
- **Text Audio Program:** The Text Audio Program contains recordings of all the listening activities in the text as well as all active chapter vocabulary. The audio activity clips are available as MP3 files and the vocabulary pronunciations can be found in the flashcards on iLrn or the Premium Website. The Text Audio Program is also available on CD. These audio materials are designed to maximize your exposure to the sounds of natural spoken Japanese and to help you practice pronunciation.
- **Student Activities Manual (SAM):** The Student Activities Manual (SAM) includes out-of-class practice of the material presented in the Student Text. Each chapter of the SAM includes a workbook section, which focuses on written vocabulary, grammar, **kanji** and writing practice, and a lab section, which focuses on pronunciation and listening comprehension, including Dict-a-Conversation dictation activities.
- **SAM Audio Program:** The SAM Audio Program corresponds to the audio portion of the SAM and reinforces your pronunciation and listening skills. You may listen to this material in the lab or on CD. The audio is also available as MP3 files on iLrn and the passkey-protected area of the Premium Website.
- **Student Premium Website:** You will find a variety of resources on the Premium Website at www.cengagebrain.com. Web quizzes give you further practice with chapter vocabulary and grammar. Audio flashcards for vocabulary, and **kanji** and pronunciation review help you monitor and assess your progress. Web links encourage further exploration of chapter themes. MP3 files for the text listening activities can also be downloaded from the site.

- **iLrn™ Heinle Learning Center:** This dynamic all-in-one diagnostic, tutorial, assessment, assignment, and course management system enhances your language-learning experience. Everything you need to master the skills and concepts of the course is built right in to this online system, including an audio-enhanced eBook, integrated textbook activities, an online Student Activities Manual, interactive enrichment activities, a trackable diagnostic study tool, an interactive VoiceBoard, and more. The new Share It! feature enables uploading and sharing of files, such as videos, for assignments and projects. Share It! also allows you to comment and rate your classmates' uploaded material.

ACKNOWLEDGMENTS

The authors and publisher would like to thank all those who reviewed *Nakama* and contributed comments and suggestions that were instrumental in shaping the second edition of *Nakama 2*. Their recommendations were invaluable during the development of this publication.

The authors are also grateful to the following people at Cengage Learning for their valuable assistance during the development of this project: Beth Kramer, Nicole Morinon, Ben Rivera, Courtney Wolstoncroft, Kim Beuttler, Gregory Madan, Lauren MacLachlan, and Lianne Ames.

They are especially grateful to Atsushi Honda and Colleen Shiels for copyediting, to Toru Ishizawa for proofreading, and to Michael Kelsey of Inari Information Services, Inc. Finally, profound thanks go to Satoru Shinagawa for his work on the Student Activities Manual and to Kazuko Yokoi for her work on the illustrations in this edition.

Preliminary Chapter

序章(じょしょう)

Image Source / Alamy

復習(ふくしゅう)
Review

Kanji Review

大学校先生山川田人上中下小日本今私月火水木金土曜何
週末休時間分半毎年好語高番方新古安友一二三四五六七
八九十百千万円店行来帰食飲見聞読書話出会買起寝作入
男女目口耳足手父母姉兄妹弟家族両親子天気雨雪風晴温
度東西南北寒暑多少冷春夏秋冬朝昼晩午前後去昨供元思
明回

Chapter 1	Greetings and useful expressions
Chapter 2	あいさつとじこしょうかい
Chapter 3	毎日の生活(かつ)
Chapter 4	日本のまち
Chapter 5	日本の家
Chapter 6	休みの日
Chapter 7	好きなものと好きなこと
Chapter 8	買い物(もの)
Chapter 9	レストランとしょうたい
Chapter 10	私の家族
Chapter 11	きせつと天気
Chapter 12	年中行事(ねんじゅうぎょうじ)

Chapter Resources

www.cengagebrain.com

Heinle Learning Center

Audio Program

かんじのふくしゅう

Kanji Review

Activity 1 Circle the character that does not belong in the group.

1. 山　川　木　水　上
2. 五　八　円　千　百
3. 父　男　弟　母　妹
4. 曜　週　年　分　何
5. 買　好　話　食　見
6. 行　出　読　来　帰
7. 休　手　目　足　耳
8. 金　月　土　上　火
9. 入　寝　度　聞　書

Activity 2 How are the **kanji** in each pair different?

1. 木　休
2. 男　田
3. 読　話
4. 耳　目
5. 入　八
6. 上　土
7. 三　川
8. 姉　妹
9. 母　毎
10. 回　口

Activity 3 下のことばを読んで下さい。

1. 山川　田中　中田　小川　大川　川中　中川　山中　上田　本田　小川　下田　中本　山本　金田　高田　高山　古川　古山　古田　友田　川口
2. 大きい　小さい　高い　一番　新しい　古い　安い　大変[へん] (な)　大丈夫[じょうぶ] (な)　好き (な)　大好き (な)　親切[せつ] (な)　寒い　暑い　多い　少ない　明るい　元気 (な)　上手 (な)
3. 時　今　三十分　何時　一時　二時　三時　四時　五時　六時　七時　八時半　九時　十時　三時間　朝　毎朝　今朝　毎晩　今晩　午前　午後　毎日　今日　明日　昨日　二日前　三日後　何曜日　日曜日　月曜日　火曜日　水曜日　木曜日　金曜日　土曜日　週末　毎週　今週　来週　先週　二週間　毎月　今月　来月　先月　春　夏　秋　冬　毎年　今年　来年　去年　昨年　今度　休みの日　誕生[たんじょう]日

4. 一本　二本　三本　四本　五本　六本　七本　八本　九本　十本　一つ
二つ　三つ　四つ　五つ　六つ　七つ　八つ　九つ　十　一人　二人
三人　何人　百円　千円　一万円　一回　二回　三回

5. 行く　来る　帰る　食べる　飲む　見る　聞く　読む　書く　話す　出る
会う　買う　起きる　寝る　作る　入る　晴れる　冷える　上がる　下がる
分かる　思う　上がって下さい　何をしますか　何ですか　一緒(しょ)に

6. 私　友達(だち)　先生　学生　留(りゅう)学生　大学院(いん)生　一年生　日本人　いい方
男の人　女の人　男の子　女の子　子供　家族　両親　兄弟　お子さん
父　お父さん　母　お母さん　姉　お姉さん　兄　お兄さん　妹さん
弟さん　ご主(しゅ)人　～番目

7. 目　口　耳　足　手　人

8. 天気　雨　雪　風　温度　何度　東　西　南　北　南東　北東　北西
南西

9. 山　川　水　木　上　下　中　本　本棚(だな)　家　大学　学校　中学　高校
大学院(いん)　中国(ごく)　～学　学生会館(かん)　銀(ぎん)行　本屋(や)　新聞　店　喫茶(きっさ)店　飲み物(もの)
和(わ)食　洋(よう)食　朝ご飯(はん)　昼ご飯(はん)　晩ご飯(はん)　電(でん)話　会話　日本語　生活(かつ)
思い出　図(と)書館(かん)

Activity 4　下のひらがなの文(ぶん)をかんじとひらがなで書いて下さい。

1. かねだ：　こんにちは。
おがわ：　こんにちは。あついですね。
かねだ：　ええ、そうですね。きょうはどこかへいくんですか。
おがわ：　ええ、いまからぎんこうにいって、そのあと、
デパートにかいものにいくんです。
かねだ：　そうですか。

2. こども：　ねえ、おかあさん。
おかあさん：　なに？
こども：　きょうのばんごはん、なに？
おかあさん：　そうね、こんばんはカレーよ。
こども：　え、またカレー？カレーよりおすしがいいな。
おかあさん：　そうねえ。おすしもたべたいねえ。でも、きょうは、
もうカレーつくったから、あしたおすしでどう？
こども：　うん、いいよ。

3. わたしは　ふるた　たかこです。こうこうさんねんせいです。わたしの かぞくは　ごにんかぞくです。ちちと　ははと　あにと　おとうとがいます。ちちは　だいがくの　せんせいで　ははは　ほんやに　つとめています。ちちは　にほんじん　ですが、ははは　ちゅうごくじんです。あにはだいがくいん　せいで、てとあしが　ながいです。　おとうとは　ちゅうがくせいです。　げんきで いいこなんですが、いちばんしたなので、 あまえんぼう (*spoiled*) です。あにも　おとうとも　だいすき　ですが、おんなの きょうだいが　いないので、おねえさんか　(*or*)　いもうとが　ほしいです。

4. やまもと：おそいね。
なかがわ：ごめん。きのうのばん、じゅうにじまで、バイトだったから。
やまもと：え、じゃあ、なんじごろうちにかえったの？
なかがわ：いちじごろだったとおもう。そのあと、しゅくだいして、さんじごろねたんだ。
やまもと：じゃあ、あまりねてないの？
なかがわ：そうだね。はちじはんにおきたから、ごじかんはんぐらいかな。
やまもと：そうだったんだ。それは、たいへんだね。

Chapter 1
Greetings and useful expressions

Activity 1 Work with a partner. Role-play the following situations.

1. It is a cold morning. You meet your teacher on your way to school.
2. Your class is over. Say goodbye to your teacher.
3. You are going out in the evening. You meet a neighbor.
4. Your neighbor gives you a Japanese fruit. Thank him/her and ask him/her the name of the fruit in Japanese.
5. Your neighbor tells you that he/she has just bought a デジカメ. You don't know what it is. Ask him/her what デジカメ means.
6. You are attending an orientation for international students at Joto University in Tokyo. You don't know the attendees sitting near you and would like to get to know them.
7. It is a sunny Sunday afternoon. You are walking in a park and run into your friend's mother.
8. You are in a teacher's office, and are about to leave.

Activity 2 What kind of requests would you make in the following situations?

1. You didn't understand what your teacher just said.
2. You are talking with a salesperson on the phone, but you can't hear her/him well.
3. You are talking with a friend on the phone who speaks too fast.
4. You want to know how your name is written in かな.
5. You are about to make an announcement to your class, so you need everybody's attention.
6. You want to know the reading of an unknown かんじ.
7. You want to know the meaning of an unknown かんじ.
8. You want your teacher to check the shape of かんじ that you have written.
9. You want to know the Japanese word for numbers.

Activity 3 Convert the following polite expressions to their casual forms.

1. あれは日本語で何といいますか。
2. ゆっくり話してください。
3. このかんじのいみは何ですか。
4. このかんじを読んでください。
5. もう一度いって下さい。
6. *Library* は日本語で何といいますか。
7. このしゃしんを見て下さい。
8. 「らくご」って何ですか。

Activity 4 Go back to situations 1 through 5 in Activity 1. You are now talking with a friend. Change what you would say accordingly.

Activity 5 Read the following titles and figure out what they say. Ask your teacher or a classmate about any unfamiliar words or **kanji**. Ask questions in both polite and casual forms.

1

2

3

4

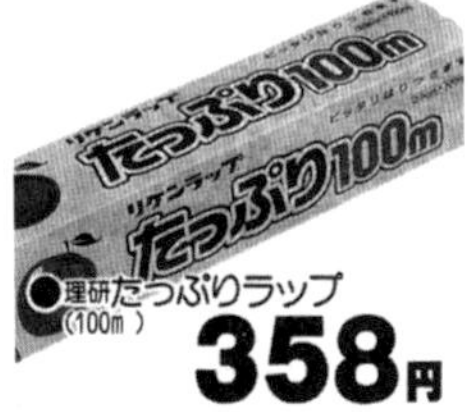

5

6

7

Chapter 2
あいさつとじこしょうかい

Activity 1 You are at a party and trying to get to know the other people there. First create a name card by selecting one of the words from each of the following categories.

名(な)前：　スミス　キム　チョー　シュミット　山中

大学：　ニューヨーク大学　シカゴ大学　シドニー大学　東京(きょう)大学

学年：　大学院(いん)　一年生　二年生　三年生　四年生

せんこう：　アジアけんきゅう　文(ぶん)学　れきし　英(えい)語

くに (*country*)：　アメリカ　日本　かんこく　中国(ごく)　オーストラリア　カナダ

Activity 2 Using the identity you have just created in Activity 1, greet and talk with as many people as you can. Remember them as you will later be asked to introduce them to others.

Example: A: はじめまして。私はスミスです。どうぞよろしく。

B: はじめまして。シュミットです。どうぞよろしく。

A: シュミットさんのせんこうは何ですか。

B: れきしです。

Activity 3 Using the names in Activity 1, ask others about the people across the room at the party. Find out their names, what they study, where they are from, etc. Remember that you are across the room from the people you are asking about.

Example: A: あの男の人はだれですか。

B: ああ、あの人はキムさんですよ。

A: キムさんの大学はどこですか。

B: 東京(きょう)大学です。

A: そうですか。キムさんはどこから来ましたか。

B: カナダから来ました。

Activity 4 You have just joined the Japan Student Association. Introduce yourself, providing appropriate information from the categories below.

名前(な)：________________________

〜年生：________________________

大学の名前(な)：________________________

せんこう：________________________

くに (*country*)：________________________

しゅみ：________________________

Activity 5 Work with a partner. Write the names of the cities in the appropriate box. Then create a conversation in which one person asks the other what time it is in each city. Write the answer.

Example: A: 東京(きょう)は今何時ですか。

B: 午前十一時ですよ。

A: そうですか。どうも。

B: いいえ。

東京(きょう)、ニューヨーク、ロンドン、ホノルル、バンコク、シドニー、デリー、モスクワ、カイロ、バンクーバー

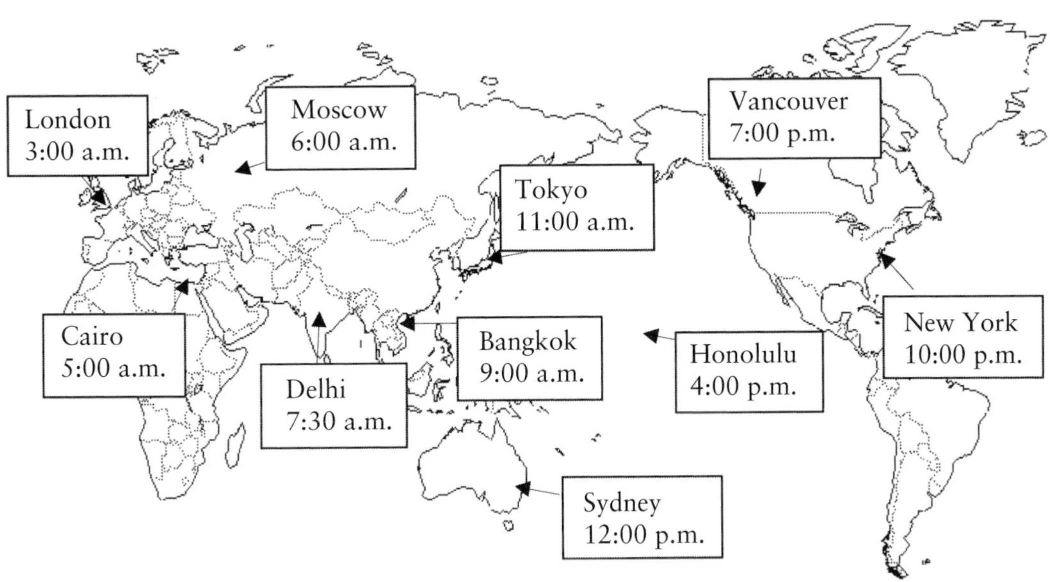

Chapter 3

毎日の生活

Activity 1 しつもんに日本語でこたえて下さい。

1. 毎朝何時ごろ起きますか。
2. 毎日何時ごろ寝ますか。
3. 朝ごはんを食べますか。何を食べますか。
4. 日本語のじゅぎょうは何曜日にありますか。
5. たいてい何時ごろ家へ帰りますか。
6. 毎日何時間ぐらいべんきょうしますか。
7. 毎日何時間ぐらい日本語のべんきょうをしますか。
8. テレビやえいがをよく見ますか。
9. おふろに入りますか。シャワーをあびますか。
10. 週末よく何をしますか。

Activity 2 Ask your classmates the questions in Activity 1, and find out what the most common answers are for each question.

Activity 3 Form groups of four. Find out what your classmates do each day of the week. What classes do they have, do they do some kind of part-time work, etc.? Who has the most classes in a single day? What do they do over the weekend?

Example:

A: ～さんは月曜日に何をしますか。

B: 私は九時と十時と三時にじゅぎょうがありますから、
大学に行きます。

A: そうですか。大変(へん)ですねえ。C さんはどうですか。

C: 私は月曜日にはじゅぎょうはありません。

D: そうですか。じゃあ、月曜日には、いつも何をしていますか。

C: そうですね。家でゆっくりしています。

名前(な)	月曜日	火曜日	水曜日	木曜日	金曜日	土曜日	日曜日
私							

Activity 4 Look at the train schedule and tell when the following trains depart from Shin-Osaka and arrive at Tokyo.

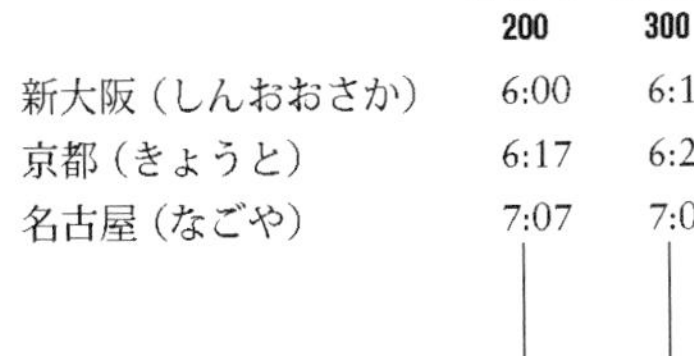
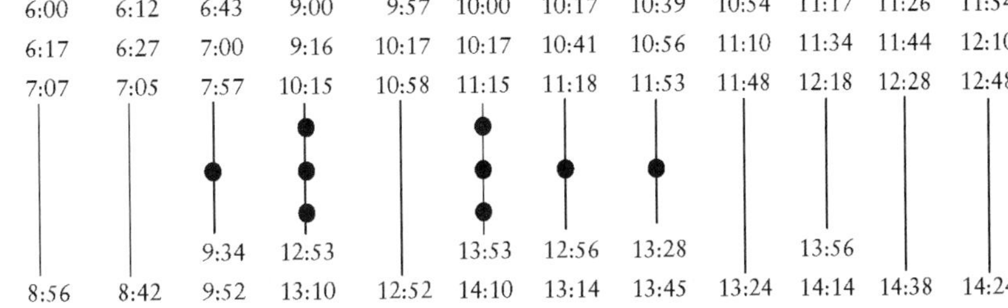

	ひかり 200	のぞみ 300	ひかり 126	こだま 404	ひかり 228	こだま 408	ひかり 032	ひかり 232	のぞみ 006	ひかり 034	ひかり 086	のぞみ 010
新大阪（しんおおさか）	6:00	6:12	6:43	9:00	9:57	10:00	10:17	10:39	10:54	11:17	11:26	11:54
京都（きょうと）	6:17	6:27	7:00	9:16	10:17	10:17	10:41	10:56	11:10	11:34	11:44	12:10
名古屋（なごや）	7:07	7:05	7:57	10:15	10:58	11:15	11:18	11:53	11:48	12:18	12:28	12:48
新横浜（しんよこはま）			9:34	12:53		13:53	12:56	13:28		13:56		
東京（とうきょう）	8:56	8:42	9:52	13:10	12:52	14:10	13:14	13:45	13:24	14:14	14:38	14:24

Example: ひかり２００ごうは六時に新大阪(しんおおさか)を出て、八時五十六分に東京(きょう)につきます (*arrive*)。

1. のぞみ 300
2. こだま 404
3. ひかり 126
4. のぞみ 006
5. ひかり 086
6. ひかり 232

Activity 5 Change the following into casual speech.

1. A: よくおふろに入りますか。
   B: いいえ、あまり入りません。
2. A: 朝ごはんを食べますか。
   B: いいえ、食べません。
3. A: 何を飲みますか。
   B: コーヒーを飲みます。
4. A: 今晩何をしますか。
   B: そうですね。テレビを見ます。
5. A: どこに行きますか。
   B: 図書館に行きます。

Activity 6 Work with a partner. Role-play the following situations.

1. You run into a friend you have not seen for a while. Greet him/her and ask what he/she is doing these days.
2. A Japanese student who has recently arrived in your country wants to know what college life is like. Explain what college students in the U.S. typically do in a day.

Chapter 4
日本のまち

Activity 1 Fill in the blanks with the appropriate words for buildings and places.

1. コーヒーを飲みに行くところは＿＿＿＿＿＿＿＿＿＿＿＿です。
2. 手紙を出しに行くところは＿＿＿＿＿＿＿＿＿＿＿＿です。
3. お金がたくさんあるところは＿＿＿＿＿＿＿＿＿＿＿＿です。
4. 日本のえきのちかくにある小さいたてものは＿＿＿＿＿＿＿＿＿＿です。
5. 本やざっしを買うところは＿＿＿＿＿＿＿＿＿＿＿＿です。
6. 本やざっしや新聞を読みに行くところは＿＿＿＿＿＿＿です。

Activity 2 Define the following words in Japanese, using the type of descriptive phrases that were used in Activity 1.

Example: カフェはコーヒーを飲みに行くところです。

1. こうえん
2. デパート
3. えき
4. アパート
5. 図書館
6. コンビニ
7. りょう

Activity 3

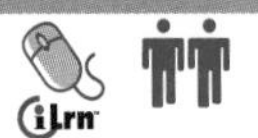

Work with a partner. You and your partner are at the police box. You are unfamiliar with this area, so you ask your partner, a police officer, for directions to go to the following places. Create a conversation using こそあど、 ～は～にあります／います and ～に～があります／います.

Example: A: あのう、すみません。

B: はい、何ですか。

A: 本屋はどこですか。

B: 本屋ですか。そこに銀行がありますね。

A: ええ。そのしろいたてものですね。

B: そうです。本屋はそのひだりですよ。

A: そうですか。どうも。

Activity 4 Work with a partner. Complete the following dialogue using こそあど words. The first one is done for you as an example.

スミス： 木村さん、<u>それ</u>は何の辞書？
木村： 英語の辞書よ。
スミス： そうなんだ。
木村： ＿＿＿＿けしゴムは、どうしたの。
スミス： ＿＿＿＿？さっき、つくえの下で見つけた (*found*) んだよ。だれのかな。
木村： さあ、分からない。あ、じゃあ、＿＿＿＿ノートも見つけたの？
スミス： ううん。＿＿＿＿は　ぼくのだよ。
木村： あ、そう。
スミス： じゃ、＿＿＿＿えんぴつは　木村さんの？
木村： ううん、＿＿＿＿は　私のじゃないけど。
スミス： そうなんだ。じゃ、＿＿＿＿ハンドバッグは？
木村： あ、＿＿＿＿は　私のよ。

Activity 5 Work with a partner. Think of food or items found at school or in a home that can be described in terms of object type, color, shape, or size. Your partner will ask questions about the object type, color, shape, size, etc., and try to figure out what the item is. Try to use the expressions in the box.

あかい	きいろい	あおい	ちゃいろい	しろい	くろい		
大きい	小さい	古い	新しい	高い	ひくい	かたい	やわらかい
まるい	しかくい	ながい	ほそながい	みじかい	あまい	にがい	

Example: A: それは食べ物(もの)ですか。
B: ええ、そうです。
A: それはしろいですか。
B: いいえ、しろくありませんね。
A: じゃあ、あかいですか。
B: ええ、あかいです。
A: 大きいですか。
B: いいえ、大きくありません。
A: じゃあ、それは、トマトですか。
B: はい、そうです。

Activity 6 Work with a partner. Role-play the following situation. Use casual speech.

You are visiting your friend's college. Ask him/her about various facilities and their locations.

Chapter 5
日本の家

Activity 1 Which of the following items might you find in the rooms or buildings listed in 1–4 below? Use casual speech.

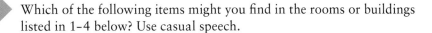

ベッド　いす　つくえ　本棚(だな)　電話(でん)　時計(とけい)　テレビ　コンピュータ
たんす　おしいれ　まど　ドア　いぬ　ねこ　ソファ　テーブル　ふとん
こくばん　ビデオ　しゃしん　え

Example: A: りょうのへやにはどんなものある？
B: そう（だ）ね。ベッドがあるよ。つくえもあるね。

1. りょうのへや
2. きょうしつ
3. 日本の家
4. 子供のへや

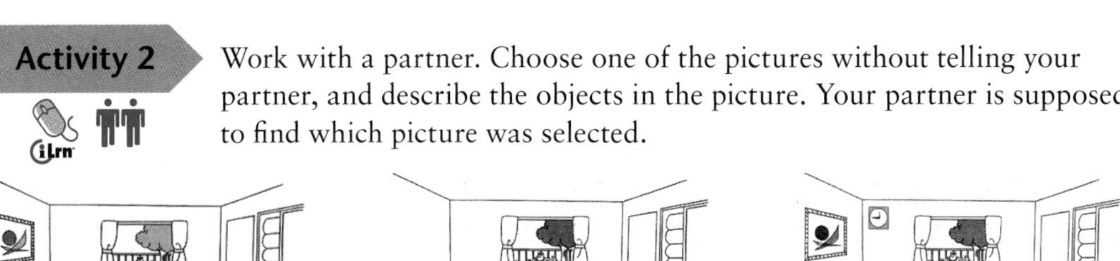

Activity 2

Work with a partner. Choose one of the pictures without telling your partner, and describe the objects in the picture. Your partner is supposed to find which picture was selected.

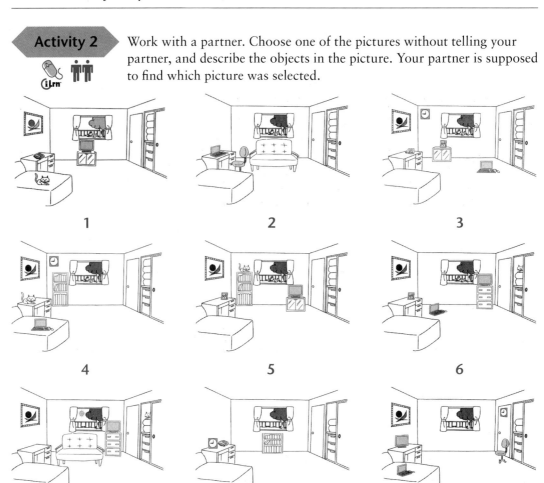

1 2

3

4

5

6

7 8 9

Activity 3

Work with a partner. You are moving into a new room with your belongings and your partner is helping you. Draw where you want to put your belongings in the following picture. Then tell your partner where to put each item in the room. Use <location> に <object> をおいて (*put*) 下さい. Your partner will draw the objects in his own picture as you tell him where to put them. Compare your picture with your partner's to see if they are identical.

ベッド　つくえ　コンピュータ　ソファ　テレビ　たんす　本棚(だな)　時計(とけい)

Example:　大きいまどの前に、つくえをおいて下さい。

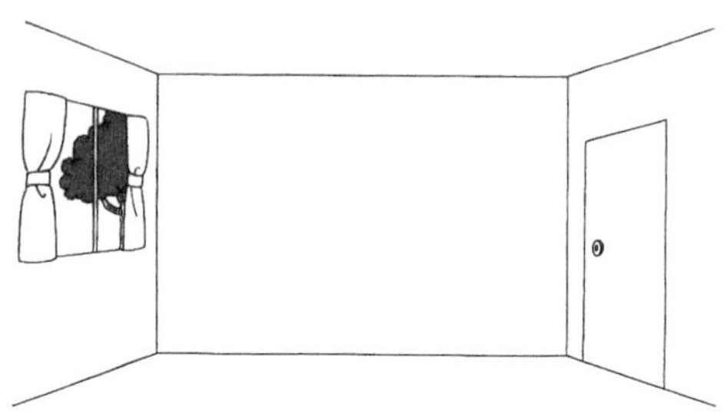

Activity 4 Change the following dialogues or statements into casual speech.

1. A: このへやのとなりに何がありますか。
   B: お手洗(あら)いがあります。
2. A: つくえの下に何がいますか。
   B: ねこがいます。かわいいですよ
3. A: そこにだれがいますか。
   B: スミスさんがいます。インターネットをしていますね。
4. あ、あそこにきれいなさかながいますよ。見て下さい。

Activity 5 Work with a partner. Role-play the following situations.

1. You are visiting a Japanese friend's house, and you have just arrived at the door. Greet your friend.
2. You are looking for an apartment. First, fill out the types of features of the apartment you want. Your friend knows a person who wants to sublet an apartment. Ask your friend about the apartment.

Number of rooms	____________	Surrounding area	____________
Size of apartment	____________	Types of rooms	____________
Old or new apartment	____________		

Chapter 6
休みの日

Activity 1 Work with a partner. Ask what your partner did last weekend and circle the activities that he/she did. Use て-form to connect activities.

Example: A: 週末は何をしましたか。
B: そうですね。土曜日は朝せんたくとそうじをして、午後出かけました。日曜日は友達(だち)を家によんで、ゲームをしました。

りょうりを作る	せんたくをする	そうじをする	しごとをする	新聞／ざっしを読む
買い物(もの)に行く	手紙(がみ)／メールを書く	日本語で話す	電(でん)話をかける	おんがくを聞く
出かける	コンサートに行く	ピクニックに行く	うんどうする	テニスをする
プールでおよぐ	ジョギングをする	友達(だち)に会う	さんぽをする	あそびに行く
ゲームをする	家でゆっくりする	おふろに入る	友達(だち)をよぶ	パーティをする

Activity 2

Work with a partner. Use the expressions below to ask your partner about his/her childhood classes and teachers. Find out why your partner thought that these classes or teachers were or were not good (interesting, difficult, etc).

Example:

A: 高校の時、どのじゅぎょうがよかったですか／よくなかったですか。

B: そうですね。アメリカのれきしのじゅぎょうがよかったです。

A: どうしてですか。

A: 先生がやさしくて、おもしろかったからです。

		どうして
いい／じゅぎょう	はい	
	いいえ	
好き／先生	はい	
	いいえ	
大変／クラス	はい	
	いいえ	

Activity 3

Change the style of the following exchanges into casual speech.

1. A: 昨日どこに行きましたか。

   B: 友達とデパートに行って、えいがを見ました。

2. A: 今日は文学のテストでしたね。テストはどうでしたか。

   B: とてもながくて、むずかしかったんです。

3. A: 昨日のジョンソンさんのパーティーにはだれが来ましたか。

   B: 田中さんや山本さんやリーさんが来ました。

4. A: 今日、えきまで何で行きますか。

   B: くるまで行って、それから、でんしゃにのります。

5. A: 明日天気がいいですから、一緒にテニスをしませんか。

   B: すみません。したいんですけど、明日はちょっとつごうがわるくて。

6. A: あ、あそこに古川さんがいますよ。

   B: そうですね。あ、中山さんもいますよ。何をしているんでしょうか。

7. A: ちょっと図書館に行きますから、ここでまっていて下さい。

   B: はい、分かりました。

Activity 4

Work with a partner. Ask your partner about his/her most memorable trip (good or bad). Use the following items to learn what your partner did on the trip and whether he/she enjoyed the activities. Use casual speech.

1. When, where, and with whom you went
2. What you did
3. How the trip was (why it was good/bad)

Activity 5

Work with a partner. You are giving a speech about the lifestyle of U.S. college students to a group of visiting Japanese students. With your partner, create a questionnaire asking about your classmates' lifestyles. Write questions about their daily lives, workload, how they spend weekends, etc. Then interview your classmates and write a speech draft with your partner based on the draft.

Chapter 7
好きなことと好きなもの

Activity 1

Work with a partner. First, write as many words as you can that belong to and/or are associated with each category. Then ask your partner what he/she has written and circle the items that both you and your partner have. Then write the words from your partner's list that you don't have.

Example: A: どんなやさいの名(な)前を書きましたか。
B: 私はレタスとにんじんを書きました。
A: 私もレタスとにんじんを書きました。そして、トマトも書きました。

1. やさい ______________________
2. にく ______________________
3. くだもの ______________________
4. 飲み物(もの) ______________________
5. スポーツ ______________________
6. おんがく ______________________
7. レジャー ______________________

Activity 2

Work as a class. Ask your classmates what kind of food and drinks they like or dislike. Determine which foods and drinks are the most and least popular in your class.

Example: A: どんな食べ物(もの)が好きですか。

B: ～や～が好きです。

A: ～はどうですか。

B: そうですね。～は～（な）ので、あまり好きじゃありません。

Activity 3

Work with a partner. Ask your partner what kind of sports or music he/she likes or dislikes and why. Use casual speech.

Example: A: どんなスポーツが好き？

B: ～が好きだよ。／～が好き。

A: ～は、どう？

B: ～（だ）から、あまり好きじゃないんだ。

Activity 4

A very rich person wants to give away a large cash prize, but only to the person who best matches his ideal. Select one person to be the donor, ask him/her about his/her favorite things. Then interview your classmates, and select the person who best matches the ideal.

Example: A: ～さんはどんなスポーツが好きですか。

B: やきゅうが好きです。

A: そうですか。テニスはどうですか。

B: テニスも好きですよ。でも、あまり上手じゃないんです。

A: そうですか。じゃあ、おんがくは何が好きですか。

Activity 5

Work with a partner. Ask your partner what he/she likes best and least among these items in each of the following categories. Rank them.

やさい　にく　くだもの　飲み物(もの)　スポーツ　おんがく　レジャー

Example: A: やさいの中で何が一番好きですか。

B: トマトが一番好きですね。

A: にんじんとレタスはどうですか。

B: にんじんもレタスも好きですが、にんじんの方がレタスより好きです／
にんじんもレタスも好きじゃないですが、にんじんの方がレタスよりまし (*tolerable*) ですね。

Chapter 8
買い物

Activity 1

Work with a partner. First, write the appropriate counter for each of the following objects. Then, your partner should write a number (not larger than 100) and call out one of the objects on the list. Say the correct number-counter expression for the number of that item. You get one point for each correct answer.

Example: Your partner writes 24 and says 「Tシャツ」 You say 「にじゅうよんまい」

セーター	ベルト	えんぴつ	ネックレス	かばん
________	________	________	________	________
さかな	いぬ	本	ざっし	りんご
________	________	________	________	________
ねこ	パンツ	けしゴム	シャツ	ノート
________	________	________	________	________

Activity 2

Work in groups of four. First, guess how much the following items cost in Japan (in yen). Then ask the other group members for their guesses. Your instructor will provide actual prices. The person who makes the most accurate guesses is the winner.

Example: A: たまごはいくらだと思いますか。

B: １００円ぐらいだと思います。～さんはいくらぐらいだと思いますか。

A: ２００円ぐらいだと思います。

	私			
たまご（12）				
テレビ（32 インチ）				
ガソリン (*gasoline*) 1 リットル＊				
おんがくの CD				
ジーンズ				

＊ 1 リットル＝ 0.264 ガロン

Activity 3

Work with a partner. Ask your partner what he/she wants to do under the following circumstances. A list of verbs is provided to assist you. ～としたら means *suppose (that)* ~ or *if* ~.

行く 帰る 飲む 入る 読む 書く 聞く 買う 作る 話す あそぶ
うたう およぐ とる 出す つつむ あびる 起きる 食べる 寝る
見る かける 出かける 入れる 見せる 来る

Example: A: 大金持ち(おおがねもち) (*rich person*) だったとしたら、どんなことがしたいですか。

B: そうですね。くるまをたくさん買いたいですね。

1. 大金持ち(おおがねもち)だったとしたら、
2. あと二か月でしぬ (*die in two months*) としたら、
3. 男・女になったとしたら、
4. 今よりかっこよくなったとしたら、

Activity 4

Work with the class. Ask your classmates what they want most right now, and find out the most interesting thing and report it to class. Use casual speech.

Example: A: ～さん、今、何が一番ほしい？

B: 日本に行くお金(かね)がほしいかな。

A: どうして日本に行きたいの？

B: 日本にかれし (*boyfriend*) がいるから会いたいの。

A: ああ、そうなんだ。

～さんは、かれしに会いたいから、日本に行くお金をほしがっています。

名前	ほしいもの

Activity 5 Work with a partner. Role-play the following situations.

1. You are at a department store. You want to know on which floor kimonos are sold. Ask the person at the information desk.
2. You are in the accessories department, and want to see a necklace in the case. Get the attention of a sales clerk and ask him/her to take it out for you.
3. You are in the woman's clothing department. You want to buy a present for your mother, but cannot decide what to get. Your budget is 10,000 yen. Get the attention of a sales clerk and explain what you need help with. Respond to questions about the size, color preference, etc. Have the clerk show you some items.
4. A sales clerk has shown you a sweater. Ask the clerk how much it is. If it is too expensive, ask for a more affordable one. Ask for ones with different colors. Ask for a bigger (or smaller) size.
5. Select the items that you want. Ask the sales clerk to put them in the box and put a ribbon on the box.

Chapter 9
レストランとしょうたい

Activity 1 しつもんに日本語でこたえて下さい。

1. 「和食」って何ですか。
2. 和食にはどんな食べ物がありますか。
3. ラーメンは何りょうりですか。
4. アメリカにはどんなりょうりがありますか。
5. メキシコりょうりにはどんな食べ物がありますか。
6. どんな飲み物が好きですか。どんな飲み物がきらいですか。

Activity 2

Work in groups of four. You are at a diner. Ask each other what you would like to have and fill out the chart. Use both formal and casual speech.

Example: A: ～さんは何にしますか。
B: 私は～にします。

A: ～さん、何にする?
B: えっと、～にする。

名前	飲み物と食べ物

Activity 3

Work with a partner who was not in your group in Activity 2. You are still in the restaurant and your partner is the server. Using the information from Activity 2, order for your group.

Example: Server: ごちゅうもんは?
A: ビールを三本おねがいします。
Server: はい、ビールを三本ですね。
A: それから、～

Activity 4

You are conducting a survey on breakfast habits. Ask your classmates if they have had anything to eat or drink today. If they have, find out what. Then determine how many people didn't have anything in the morning and what the most popular breakfast was for the class.

Example: A: キムさん、今朝、何か食べましたか。
B: いいえ、何も食べませんでした。
A: 何か飲みましたか。
B: ええ、コーヒーとオレンジジュースを飲みました。

名前(な)	食べ物(もの)	飲み物(もの)
キム	-------	コーヒー、オレンジジュース

Activity 5 Work as a class. Look at the event calendar below. Choose three things you would like to see or do and invite your classmates to go with you.

Example: A: ～さん、来週の水曜日に大学のスタジアム (*stadium*) でコンサートがあるんだけど、一緒(しょ)に行きませんか。

B: 水曜日ですか、いいですね。／
すみません、木曜日にテストがあるから、水曜日はちょっと。

月曜日 ジャズコンサート（Jay's Cafe、十時）
火曜日 「Cats」ミュージカル（大学のコンサートホール、七時半）
水曜日 ロックコンサート（大学のスタジアム、九時）
木曜日 バスケットボールのしあい (*game*)（大学のスタジアム、六時）
金曜日 クラシックのコンサート（大学のコンサートホール、八時）
土曜日 ブックセール（まちの図(と)書館(かん)、十二時）
日本のえいが（スミスホール、四時と七時）
日曜日 バザー (*bazaar*)（キャンパス、一時～五時）

Activity 6 Look at the following pictures and give your visual impression using ～そうです.

1 2 3

4 5 6

Activity 7 Work with a partner. Role-play the following situations, inviting your partner to join you, then discover the details of what you will do with your partner. Use question word + か／～ませんか／～ましょうか／～ましょう.

Example: You are with your partner and you are thirsty.

A: ～さん、何か飲みませんか。

B: ええ、いいですよ。じゃあ、どこかカフェに行きましょうか。

A: ああ、いいですね。あそこはどうでしょうか。

B: いいですね。あそこにしましょう。

1. You and your friend are walking on the street. You feel hungry.
2. You are free this weekend and want to go somewhere fun.
3. You are at your friend's house. You think you would like to see a movie. Check the website to see what is playing, and discuss which movie you would like to see, and when, with your partner.

Chapter 10
私の家族

Activity 1 Look at the figures labeled in the family tree below. You are Chris. Identify each person using an appropriate kinship term and ordinal number.

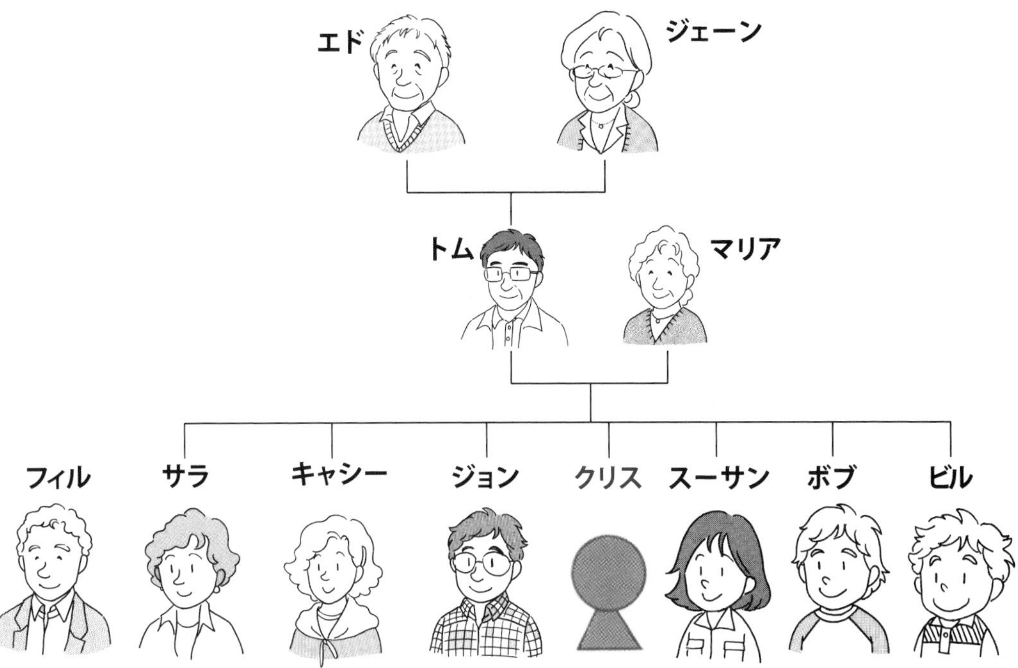

Example:　キャシーは私の姉です。上から二番目の兄弟です。

Activity 2 しつもんに日本語でこたえて下さい。

1. ～さんのクラスには学生が何人いますか。
2. ～さんの大学には学生が何人ぐらいいますか。先生は何人ぐらいいますか。
3. ～さんは友達(だち)が何人いますか。
4. このクラスで年が一番下の人は何さいですか。
5. ～さんは兄弟が何人いますか。～さんの家族は何人家族ですか。
6. ～さんは何さいですか。～さんは上から何番目ですか。下から何番目ですか。

Activity 3

Work with a partner. Ask your partner about his/her family members (their physical characteristics, occupations, residences, etc.). Use ～ている and ～は～が.

Example: A: ～さんのご家族は何人家族ですか。
B: 五人家族です。
A: そうですか。お父さんはどんな方ですか。
B: 目が大きくて、せが高いです。
A: めがねをかけていますか。
B: ええ、かけています。
A: どんなしごとをしていますか。
B: 大学の先生です。
A: そうですか。どこにすんでいますか。
B: ロサンゼルスにすんでいます。

Activity 4

Work with a new partner. Discuss with each other what you consider to be your instructor's dream partner in terms of physical characteristics, personality, skills, occupation, etc. Take notes. Use ～ている, ～は～が, and the て-form of verbs.

Example: A: 先生はどんな人が好きだと思いますか。
B: そうですね。先生はせが高いから、せが高い人が好きだと思います。
A: そうですか。かおはどんなかおがいいと思いますか。
B: 目が大きくて、はなが高い人がいいと思います。
A: じゃあ、せいかくはどうですか。
B: そうですね。明るくて、やさしい人がいいと思います。
A: 何が上手な人がいいでしょうか。
B: 先生はテニスが好きだから、テニスが上手な人がいいでしょう。

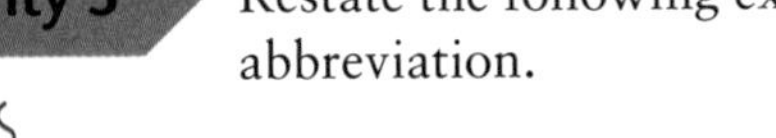

Activity 5 Restate the following exchanges in casual speech using this type of abbreviation.

Example: A: リンダさんはいつもきれいなふくをきていますね。
B: あの人はモデルなんですよ。

A: リンダさん、いつもきれいなふく、きてるね。
B: あの人、モデルなんだ／なのよ。

1. A: お父さんはニューヨークにすんでいるんですか。
   B: いいえ、フィラデルフィアにすんでいます。
2. A: あの人はとてもやせていますね。
   B: ええ、それにとても足がながくて、かっこいいですね。
3. A: あそこで日本人の学生が話していますね。山本さんはどの人ですか。
   B: めがねをかけていて、かみがみじかい人ですよ。
4. A: 学食の前でスミスさんと話している人はだれですか。
   B: ああ、あれは高田さんの妹さんだと思いますよ。

Activity 6 Work with a partner. Your partner will select a celebrity. Quiz your partner about physical characteristics, job, place of residence, clothing, etc., to figure out who the celebrity is.

Example A: その人、かみながい？
B: うん。
A: じゃあ、何をするのが上手？
B: うた、うたうの。
A: どこにすんでるの？
B: ハリウッドにすんでると思う。
A: ビヨンセ？
B: うん、そう。／ううん、ビヨンセじゃないよ。

Chapter 11
きせつと天気

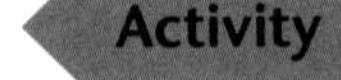

Activity 1 Give the readings of the following weather symbols

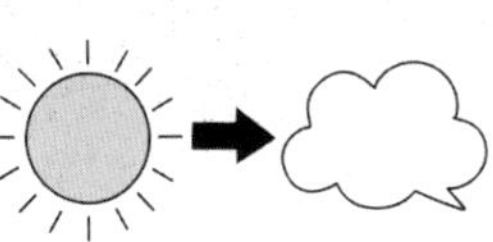

1 ______ 2 ______ 3 ______ 4 ______ 5 ______ 6 ______

Activity 2

Work in groups of four. Each person should choose five different verbs and write a sentence using them. Then take turns acting out the verb phrase. The group will try to guess what he/she is doing.

飲む	読む	書く	聞く	買う	作る	話す	あそぶ	べんきょうする
およぐ	とる	出す	あびる	起きる	食べる	寝る	する	あるく
まつ	うたう	入れる	見せる	見る				

Example: B is doing laundry:

A: あそんでいますか。

B: いいえ、そうじゃありません。

C: せんたくをしていますか。

B: はい、そうです。

Activity 3

Describe the following weather conditions using adverbial forms of adjectives and ている .

Example: 風がつよくふいています。

Activity 4 The following chart shows the weather forecast for five locations around the world. Describe the weather.

Example: 東京(きょう)は明日はくもりでしょう。気温は15度ぐらいで、あたたかくなるでしょう。雨はふるかもしれませんが、ふらないかもしれません。

	東京(きょう)	アラスカ	ニューヨーク	シドニー	ロサンゼルス
天気	くもり	雪	くもりのち雨	晴れ	くもり時々(ときどき)晴れ
気温	59° F 15° C	-4° F -20° C	41° F 5° C	91.4° F 33° C	77° F 25° C
雨	50%	0%	80%	0%	30%
雪	0%	100%	15%	0%	0%

Activity 5 Describe the seasons in your area, using 〜は〜が and other appropriate phrases.

Example: 春はとてもあたたかくて、天気がいいです。六月と七月はとても雨が多いです。夏は天気がいい日が多いですが、とてもむし暑くなります。秋はすずしくて、雨は少ないです。でも、朝と晩は寒いです。冬は雪がたくさんふって、とても寒くなります。

Activity 6 Change the following conversations into casual speech.

Example: A: おはようございます。
B: おはようございます。

A: おはよう。
B: おはよう。

1. A: 今日は、朝からちょっと寒いですね。
   B: ええ、本当(とう)に寒いですね。北からふいている風もつよいですから。
   A: そうですね。くもっていますが、今晩、雪になるでしょうか。
   B: そうですね。この天気は、雪になるかもしれませんね。

2. A: だれか、ちょっと、ここに来てくれませんか。

 B: いいですよ。今、行きますよ。

3. A: 学生会館(かいかん)の前で電(でん)話で話している人はだれですか。

 B: 小川さんですよ。金田さんをまっているんだと思います。

4. A: 今日は朝からいそがしそうですね。

 B: ええ、明日から出かけますから、今日はすることがたくさんあったんですよ。

Chapter 12
年中行事(ねんじゅうぎょうじ)

Activity 1 しつもんに日本語でこたえて下さい。

1. 夏休みは何月何日から何月何日までありますか。冬休みはどうですか。春休みは？
2. 今学期(き) (*this semester*) は何月何日にはじまって、何月何日におわりますか。来学期(き)はどうですか。
3. 今日は何月何日ですか。昨日は何月何日でしたか。おとといは何月何日でしたか。
4. 明日は何月何日ですか。あさっては何月何日ですか。
5. ご家族の誕生(たんじょう)日は何月何日ですか。
6. 一か月前は何月何日でしたか。半年前は何月何日でしたか。
7. 一学期(き) (*one semester*) は何か月ありますか。夏休みは何か月ありますか。

Activity 2 Work in groups of four. Make a guess about how often or how long students in Japan do the following activities and tell your group. Then check with your instructor to find out who made the most accurate guesses. Use plain form + 〜と思います (*I think that . . .*).

Example: A: 日本の高校生は一日に何時間ぐらいテレビを見ると思いますか。

 B: そうですね。一時間ぐらい見ると思います。

 C: 私は二時間ぐらい見ると思いますよ。

 D: そうですか。私は三時間ぐらい見ると思います。

	Your guess	～さん	～さん	～さん
1. テレビを見る／一日／時間	________	________	________	________
2. べんきょうする／一日／時間	________	________	________	________
3. 寝る／一日／時間	________	________	________	________
4. アルバイトをする／一週間／日	________	________	________	________
5. 本を読む／一か月／さつ	________	________	________	________
6. えいがを見に行く／一か月／度	________	________	________	________

Activity 3

Work as a class. First, check off the experiences you have had in the past, and write your approximate age or the time when you experienced them. Then ask your classmates whether they have had these experiences. If so, ask when. Use casual speech.

Example: A: 日本に行ったことがある？
B: うん、あるよ。
A: そう。いつ行ったの？
B: 高校三年生の時（かな）。／二か月前（くらい）。

	はい	いつ	～さん	いつ
日本に行く				
ミュージカルを見る				
きものをきる				
ハワイのうみでおよぐ				
ゆうえんちであそぶ				
キャンプをする				
ボートにのる				
がいこくに行く				
おさしみを食べる				

Activity 4

Work in groups of three. One member should choose a place from the box below, and define it using the ～たり～たりする form. The other members should try to figure out which place was selected. The person who guesses correctly gets a point. Take turns.

高校　こうえん　カフェ　ゆうえんち　銀行　はくぶつかん　どうぶつえん
うみ　びじゅつかん　水族館　スーパー　デパート　コンビニ　えき
図書館　教会　山　川　びょういん　ゆうびんきょく　たいいくかん
レストラン

Example:
A: 友達とべんきょうしたり、あそんだりするところです。
B: 図書館ですか。
A: いいえ。

Activity 5

Work with a partner. Ask your partner what he did or didn't do as a child.

Example:
A: 子供の時どんなものをよく食べましたか。
B: ドーナツ (*donuts*) をよく食べました。
A: どうしてドーナツをよく食べたんですか。
B: 母がいつも買って来たんです／買って来たからです。

	～さん
子供の時よく食べたもの	
子供の時あまり食べなかったもの	
子供の時よくしたこと	
子供の時あまりしなかったこと	
子供の時よく一緒にあそんだ人	

Activity 6

Work with another partner. Report what your partner did or didn't do in Activity 5, using the ～そうです (hearsay) form. Also, use noun modification.

Example: ～さんが子供の時よく食べたものは、ドーナツだそうです。

Chapter 1

第一課(だいいっか)

AP Photo/Uchida Hospital, Chikako Funamoto, HO

健康(けんこう)
Health

Objectives		Expressing physical conditions, asking for help, making polite requests, giving suggestions
Dialogue		熱(ねつ)があるんです。*I have a fever.*
Vocabulary		Physical symptoms; at the hospital
Japanese Culture		Longevity and Japanese hospitals
Grammar	I.	Expressing capability using the potential form of verbs
	II.	Expressing excessiveness using ～すぎる
	III.	Giving suggestions using ～たらどうですか and ～方がいいです
	IV.	Describing what efforts are being made to attain a specific goal using ～ように
	V.	Making a negative request using ～ないで下さい; expressing unacceptable actions or situations using ～てはいけない; asking for and giving permission using ～てもいい
Listening		Using the setting as a cue
Communication		Talking to a doctor
Kanji		Left-side component shapes of **kanji** 病 院 医 者 体 歯 変 熱 薬 顔 色 指 切 歩 走 勉 強 忘 早 持 痛 頭
Reading		Using your knowledge of the real world, 父の病気(びょうき)

Chapter Resources

www.cengagebrain.com

Heinle Learning Center

Audio Program

Flashcards

単語(たんご)

Nouns

アレルギー		allergy
いき	息	breath
いしゃ	医者	medical doctor, お医者さん , doctor
おなか		stomach
かおいろ	顔色	facial skin tone, complexion
かぜ	風邪	cold, かぜをひく to catch a cold; かぜ (wind) is written with the single character 風 .
からだ	体	body
きぶん	気分	feeling, spirits, mood, きぶんがわるい, to feel annoyed, feel sick/ill/unwell.
きもち	気持ち	feeling, sensation, きもちがわるい, to feel nausea, feel unpleasant, feel weird, feel revolted
くすり	薬	medicine, drug, ointment
くび	首	neck
けが	怪我	injury
こし	腰	lower back
しょうじょう	症状	symptom
ストレス		stress
せき	咳	cough
せなか	背中	back, upper back
ダイエット		diet
たばこ／タバコ	煙草	cigarette
ねつ	熱	fever, (high) temperature
のど	喉	throat
は	歯	tooth
びょうき	病気	sickness
マッサージ		massage
むね	胸	chest, breast

むり	無理	overwork, overstrain, むりをする to overwork, to overdo it
ゆび	指	finger

う -verbs

うごかす	動かす	to move (something) (transitive verb)
うごく	動く	(for someone/something) to move
きる	切る	to cut
こる	凝る	to have stiffness, かたがこる (to) have stiff shoulders
すう	吸う	to inhale, たばこをすう to smoke
だす	出す	to take out, to prescribe, to submit, くすりをだす to prescribe medicine, 学生がしゅくだいをだす to submit homework, 先生がしゅくだいをだす to assign homework
つまる	詰まる	to clog, はながつまる to be stuffed/stopped up
はかる	計る	to measure, ねつをはかる to check one's temperature
はく	吐く	to exhale; to throw up
はしる	走る	to run
はたらく	働く	to work
ひく		to catch (a cold), かぜをひく to catch a cold
やすむ	休む	to rest, to be absent, じゅぎょうをやすむ to be absent from class

る -verbs

あける	開ける	to open
あげる	上げる	to raise (something) c.f. あがる to rise
さげる	下げる	to lower (something) c.f. さがる to go down
つける	付ける	to attach, apply (medicine)
つかれる	疲れる	to become tired, つかれている to be tired
でる	出る	to come out, せきがでる to cough, ねつがでる to run a fever
とめる	止める	to stop (something)
わすれる	忘れる	to forget

Irregular verb

にゅういんする	入院する	to be hospitalized, びょういんににゅういんする

い-adjectives

いたい	痛い	hurt, painful
かゆい	痒い	itchy
ひどい		serious (injury), ひどいけが serious injury
わるい	悪い	bad, かおいろがわるい look pale

な-adjectives

いろいろ（な）	色々（な）	various
けんこう（な）	健康（な）	healthy, けんこうな人 healthy person can be used as a noun けんこうのため for the sake of health

Adverbs

すぐ		immediately, right away

Particles

を		from, じゅぎょうをやすむ be absent from a class 大学をそつぎょうする to graduate from college

Expressions

ええっと／すみません、それはちょっと（こまるんですが）。		Well, uh, I'm sorry but . . . (that presents some problems.)
おだいじに	お大事に	Please take care of yourself.
～てもいいですか。		May I ～?, Is it OK to ～?
どうしましたか。／どうしたんですか		What's wrong?
どうしたらいいですか。		What should I do?
はい／ええ、かまいません。		I don't mind. (= yes, please)
はい／ええ、どうぞ。		Yes, please.
はい／ええ、もちろん。		Yes, of course, sure.
はじめてなんですが。	初めてなんですが。	This is my first time. . .
むりをする	無理をする	to overstrain, overwork
よこになる	横になる	to lie down
よるおそくまで	夜遅くまで	until late at night

単語(たん)の練習(れんしゅう)

A. 体(からだ)にいいことわるいこと、体(からだ)にいいものわるいもの

Things that are good for one's health and things that are bad for one's health.

けんこうに気をつける	to pay attention to your health, take care of yourself
ダイエットをする	to go on a diet
マッサージをする	to (get a) massage
休(やす)む	to rest
よこになる	to lie down
はたらく	to work
たばこをすう	to smoke
よるおそくまで起きている	to stay up late at night
むりをする	to overstrain
ストレスがある	to be stressed (out)
すぐ色々(いろいろ)なことを忘(わす)れる	to forget immediately about various things

おぼえていますか。

うんどうする　ゆっくりする　しずか（な）　早(はや)く起きる　早(はや)く寝る　シャワーをあびる歩(ある)く　ふとる　きゅうにやせる　あそぶ　出かける　ジョギング　散歩(さんぽ)　生活(かつ)　しごと　元気（な）　アルバイト

NOTE

元気 is sometimes confused with けんこう. Both can be nouns or な-adjectives. けんこう／けんこうな, however, refers to one's physical condition, as its core meaning is "health." On the other hand, 元気 means *spirit* or *energy*, so it can refer to both mental and physical conditions. For example, 元気だ means that a person is energetic and/or high-spirited, so even a sick person who is happy can be 元気. Conversely, 元気じゃない means that the person does not have any energy. He/she may be physically tired or unhappy. In addition, 元気がない means that someone is in low spirits or feeling downhearted.

Activity 1

Work with a partner. Classify the expressions on the previous page based on whether they indicate good or bad health conditions, and write them in the appropriate columns in the following chart.

体(からだ)にいい	体(からだ)にわるい

Activity 2

Work with a partner. Ask your partner whether any of the following statements applies to them, and if so how frequently, then circle the correct response.

Example: A: いつもけんこうに気をつけていますか。
B: ええ、いつも気をつけています。
A: じゃあ、どんなことをしていますか。
B: よくやさいを食べています。

	パートナーのこたえ			
けんこうに気をつけている	いつも	よく	あまり	ぜんぜん
ダイエットをしている	よく	ときどき	あまり	ぜんぜん
マッサージをする	よく	ときどき	あまり	ぜんぜん
休(やす)む	よく	ときどき	あまり	ぜんぜん
よこになる	よく	ときどき	あまり	ぜんぜん
はたらく	よく	ときどき	あまり	ぜんぜん
たばこをすう	よく	ときどき	あまり	ぜんぜん
よるおそくまで起きている	たいてい	ときどき	あまり	ぜんぜん
むりをする	よく	ときどき	あまり	ぜんぜん
ストレスをかんじる (*to feel*)	よく	ときどき	あまり	ぜんぜん

B. 体(からだ) The body

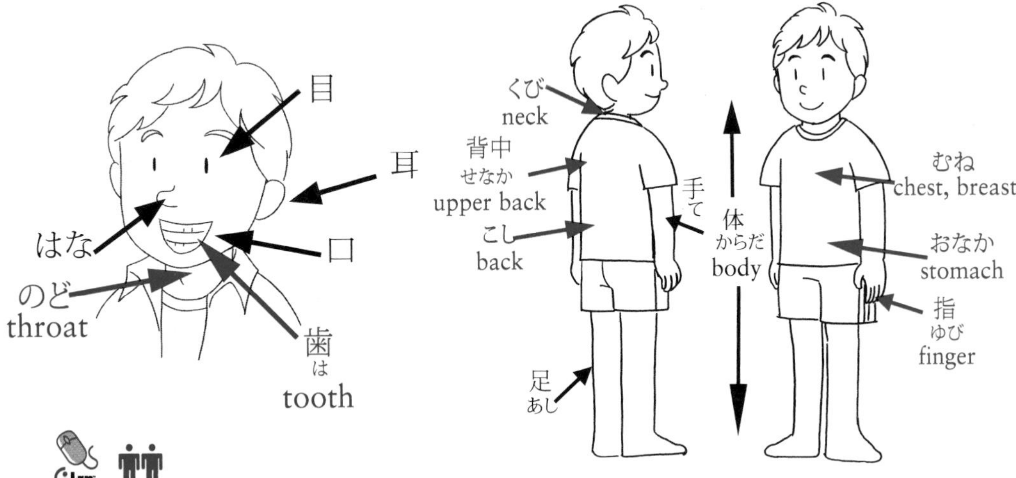

Activity 3 Work with a partner. As soon as your partner calls out a part of the body, point to the corresponding part on your own body. Take turns.

Activity 4 Work with a partner. Clap your hands together twice, then play "rock-paper-scissors" in Japanese. The person who wins should name a part of the body. The other person points to the corresponding part on his/her own body. Then play it again as fast as you can.

Supplementary Vocabulary 体(からだ) (Other parts of the body)

あしくび	足首	ankle	かた	肩	shoulder
い	胃	stomach	つめ	爪	nail
うで	腕	arm	てくび	手首	wrist

C. 体(からだ)のもんだいとしょうじょう
Physical problems and symptoms

熱(ねつ)がある・出(で)る
to have a fever

風邪(かぜ)をひく
to catch a cold

けがをする
to have an injury

指(ゆび)を切(き)る
to cut a finger

はく
to vomit

はながつまる
to have a stuffy nose

かたがこる
to have stiff shoulders

おぼえていますか。

(熱(ねつ)が) 上がる　(熱(ねつ)が) 下がる　強(つよ)い　よわい

Activity 5 しつもんに日本語でこたえて下さい。

1. 体(からだ)は強(つよ)い方ですか。よわい方ですか。
2. アレルギーがありますか。何のアレルギーですか。
3. アレルギーのしょうじょうにはどんなものがありますか。
4. よく風邪(かぜ)をひきますか。
5. 風邪(かぜ)のしょうじょうにはどんなものがありますか。
6. しごとや勉強(べんきょう)をたくさんした後、どうなりますか。

Activity 6 Work with a group. One person acts out one of the situations below and the rest of the group identifies what situation is being acted out. Complete all of these as fast as you can. The first group to finish wins.

頭(あたま)が痛(いた)い　目がかゆい　指(ゆび)を切(き)る　こしが痛(いた)い　背中(せなか)がかゆい　かたがこる
せきが出(で)る　くびがこる　熱(ねつ)がある　足が痛(いた)い　はながつまる　気持(きも)ちがわるい
おなかが痛(いた)い　風邪(かぜ)をひく　つかれる

Supplementary Vocabulary けがとしょうじょう (Other injuries and symptoms)

あたまががんがんする	頭ががんがんする	to have a pounding headache
きりきりする		to have a sharp pain
げりする	下痢する	to have diarrhea
ずきずきする		to have a throbbing pain
はきけがする	吐き気がする	to feel nausea
はなみずがでる	鼻水がでる	to have a runny nose
はれる	腫れる	to swell
ひりひりする		to have a stinging pain
ふるえる	震える	to tremble
ほねをおる	骨を折る	to break a bone
めまいがする		to feel dizzy

D. 病気(びょうき)の時にすることしないこと
Things you do or don't do when you are sick

薬(くすり)を飲む
to take(drink) medicine

薬(くすり)をつける
to apply medicine

医者(いしゃ)に行く
to go to a doctor

入院(にゅういん)する
to be hospitalized

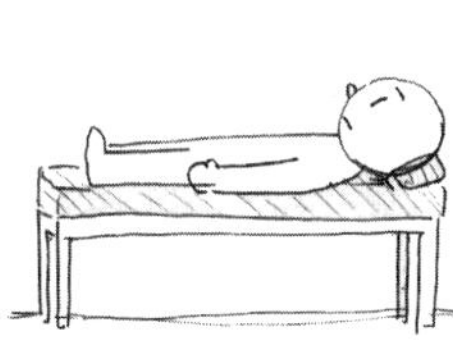

よこになる
to lie down

口をあける
to open one's mouth

熱(ねつ)をはかる
to take one's temperature

体(からだ)をうごかす
to move one's body

いきをすう
to inhale

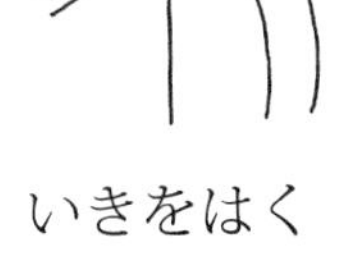

いきをはく
to exhale

いきをとめる
to hold one's breath

うごく
to move

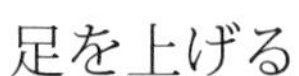

足を上げる
to raise one's legs

足を下げる
to lower one's legs

学校を休(やす)む
to be absent from school

走(はし)る
to run

おぼえていますか。

しずかにする

Activity 7 Work with a partner. You are a doctor and your partner is a patient. Give a command in the following situations and your partner will act it out.

1. You want to check his/her pulse.
2. You want to examine his/her throat.
3. You want to examine his/her stomach.
4. You want to take his/her chest X-ray.
5. You want to check his/her temperature.
6. You want to see if he/she feels any pain when moving his/her arms and legs.

Activity 8 しつもんに日本語でこたえて下さい。

1. あなたはおなかが痛(いた)い時、何をしますか。あなたの国(くに) (*country*) の人はどうですか。
2. あなたは頭(あたま)が痛(いた)い時、何をしますか。あなたの国(くに) (*country*) の人はどうですか。
3. 一年にどのぐらい医者(いしゃ)に行きますか。どんな時、医者(いしゃ)に行きますか。
4. 入院(にゅういん)したことがありますか。いつ入院(にゅういん)しましたか。どうして入院(にゅういん)しましたか。

Supplementary Vocabulary: Expressions doctors and nurses use

ここはどうですか。	How does it feel here?
大きく口をあけて下さい。	Please open your mouth wide.
上だけぬいで下さい。	Please take off your top (shirt, blouse, etc.).
後ろをむいて下さい。	Please turn around.
あおむけになって下さい。	Please lie on your back.
うつぶせになって下さい。	Please lie face down.
大きくいきをすって下さい。	Please take a deep breath.

ダイアローグ

はじめに

しつもんに日本語でこたえて下さい。

1. 病気(びょうき)の時何をしますか。
2. 風邪(かぜ)はどんなしょうじょうですか。

熱(ねつ)があるんです。 *I have a fever.*

The order of the following **manga** frames is scrambled. Read the dialogue and unscramble the frames by writing the correct number in the box in each frame.

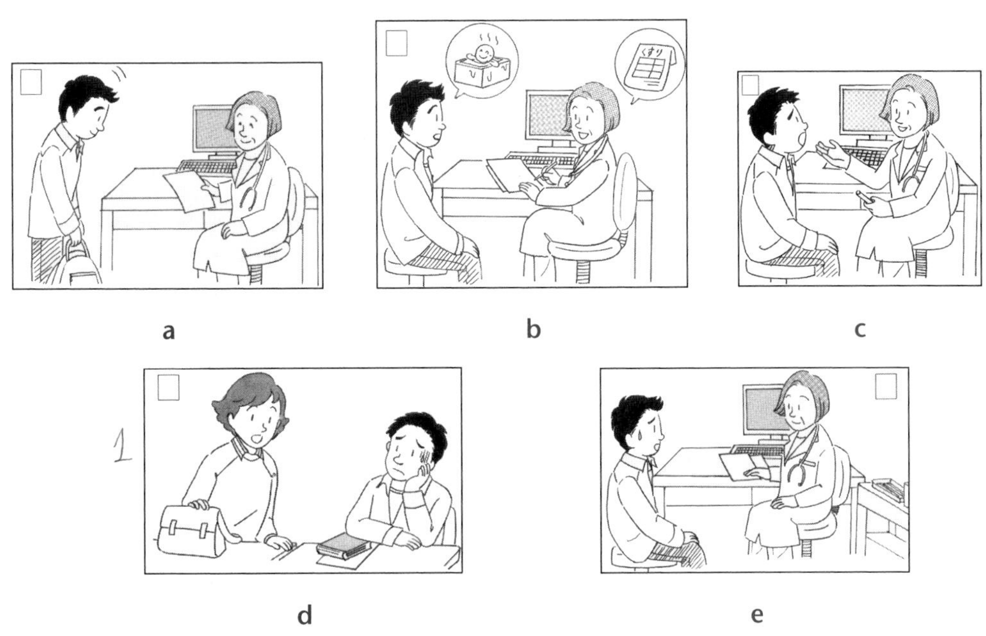

上田さんは石田(いし)さんに大学で会いました。

上田： あ、石田(いし)さん、おはよう。

石田(いし)： おはよう。

上田： どうしたの、石田(いし)さん、ちょっと顔色(かおいろ)がわるいけど。

石田(いし)： ああ、昨日から気分(きぶん)がわるくて、何も食べられないんだ。

上田： 大変(へん)。病院(びょういん)行ったの？

石田(いし)： ううん、まだ。

上田：　じゃあ、早(はや)く行った方がいいよ。

石田(いし)：　でも、今日はテストがあるから。

上田：　だけど、むりしすぎてわるくならないように、早(はや)く行った方がいいよ。

石田(いし)：　そうかな。じゃあ、後で行くよ。

石田(いし)さんは病院(びょういん)に来ました。

医者(いしゃ)：　どうしましたか。

石田(いし)：　朝から、気分(きぶん)がわるいんです。

医者(いしゃ)：　そうですか。じゃあ、ちょっと熱(ねつ)をはかりましょう。

お医者(いしゃ)さんは石田(いし)さんの熱(ねつ)をはかりました。

医者(いしゃ)：　八度五分(ぶ)ありますね。じゃあ、口を大きくあけて下さい。

石田(いし)：　はい。

石田(いし)さんは口をあけます。

医者(いしゃ)：　だいぶあかいですね。せきは出ますか。

石田(いし)：　いいえ、せきはないんですが、のどが痛(いた)くて、食べられないんです。

医者(いしゃ)：　そうですか。じゃあ、薬(くすり)を出(だ)しますから、それを飲んで二、三日家でよく休(やす)んで下さい。

石田(いし)：　あのう、先生、おふろに入ってもいいですか。

医者(いしゃ)：　おふろですか、入らない方がいいですね。シャワーはいいですよ。

石田(いし)：　はい、分かりました。どうもありがとうございました。

医者(いしゃ)：　いいえ、それじゃあ、お大事(だいじ)に。

Dialogue Phrase Notes

- ううん、まだ means *no*, *not yet*.
- 八度五分(ぶ) is 38.5℃, which is 101.3°F.
- だいぶ means *fairly*.

ダイアローグの後で

A. しつもんに日本語でこたえて下さい。

1. 石田さんはどうして病院に行ったんですか。
2. どんなしょうじょうでしたか。
3. 石田さんの病気は何だと思いますか。
4. 石田さんはおふろに入れますか。
5. 石田さんは何をしてもいいですか。

B. You are Alice Ueda. Complete the following entry in her diary by filling in the appropriate phrases.

今朝、石田さんに会った。石田さんは、____________わるくて、____________そうだった。だから、石田さんは病院に____________と思った。

amana images inc. / Alamy

Young nurse and doctor listening to senior doctor

© Everett Kennedy Brown/epa/Corbis

Japanese man wearing mask outside the Japan Red Cross Hospital near Tokyo's Narita International Airport where the first confirmed swine influenza patients in Japan are being hospitalized, Narita city, Chiba province, Japan, 09 May 2009.

amana images inc. / Alamy

Japanese nurse and doctor at the pharmacy in hospital

日本の文化 (ぶんか)

長生き (ながい) Longevity

The 2007 UN Human Development Report states that the Japanese have the longest lifespan in the world. According to 2006 statistics from the Ministry of Health and Labor, the average lifespan of Japanese men is 79.0 years and that of Japanese women is 86.81 years. This is considerably higher than the average life span of Americans (76.2 years for men and 80.4 years for women). In addition, Japan has one of the lowest infant mortality rates (2.8 infants per 1,000 infants) in the world. It is slightly higher than Singapore (2.3/1,000) and Sweden (2.76 /1,000) but much lower than countries like the U.S. (6.3/1000), Canada and England (4.8/1,000), and France and Spain (4.2/1,000). Let's look at what's behind these numbers for Japan.

The World Health Organization (2000) reported that Japan provides one of the best healthcare systems in the world among 191 member countries. Virtually all residents of Japan are covered with one of many insurance programs, regardless of any pre-existing conditions they have or any actuarial risk of succumbing to illness. Premiums are affordable because they are based on income and ability to pay. The poorest can be supported by the national health insurance program offered by the government, which allows them to see the doctor without worrying about cost. National health insurance, which covers approximately 80 percent of all medical expenses, is available to both Japanese and foreigners who plan to stay in Japan for more than a year. Application forms are available at local ward or municipal offices. Those who plan to stay in Japan for less than a year can be easily covered by one of many private insurance programs. Japanese companies provide their employees with medical insurance regardless of nationality.

Another reason for the longevity is in the Japanese diet. Japanese people are generally very conscious about health benefits. Their eating habits are often based on asking questions like "What would be good for me?" rather than "What do I feel like eating?" As a result, the Japanese have the lowest consumption rate of saturated fat among more developed countries.

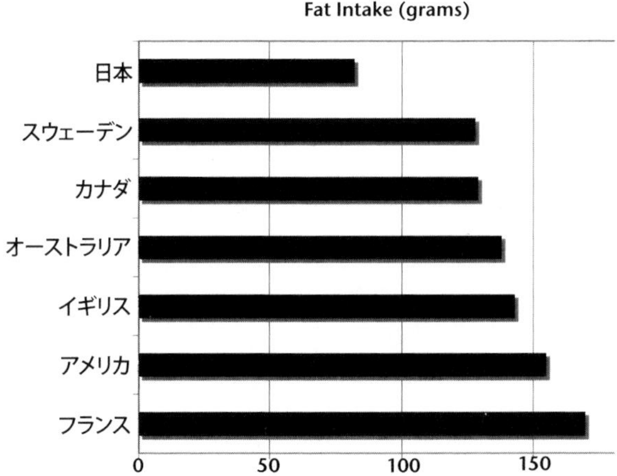

(Food and Agricultural Organization of the United Nations, 2001)

The Japanese eat more fish than red meat, which lowers the risk of heart attacks. Also, they consume a variety of soy products—a great source of protein that reduces heart disease and high blood pressure. In addition, Japanese green tea has numerous health benefits because it contains powerful antioxidants and inhibits the growth of cancer cells. Moreover, the Japanese eat small portions of food. Most Japanese portions are half the size of portions in the U.S. As a result, most Japanese men and women are thin, and it is rather uncommon to see overweight people.

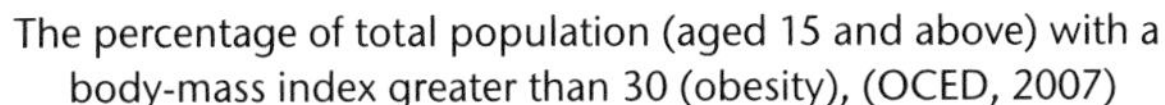

The percentage of total population (aged 15 and above) with a
body-mass index greater than 30 (obesity), (OCED, 2007)

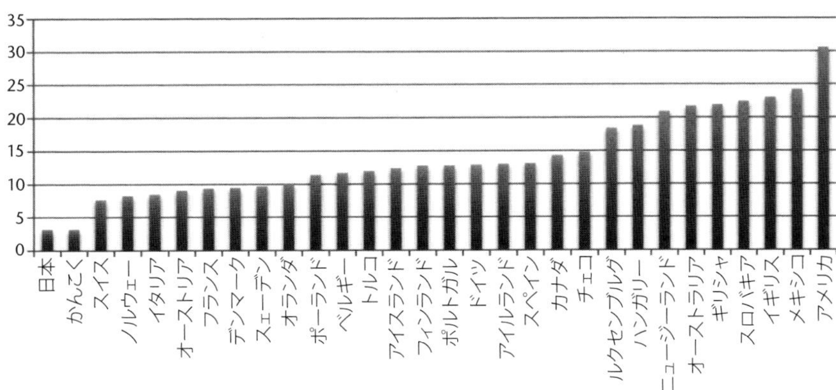

日本の病院(びょういん) Japanese hospitals

There are two types of hospitals in Japan: general hospitals and private clinics. General hospitals handle a full range of medical problems and are equipped with the latest medical technology as well as complete hospitalization facilities. A patient, however, cannot choose a certain doctor or expect to see the same doctor each time. Also, general hospitals tend to be very crowded.

Private clinics are usually run by one or two doctors. Each doctor treats patients in his/her area of specialization and handles less complicated surgeries and routine illnesses. More complicated procedures are referred to specialists at general hospitals. With a smaller clientele, doctors at private clinics see patients on a long-term basis and are also available for informal consultations. These doctors play a role similar to that of a family doctor in the U.S.

Many Japanese doctors do not speak English, though some are able to understand it or write medical terms in English. Schools, embassies and consulates generally maintain lists of hospitals or clinics with personnel who speak English and other languages.

When a patient is diagnosed as having a terminal illness, the doctor often does not tell the patient before consulting the patient's family first. Traditionally, it has been considered cruel for a doctor to tell a patient the truth about a terminal illness, and it is left up to the family to decide whether or not to tell the patient.

In Japan, a medical doctor is addressed as 先生. The term 先生 can be used for any figure of authority whether he/she is a school teacher, master craftsman, religious leader, political leader, lawyer, or instructor in general. The term is not used within companies or business organizations. Instead, rank titles such as section head or department chief are used.

文法(ぶんぽう)

I. Expressing capability using the potential form of verbs

The potential form of verbs expresses what a person can do or what is possible. The direct object particle を is replaced by が when the verb is in the potential form.

		Particle	Verb potential form (negative)
かたが痛(いた)くて	手	が	うごかせません。

I have a shoulder ache, so I cannot move my hands.

田中：どうしたんですか。 *What's wrong?*
友田：歯(は)が痛(いた)くて寝られなかったんです。 *I had a toothache, so I couldn't sleep.*
田中：そうですか。それは大変(へん)ですね。 *Is that so? I'm sorry to hear that.* (lit., *That is awful/terrible, isn't it*)

医者(いしゃ)： 右(みぎ)手が上げられますか。 *Can you raise your right hand?*
かんじゃ (*patient*)： はい、上げられます。 *Yes, I can.*
医者(いしゃ)： じゃあ、左(ひだり)手はどうですか。 *How about the left hand?*
かんじゃ (*patient*)： 痛(いた)くて、上げられません。 *It's too painful to raise.*

う -verbs

The potential form of a う-verb is formed by changing /u/ sound in the dictionary form to /e/ る.

Dictionary form	Potential forms			
	Plain present		Polite present	
	Affirmative	Negative	Affirmative	Negative
すう (*to inhale*)	すえる	すえない	すえます	すえません
走(はし)る (*to run*)	走(はし)れる	走(はし)れない	走(はし)れます	走(はし)れません
はたらく (*to work*)	はたらける	はたらけない	はたらけます	はたらけません
休(やす)む (*to rest*)	休(やす)める	休(やす)めない	休(やす)めます	休(やす)めません

る -verbs

The potential form of a る-verb is formed by replacing る with られる.

Dictionary form	Potential forms			
	Plain present		Polite present	
	Affirmative	Negative	Affirmative	Negative
忘れる (*to forget*) わす	忘れられる わす	忘れられない わす	忘れられます わす	忘れられません わす
起きる (*to wake up*)	起きられる	起きられない	起きられます	起きられません
つける (*to put on*)	つけられる	つけられない	つけられます	つけられません

Irregular verbs

Dictionary form	Potential forms			
	Plain present		Polite present	
	Affirmative	Negative	Affirmative	Negative
する (*to do*)	出来る でき	出来ない でき	出来ます でき	出来ません でき
来る (*to come*) く	来られる こ	来られない こ	来られます こ	来られません こ

Note: Potential forms of all verbs conjugate as る-verbs.

Verb types	Dictionary form	Potential forms				
		Plain Present		Plain Past		て -form
		Affirmative	Negative	Affirmative	Negative	
う -verb	飲む (*to drink*)	飲める	飲めない	飲めた	飲めなかった	飲めて
る -verb	寝る (*to sleep*)	寝られる	寝られない	寝られた	寝られなかった	寝られて
Irregular	する (*to do*)	出来る でき	出来ない でき	出来た でき	出来なかった でき	出来て でき

Note: there is no potential form for わかる .

話してみましょう

Form a sentence describing what each person is able to do. Be sure to choose the correct verb from the box and use が to make the direct object.

Example: ジョンソン おすし

ジョンソンさんはおすしが食べられます。

食べる 飲む

1.	ハモンド	日本語の手紙(てがみ)
2.	クラーク	朝五時
3.	木村(むら)	テニス
4.	ジョーンズ	スペイン語
5.	キム	天ぷら
6.	スペンサー	いやなこと

起きる	切(き)る	する	書く	話す	忘(わす)れる	作る

Activity 2

Work in groups of three or four. Think of a place and describe what a person can or cannot do there. The other members of the group will try to guess what the place is. Use casual speech.

Example: A: ここでは安いコーヒーが飲めたり、安い食べ物(もの)も食べられたりするよ。

B: 学食かな。

A: うん、そう。

Activity 3

Using the following sentences as reasons, make statements about what one is not able to do as a result.

Example: 風邪(かぜ)をひきました。

風邪(かぜ)をひいたから、学校に行けないんですね。

1. せきが出ます。
2. 熱(ねつ)があります。
3. アレルギーがあります。
4. はながつまっています。
5. 歯(は)が痛(いた)いです。
6. 指(ゆび)を切(き)りました。
7. つかれています。

Activity 4

Work with a partner. Using the cues below, create a conversation in which one person wonders why the other person has not performed a specified action, and the other person explains why.

Example: 食べる

A: あ、食べないんですか。

B: ええ、食べたいんですが、たまごはアレルギーで食べられないんです。

A: そうですか。ざんねんですね。

1. 朝早(はや)く起きる
2. 口を大きくあける
3. 薬(くすり)をつける
4. やせる
5. 手をうごかす
6. うごく
7. 入院(にゅういん)する
8. よこになる
9. はたらく
10. じゅぎょうを休(やす)む

II. Expressing excessiveness using ～すぎる

When すぎる is added after the stem of a verb, い-adjective, or な-adjective, it implies that something is excessive. The correct form for いい when used with すぎる is よすぎる.

薬(くすり)をつけすぎました。	*I applied too much medicine.*
寝すぎました。	*I slept too much.*
山本さんは話しすぎる。	*Ms. Yamamoto talks too much.*
このけがはひどすぎる。	*This injury is incredibly serious.*
このレモンはすっぱすぎる。	*This lemon is too sour.*
あの人は元気すぎる。	*That person is too hyper.*
このしごとは大変(へん)すぎる。	*This job is too tough.*

すぎる itself is a る-verb and follows the conjugation pattern of る-verbs:

勉強(べんきょう)をしすぎる	*does study too much*
勉強(べんきょう)をしすぎない	*does not study too much*
勉強(べんきょう)をしすぎます	*does study too much*
勉強(べんきょう)をしすぎて	*does study too much and ～*

リン：	どうしたんですか。	*What's wrong?*
山本：	歩(ある)きすぎて、足が痛(いた)いんです。	*I walked too much, so my feet hurt.*
リン：	大丈夫(じょうぶ)ですか。	*Are you OK?*
山本：	いや、痛(いた)すぎて、くつがはけません。	*No, it hurts too much to put on my shoes.*

話してみましょう

Activity 1 Excessive behavior can cause problems. Describe what type of behavior could cause the following problems, using the verb stem + すぎる.

Example: よる、寝られない

インターネットをしすぎて、よる、寝られないんです。

1. 頭(あたま)が痛(いた)い
2. ストレスがある
3. つかれた
4. 朝早(はや)く起きられない
5. いきが出来(でき)ない
6. 気分(きぶん)がわるい
7. 足が痛(いた)い
8. うごけない

Activity 2 Work with a partner. Use the pictures as a basis to make conversations between two friends. Use the example conversation below.

Example:

A: どうしたの?

B: 食べすぎて、おなかが痛(いた)いんだ/の。

A: 大丈夫(だいじょうぶ)?

B: ええ、まあ (*so-so*)。

Activity 3

Work with a partner. One person is a customer and the other person is a store clerk. Have a conversation based on the information provided about the items in the chart below. Be sure to talk about the size, length, and price of the items.

Example: セーター

店の人：いかがですか。

おきゃくさん：色(いろ) (*color*) は好きなんですけど、ちょっと大きすぎますね。
もう少し小さいのはありませんか。

店の人：はい、ございます。こちらはいかがでしょうか。

おきゃくさん：いいですね。これにします。

もの	色(いろ)	大きさ・サイズ	ながさ (*length*)	ねだん (*cost*)
シャツ	OK	too small	OK	OK
パンツ	OK	OK	too long	OK
ジャケット	too bright	OK	too short	OK
かばん	OK	too big	OK	too expensive

III. Giving suggestions using ～たらどうですか and ～方がいいです

The expressions ～たらどうですか and ～方がいいです are used for making suggestions or giving advice. ～方がいいです (*it's better to* ～, *you should* ～) is stronger than ～たらどうですか (*How about doing* ～, *why don't you* ～).

A. ～たらどうですか

The form ～たらどうですか is made by adding ら to the plain past affirmative form of a verb. ～たら is called the conditional form of the verb and has many functions which you will learn in later chapters. Using でしょうか instead of ですか softens the entire expression and makes it sounds more polite.

よこになったらどうですか。 *How would it be if you lie down?* *(How about lying down?)*

入院(にゅういん)したらどうですか。 *How about checking into a hospital?*

薬(くすり)を飲んだらどう？ *How about taking some medicine?*

リー：どうしたの？ *What's wrong?*

山口：足が痛(いた)くて歩(ある)けないの。 *My feet hurt, so I can't walk.*

リー：少し休(やす)んだらどう？ *Why don't you take a rest?*

B. 〜た方がいいです／〜ない方がいいです

The plain past affirmative or plain present negative of a verb with 方がいいです means *you should or should not do* 〜.

バスにのった方がいいです。	*It's better to ride the bus. (You should ride).*
バスにのらない方がいいです。	*It's better not to ride the bus. (You shouldn't ride.)*
薬(くすり)をつけた方がいいです。	*It's better to apply some medicine. (You should apply some medicine.)*
薬(くすり)をつけない方がいいです。	*It's better not to apply any medicine. (You should not apply any medicine.)*

パク： どうしたの？
What's the matter?

東山： 足がすごくかゆいのよ。
My feet itch badly.

パク： 見せて。ああ、これは、ちょっとひどいね。薬(くすり)をつけた方がいいよ。
Show me. It looks really bad. You should put on some medicine.

東山： 今、持(も)っていないの。
But I don't have any.

パク： あそこにコンビニがあるから、買いに行ったらどう？
There's a convenience store over there, so how about going to get some?

話してみましょう

Activity 1 Change each of the following into a suggestion using 〜たらどうですか.

Example: 早(はや)くしゅくだいを出(だ)す
早(はや)くしゅくだいを出(だ)したらどうですか。

1. マッサージに行く
2. 体(からだ)をうごかす
3. はく
4. 薬(くすり)をつける
5. 入院(にゅういん)する
6. 熱(ねつ)をはかる
7. よく寝る
8. 学校を休(やす)む

Activity 2 Work with the class. Think of a physical condition such as having a cold or not being able to sleep. Get suggestions from your classmates in casual speech and report them in formal speech.

Example: A: どうしたの？

B: 風邪(かぜ)をひいて、熱(ねつ)があるんだ／の。

A: そう。じゃ、家に帰ってよく休(やす)んだらどう？

B: そう（だ）ね。じゃあ、そうする（ね）。

A: お大事(だいじ)に。

to class:

家に帰ってよく休(やす)んだらいいそうです。

Activity 3 Make suggestions for each of the following conditions, using the list in the box. Make both positive and negative suggestions.

Example: おなかが痛(いた)い時

薬(くすり)を飲んだ方がいいですよ。それから、あまり食べすぎない方がいいですよ。

薬(くすり)を飲む	薬(くすり)をつける	病院(びょういん)に行く	歩(ある)く
友だちとあそぶ	勉強(べんきょう)する	むりをする	家でよく寝る
体(からだ)に気をつける	うんどうする	ゆっくりする	(other verbs)

1. のどが痛(いた)い時
2. こしが痛(いた)い時
3. 目が痛(いた)い時
4. アレルギーの時
5. 風邪(かぜ)のしょうじょうがある時 (*when you have*)
6. 足のけががある時 (*when you have*)

IV. Describing what efforts are being made to attain a specific goal using ～ように

The clause preceding ように takes the plain present form of the verb. It indicates a situation or state which the speaker hopes to attain, so the verb preceding ように tends to be in the negative form, the potential form, or to be a verb that does not indicate an intentional action. The main clause describes the efforts being made to attain that state.

風邪(かぜ)をひかないように、あたたかくする。
I will keep myself warm so as not to catch a cold.

熱(ねつ)が早(はや)く下がるように、薬(くすり)を出(だ)しましょう。
I will prescribe some medicine so that the temperature will go down quickly.

きれいにやせられるように、ダイエットをします。
I will go on a diet so that I can lose weight nicely.

かたがこらないように、毎日うんどうします。
I will do exercises every day to prevent stiff shoulders.

スミス： 山川さんは本当(とう)にけんこうですね。
何かしているんですか。
Mr. Yamakawa, you are really healthy, aren't you?
Are you doing something to stay that way?

山川： ええ、病気(びょうき)にならないように、よく寝て、よく食べて、
よくうんどうしています。
Well, I sleep well, eat well, and exercise a lot in order not to get sick.

話してみましょう

Activity 1 Match the sentence halves in Column A and Column B to make sentences using ～ように　～ます。

Example: 1. 日本語が上手になります ／ g. 毎日日本人と話します
日本語が上手になるように、毎日日本人と話します。

Column A	Column B
1. 日本語が上手になります	a. 毎日千メートルおよぎます
2. 寒い日に風邪(かぜ)をひきません	b. 少し休(やす)みます
3. 早(はや)くやせられます	c. セーターとコートをきます
4. つかれません	d. ノートに書きます
5. 明日のしごとのことを忘(わす)れません	e. たくさん勉強(べんきょう)します
6. 晩御飯(ごはん)がおいしく食べられます	f. 今は何も食べたくありません
7. 先生のしつもんにこたえられます	g. 毎日日本人と話します

Activity 2

Work with a partner. You are radio talk hosts discussing various concerns sent in by your listeners. Assuming that you are on-air, read each of the concerns and discuss possible solutions.

Example: 私の子供はやさいが食べられません。

A: この人のお子さんはやさいを食べられないそうですね。

B: やさいが食べられるように、カレーに入れたらどうでしょうか。

A: いいですね。

B: A さんはどう思いますか。

A: そうですね。分からないように、小さく切(き)ったらどうですか。

1. 私の妹ははやく走(はし)れません。
2. 私の弟はじてんしゃにのれません。
3. 私の父はおさけがやめられません。(やめる = *to quit*)
4. 私の母はおよげません。

Activity 3

Work with the class. First write down what kind of preventative care you take against the following conditions. Then ask your classmates about what they do, and tally the results. Use casual speech.

Example: A: 病気(びょうき)にならないように、どんなことに気をつけているの?

B: そう(だ)ね。私は毎朝ジョギングしてるよ。

	私	クラスメート
病気(びょうき)になる		
ふとる		
元気がなくなる		

V. Making a negative request using ～ないで下さい; expressing unacceptable actions or situations using ～てはいけない; asking for and giving permission using ～てもいい

て-forms are used in a variety of structures. ～ないで下さい expresses a negative request, and it means *please don't do* ～. ～てはいけない means *it is not OK to do* ～ and is used to express prohibition. ～てもいい, on the other hand, means *it is OK to do* ～ and is used to ask for and give permission.

A. Making a negative request using ～ないで下さい

The negative form of a verb + で下さい expresses a polite negative request. In casual speech, 下さい is dropped.

風邪(かぜ)のしょうじょうがある時は、お風呂(ふろ)に入らないで下さい。
Don't take a bath when you have cold symptoms.

病気(びょうき)の時は、うんどうしないで下さい。
Don't exercise when you are sick.

こしが痛(いた)い時は、うごかないで下さい。
Don't move when you have a backache.

つかれている時にはむりをしないで。
Don't overstrain yourself when you're tired.

かさを持って行くのを忘(わす)れないで。
Don't forget to bring your umbrella.

B. ～てはいけない

The て-form + はいけない／だめ indicates that something is not allowed. This structure is commonly used to talk about rules. The colloquial form of ～てはいけない is ～ちゃ／じゃいけない.

このへやに一人で入ってはいけません。 *You may not enter this room by yourself.*

学校を休(やす)んではいけません。 *You must not be absent from school.*

レポートを忘(わす)れたりおそく出(だ)したりしてはいけません。 *You must not forget your paper and turn it in late.*

おそくまで起きていちゃだめです。 *It is not acceptable to stay up late.*

だれともあそんじゃいけないよ。 *You may not play with anyone.*

じゅぎょうにおくれちゃだめだよ。 *It is not acceptable to be late for class.*

健二(けんじ)： ぼく、くるまで行くよ。

I will go by car.

高子： おさけ飲んでるから、うんてん (*drive*) しちゃだめよ。

No, you shouldn't drive because you drank alcohol.

〜てはいけない takes the て-form of verbs and adjectives.

	Plain Present Forms	〜てはいけない／だめ 〜くちゃいけない／だめ	Meaning
Copula verb	この薬(くすり)だ	この薬(くすり)では・この薬(くすり)じゃいけない／だめ	*must not be this medicine*
な-adjectives	きらいだ	きらいでは・きらいじゃいけない／だめ	*must not dislike*
い-adjectives	よわい	よわくては・よわくちゃいけない／だめ	*must not be weak*
Irregular verbs	来る	来ては・来ちゃいけない／だめ	*must not come*
	する	しては・しちゃいけない／だめ	*must not do*
う-verbs	休(やす)む	休(やす)んでは・休(やす)んじゃいけない／だめ	*must not rest/take a day off*
る-verbs	いる	いては・いちゃいけない／だめ	*must not stay*

Note

- When answering a question with the て-form + は　いけませんか／だめですか, use ええ、いけません／だめです to prohibit an action. Use いいえ、いいです to permit the action.

田中：この薬(くすり)を飲んではいけませんか。

Can't I take this medicine?

医者(いしゃ)：ええ、（飲んでは）いけません。

No, you may not.

or　いいえ、（飲んでも）いいですよ。

Yes, you may.

C. 〜てもいい It is OK to~, can, may

The て-form of verbs + もいいですか／いいでしょうか／かまいませんか is used to ask for permission. 〜てもいいでしょうか is more tentative and thus more polite than 〜てもいいですか, but it can also be used toward someone in one's peer group. 〜てもかまいませんか

is as polite as ～てもいいでしょうか. Although it ends in the negative, the way you answer is the same as ～てもいいでしょうか.

うごいてもいいですか／うごいてもいい？	*Is it okay for me to move?* (more casual)
うごいてもいいでしょうか／うごいてもいい？	*May I move?*
うごいてもかまいませんか／うごこいてもかまわない？	*May I move?*

学生：先生、今日は早(はや)く帰ってもいいでしょうか。
Professor, may I go home early today?

先生：え、どうしてですか。
Oh, why?

学生：気持(きも)ちがわるくて、はきそうなんです。
I don't feel good; I feel like I'm going to vomit.

先生：そうですか。じゃあ、今すぐ帰ってもいいですよ。
Oh, is that so? That's fine./You may go home right away.

学生：ありがとうございます。
Thank you very much.

先生：お大事(だいじ)に。
Take care.

Notes

- The following are common ways to respond positively to a request.

  はい／ええ、どうぞ。
  Yes, please go ahead.

  はい／ええ、かまいません／かまわない（よ）。
  That's fine. I don't mind.

  ええ、もちろん。
  Yes, of course.

  Although はい、いいです is grammatically correct, it would only be used when a superior is granting permission to a social inferior.

- Answering negatively can be awkward. Think of how you would deny a request in your own language. Using ～てはいけない may be one way to respond, but it can also sound rude, unless you are in position of authority or you are explaining a rule. As in many other countries, the Japanese tend to avoid direct statements of prohibition such as "No, you may not" and use instead phrases such as:

  すみませんが、ちょっと。
  I am sorry.

ええっと、それはちょっと。
Well, that would be a bit . . .

すみません、それはちょっとこまります。
I am sorry. That would be a little troublesome.

In such situations, the word ちょっと serves to deflect whatever tension may arise from withholding permission. It also saves the respondent from spelling out his/her reasons for denying permission.

話してみましょう

Activity 1 Look at the pictures of people suffering from certain physical ailments. You are a doctor. Tell the patients what not do using 〜ないで下さい and 〜て下さい.

Example:

ひどいせきが出ていますから、今日はどこにも出かけないで下さい。

出かけないで下さい。薬(くすり)を飲んで下さい。

Activity 2

Change each sentence to a question asking for permission using ～たい and ～てもいいですか／いいでしょうか／かまいませんか. You will need to come up with the context for each request.

Example: ゆっくりする

<u>つかれたので、ゆっくりしたいんですが、ゆっくりしてもいいですか／いいでしょうか／かまいませんか。</u>

1. 家に帰る
2. 足を上(あ)げる
3. 一緒(しょ)に行く
4. 熱(ねつ)をはかる
5. じゅぎょうを休(やす)む
6. よるおそくまで起きている
7. えんぴつで書く
8. よこになる

Activity 3

State what is or is not acceptable in each of the following places, using the expressions provided and ～てもいいです／～てはいけない／～ないで下さい.

Example: りょうのラウンジ (*lounge*) ではコーヒーを飲んでもいいですが、たばこをすってはいけません／たばこはすわないで下さい。

1. きょうしつ
2. 病院(びょういん)
3. 図(と)書館(かん)
4. じんじゃやおてら
5. おばあさんの家
6. レストラン

Activity 4

Work with a partner. Think of three places and write them in the boxes labeled 1, 2, and 3. Your partner does the same. Now you and your partner will try to figure out what each of the three places is by asking questions using ～てもいいですか／いいでしょうか／かまいませんか. You may ask only one question and make one guess at a time. The first one to reach ゴール (*goal*) wins.

Example:
A: ここでテレビを見てもいいですか。
B: いいえ、見ない方がいいですよ。
A: きょうしつですか。
B: いいえ、そうじゃないんですよ。

パートナー [1] → [2] → [3] → ゴール！

聞く練習(れんしゅう)

上手な聞き方

Using the setting as a clue

What you know about a setting gives you a lot of clues about the type of speech you hear. For example, the content of a conversation will be very different if you are in a doctor's office, at school, or in a restaurant. Also, you will use different phrases and words for the same topic depending on if you are at school or at home. The setting gives you clues about the content of a conversation, choice of words and phrases, and much more. The setting not only implies different places but also different times of the day. A conversation in the morning may be very different from one in the afternoon in context and in effectiveness, even if you are talking to the same person.

いつどこで何がありましたか。

Listen to each conversation and try to identify where it took place. Circle the place name. Then write what happened in the blank.

1. 学校　　病院(びょういん)　　デパート　　家

____

2. 病院(びょういん)　　デパート　　学校　　レストラン

____

3. 病院(びょういん)　　レストラン　　学校　　デパート

____

病院(びょういん)で

聞く前に

A. 下のしつもんに日本語でこたえて下さい。

1. 病院(びょういん)のうけつけ (*reception desk*) でどんあことを言いますか。
2. しんかん (*new patient*) の人は病院(びょういん)のうけつけ (*reception desk*) で何をしますか。
3. かふんしょう (*hay fever*) にはどんなしょうじょうがありますか。
4, かふんしょう (*hay fever*) の人はどんなことをしてはいけませんか。
5. かふんしょう (*hay fever*) の人はどんなことをしたらいいでしょうか。

B. 下のえを見て、何がおきているのかいって下さい。(*Say what is happening*)

聞いた後で

A. Rearrange the above pictures based on the order in which the actions have taken place.

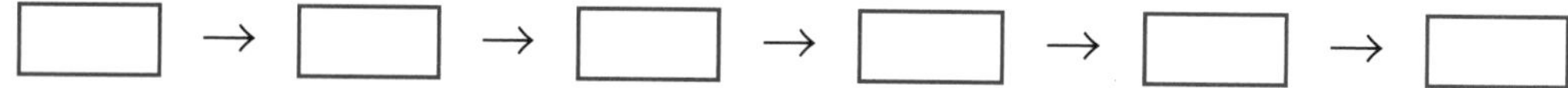

B. もう一度、会話(かいわ) (*conversation*) の前半(ぜんはん) (*first half*) を聞いて、しつもんに日本語でこたえて下さい。

1. 女の人はパーカーさんです。パーカーンさんはどうして病院(びょういん)に来ましたか。
2. 「ようし」って何ですか。
3. パーカーさんは何が出来(でき)ないのですか。

C. もう一度、会話(かいわ) (*conversation*) の後半(こうはん) (*last half*) を聞いて、しつもんに日本語でこたえて下さい。

1. 医者(いしゃ)はパーカーさんにどんなしつもんをしましたか。
2. 医者(いしゃ)によると、かふんしょう (*hay fever*) はどんな病気(びょうき)だそうですか。
3. パーカーさんは何をしてはいけませんか。

聞き上手　話し上手

医者と話す

Going to a hospital can be nerve-wracking, especially when you are not familiar with the language. Even for native speakers, Japanese medical terms can be difficult to understand, so it is important to ask for clarification. Some useful phrases are:

はじめてなんですが。	I'm a new patient. (lit.: *this is my first time.*)
（日本語が）よく分からないんです。	I don't understand (Japanese) well.
もう少しやさしいことばで言って下さい。	Please say it with easier words.
これは何の薬ですか。	What is this medicine for?
一日に何回飲みますか。	How many times a day should I take it?

A. Your instructor will be the doctor or a receptionist at a hospital and ask you questions or make requests. Respond accordingly.

B. Look at the pictures on page 52. Your instructor will be the nurse. Think about a physical problem you may want to discuss with a nurse, then tell the nurse about it and ask whether you can or cannot do the things illustrated on page 52.

漢字(かんじ)

Left-side component shapes of kanji

As mentioned in Chapter 7 of *Nakama 1*, component shapes appearing on the left side of **kanji** indicate a rough semantic category of **kanji**. The following chart shows some common left-side component shapes that you've seen so far. Examples in parentheses show the use of the component shape in a different location, or cases where a radical is used as a character by itself. If the component shape is a traditional radical, the name of the radical is listed. Component shapes that are not radicals do not have particular names. We use the concept of component shapes strictly as a pedagogical tool, and there might be discrepancies between the explanations in this book and those in traditional **kanji** dictionaries.

Names		Meaning	Examples	Related kanji
さんずい	氵	water	泳(およ)ぐ　海(うみ)　湖(みずうみ)　泊(と)まる	川
つちへん	土	land, soil	地(ち)	土
にんべん	亻	person	何　休　体(からだ)　住(す)む	人
てへん	扌	hand	指(ゆび)　持(も)つ　拾(ひろ)う (*to pick up*)　払(はら)う (*to pay*)	手
にちへん・ひへん	日	day, sun	明るい　昨日　晩　時　晴　暗(くら)い　日曜日	日　朝
しめすへん・ねへん	礻	god, shrine	お礼(れい)　神社(じんじゃ)　お祝(いわ)い	
きへん	木	tree	校　林(はやし)　机(つくえ)　橋(はし)　枚(まい)	木　本　東　来　末　親
しょくへん	飠	eating	飲　ご飯(はん)　体育館(たいいくかん)	食
ゆみへん	弓	bow	引く　強(つよ)い	弱(よわ)い　弟
かねへん	金	metal, gold	銀行(ぎん)　鉄(てつ) (*iron*)　鉱(こう) (*mineral*)	金
おんなへん	女	female	好き　姉　妹　結婚(けっこん)	女
かたへん	方	direction	家族　旅行(りょ)	方
ぎょうにんべん	彳	way	行く　後　待(ま)つ	
ごんべん	言	say, language	話　語	言う
のぎへん	禾	crop	私　秋	

いとへん	糸	thread	紙　予約(よやく)　結婚(けっこん)	糸(いと) (*thread*)
たへん	田	rice field	町	田　畑(はたけ) (*field*)
つきへん	月	moon	服(ふく)	月　朝
にくづき	肉	meat	胸(むね)　脚(あし)　腹(ふく)　脱(ぬ)ぐ	肉(にく)
こへん	子	child	孫(まご)	子

Flashcards

Kanji	Meaning	Readings	Examples
病	sickness	やま(い)　ビョウ	病気(びょうき)になる。病院(びょういん)に行く。
院	institution	イン	入院(にゅういん)する。大学院(いん)をそつぎょうする。
医	medical	イ	医者(いしゃ)になる。山田医院(いいん)は大きい病院(びょういん)です。
者	person	もの　シャ	今日は歯医者(はいしゃ)に行きます。
体	body	からだ　タイ・テイ	体(からだ)が大きい。体(からだ)がうごかない。
歯	tooth	は　シ	歯(は)が痛(いた)い。歯医者(はいしゃ)に行く。
変	strange, to change	か(わる)　ヘン	大変(たいへん)です。変(へん)な人がいます。
熱	heat, fever	あつ(い)　ネツ	熱(ねつ)がある。熱(あつ)いコーヒー
薬	medicine, chemical	くすり　ヤク	これはいい薬(くすり)です。

Kanji	Kanji	Meaning	Readings	Example
顔	顔	face	かお　ガン	顔色(かおいろ)がわるい。
色	色	color	いろ　ショク・シキ	顔(かお)の色(いろ)がくろい。
指	指	finger	ゆび　シ	指(ゆび)がながいですね。 親指(おやゆび)はthumbです。
切	切	to cut	き(る)　セツ	あっ、痛(いた)い、指(ゆび)を切(き)った。
歩	歩	to walk	ある(く)　ホ	家まで歩(ある)いて帰る。
走	走	to run	はし(る)　ソウ	毎日１０キロ走(はし)っています。
勉	勉	exertion	つと(める)　ベン	日本語を勉強(べんきょう)する。
強	強	strong	つよ(い)　キョウ	この薬(くすり)は強(つよ)いです。
忘	忘	to forget	わす(れる)　ボウ	走(はし)って、ストレスを忘(わす)れます。
早	早	early	はや(い)　ソウ	朝早(はや)く起きる。
持	持	to hold, to have	も(つ)　ジ	指(ゆび)を切(き)ったので、かばんが持(も)てません。

痛	痛	to hurt; pain いた(い)　ツウ	昨日走り(はし)すぎて、足が痛(いた)い。

頭	頭	head あたま　ズ	頭(あたま)が痛(いた)い。　山田さんは頭(あたま)がいい。

読めるようになった漢字(かんじ)

病院　病気　入(にゅう)院する　大学院　医者　体　体育館(たいいくかん)　歯　大変　熱　熱い　薬　顔　顔色　色々(いろいろ)　黄色(きいろ)い　茶色(ちゃいろ)い　指　指輪(わ)　切る　親切(しんせつ)　歩く　散歩(さんぽ)　走る　勉強　強い　忘れる　早い　お大事(じ)に　風邪(かぜ)　気分　気持ち　背中(せなか)　休む　上げる　下げる　出る　出す　思い出　持つ　痛い　頭

練習(れんしゅう)

Read the following sentences aloud.

1. 弟は熱が３８度あって体も熱かったので、家で休みました。
2. 気分がわるくて、顔色もよくなかったので、学校を休んで朝早く病院に行きました。
3. 一日に三回色々な薬を飲んでいるのは、私の父です。
4. 体がとてもつかれていて、歯も痛くなってきて、もう歩けません。
5. 母が去年から病気で入院しているから、私の家は大変です。
6. 指を切って、えんぴつが痛くて持てないので、医者に行った。
7. リンさんは、きのう、おそくまで勉強したけど、しゅくだいを家に忘れました。
8. 体が強くなるように、毎日えきまで歩いたり、こうえんを走ったりしています。
9. 薬を飲んで、頭が痛くなくなりました。

読む練習
れんしゅう

上手な読み方

Using your knowledge of the real world

As mentioned earlier in the textbook, you should always look at the title, subtitles, pictures and captions to determine what a reading is about before you start. Then think about what you know about the particular topic. This chapter is about illnesses, so you should try to remember what you know or have experienced concerning illnesses and hospitals in your country and apply your knowledge.

Most Japanese clinics and hospitals have their own pharmacies. A prescription drug is usually put in a small packet with instructions. Now look at the pictures and try to guess which one is a pharmacy packet.

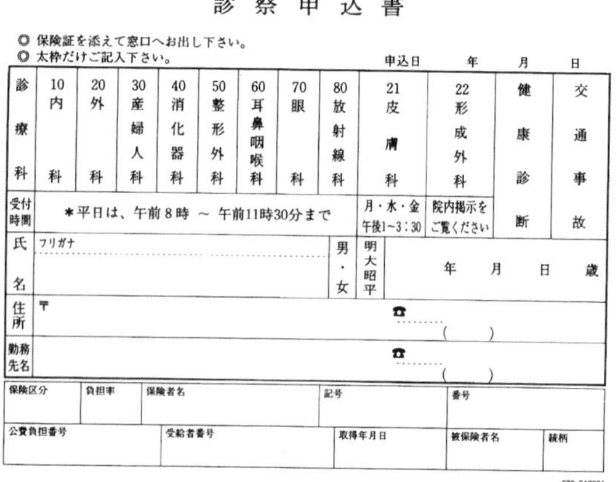

診 察 申 込 書

◎ 保険証を添えて窓口へお出し下さい。
◎ 太枠だけご記入下さい。　　申込日　年　月　日

診療科	10 内科	20 外科	30 産婦人科	40 消化器科	50 整形外科	60 耳鼻咽喉科	70 眼科	80 放射線科	21 皮膚科	22 形成外科	健康診断	交通事故
受付時間	＊平日は、午前8時 ～ 午前11時30分まで								月・水・金 午後1~3:30	院内掲示をご覧ください		

氏名	フリガナ	男・女	明大昭平	年 月 日 歳
住所	〒			☎ (　)
勤務先名				☎ (　)

保険区分	負担率	保険者名	記号	番号

公費負担番号	受給者番号	取得年月日	被保険者名	続柄

030-042001

1

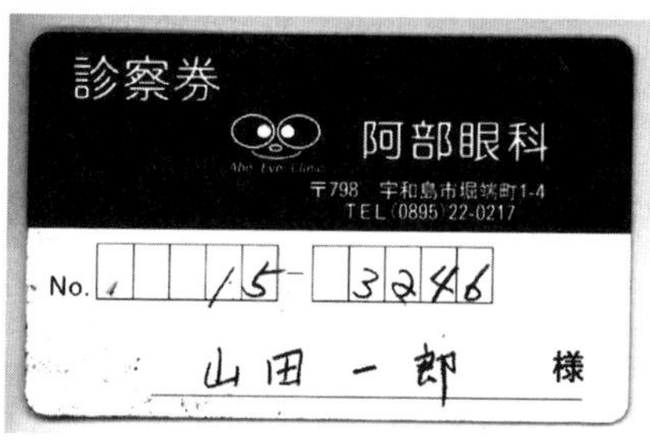

2

内 用 薬

山田 一郎 殿

○裏面を御覧下さい

用法

1日 1回 7日分

食前 食後 食前後 食間

時間毎・朝・昼・夕・就寝前 服用

飲剤は1回 包宛服用

カプセルは1回 1 個宛服用

錠剤は1回 1 錠宛服用

平成5年8月8日

清 水 医 院

東京都台東区根岸1丁目20番1号
電話 (3876) 1234

3

父の病気

言葉のリスト

心配です　worried

読む前に

1. 日本のサラリーマン (*business man*) はどんな生活をしていると思いますか。
2. つかれた時は (*when you are very tired*)、どんなしょうじょうがありますか。
3. どんな時に、ごはんがあまり食べられませんか。

これはインターネットの人生相談 (*advice column*) の手紙です。

私の父はたばこが大好きで一日に二十本ぐらいすっています。ちょっとすいすぎだと思います。そして、仕事でよくお酒を飲みに行って、毎晩十二時ごろまで家に帰れません。ですから、このごろとても顔色が悪くて、ごはんもあまり食べられないそうです。それはとてもよくないことだと思います。父は仕事が大好きで、家にいるのはあまり好きじゃないので、病気で会社を休んだことはありません。でも、私も母もとても心配です。一週間ぐらい前に父と話しましたが、父は仕事は休みたくないそうです。話を聞かない父が元気になるように、私と母は、どうしたらいいんでしょうか。

読んだ後で

1. お父さんのけんこうはどうでしょうか。
2. お父さんは何をするのが好きなんですか。
3. お父さんはどのぐらいたばこをすっていますか。
4. お父さんは何がきらいなんですか。
5. お父さんは仕事を休みたがっていますか。
6. この人 (*author*) にアドバイス (*advice*) をして下さい。

総合練習
そうごうれんしゅう
Integration

けんこうですか。

Work with a partner. Your partner should not look at the flow chart. Ask him/her about various habits and follow the flow chart according to the answers. If your partner's physical condition is not perfect, make some suggestions.

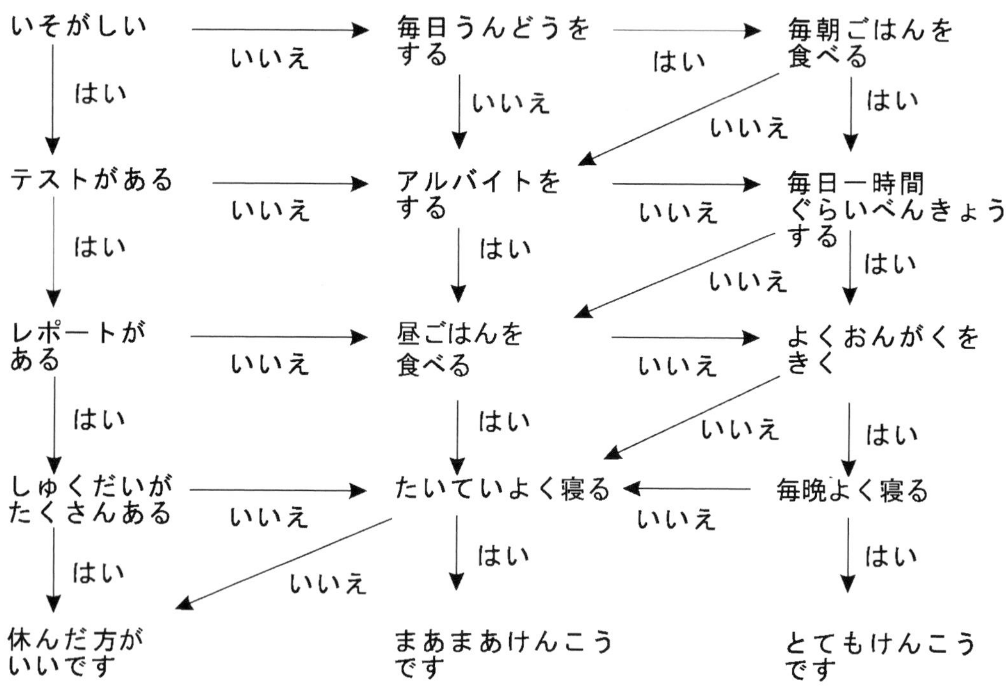

Example: A: 一日に三回ごはんを食べていますか。
B: はい。
A: ～さんはあまりけんこうじゃなさそうですね。
B: そうですか。
A: 少しうんどうをした方がいいですよ。
それから、たばこはすわない方がいいですね。

ロールプレイ

1. You are at a hospital. You are a new patient and have to tell the staff at the reception desk what kind of problem you have.
2. You started feeling sick in the middle of class. Ask your instructor if you can excuse yourself.
3. Your friend looks sick. Ask what's wrong and give several suggestions.
4. You are going on a trip tomorrow, but you feel sick. Tell a doctor what you want to do during the trip, and ask for advice.

Chapter 2

第二課（だいにか）

Courtesy of the author

旅行の計画（りょこうのけいかく）
Travel Plans

Objectives Making and describing travel plans and work plans

Vocabulary Travel, travel preparations, number of days and nights, transition devices

Dialogue 今度の休み *Upcoming vacation plans*

Japanese Culture Traveling in Japan

Grammar

I. Expressing occasion and time using 時

II. Expressing intention using the volitional form of the verb +と思う

III. Expressing intention and plans using the plain present form of verb + つもり or 予定（よてい）

IV. Using もうand まだ

V. Expressing conditions and sequence using ～たら

Listening Using transition devices, and the difference between the そ-series and the あ-series

Communication Making and receiving phone calls

Kanji Right-side component shapes of **kanji**

海 外 国 旅 館 予 定 約 計 画

荷 物 答 知 泊 乗 着 名 空 森 林

Reading Using transition devices, ハワイ旅行（りょ）

Chapter Resources

www.cengagebrain.com

Heinle Learning Center

Audio Program

Flashcards

単語
たん

Nouns

(お) かね	お金	money
(お) みやげ	お土産	souvenir
おんせん	温泉	hot spring
かいがい	海外	overseas, かいがいりょこう overseas travel
ガイドブック		guidebook
かんこう	観光	sightseeing, かんこうする to go sightseeing, かんこうバス chartered bus for sightseeing, かんこうりょこう sightseeing trip, かんこうきゃく tourist
きっぷ	切符	ticket, でんしゃのきっぷ train ticket
くうこう	空港	airport
くに	国	country
クレジットカード		credit card
けいかく	計画	plan
けしき	景色	scenery, けしきがいい nice scenery
こくない	国内	domestic, こくないりょこう domestic travel
ことば	言葉	language, words, expressions
じかん	時間	time, じかんがある to have time, じかんがない to not have time
じゅんび	準備	preparation, じゅんびする to prepare じゅんびができる preparations are done
スーツケース		suitcase
ツアー		tour
つもり		intention
デジカメ		digital camera, デジタルカメラ
にもつ	荷物	one's belongings, luggage
ばしょ	場所	location
パスポート		passport
ひがえり	日帰り	day trip
ふね	船	ship, boat

ボート		boat
よてい	予定	schedule, plan, よていをたてる to make plans
よやく	予約	reservation, きっぷのよやくをする／きっぷをよやくする to reserve a ticket
みずうみ	湖	lake
りょかん	旅館	Japanese-style inn

な -adjective

べんり（な）	便利（な）	convenient

う -verbs

あつまる	集まる	to get together, to gather, (place) に　あつまる
さがす	探す／ 捜す	to look for. Use 捜す to look for something that has been lost. Otherwise, use 探す.
つかう	使う	to use
つく	着く	to arrive, (place) に　つく
とまる	泊まる	to stay, (place) に　とまる
はらう	払う	to pay
もつ	持つ	to hold, もっている to be holding, to own
もっていく	持って行く	to take, to bring something

る -verbs

こたえる	答える	to answer, しつもんにこたえる to answer a question
きめる	決める	to decide, ～に　きめる to decide on, ～を　きめる to decide something
しっている	知っている	to know. Use しらない to express do not know. しる means come to know, and it is a う -verb.
しらべる	調べる	to check, investigate, explore
たてる	建てる／立てる	to build, establish, make. Use 建てる to build something. Otherwise, use 立てる.
でる	出る	to leave, うちをでる to leave home, 熱がでる to have a fever

Adverbs

とくに	特に	especially, in particular
もう		already, yet, any more
まだ		still, yet

Suffixes

～はく（ぱく）	～泊	～ nights, ～はく（ぱく）～日 nights and days いっぱくふつか one night and two days

Conjunctions

けれども		however
そして		and, then
そのあいだ（に）	その間に	during that time
そのあと（で）	その後で	after that
そのまえ（に）	その前に	before that
そのとき（に）	その時に	at that time
それで		then, so
だから		so
だけど		but
つぎに	次に	next
ですから		therefore, so
というのは		it's because
ところで		by the way
まずはじめに	まず始めに	first (of all)
また		also

Expressions

～について		about ～， そのりょこうについて about the trip
もしもし		Hello (on the phone)
いいえ、ちがいます（よ）。	いいえ、違います（よ）	No, you have the wrong number. (literally: No, it's not correct.)

単語の練習（たんご れんしゅう）

A. 旅行（りょこう） Travel

Look at the illustration below. When your instructor gives you the number of one of the individual components of the illustration, respond by giving the name of the component in Japanese. Use the vocabulary list below.

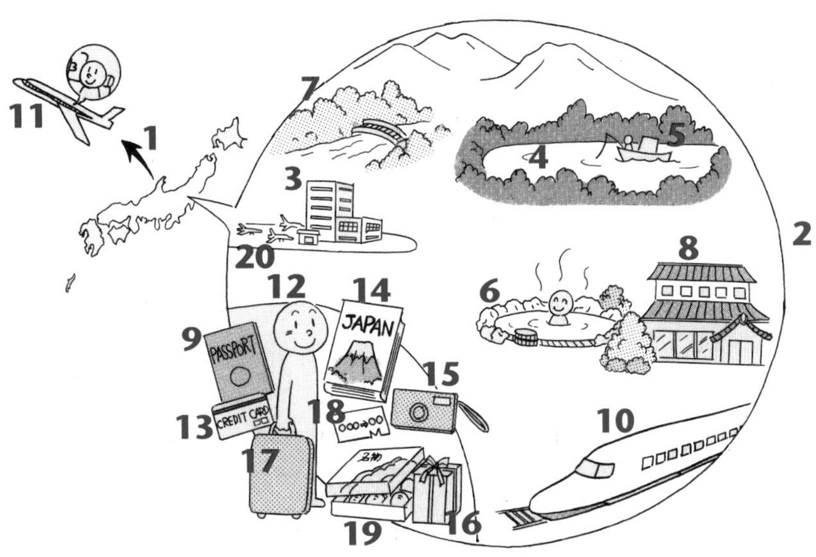

かんこう	sightseeing	乗り物（のりもの）	transportation
海外（かいがい）	overseas	でんしゃ	train
国内（こくない）	domestic	ふね	ship
ツアー	tour	切符（きっぷ）	ticket
ばしょ	location	パスポート	passport
ホテル	hotel	クレジットカード	credit card
旅館（りょかん）	Japanese-style inn	ガイドブック	guidebook
温泉（おんせん）	hot spring	荷物（にもつ）	luggage
みずうみ	lake	スーツケース	suitcase
景色（けしき）	view, scenery	デジカメ	digital camera
空港（くうこう）	airport	（お）土産（みやげ）	souvenir
かんこうきゃく	tourist	ことば	word, language

おぼえていますか。

しごと　会社(しゃ)　家族　かばん　きせつ　ところ　店　山　川　海(うみ)　国(くに)　くるま
しゃしん　じんじゃ　おてら　動物園(どうぶつえん)　博物館(はくぶつかん)　美術館(びじゅつかん)　水族館(すいぞくかん)　ゆうえんち
ホテル　おまつり　飛行機(ひき)　教会(きょう)　かぶき　外国(がいこく)　思い出　買い物(もの)　レストラン
ビジネス　スペイン　フランス　イギリス　韓国(かんこく)　中国(ごく)　たいわん
オーストラリア　カナダ　アメリカ　メキシコ

Supplementary Vocabulary 旅行(りょ)にかんすることば (Other travel-related expressions)

あんない（する）	案内（する）	to guide, to show (someone) around
あんないしょ	案内所	information center
えはがき	絵葉書	picture postcard
もくてき	目的	purpose
もくてきち	目的地	destination
ガイド		guide
クルーズ		cruise
じゆうこうどう	自由行動	free time, free activity
しゅうゆうけん	周遊券	(travel) pass
しゅくはくち	宿泊地	place to stay overnight
～つき	～付き	included, equipped with シャワーつき equipped with shower, ちゅうしょくつき lunch included
トラベラーズチェック		traveler's check
ビザ		visa
ペンション		western-style private guesthouse, B&B
ほけん	保険	insurance
やど	宿	inn
ユースホステル		youth hostel

Activity 1 Guess the Japanese words for the following terms.

Overseas travel ____________________
Sightseeing trip ____________________
Overseas tour ____________________
Domestic tour ____________________
Travel agency ____________________
Airport limousine ____________________

Activity 2 Guess the meaning of the following words.

旅(りょ)行ガイド	____________
家族旅(りょ)行	____________
温泉旅(おんせんりょ)行	____________
温泉旅館(おんせんりょかん)	____________
かんこうバス	____________
かんこうきゃく	____________
ビジネスホテル	____________

Activity 3 Find a word that corresponds to the following descriptions. Some of the items have more than one answer.

1. 飛(ひ)行機(き)が出るところです。
2. お土産(みやげ)を買うところです。
3. 旅(りょ)行の時に読むものです。
4. 旅(りょ)行の時に、ここで寝たりごはんを食べたりします。
5. 旅(りょ)行の時に買うものです。
6. おもしろいところやきれいなところに行ったりすることです。
7. 旅(りょ)行の時に、これで色々(いろいろ)な物(もの)が買えますが、お金(かね)じゃありません。
8. 外国(がいこく)人が持(も)っている物(もの)です。
9. これを買って、でんしゃや飛(ひ)行機(き)に乗(の)ります。
10. これでしゃしんがとれます。
11. ここでよく小さいボートを見ます。

Activity 4 Complete the following sentences using the appropriate words.

1. このへやは__________がいいですね。山や海(うみ)がとてもきれいですね。
2. 海外旅(かいがいりょ)行に行く人は、__________をとって下さい。
3. 海外(かいがい)では、__________が分からなくて、とても大変でした。
4. 日本では、__________ではなくて、__________に泊(と)まりたいです。

B. じゅんびをする Preparation

計画(けいかく)をたてる	to make plans
有名(ゆうめい)なホテルに泊(と)まる	to stay in a famous hotel
じゅんびをする	to prepare
～をつかう	to use
～をしらべる	to check
～を知(し)っている / 知(し)らない	to know/ to not know
予約(よやく)する	to make a reservation
お金(かね)をはらう	to pay money
～を持(も)って行く	to bring something
～に着(つ)く	to arrive at
時間がかかる	to take time
～があつまる	to get together, to gather
～をさがす	to look for
～に答(こた)える	to answer, to respond

おぼえていますか。

しつもん　ところ　店　それから　出かける　家を出る　話す　まつ　会う
りょうり　明るい　くらい　せまい　早い　ひろい　きれい（な）　有名(ゆうめい)（な）

Activity 5

新しいことばをつかって、旅(りょ)行の前にすることを書いて下さい。
(Write down some of the things done before a trip. Use the new words you have learned.)

Activity 6

Choose the appropriate words from the above list to complete the following sentences.

1. 今旅(りょ)行の計画(けいかく)を＿＿＿＿＿＿て、明日ホテルを＿＿＿＿＿＿しましょう。
2. 日本のレストランではチップ (*tip*) は＿＿＿＿＿＿。
3. かんこうルート (*route*) をガイドブックで＿＿＿＿＿＿。
4. 勉強しなかったけど、先生のしつもんに＿＿＿＿＿＿。
5. 夕(ゆう)方の六時に東京(きょう)に＿＿＿＿＿＿から、その日は東京(きょう)えきのちかくのホテルに＿＿＿＿＿＿。

6. お金がないから、安いホテルを＿＿＿＿＿＿。

7. 林田さんは大きいスーツケースを＿＿＿＿＿＿ので、えきまでタクシー (*taxi*) を＿＿＿＿＿＿。

8. 九時のでんしゃに乗るから、八時半に＿＿＿＿＿＿下さい。十時には東京に ＿＿＿＿＿＿。

C. 〜泊〜日 Number of days and nights

日帰り	ひがえり	day trip
一泊二日	いっぱくふつか	two days, one night
二泊三日	にはくみっか	three days, two nights
三泊四日	さんぱくよっか	four days, three nights
四泊五日	よんはく（ぱく）いつか	five days, four nights
五泊六日	ごはくむいか	six days, five nights

Note

- 〜泊〜日 is not commonly used when the stay is longer than one week. In this case, use 〜日（間）泊まる.（八日（間）泊まる）

おぼえていますか。

〜日

Activity 7 Say the length of each trip using the number of days and nights that match the following expressions.

Example: 火曜日に行って、水曜日に帰ります。
一泊二日の旅行

1. 月曜日に来て、金曜日に出ます。 ＿＿＿＿＿＿の旅行
2. 明日来て、明後日帰ります。 ＿＿＿＿＿＿の旅行
3. 一昨日来ました。明日帰ります。 ＿＿＿＿＿＿の旅行
4. 月曜日の午後から土曜日の朝までいます。 ＿＿＿＿＿＿の旅行
5. 今日行って、明後日帰ります。 ＿＿＿＿＿＿の旅行
6. 明日行って、明日帰ります。 ＿＿＿＿＿＿の旅行

Activity 8

Work with a partner. One person should make a sentence similar to those in activity 7 and the other should say how many nights and days are being referred to.

Example: A: 水曜日に行って、金曜日に帰ります。
B: 二泊(はく)三日の旅行でしょう。

D. せつぞくし Conjunctions

だけど	but	その前（に）	before that
けれども	however	その時（に）	at that time
というのは	it's because	その間(あいだ)（に）	during that time
（まず）はじめに、まず	first, first (of all)	それで	then, so
つぎに	next	ですから	therefore, so
ところで	by the way	だから	so
その後（で／に）	after that	また	also

おぼえていますか。

そして　それから　でも

Activity 9

Use the appropriate conjunctions to improve the flow between the following sentences.

Example: 高男くんは十五さいです。ビールは飲めません。
高男くんは十五さいです。だから / ですから、ビールは飲めません。

1. 私はバレーボールをしました。山田さんは寝ていたそうです。
2. 旅行(りょ)の計画(けいかく)をたてます。安い旅館(りょかん)をさがします。旅館(りょかん)の予約(よやく)をしたいと思います。
3. 山本さんは病気です。今日は来られないそうです。
4. クレジットカードでお金(かね)をはらいました。お金(かね)がなくなったからです。
5. 歯をみがきます。よる、寝ます。（みがく = *to brush*）
6. ハワイにはおもしろいツアーがたくさんあります。金田さんは来られなくてざんねんです。

ダイアローグ

はじめに

A. しつもんに日本語で答(こた)えて下さい。

1. どんなところに旅(りょ)行に行ったことがありますか。
2. 何日ぐらい行きましたか。(Use ~days~nights)
3. どんなことをしましたか。 (Use 〜たり〜たりする)
4. 旅行(りょ)の前にどんなことをしますか。
5. 旅行(りょ)に行く時、どんなものを持(も)って行ったらいいと思いますか。
6. 海外旅行(かいがいりょ)はどこへ行きたいですか。どうしてですか。
7. 国内旅行(こくないりょ)はどこへ行きたいですか。どうしてですか。

今度の休み *Upcoming vacation plans*

The order of the following **manga** frames is scrambled. Read the dialogue and unscramble the frames by writing the correct number in the box in each frame.

a b c d e f g

先生がリーさんと上田さんに今度の休みについて聞いています。

先生： 今度の休みはどうしますか。

上田： 北海道(ほっかいどう)に行く予定(よてい)です。

リー： 北海道(ほっかいどう)？

上田： うん、さっぽろは雪まつりがあるから、見に行こうと思ってるの。

リー： 雪まつり？それ、おまつり？

上田： ええ、雪で作った建物（たてもの）や動物（どうぶつ）がたくさん見られるの。

リー： へえ、そうなんだ。おもしろそうだね。

先生： でも、二月の北海道（ほっかいどう）はまだ寒いから、あたたかくして行った方がいいですね。

上田： ええ、ですから、今度買い物（もの）に行った時に、新しいコートを買うつもりです。

先生： そうですか。ところで、リーくんの予定（よてい）は？

リー： ぼくは、たいわんへ帰るつもりです。

先生： そうですか。いつ帰るんですか。

リー： 今学期（がっき）がおわったら、すぐ出ようと思っています。

上田： そう、じゃあ、もうすぐね。

リー： うん。だから、今週の週末は、お土産（みやげ）とスーツケースを買いに行こうと思ってるんだ。あ、先生、それで、レポートのことなんですが。

先生： はい、何ですか。

リー： 十五日に出るかもしれませんので、十四日に出（だ）してもよろしいでしょうか。

先生： ああ、もちろんいいですよ。

Dialogue Phrase Notes

- さっぽろ is the capital city of the northernmost major island, 北海道（ほっかいどう）.
- 今学期（がっき） means *this semester* or *this quarter.*
- よろしい is the polite form of いい.

ダイアローグの後で

A. 上田さんとリーさんの休みの計画(けいかく)を下のひょう (*chart*) に書いて下さい。

	上田さん	リーさん
行くところ		
行った時にすること		
行く時にすること		

B. しつもんに日本語で答(こた)えて下さい。

1. 上田さんは何をしに出かけますか。
2. 雪まつりとはどんなおまつりですか。
3. リーさんはどうして十四日にレポートを出(だ)すつもりですか。

C. Identify whom each of the speeches is directed at in the dialogue. Pay attention to the level of formality used.

D. Identify the phrases that introduce a new topic.

日本の文化

国内旅行 Traveling in Japan.

Among domestic airlines, a highway system, and several types of rail systems, the best way to travel in the country is probably by train. Various discount tickets and railway passes are available for travelers, but some of them must be purchased before arriving in Japan. For example, Japan Railways (JR), a group of the nation's largest railroad companies, sells a pass that allows unlimited travel on its trains anywhere in Japan. The pass is available to travelers who stay in Japan for more than a week, and it must be purchased before arriving in Japan. JR trains include most local trains, the airport express, and the 新幹線 (bullet train). Some local stations are not equipped with an elevator or an escalator, though, so it is not a good idea to carry heavy luggage. There are, however, very good delivery services called 宅配便 available if you want to ship a large amount of luggage within Japan. You can even send luggage to and from the airport.

© Kenneth Hamm / Photo Japan

One of the pleasures of traveling by train is 駅弁 , or a station lunch box. These packaged lunches are sold in trains and stations all over Japan. They usually contain some regional specialty, making them popular with travelers. Most cost between 500 and 1,000 yen.

Walter Pietsch / Alamy

If you do not use a railway pass, you may want to check domestic airfares. Airline companies offer highly competitive prices for tickets purchased in advance. Both airlines and JR offer inexpensive packages that include transportation and hotel accommodation. You may find packages that are cheaper than a round-trip air or train ticket.

There are all kinds of accommodations available in Japan. Western-style hotels (ホテル) are usually more expensive than others, though they are more likely to have staff who speak English. Also, they often have English newspapers, maps and other services. Business hotels (ビジネスホテル) are budget hotels for those who wish to travel affordably. The rooms are extremely small, but they are very inexpensive, provide essential amenities, and serve breakfast.

Another option is 旅館, Japanese-style inns.

The cost of these can vary from very inexpensive to expensive. Although some 旅館（りょかん） have western-style rooms, many have only Japanese-style rooms. Also, a Japanese-style breakfast and dinner are included in the price. Hotel personnel come to your room to lay out or put away ふとん , and to serve meals, tea, and snacks. This may be one of the few instances in Japan where tipping is accepted. (Tips are not necessary for most services, such as in restaurants and taxis.) Some 旅館（りょかん） have rooms with a bathroom, but many of them have communal baths and restrooms which are segregated by sex. They also provide bathrobes called ゆかた . It is perfectly acceptable for guests to walk around 旅館（りょかん） wearing ゆかた .

Private guest houses such as 民宿（みんしゅく） (Japanese-style inns) and ペンション (western-style inns) are usually less expensive than hotels or 旅館（りょかん） , and are popular among young people and students. Both 民宿（みんしゅく） and ペンション serve breakfast and dinner in the dining area, but no special room service is provided, and the bathrooms and restrooms are communal.

DAJ/Getty Images

文法

I. Expressing occasion and time using 時

In Chapter 12 of Nakama 1, 時 is used with nouns and adjectives as in 病気の時, 小さい時 and 元気な時. 時 can be combined with verbs, but the relationship between the main clause and the 時 clause is different depending on the verb tense in the 時 clause.

A. Plain present form + 時 (uncompleted action)

When 時 is combined with an action verb, the tense in the 時 clause indicates whether the action in this clause was completed by the time the action in the main clause takes place. Thus, the present form indicates that the action in the 時 clause had not been not completed when the action in the main clause takes place.

家を 出る時、電話して下さい。 *Please call me when you leave home.*

本を 読む時、めがねをかける。 *I put on glasses when I read a book.*

空港に 行く時、バスで行きます。 *I take the bus when I go to the airport.*

お金をはらう時、クレジットカードをつかった。 *I used a credit card when I made a payment.*

B. Plain past form + 時 (completed action)

Use of the past tense in the 時 clause indicates that the event in this clause has been completed by the time the event in the main clause takes place.

そのさかなを 食べた時、おなかが痛くなりました。
I had a stomachache when/after I ate the fish.

ホテルに 着いた時、電話して下さい。
Call me when/after you arrive at the hotel.

切符を 予約した時、お金をはらいませんでした。
I didn't pay when I reserved the ticket.

これはハワイに 行った時に、買った。
I bought it when I went to Hawaii.

Note that regardless of the tense in the 時 clause, the tense in the main clause indicates when the entire event took place.

日本に　　行く時、母に電(でん)話します。 *I will call my mother when/before I go to Japan.*

日本に　行った時、母に電(でん)話します。 *I will call my mother when/after I go to Japan.*

日本に　　行く時、母に電(でん)話しました。 *I called my mother when/before I went to Japan.*

日本に　行った時、母に電(でん)話しました。 *I called my mother when/after I went to Japan.*

Notes

- The form of adjectives, verbs and nouns before 時 is the same as it is for noun modification. The use of 時 with nouns and adjectives was introduced in Chapter 12 of *Nakama 1*. It is not necessary to use the past tense when pairing 時 with nouns, adjectives, and verbal expressions which express a state such as ある, いる, ～ている, or ～ない.

日帰(ひがえ)りの時、たいてい飛(ひ)行機(き)をつかいます。
I tend to go by plane for a day trip.

日帰(ひがえ)りじゃない時は、でんしゃで行きます。
I go by train when it is not a day trip.

ひまな時は、かんこうをしました。
I went sightseeing when I had free time.

ひまじゃない時は、あまりかんこうは出(で)来ませんでした。
I could not do much sightseeing when I didn't have any free time.

いそがしい時は、あまり出(で)かけられませんでした。
I couldn't go out much when I was busy.

いそがしくない時、よく映画(えいが)を見ました。
I often watched movies when I wasn't busy.

旅館(りょかん)に泊(と)まっている時、パスポートがなくなった。
I lost my passport when I was staying at the inn.

お金(かね)がある時、よくおいしいりょうりを食べに行った。
I often went out for good food when I had money.

ことばが分からない時、辞(じ)書でしらべる。
When I don't understand a word, I look it up in the dictionary.

- The particle に is optional when expressing time and ～時 can appear in the forms ～時に、～時は、～時には.

  ホテルをさがす時には、よくインターネットをつかいます。
  I often use the Internet to look for a hotel.

  知(し)っている時には、答(こた)えられるけど、知(し)らない時は答(こた)えられない。
  I can answer your question when I know the answer, but not when I don't know it.

- Use が to mark the subject of the 時 clause, if it is different from that of the main clause.

  林(はやし)さんが来た時、川口さんも来ました。
  When Mr. Hayashi was here, Ms. Kawaguchi came as well.

  でんしゃが東京についた時、そとはもうくらかったです。
  When the train arrived, it was already dark outside.

  雨がふった時、かさを持(も)っていませんでした。
  I didn't have an umbrella when it rained.

話してみましょう

Activity 1 Choose the correct main clause for each of the 時 clauses.

Example: おなかが痛くなった時、薬を飲みました。

1. おなかが痛くなった時
2. 家に帰る時
3. 旅行(りょ)に行く時
4. 旅行(りょ)に行った時
5. 計画(けいかく)をたてる時
6. 家に帰った時
7. こうえんに行った時
8. こうえんに行く時

a. いぬとあそびました。
b. 友達(だち)があそびに来ていました。
c. バスで帰りました。
d. 時間がかかりました。
e. 薬を飲みました。
f. お土産(みやげ)を買いました。
g. ホテルの予約(よやく)をしました。
h. サンドイッチを持(も)って行きました。

Activity 2 Complete the following sentences by supplying the 時 clause.

Example: <u>海外旅行(かいがいりょ)に行った時</u>、お土産(みやげ)を買いました。

1. ______________________、べんりなホテルをさがしました。
2. ______________________、景色がいいへやを予約したいです。
3. ______________________、デジカメでとりました。
4. ______________________、ガイドブックを読みました。
5. ______________________、パスポートをとりました。
6. ______________________、温泉へ行きました。
7. ______________________、ばしょが分かりませんでした。
8. ______________________、みずうみでふねに乗りました。

Activity 3

Work with a partner. Discuss what you will do before, during, or after a trip to a foreign country, using 〜時 . Use casual speech. Then report your discussion to the class using polite speech.

Example: A: 海外旅行に行くんだけど。

B: いいね。海外旅行に行く時は、その国の人と少し話せるように、その国のことばを少し勉強した方がいいと思うよ。

A: そう。じゃあ、旅行に行く時、何を持って行ったらいいかな。

B: 薬と大きいかばんを持って行ったらいいと思うよ／けど。

A: じゃあ、旅行に行った時は、何する?

B: たくさん買い物するね。

A: そう。じゃあ、旅行から帰った時は、何する?

B: 友達に電話をするよ。

海外旅行に行く時には、その国のことばを少し勉強して行きます。そして、出かける時には薬を持って行きます。旅行に行った時は、たくさん買い物をして、旅行から帰った時に、友達に電話をします。

II. Expressing intention using the volitional form of the verb + と思う

There are various ways of expressing one's intention, depending on how strongly you feel. This chapter introduces three forms of intention. The first form, the volitional forms of verbs + と思う, expresses a tentative intention.

温泉に 入ろうと思います。 *I'm thinking of taking a bath at a hot spring.*

ふねに 乗ろうと思います。 *I'm thinking of taking a ship.*

今、じゅんびしようと思う。 *I'm thinking of starting preparations now.*

Volitional form of verbs

Verb types	Dictionary form		Formation	Volitional form
う -verbs	さがす	*(to look for)*	さが＋そ＋う	さがそう
	つかう	*(to use)*	つか＋お＋う	つかおう
る -verbs	答(こた)える	*(to answer)*	答(こた)え＋よう	答(こた)えよう
	しらべる	*(to check)*	しらべ＋よう	しらべよう
Irregular Verbs	する	*(to do)*		しよう
	来る	*(to come)*		来(こ)よう

森山(もりやま)： どこかに海外旅行(かいがいりょ)に行こうと思うんだけど。
I'm thinking of going somewhere on an overseas trip.

山本： いいね。どこに行くの。
Sounds good. Where are you going?

森山(もりやま)： まだ、分からないけど、ハワイかな。
I don't know yet, but I am thinking of going to Hawaii.

山本： じゃあ、パスポートをとった方がいいよ。
Then you should get a passport.

When the subject is the speaker, the use of 思っています indicates that the speaker has been thinking of doing something for some time, while 思います merely indicates the speaker's current thinking.

もうすぐ出かけようと思います。
I am thinking of going out soon.

夏休みに日本の友達(だち)に会いに行こうと思ってるから、アルバイトをしてるんだ。
I am thinking of going to Japan to meet my friend next summer vacation, so I am working part-time.

Notes

- When the subject is someone other than the speaker, 思っています must be used to express his/her current thinking as well as his/her thinking over time.

  妹は、行きたいところにすぐに行けるように、ガイドブックでばしょをしらべようと思っています。
  My younger sister is thinking of checking a guide book so she'll be able to go straight to where she wants to go.

  しほさんはクレジットカードでお金(かね)をはらおうと思っている。
  Shiho is thinking of paying with a credit card.

- The volitional form above indicates the speaker's willingness to do something. It is the plain form of ましょう, which means *Let's* ～.

  夏休みの計画(けいかく)をたてましょう。 *Let's make plans for the summer.* (polite)

  夏休みの計画(けいかく)をたてよう。 *Let's make plans for the summer.* (casual)

- The volitional form of a verb must be used before ～かしら or ～かな to express the speaker's monologue question about what he /she should do.

  明日出かけようかな。 *I wonder if I should go out tomorrow.*

  今日は何をしようかな。 *I wonder what I should do today.*

- The form ～たいと思います is often used to express desire. This is less direct than ～たいです, and thus, it sounds more formal and polite.

  いつか日本にすみたいと思います。
  I would like to live in Japan someday. (more polite and formal)

  いつか日本にすみたいです。
  I want to live in Japan someday. (direct)

話してみましょう

Activity 1 Work with a partner. Ask your partner whether he/she is thinking of doing in the next vacation. Your partner will answer using the picture cue and ～ようと思います.

Example:

A: 休みになったら何をしようと思いますか。

B: 海外旅行(かいがいりょ)をしようと思います。

Activity 2 Work as a class. Ask if your classmates have any plans tomorrow and what they will do. Use casual speech.

Example: A: 明日、何か予定(よてい)ある?

B: うん、家でパーティしようと思ってるんだけど。

or いや、とくに何もないけど。

名前(な)	明日の予定(よてい)

Activity 3 Work as a class. First, each person should decide on one social activity for the weekend, and write the time and location on the following schedule sheet. Then, each person should invite his/her classmates to this activity. If you decide to accept a classmate's invitation, add it to your schedule. If you decide not to accept an invitation due to a schedule conflict or lack of interest, politely refuse the invitation. Try to make your schedule as full as possible.

Example A: 今週の土曜日はいそがしいですか。

B: 朝はいそがしいですけど、午後はひまですよ。

A: そうですか。テニスをしようと思ってるんですが、一緒(しょ)にどうですか。

B: 何時からですか。

A: 一時から五時ごろまでです。

B: そうですか。いいですよ。

(write テニス from 1:00 p.m. to 5:00 p.m. on Saturday.)

or すみません。三時からはちょっとようじがあって。

	土曜日	日曜日
8時		
9時		
10時		
11時		
12時		
1時		
2時		
3時		
4時		
5時		
6時		
7時		
8時		
9時		
10時		
11時		
12時		

III. Expressing intention and plans using the plain present form of the verb + つもり or 予定(よてい)

A. Expressing intention using つもり (*intend to* ～)

つもり also expresses the intention of the speaker or someone close to the speaker. Compared to the volitional form of verbs +と思う, つもり expresses a stronger intention.

私は海外(かいがい)ツアーに出かけるつもりです。 *I intend to take an overseas tour.*

母はパスポートをとるつもりです。 *My mother intends to get a passport.*

お土産(みやげ)を買うつもりです。 *I intend to buy a souvenir.*

今度は国内旅行(こくないりょ)にするつもり（だ）。 *I intend to decide on domestic travel this time.*

ツアーをつかうつもり（だ）。 *I intend to take* (lit.: *use*) *a tour.*

あつ子：旅館(りょかん)に泊(と)まるの？ *Are we staying in a Japanese-style inn?*

ウィル：うん、そのつもり。 *Yeah, we intend to do so.*

Notes

- つもり is a dependent noun and thus follows the plain present forms of verbs. It can also follow the demonstrative word その, as in そのつもり, which means to intend to do so.

  先生に話すつもりです。 *I intend to speak to the teacher.*

  先生に話さないつもりです。 *I intend not to speak to the teacher.*

  私の一番上の姉もそのつもりです。 *My oldest sister intends to do so, too.*

- Use the copula verb です／だ after つもり to indicate the presence of intention or a plan or just end the sentence with つもり. Use ～つもりはありません／ない to indicate a lack of intention or plan.

  ガイドブックを持(も)って行くつもりです。
  I intend to take a guidebook. (polite)

  ガイドブックを持(も)って行くつもり（<u>だ</u>）。
  I intend to take a guidebook. (casual)

  ガイドブックを持(も)って行くつもり<u>はありません</u>。
  I don't intend to take a guidebook. (polite)

  ガイドブックを持(も)って行くつもり<u>はない</u>。
  I don't intend to take a guidebook. (casual)

B. Expressing plans using 予定(よてい) (*plan to* ～)

Used without a modifier, 予定(よてい) is a noun meaning *plan.*

今日の予定(よてい)は何ですか。 *What is the plan for today?*

今日は予定(よてい)がありません。 *I don't have any plans today.*

予定(よてい) follows the plain present form of a verb when it is used with a modifier to indicate a specific plan. 予定(よてい) is followed by the copula verb です・だ . The subject of a statement with 予定(よてい) can be any person.

六時の飛行機(ひこうき)で出る予定(よてい)です。 *I plan to leave here by plane at six o'clock.*

ホテルには泊(と)まらない予定(よてい)だ。 *I plan on not staying in any hotel.*

リーさんは今年の冬に中国(ごく)に帰る予定(よてい)です。 *Mr. Li plans to go back to China this winter.*

スミス： 今度の休みに何か予定(よてい)がありますか。
Do you have some kind of plan for your next day off?

森(もり)： ええ、上野(うえの)の美術館(びじゅつかん)に行く予定(よてい)です。スミスさんは？
Yes, I plan to go to the art museum in Ueno. How about you, Mr. Smith?

スミス： とくに予定(よてい)はありませんが、どこかへ出かけようと思っています。
I don't have any particular plans, but I am thinking of going somewhere.

Note:

- Use ～予定はありません・ない to indicate the lack of a plan.

かんこうする予定(よてい)はありません。	*I don't plan to go sightseeing.*
みずうみに行く予定(よてい)はないよ。	*We don't plan to go to the lake.*

話してみましょう

Activity 1

You are a tour guide, taking a group of tourists to Lake Yamanaka, near Mt. Fuji. The following is the tour schedule. Explain your plans to the tour bus driver, using 予定(よてい).

© Kenneth Hamm / Photo Japan

一日目	７時３０分	バスターミナルにあつまる
	８時００分	バスで山中湖(やまなかこ) (*Lake Yamanaka*) へ
	１０時３０分	山中湖(やまなかこ)に着(つ)く
	１０時３０分～１２時	フリー・タイム
	１２時	ランチ （ホテル　マウントふじ）
	１時３０分	文学(ぶんがく)の森公園(もりこうえん)ツアー
	３時	山中湖(やまなかこ)プラザホテル
	３時	フリー・タイム
	６時	夕食(ゆうしょく) (*Dinner*)
二日目	９時	朝食(ちょうしょく) (*Breakfast*)
	１０時３０分	フロントにあつまる
	１１時	バスで東京(とうきょう)へ
	１時３０分	バスターミナルに着(つ)く

Example: 7時半にバスターミナルにあつまる予定(よてい)です。

Activity 2

The following chart shows Ms. Ueda and her family's plans for this summer. A double circle (◎) indicates a definite plan, and a single circle (○) indicates an intention. A question mark (?) indicates a tentative plan. You are Ms. Ueda. Describe each family member's plans and intentions using the volitional form of verb + と思う, the plain present form of verb + つもり or 予定(よてい), and appropriate transition devices.

Example: 父は高校の時の友達(だち)とあつまる予定(よてい)です。それから、家をさがすつもりです。というのは、父は家を買おうと思っているんです。

お父さん	お母さん	パム（妹）	私（アリス）
○ 家をさがします。	◎ 日本に来ます。	◎ フランスに行きます。	○ 海外旅行(かいがいりょ)をします。
? 家を買います。	? きょうとかんこうをします。	○ フランス人の友達(だち)を作ります。	◎ 日本語を勉強します。
◎ 高校の時の友達(だち)とあつまります。	○ 旅館(りょかん)に泊(と)まります。	? フランスでアルバイトをします。	? 安いツアーをつかいます。

Activity 3

Work with a partner. Write down your plans for this week, including both plans that are fixed and things that you intend to do. Then ask your partner about his/her plans. Decide which of you is busier. Use casual speech.

Example

A: 月曜日と火曜日の予定(よてい)はどうなってるの？

B: 九時から十二時までじゅぎょうに出る予定(よてい)（だ）よ。
火曜日は九時から五時までバイトする予定(よてい)なんだ。

A: いそがしそう（だ）ね。週末もいそがしいの？

B: あ、土曜日は日帰(ひがえ)りで温泉(おんせん)に行くつもり（だ）よ。

A: そう。それはいいね。

例	予定(よてい)	月曜日、水曜日、 金曜日　（九時から十二時）じゅぎょう 火曜日（九時から五時まで）バイト
	つもり	土曜日　友達(だち)と日帰(ひがえ)り旅(りょ)行（温泉(おんせん)）
私	予定(よてい)	
	つもり	
パートナー	予定(よてい)	
	つもり	

Activity 4

Work with a partner. Each partner should decide on his/her next vacation. Ask your partner about his/her vacation plans and take notes, using the table below. Your partner should respond using ～ようと思っている, つもり, or 予定(よてい) depending on how firm his/her plans are. Use casual speech. Then report to the class using polite speech.

Example

A: 今度の休みはどうするの？

B: 家族でオレゴンに旅(りょ)行に行く予定(よてい)なんだ。

A: いいね。何日ぐらい行くの。

B: 三泊(ぱく)四日の予定(よてい)だけど。

A: どこに泊(と)まるの？

B: まだ、分からないけれど、べんりなばしょにするつもりなんだ。

A: そう。それで、オレゴンではどんなことしようと思ってるの。

B: そうだね。つりをしたり、キャンプしたりしようと思ってるんだ。

A: そうなんだ。それはたのしそうだね。

私のパートナーは～さんです。～さんは三泊(ぱく)四日でオレゴンに行く予定(よてい)です。～さんはべんりなところに泊(と)まるつもりだそうです。オレゴンでは、つりをしたりキャンプをしたりしようと思っているそうです。

	__________さんの旅(りょ)行の計画(けいかく)
行くところ	
～泊(はく)～日	
泊(と)まるところ	
すること	

IV. Using もう and まだ

The words もう and まだ are adverbs which are often used to indicate the progress or lack of progress of an activity. The English equivalents of もう or まだ are *already*, *yet*, *now*, *still*, and *(not) yet*, depending on the verbal endings. This chapter introduces how these adverbs are used in Japanese.

A. Using もう

The adverb もう indicates that a situation which existed some time ago no longer exists. For example, 山田さんはもう出かけました (*Ms. Yamada has already left*) implies that Ms. Yamada was here some time ago, but she is not here now. Similarly, もう食べられません (*I can no longer eat*) implies that I was able to eat some time ago, but this state no longer exists. In English, もう corresponds to *already* or *now* in affirmative declarative sentences, to *yet* or *already* in affirmative interrogative sentences, and to *(not) anymore* or *(not) any longer* in negative sentences.

じゅんびはもうしました。	*I've already finished the preparations.*
予定(よてい)、もう知(し)ってる。	*I already know the plan.*
乗(の)り物(もの)はもうきめましたか。	*Have you decided on transportation yet?*
りかちゃん、もう空港(くうこう)に着(つ)いた？	*Has Rika arrived at the airport yet?*
もう計画(けいかく)はたてたくありません。	*I don't want to make any more plans.*
もう食べられません。	*I can't eat any more.*

お母さん：	お土産(みやげ)はもう買ったの？	*Have you bought souvenirs yet?*
子供：	うん、もう買ったよ。	*Yeah, I already did.*
お母さん：	じゃあ、荷物(にもつ)はもうかばんに入れた？	*Well, have you put your things in the bag?*
子供：	あ、忘れてた。	*Oh, I forgot.*

B. Using まだ

The adverb まだ indicates that a state that existed some time ago still remains. For example, 子供はまだ寝ています (*The child is still sleeping*) implies that the child was sleeping some time ago and this state still exists now. Also, 山田さんはまだ来ていません (*Ms. Yamada has not come here yet*) implies that Ms. Yamada was not here some time ago and is not here now. In English, まだ means *still* in affirmative sentences, and *yet* or *still* in negative sentences.

まだ計画(けいかく)をたてています。	*I am still planning.*
まだばしょをしらべてる。	*I am still looking into the place.*
まだつかっていますか。	*Are you still using it?*
あいちゃん、まだ、ねこ、さがしてる？	*Is Ai still looking for her cat?*

When まだ is followed by an action verb +ていません, it expresses *have not done ~ yet*. If まだ is used with the simple negative form of an action verb, it means *won't do ～for a while*.

その計画(けいかく)はまだ見ていません。	*I haven't seen that movie yet.*
その計画(けいかく)はまだ見ません。	*I won't see that movie for a while.*
林(はやし)さんはまだ帰っていません。	*Ms. Hayashi has not come back yet.*
林(はやし)さんはまだ帰りません。	*Ms. Hayashi won't come back for a while.*
c.f. まだ知りません。	*I don't know yet.*

Notes

- まだです can be used to mean *not yet*.

早川：レクチャーはもうはじまりましたか。
Has the lecture started yet?
ブラウン：いいえ、まだです。
No, not yet.

森山(もりやま)：旅館(りょかん)はもうきめたの？
Have you chosen an inn yet?
山本：いいえ、まだきめてないよ。
No, I haven't decided yet.

先生：まだしゅくだいが出ていませんね。
You haven't turned in your homework yet.
学生：すみません。今度のしゅくだいはむずかしいので、まだしらべているんです。
I am sorry but this homework is difficult, so I'm still doing research.

話してみましょう

Activity 1

The chart below contains today's schedules for Mr. Miller, Ms. Hayashi, and Ms. Cheng. The time now is 12 p.m. Answer the questions using もう or まだ.

Example: 林(はやし)さんはもう学校に行きましたか。
いいえ、まだ、行っていません。

	ミラー	はやし	チェン
午前６時	家に帰る		
７時	寝る		起きる
８時		起きる	朝御飯(ごはん)を食べる
９時		朝御飯(ごはん)を食べる	学校に行く
１０時			
午後１２時			
１時		学校に行く	
４時	起きる		家に帰る
５時	食事(じ)をする		勉強する
６時			
８時	しごとに出かける	家に帰る	

1. ミラーさんは、もう朝御飯(ごはん)を食べましたか。
2. 林(はやし)さんは、もう起きましたか。
3. ミラーさんは、もう起きましたか。
4. チェンさんは、もう学校に行きましたか。
5. ミラーさんは、もう家に帰りましたか。
6. チェンさんは、もう家に帰りましたか。
7. 林(はやし)さんは、まだねていますか。

Activity 2

Work with a partner. You and your partner are going on a trip, and you're dividing the tasks to prepare for the trip. The following is a checklist for each of you. Put a checkmark next to some of the items to indicate that you have competed them. Leave some of the items blank. Ask each other which preparations are done and which are not done. Use casual speech.

Example: A: もうホテルの予約(よやく)をした？
B: うん、もう、したよ。or ごめん。まだ、してない。

私		パートナー	
	ホテルの予約(よやく)をする		でんしゃの時間をしらべる
	ガイドブックを買う		でんしゃの切符(きっぷ)を買う
	おもしろいツアーをさがす		あつまるばしょをきめる
	レストランをきめる		レンタカーをかりる (*to rent a car*)
	銀(ぎん)行でお金(かね)をおろす (*to withdraw*)		デジカメをかばんに入れる

Activity 3

Work with a partner. Ask your partner about something that he/she started when he/she was young and is still doing now, or something that he/she started when he was young but is no longer doing, and doesn't want to do any longer. Ask for reasons why.

Example: A: 子供の時、よく何をしましたか。
B: やきゅうをしました。
A: 今もまだしているんですか。
B: ええ、好きだからしていますよ。
or いいえ、下手だからもうしていません。やきゅうは、もうしたくないですね。

V. Expressing conditions and sequence using ～たら

There are several types of conditional sentences in Japanese. The conditional たら is formed with the plain past form of a verb/adjective + ら.

雨が	ふったら、	*If it rains,*
雨が	ふらなかったら、	*If it does not rain,*
けしきが	よかったら、	*If the view is good,*
けしきが	よくなかったら、	*If the view is not good,*
	べんりだったら、	*If it is convenient,*
	べんりじゃなかったら、	*If it isn't convenient,*
きゃく	だったら、	*If (a person) is a customer,*
きゃく	じゃなかったら、	*If (a person) is not a customer,*

The condition expressed in the たらclause must be completed (or satisfied) before the action/event in the main clause can take place. Therefore, you can say 手紙を書いたら、ゆうびんきょくに持って行って下さい, (*After you write the letter, please take it to the post office*) but you cannot say ~~手紙を書いたら、えんぴつで書きます。~~ (*After I write a letter, I write it with a pencil*). This is because the use of たら here implies that one act is completed before the other takes place.

寒くなかったら、プールに行きましょう。 *If it is not cold, let's go to a pool.*

日本に行ったら、富士(ふじ)山が見たいです。 *If I go to Japan, I want to see Mt. Fuji.*

もっと勉強したら、上手になります。 *If you study harder, you will get better.*

私が山田さんだったら、先生に話すでしょう。 *If I were Mr. Yamada, I would talk to the teacher.*

お金(かね)がなかったら、日本へは行きません。 *If I didn't have money, I wouldn't go to Japan.*

明日天気がよかったらいいですね。 *It would be great if the weather were nice tomorrow.*

The たら clause can also express an actual sequence of events without introducing a condition. In this case, the event/action in the たら clause takes place before the event/action in the main clause.

家に帰ったら、電話(でんわ)します。 *I'll call after I get home.*

旅館(りょかん)に着(つ)いたら、温泉(おんせん)に入ります。 *I will soak in the hot spring when I get to the inn.*

ごはんを食べたら、出かけます。 *I will leave after I eat.*

If the main clause is in the present tense, it can be used to express the speaker's intention, request, obligation, etc. However, it cannot express an event that has already transpired.

五月になったら、しごとをするつもりです。 *I intend to have a job from May.* (lit.: *When it is May, I intend to work.*)

じゅんびが出来たら、よんで下さい。 *Call me when the preparation is done.*

お金(かね)があつまったら、持(も)って行きます。 *I'll bring the money over when it has been collected.*

When the main clause is in the past tense, the event in the main clause expresses a situation which is uncontrollable to the speaker. Thus, the main clause tends to express surprise or a realization. (an unexpected event)

おさけを飲んだら、気分がわるくなった。 *I didn't feel well after I drank the* sake.

家に帰ったら、ねこがへやにいた。 *When I got home, there was a cat in my room* (and it surprised me).

アパートに行ったら、ウィルはいなかった。 *When I went to his apartment, Will was not there.*

話してみましょう

Activity 1 Complete the following sentences.

Example　日本に行ったら、富士(ふじ)山に行きたいですね。

1. でんしゃの方がべんりだったら、＿＿＿＿＿＿＿＿＿＿＿＿＿＿＿＿。
2. お金(かね)をはらったら、＿＿＿＿＿＿＿＿＿＿＿＿＿＿＿＿。
3. 知(し)っていたら、＿＿＿＿＿＿＿＿＿＿＿＿＿＿＿＿。
4. 時間がかかったら、＿＿＿＿＿＿＿＿＿＿＿＿＿＿＿＿。
5. その映画(えいが)がよかったら、＿＿＿＿＿＿＿＿＿＿＿＿＿＿＿＿。
6. ＿＿＿＿＿＿＿＿＿＿＿＿＿＿＿＿、答(こた)えて下さい。
7. ＿＿＿＿＿＿＿＿＿＿＿＿＿＿＿＿、三泊(ぱく)四日ぐらいがいいですね。
8. ＿＿＿＿＿＿＿＿＿＿＿＿＿＿＿＿、スーツケースを持(も)って行きましょうか。
9. ＿＿＿＿＿＿＿＿＿＿＿＿＿＿＿＿、景色(けしき)がいいへやをさがして下さい。

Activity 2

Describe the following sequence of events using ～たら .

Example:　家を出たら、雨がふっていました。

1

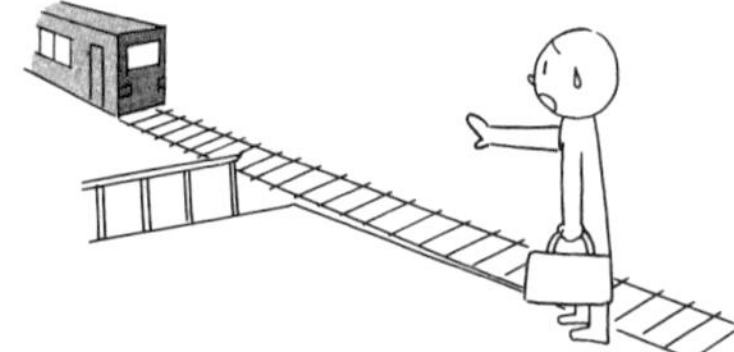

2

Activity 3 Work with a partner. Ask your partner what he/she would want to do if he/she were in the following situations:

Example: そつぎょうする (*to graduate*)

A: そつぎょうしたら、何をしようと思いますか。

B: 日本でしごとをしようと思います。

1. スペインに行ける
2. 日本語が上手
3. クレジットカードがつかえなくなる
4. 先生のしつもんに答(こた)えられない
5. 外国(がいこく)の文(ぶん)学についてよく知っている
6. 有名(ゆうめい)なホテルに泊(と)まる

Activity 4

Work with the class. Ask your classmates where they would want to go if they had a lot of money, and what they would want to do there.

Example:

A: お金(かね)がたくさんあったら、どこへ行きたいですか。

B: 日本に行こうと思います。

A: 日本で何をしようと思いますか。

B: 日本に行ったら、秋葉原(あきはばら)でデジカメを買おうと思います。

名前(な)	ばしょ	したいこと

聞く練習(れんしゅう)

上手な聞き方

Using transition devices, and the difference between the そ -series and the あ -series

As with written material, conversation is full of transitions. Transition devices are used to cooperatively form a cohesive discourse among two or more speakers. In particular, the speaker often uses そ -words (for example, それ , in comments like それはよかったですね) to refer to what is being said. Occasionally, the speaker chooses あ -series instead of そ -words. The difference between the two is that そ -series words are used when either the speaker or the listener is unfamiliar with what is being discussed, and あ -series words are used to refer to matters which both the speaker and the listener are familiar with and share knowledge about. For example, その in the following dialogue indicates that 大木さん does not know much about the 旅館(りょかん), but あそこ implies that 木村(むら)さん has previously stayed in, worked at, or checked up on the 旅館(りょかん), and 木村(むら)さん is expressing the fact that he shares the knowledge about it with 山田さん .

山田： 森下旅館(もりしたりょかん)に泊(と)まったんですよ。
大木： その旅館(りょかん)はどこにあるんですか。
木村(むら)： 京都(きょうと)にあるんですよ。あそこはとてもいい旅館(りょかん)ですね。

どの「こそあど」言葉(ことば)

Listen to the dialogues, circle the demonstrative words used in the conversation, and write what each refers to. Then explain why these particular demonstrative words are used, and why the speaker chose そ or あ .

Example　それ／その／そこ／あれ／あの／あそこ　　黒田(くろだ)さん
男の人は黒田(くろだ)さんを知(し)らないからです。

1. それ／その／そこ／あれ／あの／あそこ　　______________

____

2. それ／その／そこ／あれ／あの／あそこ　　______________

____

3. それ／その／そこ／あれ／あの／あそこ　　______________

____

どのツアーにしようと思いますか。

聞く前に

下のツアーのスケジュールを読んで、しつもんに答(こた)えてください。Note the **kanji** words 大阪(おおさか) and 名古屋(なごや).

1. 一番安いツアーはどれですか。
2. スケジュールが大変なツアーはどれですか。
3. 夏休みに行くツアーはどれがいいですか。

ニューヨーク ６日間　149,000 円より		
スケジュール（６日間）		
1	夕刻：大阪発 → ニューヨークへ 夜：ニューヨーク着　ホテルへ	ニューヨーク泊
2	終日：ニューヨーク市内観光	ニューヨーク泊
3・4	終日：自由行動	ニューヨーク泊
5	午後：ニューヨーク発　帰国の途へ	機中泊
6	夕刻：大阪着	

ケアンズ ５・６日間　169,000 円より			
スケジュール（５・６日間）			
1		午後：大阪→名古屋→ケアンズへ	機中泊
2		早朝：ケアンズ着 着後：ホテルへ	ケアンズ泊
3		終日：自由行動	ケアンズ泊
4	4	終日：自由行動	ケアンズ泊
	5	終日：自由行動	ケアンズ泊
5	6	午後：ケアンズ発 → 名古屋へ 夜：名古屋 → 大阪着	

イタリアの休日 ９日間　253,000 円より		
スケジュール（９日間）		
1	午前：大阪発→夜：ローマ着	ローマ泊
2・3	終日：自由行動	ローマ泊
4	午前：自由行動 午後：ローマ→フィレンツェ	フィレンツェ泊
5	午前：フィレンツェ市内観光 午後：自由行動	フィレンツェ泊
6	午前：自由行動 午後：フィレンツェ→ミラノ	ミラノ泊
7	終日：自由行動	ミラノ泊
8	午前：ミラノ発→帰国の途へ	機中泊
9	午後：大阪着	

ロンドンとローマとパリ １０日間　178,000 円より		
スケジュール(１０日間)		
1	夜：大阪発→ローマへ	機中泊
2	午前：ローマ発 着後：自由行動	ローマ泊
3	終日：自由行動	ローマ泊
4	午前：ローマ→パリへ 午後：パリ着→着後：自由行動	パリ泊
5・6	終日：自由行動	パリ泊
7	午前：パリ→ロンドンへ 着後：自由行動	ロンドン泊
8	終日：自由行動	ロンドン泊
9	午後：ロンドン発→帰国の途へ	機中泊
10	午後：(東京乗継ぎ) 大阪着	

シドニーとゴールドコースト ６・７・８日間 199,000 円より				
スケジュール(６・７・８日間)				
1			夕刻：大阪発→ブリスベンへ	機中泊
2			午前：(シドニー乗継ぎ) →ブリスベンへ 着後：ドリームワールドへ	ゴールドコースト泊
3	3・4		終日：自由行動	ゴールドコースト泊
4	5		午前：ブリスベン発→シドニーへ 着後：シドニー市内観光	シドニー泊
5	6	7・8	終日：自由行動	シドニー泊
6	7	8	午前：シドニー発→帰国の途へ 午後：大阪着	

サンフランシスコとロスアンゼルス ６日間　135,000 円より		
スケジュール（６日間）		
1	夕刻：大阪発→サンフランシスコへ 午後：サンフランシスコ市内観光	サンフランシスコ泊
2	終日：自由行動	サンフランシスコ泊
3	午前：サンフランシスコ発→ロスアンゼルスへ 着後：ロスアンゼルス市内観光	ロスアンゼルス泊
4	終日：自由行動	ロスアンゼルス泊
5	午前：ロスアンゼルス発→帰国の途へ	機中泊
6	夕刻：大阪着	

聞いてみましょう

A. ダイアローグを聞いて、女の人が行くツアーの名前を書いて下さい。それから、行くきかん (*duration*) も書いて下さい。Ignore other details in the conversation.

	ツアーの名前	～泊（～日）
1		
2		
3		

B. Now answer the following questions about the people who appear in the dialogues.

1. 1の女の人が行くツアーについて、しつもんに答えて下さい。

1. この女の人はいつツアーに行きますか。
2. どうしてそのツアーにしましたか。
3. この女の人と男の人のかんけい (*relationship*) は何ですか。

2. 2の人のツアーについてしつもんに答えて下さい。

1. 女の人はいくらぐらいお金がありますか。
2. どうしてそのツアーにしましたか。
3. この女の人と男の人のかんけい (*relationship*) は何ですか。

3. 3の人についてしつもんに答えて下さい。

1. きせつはいつですか。
2. 女の人はどうしてそのツアーにしましたか。

聞いた後で

A. Work with a partner. One person is a student living in Japan and thinking about going on a trip during summer or winter break. The other person is a travel agent. The student should decide on the budget and length of the trip. Explain your travel preferences to the agent. The travel agent should make suggestions.

B. Work with a partner. Both of you work for a travel agency. Plan a trip to your country for Japanese college students during their summer or winter break.

聞き上手　話し上手

電話をかけたりうけたりする。
でん

In every language there are specific ways to make and answer phone calls, and to initiate a conversation. Cell phones and e-mail are the most common methods of communication among young adults. In Japan, cell phones are so common that it is difficult to find a public phone in many places. So it is a good idea to rent a cell phone in Japan if you plan to visit.

In cell phone conversations the caller can assume that the receiver is the one who answers the call, and the receiver sometimes know who the caller is. This chapter introduces basic cell-phone manners. In Conversation A, もしもし functions very much like *hello* or *excuse me* in English. It is used to start a phone conversation, or to address a stranger on the street, as in "Excuse me, but isn't this your wallet?" In Conversation B, Mr. Smith, who answers the phone, says はい. You can use もしもし as well, although etymologically speaking, only the caller uses that phrase.

Conversation A: How to make a telephone call

スミス：　もしもし。

森田(もりた)：　あのう、森田(もりた)ですが、スミスさんですか？

スミス：　ああ、森田(もりた)さん、こんにちは。

Conversation B: What to do when you have called the wrong number by mistake

Situation: You are making a phone call to Ms. Ueda, but you dial the wrong number.

だれか：　はい。

スミス：　あのう、スミスですが、上田さんですか。

だれか：　いいえ、ちがいますよ。

スミス：　あ、すみません。

Japanese people tend to say ええ and はい more often than speakers of English say *Uh-huh* or *OK*. This often affects phone conversations between a Japanese person and an English speaker in two ways. One is that the English speaker may begin to feel pressured upon hearing ええ or はい too often. The other is that the Japanese person speaking with a native speaker of English may start feeling unsure about whether the other party is still on the line, because the person does not receive enough listening feedback. The Japanese person may start saying もしもし, which, in this case, is equivalent to *Are you there?*

A. Work with a partner. Practice making a phone call in the following situation: you call Ms. Hiroko Suzuki (or Mr. Hiroshi Suzuki). Your partner answers the phone as Ms./Mr. Suzuki

B. Work with a partner. Practice making a phone call in the following situation: you got Ms. Suzuki's phone number from one of your friends, so you call her. But the phone number is incorrect.

漢字

かんじ

Right-side components of kanji

Component shapes appearing on the right side of **kanji** often indicate their pronunciation. In this case, "pronunciation" refers to the pronunciation of the character in Chinese at the time the character was adapted for use in Japan. Those pronunciations are still reflected in the Japanese **on**-reading. For example, the component 工 gives a **kanji** the **on**-reading コウ. 江, 紅, 虹, 釭, and 舡 all have the **on**-reading コウ, but they are not necessarily related in meaning. The component 青gives a **kanji** the **on**-reading セイ. The characters 晴, 情, 清, 精, and 請 all share the same **on**-reading, セイ. The component 青 by itself has the meaning of *blue*, but these **kanji** do not necessarily share this meaning. Even if the phonetic component of a compound has a meaning, it is the pronunciation and not the meaning of the component that has significance in the character. The historical background of **kanji** is another tool to organize your knowledge of **kanji**. Possessing this knowledge makes it possible, to some extent, to guess the meaning.

Try the following:

1. Group the **kanji** you know by looking for common component shapes.
2. Find some shared properties in their meanings and pronunciations.

Name		Pronunciation	Meaning	Examples	Related kanji
りっとう	刂		cut	刈 刊 列 判 別 利 刻 制 到	
おおがい	頁		face	頭 顔 願 題	
おおざと	阝		community	部 郵 郊 郎 郡 郭 郷 都	
ぼくづくり・のぶん	攵		to hit	散 改 放 敗	
ちから	力		power	助 動 効 勉	力
あくび	欠		open mouth wide	歌 欲	欠
ふるとり	隹		bird	雄 雅 雑 雌 難 離	
みる	見		see	親 規 視 観	見
また	又		hand movement	取 収 双	又
ほこづくり	戈		fight	戦 戯	
おのづくり	斤		cut into two pieces	新 断	
つき	月		date	朝 期 朗 明	月
てら	寺	ジ	temple	時 待 持	寺
	青	セイ	blue	請 晴 清 情	青

	工	コウ	factory	江 紅	工
	冓	コウ		溝 講	
まじわる	交	コウ	intersection	校 効	交

Flashcards

海 海
sea, ocean
うみ　カイ　　海(うみ)が好きです。　海外旅行(かいがいりょ)

外 外
outside, other
そと　ガイ　　家の外(そと)　外国人(がいこくじん)

国 国
country, nation
くに　コク・ゴク　　小さい国(くに)　中国(ちゅうごく)

旅 旅
travel, trip
たび　リョ　　旅(りょ)行が好きです。

館 館
(large) building, hall
カン　　旅館(りょかん)　図書館(と　かん)　学生会館(かいかん)

予 予
in advance
あらかじ(め)　ヨ　　予定(よてい)があります。　ホテルの予約(よやく)。

定 定
decide, determine
さだ(める)　テイ　　明日は病院に行く予定(よてい)です。

約 約
promise, approximately
ヤク　　旅館(りょかん)を予約(よやく)した。

計 計
measuring, plan
はか(る)　ケイ　　旅(りょ)行の計画(けいかく)をたてる。　高い時計(とけい)ですね。

画 画
picture, painting
カク　ガ　　来年の計画(けいかく)はまだありません。

荷	load, cargo, baggage	ニ・カ	大きい荷物(にもつ)を持(も)って行く。
物	object, thing	もの　ブツ・モツ	荷物(にもつ)　食べ物(もの)　飲み物(もの)
答	to answer, answer	こた(える)　トウ	しつもんに答(こた)える。
知	to know	し(る)　チ	名前(な)を知(し)っています。　知(し)らない人
泊	to stay overnight	と(まる)　ハク・パク	二泊三日(にはくみっか)の旅行(りょ)　ホテルに泊(と)まる。
乗	to ride, get on	の(る)　ジョウ	タクシーに乗(の)る。
着	to arrive, to put on	つ(く)　き(る)　チャク	日本に着(つ)く。　シャツを着(き)る。
名	name	な　メイ・ミョウ	お名(な)前は何ですか。
空	sky	そら　クウ	成田空港(なりたくうこう)に行きます。　空(そら)がきれいです。
森	forest	もり　シン	これは森田(もりた)先生の荷物(にもつ)です。
林	woods	はやし　リン	林(はやし)さんは旅館(りょかん)に泊(と)まりました。

読めるようになった漢字

海　海外　外　外国　国　中国　国内　韓国　旅館　映画館　旅行　予定　予約
天気予報　計画　計る　映画　時計　荷物　食べ物　飲み物　買い物　建物
動物　動物園　図書館　博物館　美術館　学生会館　答える　知る　持つ
持っていく　泊まる　二泊　乗る　着く　着る　着物　名前　有名　温泉　切符
空港　森田　林

Read the following sentences aloud.

1. 森田先生は来月、四泊五日の海外旅行に出かける予定です。行ったことがない国に行きます。
2. その海の近くの温泉旅館に泊まりたいので、今から予約をしようと思います。
3. 林さん、荷物はもうスーツケースに入れましたか。
4. 雨がふって、計画していた日帰り旅行はだめになりました。
5. その高そうなシャツを着ている男の人の名前を知らなかったから、となりの人に聞いた。
6. 切符を持って行かなかったので、ふねに乗れませんでした。
7. ホテルに着いたら、少し休みたいと思っています。

読む練習

上手な読み方

Using transition devices

Transition devices, such as conjunctions and clause connectors, help clarify the relationships among sentences and paragraphs. Paying attention to these connectors will help you understand how a text is organized, and provide clues for finding important information. There are many expressions that use そ-series of demonstrative expressions such as そこ, その後, その前, その時, and その人. When they are used to refer to something that the speaker cannot physically see, they refer to something previously mentioned. In this sense, they are similar to *the* or *that* in English.

昨日、レストランに行きました。そこはとても大きい。。。。

昨日、レストランに行きました。その後で、。。。。

A. Fill in the blanks with the appropriate transition devices.

そして　それから　その後で　その前に　それに　それで　その間（に）
つぎに　まずはじめに　というのは　ですから　でも　ところが

1. 昨日、こうえんへ行きました。__________森山さんの家に行きました。__________森山さんはいませんでした。__________家へ帰りました。
2. 日本に行く時には、行きたいところがすぐにわかるようにガイドブックを買って読んだ方がいい。_____________いい旅行会社をさがした方がいい。________安い飛行機の切符を買った方がいい。__________二か月ぐらい前に予約をした方がいい。
3. 昨日は学校に行けませんでした。____________ルームメートが病気になったので、一緒に病院へ行ったのです。

ハワイ旅行 (Trip to Hawaii)

読む前に

1. ハワイに行ったことがありますか。
2. ハワイは何月がいいと思いますか。
3. ハワイではどんなことが出来ると思いますか。
4. ハワイではどんなお土産(みやげ)が買えると思いますか。
5. Skim the following text and tour information. そして、この人に一番いいツアーを下の旅行計画からさがして下さい。

言葉(ことば)のリスト

～島(とう)	island
ポリネシア文化(ぶんか)センター	Polynesian Cultural Center
内容(ないよう)	contents
宿泊地(しゅくはくち)	accommodation
自由行動(じゆうこうどう)	free activity

今年の冬は大阪(おおさか)からハワイに遊(あそ)びに行くつもりです。休みは十二月十九日から一月八日までなので、その間(あいだ)に五泊六日ぐらいの旅行に行こうと思います。ハワイ島(とう)には行ったことがありますが、オアフ島(とう)とマウイ島(とう)にはまだ行ったことがないので、そこに行きたいと思っています。それから、ポリネシア文化(ぶんか)センターはおもしろいそうなので、ハワイに行ったら、そこにも行きたいと思います。お金があまりないから、安いツアーをさがしています。

旅行日数			内容・宿泊地
5	6	7	
1-2	1-2	1-2	夜 : 大阪発→ホノルルへ (日付変更線通過) 午前 : ホノルル着 (レイ・グリーテイングはありません。) 着後 : バスにてワイキキへ。トラベル BOX にて滞在中の説明会 (昼食は各自でお取り下さい。) 午後 : ホノルル市内・近郊観光 ホテルチェックインは観光後になります。 ワイキキ
3	3-4	3-5	終日 : 自由行動 (各種オプショナルツアー) ワイキキ
4	5	6	朝：バスにて空港へ 午前：ホノルル発→大阪へ (日付変更線通過) 機中
5	6	7	午後 : 大阪着

オプショナルツアー
OPTIONAL TOUR

マウイ島日帰り観光
コース No. 3097-1
約 1 1 時間。毎日 06:30 前後発。昼食付き
最小催行人員 1 名 . 大人 28,000 円、子供 22,000 円
く主催 : トラベルプラザ >

カウアイ島日帰り観光
コース NO.3 日 7-2
約 1 1 時間。毎日 7:40 前後発。昼食付き
最小催行人員 1 名 大人 28,000 円、子供 22,000 円
< 主催 : トラベルプラザ >

ハワイ島日帰り観光
コース No.3097-3
約 1 1 時間。毎日 7:40 前後発 昼食付き
最小催行人員 1 ~2 名・大人 28,000 円、
子供 22,000 円
< 主催 : トラベルプラザ >

旅行代金 1おとな・こども同類

	ブーゲンビリアコース		
	5 日コース	6 日コース	7 日コース
出発日	食事なし	食事なし	食事なし
	3110-0 MC	3105-0 MC	3115-0 MC
11/21, 22, 23, 25, 26, 27, 28, 29, 30	95,000	99,000	105,000
12/21	108,000	111,000	115,000
12/19, 20, 22, 23	114,000	116,000	120,000
1/5, 6, 7, 8, 9, 10, 12, 13, 14, 15, 16	139,000	143,000	149,000
2/1, 2, 3, 4, 5, 6, 7, 8, 9, 10, 11, 12	150,000	154,000	160,000
3/16, 17, 18, 19, 20, 22, 23, 24, 25	161,000	165,000	171,000
1/11, 2/15	178,000	182,000	188,000
3/15, 21	202,000	206,000	212,000

デラックス・ポリネシア文化
センターコース
No. 1098-1
約 9 時間半 日曜日を抜く
毎日 13:50 前後発
夕食付き・最小催行人員 1 名
大人 15, 000 円、子供 13,000 円
< 主催 : トラベルプラザ >

シーライフ・パーク・ツアー

約 4 時間半 毎日 最小催行 人員 1 名
大人 5,000 円、子供 4,000 円
< 主催 : トラベルプラザ >

読んだ後で

A. 下のしつもんに日本語で答えて下さい。そして、せつぞくし (*transition device*) をつかって、旅行計画を書いて下さい。

1. 何日に大阪(おおさか)を出たらいいと思いますか。
2. 何日にホノルルを出たらいいでしょうか。
3. ポリネシア文化(ぶんか)センターにはいつ行けますか。
4. マウイ島(とう)へはいつ行ったらいいと思いますか。
5. お金はいくらぐらいかかると思いますか。

B. 下の旅行計画を読んで下さい。Underline the transition devices in the text. Then see what the differences are between your plan and this plan.

一月一日の晩に大阪(おおさか)を出て、一日の朝、ホノルルに着く予定です。その後、ホノルルのまちをバスで観光(かんこう)して、ホテルに行きます。昼ご飯(はん)はホテルに着いた時に食べて下さい。二日は朝十一時半にホノルルを出て、ポリネシア文化(ぶんか)センターに行く予定です。ポリネシア文化(ぶんか)センターでは、自由行動(じゆうこうどう)ですが、午後八時から十時まで、ショーがありますから、七時半までにセンターの入口(いりぐち)にあつまって下さい。ショーが終わったら、バスでホテルへ帰ります。三日目と四日目は自由行動(じゆうこうどう)です。五日の晩、ホノルルを出て、つぎの日に大阪(おおさか)に着く予定です。

総合練習

そうごうれんしゅう

ツアーの計画

Work in groups of four. You are travel agents who want to attract young Japanese tourists. Choose some travel destinations within your country and make a tour plan. Then present your travel plan.

Example: A: 日本からどこへ行ったらいいかな。

B: ニューヨークとボストンはどう？

C: いいね。何泊ぐらいしようかな。

D: そうだね。日本からニューヨークまで何時間ぐらいかかるかな？

C: 東京から十六時間ぐらいだと思うけど。

ロールプレイ

1. You are in Tokyo and thinking of going to Hiroshima. Tell a travel agent where you want to go and what you want to see there, and ask what is the best way to get there.
2. You want to make a hotel reservation in Kyoto. Call the hotel, tell the clerk that you need to make a reservation and find out if there is a room available. Ask the clerk to speak in easy Japanese rather than using the very polite forms. (Most hotel clerks use very polite speech.) You need to specify the type of room (シングル、ダブル), and your arrival and departure dates.
3. You are talking to a Japanese friend. Tell your friend about the most memorable trip you have taken. Describe where you went, what you did, and what happened.
4. You are talking to a Japanese friend who is thinking of going to the United States this summer. Tell your friend what to do before, during, and after visiting the United States.

Chapter 3

©Tatsuyuki Tayama / Fujifotos / The Image Works

将来(しょうらい)のために
Preparing for the Future

Objectives		Expressing future plans and current states; expressing what to do to achieve future objectives.
Vocabulary		Lifestyles and one's future life, parties and ceremonies, vocations, transitive/intransitive verbs
Dialogue		本田先生のけんきゅうしつで *At Professor Honda's office*
Japanese Culture		Changes in family structure, Japanese economy and employment practices
Grammar	I.	Expressing chronological order using 前 and 後
	II.	Talking about preparations using 〜ておく; expressing completion, regret and the realization that a mistake was made using 〜てしまう
	III.	Using transitive and intransitive verbs; expressing results of intentional actions using〜てある
	IV.	Expressing purpose and reason using the plain form + ため
	V.	Expressing obligation using 〜なければ／なくては　ならない／いけない; expressing lack of obligation using 〜なくてもいい
Listening		Paying attention to speech styles, 将来(しょうらい)の計画
Communication		Making confirmations and checking comprehension
Kanji		Top component shapes of **kanji** 言 葉 漢 字 質 問 卒 業 授 仕 事 結 婚 式 社 同 違 留 達 電 英 客
Reading		Using prefixes and suffixes, 日本人と結婚(けっこん)

Chapter Resources

www.cengagebrain.com

iLrn Heinle Learning Center

Audio Program

単語
たん

Flashcards

Nouns

エンジニア		engineer (as in electrical engineer)
かいじょう	会場	meeting place
けんきゅう	研究	research, けんきゅう（を）する to do research
けんきゅうしゃ	研究者	researcher
さいふ	財布	wallet, purse
しき	式	ceremony
じぶん	自分	self, oneself, I
しゃちょう	社長	company president
じゆう	自由	freedom, じゆう（な）is a な -adjective meaning *free*
しゅうしょく	就職	getting a job, ～にしゅうしょくする to get a job at ～
しょうたい	招待	invitation, ～を～にしょうたいする to invite
しょうたいじょう	招待状	invitation (letter or card)
しょうらい	将来	future
そうべつかい	送別会	farewell party
そつぎょう	卒業	graduation, ～をそつぎょうする graduate from ～
たんじょうかい	誕生会	birthday party
でんき	電気	electricity, electric light
どうそうかい	同窓会	reunion party
とし	年	year, age, 年をとる to become old, 年が上 older
にゅうがく	入学	entering a school, ～ににゅうがくする to enter ～
ひっこし	引っ越し	moving (house, residence, etc.), ひっこし（を）する to move (house, residence)
ふつう	普通	ordinary, regular
べんごし	弁護士	lawyer
ぼうえき	貿易	trading, ぼうえきがいしゃ trading company
ゆ	お湯	warm water, hot water (see わかす and わく)
りゅうがく	留学	study abroad, りゅうがく(を)する to study abroad, りゅうがくせい international student

う -verbs

あく	開く	(for something) to open
おこす	起こす	to wake up (someone)

おちる	落ちる	(for something) to fall
おとす	落とす	to drop (something)
おわる	終わる	(for something) to end
かかる		(for a telephone) to ring
かわる	変わる／替わる	(for something) to change
がんばる	頑張る	to try to do one's best, to hang on
きまる	決まる	(for something) to be decided
けす	消す	to turn off
しまる	閉まる	(for something) to close
しぬ	死ぬ	to die
ちがう	違う	to be different, A とBはちがう A and B are different. A はBとちがう A is different from B.
つく	付く／点く	(for something) to turn on
なおす	直す	to fix, to repair (something)
なおる	治る／直る	(for something) to heal, to be fixed
なくなる	亡くなる	to pass away, to die
ぬぐ	脱ぐ	to take off (shoes, clothes)
のこす	残す	to leave (something)
のこる	残る	(for something) to be left, to remain
はじまる	始まる	(for something) to begin
ひっこす	引っ越す	to move (house, etc.), to relocate
ひやす	冷やす	to chill, to let (something) cool down
まちがう	間違う	(for someone) to be mistaken, commonly used as まちがえている
よごす	汚す	to make (something) dirty
わかす	沸かす	to bring (water, bath) to boil, (お)ゆをわかす bring water to boil
わく	沸く	(for water, bath) to be boiled, (お)ゆがわく water is boiling

る -verbs

あける	開ける	to open (something)
あつめる	集める	to collect (something/someone)
うまれる	生まれる	(for someone/something) to be born
おえる	終える	to end (something); to finish (something)
かんがえる	考える	to think intellectually; to take (something) into consideration

きえる	消える	(for something) to go out, to go off
しめる	閉める	to close (something)
つける		to turn on (a TV, a light, etc.)
つづける	続ける	to continue (something)
のせる	乗せる	to give a ride (to someone) 〜を〜にのせる
はじめる	始める	to begin (something)
ひえる	冷える	(for something) to cool down
まちがえる	間違える	to miss (something), to make a mistake
やめる	止める	to quit, to stop
よごれる	汚れる	(for something) to become dirty

い -adjectives

わかい	若い	young, わかい used to describe teenagers and young people older than teenagers, but not small children.

な -adjectives

おなじ	同じ	same, AとBはおなじ A and B are the same AはBとおなじ A is the same as B. な must be deleted before a noun, as in おなじ人
じゆう (な)	自由 (な)	free, じゆうな生活(かつ) free (independent) lifestyle
だいじ (な)	大事 (な)	important

Particles

か		or, either or, 晴れか雨 rain or shine
までに		by, 五時までに帰る I will come back by 5 o'clock

Suffixes

〜かい	〜会	party, どうそうかい reunion, そうべつかい farewell party, たんじょうかい birthday party
〜しき	〜式	ceremony, そつぎょうしき graduation ceremony, にゅうがくしき matriculation ceremony, けっこんしき wedding
〜や	〜屋	owner of, 〜 retail store, さかなや fish market owner, にくや butcher, はなや flower shop owner, ほんや bookstore owner

単語の練習

A. ライフスタイルと将来の生活 Lifestyle and one's future life

自分 self, I	ふつう ordinary, average	人と同じ same as other people	人と違う to be different from others
じゆう（の／な） freedom, free	わかい young	かんがえる to think	がんばる to hold on, to do one's best
生まれる to be born	入学する to enter a school	卒業する to graduate	留学する to study abroad
けんきゅうする to do research	ひっこす to relocate, move	ひっこし moving, relocation	会社にしゅうしょくする to get a job at a company
店を持つ to own a store	やめる to quit/stop	年をとる to age	しぬ to die

おぼえていますか。

結婚する　つとめる　仕事　外国にすむ　生活　家を買う　アルバイト　大学院に入る　さがす　はたらく

Activity 1 Give the words and expressons that correspond to the following pictures.

Example:

Activity 2 Work in groups. Find out who identifies with the categories in the chart below. Write their names in the chart.

Example: A: ～さんは、自分(じぶん)はふつうの人だと思いますか。

B: ええ、たぶんそう思います。

Or いいえ、自分(じぶん)はちょっとふつうの人とは違(ちが)うと思います。

自分(じぶん)は～と思う	名前
ふつうの人	
人と違(ちが)うより同(おな)じ方が好き	
じゆうなライフスタイルが好き	
何でも (*everything*) よくがんばる方	

B. パーティと式(しき) Parties and ceremonies

入学式(にゅうがくしき) entrance ceremony	卒業式(そつぎょうしき) graduation ceremony	結婚式(けっこんしき) wedding ceremony	同窓会(どうそうかい) reunion	誕生会(たんじょうかい) birthday party
そうべつ会(かい) farewell party	会場(かいじょう) meeting place	しょうたいする to invite	しょうたいじょう invitation (letter)	

おぼえていますか。

ばしょ　教会(きょうかい)　よぶ　しらべる　予約する　電(でん)話をかける　計画をたてる

Supplementary vocabulary

いろいろなあつまり **Various gatherings**

かんげいかい	歓迎会	welcome party
こんしんかい	懇親会	social gathering
しんねんかい	新年会	beginning-of-the-year party
(お) そうしき	(お) 葬式	funeral
ぼうねんかい	忘年会	year-end party

新年会 is a party held sometime during the first two weeks of the new year.

Activity 3 質問(しつもん)に日本語で答えて下さい。

1. どんな時にしょうたいじょうを出しますか。
2. 今までどんな式(しき)やパーティに出たことがありますか。
3. 自分(じぶん)の結婚式(けっこんしき)にだれをしょうたいしたいですか。誕生会(たんじょうかい)はどうですか。
4. どの式(しき)に両親をよびたいと思っていますか。

C. 仕事(しごと) Vocations

エンジニア engineer

べんごし lawyer

けんきゅうしゃ researcher

社長(しゃちょう) company president

おぼえていますか。

会社員(かいしゃいん)

先生

医者

さかな屋(や)

本屋(や)

旅行会社(がいしゃ)

Supplementary Vocabulary　しょくぎょう　Occupations

かいけいし	会計士	accountant
きょうし	教師	teacher, instructor (more formal than 先生)
きょうじゅ	教授	professor
ぎんこういん	銀行員	bank employee
ぐんかんけい	軍関係	military-related (field)
けいさつかん	警察官	police officer
こうむいん	公務員	public officer; civil servant
コンサルタント		consultant
サラリーマン		businessman
じえいぎょう	自営業	self-employment
しょうぼうし	消防士	firefighter
しゅふ	主婦	housewife
じむいん	事務員	business clerk
せいじか	政治家	politician
とうしか	投資家	investor
のうか	農家	farmer

Activity 4　下の言葉(ことば)のいみは何だと思いますか。

飲み屋(や)　くつ屋(や)　食べ物屋(や)　とうふ屋(や)　ケーキ屋(や)　じてんしゃ屋(や)

Activtity 5　質問(しつもん)に日本語で答えて下さい。

1. ご両親は、どんな仕事(しごと)をしていますか。
2. 将来(しょうらい)、お父さんやお母さんと同(おな)じ仕事(しごと)をしたいですか。違(ちが)う仕事(しごと)の方がいいですか。
3. どんなところにしゅうしょくしたいと思いますか。
4. 自分(じぶん)が出来る仕事(しごと)は、どんな仕事(しごと)だと思いますか。
5. わかい時はどんな仕事(しごと)がいいですか。年(とし)をとったら、どんな仕事(しごと)がいいですか。
6. 何さいぐらいで仕事(しごと)をやめたいと思いますか。

Activity 6 Match the phrases in Columns A and B.

Column A	Column B
1. 十二さいから三十さいぐらいまでの人	a. エンジニア
2. 六十さいぐらいの人	b. やめる
3. 私のこと	c. けんきゅうしゃ
4. こまった 時 (*when you have a problem*) に話しに行く人	d. 年をとった人
5. きかいや電気(でんき)についてよく知っている人	e. 自分(じぶん)
6. 違(ちが)わないこと	f. 社長(しゃちょう)
7. 大学の先生がすること	g. けんきゅう
8. 新しいことを勉強する人	h. わかい人
9. 何かをしなくなること	i. べんごし
10. 会社の中で一番お金をもらう人	j. 同(おな)じ

D. じどうしとたどうし Intransitive verbs and transitive verbs

Transitive verbs		Intransitive verbs	
まどをあける	to open the window	まどがあく	the window opens
ドアをしめる	to close the door	ドアがしまる	the door closes
電気(でんき)をつける	to turn on the light	電気(でんき)がつく	the light is on
電気(でんき)をけす	to turn off the light	電気(でんき)がきえる	the light is off
電話(でんわ)をかける * 時間をかける *	to make a phone call to take time	電話(でんわ)がかかる 時間がかかる	the phone rings it takes time
映画(えい)をはじめる	to begin the movie	映画(えい)がはじまる	the movie begins
授業(じゅぎょう)をおえる	to finish the class	授業(じゅぎょう)がおわる	the class ends
子供を起こす	to wake up the child	子供が起きる *	the child wakes up
子供をくるまに乗せる	to put the child in the car	子供がくるまに乗る *	the child gets in the car
お金を出(だ)す	to pay (literally, to take out money)	お金が出る *	it will be paid (literally, the money comes out)
おゆをわかす	to bring the water to boil	おゆがわく	the water boils/is boiled
ジュースを冷(ひ)やす	to chill juice	ジュースが冷(ひ)える	the juice is chilled
くるまをガレージにもどす	to return the car to the garage.	くるまがガレージにもどる	the car returns to the garage
仕事(しごと)をつづける	to continue the work	仕事(しごと)がつづく *	the work continues
人をあつめる	to gather people	人があつまる *	people get together
会場(かいじょう)をきめる *	to decide on a meeting place	会場(かいじょう)がきまる	a meeting place is decided
ばしょを変(か)える	to change the place	ばしょが変(か)わる	the place changes
病気をなおす	to cure an illness	病気がなおる	the illness is cured
さいふをおとす	to drop a wallet	さいふがおちる	the wallet is dropped
食べ物をのこす	to leave some food	食べ物がのこる	the food remains
漢字(かんじ)を間違(まちが)える	to make a **kanji** mistake	漢字(かんじ)が間違(まちが)っている	the **kanji** is wrong
ふくをよごす	to soil the clothes	ふくがよごれる	the clothes become dirty

Notes

- Words with astericks (*) have been introduced in previous chapters.
- The commonly used form of 間違(まちが)う is 間違(まちが)っている .

おぼえていますか。

あつまる　きめる　起きる　乗る　電話をかける　出る　入れる　入る　帰る
きめる　上がる　上げる　下がる　下げる

Activity 7 下線 (*underline*) に、てきとうな (*appropriate*) 言葉を書いて下さい。

1. 風でまどが＿＿＿＿＿＿＿て、雨が家の中に入って来ました。だから、まどを＿＿＿＿＿＿＿下さい。
2. この漢字は違うから、＿＿＿＿＿＿＿方がいいですね。
3. ケーキが少し＿＿＿＿＿＿＿から、食べませんか。
4. 学生が＿＿＿＿＿＿＿ら、映画を＿＿＿＿＿＿＿。
5. けんたろうくんはまだ寝ています。授業におくれるから、＿＿＿＿＿＿＿方がいいですね。
6. さいふをどこかで＿＿＿＿＿＿＿ので、今、お金がありません。
7. 午後九時ですが、さやかさんのへやの電気が＿＿＿＿＿＿＿から、さやかさんは今晩はどこかに出かけているんでしょう。
8. 仕事が＿＿＿＿＿＿＿ので、家を新しいところに＿＿＿＿＿＿＿。
9. いい仕事がないから、今の仕事を＿＿＿＿＿＿＿つもりです。
10. せいせき (*grade*) を＿＿＿＿＿＿＿んですか。じゃあ、もっと勉強した方がいいですね。
11. 私の予定はもう＿＿＿＿＿＿＿から、高山さんの予定を＿＿＿＿＿＿＿下さい。
12. 昨日は朝まであつ子さんのへやの電気が＿＿＿＿＿＿＿、朝まで勉強していたんでしょう。
13. このへやはちょっとくらいから、電気を＿＿＿＿＿＿＿下さい。それに、暑いから、まどを＿＿＿＿＿＿＿くれませんか。
14. リーさんが会う時間を＿＿＿＿＿＿＿ので、さとみさんは一時間まったけど、家に帰りました。

Activity 8

Work with a partner. One person should select a verb pair from the chart above and create a phrase using either the transitive or intransitive verb from the pair. The partner then should then create a corresponding phrase with the remaining verb.

Example: A: まどをあけます。

B: まどがあきます。

Activity 9

Work with a partner. One person makes a set of cards with transitive verbs. The other person makes a set with cards with intransitive verbs. Combine the cards and mix them up. One person picks up a card and reads the verb on the card. The other person tries to say the corresponding verb. If the person can say the verb correctly, he/she gets the card.

Example: A: picks up a card with あく written on it and reads it.

B: あける

ダイアローグ

はじめに

A. 質問(しつもん)に日本語で答えて下さい。

1. 今、何のために日本語を勉強していますか。
2. 大学を卒業(そつぎょう)したら、どんな仕事(しごと)をしたいと思いますか。
3. そのために、どんなことをしようと思います。

B. 下のことをするためにはどんなじゅんびをしておかなければなりませんか。

1. 卒業式(そつぎょうしき)のパーティをします。
2. 冬休みにクラスで日本に行きます。
3. 高校の同窓会(どうそうかい)をします。

本田先生のけんきゅうしつで *At Professor Honda's office*

The order of the following **manga** frames is scrambled. Read the dialogue and unscramble the frames by writing the correct number in the box in each frame.

a

b

c

d

e

f

上田さんは、けんきゅうしつでゼミ (*seminar*) の先生の本田先生と話しています。

先生：　上田さんは日本に来てどのくらいになりますか。

上田：　一年半になります。来年の八月にはアメリカに帰ります。

先生：　早いですね。もう一年半ですか。で、アメリカに帰ったら、どうするんですか。

上田：　卒業(そつぎょう)までにまだ一年ありますから、大学にもどります。

先生：　そうですか。じゃあ、その後は？

上田：　まだよく分かりませんが、卒業(そつぎょう)した後は、また日本にもどりたいですから、日本語がつかえる仕事(しごと)をさがそうと思います。

先生：　そうですか。がんばって下さいね。

上田：　どうもありがとうございます。

上田さんは本田先生のけんきゅうしつの外で石(いし)田さんに会いました。

石(いし)田：　あ、上田さん、ちょうどよかった。今度のゼミの懇親会(こんしんかい)のこと、本田先生に話した？

上田：　あ、ごめん。忘れちゃった。

石(いし)田：　じゃ、まだ話してないんだね。じゃ、いいよ。ぼくも、後で先生に会うから、話しとくよ。

上田：　ありがとう。それで、もうじゅんびはおわったの？

石(いし)田：　うん。レストランの予約とりょうりのちゅうもんも、してあるよ。

上田：　じゃあ、みんなにメールは？

石(いし)田：　うん、先週出しといたから、そろそろへんじが来ると思うけど。

上田：　すごい、石(いし)田さん。何から何までありがとう。

Dialogue Phrase Notes

- ゼミ is short for "seminar." It refers to a class taken by college seniors with their advisors.
- 懇親会(こんしんかい) is a type of social gathering at which participants get to know each other and strengthen relationships among themselves. It often involves a sit-down dinner and drinking.
- そろそろ means *pretty soon*, and へんじ means *reply.*
- 何から何までありがとう means *thank you for everything.*

ダイアローグの後で

A. Complete the following paragraph based on the dialogue.

上田さんは＿＿＿＿＿＿＿＿＿＿にアメリカに帰る予定です。そして、＿＿＿＿＿＿＿＿＿＿ために、大学にもどって勉強するつもりです。大学を卒業（そつぎょう）した後、＿＿＿＿＿＿＿＿＿ために、日本語をつかえる仕事（しごと）をさがそうと思っています。

B. ゼミの懇親会（こんしんかい）について下の質問（しつもん）に日本語で答えて下さい。

1. 懇親会（こんしんかい）のために、どんなことがしてありますか。
2. まだ、何がしてありませんか。
3. しょうたいのメールが来た人は何をしておかなければならないと思いますか。

C. Underline the sentences or phrases in the dialogue where the speaker is confirming what has been said.

D. Change the conversation between Ms. Ueda and Professor Honda by substituting Mr. Ishida for Professor Honda and by using casual speech for those dialogue lines.

日本の文化

家族構成の変化 Changes in family structure

In Japan, the wife has traditionally stayed at home to take care of the children while the husband works outside of the home. It is also traditional for the eldest son to live with and take care of his parents. However, this traditional family structure is changing, as discussed in Chapter 10 of *Nakama 1*. According to a recent government survey, the percentage of people who prefer the traditional family structure declined from 52.3% in 2003 to 41.1%. Conversely, the percentage of people who oppose the traditional structure grew from 47.7% to 58.9%. Moreover, over 65% of those under 50 are against the division of roles between husband and wife.

The average size of a Japanese family declined from 5.97 in 1955 to 2.47 in 2007. The number of single-person households grew from 5.3% in 1960 to 29.0 % in 2005, and the average number of children in a family went down to 1.25 in 2005, the lowest since 1898. The percentage of children under 15 years old decreased to 13.7% in 2006. Although the birth rate recovered slightly, to an average of 1.32 in 2007, the average must now rise above 2.5 to stop the population decline.

The population decline is partly happening because more people postpone marriage until their late twenties, and consequently have fewer children. Traditionally, the Japanese have considered young people as fully independent adults only after they get married, but this idea no longer holds much importance. Instead, a growing number of young adults view marriage as constraining.

© Eric Kotara / Alamy

In addition, the ratio of the divorce rate to the marrige rate increased from 8% in 1960 to 35.4% in 2007, although it is still smaller than rates in the United States (45.8%), England (42.6%), or Australia (46.0%) in 2002. Accordingly, the percentage of single-parent households with children grew to 14.7 in 2005 (Public Opinion Poll on Statistics Survey, Cabinet Office, Government of Japan, 2006).

As the world's healthiest nation, the number of elderly people in Japan is also on the rise. The percentage of people over 60 years old was 26.4% in 2006, and the percentage of those older than 65 was 19.7%. Elderly people are financially more stable compared to fifty years ago, thanks to post-war economic growth and a better social security system. Older adults often choose to live apart from their children, as long as they remain healthy.

日本の経済と採用傾向 The Japanese economy and employment trends

Japan has suffered from a severe economic slow-down since the "bubble economy" (バブル経済) burst in the late 1980s. This bubble economy was based largely on overpriced real estate. As a small country with a large population, Japan placed a high

© amana images inc. / Alamy

value on real estate, and the price of real estate and stocks surged during the 1980s. People started investing in real estate as well as stocks for short-term profits. This resulted in unreasonably high prices for real estate, hence the term "bubble economy." During this period, banks made a number of loans taking overvalued real estate as collateral. The abrupt plunge in the price of real estate resulted in an economic slump. This was referred to as バブルがはじける (The bubble bursts.). Banks still have a large amount of bad loans that cannot be recovered.

The bursting of the bubble economy resulted in many businesses going through organizational restructuring (リストラ). Japan's employment system has been in transition since. Although it was once popular to identify the practice of lifetime employment (終身雇用) as a major characteristic of Japanese employment, this practice has become less prevalent. And the emphasis placed on the life-long employment system was always suspect, because this system was never the only or even the most prominent employment system in Japan. In reality, employees of large corporations (大企業) are the only people who enjoyed a high level of job security. Workers at smaller businesses (中小企業、零細企業) have never had this type of job security.

Seniority (年功序列), traditionally the main determining factor for job promotions in Japan, is now sometimes abandoned in favor of merit-based promotions. This shift has made it more acceptable for people to change jobs on their own initiative, and has also made it more economically viable, as well—people now have the chance to be hired at positions equivalent to the ones they have given up at their old companies, instead of at entry-level positions, as was once the case.

The burst of the bubble economy also resulted in a significant increase in the number of businesses using temporary workers instead of regular employees. Temporary workers are employed on an hourly basis, and their contracts are renewed every three months to one year. Even those temporary workers who remain with the same company for a long time are not eligible for benefit packages as the permanent employees are.

As Japan's economy recovers, the government has been trying to help more temporary and female workers to obtain regular employment. This is because Japan's population started declining in 2005, due to the low birth rate. Also, a large number of baby boomers have begun to retire and expect to be out of the workforce in the next ten years. As a result, the number of job openings has increased dramatically since 2005, and the number of female workers is also increasing. In 2007, 59.5% of women between 15 and 64 years of age held a job. The government plans to further increase the percentage of married women who hold jobs outside of the home and has set a goal of 70% employment for the year 2017.

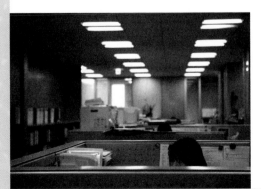
© Paolo Patrizi / Alamy

文法(ぶんぽう)

I. Expressing chronological order using 前 and 後

In Chapter 5 of *Nakama 1*, 前 and 後ろ are introduced to indicate special relationships, such as つくえの前 (*in front of the desk*) and つくえの後ろ (*behind the desk*). In Chapter 12 of *Nakama 1*, duration of time + 前 and 後 are used to indicate time, such as 三年前 (*three years ago*) and 四年後 (*four years later, four years from now*). This chapter introduces expanded usage of 前 and 後 to indicate chronology. Both 前 and 後 are nouns that can be used with nouns and verbs. Be careful to pronounce 後 in this usage as あと.

A. Noun の前 (に) ／ the dictionary form of verbs + 前 (に), *before* ～

The particle に to express time is optional with ～前. As it can be used as a topic, 前 can be combined with は as in 前は or 前には.

授業(じゅぎょう)の前に、話があります。	*I have to talk to you before class.*
ひっこしの前に、くるまをなおします。	*I will fix the car before moving.*
しけんの前は、あまり寝られない。	*I cannot sleep well before an exam.*
旅行に行く前には、計画をたてた方がいいですよ。	*You should make plans before you go on a trip.*
家を出る前に、 電話(でん)したよ。	*I called before I left home.*
卒業(そつぎょう)する前に、 やりたいことがある。	*I have something that I want to do before graduation.*

The form should be noun + の + 前 or the dictionary form of verb + 前. The use of the dictionary form in a subordinate clause such as 前 indicates that the event in the subordinate clause was not completed before the performance of the event in the main clause. Since the event in the 前 clause cannot be completed until after the event in the main clause, the verb preceding 前 must be in the present form regardless of the tense used in the main clause.

結婚(けっこん)する前に、家を買いたいです。	*I want to buy a house before getting married.*
結婚(けっこん)する前に、家を買いました。	*I bought a house before getting married.*

南： もう帰るの？	*Are you going home?*
大川： うん。	*Yeah.*
南： じゃあ、帰る前にこれ見て。	*Well, look at this before you go.*

Notes

- If the subject of the 前 clause is different from the main clause, it must be marked with the particle が.

  母が来る前に、へやをそうじしました。

  I cleaned my room before my mother came.

- 前に can also be used as an independent expression.

  この会場(かいじょう)には、前に来たことがあります。
  I have come to this meeting place before.

  あのみずうみは、前はとてもきれいだった。
  That lake was very clean before.

B. Noun の後(あと)（で）／the plain past affirmative form of verbs + 後(あと)（で）, after ～

The particle で to express time is optional with ～後(あと). Because it can be used as a topic, 後(あと) can be combined with は as in 後(あと)は or 後(あと)では.

そうべつ会(かい)の後(あと)で、ひっこした。	*I moved after the farewell party.*
卒業式(そつぎょうしき)の後(あと)で、友達(だち)と写真をとった。	*I took a picture with my friend after the graduation ceremony.*
日本に留学(りゅう)した後(あと)で、その人と会った。	*I met the person after I went to Japan for a study abroad.*
しゅうしょくした後(あと)で、結婚したい。	*I want to get married after I get a job.*

Use of the plain past form in a subordinate clause indicates that the event in the subordinate clause was completed before the event in the main clause. The completion of the event in the 後(あと) clause is necessary for the performance of the event in the main clause, the verb in the 後(あと) clause must be in the past tense regardless of the tense of the main clause.

木山：小山さんのそうべつ会(かい)、行った？
Did you go to Ms. Koyama's farewell party?
キム：うん、バイトがおわった後(あと)で行ったから、少しおそくなったけど。
Yeah, but I was a bit late because I went after I finished my part-time job.

お母さん：いつそうじするの？	*When are you going to clean up* (your room)?
子供：学校から帰った後(あと)でするよ。	*I will do it after I come back from school.*

If the subject of the 後(あと)で clause is different from that of the main clause, it must be marked with the particle が.

田中さんは、子供が生まれた後(あと)で、仕事をはじめた。	*Mr. Tanaka started working after his child was born.*
授業(じゅぎょう)がおわった後(あと)で来て下さい。	*Please come after the class is over.*

後(あと) can be used independently, with no clause.

後(あと)で来て下さい。　*Please come later.*

話してみましょう

Activity 1 Describe the following schedule for the day of the wedding using 前（に）and 後(あと)（で）.

Example: ホテルに着いた後(あと)で、少し休みます。

レストランで食事(じ)をする前に、少し休みます。

午前十一時	ホテルに着きます。
	少し休みます。
午後十二時	ホテルのレストランで、食事(じ)をします。
一時	ヘアサロン (*hair salon*) に行きます。
三時	結婚式(けっこんしき)があります。
五時半	ひろうえん (*reception*) がはじまります。
七時	ひろうえん (*reception*) がおわります。
八時	二次会(にじかい) (*second party*) に行きます。
十時	ホテルにもどります。

Activity 2 Answer the questions using 前 and 後(あと).

Example: いつしゅくだいをしますか。

家に帰った後(あと)します。

寝る前にします。

1. いつ勉強しますか。
2. いつメールをつかいますか。
3. いつご両親に電(でん)話しますか。
4. いつ海外旅行に行きたいですか。
5. いつごろ、結婚(けっこん)しようと思いますか。
6. いつ、今すんでいるところから、ひっこしをしたいですか。

Activity 3 Work with a partner. Ask your partner what he/she wants to do before or after the following occasions. Then report your partner's response to the class.

Example: A: 卒業(そつぎょう)する前にどんなことがしたいですか。

B: そうですね。日本に留(りゅう)学したいですね。

～さんは卒業(そつぎょう)する前に日本に留(りゅう)学したいそうです。

	～前にすること	～後ですること
卒業(そつぎょう)します		
しゅうしょくします		
結婚(けっこん)します		

II. Talking about preparations using ～ておく; expressing completion, regret, or the realization that a mistake was made using ～てしまう

The て-form of verbs can be combined with many types of auxiliary verbs to express different nuances. For example, you have learned that ている expresses ongoing action, continued existence of a result of an action, and habitual action. There are many other types, such as ておく (*do ~in advance*) , てしまう (*finish doing ~*) , てある (*has been done*), てみる (*try doing ~*) , てもいい (*can do~*), てはいけない (*must not do*) and so on. This chapter introduces three of them: ～ておく, ～てしまう, and ～てある. In this section, the first two of these constructions are introduced.

A. Talking about preparations using ～ておく , do ～ in advance

The て-form of the verb + おく is used when someone does something for a future purpose or leaves the current state as is for a future purpose. For example, the act of checking out graduate schools is done as preparation or precaution in the following sentence.

卒業式(そつぎょうしき)の前に、ばしょをチェックしておく。	*I will check places before the graduation ceremony.*
ひっこしのじゅんびをしておきます。	*I will make preparations for moving.*

～ておく／～でおく becomes ～とく／～どく in casual speech.

Formal speech	Casual speech	Meaning
食べ物をのこしておきます	食べ物、のこしとく	*to leave some food for someone*
おゆをわかしておきます	おゆ、わかしとく	*to boil water in advance*
薬を飲んでおきます	薬、飲んどく	*to take medication in advance*

今晩友達(だち)が来るから、ワインを冷(ひ)やしときましょう。
I will chill wine (in advance) since my friends are coming over tonight.
しゅくだいをはじめる前に、ゲームで遊んどこう。
Let's play some more games before I start doing homework.

大学院生： 先生、ドア、しめましょうか。
Shall I close the door?
先生： いや、学生が来ますから、あけておいて下さい。
No, a student's coming, so please leave it open.

お父さん： げんかんの電気(でんき)、けそうか。
Shall I turn off the light in the entrance?
お母さん： あ、つけといて。まだ、大輔(だいすけ)が帰ってきてないから。
Leave it on. Daisuke's not home yet.

Notes

- 〜ておく conjugates as an う-verb.

書いておかない	書いとかない
書いておきます	書いときます
書いておく	書いとく
書いておこう	書いとこう
書いておいて	書いといて

B. Expressing completion, regret, and the realization that a mistake was made using 〜てしまう

The て-form of the verb + しまう can have two interpretations. The first emphasizes the completion of an action. In this interpretation, 〜てしまう indicates that the speaker has finished doing something more clearly than the simple verb form does. For example, ごはんを食べてしまった emphasize the idea that the speaker has finished the meal, as opposed to ごはんを食べた, which merely reports that the speaker performed the act of eating a meal.

明日までに履歴書(りれきしょ)をかいてしまいます。
I will finish writing the resume by tomorrow.
古くなったら、おいしくないから、今食べてしまった方がいいよ。
It won't taste good if it gets old, so you should finish it now.
その DVD はもう見てしまいました。
I have already seen that DVD.

〜てしまう / でしまう becomes 〜ちゃう / じゃう in casual speech.

Formal speech	Casual speech	Meaning
テストで間違(まちが)えてしまいました	テストで間違(まちが)えちゃった	*I made a mistake on the exam.*
その本はもう読んでしまいました	その本もう読んじゃった	*I already finished reading the book.*

今日は、もうジョギングをしてしまった。 *I have already gone jogging today.*
リーさんへのプレゼント、もうつつんじゃったよ。 *I have already wrapped Mr. Li's gift.*

お母さん： しゅくだいはおわったの。 *Is your homework finished?*
子供： うん、もうしちゃったよ。 *Yes it's finished.* (lit.: *I've finished it.*)

The second usage of ～てしまう indicates that something that should not have happened took place, or that someone did something that he or she should not have done. In this case, the て-form of the verb + しまう often conveys regret. Whether the て-form- of the verb + しまう indicates completion or regret depends on the context.

Expressing regret and the realization that a mistake was made

大事(だいじ)なレポートを おとしてしまった。 *I accidentally lost an important report.*

いぬがしんでしまった。 *My dog has died.*

あ！きょうかしょ忘れちゃった！ *Oh! I forgot my textbook.*

田中： どうしたんですか、その足。 *What's wrong with your foot?*
上田： かいだんからおちちゃったんです。 *I fell down the stairs.*

すみません、田中さんのケーキは私が食べてしまったんです。
I'm sorry, but I ate Mr. Tanaka's cake.

NOTES

- ～てしまう conjugates as an う verb.

食べてしまわない	食べちゃわない
食べてしまいます	食べちゃいます
食べてしまう	食べちゃう
食べてしまおう	食べちゃおう
食べてしまって	食べちゃって
食べてしまった	食べちゃった

話してみましょう

Activity 1

Make a sentence by choosing the appropriate main clause of the subordinate clause, then changing the appropriate verb in the main clause to ～てしまう.

Example: 1. ケーキが少しのこっているから、／ a. 食べましょう。
ケーキが少しのこっているから、食べてしまいましょう。

1. ケーキが少しのこっているから、
2. かんがえる前に、
3. 五時におきゃくさんが来るから、
4. 二十五さいになる前に、
5. 子供が生(う)まれる前に、
6. 今度の同窓会(どうそうかい)は 人がたくさん来るから、
7. 社長(しゃちょう)が知る前に、

a. 食べましょう。
b. した方がいいです。
c. 社長(しゃちょう)に話したらどうでしょうか。
d. 今のアパートから大きい家にひっこします。
e. 早く会場(かいじょう)をきめましょう。
f. 大事(だいじ)なものをはこに入れましょう。
g. 大学を卒業(そつぎょう) したいです。

Activity 2 You inadvertently did the things listed in 1–6 below, and need to apologize. Make an apology using the phrases in 1–6 and 〜てしまう.

Example: マクレーさんにかりた本をなくす (*to lose*)。
<u>すみません。マクレーさんにかりた本をなくしてしまったんです。</u>

1. 昨日メールを出したけど、メールアドレスを間違(まちが)えていた。
2. (友達(だち)) の大事(だいじ)な CD がだめになった。
3. バスの時間を間違(まちが)えて、授業(じゅぎょう)におくれた。
4. さいふを家に忘れて来た。
5. (友達(だち)) と話す前に、一人できめた。
6. 山田さんのプレゼントを私のだと思って、あけた。

Activity 3 Work with a partner. Create dialogues in which you must tell someone that you have done something unfortunate, then ask that person for help. Use the following situations and 〜てしまう . Share your dialogues with the class by acting them out.

Example: コンタクトレンズがおちた。
A: あ、キムさん。どうしたの?
B: コンタクトレンズがおちちゃったんだ。
A: それは大変!じゃあ、一緒(しょ)にさがそうよ。

1. 電車(でんしゃ)の中で寝ていて、かばんを忘れた。
2. 200ドル入っているさいふをおとした。
3. 仕事(しごと)がいやになって、やめた。
4. ノートに書いていたけれども、テストの日を間違(まちが)えた。
5. コンピュータをつかいすぎて、手が痛くなった。
6. 友達(だち)のふくをよごした。

Activity 4

Answer the following questions using the て-form of verbs + おく and the expressions in the box.

Example: 結婚式(けっこんしき)の前に何をしますか。

友達(だち)にしょうたいじょうを出しておきます。

友達(だち)にしょうたいじょうを出す	お金をあつめる	電気(でんき)をつける	後(あと)のことをよくかんがえる
先生に電(でん)話をかける	いろいろなことをする	まどをしめる	ホテルの予約をする
新しい仕事(しごと)をさがす	かぜをなおす	飲み物を冷(ひ)やす	メールをする

1. 友達(だち)があそびに来る前は、何をしておきますか。
2. 授業(じゅぎょう)を休む前に、どうしますか。
3. 出かける時、どうしますか。
4. 今の仕事(しごと)をやめる前に、何をしておいた方がいいですか。
5. 旅行に行く前に、何をしておいた方がいいですか。
6. 寝る前に、何をしておきますか。
7. 家を買う前に、何をしておきますか。
8. 送別会(そうべつかい)の前に、どんなじゅんびをしておきますか。
9. しぬ前に、どんなことをしておきたいと思いますか。

Activity 5

Work with a partner. Think about three activities for which some preparations are necessary. Then write as many preparations as needed for each activity.

Example: 日本語のしけん

漢字(かんじ)を勉強しておく。友達(だち)と話す練習(れんしゅう)をしておく。

CD をよく聞いておく。教科(きょうか)書をよく読んでおく。

Main activities	じゅんび
1	
2	
3	

III. Using transitive and intransitive verbs; expressing results of intentional actions using ～てある

A. Using transitive and intransitive verbs

Transitive verbs are verbs that express action taken directly on an object by someone. The object, known as a direct object, is marked with the particle を in Japanese: 私はドアをあけた (*I opened the door*).

Intransitive verbs do not take a direct object, but rather are used in situations where the object acts on its own. An example would be ドアがあいた (*The door opened* [on its own]). English has similar verb pairs such as *to raise* and *to rise* (*Bob raised the flag* vs. *the flag rose*). However, native English speakers are often unaware of the differences between transitive and intransitive verbs, partly because the same verb can often be used in both transitive and intransitive constructions. The verb *to open* in the example above is one such verb. Japanese verbs, on the other hand, often come in transitive/ intransitive pairs, such as あける／あく, and the same verb cannot be used for both functions in Japanese.

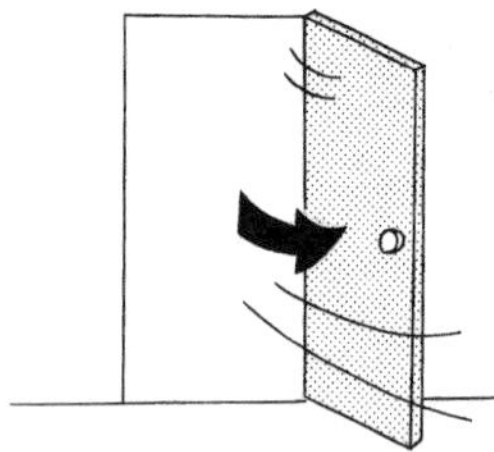

ドアが　あいた。
The door opened (on its own) .

ドアを　あけた。
I opened the door.

お母さんは子供を八時に起こします。
The mother wakes the child up at eight o'clock.

子供は八時に起きます。
The child wakes up at eight o'clock

Use a transitive verb when the focus is on the person who performs the action. Use an intransitive verb when the focus is on the event/action itself.

私は　電話を　かけています。	*I am making a phone call.*
電話が　かかりました。	*The phone is ringing.*

Except for some verbs like 入る, which can take an animate subject, as in 私はおふろに入る, many intransitive verbs of transitive/intransitive verb pairs take an inanimate subject and do not express the speaker's intentional action. When they are used with the て-form of verbs + いる structure, they express a resultant state as introduced in Chapter 9 of *Nakama 1*.

電気がついています。　*The light is on.*
まどがしまっています。*The window is closed.*

山本：このくつ、よごれていますね。　*These shoes are dirty.*
時田：ええ、子供がよごしてしまったんですよ。　*Yes, my child soiled them* (lit.: *got them dirty*).

先生：スミスさんのしゅくだいが出ていませんね。
Mr. Smith, you haven't turned in your homework. (lit.: *Mr. Smith's homework has not been turned in.)*

スミス：すみません。まだしていないんです。明日出します。
I am sorry. I have not done it yet. I will turn it in tomorrow.

大川：まだケーキがのこっていますよ。だれか食べませんか。
Some cake is still left. Would anybody like to eat it?

リー：あ、それはキムさんのケーキですから、のこしておいたんです。
Ah, since that is Ms. Kim's cake, I left it for her.

山田：この漢字、間違ってるよ。
This kanji is wrong.

上田：あ、本当だ。この漢字はむずかしいから、よく間違えるんだ。
Oh, you're right. This kanji is difficult, so I often make a mistake.

B. Expressing results of intentional action using 〜てある

〜てある expresses a state that results from someone's intentional action. It is usually used to express a situation where someone has done something for some purpose and the speaker wants to talk about the state resulting from that action. Therefore, 晩ごはんが作ってある in the following sentence indicates that the dinner has been cooked for a purpose and it is ready.

晩ごはんが作ってありますから、後で食べて下さい。
I made dinner for you, so please eat it later. (lit.: *Dinner has been made, so please eat it later.*)

The verb in the 〜てある construction can be transitive or intransitive, but it must express an intentional action.

雨がふりそうだから、まどがしめてあります。
Since it looks as if it will rain, the windows have been closed.

たくさんトレーニングはしてあるから、マラソンでいいタイムが出せるでしょう。
Since I trained a lot, I should have a good time in the marathon.

When the main verb is transitive, the direct object can be marked with either が or を. The particle を tends to be chosen when the action was performed by the speaker.

たくさん食べ物が　買ってあります。　*A lot of food has been purchased.* (by me or others)
たくさん食べ物を　買ってあります。　*A lot of food has been purchased* (by me).

In the case of transitive and intransitive verb pairs, transitive verbs indicate an intentional action. So the て-form of transitive verbs + ある is used to express a state resulting from an intentional action. In contrast, intransitive verbs in the transitive/intransitive verb pairs usually express non-intentional action, except for verbs such as 入る and のる, so they are not used in 〜てある constructions. Instead, they are used in 〜ている constructions to express a resultant state.

ビールを冷やしてあります。　*The beer has been chilled.*
ビールが冷えています。　*The beer is cold.*
おゆをわかしてあります。　*The water has been boiled.*
おゆがわいています。　*The water is boiling.*

トム：　どうしてまどがあいているの？　*Why is the window open?*
かおり：　暑いから、あけてあるの。　*Since it's hot, I have left it open.*

川口：　来週のじゅんびはもうおわりましたか。
Are you ready for the trip? (lit.: *Have preparations been finished?*)
北山：　ええ、ホテルの予約もしてあるし、飛行機の切符も買ってありますよ。
Yes, the hotel reservation has been made, and plane ticket has been purchased.

タクシーをよんであるから、もうすぐ来ます。
I've called a cab already, so it should be here soon. (lit.: *Since a cab has been called, it should be here soon.*)

そのことについては私から先生に少し話してあるから、そうだんしてみたらどうですか。
I've spoken to the teacher a little bit about it, so why don't you talk with him?

高山：　朝早かったから大変でしょう。
Since you had to get up early this morning, it might be tough, won't it?
石田：　いいえ、よく寝てありますから、大丈夫ですよ。
No, since I (have) slept well (since I got a good sleep), I'll be OK.

話してみましょう

Activity 1 Make a sentence using the nouns and verbs presented.

Example:　水／出る
水が出ます。

1. 水／出す
2. 仕事／かわる
3. 電気／つく
4. くるま／乗せる
5. バイト／つづく
6. 時間／間違える
7. さいふ／おとす
8. へや／よごれている
9. お金／あつまる
10. 電気／きえる
11. ジュース／のこる
12. 電話／かかる
13. 病気／なおす
14. 卒業式の日／きまる
15. 授業／おえる

Activity 2 Work in groups of four. Make a pile of cards using transitive and intransitive verbs. One person selects a card and creates a phrase using the verb written on it. The other three should try to say a phrase using the corresponding transitive or intransitive verb. The first person to correctly make a phrase wins the round.

Example:　A:　(The card has あく written on it.) まどがあきます。
B:　まどをあけます。

Activity 3

Look at the picture of Mr. Ishida's room. Describe his room using intransitive verbs.

Example: 電気（でんき）がついています。

Activity 4

Mr. Ishida's parents are visiting him today, so he cleaned his room. It is a very hot day today. Now describe his room in the following picture using the て-form of verbs + ある. Note that はな means *flower.*

Example: まどがあけてあります。

Activity 5

Work with a partner. What kind of preparations should you finish before the following events? Make a dialogue using the phrases in 1-5 below with ~てしまう and ~てある. Use casual speech.

Example: 誕生会（たんじょうかい） / お母さんに話す / お父さんに言（い）う

A: 今度の誕生会（たんじょうかい）のことなんだけど。

B: お母さんに話してあるの？

A: うん。もう話しちゃったよ。

B: あ、そう。じゃあ、お父さんにも言（い）ってあるの？

A: それはまだ。明日言（い）うつもり。

1. 旅行／切符(ぷ)を買う／旅館の予約をする
2. 卒業式(そつぎょうしき)／ガウン (*gown*) を買う／先生をよぶ
3. 母の日／カードを書く ／カーネーション (*carnation*) を買う
4. 同窓会(どうそうかい)／会場(かいじょう)をきめる／しょうたいじょうを出す
5. 入学式(にゅうがくしき)／両親に言(い)う／新しいふくを買う

IV. Expressing purpose and reason using the plain form + ため

The ます stem of the verb + に (*Nakama 1*, Chapter 6,) expresses purpose, but this construction must be used when the main verb is a motion verb such as 行く, 来る, and 帰る. This chapter introduces the dependent noun ため, which expresses a purpose and can be used with a wider variety of verbs. In addition, ため can be used to express reason. Whether ため expresses a purpose or a reason depends on the type of verb and adjective used with ため and the type of main verb.

A. Expressing purpose, using the plain form of the verb + ため, *in order to* ～, for ～

The plain form of the verb + ため expresses purpose (*for the purpose of* ～) or reason/cause (*because*). When the plain form of verb + ため indicates a purpose, the main clause expresses an action or event that is controlled by the speaker. Also, ため is often preceded by a noun + の or a plain present affirmative form of a verb which expresses an action or event that can be controlled by the speaker. For example, in order to express the idea of someone standing up in order to open a door, ドアをあける, which is controlled by the speaker, is used rather than ドアがあく, which is not controlled by the speaker. Therefore, the sentence should be ドアをあけるためにたった.

エンジニアになるために、勉強しています。 *I am studying in order to become an engineer.*

けんきゅうするために、来ました。 *I have come to do research.*

自分(じぶん)のためになる仕事(しごと)がしたい。 *I want to do work that is good for myself.*

何のために、その会社(かいしゃ)にしゅうしょくするんですか。 *Why are you taking a job at that company?*

留(りゅう)学するために、アルバイトをする。 *I work part-time to study abroad.*

将来(しょうらい)のために、わかい時は色々(いろいろ)なことをした方がいい。 *For your future, you should experience various things while you're young.*

Notes

- When ため is used with a motion verb such as 行く, 来る, and 帰る, ため expresses a rather important purpose. On the other hand, the ます-stem of verbs + に can be used without a directional phrase, and the purpose does not have to be important.

しけんの勉強をするために図書館に行きました。
I went to the library to study for the exam.

しけんの勉強をしに図書館に行きました。
I went in order to study for the exam.

コーヒーを飲むために来ました。 *I came to have some coffee.*

コーヒーを飲みに来ました。 *I came to have some coffee.*

- Also, ため can be followed by the particle に (when it modifies a verbal phrase) or の when it modifies a noun. The particle に can be optionally deleted.

日本に留学するため（に）アルバイトをしているんです。
I'm working part-time in order to go to Japan to study.

これは、新しいくるまを買うためのお金です。
This is the money to buy a new car.

体育館は、うんどうするための建物です。
A gym is the place where people exercise.

B. Expressing reason or cause, using the plain form + ため

The plain form of verbs + ため indicates a reason or cause (1) when ため is preceded by an adjective or the past plain form of a verb and adjective, or (2) when the main clause expresses an action or event that cannot be controlled by the speaker.

Past tense + ため (*because* ～)

祖父がなくなったため、学校に来られませんでした。
I couldn't come to school because my grandfather died.

仕事をやめたために、生活が大変になってしまった。
Life got tough because I quit my job.

Adjective + ため (*because* ～)

アルバイトが大変なために、毎晩おそく帰る。
I go home late every night because my part-time job is demanding.

博物館はここからとおいため、くるまで行った方がいいでしょう。
You should probably go to the museum by car because it's far away from here.

Uncontrollable event in the main clause (*because* ～)

しゅうしょくがきまらないため（に）、毎晩寝られない。
I cannot sleep every night because I have not gotten a job.

けんきゅうのため、今日は家に帰れません。
I cannot go home today because of my research.

雪のため、電車がおそく来た。
The train arrived late because of the snow.

Grammatically, ため is a noun, so the form of an adjective or a verb that precedes ため is the same as noun modifying clauses.

	Category	Example	Meaning
い-adjectives	いい (*good*)	いいため	*because it is good*
		よくないため	*because it isn't good*
		よかったため	*because it was good*
		よくなかったため	*because it wasn't good*
Copula verbs	留(りゅう)学生 (*foreign student*)	留(りゅう)学生のため	*for the sake of the foreign student; because of the foreign student*
		留(りゅう)学生じゃないため	*because he/she isn't a foreign student*
		留(りゅう)学生だったため	*because he/she was a foreign student*
		留(りゅう)学生じゃなかったため	*because he/she wasn't a foreign student*
な-adjectives	大事(だいじ)な (*important*)	大事(だいじ)なため	*because it is important*
		大事(だいじ)じゃないため	*because it isn't important*
		大事(だいじ)だったため	*because it was important*
		大事(だいじ)じゃなかったため	*because it wasn't important*
Verbs	なおす (*to fix*)	なおすため	*in order to fix something; because he/she fixes something*
		なおさないため	*because he/she doesn't fix something*
		なおしたため	*because he/she fixed something*
		なおさなかったため	*because he/she didn't fix something*

NOTES

- When the plain form + ため expresses a reason or cause, it can be replaced by から and ので. But ため is more formal than から or ので, so it is rarely used in casual speech.

  あの子供は、けががなおらないため、まだ入院している。
  The child is still hospitalized because the injury has not healed.

  しけんのために、今日はアルバイトに行けません。
  I cannot go to my part-time job because I have an examination.

話してみましょう

Activity 1 Choose a phrase in Column A and form a clause with ため indicating a reason. Then choose a phrase that expresses the corresponding result from Column B, and make a sentence expressing the reason and result.

Example: Column A ドアがしまっています／Column B 中に入れません。
ドアがしまっているため、中に入れません。

Column A	Column B
1. お金があつまりません	a. よく外国に行きます。
2. 大きい会社(かいしゃ)は好きじゃありません	b. 間違(まちが)えることも多いですが、仕事(しごと)は早いです。
3. 人と同(おな)じなのはきらいです	c. お金がかかるけんきゅうは出来ません。
4. 年(とし)をとりました	d. 私もべんごしになりました。
5. まだわかいです	e. 違(ちが)う病院に行ってみようと思っています。
6. ぼうえき会社につとめています	f. 足がよわくなりました。
7. 父がべんごしでした	g. このふくを着ています。
8. 病気がなおりません	h. この会社(かいしゃ)ではたらいています。

Activity 2 Define each of the following objects using the plain form + ための ～.

Example: はし
食べるためのものです。／食べるためのもの（だ）よ。

1. ファックス
2. iPod
3. えんぴつ
4. コンピュータ
5. たんす
6. コート
7. くるま
8. さいふ

Activity 3 Work as a class. Ask your classmates what they study and why, using ～ために. Also, ask why they study Japanese. Use casual speech.

Example: A: せんこうは何？
B: けいえい学だよ。
A: あ、そうなんだ。どうしてけいえい学をべんきょうしてるの？
B: ぼうえき会社(がいしゃ)にしゅうしょくするため（だ）よ。

A: そう。じゃあ、日本語もぼうえき会社(がいしゃ)にしゅうしょくするために勉強してるの？

B: いや、日本語はしゅうしょくのためじゃないよ。自分(じぶん)の勉強のため（だ）よ。

勉強していること	何のため

V. Expressing obligation using ～なければ／なくてはならない／いけない ; expressing a lack of obligation using ～なくてもいい

In Japanese, verbs and adjectives can be combined with other phrases to express new meanings. You have already learned that the て-forms of verbs are used extensively in this regard. Similarly, the stem of the negative form (the part preceding ない) can be used with other phrases to express new meanings. This chapter shows how negative stems are used to express obligation or lack thereof.

A. ～なければならない／なくてはならない／なければいけない／なくてはいけない , *must ~*

The negative form with ～なければならない／なくてはならない／なければいけない／なくてはいけない expresses obligation and ~なくてもいい expresses a lack of obligation. Study the following four sentences.

明日、入学式(にゅうがくしき)に出なければならない。 *I/you must attend the entrance ceremony tomorrow.*

明日、入学式(にゅうがくしき)に出なくてはならない。 *I/you must attend the entrance ceremony tomorrow.*

明日、入学式(にゅうがくしき)に出なければいけない。 *I/you must attend the entrance ceremony tomorrow.*

明日、入学式(にゅうがくしき)に出なくてはいけない。 *I/you must attend the entance ceremony tomorrow.*

Although the above four sentences are are virtually interchangeable, いけない carries a stronger sense of obligation than ならない. When one talks about general obligations or necessities, ～なければならない or ～なくてはらない tends to be used. ～なければいけない or ～なくてはいけない tends to be used for specific cases of obligations or necessities.

～なければならない／なくてはならない／なければいけない／なくてはいけない can be used with the negative stem of verbs and adjectives. The combination of any of these forms and a verb indicates one must or has to do something. When they are combined with an adjective or the copular verb, the sentence indicates one is expected to be a certain way.

もっと勉強しなければならない。	*I/you have to study harder.*
送別会(そうべつかい)を休まなくてはいけない。	*I/you must excuse my/yourself from the farewell party.*
ここにいなければいけません。	*I/you must stay here.*
二十一さいじゃなければならない。	*I/you must be 21 years old.*
子供は元気じゃなければならない。	*The children are expected to be healthy.*
ゆうえんちは、たのしくなければならない。	*The amusement park ought to be fun.*

なければ／なくては is derived from the negative ending 〜ない.

	Dictionary	Negative form	negative stem + なければ／なくては
Copula verbs	医者だ (*doctors*)	医者じゃない	医者じゃなければ／医者じゃなくては
な -adjectives	しずかだ (*quiet*)	しずかじゃない	しずかじゃなければ／しずかじゃなくては
い -adjectives	やさしい (*kind*)	やさしくない	やさしくなければ／やさしくなくては
る -verb	つづける (*to continue*)	つづけない	つづけなければ／つづけなくては
う -verb	ぬぐ (*to take off*)	ぬがない	ぬがなければ／ぬがなくては
Irregular verbs	来る (*to come*)	来(こ)ない	来(こ)なければ／来(こ)なくては
	する (*to do*)	しない	しなければ／しなくては

In casual speech, the following contracted forms are used. Also, ならない／いけない can be omitted or replaced by だめ.

Formal speech	Casual speech
〜なければならない／いけない	〜なきゃ（なんない／いけない／だめ）
〜なくてはならない／いけない	〜なくちゃ（なんない／いけない／だめ）
知らなければなりません／いけません	知らなきゃ（なんない／いけない ／だめ）
知らなくてはなりません／いけません	知らなくちゃ（なんない／いけない ／だめ）

誕生会(たんじょうかい)に出るためには、今、もどらなければなりません。
I must go back now in order to attend the birthday party.

同窓会(どうそうかい)のお金をあつめなければならない。	*I have to collect money for the reunion.*
その子をくるまに乗せなくちゃならない。	*I have to give a ride to the child.*

西川： もう帰るんですか。
Are you going home already?

山本： ええ、明日は東京に行かなければならないんです。
Yes, I must go to Tokyo tomorrow.

かおる： どこ行くの？
Where are you going?
健一(けんいち)： ゆうびんきょく。この手紙(がみ)、出さなきゃならないんだ。
The post office. I must mail this letter.

お母さん： つかった後は、トイレのドアはしめなきゃだめよ。
After using the bathroom, you must close the bathroom door.
子供： はい。
OK.

Notes

- Because the negative form of the verb ある is ない, なければ／なくては　ならない／いけない by themselves mean *something must exist* or *one must have something.*

  ここに先生のサインがなければいけない。
  You must have a teacher's signature here.

  学生証(しょう)がなければいけませんよ。
  You must have a student ID.

- To answer questions with なければ／なくては　なりませんか／いけませんか, use ええ、～なければ／なくては　いけません to express an obligation. Use いいえ、～なくてもいいです to express the lack of an obligation.

B. Expressing the acceptability of an action or state using the negative stem + なくてもいい

The negative stem of verbs and adjectives + なくてもいい means that one does not have to do something or something does not have to be in a certain way. It is the opposite of the negative stem + ～なければならない・なくてはならない・なければいけない・なくてはいけない. The negative stem + なくてもいい is also derived from the negative ending ～ない.

やめなくてもいいです。	*You don't have to stop.*
違(ちが)わなくてもいいです。	*It does not have to be different.*
同じじゃなくてもいいです。	*It does not have to be the same.*
わかくなくてもいいです。	*He/she does not have to be young.*

スミス： 会場(かいじょう)を変えなければなりませんか。 *Do we have to change the meeting place?*
山本： いいえ、変えなくてもいいですよ。 *No, you don't have to change it.*

明(あきら)： ネクタイしなきゃいけないの？ *Do I have to wear a tie?*
ケイト： いや、しなくてもいいよ。 *No, you don't have to wear one.*

学生：	同(おな)じのでなければなりませんか？	*Does it have to be the same one?*
先生：	いや、同(おな)じのじゃなくてもいいよ。	*No it does not have to be the same one.*
	違(ちが)うのでもいいよ。	*You can use a different one.*

Notes

- The negative stem + なくてもいい by itself means something does not have to exist or one does not have to have something.

  パスポートがなくてもいいですよ。
  You don't have to have your passport.

- Instead of the negative stem + なくてもいい, the negative stem + なくてもけっこうです and the negative stem + なくてもかまいません are used in polite speech. Store clerks, bank tellers and post office clerks commonly use this more polite version.

  学生証(しょう)は、なくてもけっこうです。
  You don't have to have your student ID.

  しょうたいじょうは、なくてもかまいませんよ。
  You don't have to have an invitation letter.

話してみましょう

Activity 1 A student asks you about the rules and regulations of your university. Answer the questions using the following academic calender. Use polite speech.

Example: 課目(かもく)とうろく (*course registration*) はいつまでにしなければなりませんか。
八月三十日までにしなければなりません／いけません。
八月三十日までにしなくてはなりません／いけません。

August 25–August 30	On-campus registration
September 1	Instruction begins
September 14	Last day to add a course or to change sections
September 20	Last day to pay tuition without penalty
October 30	Last day to drop a course
November 30	Last day to submit the graduation request
December 5	Instruction ends
December 8–14	Final examination

1. セクションは、いつまでに変えなければなりませんか。
2. 卒業(そつぎょう)する人は、いつまでに卒業申込書(そつぎょうもうしこみしょ) (*application*) を出さなくてはいけませんか。
3. 授業料(じゅぎょうりょう) (*tuition*) は、いつまでにはらわなくてはいけませんか。
4. コースをおとしたい時は、いつまでにおとさなければなりませんか。
5 期末(きまつ) (*final*) しけんは、いつまでにうけなければなりませんか。

Activity 2

Work with a partner. Ask each other the course requirements for your Japanse class.

Example: 毎日漢字(かんじ)を勉強する

A: 日本語の授業(じゅぎょう)では毎日漢字(かんじ)を勉強しなければなりませんか。

B: はい、しなければなりません。

or いいえ、しなくてもいいです。

1. 毎日、日本語で話す
2. 日本人にインタビューする
3. 毎日、単(たん)語テストをうける
4. 毎週、先生のけんきゅうしつに行く
5. 日本語でブログを書く
6. 日本語のウェブページを読む

Activity 3

Respond to the following questions, requests, or invitations using ～なければ／なくてはならない／いけない and the appropriate phrase. Use casual speech. ごめん is the casual expression for an apology .

Example: 映(えい)画を見に行く／アルバイトをする

A: 今日の午後、映(えい)画、見に行かない?

B: 行きたいんだけど、今日の午後はバイトに行かなくちゃなんないから、ごめん。

1. テニスをする／病院に行く
2. ゲームをしに来る／レポートのデータをあつめる
3. あそびに来る／今日は早く家に帰る
4. 食事(しょくじ)に行く／会社(かいしゃ)にのこって仕事(しごと)をする
5. 今晩、家に泊まる／明日までにレポートをおえる

Activity 4 State as many things as you can do in advance to achieve the following goals, using the て-form of verbs + おく.

Example: テストでいいせいせき (*grade*) をとります

テストでいいせいせきをとるために、前の日によく勉強しておかなければなりません。

1. 卒業(そつぎょう)した後(あと)も日本語の勉強をつづけます
2. 五十さいぐらいで仕事(しごと)をやめます
3. 日本に留学(りゅう)します
4. 社長(しゃちょう)になります
5. 将来(しょうらい)、日本で自分(じぶん)のレストランを持ちます
6. ハワイですてきな結婚式(けっこんしき)をします

Activity 5 Work with a partner. One person plays the role of a student and the other person should be his/her Japanese instructor. The student asks the instructor what he/she is or is not required to do in the Japanese course or other related situations, and the instructor answers the questions. Create a dialogue for the following situations. Use the course syllabus of your Japanese class if necessary. Use polite speech.

Example:
A: 先生、あのう。日本語のレベル３の授業(じゅぎょう)をとりたいんですが。
B: はい。
A: どんなことをしなければならないでしょうか。／何をしたらいいでしょうか。
B: そうですね。しけんをうけなければなりませんね。
A: じゃあ、どんなじゅんびをしたらいいでしょうか。
B: 何もしなくてもいいですよ。

1. 来年の夏に日本に留学(りゅう)する
2. けんきゅうレポートのしりょう (*data*) を日本語であつめたい
3. 病気で一週間休んだので、授業(じゅぎょう)が分からない
4. 日本語でブログを書きたい
5. 今度のしけんで、もっといいせいせきがとりたい

聞く練習(れんしゅう)

上手な聞き方

Paying attention to speech styles

The use of appropriate speech style is very important in one's career in Japan. In many cases, language skills are considered a type of competence, so Japanese college students are often explicitly taught how to use polite language before they start looking for a job. If a job candidate cannot use polite language he/she will not be considered for the job regardless of how competent he/she is. For this reason, paying attention to how people use polite and casual speech styles depending on the context of a conversation is essential to understanding how communication works.

A company is looking for a person who can do the following.

月曜日から金曜日、午前朝九時から十二時まではたらける人
土曜日も仕事(しごと)に来られる人
ひょうけいさんソフト (*spreadsheet software*) がつかえる人

Listen to three job interviews and decide who is the best candidate for the job. Explain your choice.

名前：____________________

どうして：____

将来(しょうらい)の計画

聞く前に

Work with a partner. Look at the chart of four college students and discuss what kinds of careers and lifestyles they may have.

名前	山田 友美(ともみ)	北川 高子	安田 春子(はるこ)	高田 友紀(ゆうき)
年	１８さい	２３さい	１９さい	２１さい
せんこう	文学	れきし	びじゅつ (*art*)	きょういく (*education*)
アルバイト	ウェイトレス	家庭教師(かていきょうし) (*tutor*)	デパートの店員(てんいん) (*clerk*)	日本語学校の先生
しゅみ	本を読む	旅行	テニス	おんがく

聞いた後で

A. Listen to three of the college students in the above chart talk about their future plans and current lifestyles. They do not reveal their names in the conversation. Then do the following:

1. Write the future plans of each, and what each is doing to achieve that plan (if any).

学生	将来(しょうらい)の計画	しておくこと／してあること
A		
B		
C		

2. Work with a partner. Try to identify the students names by comparing the description you have just listened to and the descriptions in the chart in 聞く前に .

Aさんの名前 ________________

Bさんの名前 ________________

Cさんの名前 ________________

B. 質問(しつもん)に日本語で答えて下さい。

1. Aさんは、卒業(そつぎょう)したら、好きなことが出来ると思っていますか。
2. Aさんは結婚(けっこん)したいと思っていますか。
3. Aさんはしゅうしょくしたいと思っていますか。
4. Bさんは来年何をするつもりですか。どうしてですか。
5. Bさんはどこでアルバイトをしていますか。
6. Bさんは結婚(けっこん)したいと思っているでしょうか。
7. Cさんは卒業(そつぎょう)したらすぐしゅうしょくするつもりですか。
8. Cさんは英(えい)語が上手ですか。
9. Cさんは英(えい)語の勉強をするために外国に行くのですか。

C. パートナーと下の質問(しつもん)について話して下さい。

1. Aさん、Bさん、Cさんの中で、自分(じぶん)はどの人に一番ちかいと思いますか。どうしてそう思いますか。
2. Aさん、Bさん、Cさんの中で、自分(じぶん)はどの人と一番違(ちが)うと思いますか。どうしてそう思いますか。
3. Aさん、Bさん、Cさんはどんな人だと思いますか。どの人と友達(だち)になりたいと思いますか。

D. Listen to the conversation between two people. One of the two people is either student A, B, or C. Using listening strategies such as key word search, your knowledge about the students, and speech style, try to guess which student is talking, where and with whom the conversation takes place, and what the conversation is about. Then summarize the content of the conversation.

学生の名前 ________________________________

学生が話している人 ________________________________

話しているところ ________________________________

トピック________________________________

ないよう (*contents*) ________________________________

____

____

E. Work with a partner. Each of you should write a short description of your future plans on a piece of paper. Include your age, interests, what you want to do in the future, what you are doing or must to do to achieve your goal. The description should not include your name. Then, exchange your description and proofread your partner's description.

F. Work in groups of six, making sure your partner in Activity E is not in your group. One person collects the descriptions written in activity A from each member, and then gives them to the other members so that nobody has his/her own paper. Each person reads a description and the rest of the group figures out the name of the person who wrote it.

聞き上手話し上手

Making confirmations and checking comprehension

Communication strategies such as asking for repetition or paraphrases, checking the other person's comprehension, and confirming what is said, are very important in sustaining conversation and preventing a breakdown in communication. Chapter 6 of *Nakama 1* introduced how to ask for repetition and paraphrase. (あのう、すみません、もう一度言って下さい and ゆっくり言って下さい) You can also use もう一度おねがいします or ゆっくりおねがいします, which is more polite than 言って下さい.

This chapter focuses on making confirmation and checking comprehension. To check someone's comprehension, you can use わかりますか (*Are you following me?* or *Do you understand what I am saying?*), or わかりましたか (*Did you understand what I meant?*). If your conversation partner does not understand you, don't immediately give up or change the subject. Try your best to paraphrase what you are trying to say. Making such an effort gives you more opportunity to try out a variety of structures and expressions. It helps you to increase your knowledge and retention as well as fluency.

Conversely, if you are not sure about your understanding of the other person's speech, you should confirm what has been said. This will help you get important information and prevent you from running into a major misunderstanding.

There are several ways of confirming information in Japanese.

1. Repeating a word or expression with rising or falling intonation.

川田：あのう、銀(ぎん)行はどこですか。／ねえ、銀(ぎん)行どこ？	*Where is the bank?*
山本：そのケーキ屋(や)の後ろです。／そのケーキ屋(や)の後ろだよ。	*It's behind that cake shop.*
川田：ケーキ屋(や)の後ろですか。／ケーキ屋の後ろ？	*Behind the cake shop?*
山本：ええ。／うん。	*Yes.*

Another strategy is to use a brief pause (which may be as long as five seconds or so), but a pause can also indicate a lack of comprehension or communication difficulty.

2. Repeat a word or expression and add ですか with a rising intonation. In casual speech, simply repeat with a rising intonation.

川田：電車(でんしゃ)は何時に出ますか。／電車(でんしゃ)、何時に出るの？	*What time does the train leave?*
山本：朝六時半に出ますよ。／朝六時半に出るよ。	*It leaves at 6:30 a.m.*
川田：六時半（に）ですか。／六時半（に）？	*6:30 a.m.?*
山本：ええ。／うん。	*Yes.*

A short rising intonation not only helps confirm information but also expresses surprise.

3. Repeat a word or expression and add ですね or ね (casual speech) with a short rising intonation. The intonation does not indicate any surprise. The use of ね, instead of か, indicates that you are convinced or satisfied with the information given to you.

川田：どこでおとしたんですか／おとしたの？
Where did you drop it?

山本：あのこうえんのちかくの高校の前で。
In front of the high school near that park.

川田：ああ、分かりました／分かった。東高校の前ですね／だね。
Oh, I see. It's in front of Higashi High School.

山本：はい、そうです。／うん、そうだよ。
Yes, it is.

4. Repeat a sentence or verb phrase using ～んですね／～んだね.

川田：ビールとワインは、ありますか。／ビールとワイン、ある？
Do you have beer and wine?

山本：ええ、買ってありますよ。／うん、買ってあるよ。
Yes, I've got them.

川田：ビールもワインも買ってあるんですね／だね。
You've got beer and wine, right?

山本：ええ。／うん。
Yes.

A. Complete the following conversations by writing confirming remarks on the blank lines.

1. A: あのう、すみません。トイレはどこにありますか。
   B: 一階のエレベータのよこにありますよ。
   A: ________________
2. A: ねえ、今週、日本の映画があるそうだけど、いつ、どこであるの？
   B: 金曜日の午後八時から、図書館の二階のラウンジであるそうだよ。
   A: ________________
3. A: あの、来年の夏、日本で勉強したいと思うんですけど。
   B: じゃあ、三階にある留学生センターのじむしつ (*office*) に行ったらどう？
   A: ________________
4. A: ビールとワインはもう買ってあるから、ジュース買っといてくれる？
   B: ________________

B. Listen to a series of short statements. Confirm what been said.

1. ________________ 5. ________________
2. ________________ 6. ________________
3. ________________ 7. ________________
4. ________________ 8. ________________

iLrn Self-Tests

C. Listen to a series of announcements about your Japanese class. Confirm what has been said, and write down the content of the announcements in Japanese.

1. ________________
2. ________________
3. ________________

D. Work with a partner. You are a reporter and your partner is a celebrity. Interview him/her, take notes, and confirm what you have written. Your partner makes sure you understand what he/she says by checking your comprehension.

漢字
かんじ

Top component shapes of kanji

Like the left component, many of the top components indicate a semantic category to which the meaning of a **kanji** belongs. Some of them, such as くさかんむり、うかんむり、and たけかんむり, appear in a large number of **kanji** while others are more limited in their use.

Name		Meaning	Examples
くさかんむり	艹	grass	英 茶 荷 菜 葉 落 薬 花 草
うかんむり	宀	housing	安 家 客 室 定 宿 寒 寝
たけかんむり	⺮	bamboo	笑 符 第 答 等 節 箱
あめかんむり	雨	rain	雪 雲 電 雷 震 霜
ひとやね	𠆢	person	全 今 会 合 令 企 余 舎 倉 傘
あみがしら / よつがしら / よこめ	罒	net	罪 署 置 罰
あなかんむり	穴	hole	空 究 突 窃 窓
やまかんむり	山	mountain	岸 岩 崇 崩 嵐
おいかんむり / おいがしら	耂	elderly, aged	考 老 者
なべぶた	亠	N/A	亡 交 京 享 亭
わかんむり	冖		冗 写 冠
はつがしら	癶		発 登

Flashcards

言	言	to say, speak い(う)・こと　ゲン・ゴン　もう一度言(い)って下さい。	、 亠 亡 亖 言 言 言
葉	葉	leaf は　ヨウ　韓国(かん)の言葉(ことば)は日本語と違(ちが)います。	一 艹 艹 艹 苹 茥 茥 葉 葉
漢	漢	Chinese カン　中西さんは漢字(かんじ)がたくさん書けます。	氵 氵 汁 汁 汼 汼 漌 漢 漢
字	字	letter ジ　漢字(かんじ)を読むのは大変です。	、 ハ 宀 宁 字 字

質	quality, matter	シツ・シチ・チ	旅行の計画について質問(しつもん)する。
問	question	と(う)・と(い)　モン	漢字(かんじ)の質問(しつもん)はありますか。
卒	to graduate	ソツ	大学を来年の五月に卒業(そつぎょう)する予定です。
業	work, industry	わざ　ギョウ・ゴウ	大学の卒業式(そつぎょうしき)　日本語の授業(じゅぎょう)
授	to confer, give	さず(ける)　ジュ	授業(じゅぎょう)を三つとっています。
仕	to serve, to do	つか(える)　シ・ジ	新しい仕事(しごと)を中国で始める。
事	abstract thing, affair	こと　ジ	来年の仕事(しごと)がいそがしい。
結	to tie, to bind	むす(ぶ)　ケツ・ケッ	来年、結婚(けっこん)する。
婚	marriage	コン	結婚式(けっこんしき)の予約をとりました。
式	style, ceremony	シキ	友達(ともだち)の卒業式(そつぎょうしき)に行く。
社	company, society	やしろ　シャ	会社(かいしゃ)の社長(しゃちょう)の仕事(しごと)は大変です。

同	same	おな(じ) ドウ	同じ(おな)本を読んだ。 高校の同窓会(どうそうかい)がある。
違	to differ, violate	ちが(う)・ちが(い) イ	この答えは間違(まちが)っています。
留	keep, stay	と(める)・と(まる) リュウ・ル	留(りゅう)学生センター
達	attain	タツ・ダチ	昨日、子供の時の友達(ともだち)と会った。
電	electric	デン	携帯電話(けいたいでんわ)の番号(ばんごう)を知りません。電気(でんき)をつける。電車(でんしゃ)
英	distinguished, England	エイ	会社(かいしゃ)の仕事(しごと)は英(えい)語でしています。
客	guest	キャク	お客(きゃく)さんがたくさん来ました。

読めるようになった漢字

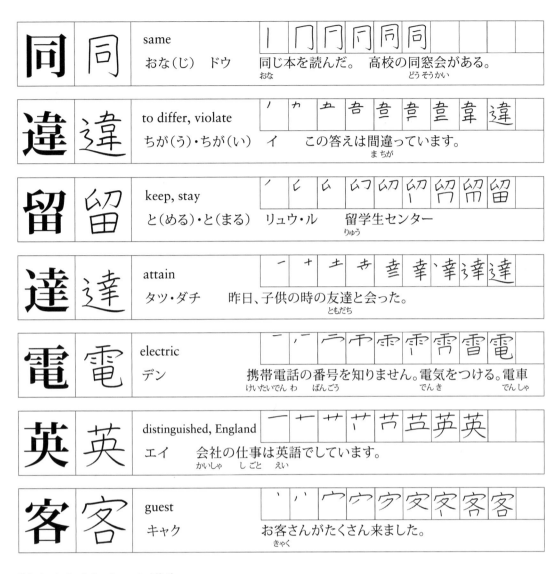

言葉　言う　漢字　質問　卒業　授業　仕事　食事　卒業式　結婚する　結婚式
会社　同じ　違う　留学生　友達　電気　電話　英語　客　大事　生まれる
会場(じょう)　年　入学　起こす　同窓(そう)会　社長(ちょう)　自(じ)分　変わる　将(しょう)来

Read the following sentences aloud.

1. 日本語を勉強して半年で、言葉は少し話せますが、漢字は、まだあまり知りません。
2. 弟の入学式と兄の卒業式には同じスーツを着て行くつもりです。
3. 質問に日本語で答えて下さい。
4. 山本さんは来年留学するので、今、会社でバイトをしています。
5. 授業で分からないことがあったので、友達に電話をかけて、質問をした。
6. 会社は同じだけど、違う仕事をする予定です。
7. 社長は新しいお客さんと話しました。
8. 今年の秋に結婚するので、早く結婚式の会場(じょう)を予約しなければなりません。

読む練習(れんしゅう)

上手な読み方

Using prefixes and suffixes

The size of a person's vocabulary is strongly correlated to his/her reading proficiency. In order to understand a text completely, a reader needs to know over 90 percent of the vocabulary in the text. For this reason, it is important to acquire vocabulary through reading. One way to achieve this is to use prefixes and suffixes to guess the meaning of a word. In this book, many suffixes and prefixes have already been introduced and practiced. Try using them to guess the meanings of new words as you encounter them.

Guess the meanings of the following expressions using your knowledge of prefixes and suffixes.

研究会(けんきゅう)　学会　大会　研究員(けんきゅういん)　教員(きょういん)　会員(いん)　学生会館　映画館(えい)　毎回　毎度　大会社　子会社

日本人と結婚

読む前に

A. In Japanese, genre, rather than formality, determines whether to use plain or polite forms in writing. For example, compositions, diaries, and newspaper articles are usually written in plain form while letters and post cards are written using polite forms. Check the writing styles of the reading materials in the previous chapters as well as other authentic materials, and determine which types of writing use the plain form, and which use the polite form.

B. 結婚について、下の質問に日本語で答えて下さい。

1. あなたの国では、男の人は何さいぐらいで結婚しますか。女の人はどうですか。
2. 結婚した後、だれが家の外ではたらきますか。
3. 結婚した後、家事(かじ) (*household work*) や子供の世話(せわ) (*care*) はだれがしますか。
4. あなたは結婚したいと思いますか。したくありませんか。どうしてそう思いますか。

C. Work as a class. You are going to conduct a survey (アンケート) about how your classmates think about marriage.

1. First, look at the following survey form, a summary sheet, and the expressions below. (The expressions in this activity will appear in the reading materials for this chapter.) Identify the types of information that you need to complete the summary sheet. Then conduct the survey and complete the survey form by classifying responses according to the gender of the interviewee.

平均(へいきん)	average	家事(かじ)	household work
年令(ねんれい)	age (formal expression)	世話(せわ)	(child) care
男性(だんせい)	formal word for 男の人	養う(やしなう)	to support (financially)
女性(じょせい)	formal word for 女の人		

Example: A: 何さいぐらいで結婚したいと思いますか。

B: 三十さいぐらいで結婚したいと思います。

質問	女性(じょせい)	男性(だんせい)
何さいぐらいで結婚したい		
家事(かじ)はだれがした方がいい		
子供の世話(せわ)はだれがした方がいい		
結婚したら、だれが家族を養(やし)った方がいい		
結婚したら、じゆうな生活(かつ)が出来ない		

2. Now complete the following summary sheet based on the results of your survey:

	男性（だんせい）	女性（じょせい）
結婚したい平均年令（へいきんねんれい）	______さい	______さい
家事（かじ）	ご主人（しゅ）______%	ご主人（しゅ）______%
	おくさん______%	おくさん______%
	ご主人（しゅ）とおくさん______%	ご主人（しゅ）とおくさん______%
子供の世話（せわ）	ご主人（しゅ）______%	ご主人（しゅ）______%
	おくさん______%	おくさん______%
	ご主人（しゅ）とおくさん______%	ご主人（しゅ）とおくさん______%
家族を養う（やしな）人	ご主人（しゅ）______%	ご主人（しゅ）______%
	おくさん______%	おくさん______%
	ご主人（しゅ）とおくさん______%	ご主人（しゅ）とおくさん______%
じゆうな生活（かつ）	出来る______%	出来る______%
	出来ない______%	出来ない______%

日本人の平均（へいきん）結婚年令（ねんれい）は毎年少しずつ上がっている。三十年前の平均（へいきん）結婚年令（ねんれい）は男性（だんせい）が25.4歳（さい）、女性（じょせい）が24歳（さい）だったが、今は男性（だんせい）が28.5歳（さい）、女性（じょせい）も26.5歳（さい）になっている。

<u>これ</u>はどうしてだろうか。１９９４年のアンケートでは男性（だんせい）の５５％が「結婚したら、したいことが出来なくなる」と答えた。結婚したら、家族のために働（はたら）かなければならないから、好きなことが出来ないと言うのだ。それに、三十年前より今の方が生活（かつ）にお金がかかるので、わかい時に結婚したら大変だと考（かんが）えているのだ。２００７年のアンケートによると、「結婚した後、家族を養（やしな）えないかもしれない」と答えた男性（だんせい）が多かった。

また、同じアンケートでは、多くの女性（じょせい）が「一人でも生活（かつ）できるし、結婚したら自由（じゆう）な生活（かつ）が出来ないから、あまり早く結婚したくない」と答えていた。日本では働（はたら）く女性（じょせい）も、結婚した後も仕事を続（つづ）ける人が多くなってきている。けれども、女性（じょせい）は、子供が生まれたら、家事（かじ）や子供の世話（せわ）をしなければならないという考（かんが）えはまだ残（のこ）っている。だから、結婚するより、就職（しゅうしょく）して好きなことをしたい、結婚したくなったらしようと考（かんが）えるのかもしれない。

読んだ後で

A. Choose the paragraph that best summarizes the above passage.

1. この文章(ぶんしょう) (*text*) は日本の男性(だんせい)と女性(じょせい)の平均(へいきん)結婚年令(ねんれい)について書いてあります。
2. この文章(ぶんしょう) (*text*) はどうして日本人の女性(じょせい)が結婚しないかについて書いてあります。
3. この文章(ぶんしょう) (*text*) はどうして日本人がはやく結婚したがらないかについて書いてあります。

B. Circle はい if the statement is consistent with the passage and いいえ if it isn't.

1. 日本人は男性(だんせい)も女性(じょせい)もはやく結婚したいと思っている。　はい　いいえ
2. 働(はたら)く女性(じょせい)は多くなった。　はい　いいえ
3. 仕事を持つ女性(じょせい)が家事(かじ)をすることが多い。　はい　いいえ
4. 日本の男性(だんせい)は結婚した後、自分(じぶん)が家族を養(やしな)わなければならないと思っている。　はい　いいえ

C. 下の質問に日本語で答えて下さい。

1. What does これ (underlined) refer to in the second paragraph of the reading?
2. What are the subjects of the following sentences?

   Fourth sentence of the second paragraph:

   三十年前より今の方が生活(かつ)にお金がかかるので、わかい時に結婚したら大変だと考(かんが)えているのだ。

   Third sentence of the third paragraph:

   結婚するより、就職(しゅうしょく)して好きなことをしたい、結婚したくなったらしようと考(かんが)えるのかもしれない。

総合練習(そうごうれんしゅう)

A. そうだんしたいことがあります

Work with a group of four. You are consultants for people with problems. Read the following statements about the worries these people have and discuss suggestions as to what steps they should take to solve their problems.

Example: マクドナルドさん

私は18さいで、スーパーではたらいていますが、仕事がおもしろくないので、仕事をかえたいと思います。高校はきらいだったので、一年前にやめたんです。でも、卒業しておいた方がよかったのかもしれません。どうしたらいいですか。

A: 高校を卒業していないから、いい仕事がないんだと思います。高校にもどった方がいいですね。

B: しけんをうけたら、どうでしょうか。

C: そうですね。そして、新しい仕事をさがす前に、大学も卒業しておいたほうがいいですね。

1. ホンさん

私は今大学二年生ですが、大学にのこった方がいいかどうか分かりません。高校の時は何でもよく出来ましたが、大学に入ってから、A がとれません。D をたくさんとってしまったんです。両親は大学を卒業した方が将(しょう)来のためにいいからやめてはいけないと言いますが、私には分かりません。

2. ジョンソンさん

日本人のガールフレンドがいるんですが、春に卒業して、日本に帰ってしまったんです。ぼくはまだ学生ですが、将(しょう)来はその人と結婚したいと思っています。でも、彼女(かのじょ) (*girlfriend*) の両親は外国人はきらいだそうです。どうして外国人がきらいなのか、よく分かりません。今度の冬には日本へ行くつもりですが、その時彼女(かのじょ)の両親に会おうと思っています。今から何をしておいたらいいでしょうか。

ロールプレイ

1. You broke your friend's computer. Tell him/her what you have done, apologize, and offer some compensation.
2. You are an organizer of a workshop. You want to make sure that everything is ready. You are talking to a Japanese assistant. Confirm with the assistant that the following things are ready.
   a. speaker's hotel reservation
   b. conference site reservation
   c. preparation for coffee and snacks
   d. name tags (バッジ)
   e. staff at the registration desk (うけつけ)
3. A Japanese friend of yours has invited you for a weekend trip, but you're not sure if you can go because you have to study for final exams and finish your final papers. Tell your friend about your situation.
4. You lost your bag on the train in Japan. Important things such as your wallet, keys, and textbooks are in the bag. Go to the lost-and-found department and explain the situation. Describe what is inside the bag and ask for help. Also, leave your telephone number and ask to be called if the bag is found.

Chapter 4

第四課（だいよんか）

Kyodo/Landov

おねがい

Asking for Favors

Objectives	Asking for favors, offering help
Vocabulary	Personal identification, words used for study at school, postal and parcel delivery services, banks
Japanese Culture	Japan Post and post offices, delivery services, Japanese addresses, banks
Dialogue	銀行口座（ぎんこうこうざ）をひらく Opening a bank account
Grammar	I. Expressing and inquiring about one's factual knowledge using the clause か（どうか）
	II. Expressing movement away from or toward the speaker through space using ～ていく and ～てくる
	III. Expressing one's desire for someone to do something using ～てもらう／いただく and ～てほしい
	IV. Expressing willingness using ～ましょう／ましょうか
	V. Expressing time limits using までに (*by ~, by the time ~*)
Listening	Knowing how to use varied request forms appropriately, 三つのおねがい
Communication	Making a request and turning down a request or an invitation
Kanji	Bottom and enclosing component shapes of **kanji**
	郵 便 局 銀 送 紙 住 所 引 練 習
	宿 題 試 験 受 教 文 法 意 味 石
Reading	Filling out forms, ホストファミリー

Chapter Resources

www.cengagebrain.com

Heinle Learning Center

Audio Program

単(たん)語

Flashcards

Nouns

ATM		automatic teller machine
いみ	意味	meaning
うんてんめんきょしょう	運転免許証	driver's license
かいわ	会話	conversation
カード		card
きって	切手	postage stamp
こうざ	口座	bank account, こうざをひらく to open a bank account
こづつみ	小包	parcel post
ざいりゅうカード	在留カード	residence card
サイン		signature, サインをする to sign
さくぶん	作文	composition
しけん	試験	examination, test
じゅぎょうりょう	授業料	tuition
じゅうしょ	住所	address
せつめい	説明	explanation, せつめいする to explain
たくはいびん	宅配便	parcel delivery service. Also called 宅急便(たっきゅうびん), a registered company trademark commonly used instead of 宅配便(たくはいびん)
たんご	単語	vocabulary
ドル		dollar
はがき	葉書	postcard
はんこ	判子	seal
ふうとう	封筒	envelope
ふつうよきん	普通預金	regular bank account
ぶんぽう	文法	grammar
ポスト		public mail collection box
ゆうびんうけ	郵便受け	mail box, to receive mail
ゆうびんばんごう	郵便番号	postal code
ようし	用紙	form
よきん	預金	bank account, よきんする to deposit money, よきんがある to have money in the bank

レポート		report, term paper, term project
れんしゅう	練習	practice, れんしゅうする to practice

う -verbs

いる	要る	to need, お金がいる to need money. The verb いる (*to need*) is an う -verb and written with the **kanji** 要る. It is different from いる (*to exist*) which is a る -verb and can be expressed in **kanji** as 居る.
おくる	送る	to send
かえす	返す	to return something
かす	貸す	to lend
つれていく	連れて行く	to take (someone somewhere)
てつだう	手伝う	to assist, help
とどく	届く	(for something) to arrive
ひきだす	引き出す	to withdraw (money)
ひらく	開く	to open, こうざをひらく to open an account
もうしこむ	申し込む	to apply, もうしこみようし application form

る -verbs

うける	受ける	to receive, to get, しけんをうける to take an exam
おしえる	教える	to tell, teach
おぼえる	覚える	to memorize, おぼえている to remember, to recall
かえる	替える / 変える	to change, セクションをかえる to change a section
かりる	借りる	to borrow, to rent (a house, apartment)
ためる	貯める	to save (money)
とどける	届ける	to deliver, send

Irregular verbs

もってくる	持って来る	to bring (something)
つれてくる	連れて来る	to bring (someone)

な -adjectives

だめ (な)	駄目 (な)	no good, impossible, hopeless; not useful; not acceptable

Suffixes

～かた	～方	how to, way of ～ ing
～しょう	～証	card (for identification), 学生証 (しょう) student identification

Expressions

ありがとう。たすかります。	有り難う。助かります。	Thank you. That helps me a lot.
ごめん（なさい）	ご免（なさい）	I'm sorry. (used only for an apology, more colloquial than すみません)
じつは	実は	Actually
たすかります。	助かります。	That will be helpful.
ちょっとおねがいがあるんですけど	ちょっとお願いがあるんですけど	I have a small favor to ask.
ほんとにいいんですか。	本当にいいんですか。	Are you sure you are OK with it?

単語の練習

A. 身分証明書　Personal identification

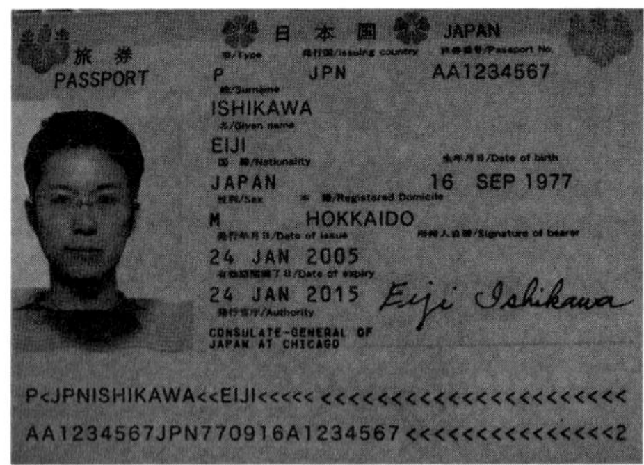

パスポート
passport

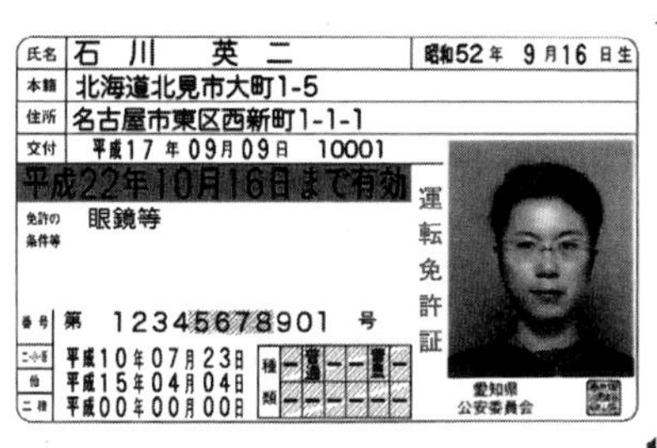

うんてんめんきょしょう
driver's license

学生証
student ID

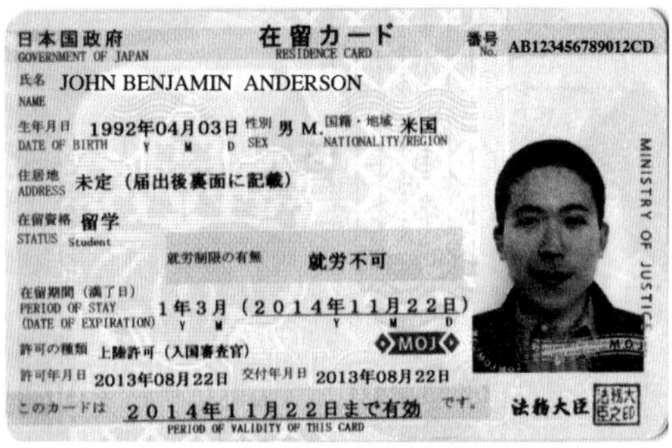

在留カード
residence card

Activity 1 Work with the class. Ask your classmates whether they have the following IDs and find out how many people have them.

Example: A: ～さんはパスポートを持っていますか。

B: ええ、持っていますよ。～さんもパスポートを持っていますか。

or いいえ、持っていません。～さんは持っていますか。

A: ええ、持っています。or いいえ、持っていません。

ID	持っている人
パスポート	
うんてんめんきょしょう	
学生証(しょう)	
ざいりゅうカード	

B. 学校で勉強する

会話(かいわ)	conversation	文法(ぶんぽう)	grammar	作文(さくぶん)	composition
レポート	report, paper	練習(れんしゅう)	exercise	意味(いみ)	meaning
試験(しけん)	examination	授業料(りょう)	tuition	単語(たんご)	vocabulary
作り方(かた)	how to make	話し方(かた)	how to talk, manner of talking	教(おし)える	to tell, teach
説明(せつめい)する	to explain	手伝(てつだ)う	to assist	試験(しけん)を受(う)ける	to take an exam
単語(たんご)をおぼえる	to memorize vocabulary				

おぼえていますか。

漢字　宿題(しゅくだい)　テスト　英語　おんがく　授業　せんこう　じゅんび　卒業する　大学　大学院
大学院生　同窓(そう)会　図(と)書館　文(ぶん)学　れきし　工(こう)学　留学する　留学生　アジアけんきゅう
学生会館　学食　学期(き)　教科書(きょうか)　教室(きょうしつ)　経営(けいえい)学　けんきゅうする　けんきゅうしゃ　高校
こくばん　答える　質問する

Activity 2 質問に日本語で答えて下さい。

1. 日本語の授業ではどんな宿題(しゅくだい)がよく出ますか。
2. 日本語の何がむずかしいですか。何がやさしいと思いますか。
3. 漢字をおぼえるために、どんなことをしていますか。どんなことをしたらいいと思いますか。
4. 単語(たんご)をおぼえるのが上手だと思いますか。
5. どうやって、単語(たんご)をおぼえていますか。
6. 英語を教(おし)えたことがありますか。
7. 英語の文法(ぶんぽう)が説明(せつめい)できますか。
8. 先生の仕事を手伝(てつだ)ったことがありますか。

Activity 3 Work with the class. Ask your classmates whether they know how to perform the actions in the following table and write the name of one person who knows how to do each.

Example: おすしを食べる

A: おすしの食べ方(かた)を知っていますか。

B: ええ、知っています。

Activity	クラスメートの名前
おすしを食べる	
日本語のメールを書く	
国際(こくさい)電話 (*international call*) をかける	
ちずを見る	
天ぷらを作る	

C. 郵便局(ゆうびんきょく)と宅配便(たくはいびん)

宅配便(たくはいびん) Parcel delivery service

切手(きって) postage stamp　ふうとう envelope　小包(こづつみ) parcel

葉書(はがき) postcard　カード card　住所(じゅうしょ) address

郵便番号(ゆうびんばんごう) postal code　送(おく)る to send　荷物をとどける to deliver a parcel

荷物がとどく a parcel is delivered　郵便受(ゆうびんう)け post box to receive mail

ポスト public mail collection box

おぼえていますか。

手紙　荷物　はらう　場所

Supplementary vocabulary 郵便局や宅配便でつかう言葉

EMS		international express mail
あてさき	宛先	recipient's address
うけとりにんばらい	受取人払い	fee paid by the recipient, COD
おくりじょう	送り状	sender's bill/shipping document
かきとめ	書留	insured mail
そくたつ	速達	express mail
ほけん	保険	insurance
りょうきん	料金	fee

Activity 4 下に説明してある単語は何ですか。

1. 手紙を入れる物です。
2. クリスマスやバレンタインデーにとどけるものです。
3. ふうとうにはる (*affix*) 物です。
4. 旅行している時、友達や家族によく送る物で、カードや手紙より安いです。
5. 小包やスーツケースをとどけるサービス (*service*) です。
6. これを書いていないと、荷物がとどきません。

D. 銀行

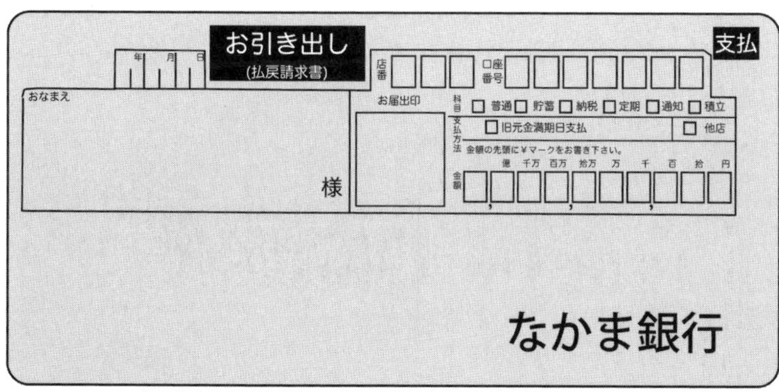

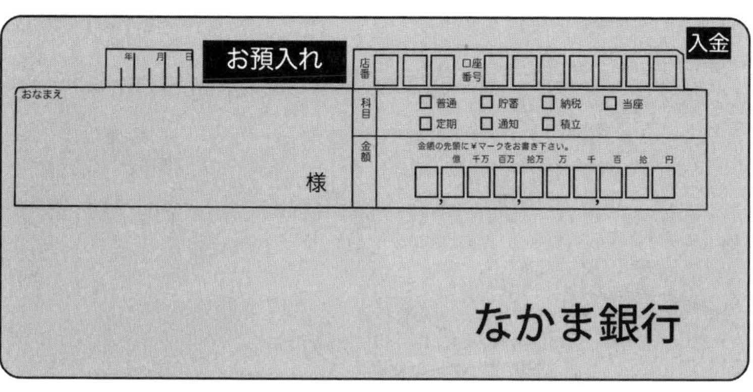

ATM	automatic teller machine	ふつう預金(よきん)	regular bank account
判子(はんこ)	seal	サイン signature	サインをする to sign
ドル	dollar	口座(こうざ)をひらく	to open a bank account
預金(よきん)する	to deposit money	預金(よきん)がある	to have money in the bank
お金を引(ひ)き出(だ)す	to withdraw money	お金をかえす	to return money
お金をかす	to lend money	お金をかりる	to borrow money
お金をためる	to save money		

Supplementary vocabulary 銀(ぎん)行でつかう言葉

がいこくかわせ	外国為替	foreign currency exchange
キャッシュカード		ATM card
ぎんこうふりこみ	銀行振込	wire transfer of funds
げんきん	現金	cash
じどう	自動	automatic
じどうひきおとし	自動引き落とし	automatic deduction of bills (from a bank account)
そうきん	送金	sending money
てすうりょう	手数料	transaction fee
つうちょう	通帳	account book
まどぐち	窓口	window (bank teller, municipal office, etc.)

Activity 5 質問に日本語で答えて下さい。

1. アメリカの銀行(ぎんこう)で口座(こうざ)をひらくとき、どんな物がいりますか。
2. ATM でどんなことが出来ますか。
3. 銀(ぎん)行の口座(こうざ)を持っていますか。どんな口座(こうざ)をもっていますか。
4. キャッシュカードとクレジットカードは何が違いますか。

Activity 6 下の言葉を日本語で説明(せつめい)して下さい。

判子(はんこ)　ドル　預金(よきん)がある　預金(よきん)する　お金をかえす

ダイアローグ

はじめに

質問に日本語で答えて下さい。

1. 銀行口座をひらく時、何がいりますか。
2. あなたの国には、判子がありますか。どんな判子がありますか。
3. パスポートを持っていますか。
4. アメリカに住んでいる外国人は、在留カードを持っていなければなりませんか。

銀行口座をひらく *Opening a bank account*

The following manga frames are scrambled, so they are not in the correct order. Read the dialogue and unscramble the frames by writing the correct number in the box in each frame.

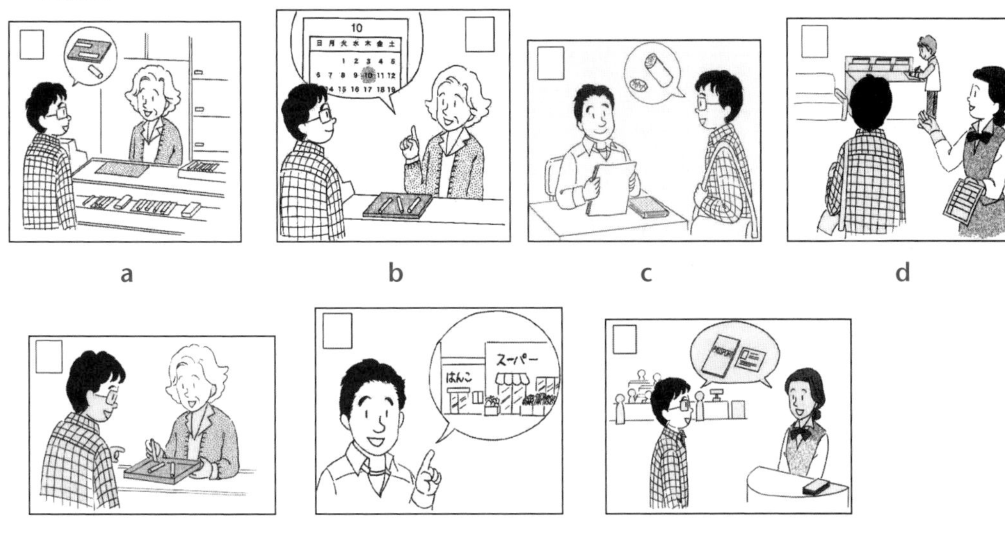

リー：　石田くん、ちょっと聞きたいことあるんだけど。

石田：　何？

リー：　判子作りたいんだけど、どこで作ってもらえるのかな？

石田：　判子は判子屋に行った方がいいよ。

リー：　そう、判子屋ってどこにあるか知ってる？

石田：　ああ、駅前のスーパーのとなりにあるよ。一緒に行こうか？

リー：　ありがとう。でも、大丈夫。今から、行ってくるよ。

リーさんは判子屋(はんこや)へ行きました。

リー：あのう、すみません。判子(はんこ)を作ってほしいんですが。

判子屋(はんこや)：色々(いろいろ)ありますけど、どんなのがいいですか。

リー：銀行口座(ぎんこうこうざ)をひらくための物なんですが。

判子屋(はんこや)：じゃあ、こんなのはどうですか。

リー：ああ、いいですね。じゃあ、これでおねがいします。

判子屋(はんこや)：名前はどうしますか。

リー：漢字で「李(り)」と書いて下さい。

判子屋(はんこや)：分かりました。

リー：いつ、取(と)りに来たらいいですか。

判子屋(はんこや)：そうですね。来週の木曜日までには出来ますよ。

リー：そうですか。じゃ、木曜日の午後取(と)りに来ます。よろしくおねがいします。

次の週の木曜日にリーさんは銀行(ぎん)に行きました。

リー：あのう、ふつう預金(よきん)の口座(こうざ)をひらきたいんですが。

銀行員(ぎんいん)：外国の方ですか。

リー：はい、そうです。

銀行員(ぎんいん)：では、パスポートと在留(ざいりゅう)カードをお持ちですか。

リー：はい、持ってます。

銀行員(ぎんいん)：では、あちらで、このもうしこみ用紙(ようし)にご記入(きにゅう)下さい。

リー：はい、分かりました。

Dialogue Phrase Notes

- 銀行員(ぎんいん) means a *banker* or a *bank teller.*
- 「李(り)」と書く means *to write Li.*
- 記入(きにゅう) means *to fill out.*

ダイアローグの後で

A. Complete the following paragraph based on the dialogue.

リーさんは＿＿＿＿＿＿を作りたいと思いましたが、＿＿＿＿＿＿を持っていませんでした。でも、どこで作ったらいいか分からなかったので、＿＿＿＿＿＿に場所(ばしょ)を聞きました。そして、スーパーの＿＿＿＿＿＿にある＿＿＿＿＿＿に、判子(はんこ)を＿＿＿＿＿＿に行きました。一週間後に＿＿＿＿＿＿が出来たので、＿＿＿＿＿＿に行って、＿＿＿＿＿＿を作ってもらいました。

B. Identify the phrases in the dialogue that Mr. Li uses to start a conversation and those he uses to introduce the topic of a conversation.

Bloomberg via Getty Images

A row of ATM machines

日本の文化

日本郵便と郵便局 (Japan Post and post offices)

Japan's postal service is very efficient. Regular postcards and letters usually reach their destinations within two days. The Japan Post (JP) offers a range of postal services including the shipping of post cards, letters, and parcels. Mail is delivered once a day except Sunday. Outgoing mail must be dropped into a public mailbox (郵便ポスト or ポスト) since private mailboxes (郵便受け) are intended only for deliveries. Japan Post also offers pick-up services although it is more common for people to go to the post offices.

There are two types of postal facilities in Japan: standard post offices (郵便局), and distribution centers (集配局). Most are 郵便局 , which are open Monday to Friday from 9 a.m. to 5 p.m. and are closed on weekends and national holidays. 集配局 are large and they are open on weekdays until 7 p.m. They may also be open on Saturdays and Sundays. They offer a wider range of services for businesses than normal post offices. JP Bank (ゆうちょ銀行) and JP Insurance (かんぽ保険) are often located within or next to the 郵便局 . This is because Japan Post also handled life insurance and banking services until it was privatized and divided into four separate companies in 2007.

The post office symbol is 〒. It can be seen both at post offices and on post boxes. It also precedes postal codes in written addresses.

宅配便 Delivery services

宅配便 is a convenient door-to-door delivery service for regular parcels, oversized boxes, fresh or frozen foods, computers, ski and golf bags, clothing that should not be wrinkled, furniture, luggage, and various other types of goods. Delivery costs are moderate, deliveries are usually made within a day or two, and desired drop-off times can be specified. Most companies also offer express options at a surcharge, which ensures expedited delivery.

Goods can be sent from and delivered to almost any address in Japan, including private homes, offices, hotels, airports, and 宅配便 service centers. Pickup times may be scheduled with the nearest service center to send goods from a private home. Alternatively, goods may be dropped off at most convenience stores, as well as a variety of other stores that display a 宅配便 sign and 宅配便 service centers. Some stores, such as souvenir shops, can arrange for purchased merchandise to be sent directly to a designated recipient. In addition, Japanese people often use 宅配便 to send their luggage from an airport to a hotel or between hotels, in order to avoid hauling heavy luggage onto crowded trains and up and down stairways. Several 宅配便 counters can be found in the arrival lobbies of airports.

Courtesy of the authors

日本の住所(じゅうしょ) Japanese Addresses

With the exception of major roads, Japanese streets are not named. Instead, cities and towns are subdivided into areas, subareas and blocks, and houses within each subarea are in the temporal order in which they are constructed. If addresses are written in Japanese, they start with the postal code, followed by the prefecture, city and subarea(s), and end with the recipient's name. As with all Japanese text, addresses may be written vertically from right to left instead horizontally. If addresses are written in English, they start with the recipient's name and end with the prefecture and postal code. A typical Japanese address looks like this:

〒 100-8558 東京(とうきょう)都(と)千代田(ちよだ)区(く)内幸町(うちさいわいちょう) 1 丁目(ちょうめ) 1-1

1-1, Uchisaiwai-cho 1-chome, Chiyoda-ku, Tokyo 100-8558

銀行(ぎんこう)

Cash cards and credit cards (クレジットカード) are the most prevalent methods of personal financial transactions in Japan, and banks do not have checking accounts for private use. Most business transactions, including payroll disbursements, are made via bank transfers (銀行振込(ぎんこうふりこみ)) or クレジットカード. Other services offered by banks include direct debit payment for utility bills (自動引き落とし(じどうひきおとし)), travelers checks (トラベラーズチェック) issuance, and bank-to-bank money transfers. Bank transfers are used to make a variety of payments such as tuition and mail order charges.

It is difficult for a short-term visitor to Japan to open a bank account because this transaction is highly restricted, to prevent crimes such as money laundering, and the use of fictitious names for bank accounts. To open a bank account, non-Japanese need to present both an ID, such as a パスポート or driver's license (運転免許証(うんてんめんきょしょう)), and a residence card (在留(ざいりゅう)カード). It is also necessary to bring an initial deposit and a personal seal or stamp (判子(はんこ) or 印鑑(いんかん)). Some banks, especially those with a foreign currency exchange service, will accept a handwritten signature to open an account, but since personal seals are so widely used in Japanese society, it's a good idea to have an inexpensive one made at a local stamp shop. Personal stamps usually have one's last name. Most bank accounts for foreigners are registered in either **katakana** or roman letters. It's also possible to use a **kanji** combination that approximates the sound of a non-Japanese last name. Banks have special teller windows for regular savings accounts (left), and foreign customers can transact business using personal stamps with their names transcribed in **katakana** (see above).

文法(ぶんぽう)

I. Expressing and inquiring about one's factual knowledge using the clause か（どうか）

To express or inquire about someone's knowledge of an event, situation or fact, a question is embedded within another sentence in English and Japanese. For example, the statement, *I don't know when John is coming* contains a question, *When is John coming.* This type of question is called an indirect question. Two types of questions, yes-no questions and information questions, can be embedded. In English, an embedded yes-no question is preceded by "whether (or not)" or "if," and an embedded information question is preceded by a question word. This chapter explains the formation of embedded questions in Japanese.

A. Indirect information question (*when, what, where,* etc.)

In Japanese, an embedded information question ends with a plain form followed by か. The only exceptions are noun + the copula verb だ and な-adjectives. In these cases, だ is deleted. Thus, the formation of the construction is the same as かもしれません and でしょう.

Indirect questions can be followed by a range of main verbs, including 知っている, 見る, 聞く, 分かる, かんがえる, 教(おし)える, 忘れる, きめる, and おぼえている.

小包(こづつみ)がいつとどくか知りません。	*I don't know when the package is arriving.* (will arrive)
どの銀(ぎん)行がいいか聞きました。	*I asked which bank is a good one.*
住所(じゅうしょ)はどこか教(おし)えて下さい。	*Please tell me where the address is.* (what the address is)
どこでその人に会ったか忘れました。	*I forgot where I met that person.*
いくらお金をかりたかおぼえていますか。	*Do you remember how much money you borrowed?*

田中：英語の試験(しけん)はいつか知ってる？
Do you know when the English exam will be?

川上：あ、来週の火曜日だよ。
Oh, that will be next Tuesday.

田中：じゃあ、どこ勉強したらいいか分かる？
Well, then do you know which part I should study?

川上：ううん、知らない。でも、先生が今日授業で話すと思うよ。
No, I don't know. But I think the teacher will talk about it in class today.

Note

- The subject of the question clause is often, but not always, marked by が, when it refers to something or someone other than the speaker. This makes it clear that the subject of the question is different from the speaker.

田中さんはどこから来ましたか。
Where is Mr. Tanaka from?

田中さんがどこから来たか知りません。
I don't know where Mr. Tanaka is from.

B. Indirect yes-know questions, whether or not ~; if ~

In order to embed a yes-no question, use かどうか instead of か.

銀行からお金をかりるかどうかまだきめていません。
I have not decided whether I will borrow money from the bank.

今、ドルを円にかえた方がいいかどうか教えて下さい。
Please tell me whether I should exchange dollars for yen now.

川田：アメリカで銀行のふつう預金の口座をひらく時、パスポートがいるかどうか知っていますか。
Do you know if I need my passport when I open a regular bank account in the US?

タン：すみません、分かりません。
Sorry, I don't know.

話してみましょう

Activity 1 Work with a partner. Say whether you know the answer to the following questions about Japan, using indirect questions.

Example: 日本では、何時まで銀行があいていますか。
何時まで銀行があいているか知っています／分かります。
or
さあ、何時まで銀行があいているか知りません／わかりません。

1. 日本では、宅配便でどんなものが送れますか。
2. 宅配便と郵便局は何が違いますか。
3. 日本では、郵便局と宅配便とどちらの方が安いですか。
4. 日本の郵便局は何時にしまりますか。
5. 日本では、ATM でいくらまでお金が引き出せますか。
6. 今、一ドル何円ですか。
7. ATM で日本から海外にお金が送れますか。
8. 日本では、銀行口座をひらく時、サインがつかえますか。
9. 日本では、宅配便は日曜日に荷物を取りに来ますか。
10. 日本では、家の郵便受けから手紙を出すことが出来ますか。
11. 日本では、コンビニで切手が買えますか。

Activity 2

Work with a partner. Ask your partner whether he/she remembers something that you have forgotten.

Example: A: 今度の漢字のテストが<u>いつあるか</u>忘れちゃったんですが、
～さんは<u>いつか</u>おぼえていますか。

B: さあ、おぼえていません。先生に<u>いつあるか</u>聞いた方がいいですね。

Activity 3

Work with the class. Think of four interesting facts that you know about Japan and create a quiz. Then quiz your classmates to find out if they know the answers. Write the name of each classmate under 知っている人 or 知らない人 , depending on whether they know. Write the answers if you find them. Use casual speech. The first three quiz questions are provided for you as practice.

Example: A: 日本にはじめて来たアメリカ人はいつ来たか知ってる?

B: いや、知らない。

or

うん、知ってるよ。1854 年だよ。

A: そのとおり (*That's right*)。すごいね！

クイズ	知らない人	知っている人	答え
Ex. 日本にはじめて来たアメリカ人はいつ来ましたか。			
1. 日本で一番古い建物(たて)はきょうとにありますか。			
2. 東京(きょう)からホノルルまで飛(ひ)行機(き)で何時間かかりますか。			
3.			
4.			
5.			
6.			

II. Expressing movement away from or toward the speaker through space using ～ていく and ～てくる

The て-form of verbs + いく and くる indicates an action or event which moves away or towards the speaker. For example, 持っていく, which consists of the verb 持つ (*to hold*) and 行く (*to go*) means *to take*, but 持ってくる means *to bring*.

A. ～ていく

～ていく is used when the direction is away from the current location of the speaker. It can be used when the speaker does something and leaves his/her current location, as in the following example.

朝御飯(ごはん)を食べていきましょう。 *Let's eat breakfast before we go.*
(lit.: *Let's eat breakfast and go/leave.*)

宿題(しゅくだい)をしていきます。 *I will do my homework before I go.*

ここで少し休んでいきましょう。 *Let's take a little break here before we go.*

単語(たんご)をおぼえていきます。 *I will memorize the vocabulary before I go.*

In the above situations, the speaker finishes something (e.g., eating, doing homework, and resting) and then goes out, so the meaning of the sentence is the same as ～て (*and*).

In addition, ～ていく is used when the speaker does something in a direction away from where he/she starts.

銀(ぎん)行にうんてんめんきょしょうを持っていきました。
I took my driver's license to the bank.

郵便局(ゆうびんきょく)までくるまに乗っていきます。
I will drive to the post office.

子供を学校につれていきました。
I took my child to school.

In these situations, the act of holding (持つ), riding (乗る), or accompanying (つれる) takes place in the direction away from where the speaker is. Thus, it expresses taking something to.

お父さん：じゃあ、行ってくるよ。
I'm leaving.

お母さん：じゃあ、この葉書(はがき)、ポストに入れていってくれない？
Well, can you put this postcard into a mailbox on your way (to your office.)

Notes

- The verbs いく and くる do not necessarily correspond to the English "to come" and "to go." For example, when called, an English speaker might respond by saying "I'm coming." In Japanese, however, the corresponding response would be すぐ行くよ. This is because the speaker's position is considered the center point. So いく is used when the speaker or someone or something else moves away from the speaker's current position. This is true when いく is used as an auxiliary verb in the て-form of the verb + いく form. Therefore, the て-form of the verb +

いく indicates an action or event which moves away from the speaker's current location.

- In casual speech, the sound い in 〜ていく may be dropped.

ごはんを作っていきますよ。
ごはん、作ってくよ。
I will cook a meal and go.

山田さんのところに持っていって下さい。
山田さんのところに持ってって。
Take (it) *to Mr.Yamada.*

晩ごはんを食べていったらどうですか。
晩ごはんを食べてったらどう？
How about eating supper before leaving?

B. 〜てくる

The て-form of verbs + くる is the exact opposite of the て-form of verbs +いく. While the use of いく implies a direction away from the current location of the speaker, くる indicates a movement toward the location of the speaker.

ふうとうを買って来ました。	*I bought some envelopes before I came* (here). (lit.: *I bought some envelopes and came.*)
作文(さくぶん)を書いてきましたか。	*Have you written a composition before coming* (here)*?*
単語(たんご)の意味(いみ)をしらべてきましたか。	*Have you checked the vocabulary meaning before coming* (to class)*?*
会話(かいわ)の練習(れんしゅう)をしてきましたか。	*Did you practice speaking before coming* (to class)*?*
判子(はんこ)を作ってきて下さい。	*Please have your seal made and come back.*
学生証(しょう)を持ってきて下さい。	*Please bring your student ID.*
友達が電話をかけてきた。	*My friend phoned before coming* (over).
弟をここまでつれて来ました。	*I brought my brother here.*

ジョン：文法(ぶんぽう)の宿題(しゅくだい)、してきた？
Did you bring your grammar homework?
さなえ：え、今日宿題(しゅくだい)あったの？
What? Did we have an assignment for today?

Notes

- Because the spatial point of reference is the current location of the speaker, 今ジュースを買ってきます and 明日ジュースを買ってきます imply slightly different situations. 今ジュースを買ってきます would mean that the person will go to the store, buy some juice, and come back. On the other hand, 明日ジュースを買ってきます means that the person will buy the juice before coming to this location.

- When verbs like いく or くる are used as auxiliary verbs, they are usually written in **hiragana**. However, in this usage the original verb meanings are retained, so you may see spellings such as 持って行く and 持って来る.

話してみましょう

Activity 1 The following diagram illustrates actions directed to certain people or places or actions that have taken place before the subject moved toward a certain place. Make sentences which express actions and directionality using ～ていく／～てくる.

Example: スミスさんは私に本をかえしてきました。
私はスミスさんの家にふうとうと切手(きって)を買っていきました。

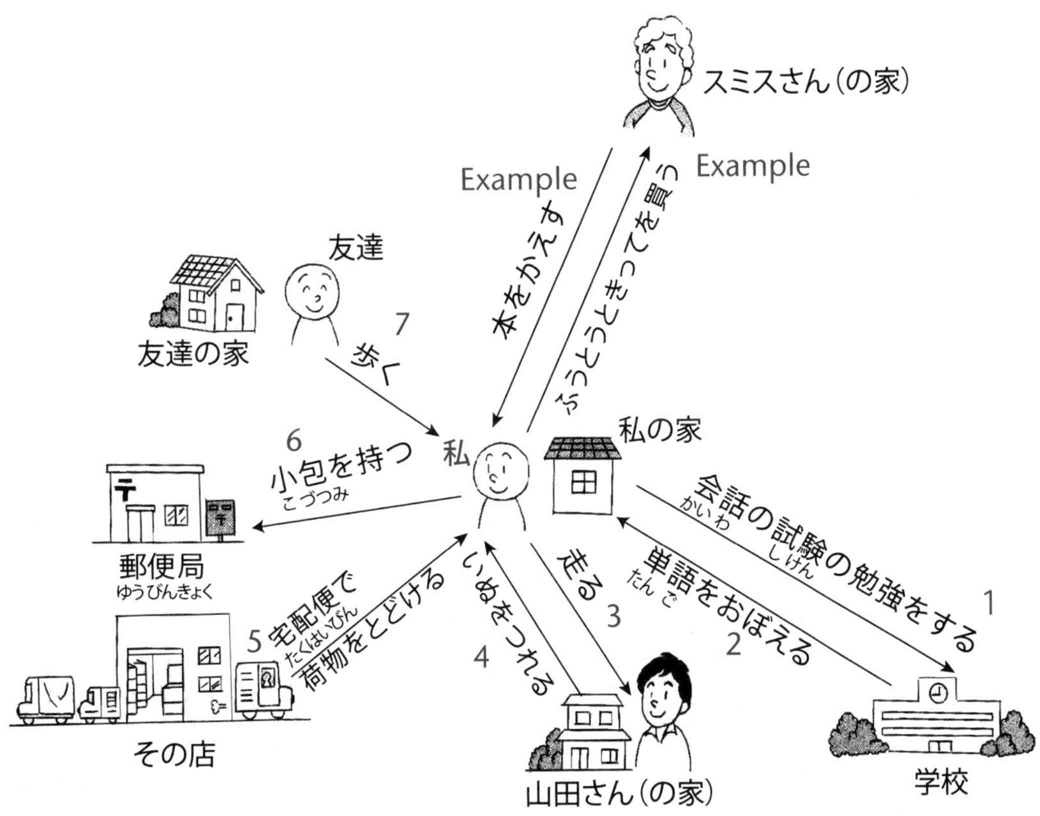

Activity 2 Work as a class. Ask your classmates what he/she has done or brought before coming to school.

Example: A: 学校に来る前に、どんなことをしてきましたか。
B: 会話(かいわ)の練習(れんしゅう)をしてきました。

Activity 3

Work with a partner. Imagine that you are roommates and that you each have a blind date this evening. Ask each other what you will do before going out using ～ていく.

Example: A: 今日のデート、何、着ていく？
B: そうだね。新しいジーンズはいていこうかな。～さんは？
A: 私は白いワンピースを着ていこうと思う。

III. Expressing one's desire for someone to do something using ～てもらう／いただく and ～てほしい

In Chapter 6 of *Nakama 1*, you learned request forms such as ～て下さい／～て下さいませんか／～てくれませんか, and that the て-form of verbs can be used for casual requests. This chapter introduce expressions that convey the speaker's desire for someone to do something, often used to make a request as well.

A. ～てもらう and ～ていただく

The combination of the て-form of verbs and もらう／いただく, which means *to receive* and たい (*want*) are used to express the speaker's desire to have someone do something. いただく is a polite version of もらう and used toward a superior and/or in a formal situation.

この荷物を とどけてもらいたい。	*I want you to deliver this package.*
お金を かしてもらいたい。	*I want you to lend me some money.*
予定を きめていただきたい。	*I would like you to decide on your plan.*
ふつう預金(よきん)の口座(こうざ)を ひらいていただきたい。	*I would like you to open a regular bank account (for me).*

在留(ざいりゅう)カードのもうしこみ方(かた)を 教(おし)えていただきたい。
I would like for you to tell me how to apply for a residence card.

Adding phrases like ～と思います makes the expression less direct and more polite while the speaker's intention is still very clear. Adding ～んです can be used to introduce a topic as shown throughout this text.

その本をかえしてもらいたいと思います。	*I would like to have my book back.*
その本かえしてもらいたいんだけど、いい？	*I would like to have my book back, OK?*
住所(じゅうしょ)を教(おし)えていただきたいと思います。	*I would like to know your address.*
住所(じゅうしょ)を教(おし)えていただきたいんですが。	*I would like to know your address . . .*

In addition, the potential form of もらう・いただく with forms such as ませんか is used to make a request.

その本をかえしてもらえませんか。	*Can I have my book back?* (lit.: *Can I receive the favor of getting my book back?*)
住所(じゅうしょ)を教(おし)えていただけませんか。	*Could you tell me the address?* (lit.: *Could I receive the favor of being taught your address?*)

スミス：あのう、高山さん。
Umm, Ms. Takayama?

高山：え、何？
What?

スミス：この漢字の書き方が分からないんだけど、書いてもらえないかな？
I don't know how to write this kanji, so can you write it for me?

高山：ああ、いいよ。
Oh, sure.

田中：すみませんが、しゃしん、とっていただけませんか。
Excuse me, could you take a picture of us?

通行人：ああ、いいですよ。
Passerby: *Sure.*

田中：ありがとうございます。
Thank you.

Notes

- If the potential form is used with the main verb, the speaker is simply asking the listener whether he/she is capable of doing something. Therefore it does not indicate a request.

  その本を<u>かえせますか</u>。
  Are you physically capable of returning that book?

  その本を<u>かえせませんか</u>。
  Are you not physically incapable of returning that book?

  その本をかえして<u>もらえませんか</u>。
  Can I have that book back?

- The level of politeness between ～てくれませんか and ～てもらえませんか is roughly the same. Similarly, ～てくださいませんか and ～ていただけませんか have a similar level of politeness. The choice between くれる and もらえる or くださる and いただく tends to depend on personal preferences, regional differences, stylistic variations, and generation.

B. Expressing a desire to have someone do something, using ～てほしい

In Chapter 8 of *Nakama 1*, the adjective ほしい as in いぬがほしい (*I want a dog*) is introduced to express one's desire for something. The combination of the て-form of the verb + ほしい is used to express the speaker's desire to have someone do something as well. The speaker, 私, and the person who actually performs the act is marked by the particle に but is usually omitted if understood from context. The て-form of the verb + ほしい cannot be used to express the speaker's desire to have a socially superior person do something. Use ～ていただきたい instead.

この荷物、ちょっと持ってほしいんだけど、いい？
I'd like you to hold this luggage, is that OK?

明日レポートを持って来てほしいんだけど、いい？
I'd like you to bring the report, is that OK?

To express a desire to have someone not do something, use ～ほしくない, ～もらいたくない, or ～ないでほしい.

この葉書(はがき)はつかってほしくないんですけど。	*I don't want you to use this postcard.*
この葉書(はがき)はつかわないでほしいんですけど。	*I don't want you to use this postcard.*
この葉書(はがき)はつかってもらいたくないんですけど。	*I don't want you to use this postcard.*

Notes

- To express a desire for a specific person other than the listener to do something, use the particle に.

山田さんに　行ってほしい。	*I want Mr. Yamada to go.*
山田さんに　行ってもらいたい。	*I want Mr. Yamada to go.*
山田さんに　行っていただきたい。	*I want Mr. Yamada to go.*

話してみましょう

Activity 1 Make polite requests to your instructor using ～ていただけませんか and ～て下さいませんか.

Example: もう一度言う。
先生、もう一度言っていただけませんか。
先生、もう一度言って下さいませんか。

1. 宿題(しゅくだい)を明日までまつ。
2. すいせんじょう (*letter of recommendation*) を書く。
3. この文法(ぶんぽう)を説明(せつめい)する。
4. DVD をかす。
5. アニメのれきしについて話す。
6. 漢字のおぼえ方(かた)を教(おし)える。
7. 作文(さくぶん)のドラフト (*draft*) を読む。

Activity 2 Work with a partner. Your partner is a roommate. Based on the pictures below, ask for favors using ～てほしい and ～もらいたい.

Example: まどの近くにいる友達にまどをあけるようにたのんでいるえ

A：あのう、～さん、暑いから、まどをあけてほしいんだけど。

B：ああ、いいよ。

A：ありがとう。

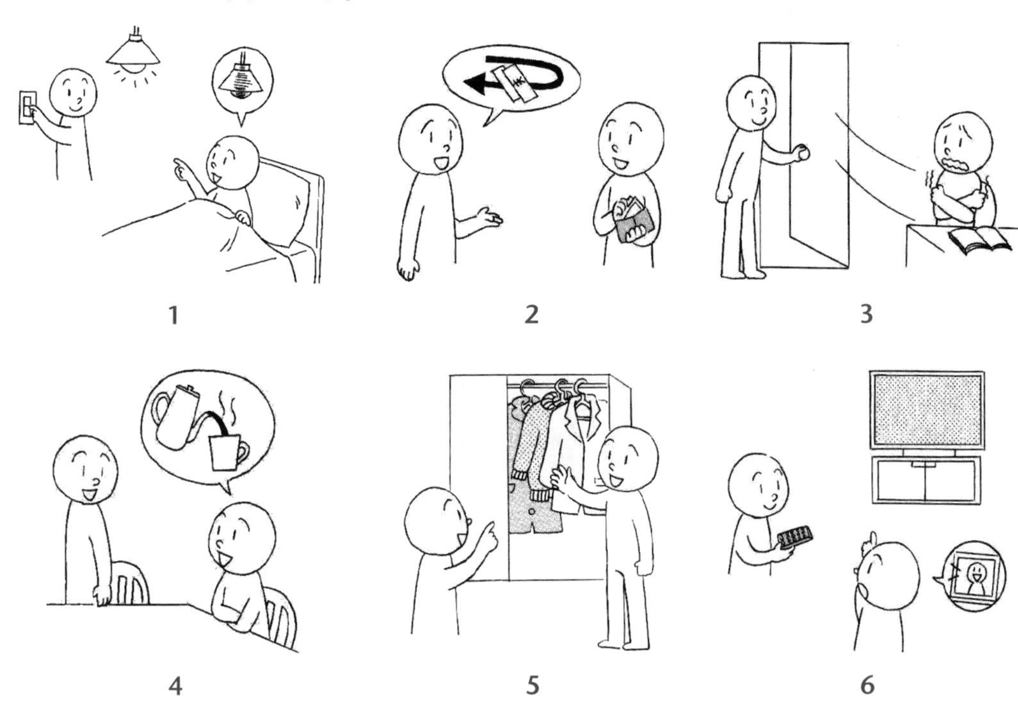

Activity 3

Work with a partner. You visit various stores and need to ask for help. In each of the following situations, make a request, using ～てもらえませんか, ～てもらいたいんですが and ～てくれませんか. Your partner is a store employee, and he/she needs to respond to your requests appropriately.

Example: デパートにいます。ほしいかばんがありますが、とても高い所にあります。

A: すみませんが、あのかばんをとってもらえませんか／とってもらいたいんですが／とってくれませんか。

B: はい、あれですね。

A: ええ、おねがいします。

1. 銀行にいます。ATM のつかい方が分かりません。
2. 銀行にいます。円をドルにかえたいです。
3. 郵便局にいます。アメリカまで手紙を送りたいんですが、切手がいくらか知りたいです。
4. 電話で宅配便の会社と話しています。明日の晩、荷物を送りたいです。
5. レストランにいます。30分まちましたが、注文したりょうりがまだ来ません。
6. さかなやにいます。たくさん買うので、少し安い方がいいと思っています。

Activity 4

Work with a partner. One person plays the role of A, and the other of B. In each case, B has a problem and asks A for help. A has the option of helping or refusing. If A decides not to help B, make sure to state the reason.

Example: B: あのう、山田さん、おねがいがあるんですけど。
A: 何ですか。
B: 明日、日本語の試験(しけん)があるんだけど。
A: ええ。
B: 分からない文法(ぶんぽう)があるので、説明(せつめい)してもらいたいんですけど。
A: ああ、いいですよ。

パートナー	私	問題 (*problem*)
Ex. 山田さん（友達）	日本語の学生	試験(しけん)があるけど、分からない文法(ぶんぽう)がある。
1. 日本人の友達	外国人学生	病院に行きたいけど、くるまがない。
2. 先生	学生	先生の授業を取(と)りたい。
3. 客	宅配便(たくはいびん)の人	住所(じゅうしょ)と電話番号が知りたい。
4. 兄／姉	弟／妹	デートするので、兄／姉のくるまを一日つかいたい。
5. 先生	学生	もうしこみ用紙(ようし)に先生のサインがいる。
6. お母さん／お父さん	子供	コンピュータを買いたいけど、お金がない。

IV. Expressing willingness using ～ましょう／ましょうか

In Chapter 9 of *Nakama 1*, ましょうか (*shall we ~*) and ましょう (*let's ~*) are used to make suggestions. The same structure can also be used to express the speaker's willingness to do something for someone else. In casual speech, you can use the plain forms of the volitional ~ましょう, such as 行こう or 食べよう. Add 私が／ぼくが to emphasize the speaker's willingness to do so.

明日電話しましょうか。	*Shall I call you tomorrow?*
明日のパーティに何を持って行きましょうか。	*What shall I take to tomorrow's party?*
私が話しましょう。	*I will talk* (with him).
晩御飯(ごはん)はぼくが作ろう。	*I'll make dinner.*

田中： 寒いですね。	*It's cold, isn't it?*
川口： じゃあ、まどをしめましょうか。	*Shall I close the windows?*
田中： 大変ですね。手伝(てつだ)いましょう。	*It looks tough* (too much for you). *I will help you.*
山本： ありがとう。	*Thank you.*

健一：	どうしたの。	*What's wrong?*
道子：	頭がとても痛いの。	*I have a bad headache.*
健一：	大変だね。薬、買ってこようか。	*That's too bad. Shall I get some medicine?*

Note

- To explicitly offer help, rather than simply show willingness to do something, use the て-form of the verb + あげましょう(か)/あげよう(か). The auxiliary verb forms あげる and あげましょう/あげよう indicate that the speaker is doing a favor for the listener. This form should not be used with a social superior, because offering a favor to a superior sounds arrogant in Japanese.

  上田： あ、ペン、忘れちゃった。
  Oh, I forgot my pen.

  石田： じゃあ、ぼくのをかしてあげようか。
  I can lend you mine.

  上田： ありがとう。
  Thank you.

話してみましょう

Activity 1

Your friend is having a problem in each of the following pictures. Offer to help or provide a solution for each of the following situations using ましょう / ましょうか . Use formal speech.

Example: 私がはらいましょう／私がはらいましょうか。

Activity 2

Work as a class. In the following chart, write three things you would like help with. Tell a classmate about one of your problems. Your classmate may or may not offer to help you. Write down the names of anyone who offers help. If someone else asks for help, offer assistance if you can.

Example: A: どうしたんですか。

B: このペン、書けなくて。

A: じゃあ、私のをかしてあげましょうか／かしましょうか。

or こまりましたね。私、今、ペン持ってないので、すみません。

	友達の名前

Activity 3

Work in groups of four. Each group should plan a party and invite classmates. Decide what to buy, what to make, etc. Then decide on volunteers to do the various tasks. Write down who will do what.

Example: A：いつ、どこでしようか。

B：土曜日の晩はどう？ぼくの家でしようよ。

C：ありがとう。じゃ、時間は七時からはどう？

D：いいね。じゃあ、食べ物はどうしようか。

A：じゃあ、私はサラダを作ろうかな。

C：じゃあ、ぼくは、飲み物を持って来よう。

V. Expressing time limits using までに (*by ~ , by the time ~*)

The particle までに specifies a time limit within which an action or event must be completed. If までに is used, the action in the main clause must be completed.

明日までに宿題をしなければならない。	*I must do my homework by tomorrow.*
十二時までに来て下さい。	*Please come by 12 o'clock.*
今度の誕生日までに１０キロやせたい。	*I want to lose 10 kilograms* (22 pounds) *by my next birthday.*

までに can be used with a clause that ends with the plain present form.

夏休みがおわるまでに、レポートを書かなければならない。
I must write a paper by the end of the summer break.

小包がとどくまでに、何日ぐらいかかりますか。
How long will it take for the package to arrive?

卒業するまでに、日本語能力試験のＮ１を取りたい。
I want to pass N1 of the Japanese Language Proficiency Test by the time I graduate.

Notes

- までに and 前に overlap in usage. While 前に merely indicates chronological sequence, までに indicates a time limit or deadline by which something must be completed. For this reason, までに often occurs with phrases such as なければならない (*must*). For example, 日本に留学する前に、１００万円ためなければならない means *I must save one million yen before going to Japan.* 日本に留学するまでに、１００万円ためなければならない also conveys the same action, but in this case, the speaker's trip to Japan is the definitive deadline to save up one million yen. This sense of a definitive deadline is not conveyed with 前に.
- Another similar expression is まで (*until*). Like までに, まで can be used with a clause ending in the plain present from as in 先生がいらっしゃるまで (*until the teacher comes*). However, there are two major differences between まで and までに. First, まで can be used with time expressions and space expressions but までに can be used only with time expressions. Second, まで indicates that the action or event must continue until the specified time. On the other hand, までに indicates that the action or event must be completed by the specified time.

  四時までまちました。
  I waited until four o'clock .

  七時までに出かけなければなりません。
  I must leave by seven o'clock.

  山田さんが着くまで、ここでまっています。
  I will wait here until Ms. *Yamada arrives.*

  山田さんが着くまでに、食べてしまいました。
  We finished eating by the time Ms. *Yamada arrived.*

話してみましょう

Activity 1

Work with a partner. You have just arrived in Japan to study at Joto University, and need to get settled quickly. But you have not done a lot of things. The calendar below indicates upcoming events. Discuss things that you need to get done before each event on the calendar.

Example: A: まだ住(す)む所(ところ)がきまっていないんですよ。
B: じゃあ、留学生オリエンテーションまでに／８日までに、アパートをさがさなければなりませんね。

1. まだ銀行(ぎんこう)の口座(こうざ)がありません。
2. まだかもくとうろく (*course registration*) をしていません。
3. まだ先生に会っていません。
4. まだ学生証(しょう)がありません。
5. まだざいりゅうカードを持っていません。

日	月	火	水	木	金	土
	1	2	3	4	5	6
7	8 留学生オリエンテーション	9	10 学部(がくぶ) (undergraduate) オリエンテーション	11	12	13
14	15 Class begins	16	17	18	19	20 Parents' visit
21	22	23	24 Last day for registration	25	26	27
28	29	30 Last day to pay tuition				

Activity 2

Work with a partner. Make a schedule on the calendar below and write five things you need to get done before certain dates. Ask your partner about his/her schedule and fill in his/her information on your calendar using a different color.

Example: A: 今週、何かしなければならないことある？
B: うん、火曜日までに作文(さくぶん)を書かなければならないんだ。
A: あ、私もそう。

日	月	火	水	木	金	土
		Example: 作文(さくぶん)を出す				

Activity 3

Work with a partner. Ask what your partner needs to get done before the following events take place. Also, ask what your partner would like to do or be doing up until the time the same events take place.

Example: A：卒業するまでに何をしておきたいと思いますか。

B：そうですね、日本語能力試験(のうりょくしけん) (*Japanese Language Proficiency Test*) の N1 をとっておきたいですね。

A：そうですか。いいですね。じゃあ、卒業するまで、どんなことをしていたいですか。

B：そうですね。たくさんあそんでいたいですね。

1. 卒業します。
2. 30 さいになります。
3. 結婚します。
4. 子供が出来ます。
5. 50 さいになります。
6. 仕事をやめます。
7. しにます (*to die*)。

聞く練習（れんしゅう）

上手な聞き方（かた）

Knowing how to use varied request forms appropriately

A request is a type of imposition from the speaker to the listener, because it normally benefits the speaker and not the listener. Depending on the context of the conversation and the relationship between the speaker and the listener, the tone, directness, and politeness of a request varies. For example, an athletic coach may make a strong request to an athlete during training. On the other hand, a business executive may make a very polite request to a representative of another company. English has a variety of expressions for making requests, such as *please ~*, *can you ~*, *could you*, *do you mind ~*, as well as the simple imperative form. Also, requests may be implied such as in the examples *Do you have an extra pen?* and *I can't find my pen.* Japanese also has a variety of ways to make a request, as you have been seen throughout this book. Knowing how to use them properly is extremely important for maintaining good social relationships, so it is essential to be aware of when and with whom to use each kind of request form.

1. Complete the following table.

Expressions	**Situations**	**Listener types**	**Social relationship**	**Directness of request**
	Casual/ Formal	Social superior/ Equal/ Social inferior	Close/ Average/ Distant	Implied/ Overt & indirect/ Overt & direct
寒いね。	Casual	Equal, inferior	Close /average	Implied
あ、まどがあいてる。				
まど、しめてくれない？				
まど、しめて。				
まど、しめてくれませんか。				
まど、しめてもらえませんか。				
まど、しめてほしいんですけど。				
まど、しめてもらいたいんですけど。				
まど、しめて下さいませんか。				
まど、しめていただけませんか。				
まど、しめていただきたいんですが。				

2. Listen to the following requests and circle the person being spoken to. There may be more than one answer.

Example: ね、早く起きて。

 子供　きゃく　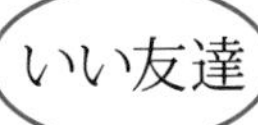 いい友達　先生

1.	クラスメート	先生	友達	客
2.	お母さん	同じアパートにすんでいる人	妹	いい友達
3.	学生	よく知らない学生	日本語の先生	先輩(せんぱい) (*a person in a grade ahead of you*)

三つのおねがい

聞く前に

There are many occasions for which you want to ask for favors in your daily life. Given the following situations and relationships, write the kind of request you might make in Japanese.

学校で　友達 ______________________________

先生 ______________________________

家で　両親 ______________________________

兄弟 ______________________________

近所(きんじょ)の人 (*person in the neighborhood*) ______________________________

みち (*street*) で　知らない人 ______________________________

友達 ______________________________

聞いてみましょう

Listen to three dialogues and complete the table below by writing the name or title of the person who has made the request, the content of the request, and the name or title of the person to whom the request is being made. Circle はい if the request is accepted. Circle いいえ if it is denied.

Example: A: 行ってきます。

B: あっ、まもる、今日はおばあちゃんが来るから、早く帰ってきてよ。

A: ああ、わかったよ。

	だれが	何を	だれが	はい・いいえ
Example	お母さん	家に早く帰ってくる	子供 or まもる	はい・いいえ
1.				はい・いいえ
2.				はい・いいえ
3.				はい・いいえ

聞いた後で

Based on the chart you have just completed in 聞いてみましょう, write a brief summary of each conversation.

聞き上手話し上手

Making a request and turning down a request or an invitation

A. Making a request

A conversation for making a request has a relatively set structure. First, use a conversation opener such as あのう or あのう、すみません to get the attention of the listener. This is optionally followed by an expression that implies that the request is on its way, such as じつは、ちょっとおねがいがあるんですけど (*Actually, I have a small favor to ask*).

スミス： あのう。
山本： 何、スミスさん？
スミス： じつは、ちょっとおねがいがあるんですけど。
山本： あ、何ですか。

Then express a desire, problem, or fact that will lead to a request, such as 明日、会話(かいわ)の試験(しけん)があるんですけど. Finally, make the request itself, like 一緒(しょ)に練習(れんしゅう)してくれませんか. If a request is a difficult one, show your concern for the listener by adding a phrase such as よかったら (*if it's OK with you*) or 時間があったら (*if you have time*).

スミス： 明日、会話(かいわ)の試験(しけん)があるんですけど、（時間があったら、）一緒(しょ)に練習(れんしゅう)してくれませんか。

Then express gratitude and appreciation. In addition to ありがとう, you may want to add ほんとに、いいんですか or たすかります (*That will be helpful*). If a request could be seen to be an imposing one, you may want to use すみません instead of ありがとう.

山本： あ、今、ちょっといそがしいけど、昼御飯(ごはん)の後だったら、いいですよ。
スミス： ありがとう。たすかります。

B. Refusing a request or an invitation

Although there are a number of situations where you might need to turn down a request or invitation, a typical refusal will begin with an expression of regret such as ざんねんですが or an apology such as すみません or ごめん（なさい）. Then state a reason. When stating a reason, it is very common not to finish the sentence. Leaving the sentence incomplete makes your refusal sound less assertive and hesitant, which in turn makes it sounds more considerate. Avoid the use of ～たくありません (*don't want to do~*), since it is considered impolite in this situation. You can suggest an alternative. It is also a good strategy to indicate your willingness to offer help on another occasion or to do something with the person at another time.

まもる：あの、今ちょっといい？
さやか：あ、いいけど。何？
まもる：あの、英語の作文(さくぶん)の宿題(しゅくだい)してるんだけど、ちょっと手伝(てつだ)って
　　　　もらえないかな。
さやか：あ、悪いけど、英語の宿題(しゅくだい)はちょっと。
まもる：そう、だめ？
さやか：う～ん。ごめん。英語はちょっと。あ、上田さんに聞いたらどう？
まもる：あ、そうだね。そうするよ。

A. Work with a partner. Practice making requests in the following situations.

1. You want to try on a pair of pants in the display case at a department store. Make a request to a store clerk.
2. You want to buy something to drink, but don't have money. Make a request to a close friend.
3. You want to use your friend's car for a date. Ask your friend for the use of the car.
4. You want your doctor to write a letter stating your physical condition so that your absence can be excused.

B. Work with a partner. Your partner will ask you to do one of the following things. Politely turn down the request.

1. to lend him/her some money
2. to explain to him/her how to do something
3. to teach him/her how to use e-mail
4. to teach him/her how to cook ____________ (choose a dish)

iLrn Self-Tests

C. Work with a partner. Your partner invites you to one of the following events. Politely turn down the invitation.

誕生(たんじょう)日パーティ　　コンサート　　映(えい)画　　食事

漢字

Bottom and enclosing component shapes of kanji

There are not as many bottom components as side components, but they tend to indicate rough meanings of **kanji**, just like the left components. For example, 心, which means *heart*, indicates that the **kanji** with this component has something to do with human emotion and thought, as in 忘 (*forget*), 思 (*think*), 悪 (*bad*), and 悲 (*sad*).

Name		Meaning	Examples
こころ	心	heart	忘 思 急 悪 忠 念 応 怠 怒 恐 恵 息 恋 患 悲 惑 意 感
れんが・れっか	灬	fire	熱 点 烈 煮 焦 然 無 照 熟 為
ひとあし	儿	walking	元 兄 光 充 先 克 児 免 党
こがい	貝	money	買 貞 負 貢 貨 貫 責 貧 賀 貴 貸 費 留 資 賃 賛 質 賞 賓 賢
いわく	曰	day	書 曹 替
ころも	衣	cloth, clothing	袋 装 裂 製 襲
はち	八	eight	六 共 兵 具 典

There are three types of enclosing components. One is called たれ and covers the left side and the top. The second one, にょう, covers the left side and bottom. And the last one, かまえ, encloses three sides or all four sides. These shapes do not provide any clues to the pronunciation of a character.

Name たれ (left and top)		Meaning	Examples
やまいだれ	疒	sickness	病 痛
まだれ	广	slanting roof	店 度 広
がんだれ	厂	cliff	原 厚 歴
Name にょう (left and bottom)		**Meaning**	**Examples**
しんにょう	辶	road	週 送 近 遠 道 運 通
えんにょう	廴	progress, extend	建 延
そうにょう	走	run	起 超

Name かまえ (three or four sides)	□	Meaning	Examples
くにがまえ	口	enclosure	四 国 回 園 図
もんがまえ	門	gate	門 問 聞 開 閉
けいがまえ	冂	N/A	円 再 冊
はこがまえ・かくしがまえ	匚	box	匠 医 区 匹
うけばこ	凵	receiving box	出 凶 凹
つつみがまえ	勹	wrap	包 勺 匁

Flashcards

Kanji	Handwritten	Meaning / Readings	Examples
郵	郵	mail ユウ	この葉書(はがき)に郵便番号(ゆうびんばんごう)を書いて下さい。
便	便	post, convenient たよ(り) ベン・ビン	郵便(ゆうびん)ポスト 宅配便(たくはいびん) 便利(べんり)な
局	局	bureau, limited part キョク	郵便局(ゆうびんきょく)に行きます。 NHKはテレビ局(きょく)です。
銀	銀	silver ギン	銀行(ぎんこう)に行きます。 きれいな銀(ぎん)のネックレスですね。
送	送	to send おく(る) ソウ・チ	メールを送(おく)る。 送別会(そうべつかい)
紙	紙	paper かみ シ	手紙(てがみ)を書きます。 コピー用紙(ようし)を下さい。
住	住	to reside, to live す(む) ジュウ	東京(きょう)に住(す)んでいます。 住所(じゅうしょ)が分かりません。
所	所	place ところ ショ	住(す)む所(ところ)がない人をホームレスといいます。

引	to pull	ひ(く)　イン	銀行からお金を引き出す。	ぎんこう　ひ　だ
練	to train, practice	ね(る)　レン	会話の練習をする。	れんしゅう
習	to learn, custom	なら(う)　シュウ	テニスを練習する。	れんしゅう
宿	lodge, inn	やど　シュク	宿題を出すのを忘れてしまった。	しゅくだい
題	title, topic, problem	ダイ	今晩、宿題をしなければなりませんか。	しゅくだい
試	to try	こころ(みる)・ため(す)　シ	日本の入学試験は二月にあります。	しけん
験	test	ケン	明日の日本語の会話試験は大変です。	かいわ しけん
受	to receive	うけ(る)　ジュ	試験を受ける。　受験する。	しけん　う　じゅけん
教	to teach	おし(える)　キョウ	天ぷらの作り方を教えて下さい。	つく　かた　おし
文	sentence, letter, writing	ふみ　ブン・モン	明日、作文と文法の試験があります。	さくぶん　ぶんぽう　しけん
法	law, method	ホウ	この文法の使い方を教えて下さい。	ぶんぽう　おし

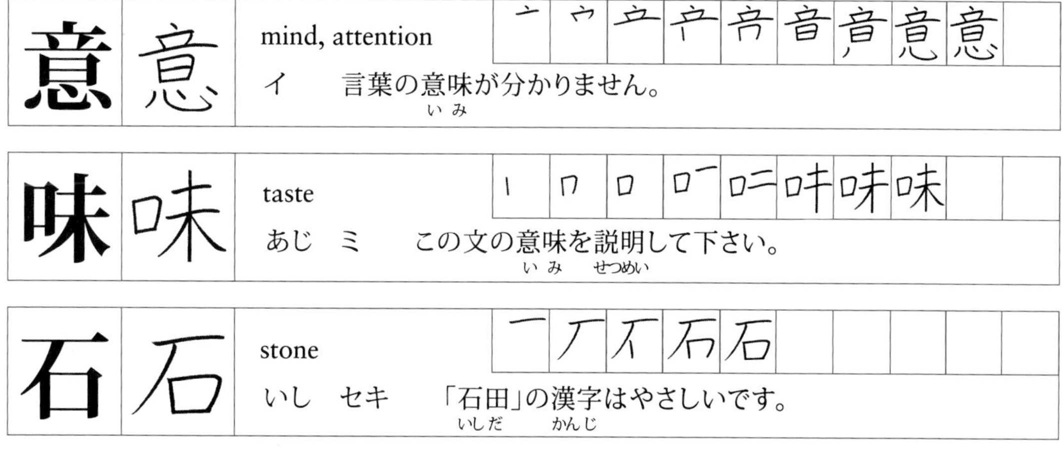

意	意	mind, attention イ 言葉の意味(いみ)が分かりません。	亠 立 音 意 (stroke order)
味	味	taste あじ ミ この文の意味(いみ)を説明(せつめい)して下さい。	口 味 (stroke order)
石	石	stone いし セキ 「石田(いしだ)」の漢字(かんじ)はやさしいです。	一 ア 石 (stroke order)

読めるようになった漢字

郵便局　郵便番号　銀行　送る　手紙　用(よう)紙　住む　所　住所　引き出す　練習
受ける　受験　宿題　入学試験　教える　文法　作文　文学　意味　石田　葉書
会話　切手(きって)　口座(こうざ)　小包(こづつみ)　説明(せつめい)　判子(はんこ)　預金(よきん)　手伝う(てつだう)　作り方　行き方

練習

1. イギリスに行く前に、英語の会話の練習をしておきます。
2. 住所と郵便番号(ごう)を教えて下さいませんか。
3. 銀行でお金を引き出して、郵便局で手紙と小包(づつみ)を送ってしまいましょう。
4. 石田さんは来月入学試験を受けなければなりません。
5. 文学の宿題が出たので、今日の午後にするつもりです。
6. 卒業した後、ニューヨークに住んだら、お金がためられるかどうか分からない。
7. この文法の意味が分からないので、答え方も分かりません。

読む練習(れんしゅう)

上手な読み方

Filling out forms

Forms such as applications forms, bank transfer forms, and delivery request forms often contain a lot of **kanji** words, but the information needed to fill out the form is restricted depending on the purpose of a given form. Therefore, consider the purpose of the form and think about what sort of information you would normally need to supply. Then look at any examples. Note the **kanji** that you've already learned, and guess the meanings of words that include them.

A. 質問に答えて下さい

1. 口座(ざ)をひらく時、どんなことを知らなければなりませんか。どんな物がいりますか。
2. お金を引き出す時、どんなことを知らなければなりませんか。どんな物がいりますか。何がなくてもいいですか。
3. 預(よ)金する時、どんなことを知らなければなりませんか。どんな物がいりますか。何がなくてもいいですか。

B. 下の言葉の意味は何だと思いますか。日本語で言って下さい。

入金　口座番号(ざ ごう)　郵便番号(ごう)　郵送(ゆうそう)　本人(ほんにん)　日付(づけ)(〜年〜月〜日)　お電話　おところ

C. Fill out the following forms.

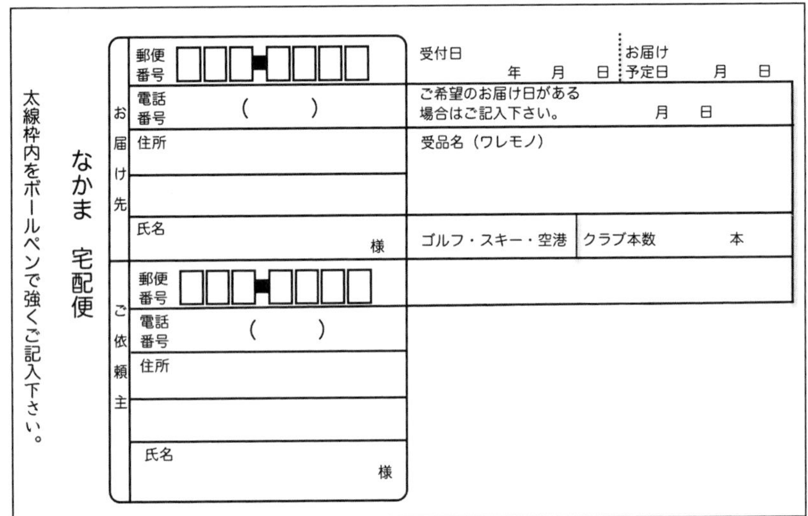

太線枠内をボールペンで強くご記入下さい。

なかま　宅配便

お届け先
郵便番号 □□□-□□□□
電話番号 (　　)
住所
氏名　様

ご依頼主
郵便番号 □□□-□□□□
電話番号 (　　)
住所
氏名　様

受付日　年　月　日
お届け予定日　月　日
ご希望のお届け日がある場合はご記入下さい。　月　日
受品名（ワレモノ）
ゴルフ・スキー・空港　クラブ本数　本

1. Parcel service

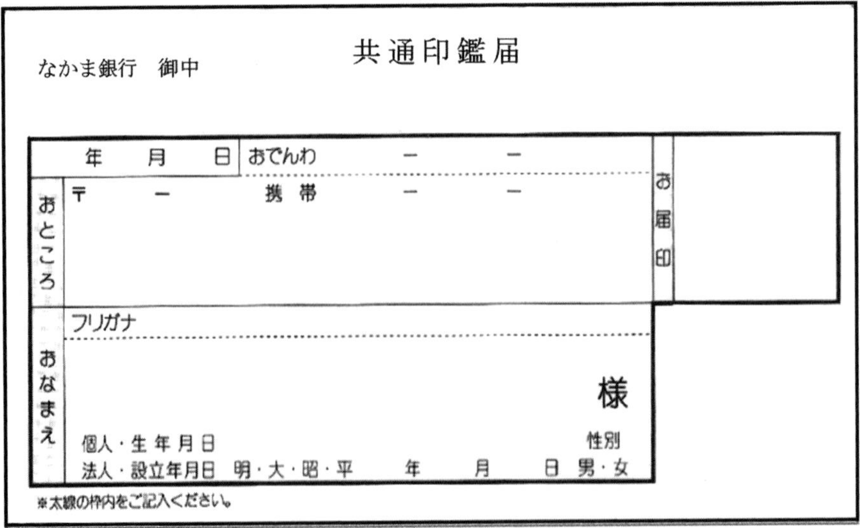

なかま銀行　御中　　共通印鑑届

年　月　日　おでんわ　－　－
おところ　〒　－　携帯　－　－
お届印
おなまえ　フリガナ
様
個人・生年月日
法人・設立年月日　明・大・昭・平　年　月　日
性別　男・女
※太線の枠内をご記入ください。

2. Seal registration for a bank

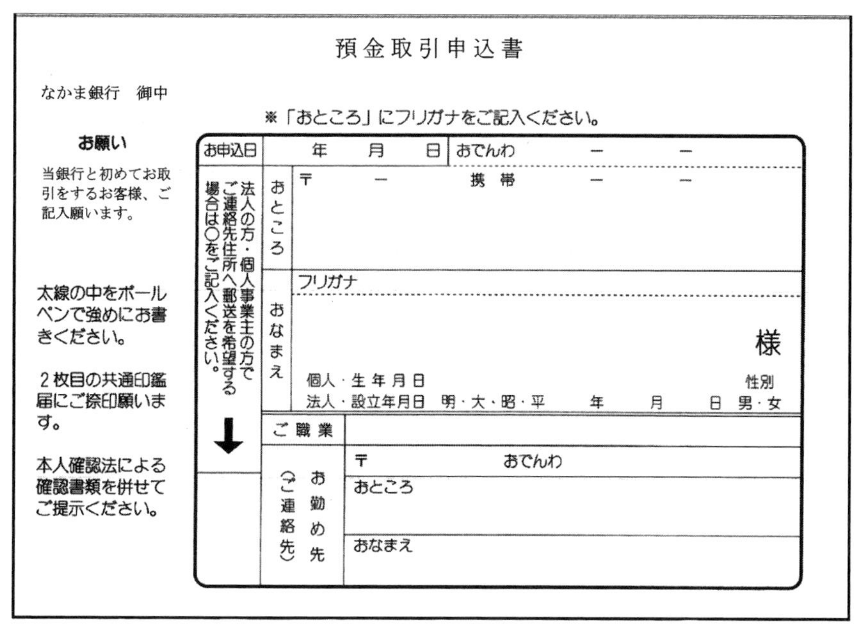

預金取引申込書

なかま銀行　御中

※「おところ」にフリガナをご記入ください。

お願い

当銀行と初めてお取引をするお客様、ご記入願います。

太線の中をボールペンで強めにお書きください。

２枚目の共通印鑑届にご捺印願います。

本人確認法による確認書類を併せてご提示ください。

法人の方・個人事業主の方でご連絡先住所へ郵送を希望する場合は○をご記入ください。

お申込日	年　月　日	おでんわ　－　－
おところ	〒　－	携帯　－　－
おなまえ	フリガナ 様 個人・生年月日 法人・設立年月日　明・大・昭・平　年　月　日	性別 男・女
ご職業		
お勤め先（ご連絡先）	〒　おでんわ おところ おなまえ	

3. Application to open a bank account

ホストファミリー

読む前に

1. アメリカのホストファミリーは外国人にどんなことをしてほしいと思うでしょうか。クラスで話して下さい。
2. 日本のホストファミリーはアメリカの大学から来た留学生に何をしてほしいと思っていると思いますか。日本人に聞いて下さい。

読んでみましょう

言葉のリスト

困る（こま）　to be in trouble　　頼む（たの）　to ask/request

私は今ホストファミリーと住んでいます。私は掃除や洗濯が好きなので、自分の服の洗濯や部屋の掃除をよくしています。それに料理も好きですから、よくホストファミリーのために料理をします。でも、最近ちょっと困っているのです。

私のホストファミリーのお母さんはとてもいい人ですが、よく色々なことを私に頼んできます。例えば、リビングルームの掃除をしたり、子供達と遊んだり、時々洗濯もします。私も出来るだけ手伝おうと思うのですが、手伝わなければならないことが多くて、勉強したり友達と遊んだりする時間が取れません。ホストファミリーのお母さんと話をしたいのですが、どう言ったらいいかよく分かりません。

読んだ後で

A. 質問に日本語で答えて下さい。

1. この人はだれと住んでいますか。
2. この人はどんなことをするのが好きですか。
3. この人はどんなことをしたいと思っていますか。
4. この人はどうしてこまっているのですか。

B. この人にアドバイス (*advice*) をして下さい。

C. 日本でホストファミリーと住む時のマナー (*manners*) について、日本人や日本に行ったことがある友達に聞いて、作文を書いて下さい。

総合練習

日本に留学する

1. Work in groups of four. Obtain catalogues or brochures for a few exchange programs or study abroad programs in Japan, and describe the programs as thoroughly as you can.

Example: このプログラムは東京の大学に留学するプログラムです。
ホストファミリーもりょうもありませんから、アパートを
さがさなければなりません。

2. Compare the programs and decide on one you like.
3. Write an e-mail in Japanese asking your Japanese instructor to write a reference letter (すいせんじょう) on your behalf. State why you want to study abroad, and why you have chosen this particular program.

ロールプレイ

1. You want to buy a present for a friend but don't have enough money because it is the end of the month. You should receive some money in a week or so. Ask another friend to lend you the money to buy the gift.
2. You are travelling with a friend. Your luggage was stolen, so you've lost everything, including your passport, cash, and laptop. Ask for help.
3. You are travelling with a friend. Your friend's luggage got stolen, so everything is lost, including his/her passport, cash, and laptop. Offer some help.
4. You are graduating in a few months and have been looking for a job but haven't gotten one yet. You are getting worried about not having a full-time job after graduation. Ask your instructor for some advice and help.

Chapter 5

第五課

amana images inc. / Alamy

道の聞き方と教え方
Asking for and Giving Directions

Objectives		Asking for and giving directions
Vocabulary		Y called X, landmarks, directions, expressions used in giving directions, stations and transportation
Dialogue		ヒルトンホテルへの行き方 *Directions to the Hilton Hotel*
Japanese Culture		Streets and addresses in Japanese cities, the Japanese train system
Grammar	I.	Expressing a route using the particle を; expressing a point of departure using the particle を; expressing scope or limit using the particle で
	II.	Expressing conditions leading to set consequences using the plain form +と
	III.	Expressing chronology using the て-form of the verb + から
	IV.	Expressing presuppositions using the plain form + はず
	V.	Expressing conditions originated by others using ～(の)なら
Listening		Announcements at stations and on trains, 駅と電車のアナウンス
Communication		How to ask for and give directions
Kanji		Importance of pronunciation in letter identification and **kanji** words 場 寺 橋 町 映 公 園 図 地 鉄 駅 育 道 部 屋 車 右 左 近 遠 通 飛
Reading		Reading maps, 東京大学へ行く

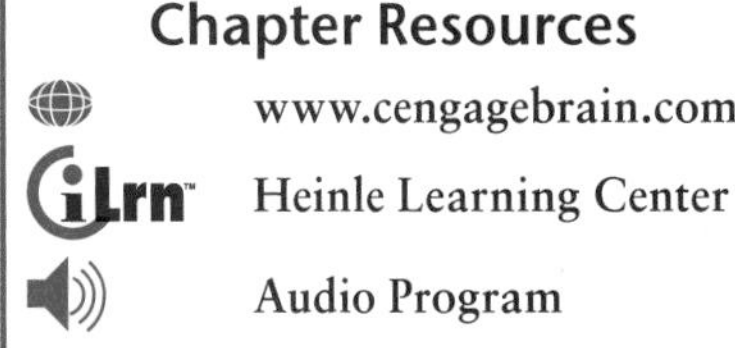

Chapter Resources
www.cengagebrain.com
iLrn Heinle Learning Center
Audio Program

単語
たんご

Flashcards

Nouns

えいがかん	映画館	movie theater
おうだんほどう	横断歩道	pedestrian crossing
かいさつ (ぐち)	改札 (口)	ticket gate
かいだん	階段	stairs
かくえきていしゃ	各駅停車	local train (literally: train that stops at every station)
ガソリンスタンド		gas station
かど	角	corner
きゅうこう (れっしゃ)	急行 (列車)	express train
こうさてん	交差点	intersection
J R		Japan Railway, pronounced as ジェイアール. Formerly government owned now privatized railway system
しやくしょ	市役所	city hall
しんごう	信号	traffic signal
たいしかん	大使館	embassy
タクシー		taxi
ターミナル		terminal, バスターミナル bus depot
ちかてつ	地下鉄	subway
ちず	地図	map
ちゅうしゃじょう	駐車場	parking lot
つぎ	次	next
つきあたり	突き当たり	at the end of the street, T-road
でぐち	出口	exit
でんしゃ	電車	train
どうろ	道路	road, street
とっきゅう (れっしゃ)	特急 (列車)	limited express train
はし	橋	bridge
バスてい	バス停	bus stop
ふつう (れっしゃ)	普通 (列車)	local train, same as かくえきていしゃ
へん	辺	area, このへん (この辺) this area
みち	道	road, street, way

あいだ	間	between
こちらがわ	こちら側	this side
さき	先	beyond, further ahead
てまえ	手前	just before
むかいがわ	向かい側	the other side, the opposite side

い -adjectives

ちかい	近い	close to, near, こうえんにちかい close to the park
とおい	遠い	far from, こうえんからとおい far away from the park

う -verbs

こむ	混む	to become crowded
とおる	通る	to go through, to pass
とまる	止まる	(for someone or something) to stop [intransitive verb]
まがる	曲がる	(for someone or something) to turn [intransitive verb]
よる	寄る	to drop by
わたる	渡る	to cross (bridge, road, etc.)

る -verbs

おりる	降りる	to get off
とめる	止める	to stop (something) [transitive verb]
のりかえる	乗り換える	to transfer, to change transportation
みえる	見える	can see ~ (literally: something is visible)

Adverbs

まっすぐ	真っ直ぐ	straight
すぐ		soon, shortly

Particles

で		limit
を		place in which movement occurs
を		out of ~, from ~

Suffixes

～いき／～ゆき	～行き	bound for ~, 東京行き (きょうゆ/い) bound for Tokyo, 京都行き (きょう と ゆ/い) bound for Kyoto

～がわ	～側	side, こちらがわ this side, むかいがわ the other side, the opposite side, みぎがわ right-hand side, ひだりがわ left-hand side
～ぐち	～口	~ entrance/exit, 西口(にしぐち) west exit
～せん	～線	~ line (train line), 山手線(やまのてせん) the Yamanote Line, 中央線(ちゅうおうせん) the Chuo Line
～つめ	～つ目	ordinal numbers, 一(ひと)つ目(め) first
～ばんせん	～番線	track number (train), さんばんせん (三番線) Track 3
～メートル		meter (distance measurement), 10 メートル ten meters

Expressions

～という		called ~
～のをたのしみにしています	～のを楽しみにしています	to be looking forward to ~, お会い出来るのをたのしみにしています I am looking forward to seeing you.
みちなりに	道なりに	following the road

単語(たん)の練習

A. X という Y　*Y called X*

大江戸線(おおえどせん)という地下鉄(ちかてつ)	a subway called the Ooedo line
ローソンというコンビニ	a convenience store called Lawson
三越(みつこし)というデパート	a department store called Mitsukoshi
スタバ（スターバックス）というカフェ	a café called Starbucks

In the expression XというY, the noun Y indicates a general category such as person, place, school, and name, and the noun X indicates a specific instance of Y. In this usage, という is usually written in **hiragana** instead of **kanji**.

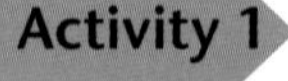

日本語で質問に答えて下さい。 

Example:　家の近(ちか)くにどんな店がありますか。
　　ファミリーマートというコンビニがあります。

1. 家の近(ちか)くにどんな店がありますか。
2. どのレストランによく行きますか。
3. よくどこでふくを買いますか。
4. どんなうたが好きですか。
5. どんなテレビ番組(ばんぐみ) (*TV program*) をよく見ますか。

B. 道(みち)しるべ landmarks

Using the words below, identify the numbered objects in the illustration.

道(みち)	street
道路(どうろ)	road
行き方	way of going
こうさてん	intersection
かど	corner
横断歩道(おうだんほどう)	crosswalk
しんごう	traffic signal
バスてい	bus stop。
バスターミナル	bus terminal
橋(はし)	bridge
映画館(えい)	movie theater
ガソリンスタンド	gas station
市役所(しやくしょ)	city hall
大使館(たいし)	embassy
駐車場(ちゅうしゃじょう)	parking lot
地図(ちず)	map

おぼえていますか。

〜かい　所　山　川　体育館(たいいく)　学生会館　アパート　駅(えき)　カフェ　喫茶店(きっさ)　銀行　公園(こうえん)　交番(こう)
このへん　コンビニ　スーパー　建物(たて)　デパート　ビル　病院　本屋(や)　郵便局　町(まち)　りょう
レストラン　動物園(どうえん)　空港(こう)　住所　場所(ば)　みずうみ　旅館　ホテル　博物館(はく)　美術館(びじゅつ)

Supplementary vocabulary　ほかの道(みち)しるべ　Other landmarks

こうみんかん	公民館	public hall, a community center
じゅうたくがい	住宅街	residential district
しょうてんがい	商店街	shopping district
ショッピングセンター		shopping mall
みなと	港	port
りょうじかん	領事館	council general

Activity 2

下の質問に日本語で答えて下さい。

1. 建物はどれですか。
2. 道(みち)という漢字がある言葉はどれですか。
3. 館という漢字がある言葉はどれですか。
4. 車(くるま)のためにあるものはどれですか。
5. 道(みち)にあるものはどれですか。

Activity 3

Supply the words that match the following descriptions.

1. 川の上にある物 ____________________
2. バスが来る所 ____________________
3. 二つの道(みち)がまじわる (*intersect*) 所 ____________________
4. 車(くるま)にガソリンを入れる所 ____________________
5. パスポートがなくなった時に行く所 ____________________
6. 道(みち)が分からない所で便利(り)な物 ____________________

C. 方向(ほうこう) Directions

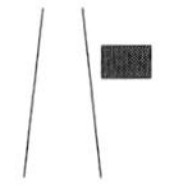

道(みち)の右側(みぎがわ)
right side of the street

道(みち)の左側(ひだりがわ)
left side of the street

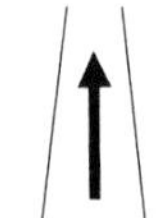

まっすぐ
straight

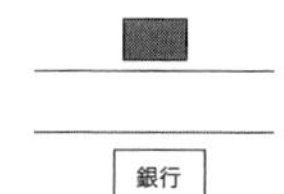

銀行のむかい(がわ)
across the street from the bank

道(みち)のこちらがわ
this side of the street

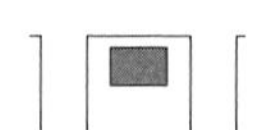

道(みち)と道(みち)の間
between the streets

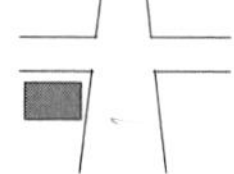

こうさてんの手前(てまえ)
in front of the intersection

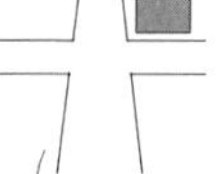

こうさてんの先(さき)
past the intersection

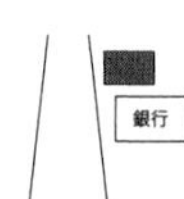

銀行のすぐ先(さき)
right after the bank

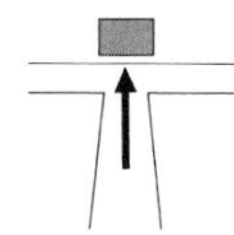

つきあたり
at the end of the street

道(みち)なりに行く
follow the road

おぼえていますか。

中　外　前　後ろ　上　下　よこ　となり　右　左　近く　東　西　南　北　方
北西　北東　南西　南東

Activity 4

Look at the following map. Two people, A and B, are at the gas station walking toward the park. Complete the following sentences, using words that indicate direction.

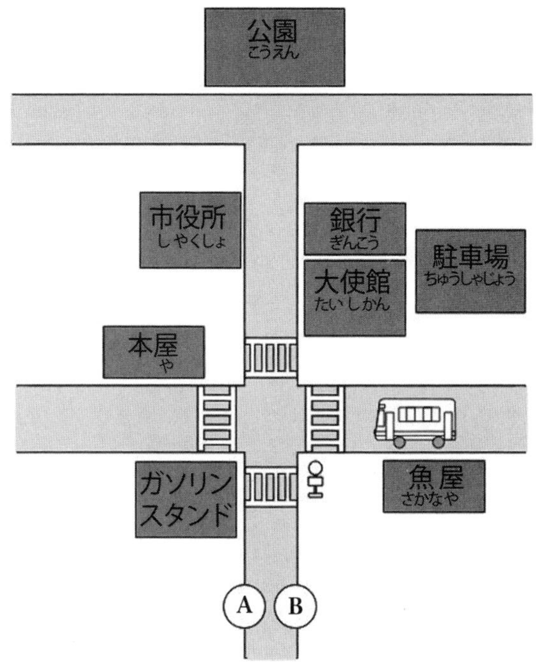

1. バスていはこうさてんの＿＿＿＿＿＿にあります。
2. 公園は＿＿＿＿＿＿行って、＿＿＿＿＿＿＿にあります。
3. 市役所は一つ目のかどと二つ目のかどの＿＿＿＿＿＿で、道路の左側にあります。銀行の＿＿＿＿＿＿です。
4. 大きい道の＿＿＿＿＿にはガソリンスタンドやバスていやさかな屋があります。
5. ガソリンスタンドの＿＿＿＿＿＿には本屋があります。
6. 大使館と銀行はこうさてんの＿＿＿＿＿＿にあります。
7. 大使館のすぐ＿＿＿＿＿＿に銀行があります。大使館のすぐ＿＿＿＿＿＿に駐車場があります。
8. 小さい道の＿＿＿＿＿に銀行があって、＿＿＿＿＿＿に市役所があります。

Activity 5

Work with a partner. Imagine that you are in front of the building where you are studying. Tell each other what buildings and facilities are around your building, using the location and direction expressions above as well as other expressions you know. Verify the information you receive.

D. 行き方を教える時につかう言葉 Expressions used in giving directions

〜をわたる	to cross ~
〜を通(とお)る	to go through/pass ~
〜がとまる	(for something) to stop ~
〜をとめる	to stop something ~
〜をおりる	to get off ~
〜を右(みぎ) / 左(ひだり)にまがる	to turn right/left at ~
〜で〜から〜に乗りかえる	to transfer from ~to ~ at ~
〜が見える	can see ~
〜に近(ちか)い	close to ~
〜から遠(とお)い	far from ~
〜メートル	~ meters
〜つ目(め)	the ~th (一つ目(め)のかど the first corner)

〜つ目(め) is not used for large numbers. The larger the number, the less likely it is to be used. Use 〜番目(め) (Chapter 10 of *Nakama 1*) for numbers larger than nine.

おぼえていますか。

行く　来る　帰る　歩く　出る　乗る　乗せる　(時間が) かかる

Activity 6 Say the following expressions.

何メートル	一メートル	二メートル	三メートル	四メートル	五メートル
	六メートル	七メートル	八メートル	九メートル	十メートル
いくつ目	一つ目	二つ目	三つ目	四つ目	五つ目
	六つ目	七つ目	八つ目	九つ目	

Activity 7 Match the phrases in the box with the pictures.

かどを右(みぎ)にまがる	しんごうでとまる	駅(えき)から遠(とお)い	バスをおりる
中央線(ちゅうおうせん)に乗りかえる	公園(こうえん)を通(とお)る	山が見える	駅(えき)に近(ちか)い
バスに乗る	橋(はし)をわたる	かいだんをおりる	公園(こうえん)に近(ちか)い
かどを左(ひだり)にまがる	道(みち)なりに歩く		

1

2

3

4

5 6 7 8

Activity 8 Draw the following directions on the street map below.

1. 一つ目(め)のかどを右(みぎ)にまがる
2. しんごうを右(みぎ)にまがって、左(ひだり)にある
3. 二つ目(め)のこうさてんを左(ひだり)にまがって、 まっすぐ行く
4. まっすぐ行って、二つ目(め)のかどの手前(てまえ)
5. 50 メートルぐらいまっすぐ行く
6. 一つ目(め)のかどを左(ひだり)にまがる
7. 公園(こうえん)を通(とお)って橋(はし)をわたる

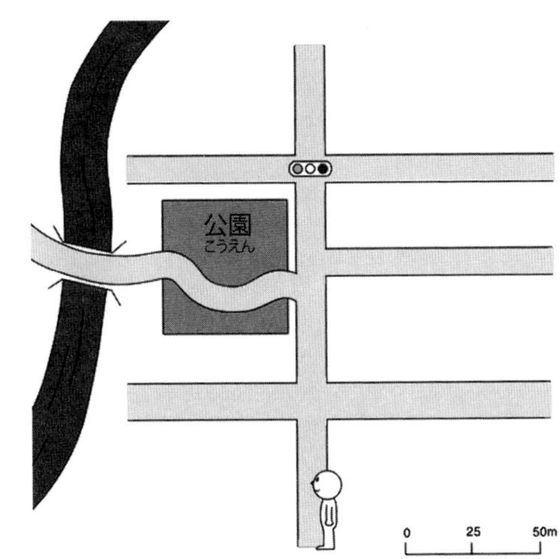

E. 駅(えき)と乗(の)り物(もの) Stations and transportation

出口(でぐち)	exit	各駅停車(かくえきていしゃ)	local train
入口(いりぐち)	entrance	普通(ふつう)(列車(れっしゃ))	local train
～口(ぐち) (北口(きたぐち)、西口(にしぐち)、南口(みなみぐち))	~ exit/entrance	急行(きゅうこう)(列車(れっしゃ))	express train
かいさつ(口(ぐち))	ticket gate	特急(とっきゅう)(列車(れっしゃ))	limited express train
地下鉄(ちかてつ)	subway	～線(せん)	~ line (山手線(やまのてせん) Yamanote line)
タクシー	taxi	～行(い/ゆ)き	bound for ~ (京都行(きょうとい/ゆ)き bound for Kyoto)
JR	Japan Railway	～番線(せん)	track number

Supplementary Vocabulary 駅で使う言葉 other expressions used in the station

かいすうけん	回数券	a coupon book for train/bus tickets
がくわり	学割	student discount (shortened form of がくせいわりびき（学生割引）)
きっぷうりば	切符売り場	ticket stand
していせき	指定席	reserved seat
じゆうせき	自由席	unreserved seat
しゅうゆうけん	周遊券	(travel) pass
ていきけん	定期券	train/bus commuter pass
わりびき（けん）	割引（券）	discount (ticket)

Activity 9 下の質問に答えて下さい。

1. 一番近くの町まで、バスでどのくらいかかりますか。タクシーではどうですか。
2. 町のバスはいくらぐらいかかりますか。
3. 一番近くの空港から家までタクシーでどのくらいかかりますか。
4. どの町に地下鉄がありますか。
5. 地下鉄に乗ったことがありますか。どこで乗りましたか。

Activity 10 下のえは上野駅から成田空港までの路線図 (train map) です。路線図を見て、日本語で質問に答えて下さい。

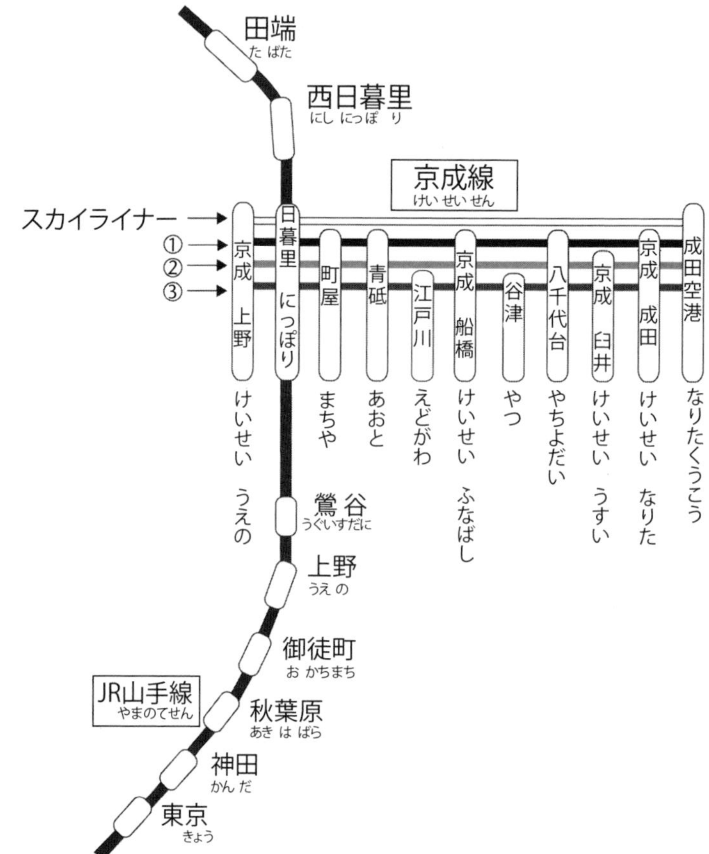

1. どれが各駅停車(かくえきていしゃ)ですか。
2. どれが急行(きゅうこう)ですか。とっきゅうですか。
3. 急行(きゅうこう)やとっきゅうがあるのは何線(せん)ですか。
4. 山手線(やまのてせん)には急行(きゅうこう)がありますか。
5. 京成上野駅(けいせいうえのえき)から成田空港(なりたくうこう) (Narita Airport) までどの電車(でんしゃ)が一番はやいですか。
6. その電車(でんしゃ)で京成上野駅(けいせいうえのえき)のつぎの駅(えき)は何ですか。

Activity 11 下の地図(ちず)は東京駅(きょうえき)のターミナルです。えを見て質問に答えて下さい。

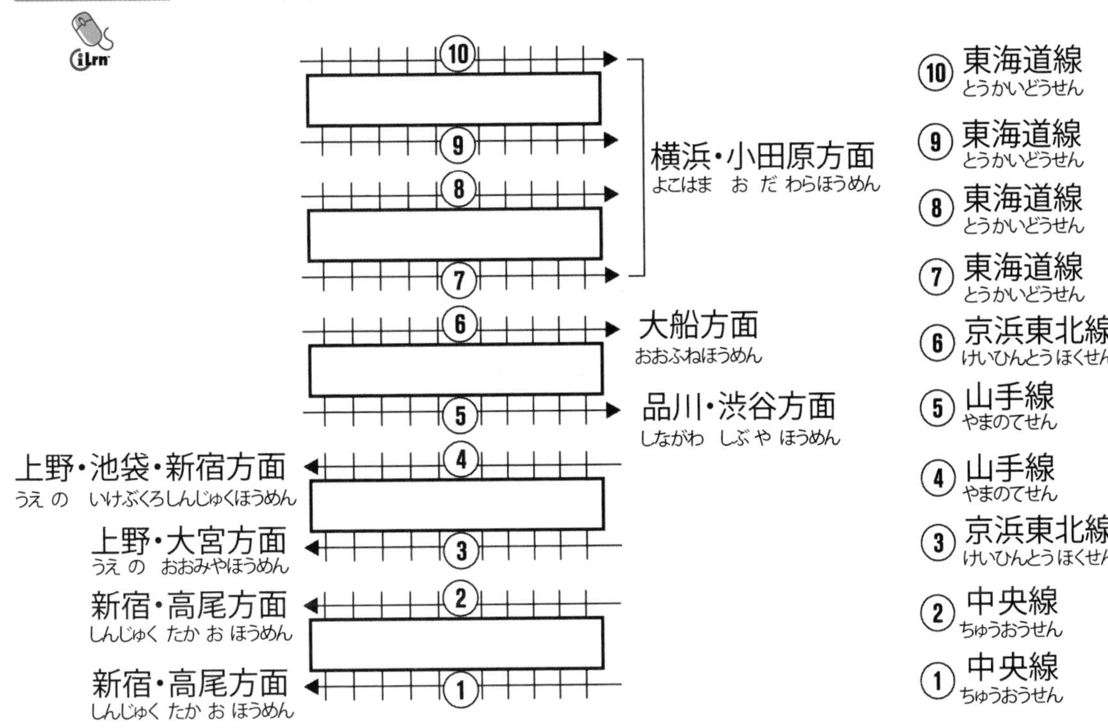

1. よこはまに行く時は何番線(せん)の電車(でんしゃ)に乗りますか。 はやいのは何番線(せん)ですか。
2. 新宿(しんじゅく)に行きたい人は何線(せん)に乗りますか。
3. いけぶくろに行く人は何番線(せん)の電車(でんしゃ)に乗りますか。何線(せん)ですか。
4. しぶやに行く人は何線(せん)に乗らなくてはいけませんか。何番線(せん)ですか。

ダイアローグ

はじめに

質問に日本語で答えて下さい。

1. 東京は電車の方が車より便利です。あなたの町ではどうですか。
2. 電車でどこかへ行く時、どんな言葉を使いますか。
3. あなたの国では道を教える時、どんな建物や物の名前をよく使いますか。
4. 道を聞く時は、どんな言葉がつかえると思いますか。

ヒルトンホテルへの行き方 *Directions to the Hilton Hotel*

The following **manga** frames are scrambled, so they are not in the order described in the dialogue. Read the dialogue and unscramble the frames by writing the correct number in the box located in the upper right corner of each frame.

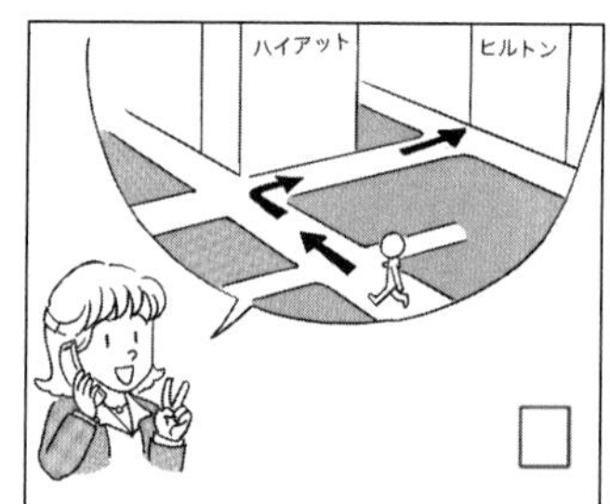

ブラウンさんはあさくさに住んでいます。明日ヒルトンホテルで道子さんと会う予定ですが、行き方が分からないので、電話で道子さんに行き方を聞いています。

ブラウン：ここからヒルトンホテルまで、どう行ったらいいの？

道子：新宿までは、行き方分かる？

ブラウン：ごめん。分からない。

道子：そう、じゃあ、まず、地下鉄の銀座線で、神田まで行くの。

ブラウン：銀座線で神田まで行って、それから？

道子：神田で中央線に乗りかえて、三つ目の駅が新宿だから、そこでおりるの。

ブラウン：OK。中央線で新宿まで行くのね。で、新宿で電車をおりてから、どこへ行くの？

道子：西口のかいさつを出て。出たら、すぐ目の前に地下道があるから、その道をまっすぐ行って。

ブラウン：西口を出て地下道をまっすぐ行くのね。

道子：うん、そう。十分か十五分ぐらい歩くと、高いビルがたくさん見えてくるはずよ。

ブラウン：ああ、あのビルがたくさんある所？

道子：そう。二つ目のかどにハイアットホテルがあるから、その手前を右にまがるの。

ブラウン：ハイアットは道の右側、左側？

道子：右側だよ。

ブラウン：分かった。じゃあ、で、ハイアットの手前を右ね。

道子：うん。で、右にまがってから、まっすぐ行くと、つきあたりにヒルトンが見えるはず。

ブラウン：分かった。で、時間はどれくらいかかるの？

道子：新宿の駅までは、十五分から二十分ぐらい、ホテルまでは歩いて二十分ぐらいだから、四十分ぐらいかかると思うけど。

ブラウン：ありがとう。じゃあ、明日一時にヒルトンのロビー (*lobby*) でね。

道子：じゃあ、明日ね。

つぎの日、ブラウンさんは神田駅にいます。

ブラウン：あのう、すみません。中央線の新宿行きは何番線ですか。

男の人：一番線ですよ。

ブラウン：あ、どうもありがとうございました。

ブラウンさんは新宿駅(しんじゅくえき)にいます。

ブラウン： あのう、西口(にしぐち)はどこですか。
女の人： ああ、西口(にしぐち)なら、あそこのかいだんをおりたところですよ。
ブラウン： どうも。

ブラウンさんはホテルに着きました。

道子(みち)： あ、ブラウンさん。ここ、ここ。道(みち)、分かった？
ブラウン： 道子(みち)さん。うん、すぐ分かった。
道子(みち)： ああ、よかった。

Dialogue Phrase Notes

- ごめん is a casual form of ごめんなさい, which means *I'm sorry.*
- 地下道(ちかどう) is an underground street or underground passageway.

ダイアローグの後で

A. Circle the stations where Ms. Brown gets on or off trains; then follow her route on the map.

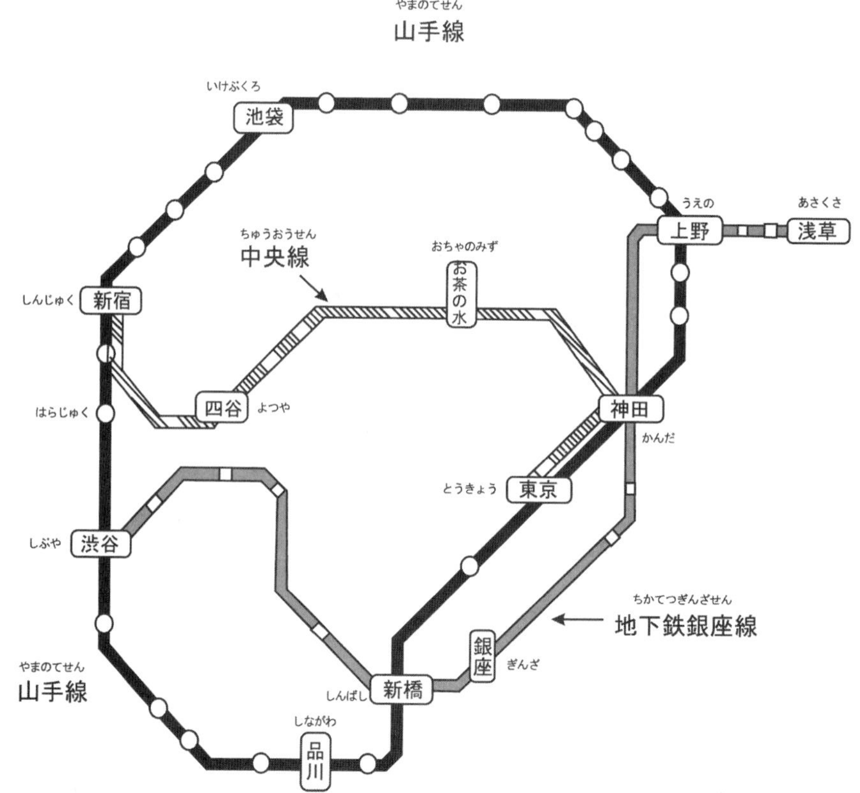

B. Follow Michiko's directions after Ms. Brown gets off the train at Shinjuku. The Hilton Hotel is building A, B, C, D, or E. Which is it?

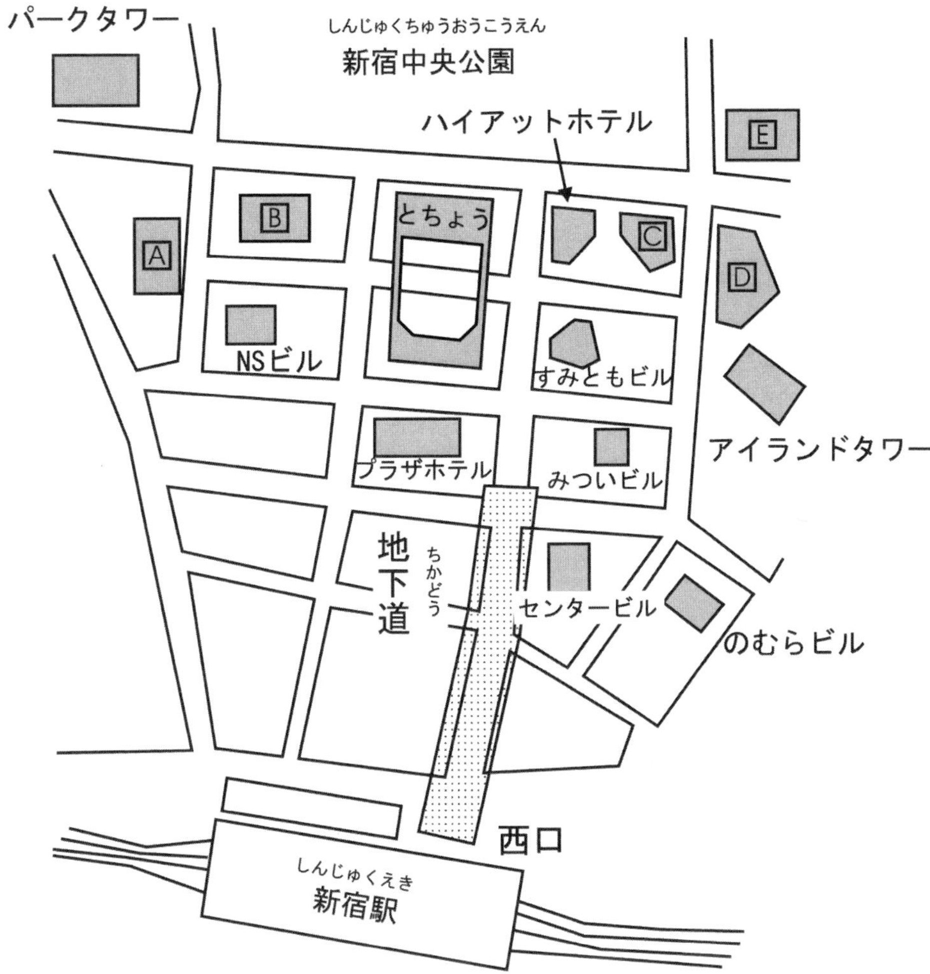

C. Identify the expressions in the dialogue where Ms. Brown confirms her understanding.

D. Suppose Ms. Brown is asking directions of her Japanese instructor. Rewrite the dialogue and make Michiko the **sensei**.

E. Explain how to go to パークタワー and the NS ビル from Shinjuku Station, using the map of Shinjuku in Exercise B.

日本の文化

日本の道と住所 Streets and addresses in Japanese cities

The Japanese address system is considerably different from that used in the United States. Because not all streets have names, it is not always possible to specify a location with a number and a street name. In Japan, addresses are expressed in terms of a sub-area within a larger area (as shown in the map below). For example,「神奈川県山田市本町 2—4—8」indicates house number 8 in neighborhood 4 of sub-area 2 in Hon-machi district, Yamada-city, Kanagawa prefecture. (Yamada-city is fictitious.)

神奈川県山田市

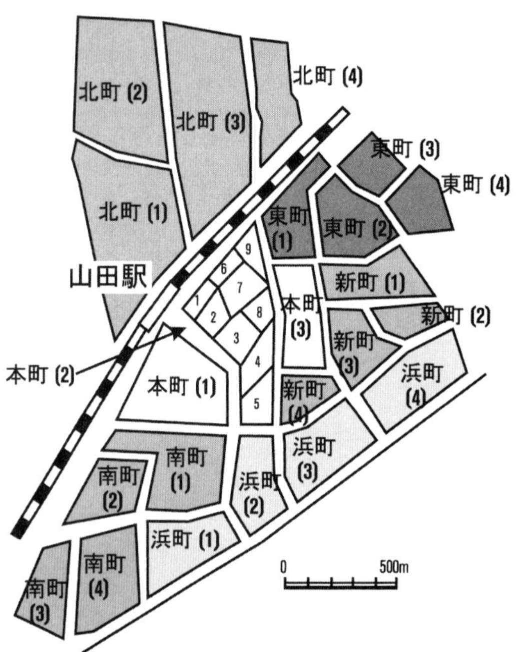

神奈川県山田市

Sub-areas are organized by number, but the order of these numbers is not consistent from one area to another. It would not be uncommon for residents of sub-area 1 to not know where sub-area 2 is. Also, house numbers are somewhat arbitrary. That is, house numbers 2 and 3 are likely to be adjacent, but house 2 could be either to the right or the left of house 3. Neighborhood maps are posted in each neighborhood to help non-residents find numbers. It can be difficult even for a Japanese person to find a given house address. For this reason, some mobile phones are equipped with a GPS or navigation system just like those in cars. When in doubt, ask a local resident or an officer at a nearby police box for assistance.

日本の鉄道 The Japanese train system

The Japanese train system, including subways, is well developed and very reliable. If a train is scheduled to arrive at 12:58, it nearly always comes at 12:58. There are many different transportation companies, all of them now private. The largest one is the JR Group, derived from Japan Railways and pronounced as ジェイアール. This is the former

Gavin Hellier/Getty Images

National Railway, now divided into six regional companies (JR東日本 , JR東海 , JR西日本 , JR九州 , JR四国 , JR北海道). Other private lines run in different directions and serve commuters in surrounding areas. The lines mentioned in this book are in Tokyo. 山手線, 中央線, and 新幹線 are JR lines; 京成線 is a private line; and 銀座線 and 丸の内線 are subway lines. The 山手線 loops around the Tokyo metro area and carries the largest number of passengers a day.

Trains in Japan do not use tokens. Instead, they use tickets and turnstiles. Passengers must retain their tickets throughout the ride because they need to reinsert them in the turnstile when exiting the station at their destination. Fares increase with distance. Because you must purchase the ticket for your specific destination, you need to figure out the fare by using a fare table or by asking others. The minimum fare is about 130 yen. Electronic train passes (IC cards) such as Suica (スイカ) and Pasmo (パスモ) are convenient alternatives to tickets in the Tokyo area. Other parts of Japan offer similar types of passes. These passes are smart cards that can be used as rechargeable debit cards for train or subway fares as well as electronic money for purchases at stores and kiosks in Japan. They can be purchased in stations at ticket vending machines. Some Japanese cell phones offer similar technology and can be converted into electronic train passes or debit cards.

JR offers a range of discount tickets for foreign travelers. One pass lets the holder ride unlimited in a certain area for a fixed number of days (e.g., one week) such as ジャパン・レール・パス or JR East Pass. If you are planning a trip to visit a series of different places, this type of ticket will save you money. There is also special IC card for foreign travelers. You can obtain detailed information from the JR Group's website (http://www.japanrail.com/)

JR also offers a 20% student discount (学生割引 or 学割) for one-way fares for distances of more than 100km. Travel agents (旅行会社) and びゅうプラザ (JR's own travel service, found in major stations) are a good source of information about the different types of discounts available.

文法(ぶんぽう)

I. Expressing a route using the particle を; expressing a point of departure using the particle を; expressing scope or limit using the particle で

So far you have learned that the particle を indicates the direct object. The particle で indicates a place of action or events as well as the means or instrument. This chapter introduces two other use of を and another use of the particle で.

A. Expressing a route, using the particle を

The particle を indicates a location when movement occurs. It takes a verb of motion such as 行く, 来る, 帰る, 歩く, 通る, 走る, or およぐ.

大使館(たいしかん)はこの道(みち)をまっすぐ行ったところにあります。
The embassy is straight ahead on this road.

第(だい)三コースをおよぎます。 *(I) swim in lane 3.*

毎日公園(こうえん)を走る。 *I run (jog) in the park every day.*

ゆみ: ここから学校までは遠(とお)いから、歩きたくない。
I don't want to walk because the school is far away from here.

まもる: そんなことないよ。あの駐車場(ちゅうしゃじょう)を通(とお)って行くと近(ちか)いよ。
It's not far. It's close if you go through that parking lot.

B. Expressing a point of departure using the particle を, (*out of ~, from ~*)

The particle を here indicates a place or vehicle from which one gets off or leaves. A noun preceding で indicates an enclosed space such as vehicles, buildings, elevators, etc.

バスをおりて、電車(でんしゃ)に乗りかえる。 *I got off the bus and transferred to a train.*

駅(えき)を出たら、すぐ右(みぎ)にまがります。 *When you leave the station, you immediately turn right.*

去年大学を卒業しました。 *I graduated from college last year.*

つぎの駅(えき)で地下鉄(ちかてつ)をおりる。 *I get off the subway at the next station.*

C. Expressing scope or limit using で

When the particle で is preceded by an expression for quantity, time, or amount, it indicates an extent or limit.

十分で帰ります。 *I will return in 10 minutes.*

あと一週間で休みです。 *Vacation starts in another week.*

そのみかんは五つで三百円です。 *Those oranges are 300 yen for five.*

このシャツはセールだったから、五百円で買ったよ。
This shirt was on sale, so I bought it for 500 yen.

話してみましょう

Activity 1

Complete the following sentences by supplying the particles を (*route*), を (*out of; from*), で (*location*), で (*limit*), に (*goal*), or から (*from*).

Example: 市役所(しやくしょ)の前 / とおる
市役所(しやくしょ)の前をとおる。

1. こうさてん / とまる
2. とっきゅう / 乗る
3. 東京駅(きょうえき) / 電車(でんしゃ) / おりる
4. 四つ目のかど / 左(ひだり) / まがる
5. 公園(こうえん) / 歩く
6. 橋(はし) / わたる
7. 三十分ぐらい / 着く
8. 横断歩道(おうだんほどう) / わたる
9. 東京駅(きょうえき) / 山手線(やまのてせん) / 中央線(ちゅうおうせん) / 乗りかえる
10. 川 / あそぶ
11. 急行(きゅうこう) / 各駅停車(かくえきていしゃ) / 乗りかえる
12. バスていの前 / とおる
13. 市役所(しやくしょ) / よる
14. かいだん / おりる

Activity 2

Work in groups of four. First, fill in the blanks with the appropriate particles. Then one person should choose an expression from the box and act it out. The other members try to guess which expression was chosen.

横断歩道(おうだんほどう)____わたる	橋(はし)____わたる	左(ひだり)____まがる	タクシー____乗る
しんごう____車(くるま)____とめる	大きい道路(どうろ)____まっすぐ行く		小さい道(みち)____歩く
先生の後ろ____とおる	かど____右(みぎ)____まがる		橋(はし)の手前(てまえ)____道(みち)____入る

Example: 横断歩道(おうだんほどう)

A: 横断歩道(おうだんほどう)をわたるんですか？
B: いいえ、ちがいます。
A: じゃ、橋(はし)をわたるんですか？
B: ええ、そうですよ。

Activity 3

Work with a partner. Choose a place in your town that your partner knows. Explain how to get there from the building you are in. Use the expressions in Activity 2 as well as other expressions when necessary, but do not use the name of the place you have in mind. Your partner may ask questions except for the name of the place. He or she should try to guess the place on the basis of your directions. Use polite speech.

Example: A: この建(たて)物を出て、横断歩道(おうだんほどう)をわたります。すぐ右(みぎ)にまがって、
10 メートルぐらい歩きます。その建(たて)物は右側(みぎがわ)にあります。
B: 大学の本屋(や)ですか。
A: はい、そうです。

II. Expressing conditions leading to set consequences using the plain form + と

The conditional と can be translated as *if*, *when*, or *whenever*, although the interpretation of a sentence with と depends on the tense of the main clause.

If the sentence ends in the present tense, と indicates a condition for which the event in the main clause is the natural or automatic consequence. Therefore, this usage tends to be for facts or statements of habit. *When* or *whenever* is the closest in meaning.

左(ひだり)にまがると、公園(こうえん)がすぐ先(さき)に見えます。	*If you turn to your left, you can see the park just ahead.*
冬になると、このへんはとても寒くなる。	*When the winter comes, it gets very cold around here.*
駅(えき)を出ると、目の前にかいだんがあります。	*When you leave the station, there are stairs in front of you.*

と is preceded by the plain present form of verbs, adjectives, and the copula verb.

	Noun	な -adjective	い -adjective	Verb
Dictionary form	山手線(やまのてせん) (*Yamanote line*)	しずか (*quiet*)	遠(とお)い (*far from*)	よる (*to drop by*)
Affirmative	山手線(やまのてせん)だと	しずかだと	遠(とお)いと	よると
Negative	山手線(やまのてせん)じゃないと	しずかじゃないと	遠(とお)くないと	よらないと

A sequence of two events connected by と expresses an inevitable or habitual cause-and-effect relationship. On the other hand, a sentence with たら conditional expresses a temporal, accidental cause-and-effect relationship. In this sense, と conditional conveys a general statement of a fact rather than any specific event. For example, in the case of 冬になると、スキーに行きます (*I go skiing when the winter comes*), the speaker always goes skiing in winter. In contrast, 冬になったら、スキーに行きます means the speaker plans to go skiing this winter. The other difference between と and たら is that the main clause in sentences containing the と conditional cannot express intention, desire, or a request, invitation, or command made by the speaker.

橋(はし)をわたると、左側(ひだりがわ)に学校が見えます。	*You will see the school on your left immediately after you cross the bridge.*
橋(はし)をわたったら、左側(ひだりがわ)に学校が見えます。	*Upon crossing the bridge, the school can be seen on your left.*

地下鉄(ちかてつ)をおりたら、電話して下さい。	*Please call me when you get off the subway.*
~~地下鉄(ちかてつ)をおりると、電話して下さい。~~	*Please call me as a result of getting off the subway.*
山田さんが来たら、行きましょう	*Let's go as soon as Yamada-san comes.*
~~山田さんが来ると、行きましょう。~~	*Let's go as a result of Yamada-san's arrival.*

When the main clause is in the past tense, と expresses an unexpected or surprising event resulting from the condition described. In these cases, と and たら are interchangeable.

家に帰ると、母が来ていた。	*When I went home, my mother was there.*
家に帰ったら、母が来ていた。	*When I went home, my mother was there.*

話してみましょう

Activity 1 Match the statements in columns A and B and connect them using と , たら , or both.

Example: 1 と f

梅雨(つゆ)になると、三日に二日雨がふります。

Column A	Column B
1. 梅雨(つゆ)になります。	**a.** シャワーをあびて下さい。
2. 好きな人が出来ます。	**b.** おそくなってしまいました。
3. うんどうをします。	**c.** とっきゅうで行きませんか。
4. 友達の家によりました。	**d.** 勉強が出来なくなります。
5. 時間がかかりそうです。	**e.** しんごうが見えます。
6. 道(みち)なりに歩いて行きます。	**f.** 三日に二日雨がふります。
7. 各駅停車(かくえきていしゃ)に乗ります。	**g.** つきあたりに映(えい)画館があります。

Activity 2 Look at the map below and describe what will be visible right after you perform the following activities.

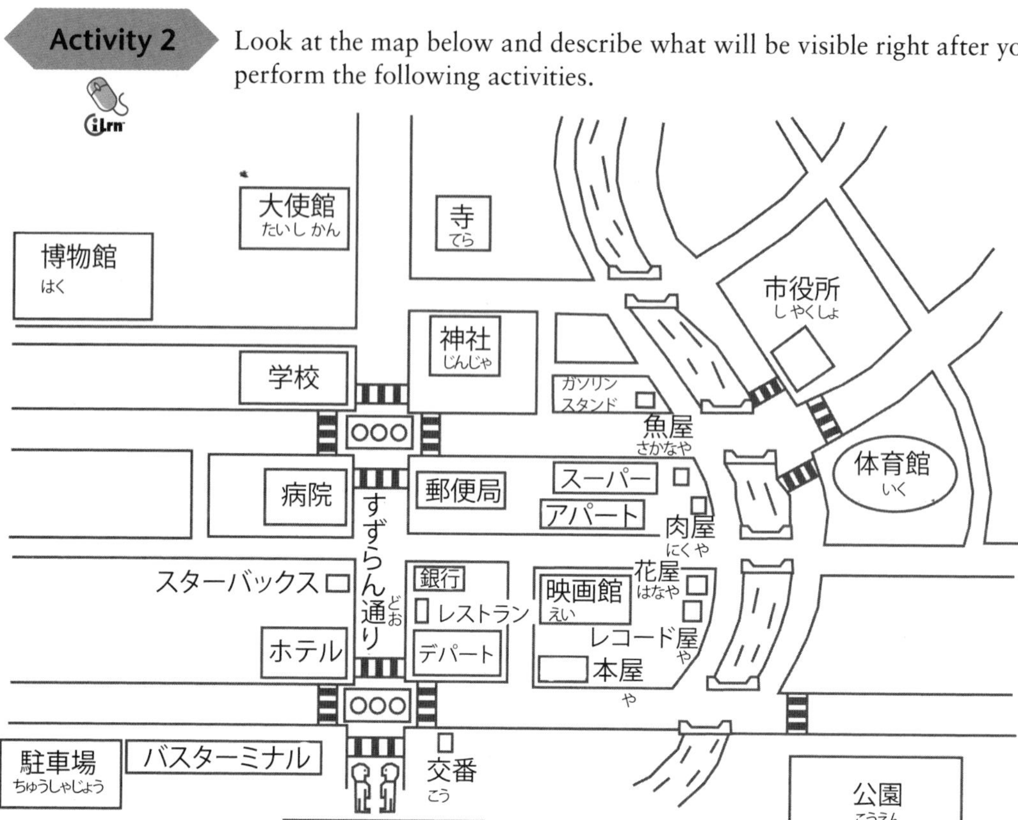

Example: 駅(えき)を出る
駅(えき)を出ると前にしんごうと横断歩道(おうだんほどう)が見えます。

1. 駅(えき)を出て、右(みぎ)にまがります。
2. 駅(えき)を出て、横断歩道(おうだんほどう)をわたります。
3. 駅(えき)を出て、左(ひだり)にまがって、まっすぐ行きます。
4. 駅(えき)を出て、すずらん通(どお)りを三つ目のかどまでまっすぐ行きます。
5. 映画館(えいが)の前の道(みち)を右(みぎ)にまっすぐ行きます。
6. 公園(こうえん)の前の横断歩道(おうだんほどう)をわたって、まっすぐ行きます。
7. デパートと本屋(ほんや)の間の道(みち)を通(とお)って、つきあたりまで行きます。

Activity 3 Work with a partner. Look at the map in Activity 2. You are at the station. Ask your partner where the following landmarks are. Your partner will answer using ~ と . Take turns.

Example: 交番(こう)
A: 交番(こう)はどこですか。
B: 駅(えき)を出ると、右側(みぎがわ)にありますよ。

1. 駐車場(ちゅうしゃじょう) 2. 公園(こうえん) 3. ホテル 4. 神社(じんじゃ) 5. 博物館(はく)

Activity 4

Work with a partner. You are at the intersection at the bottom of the map below. You would like to know where the following are: bus stop, subway station, public phone, gas station, and parking lot. Ask your partner, who is a passerby, the locations of these objects and places. Your partner will have randomly assigned the numbers 1 through 5 to the places and will describe how to get to the location you ask about using ～と . Then tell your partner the number he/she assigned to the location.

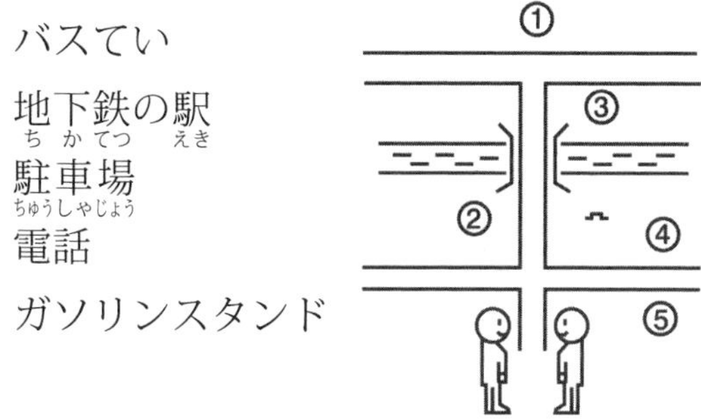

Example: B has chosen location 1 for the public phone.

A: このへんに電話がありますか。

B: ええ、まっすぐ行くと、橋(はし)がありますから、橋(はし)をわたって下さい。わたると、目の前にあります。

A: じゃあ、この地図(ちず)だと、一番ですか。

B: ええ、そうです。

III. Expressing chronology using the て -form of the verb + から

The て-form of the verb + から means *after doing ~*. Because から originates in the particle から (from), the event in the てから clause tends to signal the beginning point at which the action in the main clause starts.

地図(ちず)で道(みち)をしらべてから、行ったらどう？	*How about if we checked the street on a map and then went?*
見てから、買うかどうかきめるつもりだ。	*I plan to decide whether to buy it after seeing it.*
一月になってから、寒い日がつづいている。	*It's been continuously cold since the beginning of January.*
家に帰ってから、どうしたんですか。	*What did you do after you got home?*

～てから is similar to ～後で, so they can be used interchangeably in some cases, but not all the time. Here are some major differences between the two. First, as mentioned before, ～てから indicates when the action in the main clause begins. On the other hand, ～後で merely indicates the sequence of two events. For example, 八月から日本語を勉強する means the speaker will start studying Japanese in August. Similarly, 日本に行ってから日本語を勉強する indicates the speaker will start studying Japanese once he/she arrives in Japan. 日本に行った後で日本語を勉強する merely indicates that the act of going to Japan precedes the act of studying Japanese. For this reason, if someone asks when you would start studying Japanese, it would be appropriate to use ～てから, but answering with ～後で is somewhat awkward.

八月から日本語を勉強する。 *I will start studying Japanese in August.*

日本に行ってから日本語を勉強する。 *I will start studying Japanese after going to Japan.*

日本に行った後で日本語を勉強する。 *I will study Japanese after I go to Japan.*

This also means that ～てから tends to imply that two events must be sequenced in that order, while 後で does not imply any inevitability about the order of two events. Therefore, it is more natural to use ～てから when the order is an important factor. For example, one must take off one's shoes before entering the house in Japan. To describe this situation, ～てから is more appropriate than 後で.

くつをぬいでから、入って下さい。 *Please enter after taking off your shoes.*

~~くつをぬいだ後で、入って下さい。~~ *Please enter (sometime) after you take off your shoes.*

On the other hand, if the order is not important, and you merely want to indicate that two events take place in a sequence, use ～後で. For example, if you ran into Mr. Tanaka after you went to the movie, it would be more natural to use ～後で. Using ～てから in this case imply that the meeting with Mr. Tanaka after watching a movie was a planned event.

映(えい)画を見た後で、田中くんに会った。 *I saw Mr. Tanaka after seeing a movie.*

映(えい)画を見てから、田中くんに会った。 *I saw Mr. Tanaka after seeing a movie* (and it was planned beforehand.)

The final difference is that ～てから can be used when the event in the main clause continues after the event in the ～てから clause has taken place. ～後で cannot be used in this case because it does not indicate continuity.

祖(そ)父がしんでから、三年になる。 *It has been three years since my grandfather died.*

~~祖(そ)父がしんだ後で、三年になる。~~ *It has been three years since my grandfather died.*

大学に入ってから、ずっと一人で住んでいる。 *I have lived alone since entering college.*

~~大学に入った後で、ずっと一人で住んでいる。~~ *I have lived alone since entering college.*

Note

- Like other subordinate clauses, the subject of clauses with てから must be marked by the particle が if it is different from the subject of the main clause.

  しんごうが青(あお)になってから、道路(どうろ)をわたった方がいいですよ。
  It's best to cross the road after the signal turns green.

  そのこうさてんで一度とまってから、左(ひだり)にまがって下さい。
  Stop at the intersection, and then turn left.

話してみましょう

Activity 1 Complete the following sentences using 〜てから , 後で , or both.

Example: ガソリンスタンドによる。家に帰ろう。
ガソリンスタンドによってから、家に帰ろう。

1. 家に帰りました。母から電話がありました。
2. 大使館(たいしかん)に着きました。もう三時間です。
3. 結婚します。家を買います。
4. 切符(ぷ)を買います。地下鉄(ちかてつ)に乗ります。
5. しんごうが青(あお)になります。横断歩道(おうだんほどう)をわたって下さい。
6. 山手線(やまのてせん)で東京(きょう)に行きます。成田行(なりたい/ゆ)きの急行(きゅうこう)に乗りかえます。
7. お土産(みやげ)を買います。空港(こう)に行った方がいいですよ。

Activity 2 Look at the map below and describe what you have to do to go from place to place as specified below using てから .

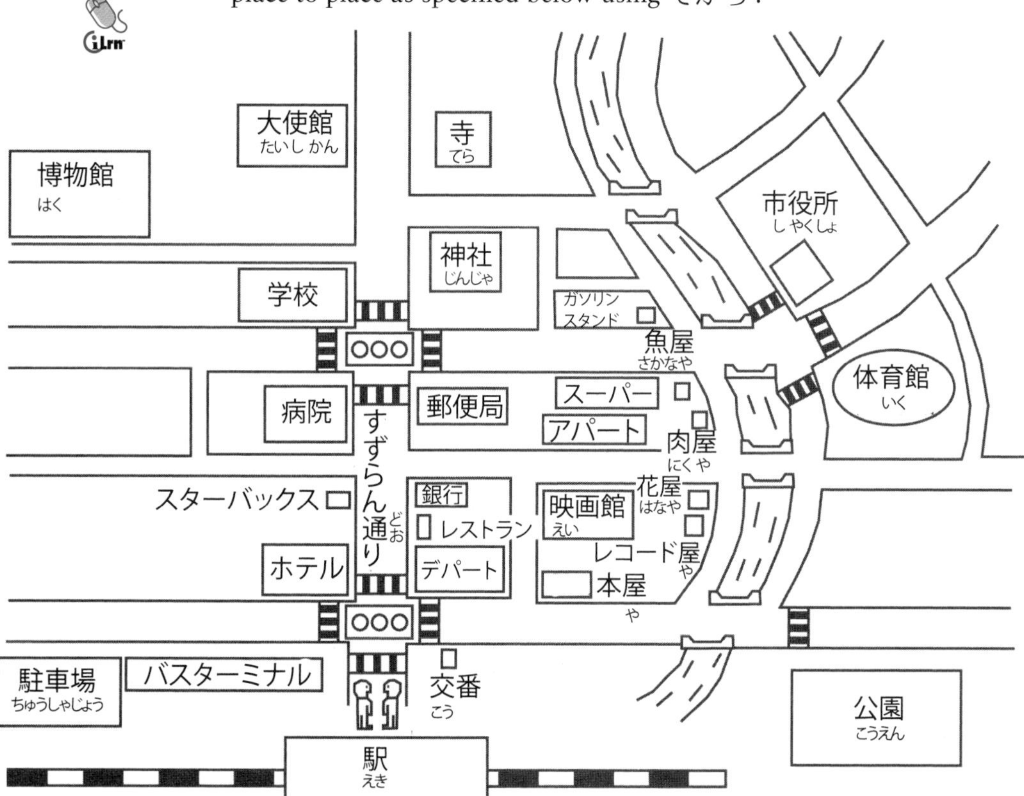

Example: 公園(こうえん)から体育館(いく)まで行く
公園(こうえん)を出て、横断歩道(おうだんほどう)をわたってから、道(みち)なりに行くと、右側(みぎがわ)にあります。

1. 駅(えき)からデパートに行く
2. スターバックスから郵便局に行く
3. 本屋(や)から公園(こうえん)に行く
4. デパートから郵便局に行く
5. 肉屋(にくや)から市役所(しやくしょ)に行く

Activity 3

Work as a class. Think of one habit you have before going to bed, and make a sentence using ～てから、寝ます。Interview your classmates about their habits and record in the chart what your classmates do.

Example: A: ～さんは、寝る前に何をしますか。
B: 私は～てから、寝ます。
A: そうですか。

名前	～てから、寝ます。

IV. Expressing presuppositions using the plain form + はず

はず indicates the speaker's judgment about the likelihood of an action or event happening, and can be translated as *I expect that ~*, *it is expected that ~*, *ought to ~*, or *~is supposed to.* The judgment is based on some objective information or knowledge. That is, the speaker thinks that the event or action ought to take place, if his or her interpretation of the information or knowledge is correct. In this sense, はず is very different from だろう, which expresses a subjective speculation.

この電車(でんしゃ)は新宿駅(しんじゅくえき)にとまるはずだ。	*This train is supposed to stop at Shinjuku Station.*
昨日は休みじゃなかったはずです。	(According to my expectations/as far as I know) *Yesterday was not a holiday. The day off was not supposed to have been yesterday.* (This makes it sound like it was a holiday even though it wasn't supposed to be.)
あの人はまだ学生のはずです。	*That person should (as far as I know) still be a student.*

はず is grammatically a noun but it never stands on its own. The preceding verb and adjective forms must be identical to those in other instances where verbs and adjectives are used to modify nouns.

	Copula verbs	な -adjective	い -adjective	Verb
Dictionary form	こちらがわ + だ (*to be this side*)	だめ (*no good*)	近(ちか)い (*close*)	こむ (*to become crowded*)
Present affirmative	こちらがわのはず	だめなはず	近(ちか)いはず	こむはず
Present negative	こちらがわじゃないはず	だめじゃないはず	近(ちか)くないはず	こまないはず
Past affirmative	こちらがわだったはず	だめだったはず	近(ちか)かったはず	こんだはず
Past negative	こちらがわじゃなかったはず	だめじゃなかったはず	近(ちか)くなかったはず	こまなかったはず

The subject of a sentence containing はず cannot be the speaker. Although it is possible to say *I'm supposed to do ~* in English, はず cannot be used in this sense. Use ～なければならない/なくてはいけない instead.

私は明日東京(きょう)に行かなければなりません。 *I must/am supposed to go to Tokyo tomorrow.*

~~私は明日東京(きょう)に行くはずです。~~ *I am supposed to go to Tokyo tomorrow.*

田中さんは明日東京(きょう)に行かなければなりません。 *Mr. Tanaka must go to Tokyo tomorrow.*

田中さんは明日東京(きょう)に行くはずです。 *Mr. Tanaka is supposed to go to Tokyo tomorrow.*

キム： 大使館(たいしかん)はこのへんでしょうか。 *Is the embassy around here?*
半田(はんだ)： ええ、この先(さき)にあるはずですよ。 *Yes, it should be just ahead.*
キム： そうですか。どうもありがとう。 *I see. Thanks a lot.*

川上(かわかみ)： つぎのとっきゅうはいつ出ますか。 *What time will the next limited express leave?*
イー： 五時二十五分に出るはずですが。 *It is supposed to leave at 5:25.*
川上(かわかみ)： じゃあ、まだ乗れます。 *Then we can still catch it.*

話してみましょう

Activity 1 Look at the following train and subway map. Answer the questions using はず.

Example: 山手線(やまのてせん)で上野(うえの)に行けますか？
ええ、行けるはずです。

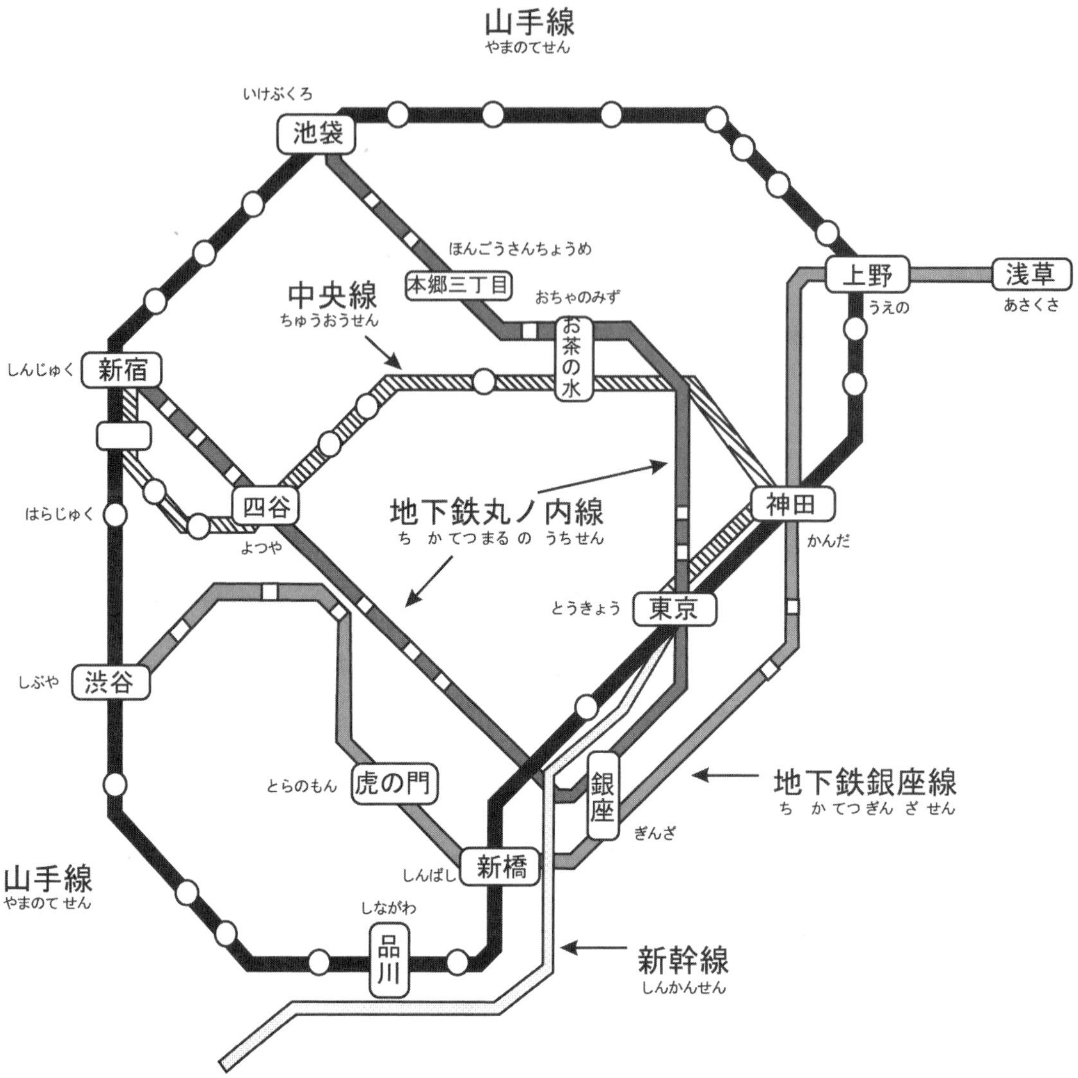

1. 山手線（やまのてせん）であさくさに行けますか。
2. 中央線（ちゅうおうせん）で神田（かんだ）のつぎの駅（えき）は何ですか。
3. まるのうち線（せん）は銀座（ぎんざ）をとおりますか。
4. 新宿（しんじゅく）でまるのうち線（せん）に乗れますか。
5. 新宿（しんじゅく）で銀座線（ぎんざせん）に乗れますか。
6. 上野（うえの）で山手線（やまのてせん）から地下鉄（ちかてつ）に乗りかえられますか。
7. 上野（うえの）で山手線（やまのてせん）から中央線（ちゅうおうせん）に乗りかえられますか。

Activity 2 Make sentences based on the following information that express an inference or judgment using はず.

Example: 天気予報（ほう）を見たら明日は晴れだと書いてありました。
明日は晴れのはずです。

1. 山田さんは昨日病気で入院しました。
2. スミスさんは日本に十年住んでいました。
3. キムさんは毎日午後九時に寝ます。
4. 京都(きょうと)は日本で一番古い町(まち)の一つです。
5. 東京(きょう)には有(ゆう)名な人がたくさん住んでいます。
6. ハワイは一年中気候(こう)がよくて、きれいです。

Activity 3

Work as a class. Ask your classmates what time they leave school and how long it takes to get from school to home. Then confirm the approximate time of arrival and complete the chart.

Example: A: 今日は何時ごろ家に帰るの？
B: 五時ごろ帰るつもり。
A: 家までどのくらいかかるの？
B: 歩いて、十五分か二十分ぐらいかな。
A: じゃあ、五時二十分ごろには家に着くはずだね。

クラスメートの名前	学校を出る時間	かかる時間	家に着く時間

V. Expressing conditions originated by others using ～(の)なら

なら is used when the speaker uses something from a previous context as a condition, and is translated as *if it is the case that ~*. Inserting the optional の or ん is before なら, emphasizes the sense of condition and is translated as *if it is indeed the case that.*

キム： このへんに駐車場(ちゅうしゃじょう)はなさそうですね。
It does not look like there is any parking lot around here.

白川(しらかわ)： 駐車場(ちゅうしゃじょう)がない（の）なら、あそこに車(くるま)をとめたらどうですか。
If there is no parking lot, how about parking over there?

イー： 朝は道(みち)がこんでいるから、時間がかかりそうです。
It will probably take time because the traffic is heavy in the morning.

木村(むら)： 道(みち)がこんでいる（の）なら、地下鉄(ちかてつ)で行きましょう。
If the roads are crowded, we can take the subway.

町田(まちだ)： 急行(きゅうこう)は、この駅(えき)にとまりませんね。
Express trains do not stop at this station.

川口： 急行(きゅうこう)に乗る（の）なら、次の駅(えき)で乗りかえた方いいでしょう。
If we are to take an express train, we should transfer at the next station.

ミラー： このへんにアメリカ大使館(たいしかん)がありますか？
Is the U.S. Embassy around here?

通行人(つうこうにん)： アメリカ大使館(たいしかん)なら、この道(みち)をまっすぐ行くと、右側(みぎがわ)にありますよ。
Passerby: *If it's the U.S. Embassy you want, go straight and you will see it on the right.*

Like ～でしょう, なら must be preceded by a clause ending with an adjective or verb in the plain form. The copula だ (for nouns and な-adjectives) is omitted from clauses followed by なら. Hence, one says 寒い（の）なら (include い), but 電車（なの）なら (omit だ).

Copula verb

出口(でぐち)だ (*exit*)	出口(でぐち)（なの／ん）なら	*if it is the case that it is an exit*
	出口(でぐち)じゃない（の）なら	*if it is the case that it is not an exit*
	出口(でぐち)だった（の）なら	*if it is the case that it was an exit*
	出口(でぐち)じゃなかった（の）なら	*if it is the case that it was not an exit*

な-adjectives

便利(べんり)だ (*convenient*)	便利(べんり)（なの／ん）なら	*if it is the case that it is convenient*
	便利(べんり)じゃない（の）なら	*if it is the case that it is not convenient*
	便利(べんり)だった（の）なら	*if it is the case that it was convenient*
	便利(べんり)じゃなかった（の）なら	*if it is the case that it was not convenient*

い-adjectives

はやい (*fast*)	はやい（の）なら	*if it is the case that it is fast*
	はやくない（の）なら	*if it is the case that it is not fast*
	はやかった（の）なら	*if it is the case that it was fast*
	はやくなかった（の）なら	*if it is the case that it was not fast*

Verbs

とめる (*to stop*)	とめる（の）なら	*if it is the case that you stop*
	とめない（の）なら	*if it is the case that you do not stop*
	とめた（の）なら	*if it is the case that you stopped*
	とめなかった（の）なら	*if it is the case that you did not stop*

なら is different from たら in the following ways:

(1) なら uses something from the previous context as a condition. In this sense, the condition usually originates from a source other than the speaker. On the other

hand, たら can be used without previous context and the condition originates with the speaker. For example, when someone says 今週の土曜日、いそがしくなかったら、家に来ませんか (*If you are not busy this Saturday, would you like to come to my house?*), the speaker does not have any information as to whether you are busy this Saturday. So the speaker can just create the condition that you aren't busy on his/her own and use it as a condition for invitation. On the other hand, the speaker must have some reason to assume that you are not busy this Saturday in order to say 今週の土曜日、いそがしくないなら、家に来ませんか (*If you are not busy this Saturday, would you like to come to my house?*). Such reason is provided by a prior context usually provided by someone other than the speaker.

(2) The condition in the たら clause must be satisfied or completed before the event in the main clause takes place. For example, おさけを飲んだら、うんてんしない (*I don't drive if I've drunk alcohol*) indicates the act of drinking must occur first in order for the speaker to decide not to drive. On the other hand, in the sentence, おさけを飲むなら、うんてんしてはいけない (*If you are going to drink alcohol, you should not drive*), the speaker does not have to drink alcohol before deciding not to drive—just the intention of drinking is enough for him/her to avoid driving. In this sense, the condition expressed in the なら clause does not have to take place before the event in the main clause takes place.

話してみましょう

Activity 1

A new student asks you the locations of various facilities on campus. The student and you are in the bottom of the picture (at the spot marked ここ). Respond to the following questions using なら.

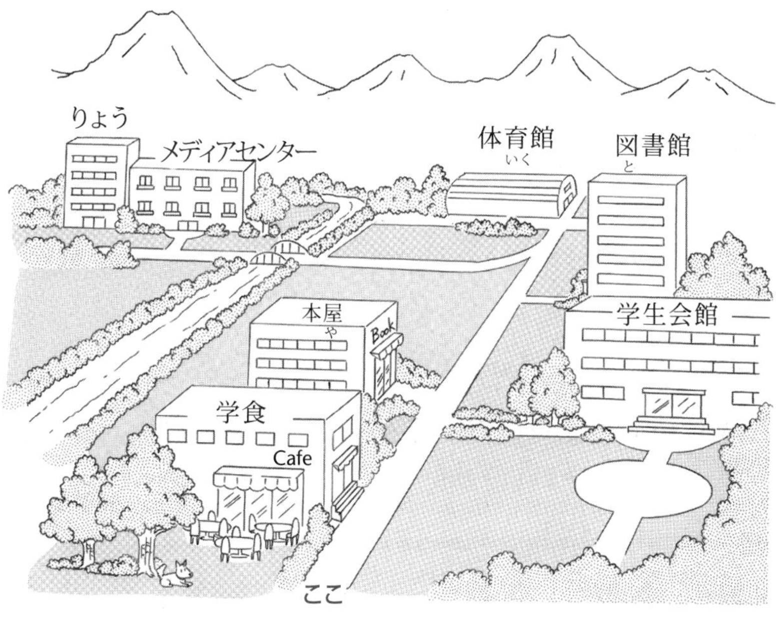

Example: 体育館(いく)はどこにありますか。
体育館(いく)なら、この道(みち)をまっすぐ行って、つきあたった所にあります。

1. 体育館(たいいくかん)
2. 学食
3. 学生会館
4. 図書館(と)
5. メディアセンター
6. りょう

Activity 2 Work with a partner. One person asks a question using the phrases given. The other person makes recommendations using ～なら .

Example: けいたい電話がほしいです。どれがいいか分かりません。

A: けいたい電話がほしいんだけど、どれがいいか分からないんだ。

B: けいたいなら、日本のがいいよ。

1. はじめての (*first*) デートです。どこに行ったらいいか分かりません。
2. お金がありません。どうしたらいいか分かりません。
3. 道(みち)が分からなくなりました。どうしたらいいか分かりません。
4. 大使館(たいしかん)に行きたいです。行き方が分かりません。
5. いそいでいます。バスに乗れるかどうか分かりません。
6. 車(くるま)をとめなければなりません。どこにとめたらいいか分かりません。

Activity 3 Work as a class. Write one thing you would like to ask for advice on. Then ask four or five classmates for suggestions and write them down. Report the best advice.

Example: A: あのう、ちょっと今いい?

B: うん、何?

A: 日本語が使える仕事をしたいんだけど、どうしたらいいかな。

B: 日本語が使える仕事をするなら、図(と)書館でアルバイトしたらどう?

聞く練習

上手な聞き方

Announcements at stations and on trains

What you know about the setting gives you a lot of clues about the type of speech you hear. For example, announcements in a train station would be different from those within a train because the purpose of each announcement is different. Being aware of purpose in these settings allows you to determine key words to listen for.

練習

A. 日本語で質問に答えて下さい。

1. 駅(えき)でどんなアナウンスを聞いたことがありますか。
2. どんなアナウンスがあったらいいと思いますか。
3. 電車(でんしゃ)の中でどんなアナウンスを聞いたことがありますか。

B. In the following chart, write down the possible reasons for an announcement on the platform and on the train, and then write possible key words.

	目的（*Purpose*）	キーワード
プラットフォーム (*platform*) ／駅	Example: delay	おくれる　～時～分
電車の中		

駅と電車のアナウンス　Announcements at stations and on trains

聞く前に

Look at the photos below, of the platform area of a train station. Tell what kind of signs you see in the picture. Also, guess why there are yellow lines on the platform.

Kenneth Hamm / Photo Japan

Kenneth Hamm / Photo Japan

聞いてみましょう

A. 日本の駅や電車の中でも色々なアナウンスがあります。次のアナウンスを聞いて、何のためのアナウンスか考えて下さい。

Example: You hear: 二番線に電車がまいります。あぶないですから、きいろい線の後ろに下がってお待ち下さい。

You say: 二番線に電車が来ます。

B. もう一度アナウンスを聞いて、下の質問に答えて下さい。

1. どんな電車(でんしゃ)が来ますか。
2. この電車(でんしゃ)はこの駅(えき)にとまりますか。
3. この電車(でんしゃ)はどこ行(い/ゆ)きですか。
4. この電車(でんしゃ)がとまる駅(えき)はどれですか。

   Circle all that apply: 四谷(よつや)　しなのまち　千駄ヶ谷(せんだがや)　代々木(よよぎ)　新宿(しんじゅく)

   この電車(でんしゃ)がとまらない駅(えき)でおりたい人はどうしますか。

聞いた後で

Mr. Chan has not understood the announcements in 聞いてみましょう, so he asks for you help. Complete the following dialogues with Mr. Chan.

Example:
チャン： あのう今のアナウンスよく分からなかったんですが。
あなた： ああ、二番線(せん)に電車(でんしゃ)が来るそうですよ。
チャン： ああ、そうですか。どうもありがとうございます。

1. チャン： あのう、今のアナウンス、何て言ったんですか。
   あなた： ______________________________
   チャン： あ、そうですか。どうも

2. チャン： あのう、どこに行く電車(でんしゃ)ですか。
   あなた： ______________________________
   チャン： 電車(でんしゃ)は東京駅(きょうえき)にとまりますか。
   あなた： ______________________________

3. チャン： あのう、今のアナウンス、よく分からなかったんですが、
   ひかり十三号はいつ出るんでしょうか。
   あなた： ______________________________
   チャン： そうですか。どうも。

4. チャン： あのう、今のアナウンスよく分からなかったんですけど、代々木(よよぎ)は
   この電車(でんしゃ)で行けますか。
   あなた： ______________________________
   チャン： そうですか。じゃあ、つぎの駅(えき)でおりなきゃならないんですね。
   どうもありがとうございます。

聞き上手　話し上手

道(みち)の聞き方と教え方　Asking for and giving directions

Japanese people do not use street names or terms like north and south when they give directions. Except for a few cities such as Kyoto, streets in Japanese cities run in various directions, so it is often difficult to orient oneself in terms of north, south, east, or west. Also, most streets do not have names. Japanese people thus use relative locational terms such as right and left, number of blocks, public facilities, large buildings, and other noticeable landmarks. Many people use trains and subways where available. It is very common to give directions that start from a train station. When it is necessary to transfer to different lines or a different means of transportation, it is also necessary to explain where the transportation being transferred to is going, where to get off, or where to transfer, as shown in the following example:

東京駅(とうきょうえき)で三鷹(みたか)行きの中央線(ちゅうおうせん)に乗って、四つ目(め)の駅(えき)が新宿(しんじゅく)ですから、そこでおりて下さい。新宿(しんじゅく)で中野(なかの)行(い/ゆ)きのバスに乗りかえて、一つ目(め)のバスていでおりて下さい。

Take the Chuo Line bound for Mitaka at Tokyo Station and get off at Shinjuku Station, which is the fourth station from Tokyo Station. Then, at Shinjuku, transfer to the bus bound for Nakano, and get off at the first stop.

Common expressions used in asking for directions:

あのう、すみません。アメリカ大使館(たいしかん)に行きたいんですけど。

Excuse me, but I want to go to the U.S. Embassy.

あのう、すみません。このへんにガソリンスタンドはありますか。

Excuse me, but is there a gas station around here?

あのう、すみません。郵便局はどこですか。

Excuse me, but where is the post office?

あのう、すみません。新宿(しんじゅく)まで行きたいんですが、どう行ったらいいでしょうか。

Excuse me. I want to go to Shinjuku. How can I get there?

Use the following expressions to ask how long it takes to get to a specified place:

東京駅(きょうえき)から新宿(しんじゅく)まで、バスで何分ぐらい / どのぐらいかかりますか。

How many minutes/how long does it take from Tokyo Station to Shinjuku by bus?

歩いてどのぐらいかかりますか。

How long does it take on foot?

大阪(おおさか)から東京(きょう)まで新幹線(しんかんせん)で何時間ぐらい / どのぐらいかかりますか。

How many hours/how long does it take from Osaka to Tokyo by the Shinkansen Express?

To ask for specific buses, lines, tracks, or terminals, use:

新宿行(しんじゅくい/ゆ)きの電車(でんしゃ)は何番線(せん)ですか。

Which tracks does the Shinjuku train leave from?

中央線(ちゅうおうせん)の新宿行(しんじゅくい/ゆ)きは何番線(せん)ですか。

Which track is the Chuo Line train bound for Shinjuku?

新宿行(しんじゅくい/ゆ)きのバスはどれですか。
Which bus goes to Shinjuku?
新宿行(しんじゅくい/ゆ)きのバスはそのターミナルから出ますか。
Does the Shinjuku bus leave from that terminal?

Finally, it is very important to confirm your understanding using the confirmatory expressions introduced in Chapter 5 as well as the あいづち in Chapters 2 and 3 in *Nakama* 1.

A. 下の地図(ちず)を見て下さい。地図(ちず)には建(たて)物がありません。話を聞いて、建(たて)物の名前を地図(ちず)に書いて下さい。

Example: A: あのう、このへんにそば屋(や)がありますか。
B: 駅(えき)を出るとすぐに大きい道路(どうろ)があります。
そば屋(や)は道路(どうろ)をわたったところの右側(みぎがわ)のかどですよ。

iLrn Self-Tests

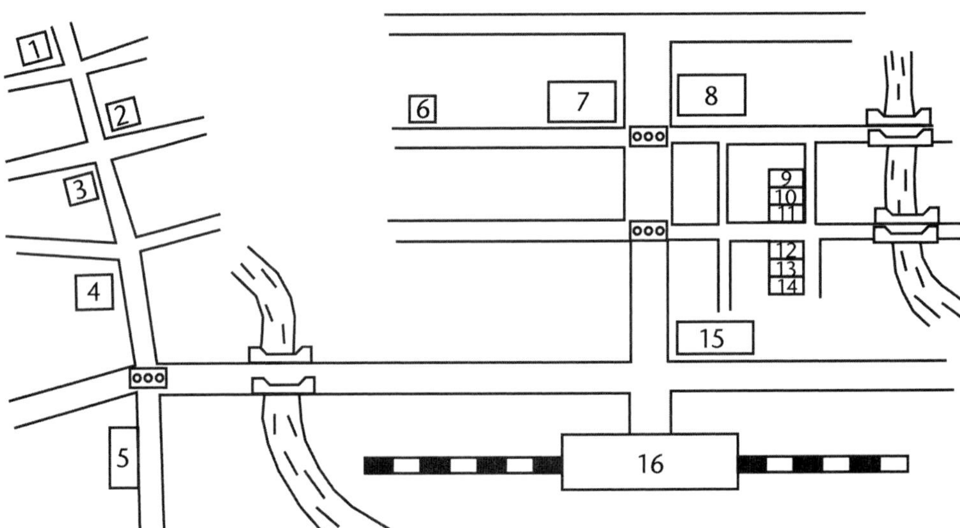

B. Listen to this series of six answers to questions. On a separate sheet of paper, make appropriate questions asking for directions that would have led to these answers.

C. Work with a partner. Ask your partner how to get from one place on the map on page 237 to another place. (Decide where to start first.) Take notes on what your partner says, but don't look at the map. Make sure to confirm your understanding. Then look at the map and verify the locations.

D. Work with a partner. Ask your partner how to get from the station to various places on the map used with Exercise C. Take notes on what your partner says, but don't look at the map. Make sure to confirm your understanding, using あいづち and other confirmatory expressions. Then use your notes to trace a route on the map to verify what you have understood.

漢字

Importance of pronunciation in letter identification and kanji words

Native speakers are implicitly aware of the sound and spelling correspondence in their language, though how the spelling and sound correspond to each other may be different depending on the language. For example, native speakers of English know the presence of the letter "e" at the end of a word may affect the vowel sound in a one-syllable words like the following:

cap	cape	mat	mate	hat	hate	pin	pine	kit	kite
win	wine	sit	site	not	note	pet	Pete	cut	cute

Native speakers of alphabetic languages such as English rely heavily on sound information when processing written letters and words. For example, it takes more time to identify pronounceable non-words than unpronounceable non-words because native speakers try to process sound information if the word is pronounceable. Similarly, word identification time correlates with the number of syllables in English.

When reading **kanji**, native English speakers tend to process them in terms of sound. This is reasonable because native Japanese speakers use sound information as well, although they rely on other sources of information such as graphic and semantic information.

In order to use sound information, readers must be sensitive to the phonetic radicals. Also, they should remember how a **kanji** is read in other words, especially those words consisting of more than one **kanji**.

Try the following:

1. Try to write the phonetic component of a kanji you know.
2. Try to guess the pronunciation of the following words:

話題　会計　水銀　英会話　朝会　親族　作家　半人前　語学　学友
親友　晴天　毎回　出番　間食　海上　漢語　医学　休日　休館　学習
英文　住人　薬局　式場　変人　英国　年度　名人　達人　留年

場	場	place ば　ジョウ	駐車場(ちゅうしゃじょう)　売り場(うりば)　場所(ばしょ)　会場(かいじょう)
寺	寺	temple てら　ジ	大きいお寺(てら)　東大寺(とうだいじ)　清水寺(きよみずでら)
橋	橋	bridge はし　キョウ	橋(はし)をわたります。　橋本(はしもと)さん　大橋(おおはし)さん
町	町	town まち　チョウ	大きい町(まち)に住んでいます。

Flashcards

映 映
to reflect, to project
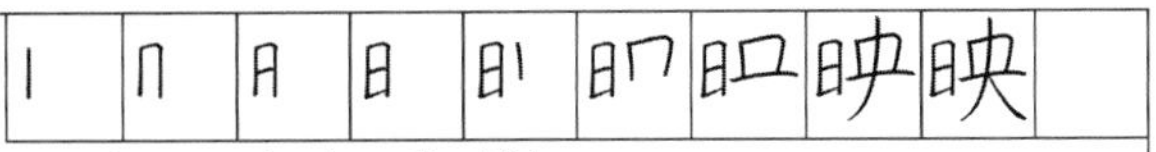
うつ(る)・うつ(す)　エイ　映画（えいが）　映画館（えいがかん）

公 公
public, official
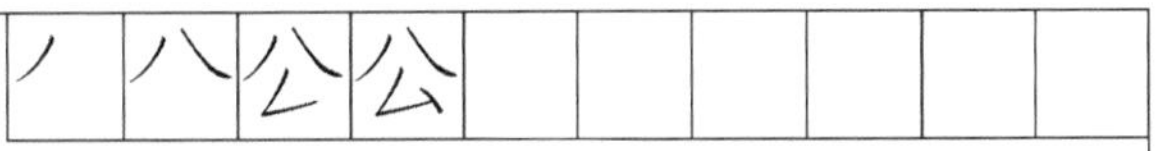
おおやけ　コウ　公園（こうえん）

園 園
garden

その　エン　動物園（どうぶつえん）じゃなくて遊園地（ゆうえんち）に行きたい。

図 図
drawing, diagram, to plan
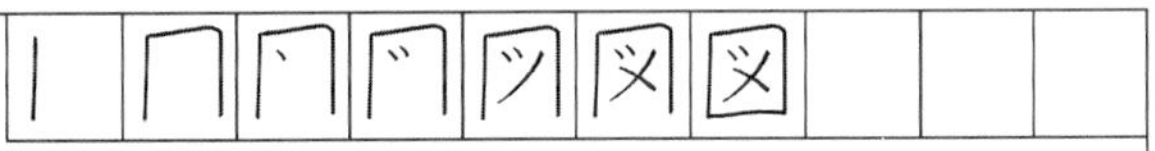
はか(る)　ズ・ト　図書館（としょかん）の近（ちか）くの地図（ちず）をみる。

地 地
Earth, land

チ・ジ　デパートの地下（ちか）　地下鉄（ちかてつ）の地図（ちず）

鉄 鉄
iron

テツ　地下鉄（ちかてつ）

駅 駅
(train) station

エキ　地下鉄（ちかてつ）の駅（えき）　電車の駅（えき）

育 育
to grow up, to raise
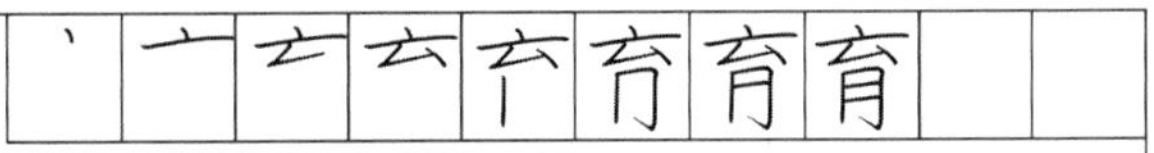
そだ(てる)・そだ(つ)　イク　体育館（たいいくかん）で遊（あそ）ぶ。

道 道
road, street, way
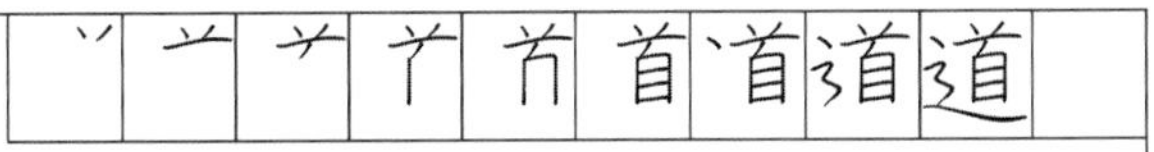
みち　ドウ　道（みち）なり　横断歩道（おうだんほどう）を歩く　道路（どうろ）

部 部
part, selection
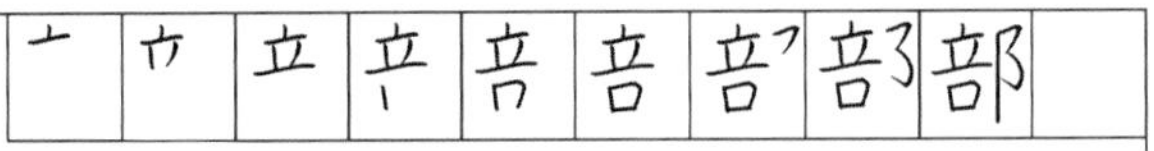
ブ・ヘ　部屋（へや）　全部（ぜんぶ）で学部（がくぶ） (department) は十あります。

屋 屋
roof, house, shop
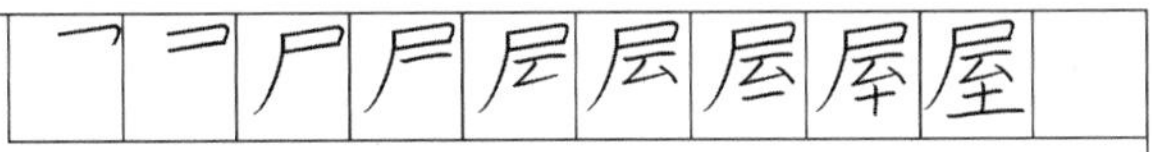
ヤ・オク　駅（えき）のそばの本屋（ほんや）　私の部屋（へや）はきれいです。

車	vehicle, wheel	くるま　シャ	車(くるま)　自転車(じてんしゃ)　電車(でんしゃ)　各駅停車(かくえきていしゃ)
右	right	みぎ　ウ	道(みち)の右側(みぎがわ)　右手(みぎて) (right hand)　右足(みぎあし) (right leg)
左	left	ひだり　サ	駅(えき)の左側(ひだりがわ)　左耳(ひだりみみ) (left ear)
近	near, close	ちか(い)　キン	大学の近(ちか)く　最近(さいきん)　遊園地(ゆうえんち)に近(ちか)い
遠	far, distant	とお(い)　エン	公園(こうえん)から遠(とお)い。
通	to go along, to pass	とお(る)　ツウ	小さい町(まち)を通(とお)って行きました。
飛	to fly	と(ぶ)　ヒ	飛行機(ひこうき)で行きます。

読めるようになった漢字

売(う)り場　駐(ちゅう)車場　場所　寺　橋　町　映画　映画館　公園　図書館　地図　地下
地下鉄　遊(ゆう)園地　駅　体育館　道　横断(おうだん)歩道　道路(ろ)　部屋　全(ぜん)部で　本屋　車
電車　各(かく)駅停(てい)車　右側(がわ)　右手　左側(がわ)　左足　近い　近く　最(さい)近　遠い　普通(ふつう)　通る

練習

Read the following sentences aloud.

1. A：この映画館のチケット売(う)り場はどこですか。
   B：このビルの前を通って、左にまがった所にあります。
2. A：この近くに地下鉄の駅はありませんか。
   B：この道路をまっすぐ歩いていって、横断(おうだん)歩道をわたった、右側にあります。
3. この町には大きい公園と新しい図書館があります。そして、古いお寺がたくさんあります。川が多いので、橋もたくさんあります。

4. 明日は遊(ゆう)園地と動(どう)物園に友達と行くつもりです。
5. 本屋で南アメリカの地図を買いました。
6. 体育館の予約をとりました。
7. 私の部屋は出口から遠いです。

読む練習

上手な読み方

Reading maps

As mentioned in the Culture Notes, Japanese streets and towns are not well organized and directions like north, south, east, and west make little sense in following directions or identifying a location. For this reason, it is important for you to be able to read maps in Japan. In fact, many people, including taxi drivers, use car navigation systems or GPS. Cell phones with navigation systems are also common.

1. Go to the English version of the MapFan Web site: http://www.mapfan.com/en/en_m.cgi, and get a map of the area around Tokyo Station.
2. There are several symbols in the map. Find out the meaning of symbols in the map by surfing the web.
3. Go to the corresponding Japanese map. Find out the names of some of the buildings and facilities located in the symbols and tell the differences between the English and Japanese versions.

東京(きょう)大学へ行く

読む前に

A. 下の新幹線(しんかんせん)の時刻表(じこくひょう) (*timetable*) を見て質問に答えて下さい。

	ひかり 200	のぞみ 300	ひかり 126	こだま 404	ひかり 228	こだま 408	ひかり 032	ひかり 232	のぞみ 006	ひかり 034	ひかり 086	のぞみ 010
新大阪(しんおおさか)	6:00	6:12	6:43	9:00	9:57	10:00	10:17	10:39	10:54	11:17	11:26	11:54
京都(きょうと)	6:17	6:27	7:00	9:16	10:17	10:17	10:41	10:56	11:10	11:34	11:44	12:10
名古屋(なごや)	7:07	7:05	7:57	!0:15	10:58	11:15	11:18	11:53	11:48	12:18	12:28	12:48
	｜	｜	○	○○○	｜	○○○	○	○	｜	｜	｜	｜
品川(しながわ)	｜	｜	9:47	13:05	｜	14:05	13:09	13:40	｜	14:09	｜	｜
東京(きょう)	8:56	8:42	9:52	13:10	12:52	14:10	13:14	13:45	13:24	14:14	14:38	14:24

1. 新大阪(しんおおさか)から東京(きょう)まで行く一番はやい新幹線(しんかんせん)はどれですか。
2. 京都(きょうと)と品川(しながわ)にとまる新幹線(しんかんせん)はどれですか。
3. 一時ごろ東京(きょう)に着くためには、何時の新幹線(しんかんせん)に乗らなければなりませんか。

B. 下の文章を読んで、日本語で質問に答えて下さい。

パークさんは大阪大学の大学院で勉強している留学生です。明後日、研究のために東京大学の大山先生に会いに行く予定です。大山先生は三時ごろ研究室にいらっしゃるはずですから、パークさんは三時少し前に東京大学に着いていなければなりません。

1. パークさんは今どこに住んでいますか。

2. パークさんはいつ東京に行く予定ですか。

3. パークさんは何時にどこに行かなければなりませんか。

読んでみましょう

下の手紙は大山先生の助手 (*assistant*) の本田さんがパークさんへ送ったファックスです。

パークさんへ

明後日の三時に大山先生が研究室でお待ちですから、東京駅から大学までの行き方を書いておきます。何か分からないことがあったら、私(本田)に電話して下さい。電話番号は 080-1234-5678 です。それでは明後日お会いしましょう。

東京駅で地下鉄丸ノ内線の池袋行きに乗り換えます。そして、本郷三丁目の駅で降りて下さい。四つ目の駅ですから十分ぐらいで着くはずです。電車を降りたら、本郷通りの方に出る改札に行って下さい。本郷通りはとても大きいので、すぐ分かるはずです。

本郷通りを左の方に行くと、大きい交差点があります。その交差点を通って、まっすぐ行くと、右側に赤い門が見えます。門の前に横断歩道がありますから、道路を渡って下さい。中に入ったら、すぐ左に曲がって下さい。大山先生の研究室は、二番目の建物です。三階の３０５号室です。本郷三丁目の駅から大学までは歩いて十分ぐらいかかります。

読んだ後で

A. 下の路線図 (*train map*) を見て、パークさんが乗る電車と駅に○をつけて下さい。おりる駅もさがして下さい。

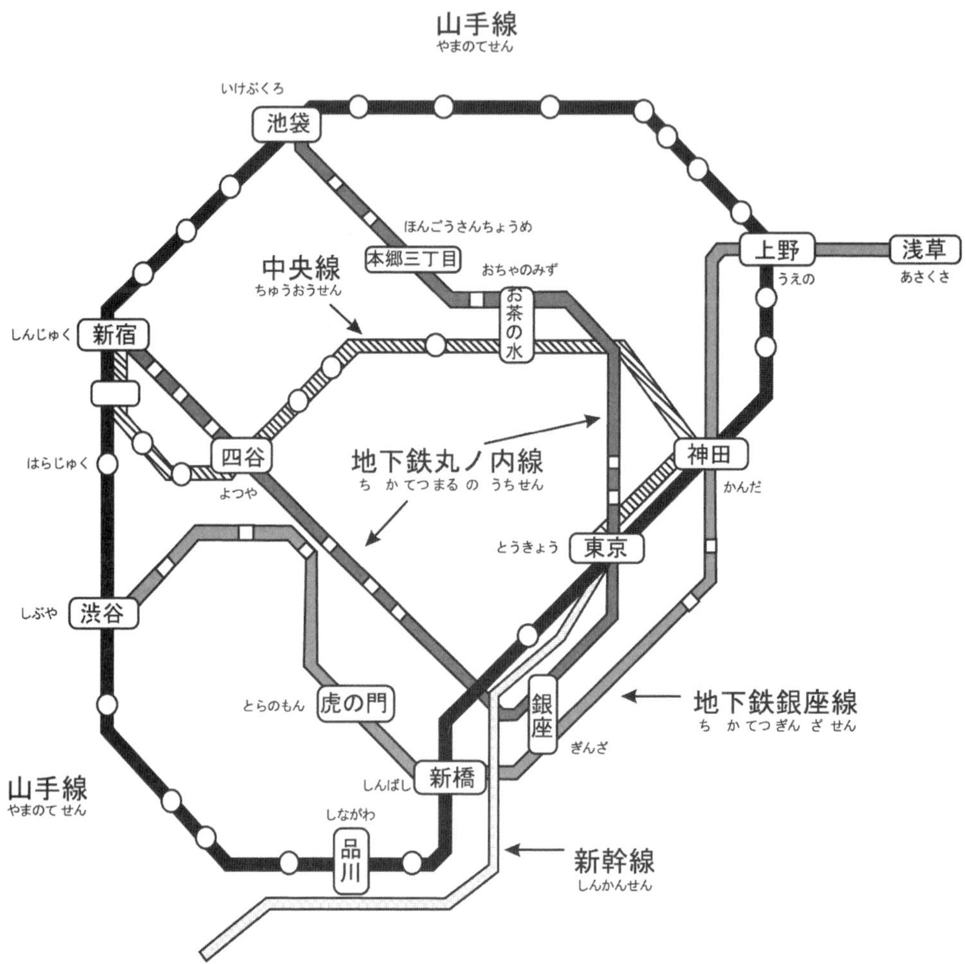

B. The picture below shows the subway station and Hongodori. Draw a line from the station to the approximate location of Professor Oyama's office.

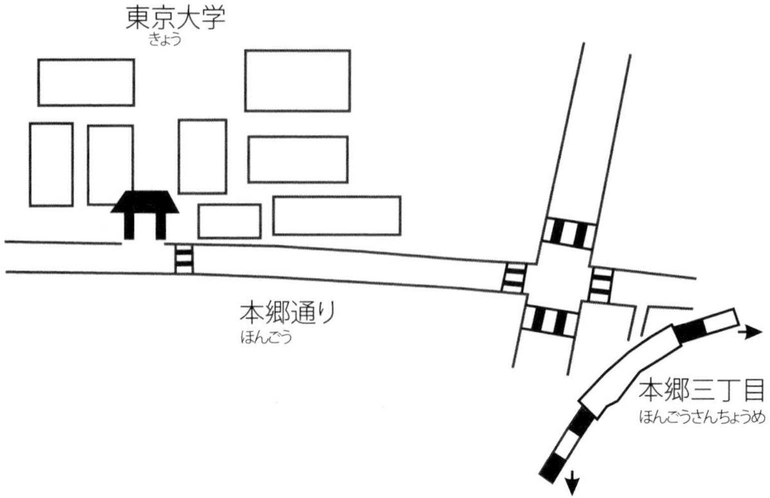

C. 地下鉄では一つの駅から次の駅まで3分ぐらいかかります。東京駅から東京大学までどのくらいかかるか言って下さい。

D. 三時に大山先生の研究室に行くためには、パークさんは何時の新幹線に乗らなければなりませんか。２５２ページの新幹線の時刻をつかって言って下さい。

E. Mr. Park needs to send a fax to Mr. Honda to thank him for the directions and to confirm his visit. Complete the fax form your instructor hands out, being sure to include the following information:

1. Date
2. Expression of thanks
3. Departure time of train from Osaka
4. Arrival time in Tokyo
5. Estimated arrival time at Tokyo University
6. What Mr. Park will do if he cannot get there on time
7. Say that he is looking forward to meeting them. (お会い出来るのをたのしみにしております。)

総合練習

A. 私の家

1. Work with a partner. Invite your partner for dinner and give him or her directions to your home. First, decide on a starting point. Draw a map and give directions as though you were in Japan, without using street names or expressions such as north, south, east, or west. Your partner should take notes while confirming the directions. Then he or she should also draw a map. Compare the two maps to verify how accurately you have given the directions.
2. Repeat the above activity, using another local place as a destination (parent's house, grandparent's house, friend's house, etc.).

B. 成田空港で (At Narita Airport)

1. Ms. Brown and Mr. Jones have just arrived at Narita Airport. Jones-san calls up his Japanese friend. Listen to the conversation between Jones-san and the friend and identify the friend's name and why Jones called her.

   名前：____________________________

   理由：____________________________

2. Listen to the conversation again and answer the following questions.

   a. ジョーンズさんはどこに行きますか。
   b. ジョーンズさんは何で（どうやって）そこに行くつもりですか。
   c. ジョーンズさんの友達によると京成線とJR線とどちらの方が便利ですか。どちらのほうがはやいですか。

3. Work with a partner. You and your partner have just arrived at Narita Airport.You are staying at the Plaza Hotel in Shinjuku (see the map on page 227). Look at the following information about the transportation services from Narita to downtown Tokyo. Discuss with your partner how you would go to Shinjuku.

成田空港 —————— 日暮里 —————— 新宿
京成アクセス特急（60 分 , 1200 円）　JR (20 分 , 190 円)

成田空港 —————— 日暮里 —————— 新宿
成田スカイライナー（36 分 , 2400 円）　JR (20 分 , 190 円)

成田空港 —————— 東京 —————— 新宿
JR 成田エクスプレス (58 分 , 2940 円)　JR (15 分 , 190 円)

成田空港 —————————————— 新宿
リムジンバス（115 分), 3,000 円

ロールプレイ

1. You are looking for a mailbox. Ask a passerby where you can find one.
2. A Japanese student wants to go to the student union and a bookstore. Give him or her directions
3. You are new to town. Ask your friends about good restaurants, shops, etc. Ask how to get to each place and how long it takes.
4. You are in Tokyo Station. You want to go to Asakusa. Ask a passerby which train to take, whether you need to transfer, and how long it takes to get there. Use the diagram showing the Tokyo Station terminal on page 254.

Chapter 6

第六課

Junichi Kusaka/Getty Images

贈り物
Gifts

Objectives Describing experiences of gift giving and receiving, expressing preferences and selections

Vocabulary Gifts, gift givers and recipients, gift-giving vocabulary, gift-giving occasions, nouns derived from い-adjectives

Dialogue 上田さんの誕生日プレゼント

Japanese Culture Gift exchanges

Grammar

I. Using verbs of giving and receiving

II. Expressing the fact that something is easy or hard to do using the stem of the verb + やすい／にくい

III. Listing actions and states, and implying a reason, using the plain form + し

IV. Trying something using 〜てみる

V. Quoting speech and words, using 〜という

Listening Shadowing and concentrating

Communication Phrases used when giving or receiving gifts

Kanji 送りがな **okurigana**

犬 花 形 服 辞 礼 祝 誕 自
転 運 動 使 写 真 絵 雑 誌 音

Reading Making strategic inferences

Chapter Resources

www.cengagebrain.com

Heinle Learning Center

Audio Program

単語
たん

Flashcards

Nouns

えさ	餌	food (for animal, fish)
おいわい	お祝い	congratulatory gift
おかし	お菓子	confectionary, sweets
おかえし	お返し	thank-you gift
おきもの	置物	ornament placed in an alcove, desk, cabinet, etc., such as figurines, clocks, pottery, and other art pieces
おくりもの	贈り物	gift
おじさん		middle-aged man, someone else's uncle, also used when speaking to one's own uncle
おじいさん		elderly man
おせいぼ	お歳暮	end-of-year gift exchange
おちゅうげん	お中元	mid-year gift exchange
おばさん		middle-aged woman, someone else's aunt, also used when speaking to one's own aunt
おばあさん		elderly woman
おみまい	お見舞い	sympathy gift
おもちゃ		toy
おれい	お礼	thank-you gift
カーネーション		carnation
キャンディ		candy
きんじょ	近所	neighborhood, 近所(きんじょ)の人 neighbor
こうはい	後輩	one's junior at a school, university, office, etc.
コーヒーカップ		coffee cup, mug
じょうし	上司	boss, workplace superior
しょうせつ	小説	novel
しょっき	食器	dishes
スイーツ		sweets
せっけん	石鹸	soap
せんぱい	先輩	one's senior at a school, university, office, etc.
タオル		towel
チケット		ticket for entertainment such as movies, theaters, and concerts
ちちのひ	父の日	Father's Day

どうりょう	同僚	co-worker, colleague
どうぶつ	動物	animal
DVD		DVD
にんぎょう	人形	doll
ぬいぐるみ		stuffed animal
パソコン		personal computer
はちうえ	鉢植え	potted plant, house plant
はな	花	flower
ははのひ	母の日	Mother's Day
ばら／バラ	薔薇	rose
ハム		ham
バレンタインデー		Valentine's Day
ぶか	部下	junior employee, subordinate
ペット		pet
フルーツ		fruit
ボール		ball
ようふく	洋服	Western clothes (not traditional Japanese attire)
リボン		ribbon, リボンをかける to put on a ribbon
ワイングラス		wine glass

な -adjectives

たいせつ (な)	大切 (な)	precious, important

う -verbs

いただく	頂く／戴く	to receive
えらぶ	選ぶ	to choose
かう	飼う	to raise, keep (an animal)
くださる	下さる	to give (from a social superior to me or a person in my in-group)
つつむ	包む	to wrap
やる		to give (to a socially inferior person)
よろこぶ	喜ぶ	to be pleased

る -verbs

あげる		to give (to a socially equal person)
くれる		to give (to a socially equal or inferior in-group person)
さしあげる	差し上げる	to give (to a socially superior out-group person)

Particles

に		from 〜にもらう （〜からもらう） to receive something from 〜

Prefixes

こ〜	子〜	baby 〜 , 子犬(こいぬ) puppy, 子猫(こねこ) kitten

Suffixes

〜いわい	祝い	congratulatory gift, 結婚祝い(いわ) wedding gift, 就職祝い(しゅうしょくいわ) gift for getting a new job, 卒業祝い(いわ) graduation gift
〜さ		suffix to convert an adjective to a noun for measurement 大きさ (size) 高さ (height) 長さ (length) 重さ (weight)

Expressions

あまりきをつかわないでください。		あまり気を遣／使わないで下さい。 Please don't put yourself out for me.
おきをつかわせてしまいまして。		お気を遣／使わせてしまいまして。 You shouldn't have gone to so much trouble for me/us.
（そんな）おきをつかわないでください。		（そんな）お気を遣／使わないで下さい。 Please don't go to so much trouble.
おすきだとよろしいのですが。		お好きだとよろしいのですが。 I hope this will be to your liking.
おれいにとおもいまして。		お礼にと思いまして。 I thought I would make this a token of my appreciation.
おめでとうございます。		Congratulations!
(そんな) しんぱいしないでください。		（そんな）心配しないで下さい。 Please don't go so much trouble.
(お) せわになる	(お) 世話になる	to be cared for or helped by somebody
たいしたものじゃありませんから		たいした物じゃありませんから It is of little value.
ほんのきもちですから	ほんの気持ちですから	Just a token of my appreciation.
ほんのすこしですから	ほんの少しですから	It's not such a big deal, Just a little bit . . .
やくにたつ	役に立つ	useful

単(たん)語の練習

A. 贈(おく)り物(もの) Gifts

他のプレゼント Other gifts

おさら	お皿	plates
かんづめ	缶詰	canned food
クッキー		cookies
グローブ		baseball glove or boxing gloves
けしょうひん／コスメ	化粧品	cosmetics
シーツ		sheets, linens
しょうひんけん	商品券	gift certificate
スカーフ		scarf
スニーカー		sneakers
ゼリー		jelly, Jello
せんざい	洗剤	detergent
(お) せんべい	(お) 煎餅	rice crackers
てぶくろ	手袋	gloves
バット		bat
ハンドソープ		hand soap
ハンドクリーム		hand cream
ふうせん	風船	balloon
ボディソープ		body soap
ポテトチップ		potato chips
ユニフォーム		uniform
ようがし	洋菓子	Western-style confectionary
マフラー		scarf, muffler
(お) まんじゅう	(お) 饅頭	steamed buns
もうふ	毛布	blanket
ひもちするもの	日持ちする物	nonperishable items
ひもちしないもの	日持ちしない物	perishable items

おぼえていますか。

お(金)　お(さけ)　コーヒー　テレビ　本　えんぴつ　かばん　けしゴム　携帯(けいたい)電話　カード　辞(じ)書　ペン　ボールペン　犬(いぬ)　絵(え)　車　自転車(じてんしゃ)　写真(しゃしん)　ソファ　たんすつくえ　テーブル　電話　時計　ねこ　ビデオ　ふとん　ベッド　本棚(だな)　物　ゲーム　雑誌(ざっし)　新聞　手紙　メール　おちゃ　オレンジ　果(くだ)物　こうちゃ　コーラゴルフ　さかな　ジュース　スキー　食べ物　たまご　トマト　にく　にんじん　バスケットボール　バナナ　ビール　水　ミルク　やさい　りんご　レタス　ワイン　アクセサリー　イヤリング　腕(うで)時計　かさ　くつ　くつした　コート　ジーンズ　ジャケット　シャツ　食品(しょくひん)　スーツ　スカート　ストッキング　ズボン　セーター　Tシャツ　ドレス　ネクタイ　ネックレス　パンツ　服(ふく)　ブラウス　文房具(ぼうぐ)　ベルト　帽(ぼう)子　指輪(わ)　アイスクリーム　あぶら　ランチ　カレーライスクッキー　ケーキ　(お) さしみ　サラダ　サンドイッチ　スープ　(お) すし　ステーキ　スパゲティ　そば　チーズ　チキン　チャーハン　チョコレート　デザート　天ぷら　ハンバーガー　パン　ピザ　フライドチキン　ラーメン　着物　プレゼント　薬　マッサージ　お土産(みやげ)　切符(ぷ)　スーツケース　デジカメ　さいふ　しょうたいじょう　趣(しゅ)味

Activity 1 下の場所にはどんな物があるか、何をよく見るか言って下さい。.

Example:　リビングルームにはたいていソファやテーブルがあります。

場所	よくある物や見る物
リビングルーム	
ベッドルーム	
お風呂	
キッチン	
げんかん	
子供の部屋	
体育館	
教室	
公園	
遊園地	
動物園	
博物館	
美術館	

Activity 2 List the words that fit in the following categories.

カテゴリー	物の名前
食べ物	
飲み物	
服	
アクセサリー	
動物	
植物 (*plants*)	
きかい (*machines*)	
文房具	
読み物	
おもちゃ	

B. 贈(おく)り物(もの)をあげる人、もらう人 Gift givers and recipients

おばさん	middle-aged woman, someone else's aunt
おじさん	middle-aged man, someone else's uncle
おばあさん	elderly woman
おじいさん	elderly man
近所(きんじょ)の人	neighbor
(お) 世話(せわ)になった人	someone who has helped me
上司(じょうし)	boss
同僚(どうりょう)	co-worker, colleague
部下(ぶか)	junior employee, subordinate
先輩(せんぱい)	one's senior at a school, university, or office
後輩(こうはい)	one's junior at a school, university, or office

おぼえていますか。

社長(ちょう)　先生　友達　家族　祖父(そふ)　祖母(そぼ)　母　父　(ご) 主人(しゅじん)　つま　姉　兄　妹　弟　お母さん　お父さん　おくさん　お姉さん　お兄さん　妹さん　弟さん

Activity 3 下にてきとうな (*appropriate*) 言葉を書いて下さい。

1. 一緒(しょ)に仕事をしている人を＿＿＿＿＿＿と言います。
2. 八十さいぐらいの女の人を＿＿＿＿＿＿と言って、同じ年の男の人を＿＿＿＿＿＿と言います。
3. 会社で自分(じぶん)より上の人を＿＿＿＿＿＿と言います。
4. 自分(じぶん)より後に大学に入学した人を＿＿＿＿＿＿と言います。
5. 高校の先生や、よく行く病院のお医者さんを＿＿＿＿＿＿と言います。
6. 会社で同じ課(か) (*section*) で自分より下の人を＿＿＿＿＿＿と言います。
7. 自分(じぶん)の家の近くに住んでいる人を＿＿＿＿＿＿と言います。
8. 自分(じぶん)より前に大学に入学した人を＿＿＿＿＿＿と言います。
9. 四十さいぐらいの女の人を＿＿＿＿＿＿と言って、同じ年の男の人を＿＿＿＿＿＿と言います。

Activity 4 日本語で質問に答えて下さい。

1. どんな人にお世話(せわ)になったことがありますか。
2. 何さいぐらいになると、「おじさん」と言いますか。
3. 何さいぐらいになると、「おばあさん」と言いますか。
4. どんな後輩(こうはい)や先輩(せんぱい)がいますか。
5. 自分(じぶん)はどんな先輩(せんぱい)だと思いますか。
6. 近所(きんじょ)にどんな人が住んでいますか。

D. 贈(おく)り物(もの)をする時に使(つか)う言葉　Gift-giving vocabulary

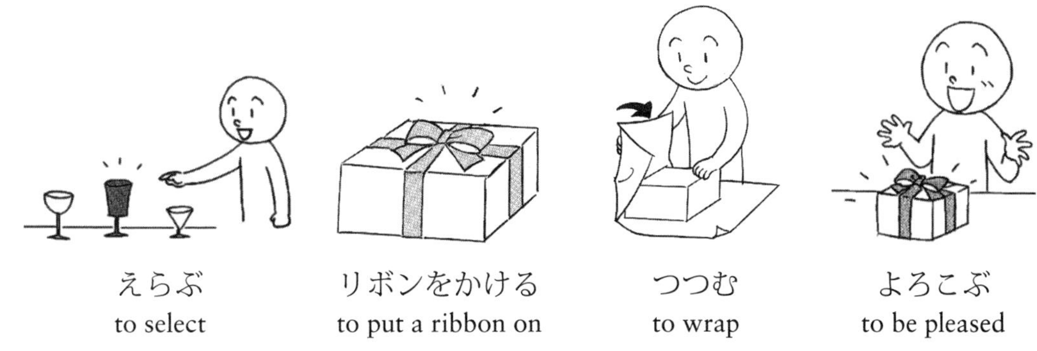

えらぶ	リボンをかける	つつむ	よろこぶ
to select	to put a ribbon on	to wrap	to be pleased

大切(たいせつ)な	precious, important
やくにたつ	useful
おめでとう（ございます）	Congratulations

おぼえていますか。

あかい　あおい　新しい　いい　大きい　黄(き)色い　くろい　しろい　高い　小さい　茶(ちゃ)色い　古い　明るい　うれしい　おもしろい　かなしい　楽(たの)しい　つまらない　おいしい　安い　あまい　からい　冷たい　温かい　かっこいい　かわいい　ながい　みじかい　わかい　つまらない　きれいな　有(ゆう)名な　りっぱな　しずかな　好きな　きらいな　便利(り)な　大事な　書く　作る　買う　とる　送る　知っている　きめる　さがす　きまる　（お金が）かかる　つける　かえす

Activity 5 日本語で質問に答えて下さい。

1. 何か大切(たいせつ)にしている物がありますか。どんな物を大切(たいせつ)にしていますか。
2. 日本語の勉強にはどんなものがやくにたちますか。
   父の日のプレゼントにどんな物をえらんだことがありますか。
3. 日本ではお祝(いわ)いをする時、「おめでとうございます」とよく言います。あなたの国では何と言いますか。
4. 何をしたら、ご両親はよろこぶと思いますか。

Activity 6 下にてきとうな (*appropriate*) 言葉を書いて下さい。

1. 誕(たん)生日プレゼントは電子(でんし) (*electronic*) 辞(じ)書にしました。この辞(じ)書は単(たん)語が多くて、とても____________________。
2. 誕(たん)生日プレゼントにリボンを____________________。
3. 誕(たん)生日ケーキに____________________と書いた。
4. その男の子は誕(たん)生日ケーキを見て、とても____________________。
5. 母は私にとって一番____________________人です。

D. 贈(おく)り物(もの)をする場面(ばめん)　Gift-giving occasions

お中元(ちゅうげん)	mid-year gift exchange	お見舞(みま)い	sympathy gift
おせいぼ	end-of-the-year gift exchange	おかえし	reciprocal gift
母の日	Mother's Day	お祝(いわ)い	congratulatory gift
父の日	Father's Day		

～祝(いわ)い　congratulatory gift for ～

結婚祝(いわ)い wedding gift, しゅうしょく祝(いわ)い gift for new job, 誕(たん)生日祝(いわ)い birthday present, 入学祝(いわ)い gift for entering school, 卒業祝(いわ)い graduation gift

おぼえていますか。

誕(たん)生日　誕(たん)生会　送別(べつ)会　同窓(そう)会　しょうたいじょう　結婚　しゅうしょく
入学　卒業　バレンタインデー　ハロウィン　クリスマス　デート　お土産(みやげ)

Activity 7

Work as a class. Ask your classmates what kinds of gifts they give in the following cases and determine the three most popular gifts for each situation.

Example: A: 母の日の贈(おく)り物(もの)には何がいいと思いますか。

B: あかいカーネーションがいいと思います。

Occasion	一番	二番	三番
母の日			
父の日			
結婚祝(いわ)い			
病気の人のお見舞(みま)い			
お世話(せわ)になった先生にするお礼(れい)			
バレンタインデー			
クリスマス			

Activity 8

下にてきとうな (*appropriate*) 言葉を書いて下さい。

1. 日本ではお世話(せわ)になった人に一年に二度贈(おく)り物(もの)をします。＿＿＿＿＿＿は七月にします。
   ＿＿＿＿＿＿は十二月にします。
2. 十二月二十五日は＿＿＿＿＿＿です。二月十四日は＿＿＿＿＿＿です。
3. ＿＿＿＿＿＿は五月の二週目の日曜日ですが、＿＿＿＿＿＿はいつですか。
4. だれかがしゅうしょくした時にする贈(おく)り物(もの)を＿＿＿＿＿＿と言います。
   大学を卒業した時にする贈(おく)り物(もの)を＿＿＿＿＿＿と言います。
5. 友達が入院したので、＿＿＿＿＿＿にフルーツを持って行きます。
6. 入学祝(いわ)いをもらったので、＿＿＿＿＿＿のカードを書きました。
7. 旅行に行ったので、会社の同僚(どうりょう)に＿＿＿＿＿＿を買いました。
8. 日本ではお見舞(ま)いをもらったら、＿＿＿＿＿＿をしなければなりません。

E. Nouns derived from い -adjectives

～さ	大きさ	高さ	ながさ	ひろさ
	size	height	length	space

Positive connotation		Negative connotation	
い -adjectives	～さ	い -adjectives	～さ
明るい	明るさ (*brightness*)	くらい	くらさ (*darkness*)
暑い	暑さ (*heat*)	寒い	寒さ (*coldness*)
大きい	大きさ (*size*)	小さい	小ささ (*smallness*)
おもい (*heavy*)	おもさ (*weight*)	かるい (*light*)	かるさ (*lightness*)
高い	高さ (*height*)	ひくい	ひくさ (*lowness*)
強い	強さ (*strength*)	よわい	よわさ (*weakness*)
はやい	はやさ (*speed*)	おそい (*slow, late*)	おそさ (*lateness*)
ひろい	ひろさ (*space*)	せまい	せまさ (*narrowness*)
ふかい (*deep*)	ふかさ (*depth*)	あさい (*shallow*)	あささ (*shallowness*)
むずかしい	むずかしさ (*difficulty*)	やさしい	やさしさ (*easiness*)

Activity 9 質問に答えて下さい。

1. 「さ」の前の言葉はどんな言葉ですか。
2. 「さ」の前の言葉はどんなかたち (*form*) を使(つか)いますか。
3. 下の言葉の意味は何だと思いますか。

よさ　ひろさ　しろさ　安さ　はやさ　むし暑さ　すずしさ　冷たさ
かっこよさ　わかさ　古さ　やさしさ　おもしろさ　いそがしさ
おいしさ　痛さ　ひどさ　かゆさ　やわらかさ　すっぱさ　にがさ
しょっぱさ　あまさ　からさ　楽(たの)しさ　さびしさ　かなしさ　うれしさ

Activity 10 Give the antonyms of the words below.

大きい　新しい　高い　ながい　ひろい　しろい　いい　明るい　はやい
多い　楽(たの)しい　暑い　あたたかい　あまい

ダイアローグ

はじめに

日本語で質問に答えて下さい。

1. どんな時に友達に贈(おく)り物(もの)をしますか。
2. 女の人にはどんなプレゼントがいいと思いますか。男の人はどうですか。
3. おじいさんやおばあさんにはどんなプレゼントがいいと思いますか。子供はどうですか。
4. 友達の誕(たん)生日プレゼントを買う時、いくらぐらいの物を買いますか。
5. 家族の誕(たん)生日プレゼントを買う時、いくらぐらい使(つか)いますか。

上田さんの誕(たん)生日プレゼント

The order of the following **manga** frames is scrambled. Read the dialogue and unscramble the frames by writing the correct number in the box in each frame.

a

b

c

d

e

f

石田さんは道子さんとキャンパスで話をしています。

石田：　あのう、道子さん、もうすぐ上田さんの誕(たん)生日だよね。

道子：　ええ、そうよ。

石田：　もうプレゼント買った？

道子：　ううん、まだ。

石田：　ぼくも、まだなんだ。自分(じぶん)でえらんでみようかと思ったんだけど、何をあげたらよろこぶか、ぜんぜん分からないんだ。

道子：　じゃあ、一緒(しょ)に買い物に行こうか。

石田：　いいの？ありがとう。

道子：　じゃあ、明後日の午後でもいい？

石田：　もちろん、いいよ。

石田さんと道子さんはデパートにいます。

道子：　予算(よさん)はいくらぐらい？

石田：　そうだね、五千円ぐらいかな。

道子：　じゃあ、おさいふはどう？　アリスが今持ってるのは古いから、新しいのがほしいって言ってたし。

石田：　どんなのがいいかな。

道子：　かわいくて、使(つか)いやすいのがいいと思うよ。

石田：　じゃあ、これはどう。

道子：　これは、色もきれいだし、かわいいけど、ちょっと大きすぎるかもしれない。

石田：　じゃあ、これはどう。大きさ、大丈夫(じょうぶ)？

道子：　ああ、これなら、使(つか)いやすそう。

店員(てんいん)：　はい、いらっしゃいませ。

石田：　あのう、このあかいさいふ、いくらですか。

店員(てんいん)：　五千円でございます。

石田：　じゃあ、これ下さい。

店員(てんいん)：　はい、かしこまりました。リボンはおかけしますか。

石田：　はい、おねがいします。誕(たん)生日プレゼントなので。

店員(てんいん)：　はい、かしこまりました。

Dialogue Phrase Notes

- もちろん means *of course.*
- 予算(よさん) means *budget.*
- 店員(てんいん) means a *store clerk.*
- でございます is an extremely polite form of です.
- かしこまりました is an extremely polite form of わかりました.
- おかけします is a humble form of かけます.

ダイアローグの後で

A. 日本語で質問に答えて下さい。

1. 石田さんは道子さんに何をしてほしかったのですか。
2. 道子さんと石田さんはどこに行きましたか。何のためにそこへ行きましたか。
3. 道子さんによると、上田さん（アリス）は何をほしがっているそうですか。それはどうしてですか。
4. 石田さんは何を買いましたか。
5. 石田さんはどんなのを買いましたか。どうしてそれにしましたか。

B. Suppose that Ishida is not a close friend of Michiko. Michiko and Ishida would then speak a little more politely than they do in the dialogue. Modify the conversation by using polite speech.

C. Suppose Michiko wants to buy a Christmas present for Mr. Li, but does not know what he likes. She asks Ishida to help her choose an appropriate present. Create a dialogue for this situation based on the dialogue above.

日本の文化

贈り物の習慣 Gift exchanges

While exchanging gifts is an intricate part of many cultures, each culture develops different social norms and expectations. In Japanese culture, the gift exchange is a highly ritualized social practice. The chart on the following page shows some of the major gift-giving occasions and special terms used for these occasions.

Among these, お中元 and お歳暮 are considered the two major gift-giving seasons. People give gifts to those to whom they feel indebted such as 上司 (company bosses) and 恩師 (former teachers and mentors). During the お中元 and お歳暮 seasons, department stores put gift packs on sale, distribute gift catalogs, and set up special sections and websites to take orders and send out gifts. The customer fills out a form with his or her name and address and the recipient's name and address, and the department stores take care of the rest. Having gifts delivered is quite acceptable in Japan, but it is a nice gesture to deliver gifts personally to close acquaintances or friends.

Money is commonly given at weddings, funerals, as New Year's gifts for children and to mark the birth of a new baby, but it must be put in a special envelope. There are a variety of special envelopes, specific to the different gift-giving occasions.

©Setsuko Suzuki / HAGA / The Image Works

Christmas in Japan is by and large a commercial event. Parents give their children special Christmas presents but there is no tradition of exchanging gifts among friends or other relatives. At the New Year holiday, parents, relatives, and friends of the family give children pocket money called お年玉. On a personal level, the Japanese usually take a gift when visiting others' homes or when they come back from trips. It is a nice gesture to bring a small gift if you have been invited to a Japanese family's home for dinner or a visit. When sending a personal gift, the Japanese often write a short message or letter congratulating the recipient on his or her wedding, birthday, or employment. Usually the letter starts with a congratulatory message such as お誕生日おめでとうございます (*Happy birthday*) or ご結婚おめでとうございます (*Congratulations on your wedding*). This is followed by the appropriate wish for the recipient's happiness and health, such as すばらしい一年であることをおいのりします (*I hope you will have a wonderful year*), お二人のおしあわせをおいのりします (*I hope you are both very happy*), or ごかつやくをおいのりします (*Wishing for your success*). The writer may then include some news about him or herself, and a message about the gift.

おかえし Reciprocation

Reciprocation is also an important aspect of gift giving in Japan. It is customary to reciprocate by spending about one half of the original amount of the gift received. This custom is called 半返し. In the case of お中元 or お歳暮, however, it is not necessary to give anything in return, though a thank-you note or phone call is important.

Occasion	Recipient	Timing	Gift
Mid-season gift お中元 (ちゅうげん)	to neighbors, friends, someone you owe a favor, boss, relatives	July 1-5 (Kanto region) July 15-August 10 (others)	Practical gift worth ¥3,000-10,000
End-of-the year gift お歳暮 (せいぼ)	to neighbors, friends, someone whom you owe a favor, boss, relatives, etc.	Dec. 1-31 (Kanto region) Dec. 13-31	Practical gift worth ¥3,000-10,000
New Year's お年玉 (としだま)	to children who visit you	Jan 1-3	¥1,000-20,000 (money)
Visiting someone's home 訪問 (ほうもん)のごあいさつ	to your host	during the visit	A gift worth ¥1,000-5,000 (usually food)
Returning from a trip お土産 (みやげ)	to family, coworkers	after the trip	Something your family will enjoy; inexpensive gift or local food to co-workers
Birthday 誕生祝い (たん いわ)	to a birthday boy or girl (usually children or an adult who is close to you.)	birthday	Something that the recipient will enjoy
Valentine's Day (from female to male) バレンタインデー	to male coworkers; to a romantic interest	2/14	Small inexpensive chocolate (ぎりチョコ) for friends, and specialty or homemade chocolate (ほんめいチョコ) for someone special.
White Day (from male to female) ホワイトデー	to a woman who has given you chocolate on Valentines' Day and to a romantic interest	3/14	Marshmallows, cookies, candies, etc.
Christmas クリスマス	to family members, boyfriend/girlfriend, etc.	12/24-25	toys, clothing, hand made items, etc., jewelry
Hospitalization 病気見舞い (み ま)	to a sick person	during a hospital visit	Practical gifts (pajamas, sheets, towels, money), fruit (but make sure the patient can eat it) , flowers (avoid potted plants and white flowers)
Wedding 結婚祝い (いわ)	to the couple	before the wedding ceremony or at the reception	¥20,000-100, 000. Avoid using the numbers 4 and 9; 8 is considered a good number
Getting a Job しゅうしょく祝い (いわ)	to someone who has just gotten a new job	when informed about the new job	Practical gift that can be used at the job (pen, tie, etc)
Graduation 卒業祝い (いわ)	to the graduate	around the time of graduation	Practical gift for future use (worth ¥3,000-10,000); if graduate is getting a job or going to another school you do not need to give a graduation gift.

文法

I. Using verbs of giving and receiving

Japanese has two sets of verbs for giving, 下さる／くれる and あげる／差し上げる／やる, and one set for receiving, いただく／もらう. Each set contains two or more verbs. The usage of these verbs is determined by the social relationships among giver, recipient, and speaker.

A. Using the verbs of giving 下さる and くれる

The first group of verbs of giving, くれる and 下さる, is used when the recipient is the speaker or a member of the speaker's in-group (someone close to the speaker such as a family member or close friend). The giver can be anyone except the speaker. The honorific verb 下さる should be used when the giver is a member of the speaker's out-group and is socially superior to the speaker. Otherwise, use くれる. くれる is normally used among family members. The social relationships involved are depicted by the following diagram:

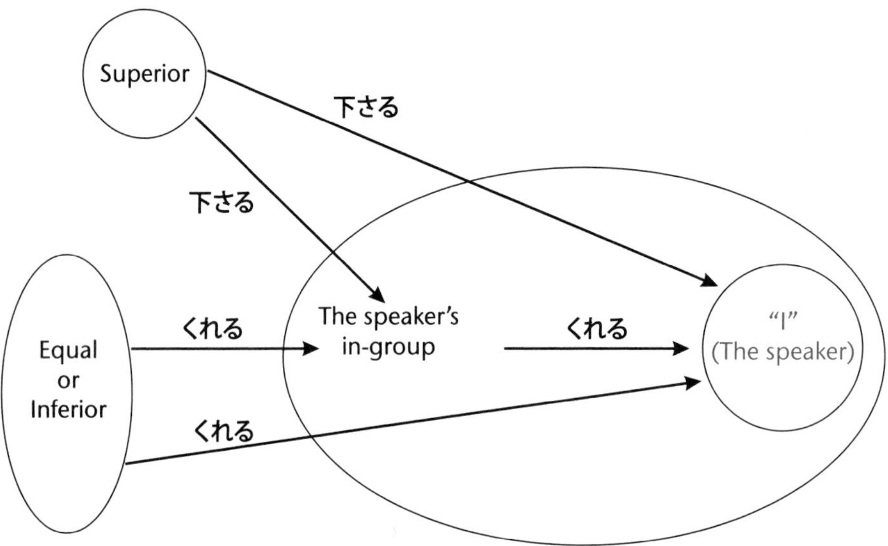

The recipient of a gift is the indirect object and is marked by the particle に, so the sentence structure is "Gift giver は recipient に Xを 下さる／くれる."

橋本先生は	私に	辞書を下さいました。	*Professor Hashimoto gave me a dictionary.*
そのおじいさんは	弟に	お菓子を下さいました。	*The elderly man gave my younger brother some sweets.*
上田さんのお父さんが	私に	人形を下さいました。	*Ms. Ueda's father gave me a doll.*
その子は	私に	フルーツをくれた。	*The child gave me some fruit.*
花子さんは	妹に	おもちゃをくれました。	*Hanako gave my younger sister a toy.*
母は	私に	洋服をくれました。	*My mother gave me clothes.*

くれる is a る-verb and 下さる is a う-verb. The polite present form of 下さる is 下さいます, not 下さります.

Dictionary form	Plain negative form	Polite affirmative form	Conditional form	Volitional form	て -form
下さる	下さらない	下さいます	下されば	下さろう	下さって
くれる	くれない	くれます	くれれば	くれよう	くれて

近所(きんじょ)の人：かわいいぬいぐるみね。 *What a cute stuffed animal!*
子供：おばあちゃんがくれたの。 *My grandmother gave her to me.*

花田(はなだ)：いい腕(うで)時計ですね。 *That's a nice watch.*
寺山(てらやま)：先輩(せんぱい)が結婚祝(いわ)いに下さったんです。 *My senior at college gave it to me as a wedding gift.*

NOTE

- The polite request ～を下さい (*please give me~*) is an extension of the use of 下さる.

B. Using verbs of giving 差(さ)し上げる / あげる / やる

The second group of verbs of giving, 差(さ)し上げる, あげる, and やる are used when the recipient is not a member of the speaker's in-group. The giver can be anyone. The verbs 差(さ)し上げる, あげる, and やる are used when the giver is the speaker. The humble verb, 差(さ)し上げる, is used if the recipient is socially superior to the speaker and is a member of the recipient's out-group. This might include professors, bosses, or older acquaintances. The verb やる is used if the recipient is socially inferior to the speaker. It includes mainly animals, plants, and one's family members. Otherwise あげる is used. The diagram below shows these relationships.

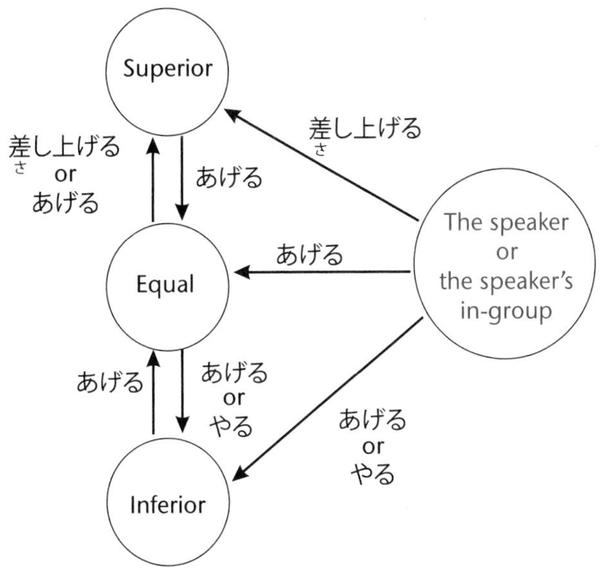

私は 高校の時の先生に お中元(ちゅうげん)を 差(さ)し上げた。	*I respectfully gave an* **ochugen** *gift to my high school teacher.*
母は 父の会社の上司(じょうし)に おせいぼを 差(さ)し上げました。	*My mother gave my father's boss an* **oseibo**.
私は 山田さんに 子犬(こいぬ)を あげた。	*I gave a puppy to Mr. Yamada.*
姉は 近所(きんじょ)のおばさんに はちうえの花(はな)を あげました。	*My sister gave a neighbor a flowering potted plant.*
キムさんは 後輩(こうはい)に ＤＶＤを あげました。	*Ms. Kim gave her junior a DVD.*
私は 花(はな)に 水を やった。	*I watered a flower. (literally: I gave water to a flower.)*
母は 子ねこに えさを やった。	*My mother gave some food to the kitten.*

差(さ)し上げる and あげる are る -verbs, and やる is an う -verb. They conjugate as follows:

Dictionary form	Plain negative form	Polite affirmative form	Conditional form	Volitional form	て -form
差(さ)し上げる	差(さ)し上げない	差(さ)し上げます	差(さ)し上げれば	差(さ)し上げよう	差(さ)し上げて
あげる	あげない	あげます	あげれば	あげよう	あげて
やる	やらない	やります	やれば	やろう	やって

けんじ： ねえ、母の日にお母さんに何かあげる？
Hey, are you going to give something to your mother on Mother's Day?

アリス： そうね。私はいつもカーネーションをあげるんだけど。ケンはどうする？
Well, I always give her carnations. What about you, Ken?

けんじ： そうだなあ。花(はな)より、あまい物か洋服(ようふく)かな。
Well, I might give (my mother) some sweets or clothes instead of flowers.

山本：	お中元(ちゅうげん)はもう送りましたか。	*Have you sent* **ochuugen** *yet?*
石川(いしかわ)：	ええ、橋本(はしもと)先生に送りました。	*Yes, I have sent one to Professor Hashimoto.*
山本：	何にしたんですか。	*What did you send?*
石川(いしかわ)：	ハムを差(さ)し上げました。	*I gave him a ham.*

Notes

- If both the giver and the recipient are members of the speaker's in-group, あげる or やる can be used more or less interchangeably with くれる. The use of くれる implies that the speaker feels closer to the recipient than to the giver and thus presents the recipient's point of view, while the use of あげる or やる implies that the speaker feels closer to the giver than to the recipient, or is at a neutral distance between them.

母が弟にお土産(みやげ)をくれた。

My mother gave my brother some souvenirs. (The speaker identifies with his brother.)

母が弟にお土産(みやげ)をあげた。

My mother gave my brother some souvenirs. (The speaker is neutral or identifies with his mother.)

- The diagram below shows these relationships.

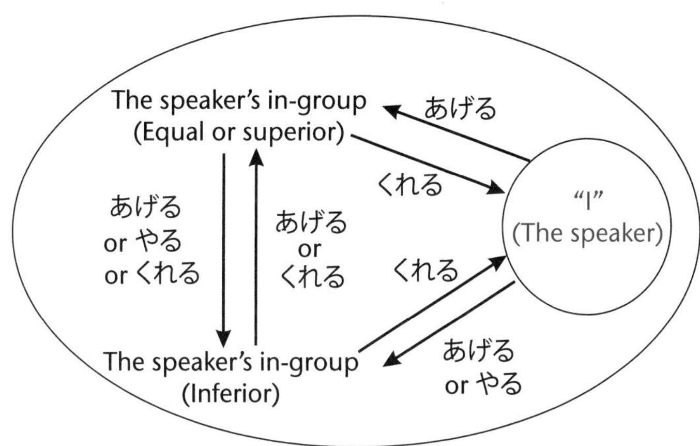

C. Using the verbs of receiving もらう and いただく

Both もらう and いただく mean to receive. They are used when the recipient is the subject of the sentence. It is important to remember that the giver cannot be the speaker, but the recipient can be anyone. The choice between もらう and いただく depends on the social relationships among the giver, recipient, and speaker. If the giver is socially superior to both speaker and recipient, use いただく. Otherwise, use もらう. The giver is marked by the particle に or から. The particle に indicates the source from which the gift originates.

兄は	先生に／から	カードを	いただいた。	*My older brother received a card from his teacher.*
私は	上司(じょうし)に／から	結婚祝(いわ)いを	いただきました。	*I received a wedding gift from my boss.*
私は	同僚(どうりょう)に／から	結婚祝(いわ)いを	もらいました。	*I received a wedding gift from my coworker.*
私は	部下(ぶか)に／から	結婚祝(いわ)いを	もらいました。	*I received a wedding gift from my subordinate.*
田中さんは	かれに	バラの花(はな)を	もらいました。	*Ms. Tanaka received a rose from her boyfriend.*
妹は	父に	人形(にんぎょう)を	もらいました。	*My younger sister received a doll from our father.*

In cases where the giver is an institution such as 大学 rather than a human being, the particle から must be used; the use of に implies that the speaker feels close to the giver.

上田さんは	大学から	メールをもらった。	*Ms. Ueda received an e-mail from the university.*
上田さんは	お母さんに	メールをもらった。	*Ms. Ueda received an e-mail from her mother.*

Both もらう and いただく are う-verbs and are conjugated as shown below. Before beginning to eat, Japanese people say いただきます (*I humbly receive*). This expression comes from the verb いただく.

Dictionary form	Plain negative form	Polite affirmative form	Conditional form	Volitional form	て -form
いただく	いただかない	いただきます	いただけば	いただこう	いただいて
もらう	もらわない	もらいます	もらえば	もらおう	もらって

話してみましょう

Activity 1 The following chart shows several gift exchanges between different people. You are the speaker. Describe each exchange using 下さる or くれる .

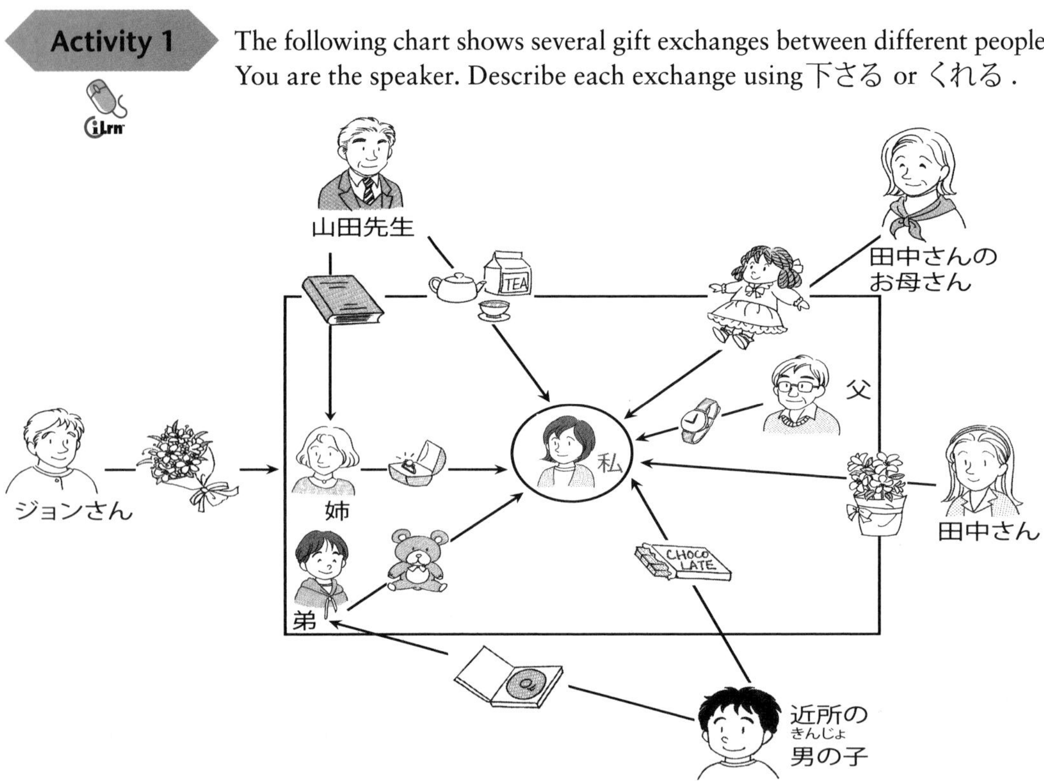

Example: 姉は私に指輪をくれました。

Activity 2 Express the same gift exchanges using the verbs of receiving いただく or もらう .

Example: 私は姉に指輪をもらいました。

Activity 3

The following chart illustrates gift exchanges among people. You are the speaker. Describe each exchange using 差し上げる, あげる , or やる .

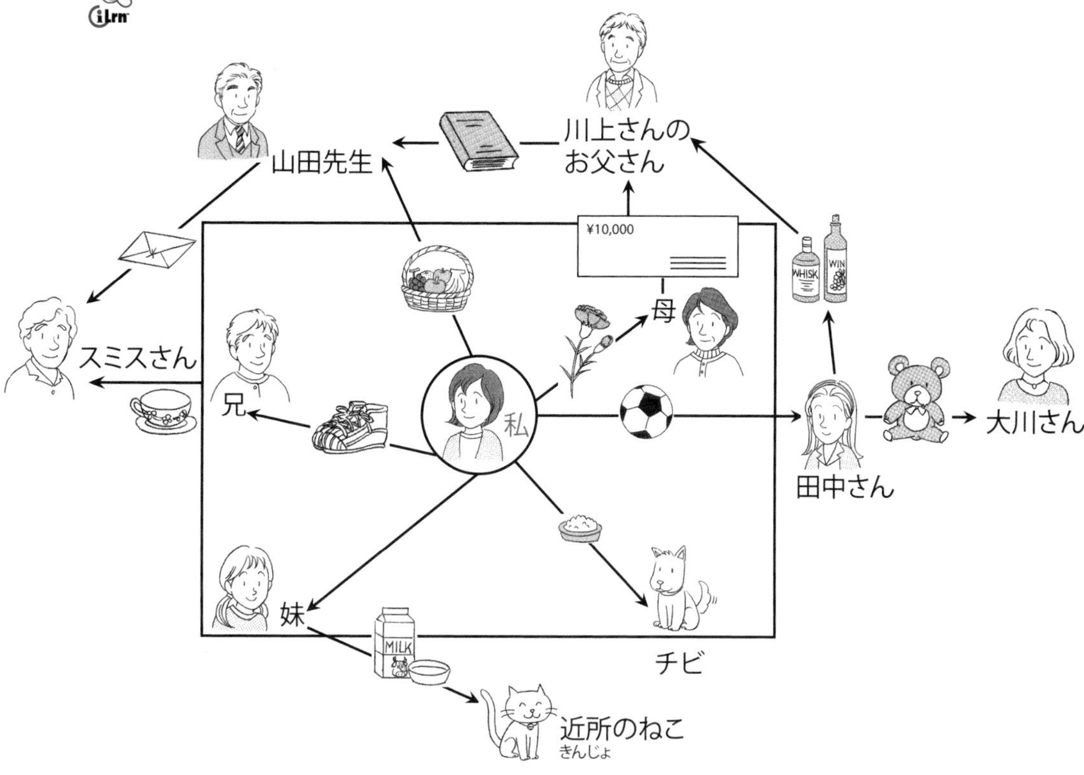

Example: 私は田中さんにサッカーボールをあげました。

Activity 4

Express the same gift exchanges as in Activity 3 using the verbs of receiving. Identify which exchanges cannot be expressed with a verb of receiving.

Example: 田中さんは大川さんにぬいぐるみをあげました。
大川さんは田中さんにぬいぐるみをもらいました。

Activity 5

Work with a partner. The two of you want to jointly give a gift on the occasions in the following table. Discuss what to give and why it will be an appropriate gift. Use casual speech.

Example:
A: 病気のお見舞(みま)いに何あげたらいいと思う？
B: そうね。スイーツはどう？
A: でも、食べられなかったら、どうする？
B: そうだね。じゃあ、雑誌(ざっし)はどう？　病院の生活(かつ)、つまらないし。
A: いいね。そうしよう。

Occasion	贈(おく)り物
病気のお見舞(みま)い	
先生の誕(たん)生日	
近所(きんじょ)の子供の入学祝(いわ)い	
大切(たいせつ)な友達の卒業祝(いわ)い	
母の日	
父の日	
バレンタインデー	

Activity 6

Work with a partner. Ask your partner what kinds of gifts he or she has received on the occasions noted in the table, and from whom. Use verbs of receiving and casual speech.

Example: A: 誕(たん)生日にだれかにプレゼントもらった？
B: うん、父に自転車(じてんしゃ)をもらった。それから、友達に置物(おきもの)をもらったよ。
A: それはよかったね。

	くれた人	くれたもの
誕(たん)生日		
クリスマス		
バレンタインデー		

II. Expressing the fact that something is easy or hard to do using the stem of the verb + やすい／にくい

やすい and にくい are い-adjectives that are combined with verbs to indicate that an act is easy or hard to perform. Both やすい and にくい immediately follow the polite stem of the verb. For example, the stem of 食べます is 食べ, so 食べやすい means *easy to eat* and 食べにくい *means hard to eat*. Similarly, the stem of 飲みます is 飲み, so 飲みやすい means *easy to drink* and 飲みにくい means *hard to drink*. The subject of the sentence is the item or person that the speaker feels is easy or hard to deal with.

この腕(うで)時計は	見やすいです。	*This wristwatch is easy to read.*
このおさけは	飲みやすいです。	*This sake is easy to drink.*
このくつは	歩きやすいね。	*These shoes are easy to walk in.*
橋本(はしもと)先生は	話しやすい先生です。	*Professor Hashimoto is an easy teacher to talk with.*

この大きさは	持ちやすいです。	*This size is easy to hold.*
この明るさは	見やすいですね。	*This brightness is easy to see.*
このコーヒーカップは	持ちにくいですね。	*This coffee cup is hard to hold.*
このいすの高さは	すわりにくいです。	*The height of this chair makes it difficult to sit in.*
日本では大きい動物(どうぶつ)は	かいにくいですね。	*Large animals are hard to raise* (as pets) *in Japan.*
この食器(しょっき)は	使(つか)いにくいと思います。	*I think this dish is difficult to use.*

話してみましょう

Activity 1 Look at the pictures and describe the objects using 〜やすい and 〜にくい.

Example: このハンバーガーは食べにくいです。

Activity 2

Work with a partner. Choose a word from the box below and explain in what way it can be easy or hard, but do not use the word itself. Your partner will try to guess which word you selected. Take turns. Once each word has been identified, see if you can make a sentence contrasting the item with an opposite, as in the example. Work through as many words as you can in five minutes.

Example: A: これは食べやすいです。

B: サンドイッチですか。

A: ええ、そうです。

<u>サンドイッチは食べやすいですが、とうふは食べにくいです。</u>

サンドイッチ　うどん　つめたいスープ　あついスープ　やきゅうのボール
りょうのベッド　日本語の文法　先生の話　日本の車　子ねこ　英語の辞(じ)書
着物　Tシャツ　携帯(けいたい)電話　バラの花(はな)　日本語の小説(しょうせつ)
スタバ（スターバックス）のコーヒーカップ

Activity 3

Work with a partner. Following the example, create a conversation between a customer and a store clerk, based on the pictures numbered 1–4 below. Use ～すぎる and ～やすい／にくい.

Example

1

2

3

4

Example: A: いかがでしょうか。

B: ちょっと大きすぎて、歩きにくいですね。もっと小さいのはありませんか。

A: では、こちらはいかがでしょう。

B: あ、この大きさだと、歩きやすいですね。

Activity 4

Work with a partner. Ask your partner what kinds of things he/she prefers to receive. Your partner responds using ～やすい.

Example: A: パソコンをもらうなら、どんなのがいい？

B: 使いやすくて、持ちやすいのがいいね。

1. パソコン
2. タオル
3. ワイングラス
4. おもちゃ
5. ペット
6. 花(はな)
7. お菓子(かし)／スイーツ
8. 置物(おきもの)

Activity 5

Work with a partner. You want to buy gifts for the following occasions. Ask your partner for suggestions. He or she will make suggestions based on the ease or difficulty of doing something.

Example: A: 友達の結婚祝(いわ)いに何かあげようと思うんですが、何がいいと思いますか。

B: 使(つか)いやすい物がいいですね。

A: じゃあ、食器(しょっき)はどうですか。

B: ああ、それはいいですね。

1. 友達／結婚祝(いわ)い
2. 先生／お中元(ちゅうげん)
3. 会社の同僚(どうりょう)／お土産(みやげ)
4. 近所(きんじょ)の子供／クリスマス
5. 会社の上司(じょうし)／お見舞(みま)い
6. お父さん／父の日
7. 友達／結婚祝(いわ)いのおかえし

III. Listing actions and states, and implying a reason, using the plain form + し

The connective particle し lists two or more mutually compatible states or facts. It can be used to list characteristics or factors that lead to a result or conclusion. The use of し is similar in some respects to the て-form, but し conveys more of a sense of making a list than て. The て-form can be used to connect states, and also to express a chronological sequence leading to a conclusion. On the other hand, the use of し suggests states that are being listed in no particular order.

A. Listing actions and states

スミスさんはやさしいし、きれいだし、 親切です。 *Ms. Smith is gentle, pretty, and kind as well.*

この石鹸(せっけん)は 安いし、使(つか)いやすいです。 *This soap is inexpensive and easy to use.*

この子ねこは元気がないし、いつも寝ています。 *This kitten is not lively and always sleeps.*

ねこもかっているし、犬(いぬ)もかっている。 *I keep a cat and dog.*

私はおさけも飲まないし、たばこもすいません。 *I don't drink, nor do I smoke.*

お見舞(みま)いに上司(じょうし)から花(はな)をいただいたし、同僚(どうりょう)からフルーツももらった。
When I was sick, I received flowers from my boss and fruit from my colleagues.

映画のチケットは買えなかったし、電車にもおくれたし、いやな一日だった。
It was a bad day because I couldn't buy a ticket for the movie, and I was late for the train.

し is preceded by the plain form of verbs and adjectives, which may be in the affirmative, negative, present tense, or past tense form.

		Present		Past	
		Affirmative	**Negative**	**Affirmative**	**Negative**
Copula verbs	お礼(れい)だ (*thank-you gift*)	お礼(れい)だし	お礼(れい)じゃないし	お礼(れい)だったし	お礼(れい)じゃなかったし
な -adjectives	大切(たいせつ)な (*precious*)	大切(たいせつ)だし	大切(たいせつ)じゃないし	大切(たいせつ)だったし	大切(たいせつ)じゃなかったし
い -adjectives	いい	いいし	よくないし	よかったし	よくなかったし
Verbs	つつむ (*to wrap*)	つつむし	つつまないし	つつんだし	つつまなかったし

し can be used to imply a reason instead of explicitly stating one.

母の日だし、今日は家でごはんを食べます。 *It's Mother's Day, so I'll eat at home today.* (indirect)

母の日だから、今日家でごはんを食べます。 *Because it's Mother's Day, I'll eat at home today.* (direct)

ペットもかいたいし、プライバシーも大事だし、アパートより家の方がいいよ。
I want to have a pet, and privacy is important, so I prefer a house to an apartment.

トム： この絵(え)、好きなんでしょ。どうして買わないの？
Why don't you buy this picture? You like it, right?

キム： でも、今あまりお金がないし。
But I don't have much money, so . . . (usage is more indirect than から *or* ので .)

Note:

- The particle も often appears with し to reinforce the meaning of し. It does not change the essential meaning.

  雨もふっているし、今日は家にいます。

  It's raining, so I'll stay home today. (stronger)

話してみましょう

Activity 1 Combine the following sentences using 〜し.

Example: スミスさんは明るいです。それに、スミスさんは親切です。ですから、スミスさんはたくさん友達がいます。

スミスさんは明るいし、親切だから、たくさん友達がいます。

1. キムさんが好きです。キムさんはバレンタインデーにチョコレートをくれました。ホワイトデー (*White Day*) にケーキをあげようと思います。
2. そのおじいさんと話したことがありません。いつも一人でさびしそうです。今度会ったら、話そうと思います。
3. 先生があまり好きじゃありません。授業もおもしろくありません。ですから、もう授業に行かないつもりです。
4. プレゼントをつつみました。リボンもかけました。カードを書いたらあげられます。
5. まどはしめました。かぎもかけました。ですから、もう出かけられます。
6. 大学の時、先生にとてもお世話(せわ)になりました。今でも時々先生に会いに行きます。けっこん式に先生をよぶつもりです。
7. 道子さんは動(どう)物が好きです。犬(いぬ)をかいたがっています。子犬(こいぬ)をあげたらいいと思います。
8. 父は、誕(たん)生日に何もくれませんでした。いつもあまりやさしくありません。好きじゃありません。

Activity 2 Work with a partner. Below there are three choices each for apartments, tours, and restaurants. Select one choice from each group. Your partner will ask what you have chosen and why. Respond to him or her using 〜し.

Example: A: どうしてアパートAをえらんだんですか。

B: このアパートは安いし、あまり古くないからです。

アパートA	駅から歩いて20分	1 DK	30,000円	築(ちく)三年
アパートB	駅から歩いて１０分	2 LDK	78,000円	築(ちく)一年
アパートC	駅から歩いて１５分	2 LDK	50,000円	築(ちく)十年

築(ちく)〜年 indicates how old the building is.

ツアー A	一泊二日	京都	食事あり	六万五千円
ツアー B	四泊五日	京都と大阪	食事なし	十万円
ツアー C	五泊六日	京都となら	食事なし	七万円

Note that ありmeans ある and なし means ない.

レストラン A	イタリアりょうり	4, 000 円から	ライブあり	バイキング (*buffet*) なし
レストラン B	メキシコりょうり	2, 000 円から	ライブなし	ランチバイキングあり
レストラン C	スペインりょうり	5, 000 円から	ライブなし	日曜日バイキングあり

Note that ライブ means *live music*.

Activity 3

Work with the class. Ask your classmates what they want to receive from their parents for their birthdays and why. Then report the results to the class.

Example: A: お誕生日にご両親からどんな物をもらいたいですか。

B: そうですね。動物が好きだし、アパートもひろいので、子犬をもらいたいです。

A: そうですか。いいですね。

名前	もらいたい物	どうして

IV. Trying something, using ～てみる

The て-form of the verb + みる is used to indicate that the speaker has done something on a trial basis (or experimentally) to see what the result would be. In this usage, みる is written in **hiragana**.

いただいたワイングラスを使ってみました。 *I tried using the wine glass that I received as a gift.* (lit.: *I used the wine glass to see what it was like.*)

この小説読んでみたらどう。 *How about trying this novel?*

日本の着物を着てみたいです。 *I want to try wearing a Japanese kimono.*

山田：このハム、おいしそうね。食べてみてもいい？ *This ham looks good. Can I try some?*

キム：いいよ。どうぞ。 *Sure. Here you go.*

山本：動(どう)物をかってみたいんだ。 *I'd like to keep an animal* (to see what it's like).

パク：ぼくもかってみたいね。 *I would like to keep one, too.*

話してみましょう

Activity 1 Answer the following questions using 〜てみたい.

Example: A: 日本へ行ったことがありますか。

B: いいえ、行ってみたいけど、行ったことはありません。

1. おすしを作ったことがありますか。
2. 日本人形(にんぎょう)をもらったことがありますか。
3. 日本に手紙を送ったことがありますか。
4. ライオン (*lion*) にえさをやったことがありますか。
5. バレンタインデーに女の人からチョコレートをもらったことがありますか。
6. 温泉(せん)に入ったことがありますか。
7. 日本のお菓子(かし)を食べたことがありますか。

Activity 2 Work as a class. Ask your classmates what they want to learn or try to do and why. Then determine what the common interests are among your classmates. Write the information down in a table.

Example: A: 〜さんはどんなことがしてみたいですか。

B: そうですね。外国に住んだことがないし、外国語も勉強したいから留学してみたいですね。

A: そうですか。

B: 〜さんは、どんなことがしてみたいですか。

A: 私は〜てみたいです。

名前	すること

Activity 3

Work with a partner. Ask your partner what he or she would like to do if he or she were a different sex or animal, and complete the chart.

Example: A: 女だったら、どんなことがしてみたいですか。

B: そうですね。ドレスがきてみたいですね。

~たら	してみたいこと
男／女	
先生の上司(じょうし)	
犬(いぬ)	
スーパーマン	

Activity 4

Work as a class. Ask your classmates whether they have ever done the things described in the following chart. If a person has performed one of the actions, write his or her name on the line at the bottom of the appropriate square below. If he or she has not, then ask whether or not he or she is interested in trying the action. Question each classmate until you receive an affirmative response, then move to the next action with a different classmate. This is a bingo game, so the first person to complete an entire row, an entire column, or a diagonal line with names is the winner.

Example: A: 日本の会社で仕事したことある？

B: いや、ないよ。

A: してみたいと思う？

B: うん、してみたいね。 or いや、してみたくないね。

日本の会社で仕事をする ______	日本のスイーツを食べる ______	飛行機(き)に乗る ______	子ねこをかう ______	自分(じぶん)の音楽(おんがく)のＤＶＤを作る ______
日本人と住む ______	たばこをすう ______	日本の学校に行く ______	スペイン語を勉強する ______	ゴルフをする ______
先生の仕事を手伝(てつだ)う ______	ハワイに行く ______	バラの花をもらう ______	日本で勉強する ______	先輩(せんぱい)の家に行く ______
おすしを作る ______	小説(しょうせつ)を書く ______	父の日にお父さんと旅行する ______	大学院に行く ______	日本のおさけを飲む ______
英語を教える ______	日本語でノートをとる ______	日本人形(にんぎょう)を買う ______	日本のうたをうたう ______	かぶきを見に行く ______

V. Quoting speech and words, using ～という

In Chapter 12 of *Nakama 1*, you learned that the plain form of verbs + そうだ expresses hearsay, as in 本屋はこの先にあるそうです。(*I hear that the bookstore is straight ahead*). This chapter introduces another form of reported speech using the quotation marker と. The particle と indicates that the preceding clause is a quoted clause or phrase. There are four usages of という, some of which have already been introduced.

A. Using direct quotes with と言う , ~ *say "~"*

In direct quotes, what was actually said is quoted without modification and placed inside the quotation marks「 and 」.

スミスさんは「すみません。」と言いました。 *Mr. Smith said, "I'm sorry."*

キムさんは「自分でえらんだんだ。」と言った。 *Mr. Kim said, "I chose it myself."*

アリス：山田さんは鈴木さんに何て言ったの。 *What did Mr. Yamada say to Ms. Suzuki?*
道子：「好きだ。」って言ったのよ。 *He said," I love you."*
アリス：それで、鈴木さんは何て言ったの。 *Then, what did Ms. Suzuki say?*
道子：「ごめんなさい。」って言ったのよ。 *She said," I'm sorry."* (This is a polite way of saying *no* in this situation.)

B. Using indirect quote X は （Y に） Clause (plain form) と言う , *X says* (tells Y) *that ~*

With indirect quotes, what is quoted is expressed in the clause preceding と, which ends with a plain form, and the typical final particles such as よ and ね are deleted at the end of the sentence. In colloquial speech, the particle と is often replaced by って. In a question, 何て is pronounced なんて.

スミスさんは　すまないと言いました。 *Mr. Smith said that he was sorry.*

キムさんは　自分でえらんだと言った。 *Mr. Kim said he chose it himself.*

山田さんは鈴木さんに　好きだと言った。 *Mr. Yamada told Ms. Suzuki that he loves her.*

上司は部下に部下のレポートは役にたつと言ったが、同僚は役にたたなかったと言った。
The boss told his subordinate that his report was useful, but the subordinate's co-worker said that it wasn't.

To quote a question, use 聞く instead of 言う in an indirect quote. To quote an answer, either 答える or 言う can be used. The plain present affirmative form of the copula verb だ must be deleted before the question particle か.

その写真は大切なのかと聞きました。 *I asked if the photograph is important.*

そのハムは安いと答えました。 *I answered that the ham is inexpensive.*

その雑誌(ざっし)はおもしろかったと答えました。 *I answered that the magazine was interesting.*

その音楽(おんがく)はきれいだと答えました。 *I answered that the music is beautiful.*

川口：絵美(えみ)さんは、田中さんは明日来るかどうか聞いていました。
Emi was asking me whether you (Mr. Tanaka) *are coming tomorrow.*

田中：ああ、明日は来ないと言って下さい。
Oh, yeah, tell her that I am not coming tomorrow.

田中：絵美(えみ)さんは、あの人はだれかと聞きました。 *Emi asked who that person is.*

川口：石田さんはキムさんだと言いました。 *Mr. Ishida said it was Mr. Kim.*

キム：田中さんに上司(じょうし)のお中元(ちゅうげん)は何にしたのって聞いたの。
I asked Ms. Tanaka what she got for a mid-season gift for the boss.

サム：そう。で、田中さん何て答えた？
I see. Then what did she say?

キム：タオルと石鹸(せっけん)のセットをえらんだって言ってたよ。
She said that she chose a towel-and-soap set.

Notes

- ～か（どうか）, introduced in Chapter 4 of *Nakama 2*, is a type of indirect quote because a question is embedded in the structure.
- The use of 言いました merely reports the fact that something was said, while 言っていました tends to emphasize the content of what was said. The form 言っています also focuses on the content, but it implies that the original statement has not been recognized by the listener or it has not been realized. The form 言います is used to quote words spoken habitually, or to indicate a future action. The tenses of the quoted clause and the main clause do not have to agree.

  スミスさんは、パソコンは使(つか)わないと<u>言いました</u>。
  Ms. Smith <u>said</u> she would not use a personal computer.

  スミスさんは、パソコンは使(つか)わないと<u>言っていました</u>。
  Ms. Smith <u>was saying</u> she would not use a personal computer.

  スミスさんは、パソコンは使(つか)わなかったと<u>言っています</u>。
  Ms. Smith <u>says</u> she did not use a personal computer .

  日本人はよく贈(おく)り物(もの)をすると<u>言います</u>。
  It <u>is said</u> that the Japanese often exchange gifts.

  明日近所(きんじょ)のおばあさんに電話をかけて、その子ねこを下さいと<u>言います</u>。
  I'll call the elderly woman in the neighborhood tomorrow and <u>say</u> that I want her to give me the kitten.

- When the particle と is replaced by って in colloquial speech, the verb 言う can be deleted if the subject of 言う is not used.

川口さんは、おさけは飲まないって。
I heard that Mr. Kawaguchi does not drink sake. (lit.: *Someone said that Mr. Kawaguchi does not drink sake.*)

C. X を Y という, *call X Y*

This usage was introduced in Chapter 1 of *Nakama 1* in the phrase 〜は日本語で〜と言います, but it can be used in a variety of sentences as shown below.

Personal computer は日本語でパソコンと言います。 *A personal computer is called* pasokon *in Japanese.*

日本人は personal computer をパソコンと言います。 *The Japanese call a personal computer* pasokon.

日本語ではこれをパソコンと言いますが、英語では personal computer と言います。
This is called pasokon *in Japanese, but it is called a* personal computer *in English.*

山田さんの名前はさとしと言います。 *Yamada-san's first name is Satoshi.*

(Looking at Japanese quotation marks, 「　」)
チェ：これを／は何と言いますか。 *What are these called?*
大木：かぎかっこと言います。 *We call these* kagikakko.

Notes

- Use とよぶ when you state the name of something you have named, such as a dog's name.

  鈴木さんはその子犬をラッキーとよんでいる。
  Mr. Suzuki calls the puppy "Lucky."

  アリスはこの子ねこをミッキーってよんでるんだ。
  Alice calls this kitten "Mickey."
- To ask a question about how to pronounce unknown characters, use 読む instead of 言う.

  (Mr. Brown is asking about the **kanji** compound 自転車.)

  ブラウン：この漢字は何と読みますか。 *How do you read these* kanji?
  山田：「じてんしゃ」と読みます。 *They are read as* jitensha.

  (A girl is asking her elder sister about a label in the box witten as お中元.)

  妹：お姉ちゃん、これ何て読むの。
  How do you read this?
  姉：ああ、これ、「おちゅうげん」って読むの。
  This is read as ochuugen.

D. X という Y, *Y called X*

In the expression X という Y, the noun *Y* indicates a general category such as person, place, school, name, etc., and the noun *X* indicates a specific instance of *Y*. In this usage, という is usually written in **hiragana** instead of **kanji**.

東京(きょう)大学という大学	*a university called the University of Tokyo*
スミソニアンという博(はく)物館	*a museum called the Smithsonian*
ウォンバットという動(どう)物	*an animal called a wombat*
バラという花(はな)	*a flower called rose*
まぐろというさかな	*a kind of fish called tuna*
This is it という DVD	*a DVD called* This is it

チケットぴあというサイトで、コンサートのチケットが買えますよ。
You can purchase concert tickets at a website called Ticket Pia (tikettopia).

山田っていう人が来たよ。　*A person called Yamada came by.*

青田：こけしという日本の人形(にんぎょう)を知っていますか。
Do you know a type of Japanese doll called kokeshi?
パク：いいえ、知りません。
No, I don't.

話してみましょう

Activity 1 Use the form ～という to ask whether someone knows about the following places and things. Use both casual and polite speech.

Example: 山田さん
山田さんという人を知っていますか。／山田さんって人、知ってる。

1. デニーズ
2. SONY
3. カーネーション
4. ペプシ
5. シーズー (*Shih Tzu*)
6. ブラジル
7. ハイアット
8. ラッコ (*sea otter*)

Activity 2 Work as a class. When you travel overseas, knowing some basic phrases in the language of the country can come in handy. Choose three expressions from the box and ask how they are said in other languages.

こんにちは　さようなら　はじめまして　すみません　お元気ですか　ありがとう

Example: A: ～さんはフランス語が分かりますか。
B: ええ、分かりますよ。
or いいえ、分かりません。
A: フランス語では「こんにちは」って何と言いますか。
or そうですか。失礼(しつれい)しました。(*Excuse me*)
B: 「Bonjour」と言います。

日本語			
ドイツ語			
中国語			
韓(かん)国語			
スペイン語			
フランス語			

Activity 3

You are thinking of going on a trip to Japan for two weeks and are gathering some information. Your friends say the following. Confirm the information using indirect quotes. Use both casual and polite speech.

Example: 飛行機(き)は ANA がいいよ。(ANA refers to All Nippon Airways.)
飛行機(き)は ANA がいいと聞きましたが、本当ですか。

1. お中元(ちゅうげん)は七月に送ります。
2. 日本では、結婚祝(いわ)いにナイフを送ってはいけません。
3. 病気のお見(み)舞(ま)いにお金をあげてもいいです。
4. 日本の携帯(けいたい)電話の方がアメリカの携帯(けいたい)電話より便利(り)です。
5. 東京にはドルが使(つか)える店があります。
6. 日本のペットショップはとても高いです。
7. 入学祝(いわ)いをもらったら、おかえしに何かあげなければなりません。

Activity 4

Work with a partner. The following street signs are used in Japan. Guess the meanings of the signs, using the example conversation as a model.

Example: A: 一番はどんな意味だと思う?
B: 郵便局って意味だと思うけど、どう?
A: うん、私もそう思う。

1

2

3

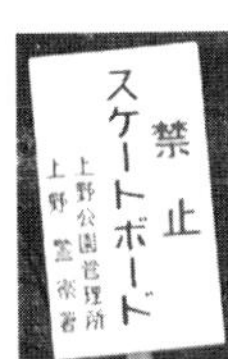

4

5

6

7

Activity 5

Work with a partner. Sit back-to-back and think of four questions about your partner's gift exchanging experience. Then ask the questions and have your partner restate them to you for confirmation. Your partner should then answer each question, and you should restate the answer for confirmation. Use both casual and polite speech.

Example:
A: 先生にお中元(ちゅうげん)をあげたことがありますか。
B: 先生にお中元(ちゅうげん)をあげたことがあるかって聞きましたか。
A: ええ、聞きました。
B: ありますよ。
A: あると答えましたね。
B: ええ、答えました。

聞く練習

上手な聞き方

Shadowing and concentrating

Listening requires a lot of concentration. If you don't pay attention to what you are hearing, you can lose information very quickly. One way to improve your listening ability is to engage in shadowing. Shadowing is a technique used to train simultaneous interpreters. This technique is found to improve both speaking and listening skills among foreign language learners because it helps them to process information faster. Shadowing also requires a lot of concentration, so it helps learners to sustain their attention to speech.

To practice shadowing, you need a relatively easy audio-recorded story. As soon as you hear the sentence, start repeating it without waiting to hear the end of the sentence. Repeat this process two or three times. You will have to pay attention to incoming words while processing the meaning of the sentence. This sounds rather difficult, and it is indeed difficult for someone who has never practiced shadowing or someone with relatively low proficiency. So, it is easier to practice shadowing with a transcript. As you become more accustomed to the practice, try to do the shadowing without a transcript. The text should be relatively short and easy, to minimize frustration.

Listen to the following stories to practice shadowing. If you would like a transcript, request one from your instructor.

1. Text 1
2. Text 2

いつどこで何がありましたか。

聞く前に

A. Listen to each short statement and write the name of the giver, receiver, and the gift.

Example: You hear: 父は私にお金をくれた。

Giver 父 Receiver 私 Gift お金

1. Giver ____________ Receiver ____________ Gift ____________
2. Giver ____________ Receiver ____________ Gift ____________
3. Giver ____________ Receiver ____________ Gift ____________
4. Giver ____________ Receiver ____________ Gift ____________
5. Giver ____________ Receiver ____________ Gift ____________
6. Giver ____________ Receiver ____________ Gift ____________
7. Giver ____________ Receiver ____________ Gift ____________

B. Describe what people in your country do on Christmas Day.

聞いた後で

iLrn Self-Tests

A. 上田さんと石田さんがクリスマスについて話をしています。 会話をよく聞いて何について話しているか、分かったことを書いてみて下さい。

B. もう一度会話を聞いて、質問に答えて下さい。

1. 石田さんによると、日本ではクリスマスにはどんなことをしますか。
2. アリスさんの家族はクリスマスによくどんなことをしますか。
3. 石田さんとアリスさんは今年のクリスマスに何をしましたか。
4. アリスさんはだれから何をもらいましたか。
5. アリスさんはだれかに何かをあげましたか。石田さんはどうですか。

C. Write a description of the most important holiday season for your family, explaining the activities that you and your family enjoy, the guests you often invite (if any), and what kinds of gifts you exchange.

D. Work with a partner. Ask your partner about the most important holiday season for his or her family. Ask him or her what his or her family does together, whether they invite friends and relatives (親戚(しんせき)), whether they exchange any gifts with each other, and what kinds of gifts have been exchanged in the past.

聞き上手話し上手

贈(おく)り物(もの)をあげたりもらったりする時に使(つか)う言葉

Phrases used when giving or receiving gifts

When a Japanese person offers a gift, he or she often uses a set phrase. In formal situations, the most common phrase is これ、つまらないものですが、どうぞ. つまらない means *worthless* or *uninteresting* and the entire phrase means *this is a thing of little worth, but please* (accept it). This expression is used even if the gift is a very valuable one. Some people choose to use other expressions, such as お好きだとよろしいのですが (*I hope this will be to your liking*), and お礼(れい)にと思いまして (*I thought I would make this a token of my appreciation*), even in formal situations. In casual situations, a simple phrase like これ、〜です。どうぞ is used.

Casual　　これ、お土産(みやげ) / お祝(いわ)いです。どうぞ。
　　　　　これ、ケーキです。みなさんでどうぞ。
　　　　　これ、母が送ってきたんです。少しですが、どうぞ。

Very casual　　これ、お土産(みやげ) / お祝(いわ)い。どうぞ。
　　　　　これ、ケーキ。みんなで食べて。
　　　　　これ、母が送ってきたの。少しだけど、どうぞ。

It is very common for the recipient of a gift to show hesitation when accepting it. This does not mean that he or she does not want the gift. Instead, hesitation indicates modesty on the part of the recipient. For example, in the following exchange, Tanaka-san says そんなしんぱいしないで下さい (*Don't go to so much trouble*) to show his hesitation.

スミス：これ、ハワイからのお土産(みやげ)です。どうぞ。
田中：そんなしんぱいしないで下さい。
スミス：いいえ、ほんの気持ちですから。 *This is a token of my appreciation.*
田中：そうですか。じゃあ、すみません。

Other phrases used to express hesitation are:

Very formal　　お気を使(つか)わせてしまいまして、もうしわけありません。
　　　　　Oh, you shouldn't have gone to so much trouble for us. That's really good of you.
　　　　　そんなお気を使(つか)わないで下さい。　*Please don't go to so much trouble.*

Formal　　あまり気を使(つか)わないで下さい。　*Please don't put yourself out for me.*
　　　　　しんぱいしないで下さい。

Casual　　そんな気を使(つか)わないで。
　　　　　そんなしんぱいしないで。

After the recipient shows hesitation, the giver can use phrases such as the following:

Very formal	ほんの気持ちですから。	*Just a token of my appreciation*
	本当につまらないものですから。	*This really is a thing of little worth.*
Formal	ほんの気持ちですから。	
	たいしたものじゃありませんから。	*It is of little value.*
	ほんの少しですから。	*It's not such a big deal.*
Casual	気持ちだから。	
	たいしたものじゃないし。	

Then the recipient will usually accept the gift by saying そうですか。じゃあ、いただきます (*Is that so? Then I will humbly receive it*) , すみませんね。 ありがとう(ございます) (*Thank you so much for your trouble*).

A. Act out the following gift exchanges.

1. A: あのう、これつまらないものですが、どうぞ。お礼(れい)にと思いまして。
B: そんな、お気を使(つか)わないで下さい。
A: いいえ、ほんの気持ちですから。
B: そうですか。じゃあ、いただきます。

2. A: あのう、これ、クッキーです。みなさんでどうぞ。
B: すみませんね。でも、しんぱいしないで下さい。
A: いいえ、たいしたものじゃありませんから。
B: そうですか。じゃあ、ありがとうございます。

B. Act out the above conversations using casual speech.

C. Work with a partner. Role-play various gift-giving situations with your partner.

漢字

送りがな Okurigana

Okurigana was introduced briefly in Chapter 9 of *Nakama 1*. **Okurigana** allows for many semantically related words with different pronunciation to be distinguished from one another. It also indicates that some words are derived from others.

The rules for **okurigana** are complex and there are many exceptions. The following are the basic guidelines set by the Japanese government in 1973.

Principle 1 — Use **okurigana** for inflected forms of words that conjugate, such as verbs and adjectives
Examples: 書く　話す　高い　and 大切(たいせつ)な

1-1. If the stem of an い -adjective ends with し, begin okurigana with し. Examples: 新しい and 楽(たの)しい.

1-2. If the stem of a な -adjective contains か, やか, or らか, begin okurigana with か, やか, or らか, respectively.
Examples: 静(しず)かだ・穏(おだ)やかだ (*calm*) 明(あき)らかだ (*obvious*)

1-3. The following are some of the exceptions:
味(あじ)わう (*to taste*) 悲(かな)しむ (*to feel sad*) 異(こと)なる (*to differ*) 明るい 危(あぶ)ない (*dangerous*) 大きい 少ない 小さい 冷たい 同じだ 幸(しあわ)せだ (*happy*)

Principle 2 Use the same **okurigana** for verbs and adjectives, with contrastive or related words, and with words containing a noun.

2-1. Transitive and intransitive verbs
動(うご)かす・動(うご)く 起こす・起きる 上がる・上げる

2-2. Adjectives and adverbs that contain the stem of the shortest words.
重(おも)たい・重(おも)い (*heavy*) 柔(やわ)らかい ・柔(やわ)らかだ (*soft*) 古(ふる)めかしい・ (*old-fashioned*)・古(ふる)い

2-3. Words that contain a noun
汗(あせ)ばむ (*to sweat*)・汗(あせ) (*sweat*) 男らしい (*manly*)・男

Principle 3 Do not use **okurigana** for nouns unless they are derived from verbs and adjectives or from the Japanese number series.
Example: 花(はな) 山 川 vs. 大きさ 高さ and 一つ 二つ

Principle 4 If a noun is derived from a verb or an adjective, use the same **okurigana** convention for the original word.
Example: 〜行き 近く 晴れ 大きさ

Principle 5 Use **okurigan**a for the last morae for adverbs and connectives.
Example: 必(かなら)ず (*for sure*) 少し 全(まった)く (*not at all*)

Principle 6 In the case of compound words, follow the rule for each of the combined words.

6-1. Compound verbs and adjectives.
申(もう)し込(こ)む 書き直(なお)す (*to rewrite*) 女々(めめ)しい (*wimpy*)

6-2. Compound nouns
落書(らくが)き (*graffiti*) 押(お)し入れ (*closet*) 教え子(ご) (*pupil*) 生(い)き物(もの) (*living being*) 行き帰り 長生(ながい)き (*longevity*) 早起(はやお)き (*early riser*)

Principle 7 Do not use **okurigana** for the following types of compound words.

7-1. Conventionally used without **furigana** in certain fields such as occupations, job titles, postal terms.
関取(せきとり) (*sumo wrestler*) 頭取(とうどり) (*bank president*) 切手 小包(こづつみ) 切符(ぷ)

7-2. Idiomatic compounds
日付(ひづけ) (*date*) 物置(ものおき) (*storage*) 建物(たて) 受付(うけつけ)

Flashcards

犬	dog	いぬ　ケン	家に犬(いぬ)がいます。　かわいい子犬(こいぬ)です。
花	flower	はな　カ	母の日の花(はな)はカーネーションです。　生け花(いばな)
形	shape, form	かたち　ケイ・ギョウ	日本人形(にんぎょう)
服	clothes, dress	フク	洋服(ようふく)　紳士服(しんしふく)　婦人服(ふじんふく)
辞	word, to resign	や(める)　ジ	お礼(れい)に辞書(じしょ)をあげました。
礼	courtesy	レイ	お礼(れい)にと思いまして。
祝	to celebrate, congratulate	いわ(う)　シュク	これはお祝(いわ)いです。
誕	birth	タン	誕(たん)生日のお祝(いわ)い
自	self	みずか(ら)　ジ・シ	自転車(じてんしゃ)　自分(じぶん)　自転車(じてんしゃ)を運転(うんてん)する
転	to roll over, to fall down	ころ(がる)・ころ(ぶ)　テン	自転車(じてんしゃ)に乗る。
運	to carry, luck	はこ(ぶ)　ウン	毎日運動(うんどう)します。　運転免許証(うんてんめんきょしょう)

動	to move	うご(く)　ドウ	手の運動(うんどう)　動物園(どうぶつえん)　足が動(うご)かない
使	to use	つか(う)　シ	大使館(たいし)　気を使(つか)う。　車を使(つか)う。
写	to photograph, to copy	うつ(す)　シャ	古い写真(しゃしん)がたくさんあります。
真	truth, exactly	ま　シン	写真(しゃしん)　真(ま)っすぐ　真(ま)ん中
絵	picture	エ・カイ	ピカソの絵(え)を買いました。
雑	miscellany	ザツ	これは日本の雑誌(ざっし)みたいですね。
誌	chronicle, magazine	シ	この雑誌(ざっし)はおもしろいですよ。
音	sound	おと　オン	日本の音楽(おんがく)
楽	music, to enjoy	たの(しむ)　ガク・ラク	音楽(おんがく)は楽(たの)しいです。
世	world, reign, age	セ・セイ	犬(いぬ)の世話(せわ)をします。
取	to take	と(る)　シュ	日本語の授業を取(と)りたいと思っています。

読めるようになった漢字

犬　子犬　花　人形　洋(よう)服　婦(ふ)人服　紳士(しんし)服　辞書　お礼　失(しつ)礼　お祝い
誕生日　自動車　自転車　自分　運動　運転　動物園　動く　使う　大使館
写真　絵　雑誌　音楽　楽しい　世話　取る お中元　大切な

練習

Read the following sentences aloud.

1. 誕生日のお祝いに、辞書と自転車をもらいましたから、お礼を言いました。
2. 動物園には犬はいません。
3. どんな音楽が好きですか。
4. この雑誌は絵や写真が多いですね。
5. 動物の世話は大変ですが、花の世話も大変です。
6. その洋服を取って下さい。
7. これは中国にある日本大使館の写真です。
8. 自動車の運転は上手ですか。

読む練習

上手な読み方

Making strategic inferences

Vocabulary knowledge is known to be the most significant factor for reading development, and language learners tend to learn vocabulary from reading. It is not beneficial to look up every unknown word you encounter while reading because it can disrupt the flow of reading. So, when you encounter an unknown word, the first thing to do is ignore it and keep reading. If the word is important, it will likely show up again. You may then be able to guess the meaning of the word from the context. If that doesn't work, figure out whether the unknown word is a noun, verb, adjective, etc. Then try to determine the general type or meaning of the word (e.g., an action) from the immediate context. Think about a possible word meaning and see if it works in context. If the sentence make sense, continue reading. Alternatively, if you wish to confirm the meaning at this point, look it up in a dictionary to see how well you have guessed.

練習

Read the following text and underline the unknown words. Try to guess the meaning of each word, using the strategies described above. Then check the meanings in a dictionary.

日本ではフォーマルな場面(ばめん)で、人の家を訪(たず)ねる時、いろいろなマナーがあります。まず、冬の寒い日はコートを着ていてもいいですが、そうではない時は、ドアのチャイムを押(お)す前にコートは脱(ぬ)がなければなりません。、チャイムがない家では、ドアの前で「ごめん下さい」と言います。ドアが開(あ)いたら、中に入って、後ろを向かないでドアを閉めます。そして、靴を脱ぐ前に、あいさつをします。「上がって下さい」と言われたら、靴を脱いで、完全に後ろを向かないようにすわり、靴の先をドアの方に向けて、端の方におきます。

贈り物のマナー The etiquette of giving and receiving gifts

読む前に

下の質問に答えて下さい。

1. あなたの国ではどんな時に贈り物をしますか。
2. 結婚祝いやしゅうしょく祝いにはどんな物をあげますか。
3. あげてはいけない物はありますか。
4. 贈り物をする時、何と言いますか。
5. 贈り物をもらう時、何と言いますか。
6. 贈り物をもらった後で、よく何をしますか。

言葉のリスト

〜によって	depending on ~	お返し（かえ）	reciprocation, return gift
仲（なか）	relationship, terms	包丁（ほうちょう）	kitchen knife
お葬式（そうしき）	funeral	値段（ねだん）	price
宗教（しゅうきょう）	religion		

Read the following passage and write, on a separate sheet of paper, the things you have to be careful about when you give or receive gifts in Japan.

日本では、贈り物をあげる時には、いろいろなマナーがあります。まず、贈り物の目的によって、あげてもいい物とあげてはいけない物があります。例えば、包丁は何かを切る物なので、結婚する二人の仲を切るという意味になりますから、結婚のお祝いにあげてはいけません。

つぎに、贈り物をもらう人がどんな人かよく知っていなければなりません。例えば、お葬式に花を贈る時にはもらう人の宗教によって、贈ってもいい花と贈ってはいけない花があります。それから、子供が多い人に何かあげる時は、たくさんある物がいいのです。

また、贈り物によってはいつあげるか決まっているものがあります。例えば、お中元は七月始めから八月十五日までに、お歳暮は十二月十日ごろから十二月三十一日までにあげなければなりません。

そしてによくお中元やお歳暮はデパートから送りますが、果物や肉など悪くなりやすい食べ物をあげる時は、いつごろ着くか電話しておきます。

それから、贈(おく)り物をもらう時にも色々なマナーがあります。まず、贈(おく)り物をくれた人がよく知っている人でなければ、その人の前で贈(おく)り物を開(あ)けてはいけません。そして、贈(おく)り物をもらったらすぐ電話か手紙でお礼を言います。最後(さいご)に、お祝いをもらったら、お返(かえ)しをしなければなりません。お返(かえ)しのためには、たいていもらったものの半分ぐらいの値段(ねだん)の物をあげます。日本では色々な時に贈(おく)り物をしますが、マナーがとても難(むずか)しいので、よく分からない時は日本人の友達に聞いたほうがいいでしょう。分かりましたか。

読んだ後で

A. Circle はい if the statement is true and いいえ if it isn't.

1. はい　いいえ　結婚式にあげてはいけない物はない。

2. はい　いいえ　お葬式(そうしき)には花をおくってはいけない。

3. はい　いいえ　子供がいる人にはたくさんある物をあげた方がいい。

4. はい　いいえ　あまり知らない人からプレゼントをもらったら、その人のでプレゼントをあけない方がいい。

B. 質問に答えて下さい。

1. 包丁(ほうちょう)にはどんな意味がありますか。

2. 食べ物をデパートから送る時、だれに電話をした方がいいのですか。

3. お返(かえ)しをする時、どんな物をあげるといいですか。

C. The reading that begins on page 302 can be divided into two major parts. Where is the division between them?

D. The first part identified in Activity C consists of more than one paragraph, and several transition words are used to signal the organization of paragraphs or sentences. Underline the words and write an outline for this part.

E. Work in groups of four. Discuss the similarities and differences in the etiquette of gift giving and receiving between your country and Japan.

F. When you receive a gift, it's a good idea to write a thank-you note. As with other letters, a thank-you note starts with a brief greeting. This is followed by an expression of thanks and a comment about the gift. Read the following letter, and identify (1) the initial greeting, (2) the expression of thanks, (3) the gift that the writer has received and her comments about it, and (4) the final closing phrase.

毎日寒いですが、お元気ですか。昨日はとてもかわいいクリスマスプレゼントをどうもありがとうございました。私はぬいぐるみが大好きなので、とてもうれしかったです。大切にします。それでは、いいお年をおむかえ下さい。みなさんによろしく。

十二月三十日

スーザン

G. Imagine that you received a new Japanese dictionary from your Japanese host family. Use the letter format in Activity B to write a thank-you note.

総合(そうごう)練習

どんなプレゼントがいいですか。

Work in groups of four. Discuss what kinds of gifts would be appropriate for each situation described below. Think of as many possibilities as you can.

Case 1: 来年一年間日本に留学します。日本ではホストファミリーと一緒(しょ)に住む予定です。ホストファミリーにはまだ会ったことがありませんが、四十五さいのお父さんと四十二さいのお母さんと中学生の女の子と十さいの男の子と七十さいのおばあさんがいます。ホストファミリーにどんな物をあげたらいいでしょうか。

Case 2: 私は今、日本の会社ではたらいています。今度の休みには二週間ぐらいアメリカに帰るつもりです。日本人は旅行に行くと、会社の人や近所の人にお土産(みやげ)をよく買うそうですね。でも、私は会社の人や近所の人にお土産(みやげ)を買ったことがないので、何をあげたらいいかよく分かりません。

Case 3: 今までお世話になった先生が、学校をやめるそうです。 クラスで何か先生にお礼をしたいと思いますが、どんなものを差(さ)しあげたらいいでしょうか。

ロールプレイ

1. You are in Japan. You want to give an **oseibo** gift to your professor, but you don't know what is appropriate. Ask a friend for suggestions.
2. Your friend took care of you when you were sick, so you want to express your gratitude by doing something for him or her. Thank him or her and offer some help or a gift.
3. You invited a Japanese friend home to spend winter vacation with your family. Your friend wants to bring a gift. Talk about your family and their favorite things and offer some suggestions.
4. You teach English to a Japanese child. Her mother has given you a rather expensive gift in addition to the tutoring fee. You feel a little uneasy about it but don't want to be rude to the mother. Ask your friend what you should do.
5. You are at a department store. You want to give a shirt to your Japanese friend on her birthday, but she is very petite and you cannot find anything small enough to fit her. Ask a clerk for help.

Chapter 7

第七課（だいなな か）

Stuart West - StockFood Munich

料理（りょうり）
Cooking

Objectives		Explaining procedures, explaining important points
Vocabulary		Ingredients for cooking, cooking expressions, kitchen equipment
Dialogue		まきずしの作り方
Japanese Culture		Food culture in Japan, convenience stores, vending machines
Grammar	I.	Expressing the performance of two actions simultaneously using ～ながら
	II.	Expressing the idea of *without doing* ~ using ～ないで
	III.	Expressing an open hypothetical condition using the ば conditional form
	IV.	Expressing possibility and capability using the dictionary form of the verb + ことが出来る
	V.	Using question word + でも～ affirmative form
Listening		Understanding signaling devices used in instructions
Communication		Giving instructions
Kanji		Statistical facts about **kanji** and learning tips 料 理 飯 野 菜 魚 鳥 肉 止 始 終 洗 悪 黒 白 赤 茶 短 長 次 焼
Reading		Understanding the characteristics of written instructions, えびだんご shrimp dumplings

Chapter Resources

- www.cengagebrain.com
- iLrn™ Heinle Learning Center
- Audio Program

単語(たんご)

Flashcards

Nouns

あじ	味	taste, あじをみる check the taste
いちご	苺	strawberry
おおさじ	大さじ	tablespoon
オーブン		oven
えび／エビ	海老	shrimp,　えびだんご shrimp dumplings
カップ		cup, けいりょうカップ measuring cup
かに／カニ	蟹	crab
キャベツ		cabbage
ぎゅうにく	牛肉	beef
きゅうり		cucumber
グラム		gram
こさじ	小さじ	teaspoon
こしょう		pepper (spice)
(お) こめ	(お) 米	uncooked rice
コーンスターチ		cornstarch
こむぎこ	小麦粉	flour
ざいりょう	材料	material(s), ingredient(s)
さとう	砂糖	sugar
(お) さら	皿	plate
サラダゆ／サラダあぶら	サラダ油	vegetable oil (lit. salad oil)
しお	塩	salt
じゃがいも		potato
ジャム		jam
しょうゆ	しょう油	soy sauce
す	酢	vinegar
すいはんき	炊飯器	rice cooker
スプーン		spoon
ソース		sauce
だし		broth
たまねぎ	玉ねぎ	onion
ちゃわん	茶碗	rice bowl

でんしレンジ	電子レンジ	microwave oven
とりにく	鶏肉／鳥肉	chicken (meat)
ドレッシング		(salad) dressing
ナイフ		knife
ねぎ		green onion
のり	海苔	seaweed
なべ	鍋	pot
はし	箸	chopstick(s)
バター		butter
ひ	火	fire
フォーク		fork
ぶたにく	豚肉	pork
フライパン		frying pan, skillet
ボウル		mixing bowl
ほうちょう	包丁	butcher knife, kitchen knife
ほうれんそう	ほうれん草	spinach
マヨネーズ		mayonnaise
ミキサー		(electric) mixer
みそ	味噌	soybean paste

う -verbs

あらう	洗う	to wash
たく	炊く	to cook, ごはんをたく to cook rice
たす	足す	to add, to make up (for a deficit)
やく	焼く	to bake, to fry, to grill
やる		to do
むす	蒸す	to steam

る -verbs

あげる	揚げる	to deep-fry
あたためる	温める	to heat up
いためる	炒める	to stir-fry, sauté (cooking)
かける		to pour
くわえる	加える	to add (an ingredient)
つける	漬ける・浸ける	to dip, to soak, to pickle
にる	煮る	to boil; to stew

まぜる	混ぜる	to mix
ゆでる	茹でる	to boil, to poach

い -adjectives

うすい	薄い	thin, あじがうすい to have little taste
こい	濃い	thick, あじがこい to have a strong taste

な -adjectives

てきとう（な）	適当（な）	appropriate

Adverbs

すこしずつ	少しずつ	little by little

Conjunctions

さいごに	最後に	lastly, at last, finally

単語(たん)の練習

A. 料理(りょうり)の材料(ざいりょう)　Ingredients for cooking

鶏肉(とりにく)／鳥肉(とりにく) chicken	豚肉(ぶたにく) pork	牛肉(ぎゅうにく) beef	海老(えび) shrimp	かに crab	のり seaweed
きゅうり cucumber	たまねぎ onion	ねぎ green onion	ほうれんそう spinach	だし broth, stock	いちご strawberry
じゃがいも potato	キャベツ cabbage	こめ uncooked rice	ジャム jam	バター butter	マヨネーズ mayonnaise
さとう sugar	しお salt	こしょう black pepper	しょうゆ soy sauce	す vinegar	味噌(みそ) soybean paste
ソース sauce	ドレッシング dressing	サラダ油(ゆ/あぶら) vegetable oil	小麦粉(こむぎこ) flour	コーンスターチ cornstarch	

おぼえていますか。

お茶(ちゃ)　オレンジ　果物(くだ)　紅茶(こうちゃ)　コーラ　魚(さかな)　ジュース　たまご　トマト　肉(にく)　人参(じん)
バナナ　ビール　水　ミルク　野菜(やさい)　りんご　レタス　ワイン　アイスクリーム　あぶら
イタリア料理(りょうり)　うどん　(お)さしみ　(お)すし　(お)ゆ　カレーライス　クッキー
ケーキ　サラダ　サンドイッチ　スープ　ステーキ　スパゲティ　ランチセット　そば
チーズ　チキン　チャーハン　中華料理(かりょうり)　チョコレート　定食　デザート　天ぷら
トースト　パン　ハンバーガー　ビーフ　ピザ　フライドチキン　ポーク　洋食
ラーメン　ライス　和食(わ)

温(あたた)かい　あつい　あまい　かたい　からい　しょっぱい　すっぱい　冷たい　にがい
やわらかい

Activity 1 Guess the meaning of the following words

トマトソース　チーズソース　チーズケーキ　クリームソース　りんごす
フレンチドレッシング　しょうゆドレッシング　赤(あか)ワイン　白(しろ)ワイン

Activity 2 質問に日本語で答えて下さい。

1. 308ページの料理(りょうり)の材料(ざいりょう)の言葉の中で野菜(やさい)はどれですか。肉(にく)はどれですか。果物(くだ)はどれですか。
2. 日本料理(りょうり)ではどんな材料(ざいりょう)をよく使いますか。中華料理(かりょうり)ではどうですか。アメリカの料理(りょうり)はどうですか。
3. 体にいいものはどれですか。体によくないものはどれですか。
4. 日本人がよく食べるものはどれですか。
5. 下の料理(りょうり)の材料(ざいりょう)を言って下さい。知らない言葉は先生に聞いて下さい。

   カレー　サラダ　ハンバーガー　ピザ　トースト　サンドイッチ
   チーズケーキ　バナナケーキ　バーベキュー (*barbecue*)

Supplementary Vocabulary 料理(りょうり)の材料(ざいりょう) Other ingredients

いか		squid, calamari
はまぐり	蛤	clam
たこ		octopus
たい	鯛	red snapper
まぐろ	鮪	tuna
ひきにく	挽肉	ground meat, ぎゅうひき肉　ground beef
むねにく	胸肉	breast meat
ももにく	もも肉	(chicken) thigh
さやえんどう		snow pea
しいたけ	椎茸	shiitake mushroom
ようなし	洋梨	pears (Asian pears are called なし)
パイナップル		pineapple
まめ	豆	beans
ブロッコリー		broccoli

カリフラワー		cauliflower
だいこん	大根	daikon radish
とうもろこし		corn
パセリ		parsley
ウスターソース		Worcestershire sauce
オリーブゆ	オリーブ油	olive oil
ケチャップ		ketchup
スパイス		spice
みりん	味醂	sweet rice wine for cooking
バルサミコす	バルサミコ酢	balsamic vinegar
かんづめ	缶詰	canned food
パンこ	パン粉	bread crumbs
はくりきこ	薄力粉	cake flour
きょうりきこ	強力粉	bread flour
ベーキングパウダー		baking powder
なまクリーム	生クリーム	whipping cream

B. 料理(りょうり)をする時の言葉

味(あじ)	taste	味(あじ)がこい	strong taste
味(あじ)がうすい	weak taste	洗(あら)う	to wash
ご飯(はん)をたく	to cook rice	ご飯(はん)がたける	rice is cooked
焼(や)く	to bake, to fry, to grill	いためる	to stir-fry, sauté
あげる	to deep-fry	ゆでる	to poach, to boil
にる	to stew, to boil, to simmer	むす	to steam
まぜる	to mix	温(あたた)める	to warm up, to reheat
かける	to pour over	つける	to dip, to soak
くわえる	to add (an ingredient)	足(た)す	to add to make up (for)

Notes

- ゆでる means to boil eggs, vegetables, or meat in water, but にる means to boil or stew in a broth, sauce, or soup.
- くわえる merely means to add something to something, but 足(た)す means to add something to make up for a deficiency. For example, if you have put salt in a soup but still don't think it is salty enough and need to add more, use しおを足(た)す. On the other hand, if you are boiling meat to make a stew and then add vegetables, use 野菜(やさい)をくわえる.
- Both 料理(りょうり)をする and 料理(りょうり)を作る refer to cooking, but they are not used in the the same way. 料理(りょうり)をする is usually used to express the action of cooking in general. On the other hand, 料理(りょうり)を作る is used to talk about cooking specific type of dishes. For example, use 料理(りょうり)をする to ask whether a person cooks at all, as in 料理(りょうり)をしますか. Use 料理(りょうり)を作る to ask what kind of dish a person makes, (どんな料理(りょうり)を作りますか。) and whether a person makes a specific type of dish (フランス料理(りょうり)を作りますか。).

おぼえていますか。

教える　わく　わかす　切る　つける　取る

Activity 3 Complete the following recipes by using the appropriate verb forms.

1. サラダを作る時は、野菜(やさい)をよく＿＿＿＿＿＿＿＿＿、ボウルに入れます。そして、ドレッシングを＿＿＿＿＿＿＿＿、よく＿＿＿＿＿＿＿下さい。
2. ステーキはよく＿＿＿＿＿＿＿＿＿＿方が好きだ。
3. スープの味(あじ)が＿＿＿＿時は、 だしを＿＿＿＿＿＿＿＿＿と、おいしくなる。
4. カレーライスを作る時は、牛肉(ぎゅうにく)とたまねぎを＿＿＿＿＿＿＿＿＿。そして、水を＿＿＿＿＿＿＿＿＿、一時間ぐらい＿＿＿＿＿＿＿＿＿＿。その後、カレーこ (*curry powder*) を＿＿＿＿＿＿＿＿＿＿。
5. 野菜(やさい)はいためるより＿＿＿＿＿＿＿＿＿方が体にいいです。
6. このスープは冷たいから、＿＿＿＿＿＿＿＿＿方がいいですね。
7. バーベキュー (*barbecue*) をする時は、肉(にく)をソースに1時間ぐらい＿＿＿＿＿＿＿＿＿とおいしいですよ。
8. 味(あじ)が＿＿＿＿＿から、もう少しさとうを＿＿＿＿＿＿＿＿＿みましょうか。

Activity 4

Work with a group. One person in the group should act out one of the verbs in B, and the rest of the group should try to guess which verb is being acted out. As soon as someone guesses the correct verb, the next person should act out another verb. Repeat this process as fast as you can until the group completes all the verbs.

Supplementary Vocabulary 料理(りょうり)をする時の言葉

Expressions used to talk about cooking

つよび	強火	high heat
ちゅうび	中火	medium heat
よわび	弱火	low heat
あえる	和える	to mix, to dress something with a sauce, dressing, etc.
あわだてる	泡立てる	to whip
いる	煎る	to roast
うつす	移す	to transfer
かきまぜる	かき混ぜる	to mix thoroughly, to beat
こねる		to knead
さます	冷ます	to let (something) cool
スイッチをいれる	スイッチを入れる	to turn on an electrical switch
とかす	溶かす	to (let something) thaw

とける	溶ける	(for something) to melt
ぬる	塗る	to spread, to paint
はかる	量る／計る	to measure, りょう (quantity) をはかる
はさむ	挟む	to pinch
ひからおろす	火から下ろす	to remove from heat
ひにかける	火にかける	to heat, to cook over heat
ひをおとす	火を落とす	to lower the heat
ふる	振る	to shake, しおをふる to salt
みずをきる	水を切る	to drain
まく	巻く	to roll (as with sushi in a roll)
まぶす		to sprinkle
むく	剥く	to peel, かわ (skin) をむく

C. 料理する時に使う物 Kitchen equipment

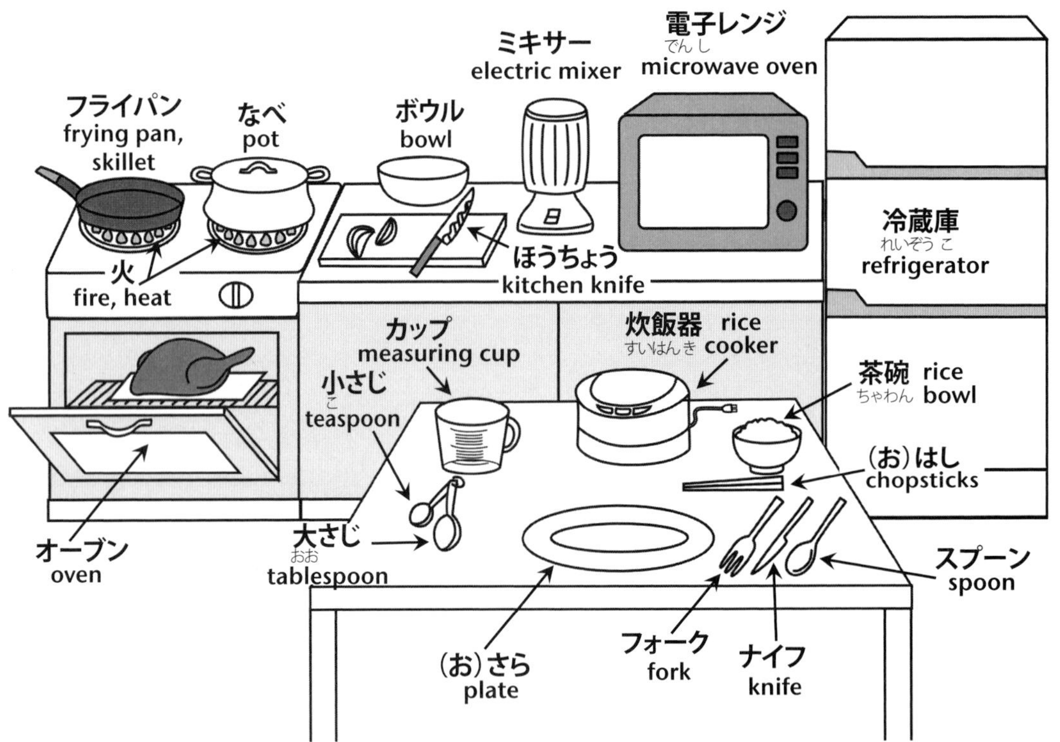

Activity 5 Based on the examples below, guess the reading and meaning of the following expressions.

Examples:	1カップ	いちカップ	one cup
	1／2カップ	にぶんのいちカップ	half a cup
	2／3カップ	さんぶんのにカップ	two thirds of a cup

1. 1／3カップ ________________ ________________
2. 1／4カップ ________________ ________________
3. 3／4カップ ________________ ________________

Activity 6 Name the items that fit the following descriptions.

1. 肉(にく)を焼(や)く時に使う物です。
2. サラダをまぜる時に使う物です。
3. 和(わ)食を食べる時に使う物です。
4. ステーキを食べる時に使う物ですが、ナイフではありません。
5. 炊飯器(すいはんき)やミキサーや電子(でんし)レンジについている物です。
6. ケーキやサンドイッチを乗せる物です。
7. 冷たい食べ物や飲み物を入れておく所です。
8. ご飯(はん)を食べる時にご飯(はん)を入れる物です。
9. 料理(りょうり)をするときに使う物です。これをつけたら、焼(や)いたり、いためたり、にたり出来ます。
10. 料理(りょうり)をするときに使う小さいスプーンで、大きいのと小さいのがあります。

Activity 7 Define the following objects using your own words.

1. ほうちょう ____________________
2. なべ ____________________
3. フライパン ____________________
4. スプーン ____________________
5. 炊飯器(すいはんき) ____________________
6. ミキサー ____________________
7. オーブン ____________________
8. 電子(でんし)レンジ ____________________

Supplementary Vocabulary 料理(りょうり)する時に使うほかの物
Additional kitchen equipment

さいばし	菜箸	long chopsticks (used in cooking, or in serving food at the table)
おたま	お玉	ladle
フライがえし	フライ返し	spatula
キッチンばさみ		kitchen scissors
タイマー		timer
はかり	秤	scale
やかん／ケトル		kettle
まないた	まな板	cutting board

ダイアローグ

はじめに

A. 質問に日本語で答えて下さい。

1. 和(わ)食のレストランに行ったことがありますか。
2. どんな日本料理(りょうり)を知っていますか。
3. どんな料理(りょうり)の作り方を知っていますか。

B. Look at the pictures below and do the following:

1. Identify the Japanese words for the cookware and kitchen utensils pictured. If you don't know the word, ask your teacher or look it up in the dialogue phrase notes.
2. Describe each picture.

Photos courtesy of the authors

まきずしの作り方 *How to make sushi rolls*

まきずし (*rolled sushi*) is a combination of the stem of the verb まく and the noun すし. Alice is interested in learning how to make まきずし. アリスが道子さんに話をしています。

上田：　ねえ、道子さん、 まきずし、作れる？

道子：　もちろん。

上田：　今度、留学生センターでパーティがあるから、まきずしを作ってみたいんだけど、作り方が分からないの。教えてくれない？

道子：　いいよ。じゃあ、明日、一緒(しょ)に作ってみようか。

上田：　ありがとう。たすかる。

つぎの日、アリスと道子さんはキッチンにいます。

道子：　まず、ご飯(はん)のたき方は知ってる？

上田：　うん。おこめを洗(あら)って、炊飯器(すいはんき)でたくんでしょ。

道子：　そうなんだけど、おすしの時は、少し水を少なくするのよ。後ですをくわえるから、少しかたい方がいいの。水が多いと、やわらかくなりすぎて、おいしくないから。

上田：　そうなんだ。

道子：　それから、おすしに入れる物を細長(ほそなが)く切っておくの。今日は、カリフォルニアまきだから、きゅうりとアボカド、切って。

上田：　分かった。で、おすしのすはどうやって作るの？

道子：　すしずね。かんたんよ。す大さじ６，さとう大さじ４、しお小さじ２をまぜるのよ。

上田：　どんなすでもいいの？

道子：　ううん。こめずって言うんだけど、おこめのすを使うの。

上田：　リンゴすやバルサミコすで作ることは出来ないの。

道子：　作ったことないから、おいしいかどうかよく分からない。今度作ってみればいいよ。

上田：　そうだね。

道子：　ご飯(はん)がたけたら、すしおけにご飯(はん)を入れるの。そして、うちわや扇風機(せんぷうき)でごはんを冷(さ)ましながら、すしずを少しずつまぜていくのよ。ほら、出来た。

上田：　じゃあ、どうやってまくの？

道子：　まず、まきすの上にのりを乗せて、

上田：　まきすって何？

道子： このたけのシートよ。

上田： あ、そうなんだ。

道子： のりの上にすし飯(めし)をひらたくのせるんだけど、むこうのはしまで、ご飯(はん)をのせないで、のりを少しのこしておくの。

上田： どうして？

道子： ご飯(はん)が先まであると、まけないのよ。ご飯(はん)の上にかにとアボカドときゅうりをのせて、こうやってまくの。

上田： 上手ね、道子さん。

道子： アリスもやってみる？

上田： うん、あ、でも、むずかしい？

道子： 少しおしながらまけば、きれいにまけるよ。

上田： 本当だ。あ、出来た。

道子： 出来たら、後は、てきとうな大きさに切るの。

上田： わかった。どうもありがとう。

Dialogue Phrase Notes

- まき means rolled まきずし means *rolled sushi*, and カリフォルニアまき means *California roll*.
- かんたん means *easy* or *simple*.
- ごはんがたける means *the rice is cooked*.
- リンゴす is apple vinegar, バルサミコす is balsamic vinegar.
- すしおけ is a special wooden bucket used to make sushi rice.
- すし飯(めし) is sushi rice.
- うちわ is a Japanese fan, and a 扇風機(せんぷうき) is an electric fan.
- 冷(さ)ます means *to let something cool down*.
- たけ is bamboo. たけのシート is a bamboo sheet.
- ひらたくのせる means *to spread*.
- のせる means *to put on*.
- はし is an *edge* or *end*.
- おす means to *press, push*. おしながらまく means *to roll while applying some pressure*.

ダイアローグの後で

A. 日本語で質問に答えて下さい。

1. すしずって何ですか。
2. こめずは何から作られますか。
3. まきすは何のために使いますか。どんな物ですか。
4. すしご飯(はん)（すし飯(めし)）をたく時、どんなことが大事ですか。
5. おすしをまく時、どうすれば上手にまくことが出来ますか。

B. Look at the pictures at the beginning of the dialogue section, which show the steps for making rolled sushi. Unscramble the pictures so that the steps are correctly shown by writing the sequence number in the box.

□ → □ → □ → □ → □ → □

C. Use these directions to try making まきずし and see if you are successful.

Heinze, Winfried - StockFood Munich

Making tekka-maki

日本の文化

日本の食文化　Food culture in Japan

The Japanese people are health conscious. According to the 2007 report by the Organization for Economic Cooperation and Development (OECD) only 3 percent of Japanese are obese. Obesity is considered a serious health problem. Partly for this reason, the amount of food served in Japanese restaurants is much less than that served in restaurants in the United States, a fact which may surprise some American visitors.

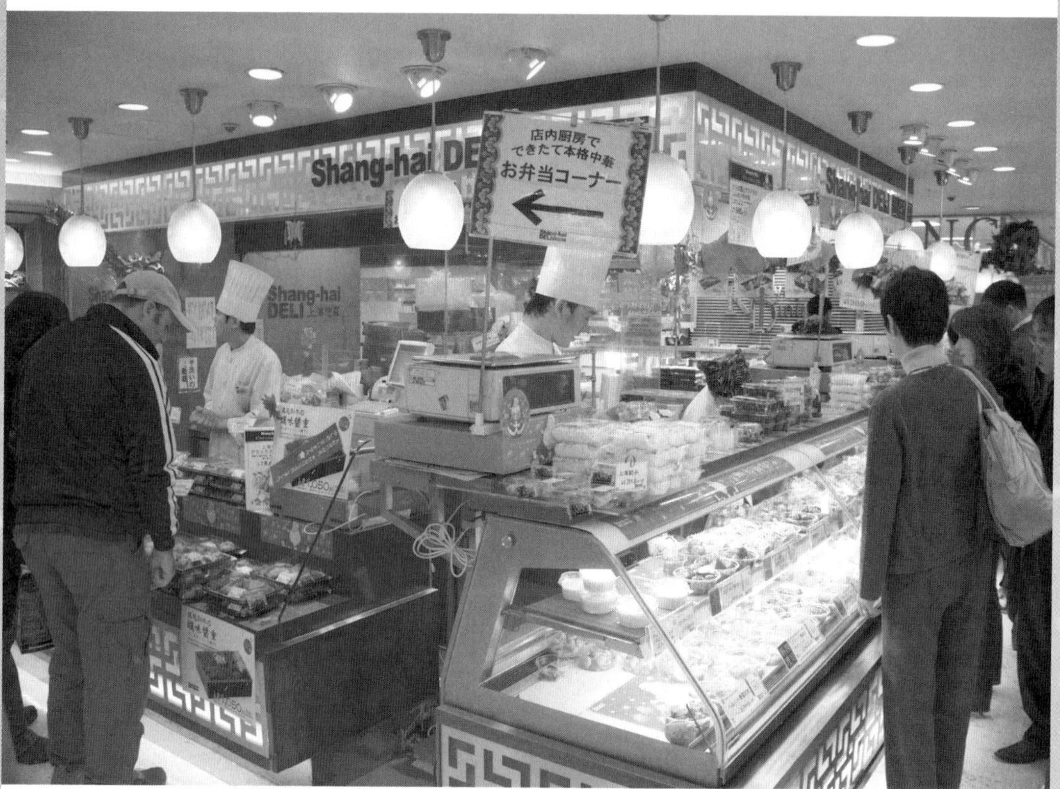

Andrew Holt / Alamy

The Japanese demand variety and quality over quantity, and they don't mind paying a high price for good food. For example, the tire company Michelin publishes gourmet restaurant guides for over 30 major cities including Paris, New York, San Francisco, and Hong Kong. Their 2009 Tokyo Guide lists more restaurants than any other city in the world.

Another characteristic of Japanese food culture is that restaurants and retail shops offer seasonal items. In the spring, many stores carry food items related to cherry blossoms, the national flower of Japan. These include cherry cookies, cherry buns, and cherry pastries. A variety of cold sweets and noodles are sold in the summer, and in the autumn, sweet items made from chestnuts and persimmons are very common. These items disappear as soon as the season is over.

The term デパ地下 is used for the basement floor of department stores, and refers to the stores' food departments. The デパ地下 is considered crucial to attract a large number of shoppers, so some department stores devote more than one floor to food.

One floor may be filled with gourmet sweets, snacks, expensive liquors, wines, or gourmet foods from around the world, while another may offer prepared food, side dishes and fruits, vegetables, and so on. In addition, department stores often offer food tasting and sales events in which a certain country, or city or region of Japan is featured. This is another way to attract a large number of customers.

コンビニ Convenience stores

Food items are usually delivered to convenience stores two to five times a day from factories, and items may change depending on the time of day. Because variety is important, these items may be sold for a couple of months and then replaced with new products. This is true even for bottled items, such as water, tea, coffee and juice. So even if you find a drink you like, there is no guarantee that it will be available for more than a year.

Rich Iwasaki / Alamy

自動販売機 (じどうはんばいき) Vending machines

Many different items are sold in vending machines in Japan. These include soda, beer, cigarettes, magazines, rice, and hot noodles, to name a few. There are large numbers of these machines in service 24 hours a day on street corners and in front of stores, and you can expect every one of them to be in good working order.

VisualJapan / Alamy

文法

I. Expressing the performance of two actions simultaneously using ～ながら

The ます-stem of verbs + ながら describes an action occurring simultaneously with another action. The actions in the ながら clause and in the main clause must be performed by the same person.

音楽を聞きながら、ご飯(はん)をたきます。 *I cook rice while listening to music.*

ソースをかけながら、まぜて下さい。 *Stir well while pouring the sauce.*

テレビを見ながら、ご飯(はん)を食べてはいけません。 *You shouldn't watch TV while eating.*

ワインをくわえながら、肉(にく)を焼(や)く。 *Fry the meat while adding wine.*

ゆみ：こんな所で何してるの？ *What are you doing here?*

さとる：田中さん、まってるんだ。 *Waiting for Mr. Tanaka.*

ゆみ：あ、そう。それで本、読んでるの？ *Oh, I see. So, you're reading a book?*

さとる：うん。ちょっと早く来たから、本、読みながら、まってるんだ。
Yes, I came here a bit early, so I'm waiting while reading.

	Dictionary form	ます -stem	～ながら
Irregular verb	する	します	しながら
る -verb	にる (*to stew, to simmer*)	にます	にながら
	あげる (*to deep-fry*)	あげます	あげながら
う -verb	洗(あら)う (*to wash*)	洗(あら)います	洗(あら)いながら
	足(た)す (*to add*)	足(た)します	足(た)しながら

来る is not normally used with ながら .

Note

- In this structure, the action expressed in the main clause is the main action, and it is accompanied by the secondary action described in the ながら clause. Thus, in the sentence コーヒーを飲みながら、話しましょう (*Let's talk over a cup of coffee*), the main action is talking, and the act of talking is done while the speaker is drinking coffee. The closest equivalent of ながら in English is while ～ ing, but in English the main action may be expressed in either the while clause or the main clause. For example, コーヒーを飲みながら、話しましょう can be translated as *let's talk while drinking a cup of coffee.* (The main action is expressed in the main clause, and the secondary action is expressed in the while clause.) It could also be translated as *let's have a cup of coffee while we talk*, where the main action appears in the while clause and the secondary action in the main clause. On the other hand, 話しながら、

食べてはいけない should be translated as *you must not talk while eating*. (The main action should be *eating*, but it is expressed in the while clause.)

話してみましょう

Activity 1 Complete the following sentences by choosing an appropriate phrase from the table below and using it with 〜ながら .

Example: お金がなかったから、アルバイトをしながら、学校に行きました。

なく	アルバイトをする	携帯(けいたい)電話で話す	本を読む	ノートをとる	下を見る
足(た)す	人に聞く	私の目を見る	地図を見る	タバコをすう	まぜる

1. マヨネーズを作る時は、____________________あぶらをくわえます。
2. ____________________歩いていたら、お金を見つけた。(*find*)
3. 行ったことがなかったので、____________________その店まで行った。
4. ____________________授業を受けた。
5. その人は____________________好きだと言った。
6. このケーキは____________________作ったんですが、あまり上手に出来ませんでした。
7. ____________________運転していたら、道を間違えた。
8. 少しずつさとうを____________________、味(あじ)を見ました。

Activity 2 Describe what the person is doing in the following pictures.

Activity 3

Work with a partner. Think of three sets of actions you can perform simultaneously. Act out each set for your partner to have him/her guess what you are doing.

Example: テレビを見ながら、キャベツをを切る。

A: (acts out a scene where you are chopping vegetables while talking on the phone.)

B: テレビを見ながら、キャベツを切っているんですか。

A: はい、そうです。

Activity 4

Work as a class. Ask your classmates what kind of things they do while they are studying, eating dinner, etc., using ～ながら . Discover what habits your classmates have in common.

Example: A: 勉強する時、よく何かしますか。

B: ええ、お菓子(かし)を食べながら、勉強します。～さんは?

A: そうですね。私はよく音楽をききながら、勉強しますね。

クラスメートの名前	～ながら、勉強する	～ながら、ご飯(はん)を食べる

II. Expressing the idea of *without doing* ~ using ないで

The negative verb form で下さい, as in 見ないで下さい, was introduced in chapter 1 in its use of indicating a negative request. When this negative form is used alone, it means *without ~ing.*

野菜(やさい)は洗(あら)わないで、ゆでてもいいです。 *It's OK to boil the vegetables without washing them.*

鶏肉(とりにく)を小麦粉(こむぎこ)につけないで、あげた。 *I deep fried chicken without dipping it into flour.*

炊飯器(すいはんき)を使わないで、ご飯(はん)をたいた。 *I cooked rice without using a rice cooker.*

練習しないで、上手になる人はいない。 *There is no one who can become good at anything without practicing it.*

キム：　おはしもナイフもフォークも使わないでご飯(はん)を食べるの？
Do you eat your meals without using a knife, a fork or chopsticks?

ラジュ：　うん、南インドでは、手で食べるんだ。
Yeah, we eat with our hands in southern India.

話してみましょう

Activity 1 Mr. Smith and Mr. Tanaka have different habits. Describe their habits using ～て and ～ないで.

Example: スミスさんはコーヒーにさとうを入れて飲みますが、
田中さんはさとうを入れないで飲みます。

Activity 2 Work with a partner. Ask your partner a choice question using the following statement. Your partner will answer the question.

Example: 毎朝ご飯(はん)を食べて出かけます。
毎朝ご飯(はん)を食べて出かけますか、食べないで出かけますか。

1. パンにバターをつけて食べます。
2. コーヒーにさとうを入れて飲みます。
3. 鶏肉(とりにく)はよく焼(や)いて食べます。
4. ほうれんそうはゆでて食べます。
5. 魚(さかな)はむして食べます。
6. ヨーグルトにジャムをまぜて食べます。

Activity 3

Work with a partner. Check the はい column for things in the following chart that you do, and the いいえ column for things that you don't do. Then ask your partner whether or not he/she does these things. Use both the casual and polite styles of speech.

Example: A: 朝御飯(ごはん)を食べて学校に行きますか。
B: いいえ、たいてい食べないで行きます。～さんは？
A: 私も食べないで行きます。

	私		パートナー	
	はい	いいえ	はい	いいえ
朝御飯(ごはん)を食べて学校に行く				
インターネットをよく使う				
パンにジャムをつけて食べる				
豚肉(ぶたにく)はよく焼(や)く				
じゃがいもは、むして食べる				
いちごはミルクをかけて食べる				
コーヒーにさとうを入れて飲む				

Activity 4

Work with a partner. The following items make our lives easier. Name some things we can do or don't have to do because of each of them.

インターネット　電子(でんし)レンジ　ミキサー　携帯(けいたい)電話　炊飯器(すいはんき)　パソコン　冷蔵庫(れいぞうこ)
DVD プレイヤー　E メール　ボウル　フライパン

Example: インターネット
これを使うと、新聞を買わないで、ニュースが読めます。

III. Expressing an open or hypothetical condition using the ば conditional form

The ば conditional clause indicates a condition necessary for the event or action in the main clause to take place. In this sense, it can be translated as if or only if. It can refer to a future condition which has not yet been realized or to a hypothetical condition that cannot be realized. This chapter introduces both types of condition.

A. Expressing an open condition using the ば conditional form.

If the ば conditional refers an event that may or may not be realized in the future it expresses the condition necessary for the event in the main clause to become true.

じゃがいもと豚肉(ぶたにく)を一緒(しょ)ににれば、おいしくなると思う。
I think it will taste good if you stew the potatoes and pork together .

味噌(みそ)とさとうとサラダ 油(ゆ/あぶら) とすをまぜれば、おいしいドレッシングが作れるよ。
You can make a delicious dressing if you mix miso, sugar, salad oil, and vinegar.

この魚(さかな)はあげれば、まだおいしいよ。
This fish will be delicious if you deep fry it.

The ば conditional form is made as follows:

1. Irregular verbs and る-verbs:
   Replace る with れば
2. う-verbs:
   Same as the potential form except that ば is used instead of る at the end of the phrase. (e.g. 歩ける→歩けば)
3. い-adjectives and the negative ending ない:
   Replace い with ければ. The negative form of the ば conditional is ～なければ which is the same as the ～なければ found in ～なければならない. All negative forms use ～なければ, regardless of what part of speech they are.
4. な-adjectives and nouns:
   Replace だ with なら(ば) or であれば. The ば in ～なら(ば) is optional.

	Dictionary form	Affirmative conditional (if ~)		Negative conditional (if ~not)	
		Formal	Colloquial		Colloquial
Copula verbs	材料(ざいりょう)だ (*ingredient*)	材料(ざいりょう)なら (ば)	N/A	材料(ざいりょう)じゃ なければ	材料(ざいりょう)じゃ なきゃ
な -adjectives	しずかだ (*quiet*)	しずかなら (ば)	N/A	しずかじゃ なければ	しずかじゃ なきゃ
い -adjectives	こい (*thick*)	こければ	こけりゃ	こくなければ	こくなきゃ
	いい	よければ	よけりゃ	よくなければ	よくなきゃ
Irregular verbs	来る	来(く)れば	来(く)りゃ	来(こ)なければ	来(こ)なきゃ
	する	すれば	すりゃ	しなければ	しなきゃ
る -verbs	温(あたた)める (*to heat up*)	温(あたた)めれば	温(あたた)めりゃ	温(あたた)めなければ	温(あたた)めなきゃ
	にる (*to stew*)	にれば	にりゃ	になければ	になきゃ
う -verbs	むす (*to steam*)	むせば	むしゃ	むさければ	むさなきゃ
	やる (*to do*)	やれば	やりゃ	やらなければ	やらなきゃ

Note

- The colloquial form of the ば construction is made by replacing ~れば, which becomes ~りゃ for い-adjectives, for the negative form ない, and for る-verbs. For う-verbs, the /-eba/ becomes /-ya/. (The dash indicates a consonant sound, such as /k-eba/ for /k-ya/.) There is no colloquial form for ~なら(ば).

キム：ボウルとなべはどこ？
Where are the bowl and pot?

まもる：分からないけど、アリスさんに聞けば分かると思うよ。
I don't know, but you should be able to find out if you ask Alice.

Note that ~ばいい can express suggestions or the speaker's hope:

道子：ちょっと味(あじ)がこいね。 *Oh, it's seasoned too much.*

健一：じゃあ、水を足(た)せばいいよ。 *It'll be fine if you add some water.*

黒田(くろだ)：まだ野菜(やさい)がかたいね。 *The vegetables are not cooked enough.* (lit.: still hard)

青山(あおやま)：少しいためればやわらかくなるよ。 *They should get tender if you stir fry them a bit.*

B. Expressing a hypothetical condition using the ば conditional form.

In this usage, the condition in the ば clause may express a counter-factual situation or a hypothetical condition.

味噌(みそ)があれば、味噌汁(みそしる)を作ったんですが。
If there were some soybean paste, I would have made some miso soup.

かにがあれば、もっとおいしかったはずです。 *It would have tasted better if we had had some crab.*

その鶏肉(とりにく)、かたくなければ食べられた。 *I could have eaten that chicken if it weren't so tough.*

～ばよかった is used to express the speaker's regret about something that the speaker wished he or she had done, or something that he or she wished had happened.

こしょうをかけすぎなければ、よかった。 *I wish I hadn't put in so much pepper.*

電子(でんし)レンジがあれば、よかった。 *I wish I had had a microwave oven.*

電話しておけば、よかったんです。 *I wish I had called in advance.*

ウスターソースを使えば、よかった。 *I wish I had used Worcestershire sauce.*

The expressions ～ばいいのに/～ばいいんだけど/～ばいいんですが are often used when the speaker wishes for something that does not or will not take place in reality.

あの人まだいるの？早く帰ればいいのに。 *Is that person still here? I wish he'd go home soon.*

石田：　ケーキ作れる？
Can you bake a cake? (lit. *make*)

上田：　もちろん。でも、この家オーブンないんだ。オーブンがあればいいんだけど。
Of course. But we have no oven here. I wish we had one.

白鳥(しらとり)：山田さん、今日は仕事でおそくなるから、来られないって。
Mr. Yamada says he can't come today because he has to work late.

黒木(くろき)：そう、ざんねんね！来られればいいのに。
That's too bad. I wish he could come.

話してみましょう

Activity 1 Change each phrase in Column A using 〜ば, and choose the appropriate result from Column B.

Example:　天気がいい

天気がよければ、歩いて行きます。

Column A	Column B
1. たまねぎです	**a.** ご飯(はん)が上手にたけます。
2. 炊飯器(すいはんき)を使う	**b.** チャーハンが出来ません。
3. 牛肉(ぎゅうにく)がかたい	**c.** ケーキが作れます。
4. いためない	**d.** マウイ・オニオンがおいしいですよ。
5. お茶碗(ちゃわん)がない	**e.** 味(あじ)がこくなりますよ。
6. フォークがない	**f.** コーンスターチにつければ、やわらかくなります。
7. ソースをまぜる	**g.** おさらを使ったらどうですか。
8. 赤(あか)いいちごがある	**h.** 木のスプーンが使いやすいですよ。

Activity 2 Work with a partner. Think about what kinds of things you could do if you were in the following situations. Tell your partner what you would do.

Example:　百万ドルあれば、新しい家が買えます。

1. 百万ドルある
2. 冬休みになる
3. 日本に住んでいる
4. 結婚する
5. 大学を卒業する

Activity 3

Work with a group of four. Choose one word from the list below and tell your group what would be possible or impossible if that item was or wasn't present. The rest of the group will try to guess what word you selected.

小麦粉(こむぎこ)　さとう　パンこ　コーンスターチ　ほうれんそう　だし　豚肉(ぶたにく)　のり　す
火(ひ)　茶碗(ちゃわん)　おはし　スプーン　フライパン　冷蔵庫(れいぞうこ)　なべ　味噌(みそ)　鶏肉(とりにく)　おはし

Example:　A:　これがあれば、ケーキやクッキーが焼(や)けます。
　　　　　　これがなければ、作れません。
　　　　B:　小麦粉(こむぎこ)ですか。
　　　　A:　はい、そうです。

Activity 4

Work with the class. Ask a classmate if there have been incidents which he/she regrets, and report to the class about what you have learned. Use the ～ばよかった form.

Example:　A: ～さん。～さんは　こうすればよかったと思うことがありますか。
　　　　B:　ええ、ありますよ。先週、新しいドレッシングを買ったんですが。
　　　　A:　ええ。
　　　　B:　おいしくなかったので、買わなければよかったと思いました。
　　　　A:　そうですか。それはざんねんでしたね。

クラスメートの名前	すれば・しなければよかったこと

IV. Expressing possibility and capability using the dictionary form of the verb + ことが出来る

The dictionary form of the verb + ことが出来る means *can* or *be able to do* in English. It is similar to the potential form, indicating possibility or capability depending on the context, but it is usually a little more formal than the potential form and tends to be used to make objective statements about whether doing something is possible or not.

さとうやぎゅうにゅうを使わないでおいしいお菓子(かし)を作ることが出来る。
It is possible to make delicious sweets without using sugar or milk.

フライパンで鶏肉(とりにく)をあげることが出来ます。　*It is possible to deep-fry chicken with a frying pan.*

オーブンで温(あたた)めることが出来る。　*You can reheat it in the oven.*

川本： 電子(でんし)レンジでケーキを焼(や)くことが出来ますか。
Is it possible to bake a cake using a microwave oven?

上田： もちろん、出来ますよ。
Of course you can.

話してみましょう

Activity 1 Answer the questions using the dictionary form of the verb + ことが出来る.

Example: アメリカでは日本のテレビ番組(ばんぐみ)が見られますか。
(テレビ番組(ばんぐみ) =*TV program*)
ええ、大きい町なら見ることが出来ますよ。

1. アメリカでは何さいで車の運転が出来ますか。
2. だれでもアメリカの大統領(だいとうりょう) (*president*) になれますか。
3. 安いチケットはどこで買えますか。
4. アメリカでは何さいでおさけが飲めますか。
5. このしゅう (*state*) では何さいで結婚出来ますか。

Activity 2 Work with a partner. Select an object from the list below and explain what can be done with that object, and have your partner guess which object you are talking about.

Example: A: これは、いろいろな物を焼(や)くことが出来る物です。
B: フライパンですか？
A: はい、そうです。

> 冷蔵庫(れいぞうこ)　車　飛行機(き)　ほうちょう　フォーク　たまご　のり　コーンスターチ
> サラダ油(ゆ/あぶら)　ソース　ボウル　ミキサー　オーブン　しょうゆ　小麦粉(こむぎこ)　味噌(みそ)
> ねぎ　(お)さら

Activity 3 Work as a class. The following are traffic signs used in Japan. Find people who know the meanings of the signs in the chart, and write their names and the meanings of the signs.

Example: A: あのう、このサインの意味は何ですか。
B: ここでタクシーに乗ることが出来るんですよ。
A: ああ、そうですか。

サイン	名前	サインの意味

V. Using question word + でも ～ affirmative form

In *Nakama 1*, Chapter 9, you learned that using a question word + か indicates an indefinite something, someone, etc., and that a question word + も followed by a negative form means *not ~any*. This chapter introduces another combination of question word and particle: question word + でも. This form can be used only in sentences ending in an affirmative form, and it means *any*, *all*, or *whatever/whenever/wherever*, etc.

木村さんは何でも食べられます。 *Kimura-san can eat anything.*

川本：だれをしょうたいしようか。 *Whom shall we invite?*

木村：だれでもいいよ。 *Anybody is fine.*

ジェフ：いつがいいですか。	*When should we go/do it?*
さなえ：明日ならいつでもいいです。	*Anytime tomorrow will be fine.*
ジェフ：どこに行きましょうか。	*Where shall we go?*
さなえ：おいしい店ならどこでもいいです。	*Anywhere will be fine as long as it serves good food.*

The following chart summarizes phrases that can be created with a question word and the particles か, も, and でも.

Question word	+ か ～ **affirmative**	+ も ～ **negative**	+ でも ～ **affirmative**
何	何か (*something*)	何も (*nothing, not at all*)	＊何でも (*anything, whatever*)
だれ	だれか (*someone*)	だれも (*no one*)	だれでも (*anybody, whoever*)
いつ	いつか (*sometime*)	＊いつも (*never*)	いつでも (*anytime*)
どこ	どこか (*somewhere*)	どこも (*nowhere*)	どこでも (*anywhere*)

Note

- ＊ When いつも is used in an affirmative sentence, it means *always*. For example, いつも朝御飯(ごはん)を食べる means *I always eat breakfast.*

The particles が and を are not used with the question word + も or でも. However, other particles such as に and と can be inserted between the question word and ～も or でも.

昨日はだれにも会いませんでした。	*I didn't meet anybody yesterday.*
こしょうはどこにもありません。	*There is no pepper anywhere.*
このソースは何とでもあいます。	*This sauce works with anything.*
仕事はいつからでも始(はじ)められます。	*I can start the job anytime.*
サラダ油(ゆ/あぶら)はどこででも買えます。	*You can buy vegetable oil anywhere.*

話してみましょう

Activity 1 Answer the questions, using the question word + も ～ negative or the question word + でも ～ affirmative.

Example 1: 朝、何か食べますか。
　　いいえ、朝は何も食べません。

Example 2: 何を作りましょうか。
　　何でもいいですよ。

1. 朝、何か飲みましたか。
2. だれかと一緒(しょ)に食事に行きますか。
3. 日本のしょうゆはどこかにありますか。
4. キャベツとえびをいためてくれる人はいませんか。
5. いつステーキを焼(や)たらいいですか。
6. いくらお金をあつめたらいいでしょうか。
7. だれをパーティによんだらいいでしょうか。
8. どこで材料(ざいりょう)を買いましょうか。
9. だれがたまねぎと人参(じん)をを切りますか。

Activity 2

Work as a class. Ask your classmates about their likes and dislikes about food.

Example: A: ～ さんはどんな食べ物が好きですか。

B: そうですね。野菜(やさい)が好きですね。

A: 野菜(やさい)なら、何でも食べられますか。

B: ええ、食べられます。／いいえ、ねぎはあまり好きじゃありません。

Activity 3

Work with a partner. You and your partner are roommates and you have decided to make dinner together. Decide what to make and what kind of ingredients you will need to prepare. Create a dialogue following the example.

Example: A: ～さん、今晩、何にしようか？

B: 何が食べたい？

A: 何でもいいよ。

B: じゃあ、天ぷらはどう？

A: いいね。じゃあ、何を買ったらいい？

B: 野菜(やさい)なら、何でもいいと思うけど。

A: じゃあ、魚(さかな)は？

聞く練習

上手な聞き方

Understanding signaling devices used in instructions

Nakama 2, Chapter 2 introduced transition devices, such as そして , その間 （に）, その後（で）, その時（に）, その前（に）, それで , だから , だけど , つぎに , ですから , というのは , ところで , まず始めに , and また . Some of these expressions—for example, まず, 始めに , つぎに , それから , and そして —are commonly used to indicate sequence. Another commonly used expression is 最後に (*lastly, finally*), which indicates the last step. It is important to pay attention to these devices because what follows them is the most important information in the instructions.

練習

A. Listen to the following two dialogues, then identify the number of steps in each set of directions.

1. ほうれんそうのおひたし (*boiled*) の作り方 ________
2. 天ぷらの作り方 ________

B. Now listen to the dialogues again. This time, try to write down each step.

1. ほうれんそうのおひたし (*boiled*) の作り方

____

2. 天ぷらの作り方

____

料理番組 *Cooking programs*

聞く前に

A. 下の質問に答えて下さい。

1. テレビで料理の番組を見たことがありますか。
2. 料理番組にはだれが出てきますか。
3. 料理番組のキッチンにはどんな物がありますか。

新しい言葉

ひらたく	同じように	ぬる	まぶす
flat	in the same way	to spread over	to sprinkle

聞いてみましょう

A. 下の材料(ざいりょう)のリストを見て、使わない材料(ざいりょう)に×をつけて下さい。

セロリ (*celery*)	________	たまねぎ	________
さやえんどう (*snow peas*)	________	す	________
チェダーチーズ	________	マヨネーズ	________
ピーマン (*green peppers*)	________	レタス	________
ベーコン (*bacon*)	________	さとう	________
たまご	________	しお	________

B. Write the quantity necessary for each ingredient in the blanks in A.

聞いた後で

料理(りょうり)のステップを書いて下さい。そして、クラスメートと答えをチェックして下さい。

聞き上手話し上手

Giving instructions

Verbal instructions in English tend to be presented in the imperative form such as do this or do that, but in Japanese they are presented in statement form, such as 〜ます and plain forms. 〜ます is often used in giving instructions because it tends to express the speaker's awareness of a public audience. Therefore, when the speaker wants to convey a message, 〜ます tends to appear even in rather casual conversations. Since the plain form alone does not imply such awareness, it is often used with expression such as 〜の (だ) and 〜んだ, which convey the nuance that the preceding sentence is an explanation/instruction. You can use the request form 〜下さい as well, but the frequent use of 下さい sounds rather strange in instructions. It is better to use a combination of ます and 下さい.

練習

Self-tests

1. Explain how to make green salad (グリーンサラダ) in Japanese.
2. Explain how to make scrambled eggs (スクランブルエッグ) in Japanese

漢字

Statistical facts about kanji

You have learned more than 250 **kanji** so far, and you may be wondering how many more you have to learn. Here are some statistical facts about the kanji used in Japan that should help you build an overall perspective.

1. There are about 50,000 characters listed in one comprehensive kanji dictionary, but most of these are not commonly used. The National Institute of Japanese Language Research conducted a study of the use of **kanji** in newspapers and magazines and found that the 200 most frequently used **kanji** accounted for about 50 percent of all **kanji** appearing in the text. The 500 most frequently used **kanji** accounted for over 80 percent of all **kanji**, and 1,000 **kanji** accounted for 90 percent of the total. The 2,000 most frequently used **kanji** accounted for about 99 percent of all **kanji** used in newspapers. Having learned 250 **kanji**, you should be able to recognize about one-half of the **kanji** appearing, for example, in a Japanese magazine. Once you learn 500, you will know 80 percent of the **kanji** you will encounter in most publications.
2. Japanese children learn about 150 to 200 **kanji** each year in elementary school. By the time they reach the sixth grade, they know about 1,000 **kanji**.
3. The most frequently read **kanji** are visually simpler (contain fewer strokes) than the less frequently used ones.
4. There are many **kanji** compounds, so it is important to build your vocabulary knowledge to improve your reading skills even if you know basic **kanji**.

Learning tips

As the number of **kanji** you have learned begins to grow, you will face the inevitable problem of retaining everything. To keep from forgetting characters, it is a good idea to create different groupings of **kanji**. One such grouping may be done according to meaning categories, while another grouping could be based on component parts. Different ways of organizing your knowledge of **kanji** should provide you with multiple ways of remembering them.

It is also a good idea to write **kanji** when you try to remember them. Writing in this case can also be done by moving your arm through the air. Research has shown that involving different parts of your body will activate more regions in your brain, resulting in a higher degree of cognitive activity, which, in turn, leads to better retention.

Flashcards can be used to practice recognition, writing, and the grouping of **kanji**. You can make flashcards with the kanji on one side and the meaning, the **on**-reading (in **katakana**), and the **kun**-reading (in **hiragana**) on the other side. Then you can practice reading by looking at the **kanji** on the front of the card and practice writing by looking at the readings and meaning on the back. You can spread your **kanji** cards out on the floor and group them according to meaning, component shape, and pronunciation.

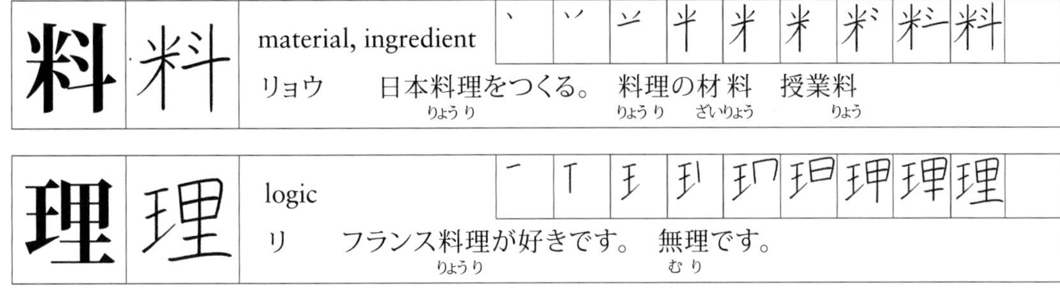

Flashcards

飯	飯	cooked rice, meal	めし　ハン	ご飯(はん)を食べる。　炊飯器(すいはんき)
野	野	field	の　ヤ	野球(やきゅう)が好きです。　野菜(やさい)を食べます。
菜	菜	vegetable	サイ	この野菜(やさい)サラダはおいしいです。
魚	魚	fish	さかな　ギョ	魚(さかな)をつる　魚料理(さかなりょうり)
鳥	鳥	bird	とり　チョウ	私は鳥肉(とりにく)を食べません。
肉	肉	meat	にく	肉(にく)を食べる。　肉料理(にくりょうり)
止	止	to stop	と(まる)　や(める)　シ	車を止(と)める　タバコを止(や)める
始	始	to begin, to start	はじ(まる)はじ(める)　シ	始(はじ)めに　学校が始(はじ)まる。
終	終	to end, to finish	お(わる)お(える)　シュウ	宿題が終(お)わる。
洗	洗	to wash	あら(う)　セン	手を洗(あら)う。　洗濯(せんたく)をする。
悪	悪	bad	わる(い)　アク	つごうが悪(わる)い。

黒	black	くろ(い)　コク	黒(くろ)い犬がいます。　黒板(こくばん)に書いて下さい。
白	white	しろ(い)　ハク	白(しろ)いねこ　雪(ゆき)は白(しろ)いです。
青	blue	あお(い)　セイ	青(あお)い海　空が青(あお)い。
赤	red	あか(い)　セキ	赤(あか)いりんご
茶	brown, tea	チャ　サ	茶色(ちゃいろ)いかばん　お茶(ちゃ)を飲む。　喫茶店(きっさてん)
短	short	みじか(い)　タン	このズボンは短(みじか)いです。
長	long	なが(い)　チョウ	長(なが)い　会社の社長(しゃちょう)
次	next	つぎ　ジ	次(つぎ)の問題をして下さい。
焼	to burn, to bake	や(く)　ショウ	ケーキを焼(や)く。　火事(かじ)で家が焼(や)ける。

読めるようになった漢字

料理　材料　授業料　朝ご飯　昼ご飯　晩ご飯　炊飯器(すいはんき)　野球(きゅう)　野菜　魚
魚料理　肉料理　鳥肉　鶏肉(とり)　止まる　車を止める　タバコを止める　始まる
始める　終わる　洗う　洗濯(たく)　悪い　黒い　黒板(ばん)　白い　赤い　茶色い　お茶
紅茶(こう)　茶碗(わん)　喫茶店(きっさてん)　短い　長い　社長　味　次　焼ける　冷ます

名前：　黒田　黒木　白鳥　赤川　青山　長田

下の文を読んで下さい。

1. 結婚式の肉料理はとてもよかったです。
2. この魚料理の材料と作り方を教えてくれませんか。
3. 牛肉より鳥肉や野菜の方が好きです。
4. これは少し長いので、短くして下さい。
5. 雪は白くて、空は青い。
6. あの茶色いセーターを着ている人はだれですか。
7. 映画は八時に始まって、十時に終わりますから、歩いて帰ります。
8. 車が銀行の前に止まりました。
9. 野菜を洗って、小さく切ったら、ここに持って来て。次に、肉を焼いて。

読む練習

上手な読み方

Understanding the characteristics of written instructions

People read written materials for various purposes. For example, you may skim newspapers to get an overall idea of what is gong on that day, or search for a particular type of house in housing ads. You may also read novels, short stories, or manga for entertainment. Furthermore, you may have to read a textbook for a test. Depending on the purpose of reading, you may scan, skim, engage in a very detailed reading, or read while taking notes. Therefore, you should be aware of why you are going to read a given text, what you want to do with it, and then think about what information you should get out of the material, and what is the most efficient way of reading it.

Written instructions are among the easiest writing styles to understand. Each step is usually separated, numbered, and often accompanied by illustrations. You can use visual cues and format to help you understand the text. Written instructions are also grammatically simple in Japanese. They are written in the present tense, and the text can be either in plain form or the formal form. The difficulty of written instructions is usually due to context-specific vocabulary and the **kanji** associated with this vocabulary. It is important to have a good idea of what vocabulary will be used before you begin reading.

練習

A. Think about when you might read a set of instructions and what you would do after reading it.

B. Suppose you are to read manuals or recipes for the following items. Identify what kind of nouns and verbs you will need to know.

DVD レコーダー　携帯(けいたい)電話　ピザ

C. The following is a typical recipe in Japanese. Identify similarities and differences in format between recipes in Japanese and recipes in English.

ひき肉のパン揚(あ)げ（１人分(ぶん)）

材料

食(しょく)パン (sliced bread)　２枚(まい)
牛(ぎゅう)ひき肉 (ground beef)　５０g
スライスチーズ　１枚(まい)
塩(しお)、こしょう　少々

作り方

1 肉に塩(しお)、こしょうをふって、味をつけます
2 食(しょく)パンと食(しょく)パンの間にバターをぬって、肉とチーズをはさみます。
3 油(あぶら)を 160 度ぐらいに温めて、ゆっくり揚(あ)げます。
4 四つに切ります。

海老団子(えびだんご) Shrimp dumplings

読む前に

A. 日本とアメリカでは材料のはかり方 (*unit of measurement*) がちがいます。

アメリカ		日本	
パウンド (*pound*)	オンス (*ounce*)	キログラム (*kilogram*)	グラム (*gram*)
2.2 lb	35 oz	1 kg	1,000 g
ガロン (*gallon*)	パイント (*pint*)	リットル（*liter*）	
1 gallon	8 pt	3.8 l	
パイント (*pint*)	カップ（アメリカ）	CC	カップ（日本）
1 pt	2 cups	473 CC	1.9 カップ
オンス (*ounce*)	大さじ	グラム (*gram*)	大さじ
0.5 oz	1 tablespoon	15 gram	大さじ 1

1. ５００グラムは、何パウンドぐらいになりますか。
2. 1リットルは、何ガロンですか。
3. アメリカの1カップは、何パイントですか。何 cc ですか。
4. 日本の1カップはアメリカの何カップですか。
5. 日本では、大(おお)さじ1は 15g で、小(こ)さじ1は 5g です。アメリカではどうですか。

B. 写真を見て、海老団子(えびだんご)の作り方を言ってみて下さい。知らない言葉があったら先生に聞いて下さい。

Photos courtesy of the authors

C. 下の材料を読んで、分からない言葉があったら、先生に聞いて下さい。AとBは何のことですか。

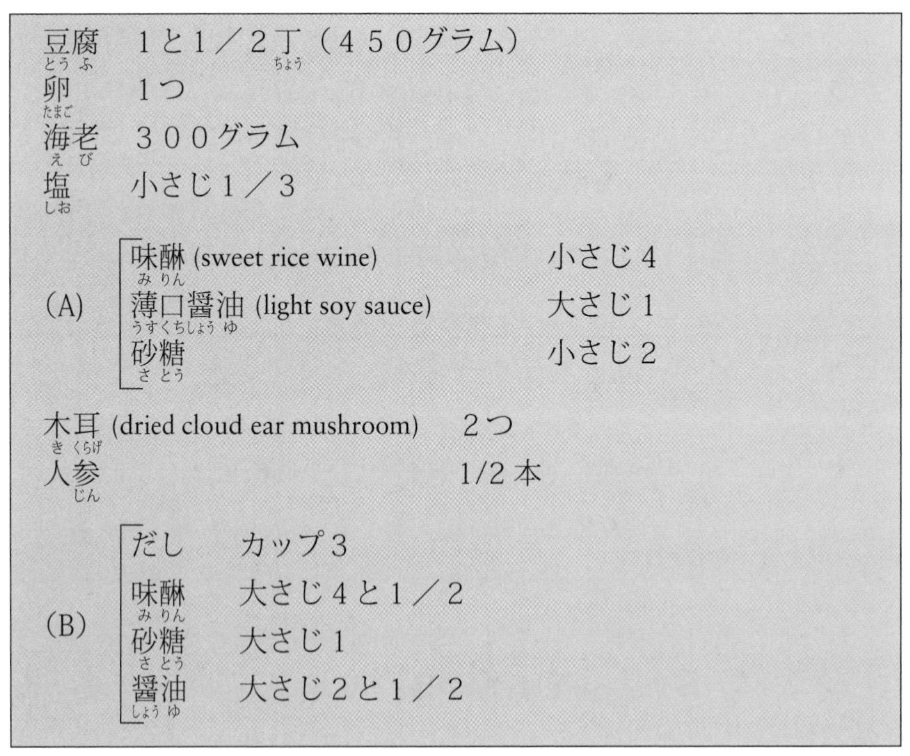

豆腐(とうふ)　1と1／2丁(ちょう)（450グラム）
卵(たまご)　1つ
海老(えび)　300グラム
塩(しお)　小さじ1／3

(A)
- 味醂(みりん) (sweet rice wine)　小さじ4
- 薄口醤油(うすくちしょうゆ) (light soy sauce)　大さじ1
- 砂糖(さとう)　小さじ2

木耳(きくらげ) (dried cloud ear mushroom)　2つ
人参(じん)　1/2本

(B)
- だし　カップ3
- 味醂(みりん)　大さじ4と1／2
- 砂糖(さとう)　大さじ1
- 醤油(しょうゆ)　大さじ2と1／2

D. The following steps are out of order. Match each step with the picture.

_1_ 豆腐(とうふ)の上におもい (*heavy*) 物をのせて、水を切る (*drain*)。

___ 人参(じん)と木耳(きくらげ)を小さく切って、２と混(ま)ぜる。

___ 揚(あ)げた団子(だんご)に熱いお湯(ゆ)をかける。

___ ３で小さい団子(だんご)を作って、油(あぶら)で揚(あ)げる。

___ ５をBのだしで１５分ぐらい煮(に)る。

___ 海老(えび)を包丁(ほうちょう)で小さくなるまでたたいて、豆腐(とうふ)と海老(えび)と卵(たまご)の黄身(きみ) (*yolk*) とAをよく混(ま)ぜる。

読んだ後で

A. 日本語で質問に答えて下さい。

1. どんな料理が好きですか。
2. どんな料理を作ったことがありますか。
3. お母さんはどんな料理が上手ですか。お父さんはどうですか。
4. どんな料理を作ってみたいと思いますか。

B. 下の質問に答えて、好きな料理の作り方を日本語で書いて下さい。

1. どんな材料を使いますか。
2. フライパンやなべを使いますか。
3. ステップはいくつぐらいありますか。
4. まず始めに何をしますか。
5. 次に何をしますか。
6. その後、何をしますか。
7. 最後(さいご)に何をしますか。

総合練習
そうごう

料理を作ろう

Choose a dish that you can make and prepare a presentation. Make a list of ingredients you will need and write the directions below the list. Then make a presentation. You can use PowerPoint, draw pictures, or bring the actual dishes if your instructor allows you to do so.

材料

作り方

1.
2.
3.
4.
5.

ロールプレイ

1. You are going to do a cooking demonstration for the Japan Cultural Association. Explain how to make rolled sushi.
2. Ask a Japanese friend to teach you an easy-to-make Japanese dish and write a recipe for it.
3. Describe mistakes in cooking that you or members of your family have made.

Jon Arnold Images Ltd / Alamy

Chapter 8

第八課(だいはっか)

うわさ
Rumors

Objectives		Describing events, making small talk, and expressing one's conjectures and opinions
Vocabulary		Unpleasant experiences, rumors, expressions that describe feelings and emotional states, animals used as metaphor
Dialogue		東京(きょう)に地震(じしん)が来るみたいです。
Japanese Culture		Natural disasters, earthquakes, and crimes
Grammar	I.	Expressing problems and events using the passive form
	II.	Expressing conjecture based on indirect evidence using ～らしい; expressing conjecture based on direct evidence using ～ようだ／みたいだ
	III.	Nのような／みたいな (*like ~*); NらしいN (*typical*)
	IV.	Expressing limited degree using だけ～ affirmative and しか～ negative
	V.	Expressing opinions indirectly using ～んじゃない（かと思う）
Listening		Expressions in oral narrative; ブタの話 *a pig's story*
Communication		Telling a story well and listening to a story well
Kanji		Using a **kanji** dictionary 笑 泣 泳 払 売 落 助 考 決 待 遊 呼 招 忙 静 暗 点 夜 心 配 困 経
Reading		Understanding the structure of narrative text, global warming

Chapter Resources

www.cengagebrain.com

Heinle Learning Center

Audio Program

単語

たん

Flashcards

Nouns

いじめ		bullying, いじめにあう being bullied
インフルエンザ		flu, influenza
うさぎ	兎	rabbit
うそ	嘘	lie, falsehood, うそをつく to tell a lie
うわさ	噂	rumor
かじ	火事	a fire
かのじょ	彼女	girlfriend, she
かみなり	雷	lightning, かみなりがおちる lightning strikes
かめ	亀	turtle, tortoise
かれ(し)	彼(氏)	boyfriend, he
クジラ	鯨	whale
くま	熊	bear
けいけん	経験	experience, 経験する to have an experience
けんか	喧嘩	a fight
こうずい	洪水	flood
こうつう	交通	traffic, こうつうじこ traffic accident
さいがい	災害	disaster, calamity
さつじん	殺人	murder
さる	猿	monkey
じこ	事故	accident, こうつうじこ traffic accident
じしん	地震	earthquake
しんぱい	心配	anxiety, anxious, しんぱいする to be worried
ぞう	象	elephant
たつまき	竜巻	tornado
とり	鳥	bird
どろぼう	泥棒	thief
はっけん	発見	discovery, はっけんする to discover
ハリケーン		hurricane
はんざい	犯罪	crime
ひがい	被害	damage, loss
へび	蛇	snake

ライオン		lion
わるくち	悪口	bad-mouthing, speaking ill of a person

う -verbs

あう	遭う／遇う	to encounter
うる	売る	to sell
おこす	起こす	to cause (something) to happen
おそう	襲う	to attack
おどろく	驚く	to be surprised, 〜におどろく to be surprised at 〜
かわる	変わる	(for something)to change
こまる	困る	to be in trouble
ころす	殺す	to kill, to murder
こわす	壊す	to destroy
しかる	叱る	to scold
だます	騙す	to deceive
ぬすむ	盗む	to steal
はやる	流行る	to spread, to gain popularity
ふむ	踏む	to step on, 足をふむ to step on somebody's foot
よぶ	呼ぶ	to invite, to call

る -verbs

いじめる	苛める	to bully
おきる	起きる	to happen, to take place
おちる	落ちる	to fall, かみなりがおちる lightning strikes
すてる	捨てる	to throw away, to discard
にげる	逃げる	to run away, to escape
ふえる	増える	to increase
ぶつける		to hit (with a machine), to crash into
ほめる	誉める	to praise
やける	焼ける	to burn
ゆれる	揺れる	to shake
わかれる	別れる	to leave, to break up

い -adjectives

こわい	怖い	frightening, scary
ひどい	酷い	serious, extensive (used in negative context)

な-adjectives

あんぜん（な）	安全（な）	safe
ふべん（な）	不便（な）	inconvenient
むだ（な）	無駄（な）	wasteful

Prefixes

おお～	大～	heavy, big, 大雨 heavy rain, 大雪 heavy snow 大火事 big fire, 大じしん big earthquake

Expressions

ええ、ええ		uh, huh
へえ、そうですか。		Oh, I see.
それで…そのあと、どうなったんですか。	それで…その後、どうなったんですか。	Well then . . . what happened after that?
それはおきのどくでしたね。	それはお気の毒でしたね。	I am sorry to hear that.
まさか。		You're kidding.
うっそー		No way! (very casual)
まじー		Are you serious? (very casual)

単(たん)語の練習

A. いやな経験(けいけん) Unpleasant experiences

さいがいが起きる disaster takes place	地震(じしん)が起きる earthquake	たつまきが起きる tornados	火事(かじ)になる a fire starts	洪水(こうずい)になる flood
大雨がふる heavy rain	大雪がふる heavy snow	ハリケーンが来る hurricane	かみなりが落(お)ちる lightning / thunder	
建(たて)物がゆれる a building shakes	家が焼ける a house burns	ひがいがある damage		
はんざい crime	殺人(さつじん) murder	ころす to kill, to murder	どろぼうがお金をぬすむ a thief steals money	おそう to attack
にげる to run away	事故(じこ) accident	交通事故(こうつうじこ)にあう get involved in a traffic accident	車をぶつける to hit a car	安全(あんぜん)な safe

Activity 1 Use the words above to identify what is happening in the illustrations.

1

2

3

4

5

6

7

8

9

10

11

おぼえていますか。

台風(たいふう)　なくなる　泣(な)く　けがをする

Supplementary Vocabulary 自然(しぜん)のさいがい Natural disasters

あらし	嵐	storm
たかなみ	高波	high tide
たつまき	竜巻	tornado
つなみ	津波	tsunami
ふぶき	吹雪	snow storm, blizzard
やまかじ	山火事	forest fire
ふんか	噴火	volcanic eruption
じすべり	地すべり	landslide

Supplementary Vocabulary はんざいと事故(じこ) Crimes and accidents

ごうとう	強盗	burglary
スリ		pickpocket
さぎ	詐欺	fraud, swindling
でんせんびょう	伝染病	infectious disease, contagious disease
ひこうきじこ	飛行機事故	airplane crash (often implies mid-air collision)
せきじゅうじ	赤十字	Red Cross
けいさつ	警察	police
パトカー		police car
きゅうきゅうしゃ	救急車	ambulance
しょうぼうしゃ	消防車	fire truck

Activity 2 List the disasters, accidents, and crimes you have seen or experienced.

	さいがい	事故(じこ)	はんざい
テレビや新聞で見たことがある			
経験(けいけん)がある (*have experienced directly*)			

Activity 3 Fill in the blanks.

1. 2008 年に中国で起きた地震(じしん)の________はとても大きかったです。
2. アメリカでは____________に人の名前をつける。
3. 家や建物(たて)が焼けることを________と言います。
4. ゴルフ場で________が________、ゴルフをしていた人がなくなったそうです。
5. 人をころすことを_________と言います。
6. ________が私のお金を________、にげました。
7. 4月から7月ごろまで、テキサスやオクラホマではよく________が________。
8. ________がふると、川が近いところでは、よく________になります。
9. アメリカの東の方は、冬になると、________のひがいがあります。
10. 昨日、横断(おうだん)歩道で___________にあいました。
11. お父さんは、車を___________、けがをした。

B. うわさ Rumors

うわさをする to start a rumor	悪口(わるくち)を言う to insult somebody	うそをつく to tell a lie
友達とけんかする to have a fight with a friend	足をふむ to step on (someone's) toes	かれし／彼女(かのじょ)とわかれる to break up with a girl/boyfriend
いじめる to bully	いじめにあう to be bullied	だます to deceive

しかる to scold	インフルエンザがはやる influenza is going around	洋(よう)服をよごす to get clothes dirty	コンピュータをこわす to break a computer

Activity 4 Use the words above to describe what is happening in the illustrations.

おぼえていますか。

仕事をやめる　結婚する　留学する　入院する　好き　きらい（な）

Activity 5 Work with a partner. Ask your partner whether he/she knows anyone who has had the following experiences. Circle his/her answers.

Example:　コンピュータをこわしたことがある人

A:　コンピュータをこわしたことがある人を知っていますか。

B:　ええ、知っています。私の父です。

or　いいえ、知りません。

経験(けいけん)がある人	Circle 知っています or 知りません	その人の名前
Example: コンピュータをこわしたことがある人	知っています・知りません	父
かれしか彼女(かのじょ)とわかれた友達	知っています・知りません	
結婚した人	知っています・知りません	
最(さい)近友達とけんかした人	知っています・知りません	
友達をだましたことがある人	知っています・知りません	
いじめにあったことがある人	知っています・知りません	
先生にうそをついたことがある人	知っています・知りません	
先生の足をふんだ人	知っています・知りません	
レストランで服をよごした人	知っています・知りません	

Activity 6 Work with a partner. List typical rumor topics for the following age groups.

	うわさのトピック
小学生	
高校生	
大学生	
40代	
50代	
60代	
70代	

C. 気持ちをあらわす言葉
Expressions that describe feelings and emotional states

こわい	むだ	不便(ふべん)	ひどい
scary	wasteful	inconvenient	serious
困(こま)る	心配(しんぱい)する	おどろく	安全(あんぜん)
to be in trouble	to worry	to be surprised	to be safe

Activity 7 Use the words above to describe what is happening in the illustrations

おぼえていますか。

うれしい　楽しい　かわいい　かなしい　ひどい　いや（な）　好き（な）
大丈夫（な）　きらい（な）　さびしい　つまらない　大変（な）　ざんねん（な）
だめ（な）

Activity 8 Answer the following questions.

1. 今までこわかった経験を教えて下さい。
2. 何かこわいものはありますか。
3. 何がないと不便だと思いますか。
4. どんなことがむだだと思いますか。
5. 今困っていることがありますか。どんなことで、困っていますか。
6. どんな時に、心配しますか。今までで一番心配した経験について話して下さい。
7. 最近何かにおどろいたことがありますか。どんなことにおどろきましたか。

D. 動物にたとえる Animals used as metaphor

おぼえていますか。

犬　ねこ　魚

Supplementary Vocabulary ほかの動物 Other animals

イルカ		dolphin
カバ		hippopotamus
カンガルー		kangaroo
キリン		giraffe
コアラ		koala
ゴリラ		gorilla
サイ		rhinoceros
さめ	鮫	shark
しか	鹿	deer
ジャガー		jaguar
チーター		cheetah
とら	虎	tiger
パンダ		panda
りす		squirrel

Activity 9 Find likely similes to describe the following people.

1. やさしい人
2. こわい人
3. 大きい人
4. 足がおそい人
5. 頭がいい人
6. かわいい人
7. 強い人
8. よわい人
9. いやな人

Activity 10 Think of an animal that characterizes you. Ask your classmates what animals they think of themselves as being like.

ダイアローグ

はじめに

日本語で質問に答えて下さい。

1. 地震(じしん)を経験(けいけん)したことがありますか。どこでしたか。
2. 地震(じしん)はこわいですか。
3. どんなさいがいがこわいですか。

東京(きょう)に地震(じしん)が来るみたいです。

The order of the following **manga** frames is scrambled. Read the dialogue and unscramble the frames by writing the correct number in the box in each frame.

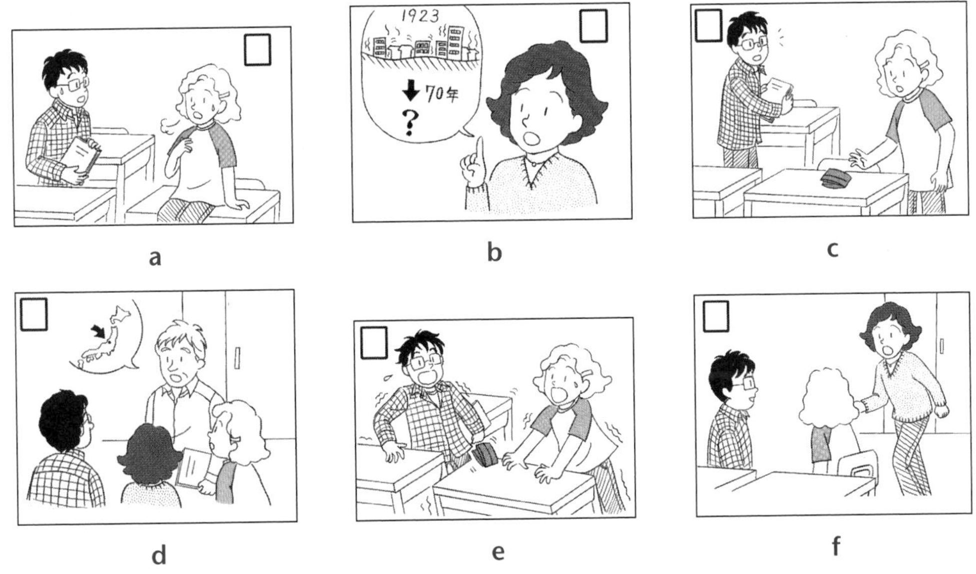

教室(きょうしつ)で。

ブラウン：あれ、こんなところにさいふがある。

リー：あ、それ、ぼくの。

ブラウン：だめだよ。こんなところにおいてたら、取られちゃうよ。

リー：あ、そうだよね。

小さい地震(じしん)が起きる。

ブラウン：何、これ？

リー：あっ、地震(じしん)だ。

ブラウン： えーっ、こわい。

リー： 大丈夫。あまり大きくないから。まだ少しゆれてるけど、すぐ終わるよ。

ゆれが止まる。

リー： ああ、止まったよ。ブラウンさん、大丈夫？

ブラウン： ああ、こわかった。日本は地震が多いって聞いてたけど、本当だったんですね。

上田さんが教室に入ってくる。

上田： 今、地震があったけど、大丈夫だった？

リー： うん、ぼくは大丈夫でもブラウンさんは、ちょっとこわかったんじゃないかな。

ブラウン： ええ、とてもこわかったです。上田さんは、大丈夫？

上田： ええ、私はカリフォルニアにいる時に、何度か経験したから、大丈夫です。

本田先生が入ってくる。

リー： あっ、先生、今地震がありましたね。

本田： ええ、新潟で地震があったらしいですよ。かなりゆれたみたいです。

リー： そうですか。東京じゃなくてよかった。

上田： うん、でも東京にも大きい地震が来るらしいですよ。

ブラウン： えっ、そうですか。うわさじゃないんですか。

上田： はい、うわさだけじゃないようですよ。東京では７０年に一度ぐらい大きい地震が起きているんですよ。だけど、１９２３年に関東大震災という 大 地震があってから、まだ地震らしい地震が起きてないそうなんです。だから、そろそろ…。

ブラウン： えー、そうなんですか。

本田： まあ、その時はその時で、何とかなるんじゃないかと思うよ。

リー： そうですよね。

ダイアローグの後で

A. 日本語で質問に答えて下さい。

1. どうしてブラウンさんはリーさんにだめだと言ったのですか。
2. ブラウンさんは地震(じしん)を経験(けいけん)したことがありましたか。
3. リーさんは地震(じしん)を経験(けいけん)したことがありましたか。
4. 上田さんは地震(じしん)を経験(けいけん)したことがありましたか。
5. いつ東京(きょう)で大きな地震(じしん)がありましたか。
6. 東京(きょう)では何年ぐらいに一度大きな地震(じしん)がありますか。
7. 将来(しょう)、東京(きょう)に地震(じしん)は来ますか。

B. Suppose Ms. Brown had experienced an earthquake before and was able to stay calm. How would you change what she says?

Dialogue Phrase Notes

- そろそろ means *it's about time* (for something to happen) . . .
- その時はその時で、何とかなる means *when that happens, we will manage.*

日本の文化

自然の災害 Natural disasters

Japan is prone to different types of natural disasters due to its location, geographical features, geological characteristics, and climate. Japan is mountainous and rivers flow rapidly. Heavy rain causes flooding and landslides. In recent years, due to housing development, landslides have accounted for a significant portion of the damage caused by natural disasters. Natural disasters in Japan include earthquakes, typhoons, heavy rain, heavy snow, floods, landslides, tsunami, and volcanic eruptions.

地震 Earthquakes

Japan lies on the edge of a continental plate and an ocean plate. Thus, it has more than 100 active volcanoes (7 percent of all active volcanoes in the world) and a higher than average share of earthquakes. About 20 percent of all earthquakes with a magnitude 6 or higher happen in Japan. Additionally, 7 percent of the active volcanoes in the world are in Japan. Since Japan occupies only 0.25 percent of the world land mass, its share of natural disasters is high. In 2007, there were more than 2,000 earthquakes powerful enough for people to feel.

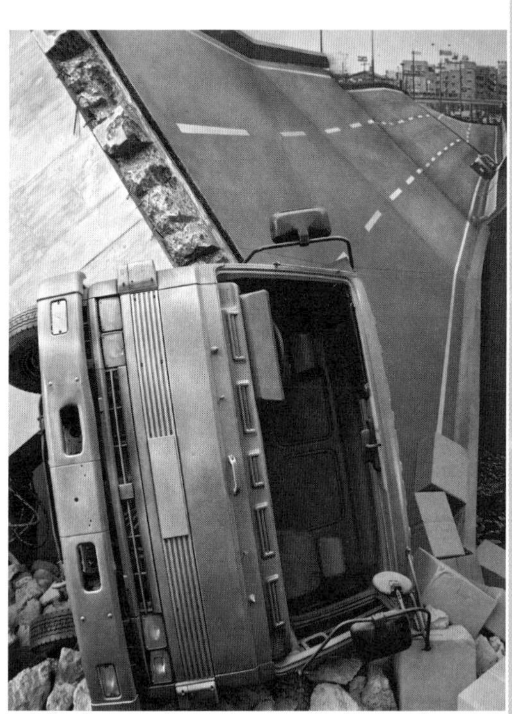

Kenneth Hamm / Photo Japan

In the Great East Japan Earthquake (東日本大震災) of 2011, more than 18,000 people were killed and 400,000 houses were completely or partially destroyed. The massive tsunami reached the East coast of Japan (Tohoku region) causing extensive damage. Due to the total loss of electricity for the cooling system caused by the fourteen-meter-high tsunami, a nuclear power plant in Fukushima experienced meltdown and hydrogen explosions. The plant is being prepared for a permanent shut down. This accident has caused the shut down of all nuclear power plants in Japan, and the very use of nuclear power is being debated. Three years after the disaster, more than 280,000 people still live in temporary housing. There has been a much higher level of awareness in preparing for emergencies. Many local municipalities have begun to play more active roles.

犯罪 Crimes

Japan is still considered to be one of the safest countries in the world, even though its crime rate is on the rise. Although it is difficult to make international comparisons on crime rates, one index published by OECD reveals the following.

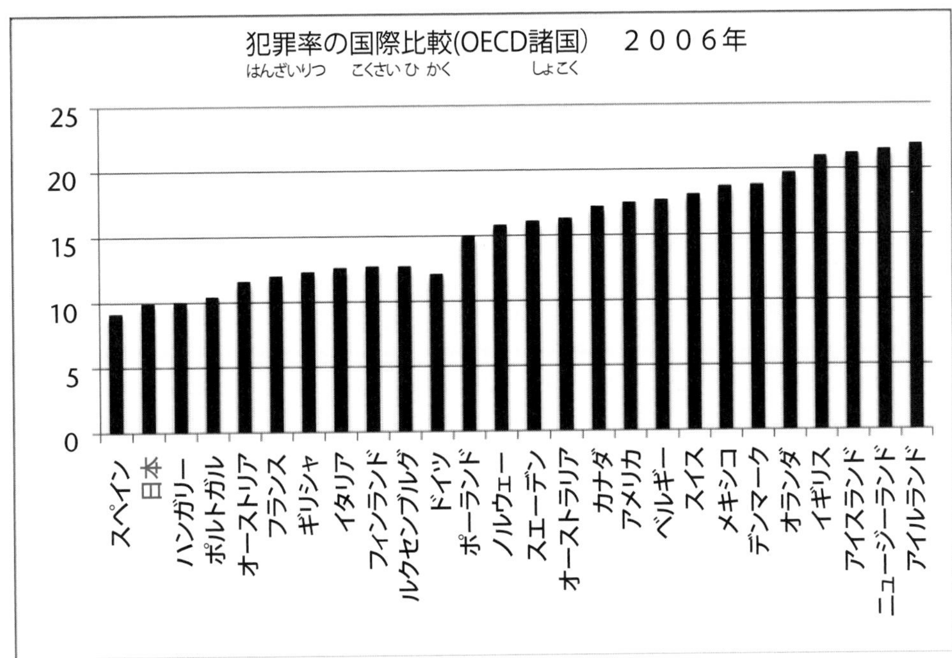

This indicates that 9.9 percent of the population of Japan were victims of at least one of the following crimes in 2006: burglary, breaking and entering or attempted breaking and entering, car theft, car vandalism, bicycle theft, sexual crime, property theft, extortion, physical violence, or motorcycle theft. Other statistics reveal that about 80 percent of crimes committed in Japan are automobile-related crimes. Violence, particularly in sexual offenses, does not get reported accurately.

Violent crimes such as murders are not prevalent. Japan has strict gun control laws, strict laws against drunk driving, and strict laws against controlled substances such as marijuana and cocaine. The use of guns is generally limited to members of organized crime gangs.

However, illegal drug use among young people such as college students has been on the rise, and the crime called いじめ, or *bullying*, has received substantial attention in educational settings. いじめ sometimes leads to suicide. Similarly, different types of bullying such as セクハラ (*sexual harassment*) and パワハラ (*power harassment*) have begun to receive social attention.

Another common crime in Japan is called 振り込めサギ (*fund-transfer scam*). It first appeared in 2003. Although scames of various sorts occur in many countries, this one has a unique form in Japan. This is a scam aimed at the elderly. There are many scenarios the scammers might use. One example is as follows. A stranger calls a house of an elderly couple. He says "It's me. I am in trouble. I hit a mob member's car and I'm being threatened with violence if I don't give them money. Please help me." This person pretends to be the son of the couple, but does not identify himself directly. He just says, オレ、オレ (*It's me, it's me*). Apparently this type of phone call creates a psychological panic in some people and leads them to falsely believe that their son is in danger. Consequently, they transfer money from an ATM machine. This sounds highly unlikely and you may wonder how such an apparently crude scam could be so successful, but during the three-month period from January to March of 2008, 5,618 incidents were reported for a total loss of 78 million dollars.

文法

I. Expressing problems and events using the passive form

A. Direct passive

The direct passive in Japanese is the equivalent to the passive construction in English. When someone does something that affects another person, the situation can be expressed from two different points of view. One is the viewpoint of the performer of the action, and the other is the viewpoint of the person affected by the action. In English, the former is expressed in active sentences such as, "Tom hit Jim," and the latter is expressed in passive sentences such as "Jim was hit by Tom." Similarly, in Japanese, an active sentence expresses the performer's point of view, and a passive sentence expresses the viewpoint of the receiving end of the action:

先生はメアリーをほめた。	メアリーは先生にほめられた。
The teacher praised Mary.	*Mary was praised by the teacher.*

A passive sentence takes the pattern: Subject は／が + agent に + passive verb form.

私は	先生に	しかられた。	*I was scolded by the teacher.*
ペットの鳥が	へびに	ころされた。	*My pet bird was killed by a snake.*
小さい時、私は	女の子に	よくいじめられました。	*I was often bullied by girls when I was little.*

私はパーティに呼(よ)ばれましたが、スミスさんは呼(よ)ばれなかったので、心配(しんぱい)していました。
I was invited to the party, but Mr. Smith was not, so he was worried about it.

イギリスにいる友達から英語で書かれた手紙が来ました。
A letter written in English arrived from my friend in England.

Verb types	Meaning	Dictionary form	Passive form		Formation
Irregular verbs	to come to do	来る する		来(こ)られる される	
る -verbs	to discard to see	すてる 見る	すて + られる 見 + られる	すてられる 見られる	Add られる to the stem
う -verbs	to deceive to invite to steal	だます 呼(よ)ぶ ぬすむ	だまさない 呼(よ)ばない ぬすまない	だまされる 呼(よ)ばれる ぬすまれる	Add れる to the plain negative stem; replace ない with れる

The particle に marks the agent (performer of the action), and the subject indicates the person who is affected by the action. (に can be replaced with から when the agent is considered as a source from which something is coming.)

私は友達に／から日本の大学について聞かれた。
I was questioned by a friend about Japanese universities.

The passive form （ら）れる conjugates as a る-verb.

negative form	いじめられない	こわされない
polite form	いじめられます	こわされます
dictionary form	いじめられる	こわされる
conditional form	いじめられれば	こわされれば
て -form	いじめられて	こわされて

The verb of a direct passive sentence must be a transitive verb. An agent is sometimes marked with によって instead of に.

村上春樹(むらかみはるき)の新しい本は色々(いろいろ)な人に読まれている。
Haruki Murakami's new book is being read by many people.

アメリカはコロンブスによって発見(はっけん)された。
America was discovered by Columbus.

The agent in a direct passive sentence can be deleted if it is understood from the context, unknown, or of no particular interest.

こんな所に子ねこがすてられている。 *Kittens are discarded in places like this.*

このお寺は１２００年にたてられました。 *This temple was built in 1200.*

あの先生は日本でもよく知られている。 *That professor is well known even in Japan.*

B. Indirect passive

Unlike English, Japanese has a second type of passive construction called the indirect passive. In an indirect passive sentence, someone does something or something happens, and the subject is adversely affected by it or troubled by the action or event. The subject has no direct involvement in the actual act or occurrence. For example, in the following sentence, the subject's TV was stolen by a burglar. In this case, the subject 私 is not directly involved in the action of stealing, but the TV was. As a consequence, however, the subject is adversely affected. The indirect passive sentence allows the subject to express negative feelings caused by the event. Direct translations of such sentences can seem very strange in English.

私はどろぼうにテレビをぬすまれた。
My TV was stolen by a thief. (lit.: *I got my TV stolen by a thief*.)

電車の中でだれかに足をふまれた。
Someone stepped on my foot in the train. (lit.: (*I*) *had my foot stepped on by someone in the train.*)

The action may be a natural occurrence or an accident, and the verbs in indirect passive sentences can either be intransitive or transitive verbs. English grammar does not allow intransitive verbs to be used in passive sentences.

私はスミスさんに悪口(わるくち)を言われた。 *Smith-san spoke ill of me .*
(lit.: *I was bad-mouthed by Smith-san.)*

雨にふられた。 *(I) got rained on.*

となりの人に服をよごされた。 *I got my clothes dirtied by the person next to me.*

だれかに車をぶつけられて、困(こま)っている。
I am annoyed because my car was hit by someone. (lit.: *I am annoyed because my car got hit by someone.*)

飛行機(き)の中で、子供に泣(な)かれて、困(こま)りました。
My child cried in the airplane, and I was embarrassed. (Lit.: *I was embarrassed because I was cried on by my baby.*)

リー： 昨日、家にどろぼうに入られちゃったんだ。
A thief broke into my house yesterday. (lit.: *Yesterday* (I had) *my house broken into by a thief.*)

山田： 何か取られたの？
Was anything stolen?

リー： うん。パソコンをぬすまれちゃったんだ。
Yes, my PC was stolen. (lit.: (I had) *my PC stolen.*)

Notes

- Unlike the direct passive, the subject of an indirect passive is always animate; that is, the subject must be capable of having feeling. Also, the agent of an indirect passive sentence is usually specific and is rarely omitted.
- One crucial difference between the direct and indirect passive is that the indirect passive tends to have a negative connotation, but the direct passive can have either a negative or a positive connotation.
- Many passive sentences in English are not necessarily expressed in passive in Japanese. For example, the verbs "to understand" and "to need" can be used in passive sentences such as "the message was understood" and "more efforts are needed." But, there is no passive form for わかる or いる (*to need*).
- The passive forms of る-verbs and 来る are identical to their potential forms. Sentence patterns, however, are very different between passive and potential sentences.

  あの動物園のさるは、フォークを使って物が食べられる。(potential form)
  The monkey at that zoo can eat things using a fork.

  さるに私のりんごを食べられた。(passive form)
  My apple was eaten by the monkey.

- The indirect passive is a is unusual in Japanese in that it is used quite often, and is used quite often. Mastery of this construction improves your Japanese significantly.

話してみましょう

Activity 1

The following statements express what happened but do not express the speaker's feeling. Change the sentences to express speaker's viewpoint more clearly using passive and add a phrase that expresses the speaker's feeling.

Example: 友達が私をだましました。
友達にだまされて、とてもかなしかったです。

1. 先生が私をほめました。
2. 台風が日本をおそいました。
3. 友達が私をパーティに招待しました。
4. 友達が私をいじめました。
5. 母が私をしかりました。
6. かみなりが私の家をこわしました。
7. どろぼうが私の家に入りました。
8. 女の人が私の足をふみました。
9. 妹が私の車をぶつけました。
10. 大雨がふりました。
11. どろぼうがにげました。

Activity 2

Work with a partner. Look at the following pictures and create a short dialogue to describe what has happened using passive constructions.

Example: A: どうしたんですか。

B: 雨にふられちゃったんです。

雨にふられました。／雨にふられてしまいました。／

Activity 3

Work with the class. Use the passive construction to ask your classmates what they would prefer that others not do. Write their names and responses.

Example: A: 人にどんなことをされたら、いやですか。

B: そうですね。うそをつかれたら、いやですね。

名前	人にされたらいやなこと

Activity 4

Work with the class. Using the passive construction, ask your classmates about things and people who have the following characteristics. Ask as many classmates as you can to find the most common answers.

Example: A: 世界(せかい) (*the world*) で一番よく知られているアメリカ人はだれだと思いますか。

B: オバマ(大統領(だいとうりょう)) (*president*) だと思います。

世界(せかい) (*world*) で一番～	クラスメートのこたえ
Well-known American	
Well-known Japanese	
Well-read book	
Frequently visited place	
Frequently spoken language	
Frequently consumed drink	
Frequently eaten food	

II. Expressing conjecture based on indirect evidence using ～らしい; expressing conjecture based on direct evidence using ～ようだ／みたいだ

A. Expressing conjecture based on indirect evidence using ～らしい (*I understand that* ～; *I hear that* ～; *the word is that* ～)

The auxiliary adjective ～らしい is used to express conjectures made by the speaker on the basis of information obtained indirectly, such as through print or word of mouth. This expression can also be used with conjectures based on visual observations, but unlike the form involving the verb or adjective stem + そうだ (*it looks like* ~), which implies a guess based on what the speaker has seen, らしい implies that the conjecture has been based on a more careful observation.

最(さい)近新しいインフルエンザがはやっているらしい。
It seems that a new (type of) influenza is spreading recently.

台(たい)風の後、まだ電気がつかなくて、不便(ふべん)らしい。
I understand that it's inconvenient because the electricity has not yet been restored since the typhoon.

気候(こう)が変わって、たつまきやハリケーンがふえているらしい。
It's my understanding that the climate has changed and there are more tornados and hurricanes.

洪水(こうずい)のひがいはあまりひどくなかったらしい。
It's my understanding that the damage from the flood was not very serious.

The word ～らしい can be combined with both adjectives and verbs. The formation is the same as for ～でしょう (*probably*) or かもしれない (*may*). That is, use a noun or な-adjective stem + らしい for the plain present affirmative form. Otherwise use the plain form + らしい.

Notes

- If the speaker's conjecture is not strong, らしい is almost the same as the hearsay expression plain form + そうだ (*I heard ~*)

  ニュースによると、中国で大きい地震(じしん)があったらしい。

  According to the news, there was a big earthquake in China.

  ニュースによると、中国で大きい地震(じしん)があったそうだ。

  According to the news, there was a big earthquake in China.

- A negative conjecture is expressed by ～ない／なかったらしい.

  あれは事故(じこ)じゃないらしい。

  The word is that that was not an accident.

  洪水(こうずい)のひがいは大きくなかったらしい。

  The word is that the damage from the flood wasn't serious.

B. Expressing conjecture based on direct evidence using ～ようだ／みたいだ (*it appears that ~*)

The auxiliary adjective ～ようだ expresses a conjecture based on first hand, reliable information (usually visual information) and the reasonable knowledge of the speaker. This expression is thus used when the likelihood of a specific action or event happening or not happening is the greatest in the speaker's mind. On the other hand, the use of verb / adjective stem + そうだ (*it looks like ~*) indicates that the speaker is making a guess based on the his or her sensory input (what the speaker sees or feels), so in this case the reliability of the speaker's guess will vary.

昨日あの店で殺人(さつじん)があったようだ。 *It appears that there was a murder at the store yesterday.*

The form ～ようだ is different from ～らしい in that ～らしい usually expresses a conjecture based on second-hand information obtained from reading or hearsay, while ～ようだ implies that the conjecture has come from first-hand information and the speaker's knowledge. Finally, it is different from ～でしょう／だろう, which is used when the speaker's conjecture is not necessarily based on any information and he or she is merely guessing.

～みたいだ is a colloquial version of ～ようだ. The degree of the speaker's confidence in his or her conjecture is less with ～みたいだ than with ～ようだ.

山本： 清水(しみず)先生は有(ゆう)名な先生のようだよ。
Apparently, Professor Shimizu is a famous professor.

高木： そうなの？あの先生、小さくてかわいくて、学生みたいだけど。
Really? She's so small and cute; she looks like a student.

A negative conjecture is expressed by ～ないようだ／～ないみたいだ／なかったようだ／なかったみたいだ.

彼女(かのじょ)とはけんかしたけど、わかれなかったようだ。
It appears that he had a fight with his girlfriend but did not break up with her.

このへん冬になるとくまがよく出てくるが、今年はまだだれも見ていないみたいだ。
There are often bears here in the winter, but apparently this year no one has seen one.

あのハリケーンで、建(たて)物のひがいは大きかったけど、なくなった人はいなかったようだ。
The structural damage from the hurricane was severe, but no one seems to have died.

Notes

- Both 〜ようだ and 〜みたいだ can be combined with adjectives and verbs. The formation of 〜みたいだ is the same as 〜らしい. That is, nouns and な-adjectives are followed by な before 〜みたいだ in the plain present affirmative form, but the plain forms of adjectives and verbs are used for other forms. Adjectives and verbs are combined with 〜ようだ in the same way that they are with 時—nouns are followed by the particle の and な-adjectives take な before 〜ようだ for the plain present affirmative form, but the plain form of adjectives and verbs are used for other forms.
- The following table shows the conjugation, source of evidence, and reliability of conjecture of らしい, ようだ, and みたいだ, as well as そうだ (it looks like) and でしょう.

<table>
<tr><td rowspan="3"></td><td colspan="2">Formation</td><td rowspan="3">Source of evidence and reliability of conjecture</td></tr>
<tr><td colspan="2">Noun うそ (lie)
な -adjective 不便(ふべん)(な) (inconvenient)
い -adjective こわい (scary)
Verbs 焼ける (to burn)</td></tr>
<tr><td>Affirmative</td><td>Negative</td></tr>
<tr><td rowspan="2">Plain form + ようだ・みたいだ
(it appears that, it seems)</td><td>うそのようだ
うそだったようだ
不便(ふべん)なようだ
不便(ふべん)だったようだ
こわいようだ
こわかったようだ
焼けるようだ
焼けたようだ</td><td>うそじゃないようだ
うそじゃなかったようだ
不便(ふべん)じゃないようだ
不便(ふべん)じゃなかったようだ
こわくないようだ
こわくなかったようだ
焼けないようだ
焼けなかったようだ</td><td rowspan="2">• First hand, reliable information
• Most reliable</td></tr>
<tr><td>うそみたいだ
うそだったみたいだ
不便(ふべん)みたいだ
不便(ふべん)だったみたいだ
こわいみたいだ
こわかったみたいだ
焼けるみたいだ
焼けたみたいだ</td><td>うそじゃないみたいだ
うそじゃなかったみたいだ
不便(ふべん)じゃないみたいだ
不便(ふべん)じゃなかったみたいだ
こわくないみたいだ
こわくなかったみたいだ
焼けないみたいだ
焼けなかったみたいだ</td></tr>
</table>

Plain form + らしい (I understand that)	うそらしい うそだったらしい 不便らしい 不便だったらしい こわいらしい こわかったらしい 焼けるらしい 焼けたらしい	うそじゃないらしい うそじゃなかったらしい 不便じゃないらしい 不便じゃなかったら こわくないらしいしい こわくなかったらしい 焼けないらしい 焼けなかったらしい	• Indirect evidence or direct observation • More reliable than stem+ そうだ
Plain form + でしょう (Probably)	うそでしょう うそだったでしょう 不便なでしょう 不便だったでしょう こわいでしょう こわかったでしょう 焼けるでしょう 焼けたでしょう	うそじゃないでしょう うそじゃなかったでしょう 不便じゃないでしょう 不便じゃなかったでしょう こわくないでしょう こわくなかったでしょう 焼けないでしょう 焼けなかったでしょう	• Evidence is not required, • Reliability varies from almost none to 100%
Adjective & verb stem + そうだ (It looks like)	不便そうだ こわそうだ 焼けそうだ	不便じゃなさそうだ こわくなさそうだ 焼けなさそうだ / 焼けそうにない	• Direct (often visual) impression • May or may not be reliable
Plain form + そうだ (I heard)	うそだそうだ うそだったそうだ 不便だそうだ 不便だったそうだ こわいそうだ こわかったそうだ 焼けたそうだ	うそじゃないそうだ うそじゃなかったそうだ 不便じゃないそうだ 不便じゃなかったそうだ こわくないそうだ こわくなかったそうだ 焼けなかったそうだ	• Hearsay, • No conjecture, because it is a reported speech

話してみましょう

Activity 1

You have overheard the following conversations between A and B. Based on what you have heard, tell your conjectures to your classmates, using ～らしい.

Example: A: 昨日どろぼうに入られたんですって？
B: ええ、家に帰ってきたら、パソコンがなくなっていたんですよ。
パソコンをぬすまれたらしいです。

1. A: 田中さん、けっこん指輪を売るんだそうですよ。
B: え、どうして？
A: ご主人とわかれるそうですよ。

2. A: 山田さんの家の近くで火事があったそうですね。
B: いいえ、火事はあったけど家からはちょっと遠かったですよ。

3. A: 先生、どうしたんですか、その足？
B: 昨日、交通事故(こうつうじこ)にあってね。

4. A: 木村(むら)さん、このごろ暗(から)いよね。
B: うん、かれとけんかしたって言っていた。

5. A: 山田さん、休みなの？
B: うん、インフルエンザだって。
A: 今月になってから、インフルエンザで休む人、多いね。

Activity 2 Using the data presented in the culture section of this chapter, express your conjectures with ～ようだ .

Example: 日本はほか (*other*) の国よりはんざいが少なくて安全(あんぜん)なようだ。

Activity 3 Work with a partner. Think about a rumor that you've recently encountered, and the source of information, and have a conversation about it.

Example: A: 東京(きょう)で大きい地震(じしん)が起きるかもしれないらしいよ。
B: え、そうなの？どうして？
A: 東京(きょう)では70年に1度大きい地震(じしん)があるけど、1923 年から大きい地震(じしん)が起きていないんだって。

III. N のような／みたいな (*like ~*); N らしい N (*typical ~*)

The conjectural expressions ～よう, ～みたい, and らしい can be used to modify a noun to express its characteristics, and when it is preceded by another noun as in Noun 1 のような／みたいな Noun 2, it means *Noun 2 that is just like Noun 1*. However, Noun 1 らしい Noun 2 expresses quite a different meaning. This section deals with the usage of these expressions when they are preceded by another noun.

A. N のような／みたいな (*like ~*)

Both Nのような and Nみたいな describe something or someone based on resemblance to something else. The resemblance tends to be visual, but not necessarily limited to that. みたい is the colloquial form of ような.

© Kenneth Hamm / Photo Japan

日本でアヒルのような電車を見ました。 *In Japan I saw a train that looks like a duck.*

日本でアヒルみたいな電車を見ました。 *In Japan I saw a train that looks like a duck.*

映画スターのような人	*a person who looks like a movie star*
クジラのようなおじさん	*a middle-aged man who looks like a whale*
花のような女の人	*a beautiful woman (literally, a woman who looks like a flower*
たつまきのような風	*a wind like a tornado*
ドラゴンボールのような頭をした人	*a person whose hairdo is like Dragon Ball* (literally: *a person who has a head like Dragon Ball*

ように and みたいに are adverbial forms of ような and みたい.

イチローのように有(ゆう)名になりたい。	*I would like to become famous like Ichiro.*
ぼくの彼女(かのじょ)は、うさぎのようにかわいい人です。	*My girlfriend is just as cute as a bunny.*
ライオンのように強くなりたい。	*I want to become strong like a lion.*

B. Noun + らしい (typical)

らしい means *having typical characteristics of* ~. Grammatically, it is an adjective. Thus, 男らしい人 is interpreted as *manly person*. This expression does not have the negative connotation found in words such as *chauvinistic*, but anyone described in this way has to be male. If the person is female, the correct Japanese is 男のような人 (*a person who acts like a man*).

子供らしい子供	*a typical child*		
女らしい人	*a ladylike person (female)*		
男らしい人	*a manly person (male)*		
女らしい女	*a ladylike woman*	女のような男	*a man who acts like a woman*
男らしい男	*a manly man*	男のような女	*a woman who acts like a man*

話してみましょう

Activity 1 Describe the following items using ～のような .

Example: ハンバーガーのようないす

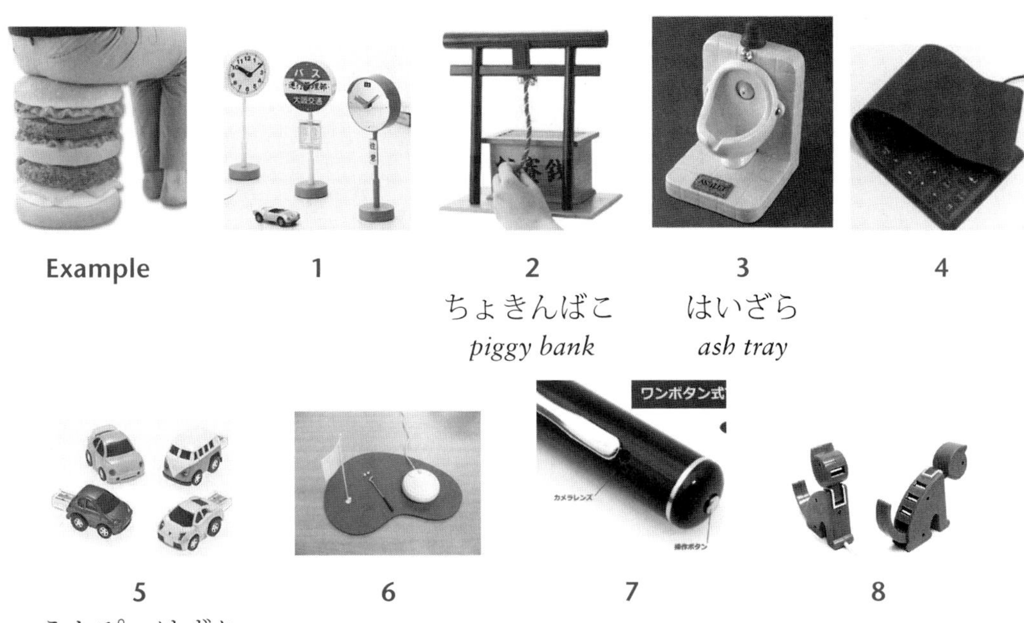

Example

1

2 ちょきんばこ *piggy bank*

3 はいざら *ash tray*

4

5 えんぴつけずり pencil sharpener

6

7

8

Activity 2 Work with a classmate. Ask what kind of person he/she wants to become in the future and write down this wish in the table. Your classmates will answer using ～のような or ～のように .

Example: A: 将来どんな人になりたいですか。

B: 私はお父さんのような人になりたいです。

or お父さんのように、強くてやさしい人になりたいです。

名前	～のような・～のように～人

Activity 3 Work with a partner. Ask your partner what he/she considers typical about the following types of people or things.

Example: 冬らしい日

A: 冬らしい日って、どんな日ですか。

B: 雪がたくさんふって、寒い日です。

～らしい人／物	パートナーの答え
1. アメリカ人らしいアメリカ人	
2. フランス人らしいフランス人	
3. 先生らしい先生	
4. 学生らしい学生	
5. 日本の車らしい自動車	
6. イタリアらしいデザイン	
7. 休みらしい休み	

Activity 4 Work with the class. Ask your classmates on what occasions they think people might exhibit the characteristics listed in the table below.

Example: 男らしい

A: どんな時、男の人を男らしいと思いますか?

B: スポーツをしている時、男らしいと思います。

～らしい	クラスメートの名前	クラスメートの答え
男らしい		
女らしい		
日本人らしい		
アメリカ人らしい		

ちょっとトリビア: The origin of the name Godzilla

One day in the Toho Studio, Mr. Tsuburaya (a special effects expert) saw a staff member who looked like a gorilla (ゴリラ) eating lunch like a whale (クジラ). ゴリラのような男がクジラのように昼ご飯を食べていた。 He combined the two words—hence, ゴジラ.

IV. Expressing limited degree using だけ〜 affirmative and しか〜 negative

The suffixes だけ and しか follow a noun or quantity expression and both of them mean *only*. However, だけ is used only with an affirmative ending, and しか is used only with a negative ending.

A. Using だけ〜 affirmative (*just; only*)

だけ follows a noun or a quantity expression to express the meaning of only.

山田さんだけが来ました。	*Only Mr. Yamada came.*
道子：まだ歩くの？	*Do we still have to walk?*
まもる：もう少しだけ。あと百メートルだけだから。	*Just a little farther. Only another hundred meters.*
高子：その話、だれかにしたの？	*Have you told the story to anyone?*
ボブ：うん、彼女(かのじょ)にだけ話した。	*Yeah, only to my girlfriend.*
山本：この駅には各(かく)駅停(てい)車だけが止まります。	*Only local trains stop at this station.*
鈴(すず)木：そうですか。次の駅は？	*I see. How about the next station?*
山本：次の駅には急(きゅう)行も止まります。	*Express trains also stop at the next station.*

昨日はつかれていたので、宿題だけしてすぐ寝ました。
Since I was tired yesterday, I only did my homework and went to bed immediately.

When だけ is used with a noun, particles such as で and に may be placed either before or after だけ Exceptions are the particles が and を. These two particles must be placed after だけ or not used at all.

動物園だけで見ることが出来ます。 or 動物園でだけ見ることが出来ます。
You can see it only in the zoo.

日本だけにあります。 or 日本にだけあります。
It is only in Japan.

かれしだけを招待(しょうたい)しました。 or かれしだけ招待(しょうたい)しました。
I invited only my boyfriend.

山田さんだけが来ました。 or 山田さんだけ来ました。
Only Yamada-san came.

B. Using しか〜 negative (only)

Like だけ, しか also means *only*, but it must be used in a sentence with a negative ending. しか is used with nouns and quantity expressions. しか implies *only* 〜 and nothing else, and sounds more exclusive than だけ. Therefore, しか is often used when the speaker expects more but finds less.

山田さんしか来ませんでした。	*Only Mr. Yamada came.* (Other people should have come.)
一万円しかありません。	*I only have 10,000 yen, and that is all.* (I should have more.)
一万円だけあります。	*I have only 10,000 yen.*

去年、台(たい)風は三つしか来ませんでした。
Only three typhoons came last year. (implies more typhoons usually come)
私は小さい地震(じしん)しか経験(けいけん)したことがありません。
I have only experienced a small earthquake.
どろぼうは家の中に５分ぐらいしかいなかったようだ。
It appears that the thief was in the house for only about five minutes .

When しか is used with a noun, the particle associated with it must precede しか. The particles が and を are omitted, but other particles remain except for the に of location, which may be deleted.

山田さんしか知りません。	*Only Mr. Yamada knows.*
肉しか食べません。	*I eat only meat.*
ここ（に）しかありません。	*It exists only here.*
私は山田さんに大学でしか会いません。	*I meet Yamada-san only on campus.*

話してみましょう

Activity 1 Answer the questions using the expressions in the parentheses and だけ or しか .

Example: 昨日たくさん人が来ていた？（高田さん）
いいえ、高田さんだけが来ていたよ。
いいえ、高田さんしか来ていなかったよ。

1. だれが知っていますか？（鈴(すず)木さん）
2. どろぼうは何人いましたか？（一人）
3. 交通事故(こうつうじこ)にあったことがありますか（一度）
4. その本はどこで売(う)っていますか。（大学の本屋）
5. 今週はずっと休みなの？（金曜日）
6. 昨日たくさん電話があった？（田中さん）
7. 何をぬすまれたんですか。（さいふ）

Activity 2

Work as a class. First write the number of each of the items below that you have in your bag or backpack. Exchange information with your classmates to find out who has more or fewer items than others. Use だけ or しか if the number of items is small.

Example: A: 私はえんぴつを三本持っています。〜さんは何本持っていますか。

B: 私は十本持っています。

C: たくさんありますね。ぼくは二本しか持っていません。

	私	クラスメート
えんぴつ		
黒か青のボールペン		
赤のボールペン		
マーカー (*marker*)		
ノート		
かぎ (*key*)		
本		
other ( )		
other ( )		

Activity 3

Work in a group of three to write as many sentences as possible using だけ and しか for each word. Take turns reading sentences to the class to see which group comes up with more sentences. Also, determine which sentence is the most creative and unique.

Example: ライオンは肉しか食べません。／肉だけ食べます。

1. 動物園のさる
2. かめ
3. 大きいさいがい
4. ハリケーン
5. 海外旅行
6. 日本語
7. 学生

Activity 4

Work with a partner. Think of a relative, a friend, or a person who has a particular habit of doing only one particular thing under certain circumstances. Then tell your partner about that person. Your partner should show an interest in what you are saying.

Example: イチローは昼にカレーライスしか食べません。

A: ねえ、聞いてくださいよ。

B: 何？

A: イチローって、昼にカレーライスだけ食べるんですよ。／カレーライスしか食べないんですよ。

B: へえ、本当！

V. Expressing opinions indirectly using ～んじゃない(かと思う)

～じゃないかと思う expresses the speaker's opinion but indicates some uncertainty.

かみなりが落ちるんじゃないかと思う。 *I think lightning might strike.*

新しいインフルエンザじゃないかと思う。 *I think this might be the new flu.*

It is similar to ～だろうと思う but is less certain.

Certain	ニュースは本当だと思う。	*I think the news is true.*
Less certain	ニュースは本当だろうと思う。	*I think the news is probably true.*
Least certain	ニュースは本当なんじゃないかと思う。	*I think the news might be true.*

～んじゃないか does of itself not indicate a negative, but merely emphasizes the uncertainty of the opinion. Use of the negative form before ～んじゃないか shows that the speaker's uncertain opinion is leaning toward the negative.

たつまきは起きないんじゃないかと思う。 *I think that a tornado will not form.*

大雨はふらないんじゃないかと思う。 *I think it won't rain heavily.*

いそがしいんじゃないかと思って、電話しなかったんだ。
I thought you'd be busy, so I didn't call you.

あの火事で田中さんの家も焼けたんじゃないかと思って、心配していたんだ。
I thought Tanaka-san's house might have been destroyed by the fire, so I was worried.

The expressions ～んじゃないですか／でしょうか, ～んじゃないかな and ～んじゃない? can be used instead of ～んじゃないかと思う to indicate that something is the speaker's opinion or that the speaker is uncertain about it.

どろぼうはにげたんじゃない？	*I think the thief has already escaped.*
どろぼうはにげたんじゃないかな。	*I think the thief has already escaped.*
変なうわさがあるんじゃないですか。	*I think there is a strange rumor.*
変なうわさがあるんじゃないでしょうか。	*I think there is a strange rumor.*

話してみましょう

Activity 1 Answer the questions using ～んじゃないかと思う .

Example: 今日雪がふるでしょうか。
さあ、よく分かりませんが、ふるんじゃないかと思います。
さあ、よく分かりませんが、ふらないんじゃないかと思います。

1. 地震(じしん)が起きた時、この建(たて)物は安全(あんぜん)だと思いますか。
2. 火事(かじ)の方が台(たい)風よりこわいと思いますか。
3. 犬は頭がいいと思いますか。
4. クジラは魚だと思いますか。
5. 日本にもくまがいると思いますか。
6. へびはライオンを食べられると思いますか。

Activity 2 Work with the class. First, write the names of the animals that you think fit the descriptions in the chart in the 私 column. Then ask three classmates about what animals they think fit the descriptions, and complete the chart.

さる　くま　クジラ　へび　かめ　ぞう　ライオン　いぬ　ねこ　ぶた　パンダ

Example: A: 中国にいないのはどの動物だと思う？
B: そうだね。クジラじゃないかと思うけど。

	私	～さん	～さん	～さん
中国にいない動物				
オーストラリアにいない動物				
動物園では見られない動物				
多すぎる動物				
少なくなっている動物				

Activity 3 Work with a partner. Ask your partner whether he or she agrees with statements 1 through 4, and why or why not.

Example: さいがいの中ではハリケーンが一番こわいです。

A: さいがいの中では、ハリケーンが一番こわいと思う？

B: ううん、ハリケーンより火事(かじ)の方がこわいんじゃない？

A: どうしてそう思うの？

B: だって ('*Cause*)、ハリケーンはいつ来るか分かるけど、火事(かじ)は分からないからね。

1. 食べるためなら、動物をころしてもいいです。
2. いじめははんざいです。
3. 人の悪口(わるくち)を言ってはいけません。
4. アメリカははんざいが多すぎます。
5. 勉強はむだです。

聞く練習

上手な聞き方

Expressions in oral narrative

Oral narratives are very common in interpersonal communication in any language. It is a part of human nature to share stories with others when something happens, whether it is good or bad. Being able to tell a story well is an important skill to have in learning a new language. The process of storytelling involves different kinds of information. For example, before you start the main plot of the story, you will need to get the attention of your listeners. Verb-past tense + んです is used frequently as an attention-getting phrase. (e.g. 「ねえ（ねえ）、聞いて（よ）。」、「〜があったんです。」) This helps to orient the audience by providing a setting and context. The main plot usually progresses chronologically. Conjunctions, such as そして, それから, それで, and the like, are used to string a chain of events. Other common expressions found in storytelling are reported speech (e.g. 「〜と言う」), and 「〜てしまう」.

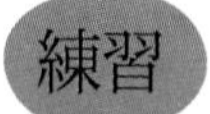

Listen to the following conversation between two people. Try to identify the common expressions used in story telling as explained above.

ブタの話

聞く前に

日本語で答えて下さい。

1. アメリカの学校では動物をかいますか。どんな動物をかいますか。
2. ブタはどんな動物だと思いますか。

聞いてみましょう

Listen to the conversation again for content.

1. 男の人と女の人のどちらが「話」をしていますか。
2. 何について話していますか。
3. 映画のタイトルは何ですか。
4. どんな映画ですか。
5. ブタは最後(さい)にどうなったと思いますか。

聞き上手話し上手

上手に話をする　上手に話を聞く
Telling a story well and listening to a story well

As explained in the previous section, when you want to tell a story you must first get the listeners' attention. Some typical opening phrases are listed below, but there are many others as well. As you can see, ねえ (or ねえねえ) is very common in casual speech.

ねえねえ、聞いて(よ)。

ねえ、昨日、おもしろいことがあったんだ。

あのう、昨日、ちょっとおもしろいことがあったんですけど。

おもしろいこと can be changed to ひどいこと, うれしいこと, かなしいこと, こと, etc.

The listener plays a very important role in the successful telling of a story. It is important for the listener to remain attentive and provide feedback to help the speaker tell the story. You learned あいづち in *Nakama 1*, Chapters 3 and 4 such as ええ, うん, あ, and そう to indicate that you are listening. You can go a step further to become a good listener. Some common phrases are listed below.

1. Indicating an interest in a conversation and maintaining the flow
   ええ、ええ。　へえ、そうですか。
2. Eliciting more information
   それで…　その後、どうなったんですか。
3. Offering a reaction
   それは大変でしたね。　それはお気のどくでしたね。　それはよかったですね。　それはうれしかったでしょうね。

4. Showing a spontaneous reaction such as surprise
   まさか。　えーっ、本当（とう）ですか。　うっそー。(very casual)
   まじー。(very casual)

As you can see, the listener is not a passive participant. However, keep in mind your initial task is to have the other person tell the entire story, and not to engage in a conversation while the story is in progress.

Try to remember incidents that made you angry, happy, sad, concerned, or surprised. Relate these to your partner as stories. Your partner should provide feedback to encourage the storytelling, as in the two examples below.

A: ねえ、ねえ、聞いて。「おくりびと」ってアカデミーしょう (*Academy award*) を取った映画らしいよ。

B: えっ、「おくりびと」って何？

A: 知らないの？何年か前の日本の映画で、なくなった人の体をきれいにしたりする人のお話よ。とてもいい映画だった。

B: そうなんだ、ぜんぜん知らなかった。かなしい映画？

A: ううん、泣（な）けるところはあるけど、かなしい映画じゃないと思う。

A: この間、かれとデートしたの。

B: うんうん。よかったじゃない。

A: でも、３０分、おくれて来たの。

B: ええ、ひどい。

A: しかも (*moreover*)、「ごめん」って言わないの。

B: うっそー。

iLrn Self-Tests

A: うん、でも、食事も映画も、全部（ぜんぶ）おごってくれたから、いいの。（おごる =*to treat someone*）

B: なんだ、ばかばかしい。(*What! That's ridiculous!*)

漢字

Using a kanji dictionary

As you begin reading more advanced materials, you will need to be able to use some sort of comprehensive **kanji** dictionary. There are several kanji dictionaries for learners of Japanese available, and most of them use variations of the traditional method to look up characters. (If you want to purchase one, you should compare them and consult with your instructor.)

Characters in a **kanji** dictionary are always grouped according to traditional radicals (部首) and ordered according to residual stroke counts within each radical group. Residual stroke counts are the number of strokes required to write a character exclusive of those needed to write the radical. Radicals themselves are ordered from the simplest to most complex in stroke counts. Thus, in order to look up a character, you must first identify its traditional radical. Then, go to the section of the dictionary that contains that radical. Lastly, count the residual strokes and look through the pages until you find the character you are looking for.

As was described in *Nakama 1*, Chapter 11, identifying a traditional radical is at times difficult, yet it is the crucial first step in using a traditional **kanji** dictionary. For example, the radical of 家 is 宀, but the radical of 字 is 子. For another example, the radical of 勝 (meaning to win) is 力, and not 月. This difficulty comes from the fact that the traditional radical system was created more than 1,000 years ago for the purpose of classifying characters, and the most salient component of the **kanji** was not necessarily assigned as the radical.

Most of the **kanji** dictionaries for learners of Japanese overcome this problem by rearranging radical groupings from traditional radicals to the most salient component shapes. In these dictionaries, you will find 家 and 字 in the same group, namely under 宀. 勝 is found in the 月 group instead of the 力 group. Once you become familiar with the idea of component shapes, it is fairly easy to identify the correct grouping in these dictionaries. The component shapes are ordered according to the number of strokes, so you need to be able to count the number of strokes correctly. The shape (宀 requires three strokes and 月 four strokes.) Some dictionaries may have a table like the one below on the inside of the front cover.

Simplified table of component shapes (or radicals)

2	亻 𠆢 亠 儿 匚 凵 冂
3	木 扌 氵 女 弓 艹 宀 囗
4	彳 方 日 心 ⻌ 疒
5	禾 罒
6	糸
7	言
8	門 雨 金 食

Once you identify the most salient component shape and its stroke count, the second step is to count the residual strokes. Since there are no short cuts for this step, you must be able to count them correctly. Within each group, there might be several characters that share the same number of residual strokes. Since they are not listed in any particular order, you will need to go through them to find the one you are looking for.

Dictionaries also have a pronunciation index for kanji at the end, so if you know or can guess either the **kun** or the **on** reading of a character, you can look it up there, also. But remember that there are many **kanji** which share the same **on** reading. Readings such as こう and せい, for example, are particularly common. Thus, if you have a choice between **on** and **kun** readings, it is better to use the **kun** reading. If an index uses Romanization for pronunciation, **on** readings are usually written in upper-case letters and **kun** readings are in lower-case letters.

Electronic dictionaries (電子(でんし)辞書)

In addition to the traditional printed kanji dictionaries, many electronic dictionaries (電子(でんし)辞書) are available on the market. These electronic dictionaries contain a large number of dictionaries such as English-Japanese, Japanese-English, Japanese-Japanese, encyclopedia, **kanji** dictionaries, and the like. With a **kanji** dictionary in an electronic format, you can search for a **kanji** by selecting its component shapes (部品検索) rather than its traditional radical (部首検索). Thus, an important skill is to break down a kanji into different component shapes. You can certainly search a **kanji** through on or kun reading as well.

Some models let you use a stylus to input **kanji** by hand (手書き入力). This type of handwriting input system is sensitive to the correct stroke order although it allows minor deviations. This is a good reason to learn the correct stroke order for the **kanji** you study.

The significant advantage of an electronic dictionary over paper dictionary is the ability to jump from one dictionary to another. Thus, you can easily go from a single **kanji** to a series of compounds, and then to a Japanese-English dictionary to find meanings.

There is dictionary software available for some game consoles. One can purchase dictionary software to use the game console as a 電子辞書.

1. Practice counting the strokes of the following components. The correct answers are provided.

a. 匚	**d.** 广	**g.** 囗	**j.** 火	**m.** 冊	**p.** 頁	**s.** 劵	**u.** 灬
b. 糸	**e.** 川	**h.** 月	**k.** 廴	**n.** 生	**q.** 己	**t.** 門	**v.** 聿
c. 日	**f.** 勹	**i.** 艹	**l.** 乂	**o.** 付	**r.** 井		

(a. 2, b. 6, c. 7, d. 3, e. 3, f. 2, g. 3, h. 4, i. 3, j. 4, k. 3, l. 2, m. 5, n. 5, o. 5, p. 9, q. 3, r. 4, s. 8, t. 8, u. 4, v. 6)

2. Now, use a **kanji** dictionary to look up the following **kanji** and the **kanji** appearing in this chapter.

   1. 勝　2. 区　3. 囲　4. 細　5. 建　6. 順　7. 府　8. 包　9. 簡　10 燃
   11. 星

3. Using the same **kanji** dictionary, find the following characters by looking them up under their **kun** and **on** readings. Compare how fast you can find them.

   1. 近 (**on:** KIN, **kun:** chikai)
   2. 習 (**on:** SYU, **kun:** narau)
   3. 会 (**on:** KAI, **kun:** au)
   4. 雪 (**on:** SETSU, **kun:** yuki)
   5. 高 (**on:** KO , **kun:** takai)
   6. 兄 (**on:** KYO, **kun:** ani)
   7. 校 (**on:** KO)
   8. 究 (**on:** KYU)
   9. 静 (**on:** SEI **kun:** shizuka)
   10. 時 (**on:** JI, **kun:** toki)

4. Write as many of the component shapes of the following **kanji** as you can.

   1. 試
   2. 験
   3. 笑
   4. 泣
   5. 泳
   6. 払
   7. 売
   8. 落
   9. 研
   10. 究

Flashcards

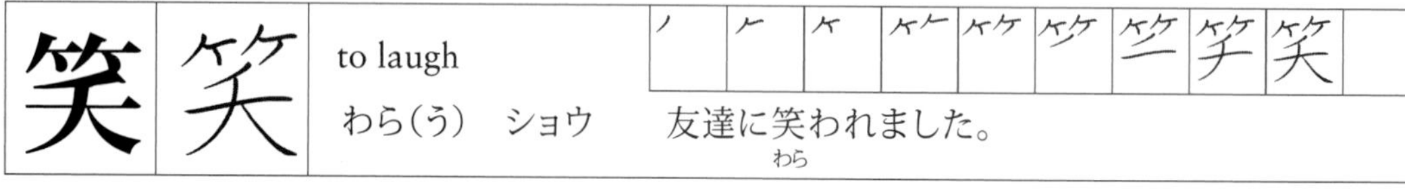

Kanji	Meaning	Readings	Example
泣	to cry	な(く)　キュウ	子供に泣[な]かれて、困[こま]りました。
泳	to swim	およ(ぐ)　エイ	魚みたいに泳[およ]ぎます。
払	to pay	はら(う)　フツ	レストランでお金を払[はら]わなかった。
売	to sell	う(る)　バイ	ネットでギターを売[う]りました。
落	to fall, to drop	お(ちる)・お(とす)　ラク	試験に落[お]ちました。
助	to help, assist	たす(かる・ける)　ジョ	とても助[たす]かります。
考	to think	かんが(える)　コウ	あの人のことしか考[かんが]えていない。
決	to decide	き(める)　き(まる)　ケツ	日本に行くことに決[き]めました。
待	to wait	ま(つ)　タイ	パーティに招待[しょうたい]されました。　待[ま]って下さい。
遊	to play, idle	あそ(ぶ)　ユウ	友達と遊園地[ゆうえんち]で遊[あそ]びました。
呼	to call	よ(ぶ)　コ	タクシーを呼[よ]んで下さい。

招	招	to invite まね(く)　ショウ	食事に招待(しょうたい)されました。
忙	忙	busy いそが(しい)　ボウ	試験があるので、とても忙(いそが)しい。
静	静	quiet, calm しず(か)　セイ	先生の家がある所はとても静(しず)かです。
暗	暗	dark くら(い)　アン	暗(くら)いから気をつけて下さい。
点	点	point, dot テン	この間の試験の点(てん)は９０点(てん)でした。
夜	夜	night, evening よる　ヤ	夜(よる)はさむくなりますよ。
心	心	mind, heart こころ　シン	母の病気のことが心配(しんぱい)です。
配	配	to deliver くば(る)　ハイ・バイ	心配(しんぱい)しないで下さい。
困	困	to be in trouble こま(る)　コン	となりの人がうるさくて困(こま)っています。
経	経	passage of time ケイ・キョウ	日本の経済(けいざい)　経済学(けいざいがく)　経験(けいけん)

読めるようになった漢字

笑う　泣く　泳ぐ　払う　売る　売り場　落ちる　落とす　助かる　考える
決まる　決める　待つ　遊ぶ　遊園地　呼ぶ　招待する　忙しい　静か暗い
点　夜　心配　困る　経験　経営(えい)学　火事　事故(こ)　交(こう)通事故(こ)　変わる　洪水(こうずい)

下の文を読んで下さい。

1. この試験は受けた経験がないので心配しています。あまりいい点は取れないと思います。
2. 赤ちゃんはすぐ笑ったり泣いたりします。
3. まだ、授業料を払っていません。
4. A: 今度の週末に遊園地に行きませんか。
   B: すみません、今週末はちょっと忙しいんです。
5. 好きな人を映画に招待することに決めました。
6. 大きい店なのに、パソコン売り場がないので、おどろいた。
7. 私は泳げないので、海では困ります。
8. さいふを落としてしまったから、友達を呼びました。
9. このへんは、夜は静かで暗くなるので、気をつけて下さい。

読む練習

上手な読み方

Understanding the structure of Japanese narrative texts

When narrating a story, an English writer often organizes the story in terms of how events are sequenced. For example,

Tomoko did not do well on the test. So her mother scolded her.

This is also the case in Japanese. However, the story also needs to be organized in terms of a single person's perspective in Japanese. Therefore, a literal translation of an English story, such as the following example, sounds awkward in Japanese. In this example, the two sentences express different perspectives: Tomoko in the first sentence and the mother in the second sentence.

ともこさんはテストが出来なかった。だから、お母さんはおこった。

In order to maintain a consisent viewpoint throughout the story, the topic of the sentence should be kept constant across sentences.

ともこさんはテストが出来なかった。だから、お母さんにおこられた。
Tomoko did not do well on the text. So she was scolded by the mother.

Another difference between English and Japanese narrative is the use of tense. In English, a writer normally stays in a single tense (i.e. present or past), but tenses can be mixed in Japanese. Writers can use the past tense to describe the foreground, or main events in a sequence. At the same time the writer can also use the present tense to express background information or to express events in a vivid, imaginative way.

Compare the following example in Japanese and in its literal translation in English.

あやかは朝起きて、空を見た。今日はとてもいい天気だ。かずおはまだ寝ている。あやかはコーヒーを入れて、かずおを起こしに行った。

Ayaka woke up in the morning and looked at the sky. It is a fine day today. Kazuo is still sleeping. Ayaka made coffee and went to wake Kazuo up.

Text A and B describes the same story, but one of them flows better than the other. Compare the text and decide which one is the better text and tell the reason.

Text A
この間、父は、おなかが痛くなって、病院に行った。そしたら、手術(しゅじゅつ) (*surgery*) をしなければならないと言われた。父は医者も病院もきらいだ。だから、手術(しゅじゅつ)はしたくない。でも、手術(しゅじゅつ)の予約をするために病院に電話したら、「明日入院して下さい。」と言われた。突然だったので、父は思わず、「今、ちょっと気分が悪いので、来週にしてもらえませんか」と言ってしまった。

Text B
父はこの間おなかが痛くなって、病院に行った。そしたら、医者が手術(しゅじゅつ)をしなければならないと言った。父は医者も病院もきらいだった。だから、手術(しゅじゅつ)はしたくなかった。でも、手術(しゅじゅつ)の予約をするために病院に電話したら、病院が「明日入院して下さい。」と言った。突然だったので、父は思わず、「今、ちょっと気分が悪いので、来週にしてもらえませんか」と言ってしまった。

地球(ちきゅう)の温暖化(おんだんか) Global warming

読む前に

A. 下の文を読んで、アンダーラインの言葉の意味は何か考えて下さい。

1. <u>地球(ちきゅう)</u>は今私たちや動物が住んでいる所で、外から見ると、青くてきれいだそうです。
2. 地球(ちきゅう)が暖(あたた)かくなることを<u>温暖化(おんだんか)</u>といいます。
3. 小さい子供のおもちゃはたいてい<u>プラスチック</u>で作られています。赤ちゃんの食べ物の入れ物もたいていプラスチックで作られています。
4. 色々(いろいろ)な国の人が会ってする大きいミーティングを<u>国際会議(こくさいかいぎ)</u>と言います。
5. トースターやオーブンやドライヤーのことを<u>電気製品(せいひん)</u>と言います。
6. 人や動物は<u>二酸化炭素(にさんかたんそ)</u>を出します。車も二酸化炭素(にさんかたんそ)を出します。

B. 質問に答えて下さい。

1. 地球は毎年暖かくなっていると言われていますが、それについてどう思いますか。
2. どうして地球は暖かくなっているのだと思いますか。
3. 地球の気温が上がるとどうして困るのですか。
4. ～さんの国ではこの問題について、どんなことをしていますか。
5. ～さんはどんなことをしたらいいと思いますか。

読んでみましょう

次の文章 (*text*) には知らない言葉がたくさんありますが、気にしないで (*without worrying*) 読んで、概要 (*gist*) だけ取って下さい。

言葉のリスト

沈む	to sink	砂漠	desert
二酸化炭素	CO_2	世界	world

　1850年頃まで、地球の温度はあまり変わらなかったそうだ。しかし、1850年から地球の温度は少しずつ上がっているそうだ。そして、1970年頃から気温の上がり方が急に高くなっていると言われていて、1900年から2100年までに地球の温度は2℃から6℃ぐらい上がるそうだ。これを地球温暖化という。

　温暖化が進むと、海面水位は60cm から1m ぐらい上がってしまうらしい。そうなると、海の中に沈んでしまう国もあるようだ。例えば、オーストラリアの北東にあるツバルという国や、ダイビングで有名なモルディブは沈んでしまうと言われている。

　温暖化の被害は他にもある。例えば、アメリカではハリケーンが、日本では台風や洪水が多くなるし、中国の北の方は砂漠が増えていくようだ。そこで、この問題について、1992年から色々な国で国際会議が開かれているようだ。

　温暖化を起こすものは色々あるが、そのうち64%は二酸化炭素である。1994年の調べでは、日本は世界で四番目に二酸化炭素を多く出していた。また、日本では、1992年から1994年までに、二酸化炭素が7%も増えていた。

　二酸化炭素(にさんかたんそ)が急に増(ふ)えたのは、人のライフ・スタイルが変わったからである。毎年、森は少しずつなくなり、畑(はたけ)や町になった。そして、歩く人は少なくなり、車に乗る人が増(ふ)えた。テレビや冷蔵庫(れいぞうこ)は大きくなり、オーブンやエアコンなどの電気製品(せいひん)を使う人も多くなった。それに、スーパーやデパートでは野菜も果(くだ)物も肉もプラスチックの入れ物に入れられているし、スプーン、フォーク、お皿(さら)など色々(いろいろ)な物がプラスチックで作られ、捨(す)てられている。
実際(じっさい)、私達が毎日出す二酸化炭素(にさんかたんそ)は全体の４５%にもなるらしい。

　温暖化(おんだんか)を防(ふせ)ぐために、国や工場(こうじょう)や大会社がしなければならないことはたくさんあるが、一人一人が自分のライフ・スタイルを変えなければならないのではないだろうか。便利(り)だから、楽だからといって、自動車や電気製品(せいひん)を使いすぎないように今からしていかなければ、この地球(ちきゅう)を守(まも)ることは出来ない。

読んだ後で

A. 下の質問に日本語で答えて下さい。

1. 地球温暖化(ちきゅうおんだんか)って何ですか。
2. この文章(ぶんしょう) (*text*) を書いた人は何が言いたいのですか。
3. ２１００年までにはどんなことが起きるかもしれませんか。それはどうしてですか。
4. この文章(ぶんしょう)を書いた人は、どうして二酸化炭素(にさんかたんそ)は多くなっていると言っていますか。

B. Read the following statements about global warming and circle はい if the statement is true according to what you read, and いいえ if it isn't.

1. はい　いいえ　温暖化(おんだんか)のげんいん (*cause*) は二酸化炭素(にさんかたんそ)だけだ。
2. はい　いいえ　電気を使うと二酸化炭素(にさんかたんそ)が多くなる。
3. はい　いいえ　温暖化(おんだんか)になると、中国で洪水(こうずい)が増(ふ)える。
4. はい　いいえ　日本では三年間で二酸化炭素(にさんかたんそ)が7パーセントふえた。
5. はい　いいえ　温暖化(おんだんか)をふせぐためには、公害(こうがい)を起こさないようにすることが一番大事だ。

C. 下のグラフは二酸化炭素(にさんかたんそ)をたくさん出している国のデータです。グラフを見て、質問に答えて下さい。

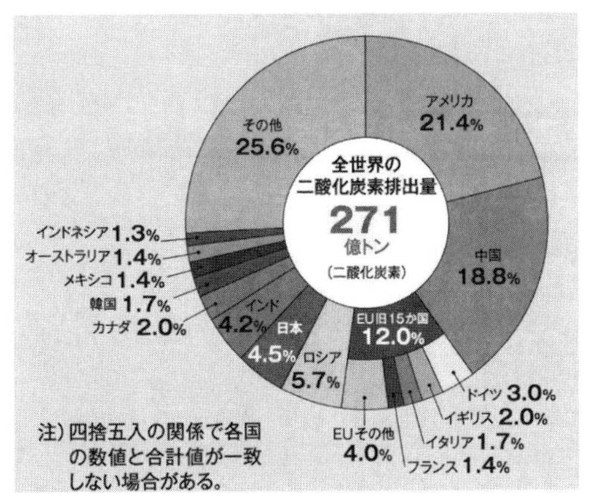

国別の二酸化炭素排出量

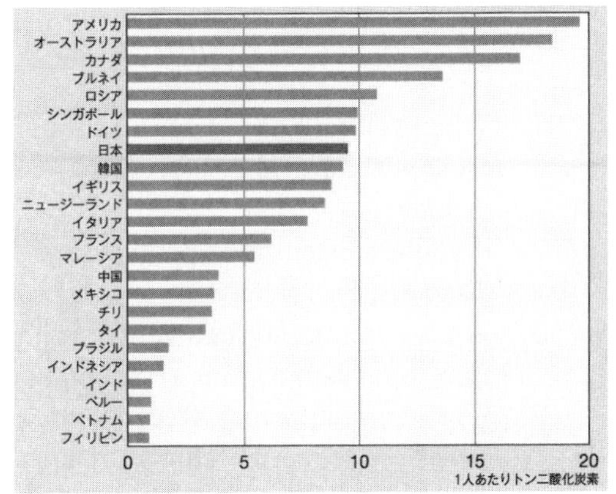

一人あたりの二酸化炭素排出量

1. 二酸化炭素を一番多く出している国はどの国ですか。
2. どの国の人達が二酸化炭素を多く出していますか。
3. この国はどうして二酸化炭素を多く出しているのだと思いますか。
4. この国はどうすれば二酸化炭素を少なくすることが出来ると思いますか。
5. 二酸化炭素を世界で二番目に多く出している国はどの国ですか。
6. この国が二酸化炭素を出しているのはどうしてだと思いますか。

総合練習

A. ゴシップをしてみよう

Work in groups of three or four. Gossip about the topics below.

ゴシップ１： えりかです。ボーイフレンドがほしいんですが、今はいません。好きなタイプはキムタクみたいな男の人です。せが高くて、イケメンが好きです。

ゴシップ２： 高橋です。来年、アメリカに行って、日本のレストランではたらこうと思っています。でも、英語がぜんぜん出来ないので、心配です。レストランのオーナーになりたいんです。

ゴシップ３： さいとうです。この間、おさけを飲みすぎてしまいました。パーティでうたをうたったり、さわいだりしたのですが、おぼえていません。朝起きたら自分のアパートで寝ていて、おどろきました。でも、どうやって帰ってきたのか分かりませんでした。

B. さいがいの経験 Experiences with natural disasters

1. When you talk about your personal experiences, or someone's experiences, with accidents, natural disasters, etc., what sort of details do you think are important to include?
2. If you are listening to people describing their experience about accidents, natural disasters, etc., what sort of questions would you ask?
3. When listening to such stories, what kind of expressions do you use to show your emotional support, interest, and understanding?
4. Work with a partner. Recall a personal experience with a natural disaster. (If you have never experienced one, relate an experience had by a family member or friend.) Try to recall all the details so you can describe them to the others. Ask questions to each other. Then write about what you have heard and describe the story to the class.

Example:

A: ～さんはさいがいを経験したことがありますか。

B: ええ、あります。私は小学校三年生の時、日本に住んでいたんですが、その時、大きい地震がありました。

A: そうですか。日本のどこに住んでいたんですか。

B: 東京です。

A: そうですか。じゃあ、その時のことをもう少し話してくれませんか。

B: ええ、いいですよ。その日は日曜日で、私は家にいたんです。

ロールプレイ

1. You heard a rumor that an earthquake is likely to happen in Tokyo in the near future. Ask your friend what to do when an earthquake happens.
2. You heard about a severe earthquake in a town where some of your Japanese friends live. You tried to call your friends but the phone lines are jammed. You would like to know more about the situation. Tell another Japanese friend about it, and ask what you should do.
3. You suspect that the nearby factory is polluting your town and causing a health problem. Tell your neighbor about your suspicion and explain why you think this. Express your anger and concern.
4. You think that you are being discriminated against by your boss because of your race (or gender). Describe your situation to your friend and ask for suggestions.
5. You have a roommate who is irresponsible. The roommate does many irresponsible things, such as staying up late, bringing friends over, not cleaning up, etc. Complain to your friend about your roommate.
6. You had your apartment broken into and some things are missing. Report the incident to a police officer.
7. You heard a rumor that a new type of influenza is spreading in the United States. You are supposed to meet a friend at Narita Airport who is coming from the United States to Japan in a few days. Ask your friend for advice.

Chapter 9

第九課

Kenneth Hamm / Photo Japan

文化と習慣

ぶんか　しゅうかん

Culture and Customs

Objectives Describing customs, regulation and expressing appreciation, and asking for permission to do something

Vocabulary Culture, customs, world religions, socializing, leave taking

Dialogue 日本で困ったこと *Problems Alice faced in Japan*

Japanese Culture An outline of Japanese history, religion and customs in Japan

Grammar

I. Expressing the performance of a favor using てあげる／くれる／もらう

II. Making or letting someone do something using the causative form

III. Requesting permission to do something using the causative て-form and request expressions

IV. Expressing the immediate future using ～る+ところ; the current situation using ～ている+ところ; and the immediate past using ～た+ばかり／ところ

V. Expressing time durations using 間 and 間に; tense in subordinate clauses

Listening Monitoring and evaluating your understanding, きせきの口紅(くちべに) *Miracle lipsticks*

Communication Leave taking

Kanji Guessing the meanings of unfamiliar **kanji**

化　治　京　説　調　集　的　失　々　難

不　利　当　期　和　重　活　弱　界　正　由　付

Reading Monitoring and evaluating your understanding, まんが

Chapter Resources

www.cengagebrain.com

iLrn Heinle Learning Center

Audio Program

Flashcards

単語

たん

Nouns

あいさつ	挨拶	a greeting, ～にあいさつ(を)する to greet ~
アドバイス		advice, アドバイスをする to advise
アニメ		animation
いけばな	生け花	flower arranging
イスラムきょう	イスラム教	Islam
いのり	祈り	prayer, おいのりをする to offer a prayer
インターネット		Internet, it can be abbreviated as ネット
おじぎ	お辞儀	bowing, おじぎをする to bow
キス		kiss, キスをする to kiss
きょういく	教育	education
きょうみ	興味	interest, ～にきょうみがある interested in ~
キリストきょう	キリスト教	Christianity
げいじゅつ	芸術	art
けいざい	経済	economy
さどう	茶道	tea ceremony
し	詩	poetry
しゃかい	社会	society
しゅうかん	習慣	custom
しゅうきょう	宗教	religion
しゅうじ	習字	calligraphy
しんとう	神道	Shinto religion
せいざ	正座	formal Japanese style sitting posture, せいざをする to sit in a formal Japanese style
せいじ	政治	politics
せかい	世界	world
そうだん	相談	consultation, ～にそうだんする to consult with ~
たのみ	頼み	request
チップ		tip
つきあい		correspondence
はいく	俳句	a Japanese verse form that consists of lines of five, seven, and five syllables.
ハグ		hug, ハグをする to hug
ぶっきょう	仏教	Buddhism

ブログ		blog
ぶんか	文化	culture
ほか	他	other, ほかの人 other people, ほかの学生 other students
マンガ	漫画	cartoon
みおくり	見送り	farewell, leave taking
み（ん）な	皆	all, everyone, みなさん（皆さん）everyone
ゆか	床	floor
ユダヤきょう	ユダヤ教	Judaism
らくご	落語	rakugo, a traditional storytelling performance
りゆう	理由	reason

う -verbs

あやまる	謝る	to apologize
いわう	祝う	to celebrate
ことわる	断る	to refuse
すわる	座る	to sit down
つきあう	つき合う	to go out with, to keep company with, to have a steady relationship
みおくる	見送る	to see someone off, みおくりに行く to send someone off

る -verbs

しんじる	信じる	to believe
たすける	助ける	to save, to help
むかえる	迎える	to welcome, むかえに行く to go to meet someone

い -adjectives

おもい	重い	heavy
こころぼそい	心細い	lonely, helpless

な -adjectives

しつれい（な）	失礼（な）	rude
ていねい（な）	丁寧（な）	polite
でんとうてき（な）	伝統的（な）	traditional

Adverbs

ぜったい（に）	絶対（に）	definitely
はっきり		explicitly

Suffixes

～てき（な）	～的（な）	suffix that converts kanji compound nouns to な -adjectives, でんとうてき traditional, せいじてき political, けいざいてき, economical しゃかいてき social, ぶんかてき cultural

Expressions

いろいろおせわになりました。	色々お世話になりました。	You've taken very good care of me. Thank you for everything.
おかげ（さま）で	お陰（様）で	thanks to ～
これからもどうぞよろしく（おねがいします）。	これからもどうぞよろしく（お願いします）。	Please stay in touch (with me) in the future, too.
そろそろしつれいします。	そろそろ失礼します。	I should be going.
どうもごちそうさま（でした）。	どうもご馳走様（でした）。	Thank you very much for the meal/drinks.
なんのおかまいもしませんで。	何のおかまいもしませんで。	We did not offer much (by way of treats).

単語の練習

A. 文化と習慣 Culture and customs

政治 politics	教育 education	経済 economy	社会 society	げいじゅつ art
生け花 flower arranging	茶道 tea ceremony	習字 calligraphy	はいく haiku poetry	落語 Japanese storytelling
し poetry	マンガ cartoon, comic		アニメ anime	インターネット Internet / ブログ blog
おじぎをする to bow	キスをする to kiss		ハグする to hug	正座する to sit in formal Japanese style
ゆかにすわる to sit on the floor	チップをはらう to tip (a waiter/waitress, etc.)		～に興味がある to be interested in	伝統的（な） traditional / 文化的（な） cultural

Activity 1 Use the words above to identify what is happening in the illustrations.

おぼえていますか。

れきし　きせつ　神社　お寺　美術館(びじゅつ)　博物館(はく)　おまつり　教会　かぶき　思い出　カラオケ　ミュージカル

Activity 2 日本語で質問に答えて下さい。

1. どれが伝統的(でんとうてき)な文化(ぶんか)ですか。どれが文化的(ぶんかてき)に新しいですか。
2. 日本の文化(ぶんか)のどんなものに興味(きょうみ)がありますか。
3. 落語(らくご)を見に行ったことがありますか。かぶきはどうですか。
4. 生け花(いけばな)や茶道(さどう)や習字(しゅうじ)をしたことがありますか。してみたいものがありますか。
5. アメリカの経済(けいざい)は今どうですか。
6. いい社会(しゃかい)って、どんな社会(しゃかい)だと思いますか。
7. 日本の政治(せいじ)や経済(けいざい)に興味(きょうみ)がありますか。ほかに、日本の何に興味(きょうみ)がありますか。
8. 教育(きょういく)と経済(けいざい)とどちらの方が大事だと思いますか。
9. アメリカにある習慣(しゅうかん)はどれですか。ない習慣(しゅうかん)はどれですか。
10. 日本にはある習慣(しゅうかん)はどれだと思いますか。ない習慣(しゅうかん)はどれだと思いますか。

伝統文化(でんとうぶんか) Traditional culture

うきよえ	浮世絵	traditional Japanese woodblock prints
おどり	踊り	traditional dance
げいじゅつ	芸術	art
げいのう	芸能	entertainment, show
こと	琴	Japanese harp, koto
しゃみせん	三味線	Japanese three-string guitar, shamisen
とうげい	陶芸	ceramic art
のう	能	Noh Play
ぶんらく	文楽	a Bunraku puppet show, a type of にんぎょうじょうるり
やきもの	焼き物	ceramics, ceramic ware, pottery

げんだい文化(ぶんか) Modern culture

あぶらえ	油絵	oil painting
えんげき	演劇	drama, play
かいが	絵画	painting
クラフト		crafts
ダンス		western style dance
バレエ		ballet

B. 世界(せかい)の宗教(しゅうきょう) World Religions

キリスト教(きょう)	イスラム教(きょう)	仏教(ぶっきょう)	神道(しんとう)	ユダヤ教(きょう)
Christianity	Islam	Buddhism	Shinto	Judaism

しんじる	おいのりをする	祝う
to believe	to offer a prayer	to celebrate

Note

- おいのりをする means literally *to do a prayer*. The noun いのり (*prayer*) is derived from the ます-stem of the verb いのる.

Activity 3 質問に答えて下さい。

1. 世界(せかい)で一番しんじられている宗教(しゅうきょう)はどれですか。二番目はどれですか。
2. ほかに、世界(せかい)にはどんな宗教(しゅうきょう)がありますか。
3. どの宗教(しゅうきょう)についてよく知っていますか。どの宗教(しゅうきょう)のことはあまり知りませんか。
4. 日本でよくしんじられている宗教(しゅうきょう)は、どの宗教(しゅうきょう)だと思いますか。

Activity 4

Work with a partner. Identify three countries which have a significant number of believers in each of the religions on the list. When you are done compare your list with other pairs.

Example: A: キリスト教(きょう)を信じている人はどの国が一番多いと思う？
B: アメリカだと思う。〜さんは？

宗教(しゅうきょう)	国
キリスト教(きょう)	
イスラム教(きょう)	
仏教(ぶっきょう)	
ユダヤ教(きょう)	

Activity 5

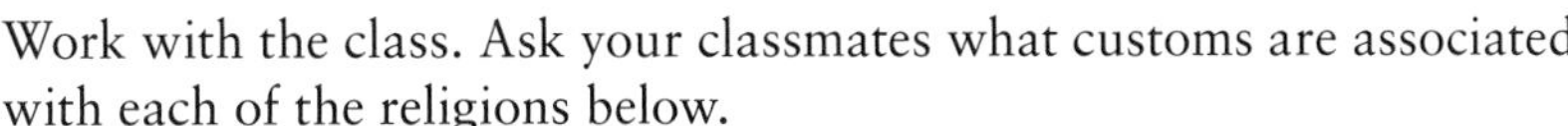

Work with the class. Ask your classmates what customs are associated with each of the religions below.

Example: A: キリスト教(きょう)にはどんな習慣(しゅうかん)がありますか。
B: 日曜日に教会へ行っておいのりをする習慣(しゅうかん)があります。

宗教(しゅうきょう)	習慣(しゅうかん)
キリスト教(きょう)	
イスラム教(きょう)	
仏教(ぶっきょう)	
ユダヤ教(きょう)	

C. おつきあい Socializing

〜とつきあう／〜につきあう
to associate with someone, to keep someone's company

あいさつをする
to greet

たのみをことわる
to refuse a favor

あやまる
to apologize

助(たす)ける
to save, to help

アドバイスをする
to advise

そうだんする
to consult with

見送(みおく)りに行く
to go to see someone off

むかえに来る
to come to greet someone

はっきり
explicitly

理由(りゆう)を言う
to say the reason

みんな
all people, everyone

ほかの人
other people

ていねい（な）
polite

失礼(しつれい)（な）
rude

Note

- 助(たす)ける means *to help someone out of a difficult situation*, such as rescuing a person, saving someone's life, saving someone from shame, or lending someone money. On the other hand 手伝う (*Nakama 2*, Chapter 4) means to *provide assistance*, such as helping someone with moving furniture or helping someone do homework.

おぼえていますか。

たのむ　手伝う　かす　かりる　つれてくる　つれていく　お礼を言う
よろこぶ　もらう　あげる　さし上げる　くれる　下さる　もらう　いただく
なれる　招待する　心配　家族　ご家族　近所の人　いじめる

Activity 6 Compare a Japanese custom with a custom in your country, using the following statements below.

Example: 日本では、バレンタインデーに女の人から男の人にチョコレートをあげる習慣(しゅうかん)があります。
アメリカでは、女の人にも男の人にもプレゼントをあげる習慣(しゅうかん)があります。

1. 日本では、クリスマスにデートをする習慣(しゅうかん)があります。
2. 日本では、お正(しょう)月に子供にお金をあげたり、神(じん)社やお寺に行ったりする習慣(しゅうかん)があります。
3. 日本では、食事の前に「いただきます」という習慣(しゅうかん)があります。
4. 日本では、ご飯を食べたら、「ご馳走(ちそう)さまでした」という習慣(しゅうかん)があります。
5. 日本では、部屋のドアをいつもしめておく習慣(しゅうかん)があります。
6. 日本的(てき)な家では、ゆかにすわる習慣(しゅうかん)があります。
7. 日本では、あやまる時、理由(りゆう)をあまり言わない習慣(しゅうかん)があります。
8. 日本では、何かをたのまれたとき、はっきりことわらない習慣(しゅうかん)があります。

Activity 7 Complete the following sentences by inserting the appropriate expressions in the blank.

1. キムさんはパクさんとつきあっていましたが、＿＿＿＿＿＿＿そうです。
2. はじめて会った人と＿＿＿＿＿＿＿時、キスをしますか。
3. 車が止まって困っている人を＿＿＿＿＿＿＿あげた。
4. 友達がガールフレンドのことで困っていたので、＿＿＿＿＿＿＿をしました。
5. スミスさんがアメリカに帰るので、空港(こう)まで＿＿＿＿＿＿＿。
6. 今日新しい先生が来るので、みんなで先生を＿＿＿＿＿＿＿行きました。

D. わかれのあいさつ

色々お世話になりました。	Thanks for all the hospitality you've shown me.
これからもどうぞよろしく（おねがいします）。	Please stay in touch in the future.
（どうも）ご馳走さま（でした）。	Thank you for the meal.
たいしたおかまいもしませんで。	We did not offer much (by way of treats).
そろそろ、失礼します。	I should be going.
おかげ（さま）で	thanks to ～

おぼえていますか。

おめでとうございます　さようなら

Activity 8 下の会話を練習して下さい。

1. 空港で

   A: 今まで色々お世話になりました。どうも有難うございました。

   B: いえ、これからもがんばって下さいね。

   B: はい、これからもどうぞよろしくおねがいします。

2. 送別会で

   A: みなさんのおかげで、とても楽しい一年でした。どうも有難うございました。

   B: 元気でね。

3. 友達のご両親の家で

   A: 今日はどうもご馳走さまでした。とてもおいしかったです。

   B: いいえ。何のおかまいもしませんで。

   A: じゃあ、そろそろ失礼します。

ダイアローグ

はじめに

質問に日本語で答えて下さい。

1. どんな所に旅行に行ったことがありますか。
2. 何日ぐらい行きましたか。

日本で困ったこと *Problems Alice faced in Japan*

The following **manga** frames are scrambled, so they are not in the order described by the dialogue. Read the dialogue and unscramble the frames by writing the correct number in the box in each frame.

石田さんと上田さんと鈴木(すず)道子さんが話をしています。

石田：　アリス、日本に来てもう二年かな？

上田：　うん、そうね。

石田：　早いね。

上田：　ええ、でも日本に来たばかりの時は、日本の文化(ぶんか)や習慣(しゅうかん)が分からなくて大変だった。

石田：　そうなんだ。

上田：　うん、お風呂(ふろ)とかおはしについては、アメリカの学校でも教えてもらったんだけど、判子(はん)をいつ使うか分からなかったから、よく判子(はん)を忘れたり、ATM の日本語が読めなくて使えなかったり。

鈴木(すず)：　ほんと、はじめは大変そうだったよね。

上田：　それにね、道が分からなくて、ホストファミリーを心配させちゃったこともある。

石田： え、何があったの？

上田： 電車を間違えて、千葉の方に行っちゃったの。でも、電車をおりたところで、帰りの電車がなくなっちゃったって分かって。

石田： で、どうしたの？

上田： で、どうしようかと思っているところに、親切な人がけいたいをかしてくれたの。それで、その電話で家に電話をかけさせてもらったの。

石田： え、けいたい持ってなかったの？

上田： まだ買ってなかったの。で、お父さんがむかえに来てくれたんだけど、待ってる間、寒くて心細かった。

石田： そりゃ、そうだよね。

上田： だから、お父さんの顔を見た時、本当にうれしかった。

鈴木： その後、すぐけいたい買わされたよね。

上田： うん、でもけいたいはぜったいいるなあって、あの時つくづく思った。

石田： たしかにそうだね。日本は公衆電話が少ないし、さがすのも大変だから、けいたいのない生活なんて、考えられないね。

Dialogue Phrase Notes

- あの時 means at that time. あの is used when both the speaker and the hearer are assumed to be familiar with an event in question as in this context. その is used when the speaker does not assume that the listener is familiar with the event.
- つくづく means *deeply* or *sincerely*.
- 公衆電話 means *public phone*.

ダイアローグの後で

A. 日本語で質問に答えて下さい。

1. 上田さんは日本に何年いますか。
2. 上田さんはホストファミリーをどんなことで困らせましたか。
3. 上田さんが電車を間違えた時、だれが何を上田さんにしてくれましたか。
4. お父さんが車でむかえに来る間、上田さんはどこで何をしていましたか。
5. ホストファミリーのお父さんは上田さんに何をさせましたか。
6. 上田さんは、日本では何がいると思っていますか。
7. 石田さんは上田さんと同じ考えですか。どうしてそう思いますか。

B. Assuming that Ms. Ueda and Ms. Suzuki are talking with Professor Tanaka instead of Mr. Ishida. Re-create the conversational styles in the dialogue using more polite expressions.

日本の文化

日本の歴史 An outline of Japanese history

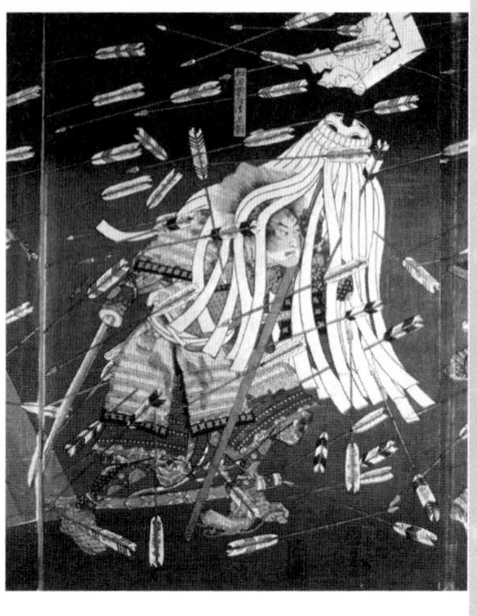

Utagawa Kuniyoshi / Getty Images

About 10,000 years ago, the Japanese islands were separated from the Asian continent. Ancient Japan was mainly agricultural. Many small states existed in Japan, but by the fourth century a political power in Yamato (Nara) ruled over Japan. During this period the Japanese imported a good deal of advanced knowledge from China, including Buddhism, Confucianism, political systems, orthography, and the like; this borrowing continued throughout early Japanese history. In 710, Nara became the first capital of Japan to be ruled by the Imperial family. In 794, a new capital, modeled after the Chinese capital city, was created in Kyoto. The society was dominated by aristocrats. Life in the capital was marked by elegance and refinement, but military families were gaining power in the outlying areas. Between 1167 and 1185, the warrior clan Heike established the first government run by members of the warrior class. Although the Heike maintained a close relationship with the aristocrats and adopted many of their customs, many scholars consider this as the beginning of the Japanese feudal period ruled by the 武士, or 侍 (*warriors*). In 1185, the Minamoto, also a warrior clan, took over the government and established a military government called 幕府 in Kamakura (near present-day Tokyo). During the 15th century, feudal lords fought among themselves for dominance and in 1603, the Tokugawa family reunited the country, establishing the 江戸幕府. Edo (present-day Tokyo) became the country's political center. The Tokugawa family adopted a policy called 鎖国 (*national isolation*), closing Japan to the outside world except for China and Holland (whose representatives were allowed contact with the country through the port of Nagasaki only). For the next 280 years, Japan was relatively peaceful. During this period, Japanese culture matured. 歌舞伎 theater, 文楽 (*puppet theater*), 浮世絵 (*wood prints*), pottery, and 俳句 are well known products of the Edo culture. Although agriculture and transportation made some advancements, technologically Japan was well behind Europe and America. In the mid-nineteenth century, European and American ships started appearing off the coast of Japan. The Tokugawa government eventually was forced to open the country, and return political authority to Emperor in 1868. During the Meiji Era (1868–1911), Japan tried to catch up with the West by modernizing society. The government's goals were economic prosperity and a strong military. The Emperor was recognized as the absolute symbol of Japan. As the military gained power, Japan began a military invasion of Asia. This led to conflict with other countries in the world. Japan launched hostilities in 1941 which led to its involvement in World War II. Japan was defeated in 1945 after the bombing of Hiroshima and Nagasaki. Under the U.S. occupation, Japan adopted a new constitution which renounced war. Japan started down the road toward economic recovery after the war and became one of the world's leading economic powers by

1980. Most of the current stereotypes of Japanese as hard workers are derived from the image of businessmen and workers during the 1950s and 1960s.

宗教(しゅうきょう)と慣習(かんしゅう) Religion and customs in Japan

The Japanese constitution guarantees freedom of religion. The country's two major religions are 神道(しんとう) (Shinto) and 仏教(ぶっきょう) (Buddhism). Shinto, which is based on belief in animistic deities known as 神(かみ), is the indigenous religion of Japan. Buddhism was introduced to Japan from China in the 6th century. Although Buddhism soon became predominant, it was always able to coexist with Shinto. This arrangement is still intact, and the Buddhist and Shinto populations are not mutually exclusive.

Christianity was brought to Japan in 1549 by Jesuit missionaries. The 16th century was a period of political unrest, and Christianity spread rapidly at first among people looking for a new spiritual symbol. It was banned in 1639 after the unification of Japan was completed, and this ban remained until the Meiji Restoration in the middle of the 19th century. About 1 percent of the Japanese population is currently Christian.

Courtesy of the author

Many Japanese people visit a Shinto shrine when a baby is born and when they get married. They also go to shrines to pray for good luck before school entrance examinations. The same people often turn to Buddhism during times of bereavement, such as for deaths. Visiting shrines and Buddhism temples on New Year is an old tradition, and about 70–80 percent of the entire population visit shrines and temples during the first three days of the year. The influence of Shinto and Buddhist beliefs is present in many rituals, festivals, and events throughout Japan year around.

There are many traditions related to both Shinto and Buddhism, and both of these religions have played crucial roles in the history of the country and its social customs, but evidence suggests that the Japanese do not view these two traditions in the same sense that religion is viewed in the West. A survey conducted by *Yomiuri Newspaper* in 2005 found that 75 percent of the people who responded said they do not believe in religion, and only 23 percent said that they do. About 60 percent of people think that religion is not important for a happy life, and only 30 percent think that it is. Even so, 81 percent of people go to shrines, temples, or churches.

日本人が考える日本のよさ

In 2006, the Internet research company Dimsdrive asked 5,003 Japanese people what made them feel lucky to have been born in Japan. The results of this survey show that the Japanese have a number of reasons for feeling good about their country. The quality of food ranked first (21.7% of respondents), and was followed by appreciation of the fact that Japan has four distinct seasons (13.3%), that it is peaceful (12.7%), that it has a low crime rate (6.7%), that it is prosperous (3.1%), that Japan has a good national character (2.5%), that it has a unique culture (1.8%), appreciation of the Japanese language (1.4%), that the Japanese enjoy freedom (1.4%), and that the country has abundant natural blessings (1.1%).

文法

I. Expressing the performance of a favor using てあげる／くれる／もらう

Chapter 6 introduced two giving verbs, あげる and くれる, and a receiving verb, もらう. These verbs can be used to express the speaker's appreciation or gratitude. That is, in Japanese, an action done for the benefit of someone else can be expressed by using the て-form with a verb of giving or receiving.

A. Expressing appreciation for a favor done for you or a member of your in-group, using 〜てくれる／下さる

Like くれる and 下さる in Chapter 6, the recipient of the favor is the speaker or a member of the speaker's in-group when 〜てくれる/下さる is used. The giver can be anyone but the speaker. 下さる is used when the giver is an out-group person who is socially superior to the speaker. The recipient of a favor can be marked by the particle に, but it does not have to be overtly marked if it is obvious.

先生は私にはいくを教えて下さいました。
My teacher taught me haiku (for my benefit).

先生がていねいな説明(せつ)とアドバイスをして下さいました。
The professor gave me a detailed explanation and advice.

上司(し)が病院にお見舞(ま)いに来て下さいました。 *My boss kindly visited me at the hospital.*

姉がマンガを買ってくれた。 *My older sister bought me a manga.*

同僚(りょう)が妹を落語(らくご)につれて行ってくれました。 *My co-worker took my younger sister to a rakugo performance.*

父は私をしんじてくれた。 *My father believed me.*

学校で一番かっこいい男の子が私とつきあってくれた。
The cutest guy in school went out with me.

道子：あ、早かったね。 *Oh, you are early.*

友子(ともこ)：うん、アリスが車でむかえに来てくれたから。 *Yeah, Alice came for me by car.*

荷物が重(おも)くて困っていた時、知らない人が持ってくれました。
When I was having difficulty with heavy luggage, a stranger carried it for me.

The in-group/out-group distinction can be applied in social contexts other than family. For example employees of the speaker's company comprise an in-group in contrast with those who are not employed by that company. In this case, use 〜て下さる when a customer regarded as a social superior to company members in a business context does something for any member of the company, including the speaker's boss or even the company president (who would be considered the speaker's superior in a strictly in-company relationship).

お客さまが社長にお祝いを持って来て下さいました。
The customer kindly brought a congratulatory gift to the president.

Note

- Request forms such as ～て下さい, ～てくれませんか, and ～て下さいませんか (*Nakama 1*, Chapter 6) are derived from this structure.

B. Expressing willingness to help using ～てあげる／やる

As is the case with the verbs あげる and やる discussed in Chapter 6, the recipient of any action expressed by ～てあげる／やる is in the speaker's out-group. If both giver and recipient are in the speaker's in-group, it is okay to use ～てくれる／あげる／やる, but the use of くれる implies identification with the recipient and the use of あげる or やる indicates neutrality or identification with the giver.

～てあげる／やる must be used if the giver is the speaker. Use やる if the recipient is socially inferior to the speaker. Social inferiors mainly include animals, plants, and one's family members. あげる can be used for both social equals and inferior.

私は　友達に　生(い)け花(ばな)を　教えてあげた。 *I taught my friend flower arrangement* (for her benefit).

私は　かれしに　しを　書いてあげた。 *I wrote a poem for my boyfriend.*

ぼくは　犬に　ボールを　買ってやった／あげた。 *I bought a ball for my dog.*

The recipient can be marked by the particle に, but the recipient is not mentioned if it is obvious from the context.

私は　黒田さんを　見送(みおく)りに行ってあげた。 *I went to see Ms. Kuroda off* (for her benefit).

私は　犬と　遊んでやった／あげた。 *I played with the dog* (for the benefit of the dog).

母は　子ねこを　お風呂(ふろ)に入れてやりました／あげました。
My mother gave the kitten a bath (for the benefit of the kitten).

道子：五時までに駅に行かなきゃいけないんだけど、おくれそうなの。
I have to be at the station by five o'clock, but it looks like I'm going to be late.

石田：じゃあ、ぼくが車で送ってあげるよ。
Well, I can take you (to the station) by car.

かばんが重(おも)そうだったので、持ってあげた。 *Since the bag looked heavy, I carried it* (for someone).

Although it is theoretically possible to use さし上げる in this structure, in reality ～てさし上げる is rarely used. さし上げる explicitly indicates that the giver is doing a favor for a superior, and such explicit remarks are considered condescending. In such cases use either a humble expression (Grammar section II of chapter 11) or the simple ます form.

私は先生のかばんを持ってさし上げました。 *I carried the professor's bag* (for his benefit).

私は先生のかばんを持ちました。 *I carried the professor's bag.*

私は先生のかばんをお持ちしました。 *I humbly carried the professor's bag.* (humble form of 持つ)

C. Expressing that someone has benefited from someone else's action using ～てもらう／いただく

As is the case when もらう or いただく is used as the sentence's main verb, the recipient of the favor is the grammatical subject and the giver of the favor is the source in the ～てもらう／いただく construction.

私は　道子さんに　その失礼(しつれい)なたのみをことわってもらった。 *I got Michiko to refuse the rude request .*

妹は　その人に　ハグをしてもらった。 *My sister got the person to hug her.*

その子は　近所の人に　ほめてもらった。 *The child got his neighbor to praise him.*

弟は　先生に　助(たす)けていただいた。 *My younger brother got the teacher to help him.*

The giver is marked by ~に or by から, but the use of から is limited to cases such as 送る, where the main verb indicates the transfer of an object.

友達に／から　本を　送ってもらった。 *I had my friend send a book.*

友達に　本を　読んでもらった。 *I had my friend read a book.*

(The particle から cannot be used.)

Sentences with ～てもらう may imply that the recipient is asking the giver for a favor. This is especially true when the verb is used in the future tense.

弟は父に理由(りゆう)を説(せつ)明してもらうつもりです。
My younger brother intends to get my father to explain the reasons to him.

鈴(すず)木さんに見てもらいたいと思っています。
I've been thinking of having Mr. Suzuki look at it.

Requests made with ～ていただける (*Nakama* 2, Chapter 4) are derived from this structure. いただける is the potential form of いただく. The expression ～ていただけませんか means *could I humbly receive the favor of your doing (this)*. The potential form of もらう, もらえる, can be used instead of いただける to express a less formal request. ～てもらえませんか means *can I receive the favor of your doing ~*, and is interchangeable with ～てくれませんか.

お金を出してもらえませんか。／お金を出してくれませんか。
Could you pay for me?

ねえ、その重(おも)そうな辞書取ってもらえる？／ねえ、その重(おも)そうな辞書取ってくれる？
Hey, could you hand me that heavy-looking dictionary?

Use ～ていただきたい to express a desire directed toward a superior. ～ていただきたい is a combination of いただく and たい. ～てもらいたい (a combination of もらう and たい) also expresses the speaker's desire and can be used interchangeably with ～てほしい. Finally, ～てほしい／もらいたい／いただきたい can be used for indirect requests, which are less forceful than ～ていただけませんか/もらえませんか/下さいませんか/ くれませんか.

今の日本の経済(けいざい)について話していただきたいんですが。
Could I ask you to talk about the current Japanese economy?

もう少していねいに教えてくれませんか。 *Could teach me with more care?*

ゴルフバッグが重(おも)いから、宅(たく)配便で送ってもらえませんか。
Since the golf bag is heavy, could you send it by a parcel service?

山田：ブログを見てもらいたいんだけど。／ブログを見てほしいんだけど。
Can I get you to look at my blog? (lit.: *I want to get you to read my blog.*)
山本：あ、ごめん。今ちょっと忙しいから、後でいい？
Oh, I'm sorry. I'm a bit tied up now—can I look at it later?

Use either the negative form of ほしい or たい (ほしくない, もらいたくない, or いただきたくない), or ないでほしい, ないでもらいたい, or ないでいただきたい to express negative desires.

田中先生にはこのレポートをまだ読んでいただきたくないんです。／読まないでいただきたいんです。
I don't want Prof. Tanaka to read this report yet. (polite)
このことはだれにも話してもらいたくないんです。／話さないでもらいたいんです。
I don't want you to tell anybody about this.
このたのみはことわってほしくないんです。／ことわらないでほしいんです。
I don't want you to refuse this request.
そんな失礼(しつれい)な質問はしてほしくない。／しないでほしい。
I don't want you to ask (me or somebody) such a rude question.

話してみましょう

Activity 1

The following chart illustrates favors done for the speaker or members of the speaker's in-group. You are the speaker. Describe each exchange using the て-form of the verb + 下さる／くれる.

Example: 弟は私にあやまってくれました。

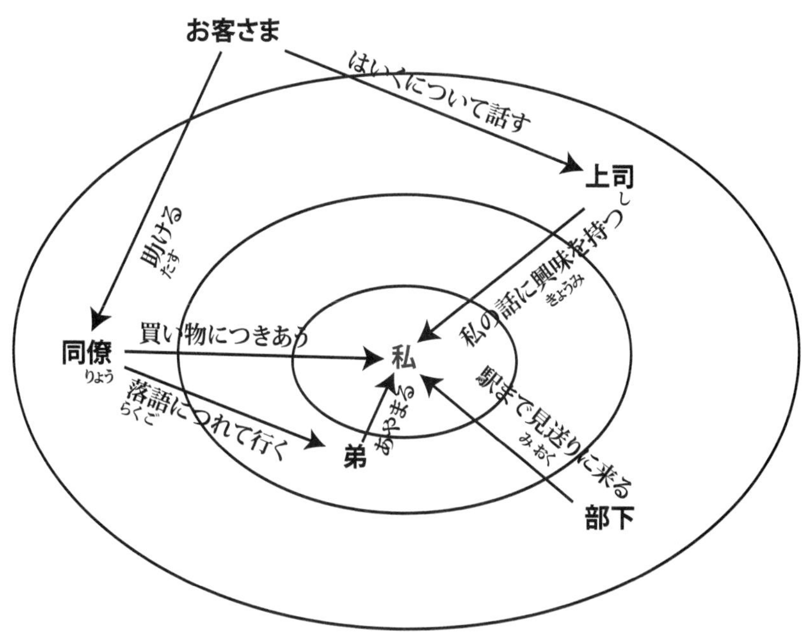

Activity 2 Express the same favors described in Activity 1, this time using the て-form of the verb + いただく / もらう.

Example: 私は弟にあやまってもらいました。

Activity 3 The following chart illustrates favors done by and for different people. Describe the exchanges using the て-form of the verb + あげる / やる.

Example: 私は友達に本をかしてあげました。

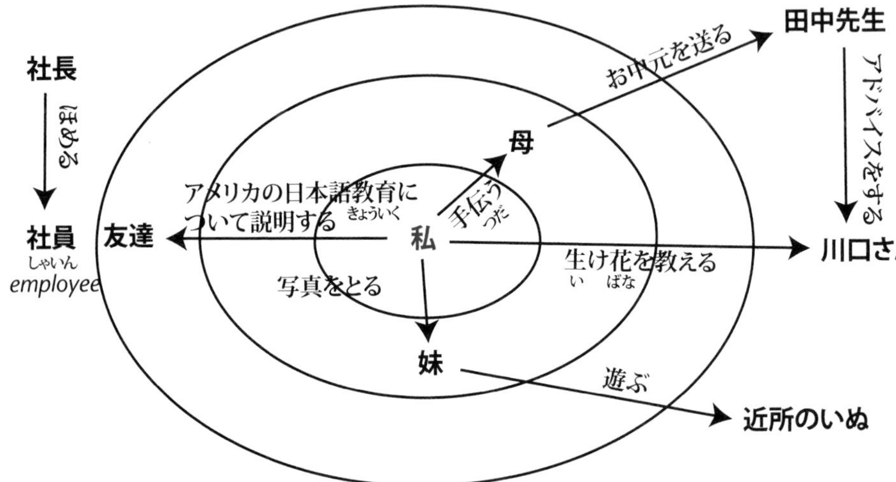

Activity 4 Express the same favors described in Activity 3, this time using the て-form of the verb + いただく / もらう. Note that not every exchange can be expressed with いただく or もらう.

Example: 私は川口さんに生(い)け花(ばな)を教えてあげました。

Activity 5 Work as a class. Write down three things that you wouldn't mind doing for your classmates. Also, write three things that you would like to ask your classmates to do for you. Ask your classmates to do one of the favors you hope to receive, and write the name of the first person who agrees to do it for you. When you have found someone to do the first favor proceed to the next, and so on. Your classmates will also ask you for favors. You are allowed to agree to do something for someone only if it is something you have written down that you wouldn't mind doing for your classmates. Find a different person to do each favor for you. Give a reason for not doing a favor if you have not marked it in the 私がしてあげること column. Use casual speech.

Example: A: あのう、１０ドルかしてくれない？

B: ごめん。かしてあげたいけど、持ってないんだ。

or B: いいよ。かしてあげるよ。

してもらいたいこと	してくれる人の名前	私がしてあげること

Activity 6 Use the results from Activity 5 to report to the class who helped you.

Example: 〜さんに 10 ドルかしてもらいました。
〜さんにノートを見せてもらいました。

II. Making or letting someone do something using the causative form

The causative construction in English is used when someone (causer) either forces or allows someone else (causee) to do something. If the causer forces the causee, the verb "make" is used, but the verb "let" is used if the causer gives the causee permission to do something, as in:

The teacher let everyone write a blog.
The teacher made everyone write a blog.

Japanese has two types of causatives as well. In both cases, the causer is the subject of the sentence just like in English, but the distinction between the make-causative and the let-causative, however, is not always from the verb forms alone.

父は　妹にいい教育(きょういく)を受けさせた。 *My father made/let my sister get a good education.*

上司(し)は部下にほかの社員(いん)とそうだんさせた。 *The boss made/let his subordinate consult with the other employees.*

先生は　学生をゆかにすわらせた。 *The teacher made /let students sit on the floor.*

The formation of causative forms is similar to passive verbs. Instead of the passive endings れる／られる, however, the endings せる／す／させる／さす are used.

Verb type	Dictionary form	Causative form
Irregular verbs	する (*to do*) 来る (*to come*)	させる or さす 来させる or 来さす
る -verbs		Replace る with させる or さす
	見る (*to see*) 食べる (*to eat*)	見る + させる／さす⇨見させる／見さす 食べる + させる／さす⇨食べさせる／食べさす
う -verbs		Replace the negative ending ない with せる or す
	すわる (*to sit*) 話す (*to talk*)	すわらない + せる／す ⇨すわらせない／すわらす 話さない + せる／す ⇨話させない／話さす

The causative construction is slightly different between transitive and intransitive verbs.

A. Intransitive verbs

When an intransitive verb is used, the cause can be marked by the particle を or に. Although both of them can be used in the let- and make-causative constructions, に tends to be used for the let-causative construction.

社長は　ほかの人を　あいさつに　行かせた。 *The president made* (let) *another person go to greet (someone)* .

社長は　ほかの人に　あいさつに　行かせた。 *The president let another person go to greet* (someone).

母は　私を　買い物に つきあわせた。 *My mother made* (let) *me go shopping with her.*

In order to explicitly mark the let-causative, combine the causative form with a verb of giving, which implies that the causer is doing the causee a favor by allowing him or her to do the action in question. In this case the use of the particle に or を does not make any difference.

上司(し)は　部下を／に　出張(しゅっちょう)にに　行かせてやった。
The president let his subordinate go on assignment.

先輩(ぱい)は　後輩(はい)を／に　すわらせてあげた。
The senior student let the junior student sit down.

母は　私を／に　買い物に　つきあわせてくれた。
My mother let me go shopping with her.

B. Transitive verbs

When the verb is a transitive verb, the causee is usually marked by the particle に. In this case, it is not possible to tell the difference between make- and let-causative constructions without context or giving/receiving verbs.

先生は　みんなに　ブログを書かせた。 *The teacher made/let everyone write a blog.*

先生は　ほかの学生に　発音(はつおん)の練習をさせた。 *The teacher made/let other students practice pronunciation.*

父は　私に　正座(せいざ)をさせた。 *My father made me sit on the floor in formal Japanese style.*

先生は　真理(まり)さんに　しを書かせてあげた。 *The teacher let Mari write a poem.*

先生は日本人の学生に神道(しんとう)と仏教(ぶっきょう)の習慣(しゅうかん)について、留学生にキリスト教(きょう)とユダヤ教(きょう)とイスラム教(きょう)の習慣(しゅうかん)について話をさせた。
The teacher made/let the Japanese students talk about Shinto and Buddhist customs, and made/let international students talk about Christian, Jewish, and Islamic customs.

話してみましょう

Activity 1 Say whether you think Japanese parents make children under 12 do the following activities. Then say what American parents would do.

Example: 毎日勉強する

日本人は子供に毎日勉強させると思います。

or 日本人は子供に毎日勉強させないと思います。

1. 九時までに寝る
2. テレビを見る
3. 習字(しゅうじ)を習う
4. 生(い)け花(ばな)を習う
5. いすにすわる
6. 一人で家にいる
7. 学校に一人で行く
8. アルバイトをする
9. けいたい電話を持つ
10. 正座(せいざ)をする

Activity 2 Describe the following situations using the causative form.

Example: 男の子が女の子にけがをさせました。

Activity 3 Work with a partner. Ask your partner what his or her parents let or didn't let him or her do when he or she was little. Make sure to insert some comments to make your conversation lively.

Example: A: 小さい時、ご両親はどんなことをさせてくれましたか。

B: そうですね。色々(いろいろ)な運動をさせてくれましたよ。

A: いいですね。だから、～さんは、色々(いろいろ)なスポーツが出来るんですね。
じゃあ、どんなことはさせてくれませんでしたか？

B: そうですね。テレビはあまり見させてくれませんでした。

A: そうですか。私もテレビは見させてもらえませんでした。

III. Requesting permission to do something using the causative て-form and request expressions

The て-form of a causative verb can be combined with a variety of endings, such as verbs of giving and receiving to indicate requests. The general meaning of these varieties is *please allow me to do~* or *please let me do ~*.

日本の政治(せいじ)について話させてくれませんか。 *Please let me talk about Japanese politics.*

日本の政治(せいじ)について話させていただけませんか。 *Please allow me to talk about Japanese politics.*

日本の政治(せいじ)について話させてほしいんですが。 *I'd like you to let me talk about Japanese politics.*

理由(りゆう)を説明(せつ)させて下さい。 *Please let me explain the reason.*

電話をかけさせて。 *Please let me make a phone call.*

帰る前にあいさつをさせて下さい。 *Please let me say hello before I go home.*

私にむかえに行かせていただけませんか。 *Would you let me go to pick* (him/her) *up?*

私にお礼を言わせてくれませんか。 *Could you let me express my appreciation?*

見送(みおく)らせてほしいんですけど。 *Can you let me send you off?*

Chapter 1 introduced a similar expression, ～てもいいですか. Although ～てもいいですか can be used in a very general and non-specific manner, the て-form of the causative form + request expression is used specifically for personal favors only.

ゆかにすわってもいいですか。 *Is it OK if I sit on the floor /Is sitting on the floor allowed here?*

ゆかにすわらせてくれませんか。 *Would you mind if I sat on the floor?*

話してみましょう

Activity 1 Suppose you would like to do the following things but need to get permission. Make a request using the causative form.

Example: 授業中にトイレに行きたいので、先生におねがいする。
先生、トイレに行かせていただけませんか。

1. 気分が悪くて、家に帰りたいので、先生におねがいする。
2. 宿題が出来なかった理由(りゆう)を先生に説明(せつ)したいので、おねがいする。
3. 友達がおいしそうに食べているケーキを、少し食べたいので、おねがいする。
4. 日本人のホストファミリーのお母さんをハグしてもいいかどうか分からないので、聞いてみる。
5. お客さんをむかえに行きたいので、上司(し)におねがいする。

Activity 2

Work with a partner. Ask each other what you would like your parents and your school to let you do and why.

Example: A: ご両親に何をさせてもらいたいと思いますか。

B: そうですね。日本に留学させてもらいたいと思っています。

A: そうですか。日本ではどんなことがしたいんですか。

B: 日本の伝統的(でんとうてき)な文化(ぶんか)について勉強したいんです。

A: いいですね。

私	させてもらいたいこと／させていただきたいこと	理由(りゆう)
両親		
先生		
パートナー	させてもらいたいこと／させていただきたいこと	理由(りゆう)
ご両親		
先生		

Activity 3

Work with a partner. Using the information in Activity 2, create dialogues in which you make requests to your parents and and to your teacher. Make sure that the conversation is natural and appropriate in terms of the sequence of topics to be introduced and the level of politeness.

Example: A: お父さん、お母さん、ちょっといい？

B: ああ、いいけど、何？

A: あのう、. . . 。

IV. Expressing the immediate future using 〜る + ところ; the current situation using 〜ている + ところ; and the immediate past using 〜た + ばかり / ところ

A. Plain affirmative verb form + ところ

ところ literally means *place*, and by extension it also means *point in time* or *moment*. It is preceded by the plain affirmative of verb form, but depending on the form of the verb preceding it, ところ can be used to describe matters or events that are just about to happen, are just happening, or have just happened. When ところ is preceded by the dictionary of a verb it means *about to do* 〜. When ところ is preceded by 〜ている, it means *to be in the middle of doing* 〜. Finally, when the plain past precedes ところ, it means *have just finished doing* 〜.

チップを　払う　　　ところです。　*I am about to leave a gratuity.*

チップを　払っている　ところです。　*I am leaving a gratuity.*

チップを　払った　　ところです。　*I have just left a gratuity.*

今出かけるところですから、後で電話して下さい。
I am just going out, so please call back later.

今、ぼくの好きなアニメが始まるところなんだよ。
My favorite anime is about to start.

習字(しゅうじ)のレッスンが終わるところです。
The calligraphy lesson is about to finish.

もう少しで、あの人の話をしんじるところだった。
I was just about to believe what he said.

今、生け花(いけばな)の練習をしているところです。
I am in the middle of practicing flower arranging.

今、魚を焼いているところだから、ちょっと待って。
I am in the middle of grilling fish, so please wait a moment.

その話は今ことわったところだ。　*I've just declined the offer* (lit.: story)

今すわったところだから、少し休ませて下さい。　*I've just sat down, so let me rest for a moment.*

和子(かずこ)：あっ、いたの？　*Oh, so you're here after all.*

正男(まさお)：うん。今帰ってきたところ。　*Yes, I've just come back.*

Notes

Note the following differences between ～ている and ～ているところ:

- Verbs in the ～ている construction can be any action verb, but verbs in the ～ているところ constructions are usually action verbs whose ～ている form suggests action in progress. For example, 勉強する can be used in both constructions because its ～ている form 勉強している (someone is studying) suggests ongoing action. On the other hand, しぬ cannot be used in the ～ているところ construction because しんでいる suggests a resultant state (someone is dead) .
- ～ている can have different interpretations such as a resultant state, a progressive action, or a habitual action, but ～ているところ does not.
- While ～ている can denote a long-term on-going process, ～ているところ only indicates an action that is taking place at this particular moment. For example, in the first sentence below, 習っている can be used when the speaker has begun taking lessons but 習っているところだ in the second sentence can mean only that the speaker is actually practicing at this moment. Therefore, the former sentence can use an adverb such as 最近, but the second sentence cannot.

  最近(さいきん)生け花(いけばな)を習っている。　*I'm learning flower arrangement nowadays.*

  生け花(いけばな)を習っているところだ。　*I'm learning flower arrangement* (right at this moment).

B. The plain past affirmative form of a verb + ばかり

ばかり is another phrase that is used to express something that has just happened. Just like ところ, it is preceded by the plain past affirmative of a verb.

ガールフレンドとわかれたばかりです。 *I've just broken up with my girlfriend.*

イスラム教(きょう)の習慣(しゅうかん)について勉強したばかりです。 *I've just studiedt Islamic customs*

Both ～ところ and ～ばかり express an event or action that has just happened. However, they are slightly different in nuance when they follow the plain past affirmative form of verbs. The word ～ところ implies that almost no time or at most a very short period of time has passed since the occurrence of the event. On the other hand, ～ばかり indicates that a relatively short time has passed since the event took place. For example, 旅行から帰ってきたところです, *I've just come back from a trip*, tends to imply that the speaker has come back today or few days ago, while 旅行から帰ってきたばかりです, *I've just come back from a trip*, can be used even if the speaker came back a month ago, so long as the speaker thinks of one month as a relatively short period of time.

話してみましょう

Activity 1 The following pictures illustrate scenes in which a person is about to do something, is doing something or has just done something. Describe each picture using ～ところ .

Example: Picture A おじぎをするところです。

Picture B おじぎをしているところです。

Picture C おじぎをしたところです。

Example: A B C

1 A B C

2 A B C

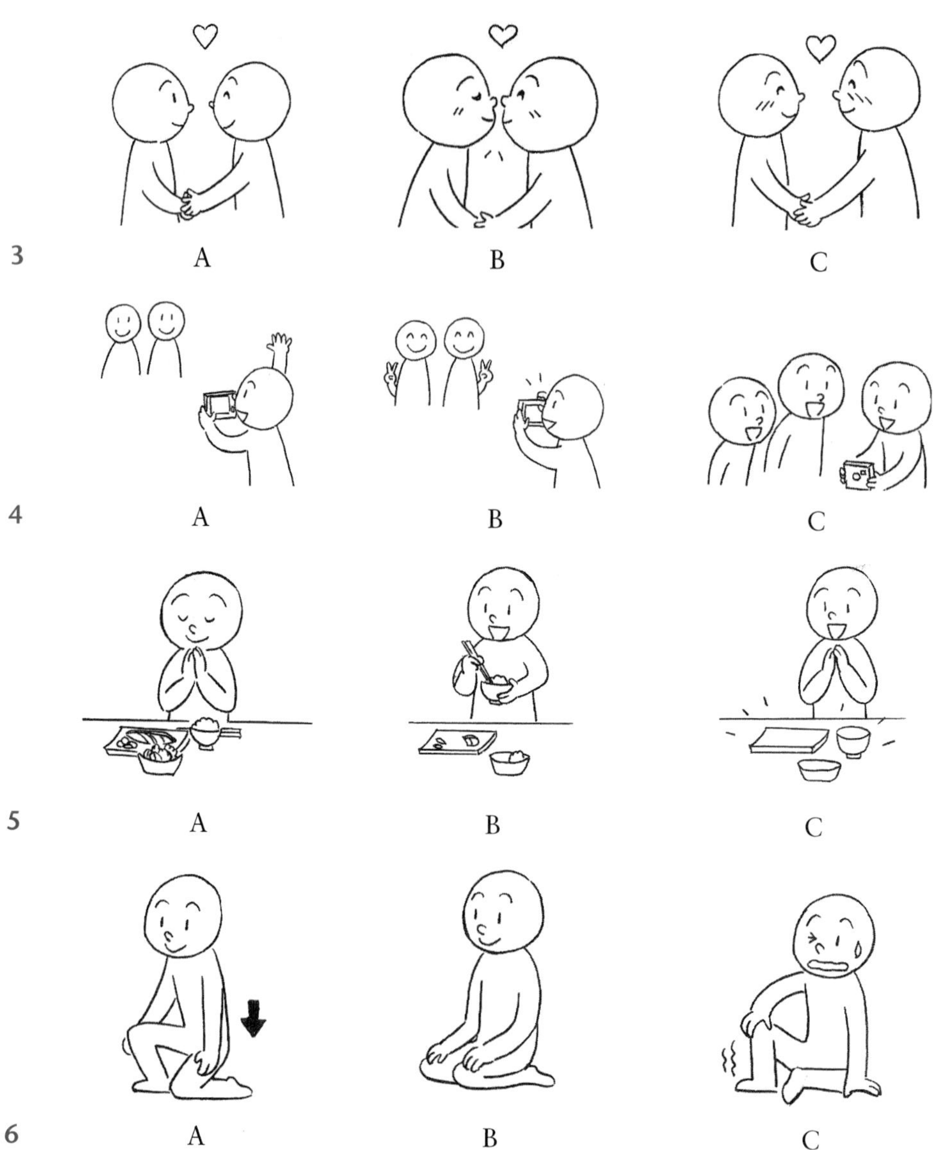

Activity 2

Work with a partner. Assume that the person in Column A of the chart has asked the person in Column B to do something. First, complete the chart by writing a few requests. Then play the role of the person in Column A, and ask a favor of your partner, who will be the person in Column B. Your partner will refuse, using ～ところ to say the timing is not convenient. If you are not satisfied with your partner's reason, ask him/her for the favor again.

Example:

Column A	Column B
お父さん／お母さん	子供

A: ちょっと、犬の散歩(さん)に行ってきて。

B: あ、だめ。今テレビ見ているところだから。

A: テレビは後で見ればいいでしょ。

	Column A	Column B
1.	お父さん／お母さん	子供
2.	ルームメート	ルームメート
3.	先生	学生
4.	上司(し)	私
5.	主人	つま

Activity 3

Work with a partner. Use 〜ばかり to ask your partner about problems encountered when he or she first started doing the following things. Then compare your partner's experience with yours and report the results to the class. Use casual speech.

Example:
A: この大学に来たばかりの時、どんなことで困った？
B: そうだね。来たばかりの時は、大学生活(かつ)になれてなかったので、何をすればいいかよく分からなかったんだ。
A: そう。ぼく／私もそうだった。
B: 〜くん／〜さんは、ほかにどんなことで困ったの？
A: ぼく／私は来たばかりの時、英語が下手で、授業が分からなかったんだ。

1. この大学に来る
2. この町に引(ひ)っ越(こ)す (*to move, change residence*)
3. 日本語の勉強を始める

V. Expressing time durations using 間 and 間に; tense in subordinate clauses

間 is a noun that means *space between*, *period*, or *duration*. The phrase 〜間 means *while ~* or *during ~*. The usage of 間 differs depending on whether it is being used alone, as in 間, or with the time particle に, as in 間に.

A. Expressing the continuation of an action or event during a specified time span using 間

When 間 is used without the time particle に the action or state described in the main clause must continue for as long as the state described in the 間 clause is in effect. In the following sentence, for example, the act of reading continues during the entire time the baby is sleeping. The tense of the 間 clause is normally present, regardless of the tense of the main clause. Like other subordinate clauses, the subject of the 間 clause is marked by the particle が if it is different from that of the main clause.

子供が寝ている間、本を読む。 *I read books while the child is sleeping*
子供が寝ている間、本を読んだ。 *I read a book while the child was sleeping*

To form an 間 clause use the ている form for action verbs. Use the dictionary form for stative verbs that indicate a state or situation, such as いる, ある, or わかる.

	Dictionary form		～間
Noun	休み (*holiday*)	Noun + の + 間	休みの間
な -adjective	ていねいな (*polite*)	Stem + な + 間	ていねいな間
い -adjective	心細い (*interesting*)	Stem + い + 間	心細い間
Verb (action verb)	ことわる (*to refuse*)	Verb ている + 間	ことわっている間
Verb (stative verb)	いる (*to exist*)	Dictionary form + 間	いる間

夏休みの間、何もしませんでした。
I didn't do anything during summer vacation.

父が元気な間は、東京で働くつもりです。
I plan to work in Tokyo as long as my father is healthy.

スミスさんは東京にいる間、茶道を習っていました。
Mr. Smith studied tea ceremony while he was in Tokyo.

話を聞いている間、ずっと正座をしていました。
I sat in formal Japanese style the whole time I listened to the story.

子供が小さい間は、あまりほかの人とつきあわなかった。
When my child was small, I didn't have a chance to associate with people outside my family.

The negative form ない + 間 can be used in this structure, but it is not as common as the affirmative form.

先生がいない間、みんなで遊んだ。 *We goofed off while the teacher was not here.*

B. Expressing the completion of an action or event in a specified time span using 間に

When 間 is followed by the particle に, which indicates a specific point in time, the action or event in the main clause must be completed within the time specified in the 間に clause. Therefore the following sentence indicates that the act of doing laundry is completed within the time in which the baby is sleeping.

子供が寝ている間に洗濯をする。 *I do laundry while my child is sleeping.*

日本にいる間に、日本のげいじゅつについて勉強した。
I learned about Japanese arts while I was in Japan.

安い間に、買ったほうがいいかもしれない。
It may be better to buy it while it's still cheap.

アメリカに留学している間に、宗教と政治に興味を持つようになった。
I became interested in religion and politics while studying in the United States.

Summary of tense in the subordinate clause

The time expressions introduced in this text are listed below. When the past tense is used in time adverbial clauses such as 時, 〜たら, or 後, the action, event, or condition of the main clause must be completed or satisfied before the action or event of the main clause can take place. On the other hand, when the present tense is used in time adverbial clauses such as 間, 間に, 前, and 時, the action, event, or condition of the subordinate clause must not be completed or satisfied before the action or event in the main clause takes place. That is, the event in the main clause may take place before the event in the subordinate clause, or the two events may take place concurrently.

1. Present tense + 間に

   日本にいる間に、落語(らくご)を見に行きたいです。

   I want to go to see Japanese storytelling while I am in Japan.

2. Present tense + 前に

   日本に来る前に、日本の文化(ぶんか)について勉強しました。

   I studied Japanese culture before I came to Japan.

3. Present tense + 間

   日本にいる間、日本の伝統的(でんとうてき)なげいじゅつについて勉強しました。

   I studied Japanese traditional art throughout the time I was in Japan.

4. Present tense + 時

   アメリカに帰る時、友達が見送(みおく)りに来てくれました。

   My friend came to say goodbye when I went back to the United States.

5. Past tense + 時

   アメリカに帰った時、両親がむかえに来てくれました。

   My parents came to pick me up when I came back to the United States.

6. Past tense + ら

   アメリカに帰ったら、高校の時の友達が会いに来てくれました。

   My high school friends came to see me after I came back to the United States.

7. Past tense + 後で

   アメリカに帰った後で、結婚しました。

   I got married after I came back to the United States.

話してみましょう

Activity 1

The following chart illustrates how Mrs. Kawano and her son spent in the afternoon yesterday. Describe Mrs. Kawano's activities with reference to the time when her son was doing something else, using ～間(に).

Example: 川野(かわの)くんが寝ている間に、お母さんは起きて朝御(ご)飯を作ります。
川野(かわの)くんが朝ご飯を食べている間、お母さんも朝御(ご)飯を食べます。

時間	川野くん	時間	お母さん
↓	寝ている	6:00	起きる。
↓		↓	朝御(ご)飯を作る
7:00	起きる	7:00	川野(かわの)くんを起こす
7:30		7:30	
↓	朝ご飯を食べる	↓	朝御(ご)飯を食べる
8:00	学校に行く	↓	
		8:00	そうじをする
			洗濯(せんたく)をする
3:00	家に帰る	2:30	茶道(さどう)を習う
↓	マンガを読む	↓	
↓			買い物に行く
4:00		3:30	家に帰る
↓	経済(けいざい)学の宿題をする	4:00	晩御(ご)飯を作る
5:00		↓	
6:00		↓	
↓	晩御(ご)飯を食べる	6:00	晩御(ご)飯を食べる
7:00		↓	
↓	お風呂(ふろ)に入る	7:00	テレビを見る
8:00		↓	
↓	インターネットで遊ぶ	↓	
↓		9:00	お風呂(ふろ)に入る
↓		↓	
11:00		10:00	日記(にっき)をつける
↓	しを書く	↓	寝る
12:00	寝る	11:00	

Activity 2

Work with the class. Survey what college students do during the following periods or seasons, using ～間（に）. Write down the number of people who do each of the following activities. Report the results to the class.

Example: A: 夏休みの間に家に帰りますか。

B: ええ、帰ります。休みの間はずっと家にいます。

A: 学校にいる間に宿題をしますか。

B: ええ、たいてい学校で宿題をします。

夏休み	学校にいる	期末(きまつ) (*final*) 試験
家に帰る	宿題をする	パーティをする
はいくを書く	寝る	マンガを読む
旅行に行く	テレビを見る	アニメを見る
おいのりをする	誕生日を祝う	友達と遊ぶ

Activity 3

Work with a group of four. Using ～間, debate on the following two topics, whether it is better to be a student or have a full-time job and whether it is best to be single or married. Two people should take each side. Fill out the following charts with the pros and cons of each position. Try to persuade your opponents, and tell your instructor which pair has won.

Example: A: 学生をつづけるのと仕事をするのとどちらがいいと思う？

B: 学生をつづけている間は、お金がないから、仕事をしている方がいいと思う。

C: そう？でも、学生でいる間は、好きなことがたくさん出来ると思うけど。

	いいこと	悪いこと
学生をつづける		
仕事をする		
	いいこと	悪いこと
一人でいる		
結婚する		

Activity 4

Work with a partner. Compare customs in Japan and your home country in terms of what is or is not considered good manners when you do the following activities. Use subordinate clauses, etc.

Example: ご飯を食べる

A: 私の国／家ではご飯を食べる前においのりをします。

B: 日本では御(ご)飯を食べる前に「いただきます」と言います。

A: じゃあ、日本ではご飯を食べている間に、してはいけないことやしてもいいことがありますか。

B: ええ、ありますよ。口の中に食べ物が入っている間は、話してはいけないんです。

1. 御(ご)飯を食べる
2. お風呂(ふろ)に入る
3. 結婚する
4. おいのりをする
5. 電車に乗っている

THE ます-STEM OF VERBS

In Japanese nouns are often derived from the ます stem of the verbs. Some common expressions are:

遊び	play, game, pastime	遊ぶ
行き	(on) the way, bound for ～	行く
いじめ	bullying	いじめる
動き	movement	動く
(お) 祝い	congratulatory gift	祝う
思い出	memory, recollection	思う＋出る
泳ぎ	swimming	泳ぐ
終わり	ending	終わる
帰り	a return	帰る
くもり	cloudy weather	くもる
答え	answer	答える
違い	difference	違う
知り合い	acquaintance	知り合う *to become acquainted with*
つかれ	fatigue	つかれる
作り	structure, construction	作る
つづき	sequel	つづく
つり	fishing	つる to fish
手伝(てつだ)い	help, helper	手伝(てつだ)う
ぬすみ	theft	ぬすむ
のこり	leftover	のこる
乗りかえ	transfer point	乗りかえる
はかり	scale	はかる
話	story	話す
晴れ	sunny weather	晴れる
間違い	mistake, error	間違う

むかえ	meeting, greeting	むかえる
見送り(みおく)	seeing someone off	見送る(みおく)
休み	holiday, day-off	休む
ゆれ	turbulence	ゆれる
よろこび	joy	よろこぶ *to be pleased*

In addition the ます -stem can be combined with other nouns or suffixes to form a more complex noun.

売り場	department section	売る + 場
おしいれ	Japanese-style closet; storage space	おす (*to push*) ＋入れる
買い物	shopping	買う＋物
着物	kimono	着る＋物
小包(こづつみ)	package, parcel	小＋包む(つつ)
つき当たり	at the end of the street, T-road	つく (*to prick, to push*) ＋当たる(あ) (*to hit*)
出口	exit	出る＋口
飲み物	drinks	飲む＋物
乗り物	transportation	乗る＋物
むかいがわ	the other side, the opposite side	むかう (*to face*) ＋がわ (*side*)
申込書(もうしこみ)	application form	申し込む(もう こ)＋書

聞く練習

上手な聞き方

Monitoring and evaluating your understanding

As you listen, it is important to monitor your understanding and form tentative hypotheses. Successful listeners are capable of revising hypotheses as they encounter information that doesn't match or notice errors or inaccurate guesses they might have made. They are also capable of setting up alternative interpretations and make selections as they continue listening. In his *Teaching Listening and Speaking: From Theory to Practice* (Cambridge University Press, 2008), Jack Richards suggests that students should work on the following self-monitoring:

General listening development	Consider your progress against a set of criteria you have specified. Check and see if you continue to make the same mistakes. Determine how close you are to achieving short-term or long-term goals.
Specific listening tasks	Check understanding during listening. Identify the source of any difficulties you are having. Check the appropriateness and the accuracy of what is understood and compare it with new information.

In addition, successful listeners self-evaluate their overall comprehension progress and assess how well they have done. This enables them to make a realistic evaluation of their comprehension while poor listeners sometimes develop a false level of confidence in their ability.

General listening development	Assess listening progress against a set of predetermined criteria. Assess the effectiveness of learning and practice strategies. Assess the appropriateness of learning goals and objectives set.
Specific listening tasks	Check the appropriateness and the accuracy of what has been understood. Determine the effectiveness of strategies used in the task. Assess overall comprehension of the text.

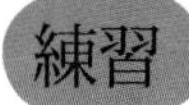
練習

Courtesy of the Author

落語(らくご) is a Japanese traditional art of comedic story telling, and 小話(こばなし) are very short stories which **rakugo** performers use at the beginning of their act to warm up the audience. Work with a partner. Listen to the following three 小話(こばなし), then do the following:

1. Write the story.
2. Underline any parts you are not sure you understand.
3. Rate your confidence level in having understood the story. (100 percent = fully confident; 0 percent = no understanding)
4. Listen to the story again and check the accuracy of your understanding.
5. Evaluate how well you understood the story in your first listening and the second listening.

A. かみさま　God

1. ____
____
____
____
____
____

3. ________ %

5. 1st listening _______ %　　2nd listening _______ %

B. **文房具屋で** At a stationary store

1. ______________________________
____
____
____
____
____

3. _______ %

5. 1st listening _______ % 2nd listening _______ %

C. **登校拒否** Refusing to go to school

1. ______________________________
____
____
____
____
____

3. _______ %

5. 1st listening _______ % 2nd listening _______ %

きせきの口紅 *Miracle lipstick*

聞く前に

質問に日本語で答えて下さい。

1. 化粧 (*makeup*) をしたことがありますか。
2. 友達によく化粧をする人がいますか。その人はいつもどこで化粧をしますか。
3. どんな色の口紅 (*lipstick*) が好きですか。

言葉のリスト

鼻	a nostril
おれる	to break off
飛び出す	to spring out
競馬新聞	newspaper for horseracing
あたる	to hit
馬券	a betting ticket
万馬券	a big winning ticket (on a horse)

聞いてみましょう

Work with a partner. View the video of the **kobanashi** entitled きせきの口紅(くちべに) (*Miracle lipstick*). This **kobanashi** is longer and more complicated than the stories you listened to in the 上手な聞き方 section above. As you listen, pay attention to the performer's gestures and form a hypothesis about the possible story line. Then verbally summarize the story to your partner and check the parts you are sure or not sure. Listen to the story again. This time, monitor your understanding, form a hypothesis, and check what you have and have not understood. Repeat this process one more time if necessary. When you feel reasonably confident, write down the story.

聞いた後で

Work with a partner. Compare your written story with your partner's production. Highlight the parts where you agree and disagree in different colors. Listen to the story again and revise if necessary.

Compare with the original text that your instructor will give you and evaluate how well you understood. Check the parts you did not understand and find out why.

聞き上手話し上手

おわかれを言う

At the beginning of *Nakama 1*, you learned expressions used in daily leave taking such as じゃあ、また , 失礼(しつれい)します and さようなら . There are other cases when you have to say good-bye, such as when you are visiting someone's house, or when you are moving away.

When you visit someone's house and are ready to leave, you can use the expression (もう) そろそろ (literally, *well, it's almost time*) to indicate that you must be leaving. The host or hostess may ask you to stay longer by saying something like まだ、いいじゃない?／まだ、いいじゃないですか。／まだ、いいじゃありませんか (*It is still early, isn't it?*) or もうちょっといいでしょう (*Stay for a while longer, OK?*). You can then give the reason you need to leave.

川口： じゃあ、もうそろそろ失礼(しつれい)します。
Well, I must be leaving now.

山本： まだ、いいじゃないですか。
It's still early. Can't you stay a little longer?

川口： ええ、でも、これからちょっと行く所がありますので。
Thank you, but I have to go somewhere now.

山本： そうですか。
I see.

You then thank them for their hospitality. The following are used to express thanks:

今日は本当(とう)に有難(ありがと)うございました。／今日は本当(とう)に有難(ありがと)う。
Thank you very much for your hospitality.

どうもご馳走(ちそう)さまでした。／どうもご馳走(ちそう)さま。
Thank you very much for the meal/drinks.

今日はとても楽しかったです。／今日はとても楽しかったよ。
I had a very good time.

The host/hostess will usually respond by saying いいえ、何のおかまいもしませんで／何もなくて (*Oh, no, it was nothing*) when you thank them for a meal.

川口： どうもご馳走(ちそう)さまでした。
Thank you very much for the meal.

山本： いいえ、何のおかまいもしませんで。
Oh, no, it was nothing.

川口： いいえ、本当(とう)に楽しかったです。じゃあ、失礼(しつれい)します。
I've had a wonderful time. Well, I must be going now.

It is customary to express your appreciation again the next time you meet the host/hostess or talk with him/her on the phone. You should write a short thank you letter if you don't think you will have a chance to thank them again.

川口： 先日は／この間はどうも有難(ありがと)うございました。とても楽しかったです。
Thanks very much for the invitation the other day. I had a good time.

山本： いいえ、どういたしまして。また来て下さいね。
Not at all. Please come again.

Another occasion for leave taking is when you move away. The following expressions are frequently used to express thanks to friends, colleagues, and neighbors when you move away:

色々(いろいろ)お世話になりまして、本当(とう)に有難(ありがと)うございました。／
色々(いろいろ)お世話になって、どうもありがとう。
Thank you very much for your help and hospitality.

これからもどうぞよろしくおねがいします。／これからもどうぞよろしく。
Please stay in touch.

練習

iLrn Self-Tests

A. Work with a partner. Listen to the conversation between Kawaguchi and Yamamoto in the explanation and practice the dialogue. Then listen to a more casual version of the same conversation and practice the dialogue.

B. Work with a partner. One person plays the role of a host/hostess and the other person is the guest. It is five o'clock now and the guest is thinking of leaving because it is dinnertime, and doesn't want to inconvenience the host/hostess. Think of a reason to leave and start taking your leave.

C. Work with a partner. One person should be a student and the other a professor. The student is graduating. The student has come to the office to express thanks to the professor and invite the professor to the graduation ceremony.

D. Work with a partner. You are in Japan and going back to your own country in a few weeks. Your partner is a neighbor who has been very nice to you. Tell the neighbor you are leaving, leave him or her your new address, and ask him/her to forward any important messages you might receive after leaving.

漢字

Guessing the meanings of unfamiliar kanji

In general, most vocabulary is learned incidentally through reading and listening, rather than by consciously memorizing it. Studies show that good vocabulary learners combine multiple strategies to guess meanings of unknown **kanji** and **kanji** compounds in texts. Two common strategies are to guess the meaning using the structure of **kanji** compounds and to guess from context. This chapter deals with guessing from context and the next chapter discusses the structure of **kanji** compounds.

It is not advisable to attempt to guess the meaning of **kanji** from context in cases where the text is hard to understand. It is very difficult to take advantage of your guessing ability when you don't understand the gist of what you are reading. Therefore, to develop this skill, choose a text that is slightly difficult, containing unknown words here and there, but easy enough for you to get the general idea. Guessing from context means not only guessing from what you have already read, but also using grammatical structure and okurigana. For example, determine the position of an unknown word in the sentence, the particle that follows it, and so on. This will give you and idea about what part of speech it is. Also, verbs often restrict the types of noun that can be used as the subject or direct object of a sentence. Finally, **okurigana** might give you a clue for a word you already know but don't know how it is written in **kanji**. Needless to say, it is also important to know the meaning of surrounding words, because grammar information alone will not tell the meaning of words. Finally, don't forget the overall context of what you have already read, the purpose of the text, and any pertinent real-world information, as these provide important clues for guessing the meaning of text, which in turn helps you to guess the meaning of unknown words.

Flashcards

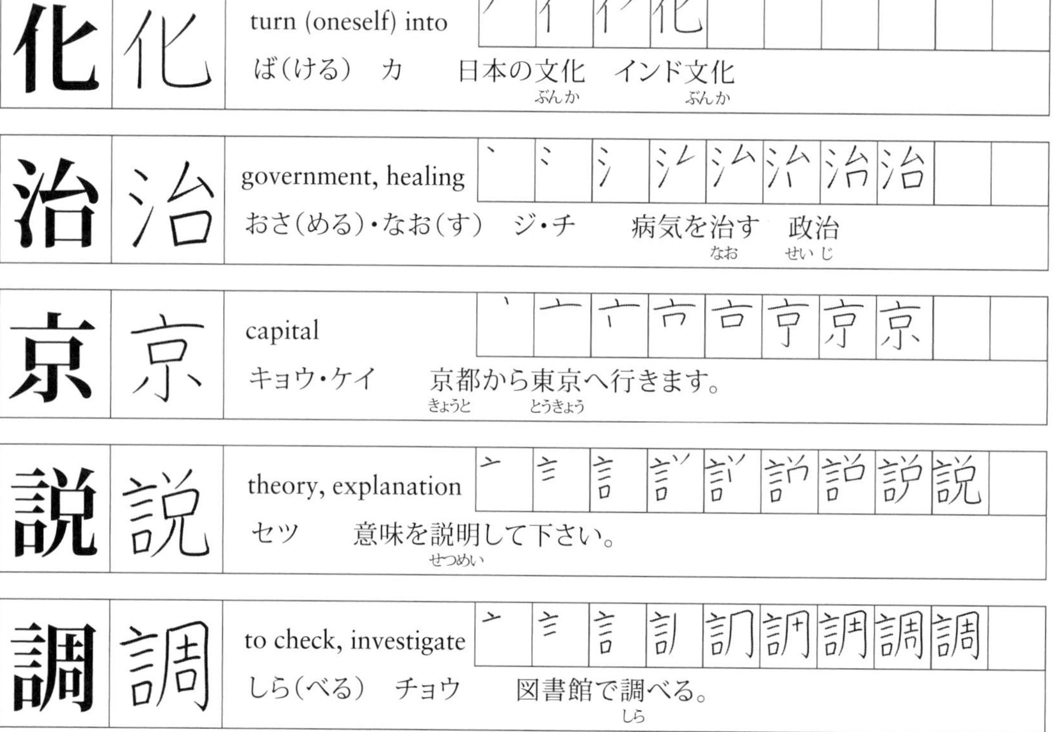

化 化	turn (oneself) into	ば(ける) カ	日本の文化(ぶんか) インド文化(ぶんか)
治 治	government, healing	おさ(める)・なお(す) ジ・チ	病気を治(なお)す 政治(せいじ)
京 京	capital	キョウ・ケイ	京都(きょうと)から東京(とうきょう)へ行きます。
説 説	theory, explanation	セツ	意味を説明(せつめい)して下さい。
調 調	to check, investigate	しら(べる) チョウ	図書館で調(しら)べる。

集	集	to collect, to gather	あつ(める・まる)　シュウ	九時に集(あつ)まって下さい。
的	的	having attribute of, target	まと　テキ	日本的(てき)な建物(たてもの)
失	失	to lose, to miss	シツ	失礼(しつれい)します。
々	々	kanji for repetition	N/A	人々(ひとびと)　色々(いろいろ)な国に行きました。　国々(くにぐに)　時々(ときどき)
難	難	difficult	むずか(しい)　ナン	説明(せつめい)が難(むずか)しかった。
不	不	not, un- (prefix)	フ	ここは不便(ふべん)です。
利	利	advantage	リ	電車を利用(りよう)する。　便利(べんり)
当	当	hit, target	あ(たる)　トウ	本当(ほんとう)ですか。
期	期	period, term, time	キ	秋学期(がっき)と春学期(がっき)　期末(きまつ)試験
和	和	Japanese, peace	ワ	和食(わしょく)　平和(へいわ) (peace)　和風(わふう) (Japanese style)
重	重	heavy, weight	おも(い)　ジュウ	重(おも)い荷物

活	活	life, activity カツ	丶 氵 氵 氵 汗 汗 浐 活 活 生活がくるしい。(せいかつ)
弱	弱	weak よわ(い) ジャク	弱 (stroke order) 体が弱い。(よわ)
界	界	world カイ	丨 冂 冊 冊 田 甲 界 界 界 世界で一番高い山(せかい) 世界旅行(せかい)
正	正	correct, right ただ(しい) セイ・ショウ	一 丅 下 正 正 正しい答えは何ですか。(ただ) 正座(せいざ)
由	由	reason, significance ユウ	丨 冂 巾 由 由 理由がわかりません。(りゆう)
付	付	to attach つ(く)・つ(ける) フ	ノ 亻 仁 付 付 会社の受付(うけつけ) 病院の受付(うけつけ)

読めるようになった漢字

文化　政治(せい)　病気を治す　京都(と)　東京　説明　調べる　集める　集まる　日本的
失礼　色々　人々　時々　難しい　不便　便利　本当　学期　期末試験　和食
重い　生活　弱い　世界　正しい　理由　付く　受付　生け花　〜教　教育
茶道　社会　習慣(かん)　宗教(しゅう)　習字　正座(ざ)　落語　心細い(ぼそ)

練習

1. 和食をたくさん食べる生活で病気が治りました。
2. 東京の文化と京都の文化は少し違うので、時々失礼になることがあります。
3. 生け花と茶道をしています。
4. 今学期の期末試験は難しかったので、答えを説明して下さい。
5. 日本の政治(せい)は、世界的に見て、まだ弱いです。
6. 社会はとても便利になりましたが、教育など色々な問題があります。
7. テニスの練習をしますから、九時に集まって下さい。
8. 荷物が重くなったので、タクシーで帰りましょう。
9. すみません、受付はどこですか。
10. 長い間、正座(ざ)をしていたので、足が痛くなりました。

読む練習

上手な読み方

Monitoring and evaluating your understanding

As is the case with listening, the effective use of monitoring and evaluation strategies should help you improve your reading skills. One way to do this is to engage in reciprocal reading.

First, focus on the purpose and title of the text you are reading. Then try to skim through the text and identify the part that is relevant for your purpose. Ignore supplementary information or any parts you don't understand. Once you get a general idea, go back to the text again, check your comprehension, and determine how well you have understood the text. Then underline any parts you have problems with and try to guess possible meanings from the surrounding context. You may have more than one possible interpretation for some sections.

Once this is done, work with another student or a group of students. In reciprocal reading, students take turns reading the text. When you read a line of text aloud, try to read it so that pauses occur at natural break points rather than in the middle of a word or inflection. If you are unable to read a text or are having trouble reading aloud, get help from a listener. When you are listening to a text being read aloud, try to predict what will come next in the text. Then check your prediction and see if your guess is correct. This helps you improve your monitoring skills. If you don't understand what is being read, ask questions about it or provide feedback about your comprehension problem. Active discussion like this is beneficial for you and other students to resolve the problems, and to learn to monitor your own learning and thinking. After going through the text once, do the same thing again, while checking the level of your understanding in this session compared to the first session. If necessary, you should repeat this process again because continuous practice is essential to gain successful reading strategies. Once you feel you have understood the text sufficiently, summarize it by yourself or with other students.

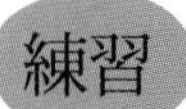

Work by yourself at first and then with a pair or a group. Read the following text using the steps described above, and summarize the main point of the text in your own words.

大衆文化は、ポピュラーカルチャー、ポップカルチャー、マスカルチャーとも呼ばれ、文学や芸術、美術などのハイカルチャーに対して、一般大衆が広く愛好する文化のことである。これとは別に、サブカルチャーという言葉があるが、これは大衆文化やハイカルチャーと違い、一部の人たちに愛されるマニアックな分野を指すものである。

しかし、時代の変化によってこれらのカルチャーの区分も変わっていくことがあるので、境界線を引くのは難しい。例えば、かつてサブカルチャーであったようなフィギュアやオタク文化が、現在では大衆文化として受け入れられているのもその一例である。

マンガ

読む前に

1. 日本のマンガを読んだり見たりしたことがありますか。
2. どんなマンガでしたか。
3. アメリカのマンガやアニメと日本のマンガやアニメはどう違いますか。
4. 日本語を勉強するために、マンガを読んだらいいと思いますか。どうしてそう思いますか。

言葉のリスト

かかわる	教養（きょうよう）	大衆（たいしゅう）	～倍（ばい）	貢献（こうけん）する
to be relevant to	education	public, the masses	~times	to contribute

日本の文化というと、歌舞伎や茶道、生け花、着物と思う人も多いだろう。確かに、これらの伝統的な文化は今でも日本人の生活に深くかかわっている。例えば、日本には社会人が趣味や教養や健康のために色々なことを習えるカルチャーセンターと呼ばれる教室があるが、どのカルチャーセンターにもたいてい茶道教室や生け花教室がある。でも、日本の文化には伝統的なものだけではなく、今の日本の社会でよく見られる大衆文化もある。

その中でもよく知られているのはマンガである。マンガは、アメリカでは子供が読むものというイメージが強かったが、日本のアニメやマンガがアメリカでも見られるようになって少しイメージが変わってきたようだ。一方、日本では、マンガは昔から子供も大人もみんなが楽しめるものである。マンガは、１９５０年代に子供を中心としてよく読まれるようになったが、その後、学生、大人のためのマンガが描かれるようになった。現在ではファンタジー、コミックはもちろん、スポーツ物、スパイ物、SF、ラブストーリー、ファミリードラマ、経済、社会問題をテーマにしたもの、料理などの趣味をテーマにしたものなど色々なものがある。そういう意味では、今のマンガは絵がついた小説のようなものだとも言えるだろう。長さも、４コママンガから、何十冊にもなる長いものまで色々で、普通の雑誌や新聞だけではなく、マンガ雑誌と呼ばれる雑誌や、マンガ本と言われるものまである。１９９５年のマンガ雑誌の売り上げは3,357億円、２５億ドルにもなる。同じように、アニメも人気が集まり、今では日本だけではなく世界中にアニメクラブがあると言われている。今や日本は世界一の「マンガ大国」なのである。

マンガは文学小説と違って、芸術的なイメージはないし、人前では読まないようにしているという人もいるようだ。けれども、本当はマンガを読むことはいいことだということを知っている人は少ない。１９９７年にライフデザイン研究所が行なったアンケートによると、マンガを読まない人の５４%は他の本も読まないが、マンガを読むが他の本は読まない人は１４%しかいなかった。つまり、マンガを読む人のほとんどがマンガではないものも読んでいるのである。マンガを読む人が増えたからだとは言えないかもしれないが、１９７５年から１９９５年の２０年間に図書館の数は２．２倍に、図書館から本を借りる人の数は５倍にも増えている。最近の日本人はテレビばかり見て、本を読まないと言われるが、そうではない。マンガという大衆文化は、日本人のリテラシーに大きく貢献しているのである。

読んだ後で

A. 上の文章の各段落 (*each paragraph*) の 一番大事なポイントを書いて下さい。

一段落目 (*paragraph 1*)

二段落目 (*paragraph 2*)

三段落目 (*paragraph 3*)

B. 下の質問に日本語で答えて下さい。

1. この文章を書いた人はマンガはいいものだと思っていますか。よくないものだと思っていますか。
2. 日本ではどんな人がマンガを読みますか。
3. 日本のアニメやマンガにはどんな物がありますか。
4. マンガはどうして「絵のついた小説のようなもの」なのですか。
5. 「マンガ大国」とはどういう意味ですか。
6. どうして人前ではマンガを読まない人がいるのですか。
7. マンガを読む人と読まない人では何が違いますか。
8. この文章を書いた人はマンガと図書館の数とはどんな関係 (*relationship*) があると思っていますか。

C. 日本のマンガを読んでみて、つぎのことを考えて下さい。

1. どうして日本人はマンガが好きなのだと思いますか。
2. マンガのどんなところがやさしいと思いますか。どんなところが難しいと思いますか。
3. 日本語を勉強する人にとって、マンガを読むのはいいことだと思いますか。

総合練習(そうごう)

A. 世界の習慣(かん)　その1

1. Work with a partner. Discuss what other people do for you and who you are allowed to do in the following situations, and make a short presentation about your culture. The example dialogue below is based on the speaker's experience.

Example: A: ～さんは大学生になった時、何かしてもらいましたか。

B: ええ、両親に新しい車を買ってもらいました。

A: わあ、いいですね。

B: ～さんは、何かしてもらいましたか。

A: 一緒(しょ)にアパートをさがしに来てもらいました。

B: そうですか。大学生になる前と後ではどう生活が変わりましたか。

A: そうですね。今は色々なことをさせてもらえますよね。
たとえば、 高校生の間はたいてい親と一緒(しょ)に住まなければならないけれど、今は、一人で住まわせてくれますね。

B: 私もそう思いますね。

	してもらうこと	させてもらうこと
大学生になる		
成人(せいじん) (*legal adult*) になる		
結婚する		

2. Interview Japanese students or students from other countries about the items you discussed in Exercise 1, and make a presentation about the differences and similarities in cultural practices in your country and theirs.

B. 私の国の習慣(かん)

1. The following chart shows some customs in Japan. Look at each custom and place a check in the column した方がいいこと if you think Japanese people would expect other Japanese to follow that custom. Check よくすること if you think Japanese people would often follow the custom even though they may not be expected to do so. Check あまりしないこと if you think Japanese people would rarely follow the custom even if there is no prohibition against it. Check してはいけないこと if this is not an acceptable thing to do in Japan.

	した方がいい	よくする	あまりしない	してはいけない
家の中に入る時、くつをぬぐ				
家の中ではスリッパ (*slippers*) をはく				
たたみの部屋でスリッパ をはく				
トイレではトイレのスリッパ をはく				
トイレのドアはいつもしめておく				
部屋のドアはいつもしめておく				
だれかの部屋に入る時はノックをする				
朝御(ご)飯にサラダを食べる				
朝御(ご)飯にあまい物を食べる				
朝御(ご)飯は和食だけだ				
食事をする時、お客さんはドアから一番遠いところにすわる				
食べ物を口に入れて話をする				
食事が終わったら、たばこをすう				
お風呂(ふろ)はお父さんが一番はじめに入る				
ゆぶね (*bath tub*) の中で体を洗う				
人の家に行く時、電話をしてから行く				
近所に引(ひ)っ越(こ)して (*to move residence*) きた人の所にあいさつに行く				
人に何かもらったら、何かをかえす				
カラオケではみんながうたう				

2. Work in groups of four. Discuss what checkmarks you assigned to each item in Exercise 1. Use casual speech. List the items that everyone agrees or disagrees with and why. Report the results to the class using polite speech.

Example: A: 日本の家ではくつをぬぐことになってるよね。

B: 今でもそうかな？今は、もうぬがなくてもいいんじゃない？

C: いや、そんなことないと思うよ。

D: うん、ぼくの日本人の友達もくつをぬぐから。くつはぬがなきゃいけないんじゃない？

私達のグループでは日本の家ではくつをぬぐことになっていると思う人が多いですが、今はぬがなくてもいいという人もいます。

3. Work with a partner. Create a similar list about customs in your country. Make copies for your classmates and ask them to mark them. Tally the results and check if your list accurately reflects what you thought would be the most likely outcome.

ロールプレイ

1. You are about to visit a Japanese friend's house. You are in front of the house. Ring the bell, greet your friend's mother, and go into the house.
2. You are visiting a Japanese friend's house. It is close to dinner time, so you should leave. Initiate the conversation to take your leave in an appropriate manner.
3. You are leaving school to help out your parents. Your friends are having a farewell party for you. Describe the memories of what you have experienced here, and express your nostalgic feelings.
4. Your Japanese friend has been invited to a wedding ceremony, and he does not know what to wear, what kind of present to give, etc. Make suggestions to your friend about customs for wedding ceremonies and receptions in your country.
5. You are in Japan. Your Japanese friends want to know what you like or don't like about Japanese culture. Express your opinions by comparing Japanese culture with your culture.
6. Your Japanese friend does not know much about religion and asks about religions in your country. Describe them to him or her.

Chapter 10

第十課(だいじゅっか)

Jon Arnold Images Ltd / Alamy

文句(もんく)と謝罪(しゃざい)
Complaints and Apologies

Objectives Expressing complaints, requesting change of behavior, expressing the intention to make a change

Vocabulary Relationships among people, annoying things, expressing complaints and annoyance, things you don't want to be forced to do

Dialogue 静かにするように言って下さい。

Japanese Culture Neighborhood relations, trash collection

Grammar
- I. Expressing complaints using the causative-passive form
- II. Expressing or requesting efforts to change behavior using the plain present form of verbs + ようにする; describing what efforts are being made to attain a specific goal using ～ように、～
- III. Expressing unchanged conditions using ～まま
- IV. Using the conditional ～ても and question word ～ても
- V. Using the plain form + のに, *despite ~*, *although ~*

Listening Annoying things

Communication Expressing complaints or anger, making apologies

Kanji Structure of **kanji** compounds

全 然 注 合 覚 歌 句 号 直

残 貸 借 返 置 急 広 最 声 開 閉 伝 横

Reading Understanding the characteristics of expository writing, いじめ

Chapter Resources

www.cengagebrain.com

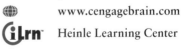

Heinle Learning Center

Audio Program

Flashcards

単語
たん

Nouns

あいて	相手	interlocutor, the other party
あかちゃん	赤ちゃん	baby
おおや	大家	landlord, landlady
おと	音	sound
おとな	大人	adult
かぎ	鍵	key, かぎをかける to lock
かべ	壁	wall
こ	子	child. こ is usually preceded by a modifier. としうえのこ (年上の子) older child, いいこ (いい子) good child
ごみ/ゴミ		trash, garbage (ごみ can be written either in **hiragana** or in **katakana**)
しりあい	知り合い	acquaintance
としうえ	年上	older
としした	年下	younger
なか	仲	relationship (among people), なかがいい to have a good relationship, なかが悪い to have a bad relationship
にっき	日記	diary, にっきをつける (日記を付ける) to keep a diary
ひ	日	day
ピアノ		piano
ひっこし	引っ越し	moving (one's residence)
ほんとう	本当	truth, ほんとうに (本当に) indeed; really
めいわく	迷惑	trouble, めいわくをかける to give (someone) problems
よなか	夜中	late at night, the middle of the night
もんく	文句	complaint, もんくをいう (文句を言う) to complain
らくがき	落書き	graffiti, らくがきをする (落書きをする) to write graffiti

Verbal nouns

ちゅうい	注意	attention, warning, ちゅういする (注意する) to warn, to call attention to, ちゅういをする (注意をする) to warn, to call attention to
そうだん	相談	consultation, そうだんする (相談する) to consult with

い -adjectives

うるさい		noisy, Shut up! (when used as a phrase by itself)
きたない	汚い	dirty
たまらない		cannot stand, unbearable
ひくい	低い	low

な -adjectives

しあわせ (な)	幸せ (な)	happy
しょうじき (な)	正直 (な)	honest
めいわく (な)	迷惑 (な)	troublesome, annoying, めいわくをかける to give (someone) trouble, to inconvenience (someone)

う -verbs

おこる	怒る	to get angry
からかう		to tease
さわぐ	騒ぐ	to make noise
たたく		to hit, to slap
ならう	習う	to learn (with a tutor)
ひく	弾く	to play (the piano/guitar, other stringed instrument), ピアノをひく to play the piano
ひっこす	引っ越す	to move residence
ゆるす	許す	to forgive

る -verbs

おくれる	遅れる	to be late
かける	掛ける	to hang, hook, かぎをかける to lock
かたづける	片付ける	to clean up, to organize

たてる	立てる	to make something stand up, おとをたてる to make noise
つける	付ける	to write (in a diary), にっきをつける（日記を付ける） to keep a diary

Expressions

いいかげんにしてよ。	いい加減にしてよ。	Give me a break. (female speech)
いいかげんにしろよ。	いい加減にしろよ。	Give me a break. (male speech)
おとをたてる	音を立てる	to make noise
きがつかなくて	気がつかなくて	I didn't realize (it).
きをつける	気をつける	to become careful, to pay attention
ごめいわくおかけして もうしわけありません。	ご迷惑おかけして 申しわけありません。	I'm sorry to cause you problems.
しかたがない	仕方がない	There is nothing one can do about it, there is no use.
じょうだんじゃないよ。	冗談じゃないよ。	You've got to be kidding.
ほっといてくれよ。		Leave me alone. (male speech)
ほっといてよ。		Leave me alone. (female speech)
やめろ		Cut it out. (male speech)
もうしわけありません。	申し訳ありません。	I'm sorry. (polite and formal)
もうしわけございません。	申し訳ございません。	I'm sorry. (very polite and formal)

単(たん)語の練習

A. 人と人とのかんけい Relationships among people

知(し)り合(あ)い	acquaintance
年上の子	older child
赤(あか)ちゃん	baby
大人(おとな)	adult
なかが悪い	to not get along with someone
年下の子	younger child
大家(おおや)（さん）	landlord, landlady
相手(あいて)	interlocutor, the other party
なかがいい	to get along with someone

覚(おぼ)えていますか。

年を取る　家族　兄弟　両親　祖父　祖母　父　母　兄　姉　弟　妹　主(しゅ)人　つま　ご家族
ご兄弟　ご両親　おじいさん　おばあさん　お父さん　お母さん　お兄さん　お姉さん
弟さん　妹さん　ご主(しゅ)人　おくさん　近所の人

Activity 1 Which words fit the following descriptions?

1. お父さんやお母さん
2. 自分よりわかい人
3. その人とつきあいたくないこと
4. 私が少し知っている人
5. ０さいの子供
6. その人といい友達でいること
7. 自分より年を取っている相手(あいて)
8. アパートや家を貸(か)す人
9. 自分の話を聞いている人
10. 子供じゃない人

Activity 2 質問に答えて下さい。

1. なかがいい人とはどんなことをしますか。知(し)り合(あ)いとはどうですか。
2. アパートを借(か)りるなら、どんな大家(おおや)さんがいいですか。
3. 年上(としうえ)の兄弟と年下(としした)の兄弟とどちらの方がいいと思いますか。
4. 赤(あか)ちゃんが好きですか。きらいですか。どうしてですか。

B. めいわくなこと Annoying things

授業におくれる
to come late for class

夜中(よなか)にさわぐ
to be noisy late at night

音(おと)をたてる
to make noise

ピアノをひく
to play the piano

たたく
to hit

かべに落書(らくが)きをする
to write graffiti on the wall

からかう
to tease

くつがよごれる
for shoes to get dirty

めいわくをかける
to give (someone) trouble, to inconvenience (someone)

覚(おぼ)えていますか。

どろぼう　殺人(さつ)　はんざい　ひがい　おそう　ころす　すてる　にげる　わかれる　けがをする　たばこをすう　さいふを落とす　しぬ　宿題を忘れる　指を切る　いじめる　けんかをする　物をこわす　洋(よう)服をよごす　人をだます　お金をぬすむ　悪口を言う　うそをつく　うわさをする　名前を間違える　間違う　仕事をたのむ　車を家の前に止める　車が止まる　バイトをやめる　お金を引き出す　笑う　しぬ　交(こう)通事故(こ)にあう　終わる　雪がふる　きらい　弱い　悪い　遠い　歌(うた)を歌(うた)う　車をぶつける　足をふむ

Activity 3 下の文に適当(てきとう)な (*appropriate*) 言葉を書いて下さい。

1. ぼくは彼(かの)女が好きだから、________てしまうんです。
2. 知(し)り合(あ)いのおじさんは車をかべに__________、こわしてしまった。
3. 年上(としうえ)の子が年下(としした)の子を____________、泣かせてしまった。
4. 赤(あか)ちゃんが寝ているので、大きい__________を______________下さい。
5. 教室のかべに________をして 、先生にしかられてしまった。
6. となりの人が夜中(よなか)にパーティをして__________ので、寝られない。
7. 雨の日に道を歩いていたら、車に服を________________。
8. 電車の中で、女の人に足を____________、とても痛かった。
9. 寝られないので、夜ピアノを____________________。
10. ______________くつをはいて、家の中に入ってはいけません。
11. あの子は毎日______________に______________ので、先生が困っている。
12. 人に____________をかけたら、あやまらなければならない。

Activity 4 質問に答えて下さい。

1. 子供がよくすることは、どんなことですか。
2. 大学生がよくすることは、どんなことですか。
3. あなたが今までにやったことは、どんなことですか。
4. やってはいけないけれど、やってみたいことは、どんなことですか。
5. どんなことで人にめいわくをかけたことがありますか。

C. 文句(もんく)を言う (Expressing complaints and annoyance)

おこる	to get angry
(〜に) 気をつける	to be careful about
注意(ちゅうい)する	to warn, to call attention to, to watch out for
そうだんする	to consult with
ゆるす	to forgive
めいわく (な)	to be annoyed, annoying
たまらない	cannot stand, unbearable
きたない	dirty
うるさい	noisy
仕方(しかた)がない	there is nothing one can do about it, there is no use
本当だ	true
ひくい	low

覚(おぼ)えていますか。

あやまる　心配する　しかる　困る　いやな　ごめん　ごめんなさい　止める
無理(むり)　無理(むり)をする　気分が悪い　ええっと／すみません　それはちょっと
残念(ざんねん)（な）　大変（な）　失礼ですが　ひどい　こわい

Activity 5 下の文に適当(てきとう)な (*appropriate*) 言葉を書いて下さい。

1. 授業におくれたので、先生に＿＿＿＿れた。
2. その話はうそじゃなくて＿＿＿＿です。
3. 友達は、変なうわさをたてられて＿＿＿＿＿、先生に＿＿＿＿＿した。
4. 友達が変なことを言ったので、＿＿＿＿＿＿、文句(もんく)を言った。
5. となりの家のピアノの音が＿＿＿＿＿、たまらない。
6. そのシャツは＿＿＿＿＿＿から、洗いました。
7. 私はせが＿＿＿＿＿から、前にせが高い人がいると、とても困るんです。
8. 道をわたる時は、右と左に＿＿＿＿＿を＿＿＿＿＿下さい。
9. 雪で私の飛行機(き)がキャンセルになりました。＿＿＿＿＿が＿＿＿＿＿ので、今日は家に帰って、明日出るつもりです。

Activity 6 質問に答えて下さい。

1. どんな時に、両親に文句(もんく)を言いますか。どんな時に両親に注意(ちゅうい)されますか。
2. どんなことについて、友達にそうだんしますか。
3. どんな時に、人にあやまりますか。どんな時には、あやまりませんか。

D. させられたくないこと Things you don't want to be forced to do

日記(にっき)をつける	to keep a diary
かたづける	to organize, to clean up
犬の散(さん)歩をする	to walk the dog
ごみを出す	to take trash out, to discard trash
引(ひ)っ越(こ)す	to move (residence)
かぎをかける	to lock (the door, the window, etc.)
ピアノを習(なら)う	to learn piano

覚(おぼ)えていますか。

勉強する　休む　はたらく　説明する　洗濯(たく)をする　そうじをする　むかえに行く　単(たん)語を覚(おぼ)える

Activity 7 Work with a group of four. One person should act out one of the actions in the list or the 覚(おぼ)えていますか section above. The rest of the group should guess what is being done. Anyone who makes a correct guess receives one point.

Activity 8 質問に答えて下さい。

1. よくすることは、どれですか。
2. 全然(ぜんぜん)しないことは、どれですか。
3. どんなことをしてみたいですか。
4. よく人にどんなことをしてもらいますか。
5. よく人にどんなことをしてあげますか。

ダイアローグ

はじめに

下の質問に日本語で答えて下さい。

1. 近所では、何か問題がありますか。
2. となりの人がうるさい時、どうしますか。
3. 近所のめいわくにならないように、どんなことに気をつけていますか。
4. どんな時に大家(おおや)さんと話をしますか。

静かにするように言って下さい。 *Please tell him to be quieter.*

The following **manga** frames are scrambled, so they are not in the order described by the dialogue. Read the dialogue and unscramble the frames by writing the correct number in the box in each frame.

a b c

d e f

リーさんはアルバイトの広告(こうこく) (*advertisements*) を見ています。そこに、上田さんが来ました。

上田： リーさん、何、見てるの。

リー： 新しいバイト、さがしてるんだ。

上田： え、どうして？前のアルバイトやめちゃったの？

リー： いや、やめさせられちゃったんだよ。最(さい)近寝られなくて、何度も仕事におくれちゃったから。

上田： 寝られないって？どこか悪いの？

リー： いや、そうじゃないんだ。となりの人がうるさくてね。

上田： となりの人？先月引(ひ)っ越(こ)してきた？

リー： うん、毎晩おそくまで大きな音(おと)でテレビを見たり、音楽聞いたり。それに、よく友達が来て夜中(よなか)までさわぐんだから、たまらないよ。

上田： 本当。ひどいね。文句(もんく)言ったの？

リー： うん、何度静かにするように言ってもだめなんだ。

上田： そう、大家(おおや)さんに言って注意(ちゅうい)してもらうようにたのんでみたら。

リー： うん、そうだね。このままだと、病気になりそうから、仕方(しかた)ないかな。

リーさんは大家(おおや)さんに電話をかけました。

リー： もしもし、あの、さくらアパートの 201 号室(ごうしつ)に住んでいるリーなんですけれども。

大家(おおや)： あ、リーさん、どうしたんですか。

リー： あのう、ちょっと おねがいしたいことがあるんですが。

大家(おおや)： 何ですか？

リー： すみませんが、となりの青木(あおき)さんに夜静かにするように言っていただけないでしょうか。

大家(おおや)： そんなにうるさいんですか。

リー： ええ。よく夜中(よなか)に、テレビやステレオの音を大きくしてさわぐので、寝られないんです。何回もたのんだんですが、聞いてくれないんです。

大家(おおや)： そう、困りましたね。じゃあ、私の方から言っておきますよ。

リー： ごめいわくおかけしてもうしわけありませんが、よろしくおねがいします。

Dialogue Phrase Notes

- 何度も means *many times.*
- そんなに means *so, that much, that many.*
- ～号室(ごうしつ) is a suffix for a room number.

分かりましたか。

A. 質問に答えて下さい。

1. リーさんは、どうしてアルバイトをさがしているのですか。
2. リーさんは、どうして寝られないのですか。
3. リーさんのとなりのアパートには、だれが住んでいますか。その人はどんな人だと思いますか。どうしてそう思いますか。
4. 上田さんは、リーさんにどうしたらいいと言いましたか。
5. 大家(おおや)さんは、リーさんのためにどんなことをしてあげるつもりですか。

B. 下の文章(ぶんしょう) (*paragraph*) は青木(あおき)さんが書いたものです。自分を青木(あおき)さんだと思って下線(かせん) (*underline*) のところに適当(てきとう)な言葉を入れて下さい。

言葉のリスト

うすい　　thin

今日大家(おおや)さんから電話があって、夜____________________ように言われた。となりの人が、______________そうだ。ぼくはテレビやステレオの音が___________とは思わなかったが、このアパートはかべがうすいのかもしれない。

C. Underline the phrases that express Li-san's annoyance and complaints.

日本の文化

Neighborhood relations

Neighborhood relations are important in any country, but are probably more complicated in Japan due to its high population density. To comprehend the amount of living space available to the Japanese people, first imagine the state of California, which has roughly the same geographical area as Japan. Now remove 80 percent of that since that much space in Japan is taken up by mountains, and is not habitable. Finally, put one-half the entire U.S. population into the remaining 20 percent of California. This is the population density of Japan. A complicating factor is that the highly populated metro areas, which take up just 1 percent of the habitable land, house one half of Japan's population. Therefore, 1m^2 of living space in Tokyo costs several times more than that in New York City. Also, many people live in high-rise apartment buildings rather than houses. Even so, the average living space per person is 30.9 m^2 in Japan, which is less than half of that in the United States. (64.0 m^2). In other words, many Japanese families live in very crowded areas.

One of the most common problems is noise. There is not much distance between houses, and thin walls separate apartments, so sound travels easily. Things that would not bother your neighbor in the United States can be a big nuisance in Japan. The sound of a chair being pulled out or someone taking a shower can be just as annoying as the sound of children running in the room. Noise prevention is thus very important. For example, it is a good idea not to take a bath or shower or do laundry early in the morning or late at night if you live in an apartment. Also, placing a stereo and musical instruments away from the wall and on a carpet can prevent sounds from traveling to your neighbors. Department stores and do-it-yourself stores sell a variety of gadgets to prevent noise.

Trash collection

Another common problem is the collection of trash and recyclables. Garbage collection is very efficient but also somewhat complicated in Japan. Garbage is classified according to type, and the classification and frequency of collection can vary from region to region. In Tokyo, for example, you first need to distinguish among combustible garbage (燃えるごみ／可燃ごみ), non-combustible garbage (燃えないごみ／不燃ごみ), recyclables (リサイクル), and large trash (粗大ごみ) such as furniture and appliances. Combustible garbage is burned, and non-combustible garbage is broken into small pieces and taken to the dump site directly. Which items are placed in which category may differ slightly depending on local laws. Garbage can be placed in trash buckets or in special plastic bags that have been approved by local authorities. Garbage placed in an unapproved container may not be collected.

Alama Images

Also, it is necessary to take garbage to the designated collection location on the day it will be collected. The collection days for each type of garbage are posted at every waste collection area. Waste must not be left overnight. Leaving uncollected garbage for a prolonged period of time in the collection area is a nuisance for people who live close to the area.

In the Tokyo metro area, combustible garbage is usually collected three times a week and non-combustible garbage is collected once a week. Recyclables (cans and bottles) are also collected once a week. These services are free for residential waste. In many cases, large waste items are collected by the department of waste management by special arrangement for a fee. In some districts, you can also take large garbage to a designated site by yourself.

種別	出せる物	具体例
燃やせるごみ	生ごみ 木くず類 紙、布類 アルミ箔 ゴム、皮革類 その他 （氷まくら、保冷剤、乾燥剤、カイロ）	生ごみ、カイロ、乾燥剤、ゴムホース（50cm以下に切る）、ハンドバッグ 小型カバン、貝がら、衣類 布類、落葉、剪定くず、アルミ、靴 履物、ボール（皮·ゴム）、ぬいぐるみ、紙おむつ（便はトイレに捨ててください）
埋立ごみ	ガラス クレヨン 絵の具 陶器くず 灰 カミソリ プラスチック製まな板	カミソリ、チャッカマン、使い切りライター、花びん、プラスチック製マナ板、クレヨン 絵の具、耐熱ガラス、ガラス製食器類、板ガラス、植木鉢（陶器製）、磁石、指定袋 灰、カセットテープ、ビデオテープ、粘土、皿
有害ごみ	蛍光管 乾電池 体温計（水銀式）	蛍光管、白熱球、乾電池、体温計（電子体温計は燃やせない粗大ごみ）
リサイクルプラ	プラスチック製 ビニール製 発泡スチロール で プラマークのあるもの	タマゴパック、ポリ袋 ビニール袋、発泡スチロール（小さく割って袋に入れる）、トレイ·ラップ·ビニール、ペットボトルのフタ·ラベル、洗剤·シャンプーなどの容器

汚れの取れないものは「燃やせるごみ」で出してください。

Types of trash. This circular from Hiroshima identifies several types of trash, including (from top) combustible trash, landfill trash, toxic trash, and recyclable plastics.

文法

I. Expressing complaints using the causative-passive form

A causative-passive sentence is a direct passive where the causee of an action is the subject and the causer is the agent of the action. Such sentences convey the viewpoint of the causee. In a causative-passive sentence, the subject (the causee) is always forced to do something by the agent (the causer).

Subject (Causee)		Agent (Causer)		Action		
Noun	Particle	Noun	Particle	Noun	Particle	Verb (causative-passive)
私	は	先生	に	本	を	読まされた。

I was made to read the book by the teacher.

When the causer is understood from the context, it can be omitted.

子供の時、毎朝運動させられた。
I was forced to do exercise every morning when I was a child.

The formation of the causative-passive is identical to the formation of the passive. However, う-verbs have two causative-passive forms, (さ)せられる and (さ)される, while る-verbs and the irregular verb する tend to have only (さ)せられる. In cases where both (さ)せられる and (さ)される are possible, the shorter causative-passive sounds more direct and more colloquial.

Verb types	Meaning	Dictionary form	Causative form	Causative-passive form
Irregular verbs	*to come* *to warn*	来(く)る 注意(ちゅうい)する	来(こ)させる 注意(ちゅうい)させる	来(こ)させられる 注意(ちゅうい)させられる
る -verbs	*to organize* *to lock*	かたづける かける	かたづけさせる かけさせる	かたづけさせられる かけさせられる
う -verbs	*to play (the piano)*	ひく	ひかせる or ひかす	ひかせられる ひかされる
	to learn	習(なら)う	習(なら)わせる or 習(なら)わす	習(なら)わせられる 習(なら)わされる
	to speak	話す	話さす	~~話させられる~~、 ~~話さされる~~＊

＊う-verbs ending in す normally do not use the short form.

子供の時、毎日部屋をかたづけさせられた。
I was made to clean up my room every day when I was a child
家の子供には、いつも心配させられる。
My child makes me worry all the time. (lit.: *I am made to worry about my child all the time.*)

小学校の時、先生に日記(にっき)をつけさせられました。
I was made to write a diary by my teacher when I was in elementary school.

Note

- Use the て+もらう／いただく if the subject is being allowed to do something by the causer.

  私は両親にピアノを習(なら)わせてもらった。
  My parents let me learn piano. (lit.: *I was allowed to learn piano by my parents.*)

話してみましょう

Activity 1

A mother is talking about what she has had her child do. You are the child and you don't like doing any of these things, but you are forced to do them anyway. Change the following statements of the mother to conform to your perspective using the causative passive construction.

Example: 私は子供に毎朝牛乳(ぎゅうにゅう)を飲ませます。
私は母に毎朝牛乳(ぎゅうにゅう)を飲まされるんです。

1. 私は子供に毎日運動をさせます。
2. 私は子供にごみを出させます。
3. 私は子供に時々近所のスーパーに買い物に行かせます。
4. 私は子供にそうじを手伝(つだ)わせるんです。
5. 私は子供に自分の部屋をかたづけさせます。
6. 私は子供に毎日日記(にっき)を付(つ)けさせるんです。
7. 私は子供にピアノを習(なら)わすんです。
8 私は子供に犬の散(さん)歩をさせるんです。

Activity 2

Work with the class. Ask your classmates what kind of things they were made to do by their parents when they were children.

Example: A: 子供の時、親にどんなことをさせられましたか。
B: おさらを洗わせられました / 洗わされました。

Activity 3

Your boss asked you to do the following things. You could not refuse his requests, so you have done them. Express your negative feelings about what you were asked to do using the causative passive.

Example: 明日大阪(おおさか)に行ってくれないか。
大阪(おおさか)に行かせられました / 行かされました。

1. コピーを100まいとっておいてくれないか。
2. 空港まで知り合いの子供をむかえに行ってもらいたいんだ。
3. 明日までにこのプロジェクトのレポートを出してほしいんだが。
4. ちょっとお茶を入れてもらえないか。
5. この荷物を持ってくれないか。
6. 今日は忙しいから、五時まで待ってくれないか。
7. 今週の日曜日は会社に来てもらいたいんだ。

Activity 4

Work with a partner. First, write the things that you want the people listed under 私 in the following chart to let you do (させてもらいたいこと) and the things you don't want other people to make you do (させられたくないこと). Ask your partner about things he or she wants them to let him or her do, or doesn't want them to make him or her do, and compare your responses to those of your partners.

Example:
A: 先生にどんなことをさせていただきたいと思いますか。
B: そうですね。英語で話させていただきたいですね。
A: 私もそう思います。
B: じゃあ、先生にどんなことをさせられたくないですか。
A: そうですね。作文を書かされたくないですね。
B: そうですか。私は毎日テストを受けさせられたくないですね。

私

～に	させてもらいたいこと	させられたくないこと
先生		
両親		
ルームメート		
主人 or つま *(current or future spouse)*		

パートナー

～に	させてもらいたいこと	させられたくないこと
先生		
両親		
ルームメート		
主人 or つま *(current or future spouse)*		

II. Expressing or requesting efforts to change behavior using the plain present form of verbs + ようにする

Expressing or requesting efforts to change behavior using ～ようにする

The plain present form of the verb +ようにする is used when such changes are expressed with a verb phrase. The meaning is *to make an effort to do ~*. The difference between a simple statement such as 早く来ます and 早く来るようにします is that the latter implies that the speaker will try to change his behavior for a prolonged period of time, but the former describes one occasion only.

交通事故に気をつけるようにします。 *I will try to be careful about traffic accidents.*

かぎをかけるようにします。 *I will try (to remember) to lock the door.*

あまり遊ばないようにします。 *I will try not to play much.*

ようにする can be used to request a change of behavior and it is often used to make a complaint.

夜中にさわがないようにしてくれませんか。
Please try to not make noise in the middle of the night.

きたない部屋ね。少しはかたづけるようにしたらどう？
What a messy room. Why don't you tidy it up a little?

赤ちゃんが寝ているから、大きい声を出さないようにして下さい。
Please try to not raise your voice because the baby is sleeping.

火曜日の朝ゴミを出すようにした方がいいですよ。
You should try to take the trash out every Tuesday morning.

授業におくれないようにして下さい。
Please try not to be late for class.

Notes

- The plain present form of verbs + ようにします implies that the speaker intends to make an effort. The plain present form of verbs + ようにしています indicates that the speaker is making such efforts, and means *I make it a rule to ~.*

  一週間に一度部屋をかたづけるようにします。
  I will make an effort to clean up the room once a week.

  一週間に一度部屋をかたづけるようにしています。
  I make it a rule to clean up the room once a week.

  めいわくをかけないようにします。
  I will make an effort to not give you any trouble.

めいわくをかけないようにしています。
I make it a rule to not give you any trouble.

- The phrases ～ようにして下さい, くれませんか, いただけませんか, etc., are less direct than ～て下さい, くれませんか, いただけませんか, etc., and imply that the speaker wants the listener to make a prolonged effort to change his/her behavior. These expressions are often used for complaints.

話してみましょう

Activity 1 Match the sentence halves in Column A and Column B to make sentences using ～ように～ .

Example: A-1 と B-g
日本語が上手になるように、毎日日本人と話すようにしています。

A	B
1. 日本語が上手になります	a. 毎日三時間ピアノをひきます
2. くつがよごれません	b. ごみの日にごみを出します
3. やせられます	c. 気をつけて歩きます
4. 近所の人のめいわくになりません	d. 大きい音(おと)をたてません
5. 赤(あか)ちゃんを起こしません	e. 授業におくれません
6. コンサートに出られます	f. 夜は何も食べません
7. 先生にしかられません	g. 毎日日本人と話します

Activity 2 Work with a partner. Imagine that you are the supervisor of a dormitory. You are writing a set of rules to maintain order. Based on a discussion with your partner, write six regulations you want students to follow, using ～ように .

Example: A: りょうの学生にどんなことをするように言ったらいいでしょうか。
B: そうですね。十時までに、りょうに帰るように言ったらどうでしょうか。

You write: 十時までにりょうに帰るようにすること

Activity 3 Work with a group of four, and create two teams of two people each. One member of each team ("A1" and "B1") should get together and decide on a location, such as a restaurant. They then return to their partners and one of them (A1) begins the game by giving his or her partner a clue to the identity of the location, using the ～ようにして下さい expression. If the partner can figure out what the location is, that team gets a point. If not, the other partner gets a guess. If it is correct, that team gets a point; if not, then "B1" must provide a clue for his or her partner, and the guessing game starts over again.

Example: A1: たばこをすわないようにして下さい。
A2: 病院ですか。
A1: いいえ。
B2: 銀行ですか。
A1: いいえ。
B1: ジャケットを着るようにして下さい。
B2: レストランですか。
B1: はい、そうです。

Activity 4

Work with a partner. The two of you are neighbors, and you are having some problems with one another. Each of you should write five things the other has been doing that you find annoying, then ask the other to stop doing these things.

Example: A: あのう、すみませんが。
B: はい、何でしょうか。
A: 家の前に止めてある白い車、～さんのですか。
B: あ、そうですが。
A: 出られなくなるから、止めないようにしていただけませんか。
B: あ、すみません。

III. Expressing unchanged conditions using ～まま

まま is a noun that expresses a lack of change in something. Literally it means *as it is*, *leave ~ as it is*, or *remain unchanged*. However, it is often difficult to translate a sentence with まま literally because it can be expressed in a variety of ways in English.

In the following example, まどを開(あ)けたまま、寝てしまった, the speaker opened the window, and it was left open when he or she went to bed. The sentence そのまま来て下さい indicates that the speaker wishes the listener to come without making any change to his/her appearance or physical state.

まどを開(あ)けたまま、寝てしまった。 *I slept with the window open.*
そのまま、来て下さい。 *Please come as you are.*

Grammatically まま works like a regular noun and it can be modified by a noun, an adjective or a verb.

Type	Formation	Example
Verbs	(plain past affirmative) + まま (plain present negative) + まま	おこったまま *stay angry* かたづけないまま *left unorganized*
い-Adjectives	い + まま	きたないまま *left dirty*
な-Adjectives	な + まま	きれいなまま *stay nice* 正直(しょうじき)なまま *stay honest*
Nouns	の + まま	知(し)り合(あ)いのまま *remain an acquaintance* このまま *stay as things are now*

このままお待ち下さい。 *Wait* (just as you are), *please.*

いつまでも、子供のままではいられない。 *You can't stay a child forever.*

この家は今のままでは売れないと思う。 *I don't think this house will sell as it is.*

この部屋は妹がいた時のままにしてある。 *This room is kept as it was when my sister was here.*

大人(おとな)になっても、せがひくいまま変わらない。 *Even though I've become an adult, I'm still as short as I always was.*

このトマト、青いままで、全然(ぜんぜん)赤くならない。 *This tomato has just stayed green, without getting red at all.*

好きなまま、何も言わなければ、何も起きないよ。 *Nothing will happen if you just keep your feelings of love to yourself without saying anything.*

何が起きたか分からないまま、ここに来た。 *I came here without knowing what had happened.*

話してみましょう

Activity 1 Express the following situations using まま.

Example: 手紙を書きましたが、その後、出していません。
<u>手紙を書いたまま、出していません。／手紙を書いたままです。</u>

1. 窓を開(あ)けましたが、その後、閉(し)めていません。
2 車をぬすまれました。その後、見つかって (*to be found*) いません。
3. 落書(らくが)きをしましたが、その後、消(け)していません。
4. 洋(よう)服がよごれましたが、その後、洗っていません。
5. 友達から手紙をもらいましたが、その後何もしていません。
6 子供の時、せがひくかったです。今もひくいです。
7. その部屋は昨日もきたなかったです。今も、きたないです。

Activity 2 Explain the situations described in the pictures using まま .

Example: まどを開けたまま、<u>出かけてしまった。</u>

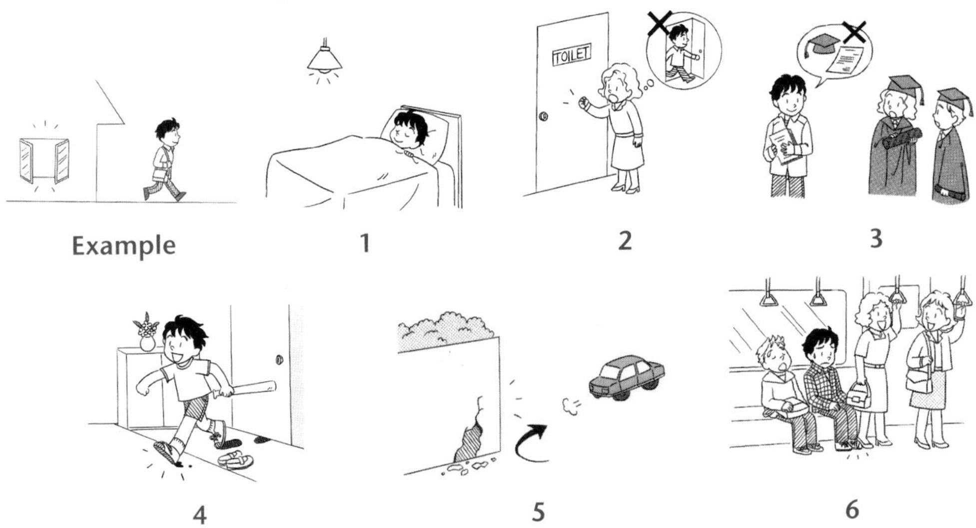

Example 1 2 3

4 5 6

Activity 3 Work with a partner. Create a short conversation using the pictures and the sentences with まま that you composed in Activity 2.

Example: A: どうしたの、この部屋は？

B: どろぼうに入られちゃった。

A: え、なんで？

B: あー、出かける時、まどを開けたままだった。

A: え、ほんと！

Example 1 2 3

4 5 6 7

IV. Using the conditional ～ても and question word ～ても

Chapter 1 of this book introduced ～てもいい, which expresses permission. This expression literally means *it is OK even if* ~, and it consists of the conditional ても and いい. This chapter introduces a more general use of this conditional phrase.

A. ～ても , even if, even though.

The conditional ても expresses future and hypothetical conditions.

好きな人なら、お金がなくても、結婚します。
If I loved a person, I would marry him even if he didn't have any money.
好きな人なら、お金がなくても、結婚していた。
If I had loved him, I would have married him even if he didn't have any money.

～ても can also be used with a factual situation. In this case, ～ても may be replaced by ～けれど or ～が, but ～ても implies a stronger affective involvement of the speaker than ～けれど or ～が.

お金がなくても、しあわせです。 *I am happy even though I don't have any money.*
お金がないけれど、しあわせです。 *I am happy though I don't have any money*
お金がありませんが、しあわせです。 *I don't have any money, but I am happy.*

This in turn means that けれど or が cannot be replaced with ても if the speaker is not expressing a strong emotion or when けれど or が has been used to introduce a topic.

日本語は話せないけれど、日本の映画を見に行きました。
I don't speak Japanese but I went to see a Japanese movie.
日本語は話せませんが、日本の映画を見に行きました
I don't speak Japanese but I went to see a Japanese movie.
~~日本語は話せなくても、日本の映画を見に行きました。~~
I went to see a Japanese movie even though I did not speak Japanese.

宿題ですけど、明日出してもいいですか。 *About the homework, can I turn it in tomorrow?*
宿題ですが、明日出してもいいですか。 *About the homework, can I turn it in tomorrow?*
~~宿題でも、明日出してもいいですか。~~ *Even if it is homework, I turn it in tomorrow?*

The て-form of a verb, adjective, or copular verb can be used in the ても conditional .

安くても、きたない所には泊まりたくない。 *Even if it is cheap, I don't want to stay in a dirty place.*
うるさくても、こわいから、何も言えない。 *Even though he is noisy, I can't say anything because I'm afraid of him.*
せがひくくても、足は長いんです。 *Even though I'm short, I have long legs.*
それが本当でも、言わない方がいいと思う。 *Even if it is true, I don't think you should say it.*

なかのいい友達でも、ゆるせなかった。	*I couldn't forgive him even though he was a good friend of mine.*
引っ越(こ)しても、私のことを忘(わす)れないで下さいね。	*Please don't forget me even after you move.*
相手(あいて)にたたかれても、おこってはいけない。	*You should not get angry even if you were hit by the other party.*
スミスさんがゆるしても、私がゆるさない。	*Even if Mr. Smith forgives you, I won't.*

Note

- To explicitly state that a condition is open, add the adverb たとえ, which also means *even if.*

  たとえしんでも、あなたのことは忘れない。
  I won't forget you even if I die.

  大人でも、泣きたい時は泣くんだ。
  Even an adult will cry when he/she wants to.

B. Question word ～ても , no matter (who/what/when/where/etc.) ~

When a question word is used within the conditional ても, it means *no matter (who/what/when/where/etc.) ~.*

最近(さい)何を食べても、おいしい。
No matter what I eat recently, it all tastes good.

赤(あか)ちゃんが何をこわしても、お母さんはおこらない。
No matter what the baby breaks, the mother does not get angry.

広田(ひろた)さんにどんな悪口を言っても、大丈夫(じょうぶ)です。
No matter how ill you speak of her, Ms. Hirota is unaffected/fine.

この料理はだれが食べても、おいしくないと言うと思う。
No matter who might eat this, I think he/she will say that it's no good.

林さんはだれといても、よく話す。
No matter whom she is with, Ms. Hayashi talks a lot.

私の大家(おおや)さんはいつ会っても、気持ちのいい人だ。
No matter when I meet him/her, my landlord/landlady is a pleasant person to be with.

この店は何曜日に来ても、閉(し)まっている。
No matter which day I come, this store is closed.

いい物なら、いくら高くても、買いますよ。
No matter how expensive it is, I will buy it if it is a quality item.

このクッキーは、いくつやいても、すぐなくなってしまう。
These cookies go very quickly no matter how many of them I bake.

何歳(さい)になっても、好きな人は好きです。
I'll love the person I love no matter how old he gets.

このマンガは何度読んでも、おもしろい。
No matter how many times I read it, this cartoon is funny.

この子は何回しかっても、またいたずらをする。
No matter how many times I scold him, this child will still get into mischief.
いくら文句(もんく)を言っても、だれも助けてくれない。
No matter how much I complain, no one will help me.
いくら泣いても、ダメなものはダメ。
No matter how much you cry, no is no.
いくら勉強しても、漢字が覚(おぼ)えられないんです。
No matter how hard I study, I cannot learn kanji.
どんなになかが悪くても、悪口を言ったり、たたいたりしてはいけない。
No matter how bad your relationship with him is, you must not speak ill of him or hit him.
どんなにしかられても、その子はあやまらなかった。
No matter how much he was scolded, the child did not apologize.
どんなにめいわくをかけても、お母さんはゆるしてくれる。
My mother forgives me no matter how much trouble I give her.
子供がどんなにほしがっても、今はお金がないから、買ってあげられない。
No matter how much the child asks for it, I can't buy it for him now because I don't have the money.

話してみましょう

Activity 1

Mr. Tom Smith and Mrs. Jane Smith are a couple and they have opposite traits. Explain Jane's characteristics using ～ても , based on the statements being made about Tom.

Example: トムさんは食べたらすぐふとります。
でも、ジェーンさんは食べてもふとりません。

1. トムさんは、運動すると、すぐつかれます。
2. トムさんは、かなしい映画を見ると、よく泣きます。
3. トムさんは、お金があると、すぐ使ってしまいます。
4. トムさんは、病気になると、すぐ病院に行きます。
5. トムさんは、新しい服を買うと、すぐ着てみたくなります。
6. トムさんは、新しい所に引っ越(こ)すと、すぐ近所の人にあいさつに行きます。

Activity 2

Work with the class. Ask your classmates what they could do if the statements in the table were true, and what they could not do even if they were true, and complete the table with at least two answers in each cell. Make sure to write the name of the respondents as well.

Example: A: 日本語が上手になったら、どんなことが出来ますか。

B: 日本語で小説が読めます。

A: そうですか。じゃあ、日本語が上手になっても、出来ないことがありますか。

B: そうですね。通訳（つうやく） (*interpreter*) にはなれないでしょうね。

	～たらできること	～てもできないこと
日本語が上手になる		
たくさん勉強する		
大学を卒業する		
日本に行く		

Activity 3

Ms. Suzuki seems to have a problem. Pretend that you are Ms. Suzuki and answer the questions using the form question word ～ても, and then write a description of the restaurant based on your answers.

Example: A: あまり食べませんね。どうしたんですか。

B: 何を食べても、おいしくないんです。

Example 1 2 3 4 5

1. この店、閉(し)まっていますね。どうしたんですか。
2. 鈴木(すず)さんは、何度も電話していますが、どうしたんですか。
3. 鈴木(すず)さんは、ダイエットしているそうですが、どうですか。
4. 鈴木(すず)さんは、英語を習(なら)っているそうですが、どうですか。
5. となりの人がよくさわぐそうですが、注意(ちゅうい)しましたか。

Activity 4

Work with a partner. A person who has recently moved into an upstairs apartment has been causing a lot of problems. You are a tenant and your partner is the manager of the apartment. Create a dialogue using a question word + ても.

Example: A: あのう、すみませんが。
B: はい、何でしょうか。
A: 私のアパートのとなりの人がとてもうるさいんです。注意(ちゅうい)していただけませんか。
B: その人と話したことはありますか。
A: ええ、何度も静かにするように言ったんですが、全然(ぜんぜん)だめなんです。
B: そうですか。わかりました。じゃあ、私が注意(ちゅうい)しておきます。

1. となりの人が夜中(よなか)にピアノをひく。
2. となりの人がゴミを出してはいけない日に、ゴミを出す。
3. となりの人のペットがにわ (*garden*) の花をふむ。
4. となりの人のペットが家の前をよごす。

V. Using the plain form + のに, *despite ~, although ~*

The conjunction のに (*although, despite*) indicates a strong contrast between two clauses. Its meaning is the exact opposite of ～ので (*because*). The のに construction is used to express a result which was not expected. In this sense, のに expresses the speaker's disbelief, surprise, regret, sorrow, frustration, or opposition to a situation that is the opposite of his/her expectations.

年上(としうえ)の子が年下(とした)の子をたたいているのに、先生は何も言わない。
Although the elder child is hitting the younger child, the teacher does not say anything.

赤(あか)ちゃんが泣いているのに、お母さんは何もしない。
Although the baby is crying, the mother does not do anything.

たくさんめいわくをかけたのに、両親はゆるしてくれました。
Although I caused my parents a lot of trouble, they forgave me.

うそをついたのに、みんな本当だと思っています。
Although I lied, everyone thinks I was telling the truth.

その子は大事にしていたおもちゃをこわされたのに、全然(ぜんぜん)おこっていません。
Although that child got his precious toy broken, he is not angry at all.

落書(らくが)きをしないように言ったのに、また落書(らくが)きをしている。
Although I told him to not write graffiti, he is writing graffiti again.

～のに is preceded by the same forms that come before ～ので or ～のです. な is used for the present affirmative tense of な-adjectives and the copula verb, and plain forms are used for all other adjectives, copulas, and verbs.

い -adjective	な -adjectives	Copula verb	Verbs
こわい	しあわせ	本当	かぎをかける
こわいのに	しあわせなのに	本当なのに	かぎをかけるのに
こわくないのに	しあわせじゃないのに	本当じゃないのに	かぎをかけないのに
こわかったのに	しあわせだったのに	本当だったのに	かぎをかけたのに
こわくなかったのに	しあわせじゃなかったのに	本当じゃなかったのに	かぎをかけなかったのに

As was the case with ～ので, the main clause can express only a statement or a question. For requests, commands, suggestions, offers, invitations, or other expressions which indicate strong feelings from the speaker, use ～け(れ)ど or ～が.

ちょっと重いですが、持ってくれませんか。 *It's a little heavy, but could you hold it?*

ちょっと重いけど、持ってくれませんか。 *It's a little heavy, but could you hold it?*

~~ちょっと重いのに、持ってくれませんか。~~ *Although it's a little heavy, but could you hold it?*

その人とはあまりなかはよくないけど、うそは言いたくありません。
Although I don't get along with him very well, I don't want to lie to him.

~~その人とはあまりなかはよくないのに、うそは言いたくありません。~~
Although I don't get along with him very well, I don't want to lie to him.

If the main clause has been omitted, the 〜のに clause is translated as *should* or *should have*. This usage is very common in conversation.

電話をかければよかったのに。 *You should have called.*

うるさいならうるさいと言えばいいのに。 *He should say so if he thinks it is noisy.*

The following compares the functions of 〜が/〜けれど, 〜ても, and 〜のに.

		が・けれども	ても	のに
1	Can be applied to a future situation	○	○	
2	Use for a current or past situation	○	○	○
3	Expresses a hypothetical situation		○	
4	Main clause can contain a phrase that expresses the speaker's feelings and opinions	○	○	
5	Expresses the speaker's surprise or critical feeling			○
6	Introducing a topic, weak "but"	○		
7	Can end the sentence without a main clause	○		○

Examples:

1 and 4 大変だけど、がんばって下さい。 *It's tough, but please do your best.*

大変でも、がんばって下さい。 *Even if it may be tough, please do your best.*

~~大変なのに、がんばって下さい~~。 *Even though it may be tough, please do your best.*

2 スミスさんに聞いたけど、分からなかった。
I asked Mr. Smith, but I didn't get the answer.
スミスさんに聞いても、分からなかった。
Even though I asked Mr. Smith, I didn't get the answer.
スミスさんに聞いたのに、分からなかった。
Even though I asked Mr. Smith, I didn't get the answer.

3 ~~スミスさんに聞いたけど、分からなかっただろう。~~
I asked Mr. Smith, but he probably would not have known the answer.
スミスさんに聞いても、分からなかっただろう。
Even if I asked Mr. Smith, he probably would not have known the answer.
~~スミスさんに聞くのに、分からないだろう。~~
Even though I asked Mr. Smith, he probably would not have known the answer.

5 たのんだけど、キムさんはしなかった。(no feeling of surprise)
たのんでも、キムさんはしなかった。 (no feeling of surprise)
たのんだのに、キムさんはしなかった。(feeling of surprise)

6 かべの落書(らくが)きのことですが、もうけしましたか。
About the grafitti, have you gotten rid of it yet?
~~かべの落書(らくが)きのことでも、もうけしましたか。~~
Although about the grafitti, have you gotten rid of it yet?
~~かべの落書(らくが)きのことなのに、もうけしましたか。~~
Even though about the grafitti, have you gotten rid of it yet?

7 私はよく知りませんが。 *I don't know much about it, but . . .*
~~私はよく知らなくても。~~ *Although I don't know much about it . . .*
私はよく知らないのに。 *Even though I don't know much about it . . .*

話してみましょう

Activity 1 Make a sentence by adding のに to the cue sentence.

Example: 日本に十年住んでいました。
日本に十年住んでいたのに、日本語が話せません。

1. 今日はゴミを出してはいけません。
2. そのうわさは本当のことじゃありません。
3. 私は落書(らくが)きをしていません。
4. ピアノを習(なら)いたくありません。
5. どろぼうにお金をぬすまれました。
6. 洋(よう)服をよごされました。
7. 足をふまれました。
8. 引っ越(こ)しました。
9. めいわくはかけていません。
10. 正直(しょうじき)に話しています。

Activity 2 Work with a partner. Look at the following pictures and tell what is odd about them.

Example: A: この絵、変(へん) (*strange*) ですね。
B: そうですね。天気がいいのに、かさをさしています。(*~has an umbrella open*)

Activity 3

Work with a partner. One person should describe a problem listed in 1 through 7 by using のに , and the other person should give advice.

Example: 何度も文句(もんく)を言いましたが、となりの人は私の家の前に車を止めます。

A: どうしたんですか。

B: となりの人が家の前に車を止めるので、困ってるんですよ。

A: そうなんですか。となりの人と話はしたんですか。

B: ええ、何度も注意(ちゅうい)したのに、全然(ぜんぜん)だめなんです。

A: そうですか。じゃあ、家の前に～さんの車を止めておいたらどうですか。

B: ああ、それはいいかもしれませんね。

1. 友達はむかえに来るといいましたが、まだ来ていません。
2. となりの人に夜中(よなか)にさわがないようにたのみましたが、全然(ぜんぜん)静かにしてくれません。
3. 主人は友達をむかえに行くと言いましたが、ゴルフに行ってしまいました。
4. いじめられたり、からかわれたりしていますが、先生は助けてくれません。
5. どろぼうにかぎをこわされたんですが、大家(おおや)さんはかぎを直(なお)してくれません。
6. うそをついたと正直(しょうじき)に話しましたが、相手(あいて)はまだおこっていてゆるしてくれません。

聞く練習

めいわくなこと Annoying things

聞く前に

Work with a partner. Discuss what kinds of annoying things people in the situations described in 1 through 5 below might tend to experience.

1. 一人で住んでいる女の人
2. りょうに住んでいる学生
3. 外国人
4. アルバイトをしている学生
5. きびしい (*strict*) 先生の授業を取っている学生

聞いてみましょう

つぎの会話を聞いて、だれについて話をしているのか書いて下さい。そして、どんな問題があるのか書いて下さい。

Example: You hear:
男の人：どうしたの。何かあったの？
女の人：家のかべに車、ぶつけられたの。
男の人：えっ？だれに？
女の人：ほら、あの、さくらアパートに住んでいる大学生。
男の人：ああ、あの、かみの長い。
女の人：そうよ。

You write: だれについて：　さくらアパートに住んでいる大学生
問題：　女の人の家のかべに車をぶつけました。

ケース１　だれについて：＿＿＿＿＿＿＿＿＿＿＿＿＿＿
問題：＿＿＿＿＿＿＿＿＿＿＿＿＿＿
ケース２　だれについて：＿＿＿＿＿＿＿＿＿＿＿＿＿＿
問題：＿＿＿＿＿＿＿＿＿＿＿＿＿＿
ケース３　だれについて：＿＿＿＿＿＿＿＿＿＿＿＿＿＿
問題：＿＿＿＿＿＿＿＿＿＿＿＿＿＿

聞いた後で

A. Work with a partner. Write two possible solutions for each of the above problems.
B. Listen to the follow-up conversations for each of the above cases, and write down the suggestions given to the person.
C. Work with the partner you worked with in Exercise A. Compare the suggestions given in Exercise B and your own suggestions, and explain what you think is the best solution and why.

聞き上手話し上手

文句(もんく)を言う、おこる、あやまる
Expressing complaints or anger, and making apologies

Complaining about people or their actions is a sensitive topic. Japanese people feel that complaints threaten the "face" of the person being complained about and can make that person feel uneasy, which is not conducive to future harmonious relationships. Therefore, it is important to make complaints carefully so as not to create an uneasy atmosphere afterwards. This is especially true if you are complaining about someone you know very well.

One way to make complaints non-threatening is to talk around the problem, stating it but not admitting to being actually bothered by it. This is often achieved by just mentioning the topic of conversation and leaving out the verbal phrase which might follow, as shown in the following example:

大木：あのう、すみませんが。	*Excuse me, but . . .*
石川：ええ、何でしょうか。	*Yes, what is it?*
大木：あのう、ちょっとテレビの音が ...。	*Well it's just the sound from your TV is . . .*
石川：あ、すみません、大きすぎましたか。	*Oh, I'm sorry. Was it too loud?*
大木：ええ、おねがいします。	*Yes, please.*

If the person does not realize what you are talking about, you can complain more explicitly.

大木：	あのう、すみませんが。	*Excuse me, but . . .*
石川：	ええ、何でしょうか。	*Yes, what is it?*
大木：	あのう、ちょっとテレビの音が ...。	*Well it's just the sound from your TV is . . .*
石川：	え？テレビの音がどうかしましたか。	*What about the sound from my TV?*

大木： あのう、少し小さくしていただけませんか。もう１１時になりますので。
Could you turn it down a bit? It's already 11:00 p.m.

石川： あ、すみませんでした。気がつかなくて。これから気をつけます。
Oh, you're right. I'm sorry. I didn't realize—I'll be more careful from now on.

大木： おねがいします。 *Yes, please do.*

In the above example, expressions such as 気がつかなくて, and これから気をつけます are useful when apologizing. The phrase 気がつかなくて expresses the absence of any ill will, and これから気をつけます indicates his intention to correct his mistake. Although what deserves apology differs from culture to culture, the Japanese apologize frequently. This is because apologies do not just mean the admittance of one's failure or guilt. Rather, apologies indicate that a person recognizes the failure to meet the expectations of others is his or her responsibility. This in turn removes blame from others, and therefore shows thoughtfulness and kindness towards others. Apologies also indicate admittance of one's weakness that deserves understanding and sympathy. Therefore, the Japanese tend to be more willing to accept apologies and more eager to apologize. The common apologies are:

ごめん。	*Sorry, Excuse me.*	(casual)
ごめんなさい。	*Sorry, Please forgive me.*	↓
すみません。	*I'm sorry.*	
もうしわけありません。	*I'm sorry.*	
もうしわけございません。	*I'm sorry.*	(polite and formal)

もうしわけありません and すみません can also used to express gratitude, as when receiving a gift. It is customary to bow when apologizing in Japan. The more sorrow you feel, the more slowly and deeply you bow.

In general, the Japanese consider showing anger in public to be childish. When two people fall out over something, they make every effort to settle the dispute amicably through discussion and sometimes by going out for drinks. However, expressions of anger are sometimes necessary, even toward strangers, to protect oneself from harassing phone calls, stalkers, etc. The following are common expressions used in such cases.

やめて（下さい）。(male/female) ／やめろ。 (male)	*Cut it out.*
何するのよ。 (female) ／何するんだよ。 (male)	*What are you doing?*
いいかげんにしてよ。 (female) ／いいかげんにしろよ。(male)	*Give me a break./ Cut it out.*
ほっといてよ。(female) ／ほっといてくれよ。(male)	*Leave me alone.*
じょうだんじゃないよ。 (male, female)	*You've got to be kidding.*

1. Work with a partner. Listen to the two versions of a conversation between Mr. Ishikawa and Mr. Oki on page 466 and practice the dialogue and act it out. Pay attention to the tone of voice.
2. Work with a partner. Your partner is your neighbor. Complain to him/her about trash, parking, noise, etc. Your partner apologizes. Before starting the conversation, listen to the model dialogue.
3. Work with a partner. One person plays the role of teacher and the other person plays the role of student. The teacher should complain to the student about forgotten homework, tardiness, etc. The student apologizes for the behavior.
4. Listen to the expressions of anger above and repeat them. Pay particular attention to the intonation and the tone of voice.
5. Work with a partner. Your partner is a very persistent salesperson who comes to your house very often and makes persistent phone calls. Express your anger and tell him/her not to contact you anymore.

iLrn Self-Tests

漢字

Structure of kanji compounds

As you have seen, two or more kanji are often combined to form a new word, known as a **kanji** compound. Different types of relationships can be found among the individual kanji in a compound, and a study of these relationships will help you better guess and learn the meanings of unknown compounds, thus increasing your vocabulary. Some of the most common relationships in compounds are described below.

1. The same **kanji** is repeated.
   人々 (*many people*) 国々 (*many countries*) (See Chapter 6 for 々.)
2. Two **kanji** with similar meanings are put together.
   教授 (*teach + give= professor*) 研究 (*study + pursue = research*)
3. Two **kanji** with opposite meanings are combined.
   男女 (*man and woman*) 朝晩 (*morning and night*) 兄弟 (*older and younger brothers = siblings*)
4. The first **kanji** is the subject of the second one, which is a verb/adjective.
   新聞 (*new + hear = newspaper*) 音楽 (*sound + joyful = music*)
5. The first **kanji** modifies the second one.
   大学 (*big + school/study = university*) 住所 (*residing + place = address*)
6. The first **kanji** is a verb and the second one is the subject/object/indirect of the first.
   有名 (*exist/have + name = famous*) 入学 (*enter + school = entering school*)
7. The first **kanji** is a prefix or the second kanji is a suffix.
   不利 (*no + profit = disadvantage*) 毎朝 (*every + morning = every morning*)

Try to classify the following **kanji** compounds into these categories. Guess the meaning of each compound.

大小　新車　入国　毎日　通行　色々　飲食　白黒　朝食　乗車　急行(きゅうこう)　父母
家族　受験　生物

Flashcards

句	句	phrase ク	あまり文句(もんく)を言わないで下さい。
号	号	number ゴウ	郵便番号(ばんごう)を書いて下さい。
直	直	to mend, to correct なお(す)　チョク・ジキ	コンピュータを直(なお)せます。　正直(しょうじき)な人
残	残	to be left, to leave のこ(る)・のこ(す)　ザン	仕事が残(のこ)っています。　残念(ざんねん)
貸	貸	to lend か(す)　タイ	本を貸(か)して下さい。
借	借	to borrow か(りる)　シャク	辞書(じしょ)を借(か)りてもいいですか。
返	返	to return something かえ(す)　ヘン	借(か)りた本を明日返(かえ)します。　返事(へんじ)
置	置	to put, to place お(く)　チ	つくえのうえに置(お)いて下さい。
急	急	sudden, steep, hurry いそ(ぐ)　キュウ	急(きゅう)に家に帰った。　急行(きゅうこう)　特急(とっきゅう)
広	広	wide, spacious ひろ(い)　コウ	広(ひろ)い家ですね。　広(ひろ)い公園
最	最	most もっと(も)　サイ	最近(さいきん)

声 声 voice
こえ セイ 大きい声で歌う。
こえ うた
開 開 to open
ひら(く) あ(く・ける) カイ まどを開ける。 開く
あ ひら
閉 閉 to close
し(める・まる) ヘイ ドアを閉める。
し
伝 伝 to report, transmit
つた(える) デン 勉強を手伝う。
て つだ
横 横 side
よこ オウ テーブルの横 横断歩道
よこ おうだんほどう

新しい読み方

全然　安全な　全部で　注意　注文する　意味　知り合い　覚える　歌　歌う
文句　番号　信号(しん)　直る　直す　正直　残る　残す　残念　貸す　借りる　返す
置く　急行　特急(とっ)　急な　宅急便(たっ)　広い　最近　声　開く　開ける　閉める
閉まる　手伝う　横断歩道(だん)　日記を付ける

練習

1. 漢字を全部で五百覚えました。
2. 友達とカラオケで大きい声で歌を歌って、のどが痛くなりました。
3. 次の練習は来週の九時ですから、時間に注意して下さい。
4. 借りた本は返す時に、そのテーブルの上に置いて下さい。
5. 知り合いに貸したお金を全然返してくれないので、とても困っています。
6. 最近、近所の人にゴミ出しのことで文句を言ってしまいました。なかがよかった人なのでとても残念です。
7. このへんにはとても広い場所がまだ残っています。
8. 私のアパートの郵便番号は 384-1205 です。
9. 銀行の横に横断歩道があります。
10. 広い部屋ですね。まどを閉めて、ドアを開けて下さい。
11. その仕事、手伝いましょうか。

読む練習

上手な読み方

Understanding the characteristics of expository writing

In English, expository text tends to have a clear structure, with a topic statement, support and conclusion. However, Japanese expository text is not always as organized as English. For example, one of the rhetorical organizations of Japanese expository writing, the Ki-Sho-Ten-Ketsu organization, presents a difficult obstacle for learners, as it is fundamentally different from the western style rhetorical organization. Expository text in Japanese frequently does not have any thesis statement, and paragraph development is often not as straightforward as it is in English. Text based on the Ki-Sho-Ten model consists of four parts: the opening; the development; the shift of a topic to an unrelated element of the previous paragraph; and the conclusion. The third section, the topic shift, creates a more esthetic flare rather than a logical development, which is a very difficult concept for western learners to grasp.

Also, pronouns are rarely used to create cohesion in Japanese. Instead, repetitions and deletion of nouns are heavily used as cohesive devices. Learning to use these devices tends to be very difficult, as neither deletion nor repetition is commonly used in English.

Go to http://www.asahi.com/ or http://www.asahi.com/english/ and look for an editorial column either in English or in Japanese. Check to see how the rhetorical organization is different from English.

いじめ

読む前に

質問に日本語で答えて下さい。

1. いじめにあったことがありますか？
2. どんな人がいじめられやすいと思いますか。
3. どんな人が人をいじめると思いますか。
4. だれかがいじめられていたら、どうしますか。

言葉のリスト

自殺（じさつ）	国際（こくさい）	行う（おこな）	場合（ばあい）	生徒（せいと）
suicide	international	conduct	the case	junior and senior high school students

日本では、１９９０年代から、いじめが問題になっている。 特に最近はインターネットのブログや 携帯(けいたい)メールに悪口を書いたりするいじめが増(ふ)えている。ネット上では、誰(だれ)がいじめをしているか分かりにくいので、誰(だれ)かがいじめを始めると、おもしろがって他(ほか)の子もいじめをしてしまう。いじめられた子は、 学校に行かなくなったりするだけではなく、 自殺(じさつ)してしまうこともある。いじめは日本だけの問題ではなく、アメリカ、イギリス、ノルウェー、オーストラリアなどでも増(ふ)えた。そのため、日本で「いじめ問題国際(こくさい)シンポジウム」が開かれたが、このシンポジウムの前に、いじめについて、一万人の小学生、中学生、高校生にアンケートが行(おこな)われた。

そのアンケートによると、日本ではいじめをする生徒(せいと)はいじめられる学生のクラスメートであるケースが７０％にもなることが分かった。また、いじめをした生徒(せいと)にどんな生徒(せいと)をいじめたかと聞くと、普(ふ)通の友達をいじめた場合(ばあい)が一番多く、その次に、仲(なか)がいい友達やあまりよく知らないクラスメートをいじめたケースが多かった。そして、「前から仲(なか)が悪かった」生徒(せいと)をいじめたと答えた生徒(せいと)は一番少なかった。つまり、いじめをした子供はそのクラスメートがきらいだから、いじめたのではない。

では、どうして子供達はきらいでもないクラスメートや仲(なか)がいい友達をいじめるのだろうか。この質問については、「いじめがおもしろいから、いじめてみたいから、いじめをするのだ。」という答えが多くみられた。いじめをした後、「おもしろかった」、「よかった」と思う子供は小学生で２０％ぐらいだが、中学生では３８％、高校生では４１％ぐらいになる。これにたいして、いじめをした後、悪いことをしたと思う生徒(せいと)は、小学生の場合(ばあい)は、８０％ぐらいいるが、中学生では７０％、高校生になると、５０％ぐらいにしかならない。

それでは、いじめられている子供はどうするのだろうか。いじめられた子供が小学生の場合(ばあい)、８０％の子供がだれかに相談(そうだん)したり、いじめる子供に止めるように言ったりするが、中学生や高校生になると、５０％の学生がだれにも言わないし、３０％ぐらいの生徒(せいと)はいじめられても何もしない。そして、先生に相談(そうだん)する子供は小学生では３０％ぐらいだが、中学生では２０％、高校生になると、８％ぐらいしかいない。

また、いじめを見ているクラスメートや友達もたいてい何もしないし、先生にも相談(そうだん)しない。これはどうしてだろうか。

アンケートによると、小学生の場合(ばあい)、先生に言ったことがいじめている子供に分かるともっといじめられるという答えが多い。中学生や高校生では、先生は何も出来ないという答えが３０％ぐらいで、いじめは自分達の問題だから先生には言わない方がいいという答えが３０％ぐらいになる。

読んだ後で

A. Circle はい if the statement is true according to the above text, and いいえ if it is not.

1. はい　いいえ　いじめの問題は日本だけの問題である。
2. はい　いいえ　いじめはクラスでよく起こる。
3. はい　いいえ　日本ではクラスメートをいじめることが多い。
4. はい　いいえ　日本では、いじめをする生徒(せいと)はたいてい自分がきらいな生徒(せいと)いじめる。
5. はい　いいえ　中学生の方が高校生よりいじめをした後、悪いことをしたと思っている。
6. はい　いいえ　高校生はいじめられた時、あまり先生に言わない。
7. はい　いいえ　いじめを見ている生徒(せいと)は、いじめられたくないから何もしない。
8. はい　いいえ　小学生は先生がいじめをやめさせることは出来ないと思っいる。

B. 下の質問に答えて下さい。

1. どうして、「いじめ国際(こくさい)シンポジウム」が開かれたのですか。
2. 日本人の子供はどうしていじめをすると言っていますか。
3. 小学生と中学生と高校生のいじめはどこがにています (*similar*) か。どこが違いますか。
4. どうして年が上になると、いじめが悪いと思わなくなるのでしょうか。
5. いじめられている子供は、どうしてほかの人にそうだんしないのですか。

C. Work in pairs or groups of four. Discuss the following situations in your country, and report your findings to the class.

1. あなたの国でも、いじめは大きい問題だと思いますか。
2. あなたの国では、どんな子供がどんな子供をいじめるケースが多いと思いますか。日本とは、どんなことが同じですか。どんなことが違いますか。
3. いじめはどうすればなくなると思いますか。学校はいじめをやめさせるために、どんなことをしたらいいでしょうか。大人はどうすればいいでしょうか。先生や友達はどうしたらいいと思いますか。

総合練習
そうごう

学生生活を楽しくしましょう Let's make college life enjoyable

Work with the class. Interview three classmates about things that make their school life difficult, based on the following categories. Ask them how they cope with these problems.

Example: A: ～さんはりょうに住んでいて、どんなことがいやですか。

B: そうですね。同じ部屋に住んでいる学生に部屋をよごされるので困ります。

A: そうですか。それで、その学生に何か言いましたか。

B: ええ、一週間に一度そうじをするように言いました。

ロールプレイ

1. Your boss makes you do a lot of things that are not part of your job. Describe things you are forced to do and complain to your co-workers.
2. Your house has been burglarized. Call the police station, describe the condition of the house, and tell the police what has been stolen.
3. Your classmate makes fun of you all the time. Tell your instructor about him, describe how he makes fun of you, and ask for help.
4. Your neighbor's son has been making a lot of noise. Complain to your neighbor.
5. You are a representative of a labor union, and you don't like the working conditions at the company. Complain to the management.

Chapter 11

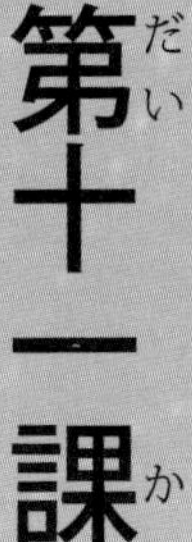

AP Photos

就職相談
しゅうしょくそうだん

Talking about Employment

Objectives Expressing respect to social superiors; expressing the outcomes of decisions

Vocabulary Honorific and humble expressions, polite expressions, expressions used in job hunting and business environments

Dialogue リーさんの相談(そうだん) *Mr. Li's consultation with Professor Motoyama*

Japanese Culture Job hunting, education

Grammar

I. Using honorific expressions to show respect

II. Using humble expressions to show respect

III. Expressing directionality in time using ～ていく and ～てくる

IV. Pronoun の, the noun こと, and ～ことになる／～ことにする

V. Expressing quantity-related emphasis using quantity expression + も

Listening A job interview

Communication Responding to compliments and expressing politeness and modesty in formal situations

Kanji Electronic tools for reading and writing Japanese

就 職 相 談 面 接 記 給 立 派 申
有 向 専 門 研 究 室 働 用 関 係

Reading Job hunting, written requests and thank-you letters

Chapter Resources

 www.cengagebrain.com

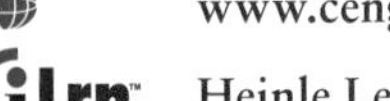 Heinle Learning Center

 Audio Program

単語（たん）

Flashcards

Nouns

エントリー		entry (the process of expressing interest in employment opportunities by requesting information from a company), エントリー・シート a form required for entry
かいぎ	会議	meeting, conference
かつどう	活動	activity
かちょう	課長	section chief
けっか	結果	result, outcome
こうこく	広告	advertisement
じこしょうかい	自己紹介	self introduction
じこ PR	自己 PR	self promotion
しめきり	締め切り	deadline
しゅうしょくかつどう	就職活動	job hunting (abbreviated as しゅうかつ（就活）in casual conversation)
じょうほう	情報	information
しょるい	書類	document
せつめいかい	説明会	a briefing session, an explanatory meeting
せんもん	専門	field of specialty
すいせんじょう	推薦状	letter of reference, recommendation
てつづき	手続	procedure
どうき	動機	a motive, しぼうどうき（志望動機）a motive for applying to a company, a school, etc.
ひっきしけん	筆記試験	a written test
プロジェクト		project
やりがい	やり甲斐	worth doing, やりがいがある it is worth doing
めんせつ	面接	interview, めんせつしけん an oral exam, interview
もうしこみようし	申込用紙	an application form
りれきしょ	履歴書	CV (curriculum vitae), resume

Verbal nouns

おうぼ	応募	application, 〜におうぼする to apply for ~
しぼう	志望	a wish, a desire, an ambition, しぼうする to desire
しゅっちょう	出張	business trip, しゅっちょうする to go on a business trip

へんじ	返事	response, へんじ(を)する to respond
れんらく	連絡	contact, 〜にれんらくする to make contact with, to get in touch with

い-adjectives

よろしい		good (polite)

な-adjectives

ひつよう(な)	必要(な)	necessary (similar to 〜がいる [to need])

う-verbs

いたす	致す	to do (humble)
いただく	頂く	to eat, to drink (humble)
いらっしゃる		to go, to come; to return; to be (honorific)
うかがう	伺う	to visit, to ask (humble)
おいでになる		to come in, to show up (honorific)
おっしゃる		to say (honorific)
おめにかかる	お目にかかる	to meet (humble)
おやすみになる	お休みになる	to sleep (honorific)
おる		to exist, to be (humble)
ござる		to exist (polite verb for ある and いる)
ごらんになる	ご覧になる	to look at (honorific)
ぞんじておる	存じておる	to know, to think (humble)
でござる		to be (polite verb for です)
なさる		to do (honorific)
まいる	参る	to go, to come (humble)
めしあがる	召し上がる	to eat; to drink (honorific)
もうす	申す	to say (humble)
やとう	雇う	to employ

る-verbs

おめにかける	お目にかける	to show (humble)
しらせる	知らせる	to notify
ぞんじる	存じる	to know (humble)
たずねる	訪ねる	to visit
もうしあげる	申し上げる	to say (humble)

Irregular verbs

はいけんする	拝見する	to look at (humble)

Expressions

おせわになっております。	お世話になっております。	I thank you for your assistance.
そういってもらえると、うれしいです。	そう言ってもらえると、嬉しいです。	I'm glad that you said so.
そうでもありません／そうでもございません。		No, not really.
そうなんですよ。		That's right
そんなことないですよ。／そんなことはありませんよ		No, that is not the case.
まあまあです。		so-so.
まだまだです。		I still have a lot to learn.
ごぶさたしております。	ご無沙汰しております。	I'm sorry to have stayed out of touch for so long.
おかげさまで	お陰様で	because of your help (common phrase when you thank for somebody for their assistance)
ざんねんながら、わたしのちからぶそくで	残念ながら、私の力不足で	Regrettably, due to the lack of my ability . . . (unfortunately I was unable to . . .)

単語の練習
たん

A. そんけい語とけんじょう語 Honorific and humble expressions

Honorific expressions are used for actions performed by people with higher social status than the speaker. Study the following special honorific verbs. Humble expressions are used for actions performed by you or a member of your in-group when these actions affect or are related to a social superior. You will learn more about these in the grammar section.

Meaning	Regular form	Honorific verbs	Humble verbs
to go	行く	いらっしゃる／おいでになる	まいる
to come	来る	いらっしゃる／おいでになる	まいる
to exist/to be	いる	いらっしゃる／おいでになる	おる
to do	する	なさる	いたす
to see/to look at	見る	ごらんになる	拝見(はいけん)する
to say	言う	おっしゃる	申(もう)す / 申(もう)し上げる
to know	知っている	ごぞんじだ	そんじておる
to eat	食べる	めし上がる	いただく
to drink	飲む	めし上がる	いただく
to sleep	寝る	お休みになる	N/A
to meet	会う	N/A	お目にかかる
to inquire	聞く	N/A	うかがう
to visit	たずねる	N/A	うかがう
to think	思う	N/A	ぞんじる
to be (copula)	だ	でいらっしゃる	N/A

- いただく is also a humble expression for もらう as introduced in Chapter 6.

覚えていますか。

さし上げる　いただく　下さる

Activity 1 下の文をそんけい語かけんじょう語を使って、書いて下さい。

1. 鈴(すず)木先生はおすしを食べました。石田先生はビールを飲みました。
2. 山田先生はこの映画をもう見ましたか。
3. 木村(むら)先生は来年オーストラリアに行きます。そして、スミス先生がオーストラリアから来ます。
4. 川上先生はゴルフをします。
5. 山下先生、先生は日本語の先生ですか。
6. 私は中村(なかむら)と言います。
7. 昨日、先生の家でビールを飲んで、おいしい料理を食べました。
8. 明日、大学で田中先生に会います。
9. 山田先生に聞いてみます。
10. 先週、先生の絵を美術(びじゅつ)館で見ました。

Activity 2

Work with a partner. Say an honorific verb, and your partner should respond with the corresponding regular verb. Once you get used to it, try it with the book closed.

Activity 3

Work with a group of three. One person should say a regular verb, and the rest of the group should respond with the corresponding honorific verb. The first person to correctly name the honorific verb gets a point.

Activity 4

Work with a partner. You are a teacher and your partner is a student. Make a simple request or a question using the regular form of a verb. Your partner will respond using the corresponding humble form. Once your partner gets used to it, try it with the book closed.

Example: A: ここに来て下さい。
B: はい、まいります。

Activity 5

Work with a group of three. One person should play the role of teacher, and make requests or ask questions. The other members of the group are students who try to respond to the teacher as quickly as possible using humble expressions. The first person to respond correctly gets a point.

B. ていねい語 Polite expressions

Meaning	Regular expression	ていねい語 (Polite expression)
to be	だ	でござる（ございます）／です
to exist	ある	ござる（ございます）
to exist	いる	おる（おります）
good	いい	よろしい
Mr./Mrs./Ms.	～さん（お客さん、山田さん）	～さま（お客さま、山田さま）
that way	そっち	そちら
that way over there	あっち	あちら
Polite prefix for nouns or adjectives		お + word (Japanese origin)
sushi	すし	おすし
customer; visitor	客	お客
gentle	やさしい	おやさしい
beautiful/pretty	きれい	おきれい
		ご + word (Chinese origin)
sickness	病気	ご病気
kind	親切	ご親切
splendid	立派 (りっぱ)	ご立派 (りっぱ)

Notes

- Polite expressions are used in any formal situation.
- そちら and あちら can be used as a polite equivalent of その人 and あの人, respectively.
- Not all adjectives or nouns take polite prefixes. For example, the following words do not take either お or ご.

  大きい　多い　黄(き)色い　新しい　四角(しかく)い　すてきな　だめな
  大丈夫(じょうぶ)な　大好きな　春　夏　秋　冬　研究室(けんきゅうしつ)

- Some words are almost always used with the particle お or ご.

  おなか　（お）茶　（お）食事　（お）すし　ご飯　（ご）主人(しゅ)
  （ご）質問

覚えていますか。 **What are their less polite equivalents?**

こちら　どちら　この方　その方　あの方　お礼　お茶　お見舞(ま)（い）　お土産(みやげ)
お辞儀(じぎ)　失礼します　おめでとうございます　お早うございます
有(あ)り難(がと)うございます　お気を遣(つか)わせてしまいまして　お気を遣(つか)わないでください
お好きだとよろしいのですが　色々お世話になりました　おかげさまで
これからもどうぞよろしくおねがいします　どうもご馳走(ちそう)さまでした
申(もう)し訳(わけ)ございません

Activity 6 Change the verbs in the following sentences into ていねい語 .

Example:　山田さんの家は立派(りっぱ)ですね。
　　　　　山田さんのおたく（a polite form of 家）はご立派(りっぱ)ですね。

1. 電話はかいだんの下にあります。
2. 婦(ふ)人服売り場は三がいです。
3. 先生の子供はとても元気だそうです。
4. 今日は休みです。
5. 気分が悪いそうです。
6. 先生の家族は何人家族ですか。
7. 駅の前に交(こう)番がある。
8. 小さくてもいいですか。
9. そっちは博(はく)物館で、あっちは図書館だ。

C. 就職活動(しゅうしょくかつどう)と会社で使う言葉

Expressions used in job hunting and business environments

手続(てつづ)き	procedure
広告(こうこく)	advertisement
じょうほう	information
エントリー	a process to express your interest to a company and request information from that company
しぼう動機(どうき)	motive for submitting an application
自己(じこ)しょうかい	self introduction
自己(じこ) PR	self promotion
履歴書(りれきしょ)	resume
すいせんじょう	letter of reference
説明会	a briefing session by a company
おうぼ（する）	application (to apply)
返事(へんじ)（する）	response (to respond)
書類(しょるい)	documents
筆記(ひっき)試験	written test
面接(めんせつ)（試験）	interview
結果(けっか)	result, outcome
知(し)らせる	to notify
課長(かちょう)	section manager
プロジェクト	project
会議(かいぎ)	meeting
出張(しゅっちょう)（する）	business trip (to go)
やとう	to employ, to hire
やりがいがある	to be worth doing

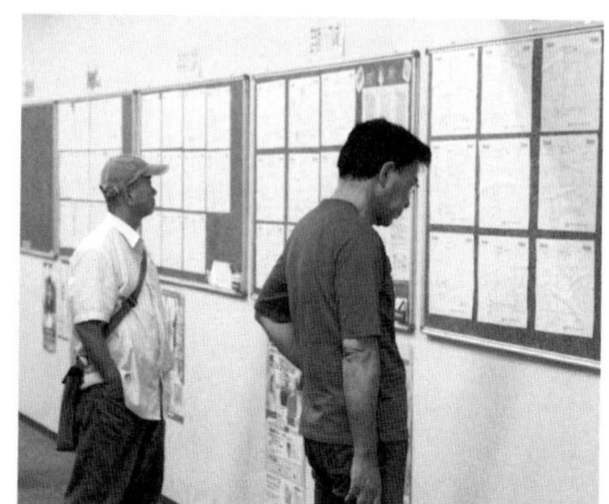
Bloomberg via Getty Images

Students check out job opening postings

覚えていますか。

上司　部下　同僚　社長　相談（する）　研究（する）　えらぶ　働く　海外
集める　決める　決まる　マネージャー　べんごし　給料　ぼうえき会社
計画（する）　さがす　就職する　じゅんびする　調べる　申し込む　年　会場
がんばる　つづける　説明（する）　会　用紙　普通　手伝う　理由ことわる
相手　バイト

会社に関する言葉 Other expressions related to businesses

きぎょう	企業	a firm, a corporation
きゅうじん	求人	help-wanted, job offer, きゅうじんこうこく help-wanted ad
しゃいん	社員	a company employee
しょるいせんこう	書類選考	document screening
しりょう	資料	material, data
せいきゅう（する）	請求（する）	request, しりょうをせいきゅうする to request materials
せんこう（する）	選考（する）	to screen
つうち	通知	notification
ないてい	内定	an unofficial decision

Activity 7 文に合う言葉を下線 (*underline*) に書いて下さい。

1. 仕事のために行く旅行です。 ________________
2. 仕事をさがす時に見るものです。 ________________
3. 質問や招待に答えることです。 ________________
4. 奨学金がほしい時に先生に書いていただくものです。 ________________
5. 会社で働いてもらうと決めることです。 ________________
6. その人に会って色々質問をすることです。 ________________
7. 自分の住所や学校や仕事について書くものです。 ________________
8. 色々な人が相談するために集まってすることです。 ________________
9. 知らない人に自分のことを知ってもらうために話すことです。 ________________
10. 自分のいいところを知ってもらうためにすることです。 ________________
11. その会社について知りたいとき集めるものです。 ________________
12. 会社がおうぼする人のために開く会です。 ________________
13. 書いて受けるテストのことです。 ________________
14. どうしてその会社で働きたいかということです。 ________________

Activity 8 Complete the following sentences with the appropriate words.

1. 仕事をさがす時には、まず会社について__________をたくさん集めることが大事だ。そして、行きたい会社を__________ら、エントリーする。
2. エントリー・シートには、__________や__________を書く。
3. エントリーしたら、会社から__________について、__________があるはずだ。
4. 会社説明会には、__________を持って行った方がいい。
5. 書類(しょるい)せんこうで__________人達は、筆記(ひっき)試験を受けることが出来る。
6. 筆記(ひっき)試験に__________ら、面接(めんせつ)がある。面接(めんせつ)では__________がとても大事だそうだ。
7. __________が多くても、__________がある仕事がしたい。
8. 面接(めんせつ)の__________について、早く__________ほしい。

Activity 9 下の質問に答えて下さい。

1. 仕事におうぼする前に、どんなことをしなければなりませんか。
2. 会社におうぼする時に、どんな書類(しょるい)がひつようですか。
3. あなたが就職(しゅうしょく)したい所では、どんな経験が大事ですか。
4. 卒業したら、どんな専門(せんもん)の仕事をやってみたいですか。
5. そこで、どんなプロジェクトをやってみたいですか。
6. やりがいのある仕事って、どんな仕事ですか。やりがいのない仕事は？

ダイアローグ

はじめに

下の質問に日本語で答えて下さい。

1. どんな仕事をしたことがありますか。
2. 仕事をさがす時、会社に何を送りますか。
3. 仕事をさがす時、だれかに相談(そうだん)しますか。どんなものを見たり読んだりしますか。
4. 大学を卒業したら、どんな仕事をしたいですか。

リーさんの相談(そうだん) *Mr. Li's consultation with Professor Motoyama*

The following **manga** frames are scrambled, so they are not in the order described by the dialogue. Read the dialogue and unscramble the frames by writing the correct number in the box in each frame.

リーさんと本山(もとやま)先生が話しています。

リー： あのう、本山(もとやま)先生、就職(しゅうしょく)のことでちょっとご相談(そうだん)したいことがあるのですが、研究室(けんきゅうしつ)にうかがってもよろしいでしょうか。

本山(もとやま)先生： ええ、いいですよ。今日は終わらせなければならない仕事があるから無理(むり)ですが、明日なら大丈夫(じょうぶ)ですよ。

リー： では、明日の何時ごろ研究室(けんきゅうしつ)にうかがったらよろしいでしょうか。

本山(もとやま)先生： 一時ごろには来ていますが、来られますか。

リー： はい、大丈夫(じょうぶ)です。では、一時ごろまいります。よろしくおねがいします。

つぎの日、リーさんは本山(もとやま)先生の研究室(けんきゅうしつ)に来ました。

本山(もとやま)先生： あ、どうぞ。

リー： 失礼します。

本山(もとやま)先生： そこにすわって下さい。

リー： はい。

本山(もとやま)先生： 相談(そうだん)したいことって何ですか。

リー： はい。再(さ)来年卒業する予定なんですが、出来たら日本で就職(しゅうしょく)したいと思っています。

本山(もとやま)先生： ええ。

リー： それで、就職活動(しゅうしょくかつどう)について教えていただけないかと思って。

本山(もとやま)先生： いいですよ。まず、3年生の秋ごろから、会社のじょうほうを集めはじめるんですね。そして、おうぼしたい会社が決まったら、その会社にエントリーします。

リー： あのう、エントリーって何でしょうか。

本山(もとやま)先生： エントリーは、自分がその会社に興(きょう)味があることを知らせて、資料(しりょう)をせいきゅうする手続(てつづ)きのことです。エントリーをしないと、会社の説明会や会社のじょうほうが送られてこないことがありますから、気をつけて下さい。

リー： そうですか。それは知りませんでした。

本山(もとやま)先生： その後、会社説明会に行って、会社に応募(おうぼ)しますから、その時は履歴(りれき)書をを持って行って下さい。そして、書類(しょるい)でえらばれたら、筆記(ひっき)試験と面接(めんせつ)があります。内定(ないてい)が決まれば、四月ごろに会社かられんらくが来ます。

リー： すいせんじょうはいらないのでしょうか。

本山(もとやま)先生： そうですね。筆記(ひっき)試験の後、すいせんじょうを送るように言ってくる会社もありますが、ないところも多いですね。

リー： そうですか。じゃあ、もしすいせんじょうがひつようになったら、先生におねがいしてもよろしいでしょうか。

本山(もとやま)先生： もちろんいいですよ。でも、ご両親はいいんですか、リーさんがたいわんに帰らなくても。

リー： ええ、両親は私の自由にしていいと言ってくれています。10年も日本語を勉強してきたから、しばらく日本で働(はたら)いてみたいと言ったら、いいよと言ってくれました。ですから、日本で仕事をさがすことにしたんです。

本山(もとやま)先生： 分かりました。じゃあ、がんばって下さい。

リー： はい、有(あ)り難(がと)うございます。

分かりましたか

A. Mr. Li is describing his discussion with Professor Motoyama. Complete the following description using the appropriate expressions.

ぼくは__________たら、日本で__________したいと思っています。それで、本山(もとやま)先生に、仕事のさがし方について_________と思って、先生の__________に_________に行きました。本山(もとやま)先生によると、日本ではまず______________。そして、会社説明会に行って、__________。会社から連絡が来たら、筆記(ひっき)試験や面接(めんせつ)を_________ことになります。でも、__________はあまりひつようではないようです。

B. 質問に答えて下さい。

1. 本山(もとやま)先生はいつリーさんに会うのですか。どうして今日はだめなのですか。
2. 日本では仕事をさがす時、どうしますか。
3. リーさんのご両親はリーさんが日本で就職(しゅうしょく)することについてどう思っていますか。

C. Underline the honorific and humble expressions used by Mr. Li. Then paraphrase them using regular polite speech.

日本の文化

Employment trends

Major Japanese companies have long followed the so-called lifetime employment （終身雇用(しゅうしんこよう)） policy, since Japan's first economic success in the 1920s. In this system, companies recruit new graduates from college, train them, and guarantee them employment for life. This provides job security and promotes company loyalty. The collapse of the Japanese asset price bubble in 1991 and economic recession did not change this practice much, although economic reform in 2003 encouraged companies to discontinue or weaken the practice of lifetime employment and hire temporary personnel. These temporary workers are called 派遣社員(はけんしゃいん) . Even so, new graduates are still recruited for a full-fledged [regular] employment positions.

Like other countries, Japanese female workers face problems with inequality in employment practices. Although the number of female workers and their net income has increased, the difference between male workers and female workers has remained larger than those in other developed countries. (The average income of female workers is 67% of that of male workers.)

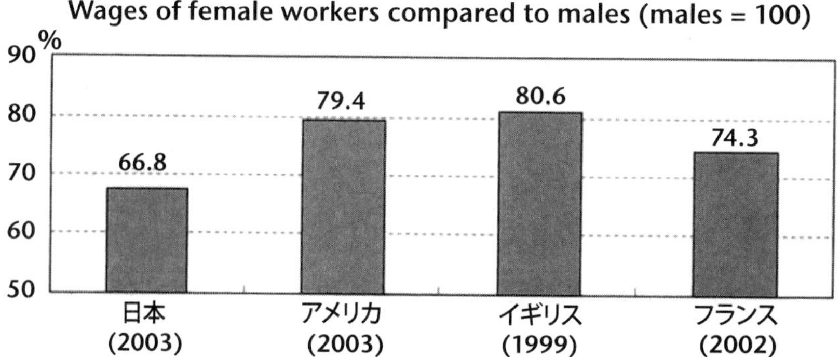

Promotions and subsequent income increases among female workers can be seen only among those who graduated from four-year colleges. However, as many as 80% of female four-year-college graduates are unable to find a full-time job whereas over 80% of male graduates are employed. (2007). Since the Japanese economy began to slow down, it has been difficult to find jobs. The group suffering the most is female graduates of four-year colleges. Female junior college graduates are doing better at finding jobs. Traditionally, women are not expected to stay in a company for a long period of time, especially after getting married or having a child. For this reason, jobs with promotional tracks are offered to male graduates instead of female graduates.

Advancement of female workers is seen in professional sectors where the traditional employment system has played a lesser role. While female workers are in the majority among pharmacists and teachers in primary and junior high schools, the number of female lawyers, public accountants, doctors, and dentists is steadily increasing. In the business world, however, a survey done by Tokyo prefecture in 2008 reports that only 8% of managerial positions are held by female employees.

Despite the passage of legislation known as 男女雇用機会均等法(だんじょこようきかいきんとうほう) (Employment equality between sexes) in the late 1980s, gender inequality in Japan remains greater than in other developed countries. The recent change in the traditional employment system may provide an opportunity for female workers who have received little advantage under the traditional system.

More non-Japanese nationals are being hired for full-time positions than was once the case, although this is still not as common as in the United States. The facts show that (1) science majors do better at getting jobs than non-science majors, (2) people with graduate degrees do better than these without, and (3) a high proficiency in Japanese language is required in most cases.

Getting a job in Japan

As in many other countries, Japanese college students start looking for a job once they become juniors. They request information about companies, attend information sessions organized by company personnel, and send applications. This is called 会社回(まわ)り, which means making the rounds of companies. There are some companies that give applicants written tests. All of them have interviews called 面接(めんせつ)試験 or simply 面接(めんせつ). The applicants typically have freshly-cut hair and wear suits that are navy blue or some other dark color.

Although hiring practices have started changing recently, there are two features which still characterize Japanese recruiting and job-hunting practices: (1) the overwhelming majority of people entering the job market in a given year do so at the same time, and (2) new recruits have little significant work experience prior to graduation. The regular employment practice is to hire college graduates in April of every year, since the academic year ends in March. Japanese universities do not have intern programs or other systems that enable their students to interact with the outside world. Also, virtually all college students maintain full-time student status throughout college. It is still rare (and difficult) for students to take, for example, a year off from college to take a job and then come back to finish school. This means that companies must rely on extensive on-the-job training (研修(けんしゅう)) for their new recruits (新入社員(しんにゅうしゃいん)). For this reason, the companies generally look for graduates from the more famous schools, because they see these graduates as being more promising "raw material" for development into full-fledged employees. This is changing, however, as Japanese companies venture further into the international world and begin to value diversity and individuality in their own workforces. Some companies even mask the names of recruits' colleges during the recruiting process. Further, there is no longer the stigma that was once attached to changing jobs, so some people in the job market may have had prior work experience.

People working for Japanese companies are paid a monthly salary (給料(きゅうりょう)). In addition, most companies pay a bonus (ボーナス) twice a year. The amount of the bonuses is determined by the financial state of the company, but usually amounts to the equivalent of two months' salary. Promotions are traditionally made by seniority; however, merit raises are getting increasingly more attention.

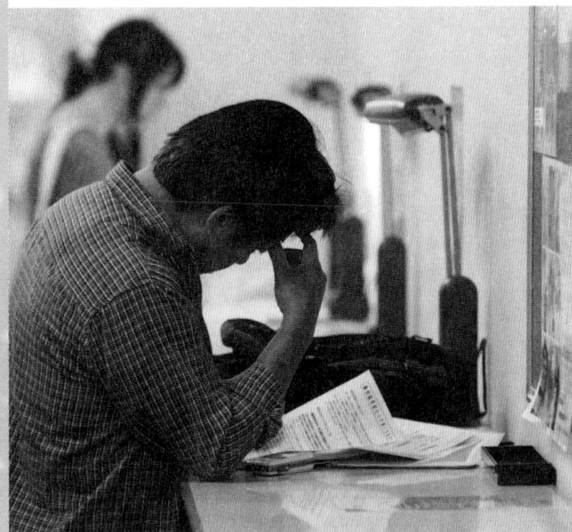

Bloomberg via Getty Images

A student checks job descriptions

文法

I. Using honorific expressions to show respect

A. Using honorific verbs to describe actions by a social superior

So far, we have learned two forms of speech: the polite form (です, the ます form of verbs) and the plain form (だ, dictionary form of verbs). These forms are used to express levels of formality and politeness toward a listener. The polite forms are used in more formal situations, often when the listener is not socially close to the speaker, and the plain form is used in more casual situations (e.g. among friends).

In this section, we will learn honorific and humble expressions, which introduce a new concept to the discussion, that of showing respect toward the topic of conversation or a socially superior listener. The topic of the conversation can be the person you are speaking with, or it can be a third person, who is not even present. This means that it is not uncommon in a Japanese conversational context for two friends talking about a teacher to use honorific and humble expressions while at the same time using the plain form of verbs. In the following example, two friends, Mr. Kimura and Mr. Li, are having a casual conversation; thus, they use plain form of verbs, but still use the honorific お帰りになる to express the actions of Professor Yamada.

木村：リーさん、山田先生、もうお帰りになった？
Mr. Li, has Prof. Yamada gone home?
リー：うん、もうお帰りになったよ。
Yes, he is already gone.

Social superiority may be measured by age, social status, experience, or the benefactor-recipient relationship. For example, a recipient of a favor usually uses honorific forms toward the giver. Furthermore, honorific forms are often used in situations where the speaker knows little or nothing about the listener. It is very common to hear telephone operators, hotel clerks, and restaurant clerks using honorific forms with their customers.

学生：山田先生は、まだいらっしゃいますか。
Is Prof. Yamada still here?
受付の人：いいえ、もうお帰りになりました。
No, he has already gone home.

学生：先生は何をめし上がりますか。
What would you like to eat? (honorific)
先生：天ぷらにします。
I'd like to have tempura.

それは先生がお書きになった本です。
That is the book the professor wrote.

山田：課長は明日の会議のことをご存知ですか。
Section Chief, do you know there is a meeting tomorrow? (honorific)
鈴木課長：ああ、知ってるよ。
Yes, I know.

今日、なかま銀行の方がおいでになって、その書類(しょるい)を持っていらっしゃいました。
A representative from Nakama Bank came today and brought this document. (honorific)

In general, honorific verbs are formed by お + the stem of the verb + に + なる. Honorific verbs with verbal nouns are formed by (お／ご) + Verbal noun + なさる. There are many irregular honorific verbs shown in the vocabulary section of this chapter.

Verb types	Dictionary form	Honorific verbs
Verbal noun + する		お／ご + verbal noun + なさる
	電話する (*to telephone*) 連絡(れんらく)する (*to get in touch with*)	お電話なさる ご連絡(れんらく)なさる
る -verbs and う -verbs		お +verb (stem) + に + なる
	やとう (*to hire*) 待つ (*to wait*) 見せる (*to show*)	おやといになる お待ちになる お見せになる

Notes

- なさる, いらっしゃる, and おっしゃる are う-verbs. Their polite forms are なさいます, いらっしゃいます, and おっしゃいます, respectively.
- When a verb is combined with an auxiliary verb such as ～ている or ～てくれる, you only need to change the auxiliary verb into its honorific form.

  読んでいる → 読んでいらっしゃる
  している → していらっしゃる
  貸してくれる → 貸して下さる
  起こしてくれる → 起こして下さる

- In the case of ～ている, there are some exceptions to this rule.

  行っている／来ている → おいでだ or いらっしゃっている
  言っている → おっしゃっている
  食べている／飲んでいる → めし上がっている／食べていらっしゃる／飲んでいらっしゃる
  寝ている → お休みだ（お休みになっている）
  着ている → おめしだ（おめしになっている）

- For some verbs, you can use お + the verb stem + です instead of ～ていらっしゃる.

  書いている → お書きだ／書いていらっしゃる
  待っている → お待ちだ／待っていらっしゃる

B. Making requests with honorifics

Honorific forms can be used in requests. In general, an honorific request is formed by お + verb (stem) + 下さい. It is customary to use honorific requests when speaking to customers in locations such as restaurants, hotels, banks, and stores. Use 下さいませんか or いただけませんか to make the request even politer .

ここでお待ち下さい。	*Please wait here.*
申込用紙（もうしこみようし）をお使い下さい。	*Please use an application form.*
この履歴書（りれきしょ）をごらん下さい。	*Please look at this resume.*
明日おいで下さいませんか／ 明日おいでいただけませんか。	*Could you please come here tomorrow?*
こちらでお待ち下さいませんか／ お待ちいただけませんか。	*Could you please wait here?*

An honorific request with a verbal noun is formed by お／ご + Verbal noun + 下さい.

Verb types	Dictionary form	Honorific verbs
Verbal noun + する		お／ご + verbal noun + 下さい
	電話する (*to call*) 連絡（れんらく）する (*to get in touch with*)	お電話下さい ご連絡（れんらく）下さい
る -verbs and う -verbs		お + verb (stem) + 下さい
	えらぶ (*to select*) 知らせる (*to notify*) 待つ (*to wait*)	おえらび下さい お知らせ下さい お待ち下さい

An honorific request using irregular honorific verbs ending with 〜になる can be formed by replacing 〜になる with 下さい.

Verbs (dictionary form)	Honorific (dictionary form)	Honorific request
行く／来る／いる	おいでになる	おいで下さい
見る	ごらんになる	ごらん下さい
寝る	お休みになる	お休み下さい
着る	おめしになる	おめし下さい

Honorific requests made from other irregular honorific verbs are formed by using the て-form of the verb + 下さい.

Verbs (dictionary form)	Honorific (dictionary form)	Honorific request
行く／来る／いる	いらっしゃる	いらっしゃって下さい
する	なさる	なさって下さい
言う	おっしゃる	おっしゃって下さい
食べる／飲む	めし上がる	めし上がって下さい

C. Using the honorific forms of adjectives

Honorific adjectives are made by adding the prefix お to the adjective. Some な -adjectives such as 立派(りっぱ) take the prefix ご instead (ご立派(りっぱ)).

社長のおくさまはおきれいな方だ。
The company president's wife is a beautiful person.

課長(かちょう)は、ゴルフがお上手です。
The section manager is good at golf. (honorific)

社長はむすめさんが結婚なさったので、毎日おさびしそうです。
The company president looks sad all the time because his daughter got married. (honorific)

あの先生は、とてもご立派(りっぱ)な方です。
That professor is a very outstanding person. (honorific)

今日は、ご病気でいらっしゃれません。
(He/She) is ill and cannot come. (honorific)

Some adjectives do not have honorific forms. For example, おもしろい , 大きい , and 有名(ゆう)な do not have honorific forms.

話してみましょう

Activity 1 Change 私 to 先生 and rewrite the sentences using the appropriate honorific forms.

Example: 明日から東京に行きます。
先生は明日から東京にいらっしゃいます。

1. 私は九時ごろ帰ります。
2. 私はそのプロジェクトについてよく知っています。
3. 私は会議(かいぎ)に出るつもりです。
4. 私は昨日十二時ごろ寝ました。
5. 私はここに来ています。
6. 私はやりがいのあるプロジェクトをしています。
7. 私はとても元気です。
8. 私はテニスが上手です。

Activity 2

Work with a group of four. You are a company president. Write five sentences you can act out. The rest of the group will try to describe what you are doing, using honorific forms. Anyone who correctly describes the action gets a point.

Example: A: *pretends to read a newspaper*
B: 社長は本を読んでいらっしゃいます。
A: いいえ、そうじゃありません。
C: 社長は新聞を読んでいらっしゃいます。
A: はい、そうです。

Activity 3

Work with a partner. You are working in the locations cited in 1–6 below and need to make various requests to the customer, as described. Your partner is the customer. Make a request using the honorific request form.

Example: レストラン／ここで少し待ってほしい
A: お客さま、こちらでお待ち下さい。
B: はい。

1. レストラン／ここにすわってほしい
2. レストラン／ジャケットを着てほしい
3. 旅行会社／クレジットカードの番号を教えてほしい
4. 旅行会社／明日までにお金を払ってほしい
5. ホテル／この用紙(ようし)に名前を書いてほしい
6. ホテル／十一時までにロビーに来てほしい

Activity 4

Work with a partner. You are an editor of a school newspaper. Your partner is a famous Japanese person who has come to the campus to give a lecture. (Decide on the topic.) Interview the person politely so that you can write an interesting article. Your instructor will give you a table containing the information you should obtain. Try to get more information about the person you are interviewing.

Example: 学生：はじめまして、スミスと申(もう)します。よろしくおねがいします。お名前を教えていただけませんか。
田中：はじめまして。東京大学の田中です。
学生：田中さまのお仕事／ご専門(せんもん)は何ですか。
田中：ロボットの研究(けんきゅう)です。
学生：そうですか。いつこちらにおいでになりましたか。／いつこちらにいらっしゃいましたか。
田中：おとといの晩に着きました。

II. Using humble expressions to show respect

Like honorifics, humble verbs and their equivalents are used to express respect for the subject of the conversation, who may or may not be the listener. While honorifics are used to describe the actions of the person who is the object of respect, humble verbs are used to describe the actions of the speaker and his/her in-group. Their intent is to show that the speaker considers himself/herself socially inferior to the person being discussed.

Humble verbs are not used unless the speaker's actions are related to or in some way affect the social superior who is the subject of the conversation. For this reason, they are often used when the speaker does a favor for the social superior.

先生：だれか、この荷物を持ってくれませんか。
Would someone hold/pick up this bag?
田中：私がお持ちします。
Yes, I will hold it (for you).

学生：先生にお話ししたいことがあるのですが、研究室(けんきゅうしつ)にうかがってもよろしいでしょうか。
I have something I would like to talk with you about. May I come to your office?
先生：ええ、いいですよ。
Yes, that is fine.

先生：ちょっと待ってくれますか。
Sorry, could you wait a little bit?
学生：はい、ここでお待ちします。
Yes, I will wait here.

Remember that in these situations, the て-form of the verb + さしあげる as in 「はい、持ってさしあげます。」and 「はい、ここで待ってさしあげます。」can be used, but this form is not preferred because it sounds rather arrogant.

In general, humble verbs are formed with お + the verb stem of the verb + する. Humble verbs with a verbal noun are formed with お／ご + Verbal noun + する.

Verb types	Dictionary form	Humble verbs
Verbal noun+ する		お／ご + verbal noun + する
	電話する (*to call*) 説明する (*to explain*)	お電話する ご説明する
る -verbs and う -verbs		お + verb (stem) + する
	知らせる (*to notify*) 見せる (*to show*) 送る (*to send*)	お知らせする お見せする お送りする

There are many irregular humble verbs included in the vocabulary section. Here are other examples of the special humble form.

つれて行く／つれて来る → おつれする
持って行く／持って来る → お持ちする

The following humble forms are also used as polite forms. That is, they are used in formal situations and the action does not have to be related to the listener or a third party. The action must be the speaker's own.

まいる (*to go*)	山田：どちらへいらっしゃるんですか。
	川口：東京へまいります。
おる (*to be/to have*)	山田：お子さんはいらっしゃいますか。
	川口：ええ、一人おります。
申(もう)す (*to say*)	山田：はじめまして。山田と申(もう)します。
	川口：はじめまして。川口と申(もう)します。
いたす (*to do*)	山田：いつも何時までお仕事なさいますか。
	川口：十時までいたします。

話してみましょう

Activity 1 Your teacher has made the following requests and questions. Respond to him/her using the humble form of the verb.

Example: いつ宿題を出すつもりですか。
<u>明日お持ちします。</u>

1. 何時に研究室(けんきゅうしつ)に来られますか。
2. 研究室(けんきゅうしつ)に来る前にれんらくして下さい。
3. 研究室(けんきゅうしつ)に来る時に履歴書(りれきしょ)を持ってきて下さい。
4. それから、私の本はもう読みましたか。
5. その会社のじょうほうをもらってきて下さい。
6. レポートはもう書きましたか。
7. 少しおそくなるかもしれませんが、何時ごろまで待ってくれますか。
8. じゃあ、後でまた会いましょう。

Activity 2 Work with a group of four. Each person should think of five requests, assuming that he/she is the president of a company and the other members are employees. Make a request and the rest of the group must respond to the request using humble forms. The person who responds appropriately to the request first scores a point.

Example: 社長：その本を取ってくれませんか。
部下：はい、お取りします。

Activity 3 Work with a partner. You are preparing for a job interview. Introduce yourself and promote yourself in one minute.

Example: はじめまして。〜と申します。〜からまいりました。大学では〜を専攻して、日本語は大学の一年生の時から勉強しております。私はチャレンジが好きなのでどんな仕事でもがんばってするつもりでおります。どうぞよろしくおねがいいたします。

Activity 4 Work with a partner. One person is a prospective employer and the other person is a student. The employer interviews the student. The student should respond to questions using humble verbs and polite speech.

Example:
A: はじめまして。山田です。
B: はじめまして。スミスと申(もう)します。どうぞよろしくおねがいします。
A: スミスさんの専攻(せんこう)は何ですか。
B: 経営(えい)学です／経営(えい)学でございます。

1. 専攻(せんこう)は何ですか。
2. この会社にしぼうした動機(どうき)は何ですか。
3. 日本語で書いたものがあれば、後で会社に送ってくれますか。
4. 出張(しゅっちょう)が多い仕事は大丈夫(じょうぶ)ですか。
5. どんな仕事がしたいですか。
6. 日本語はどのぐらい勉強しましたか。

III. Expressing directionality in time using 〜ていく and 〜てくる

In Chapter 4, you learned that the て-form of the verb + いく or くる indicates an action or event which moves away from or toward the speaker. For example, 持っていく, which consists of the verb 持つ (*to hold*) and 行く (*to go*) means *to take*, but 持ってくる means *to bring*. The same construction can be used to indicate movement along a time line.

A. Expressing the continuation of a currently on-going action (or situation) into the future using 〜ていく and the process of change to an event or an action experienced by others using 〜ていく

The following example sentences illustrate a situation where the current location is temporal, not spatial. For example, in the first sentence, the speaker is expressing his/her intention of continuing to look for a job.

これからも日本での就職活動(しゅうしょくかつどう)をつづけていくつもりです。
I intend to continue to look for a job in Japan.

これからは夜が長くなっていくよ。
Nights will start getting longer now.
これからも課長の下で仕事をしていきたいと思います。
I would like to continue working under the section chief.

In the next example sentences, the auxiliary verb いく indicates the process of change of state but does not express spatial or temporal movement. Rather, it indicates that the speaker views this process as something psychologically distant from himself. Therefore, this use of ～ていく describes an objective or impersonal situation and is often used for a change of process that does not involve the speaker or someone close to the speaker.

その人は、お金を少しずつ返していった。
He returned the money little by little.
その時から、会社は少しずつ大きくなっていきました。
From that time, the company gradually began to grow larger.

いく is considered an auxiliary verb because it no longer retains the meaning *to go*. For this reason, いく is written in **hiragana** in this usage.

B. Expressing continuation of an action or event that began in the past and continues to the present day using ～てくる and expressing the beginning of a process experienced by the speaker or someone close to the speaker using ～てくる

The following examples indicate that the action or event started in the past and has continued to the point where it has reached the present. In this usage, the auxiliary verb くる is usually in the past tense.

日本語を十年間勉強してきました。
I have been studying Japanese for 10 years now.
今までがんばって働いてきたんだから、これからもつづけていこうと思う。
I have worked hard until now, so I think I will continue to do so.

The following sentences indicate the beginning of a process.

元気が出てきた。	*I have begun to feel better.*
あっ、雨がふってきたよ。	*Oh, it has begun to rain.*
仕事がおもしろくなってきました。	*My job is starting to get more interesting.*
手続きが分かってきた。	*I have begun to understand the procedure.*
風がふいてきた。	*The wind has just begun to blow.*

In these cases, the verb くる no longer has the meaning of coming, but instead acts as an auxiliary verb. Therefore, it is often written in hiragana.

Note

- When the て-form of the verb + くる indicates a change of process as in A below, the subject must be the speaker or someone close to the speaker.

Therefore, it expresses the speaker's psychological involvement or subjectivity. In the following sentences, やせてきた indicates that the speaker began to lose weight. One the other hand やせていった indicates someone else's process of losing weight and does not indicate the beginning of a process or that the process involves the speaker or someone close to him/her.

やせてきた。 *I have begun to lose weight.*

高木さんは、やせていった。 *Mr. Takagi lost weight* (over time).

話してみましょう

Activity 1 Look at the following pictures and describe what is beginning to take place.

Example: あ、空が晴れてきましたよ。

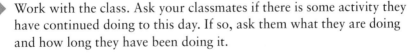

Activity 2 Work with the class. Ask your classmates if there is some activity they have continued doing to this day. If so, ask them what they are doing and how long they have been doing it.

Example: A: 何か今までつづけてきたことがありますか？

B: ええ、ゴルフをしてきました。

A: どのぐらいしてきたんですか？

B: 小学校一年の時からです。

A: それはすごいですね。

名前	してきたこと	どのぐらい

Activity 3 Write what the following famous people would say using ～ていく when they are interviewed about their future plans.

Example: イチロー

これからもヒットをたくさんうっていこうと思っています。

イチロー	バラク・オバマ (Barack Obama)	トヨタの社長
バットマン	ブラッド・ピット (Brad Pitt)	みやざきはやお
アウンサンスーチー (Aung San Suu Kyi)	アル・ゴア (Al Gore)	

Activity 4 Work as a class. Ask your classmates what they want to accomplish in the future, what they have been doing to achieve their goals, and whether they think they will continue to do so. Note that そのために means *for that purpose*.

Example: A: 将来(しょうらい)何をしたいと思いますか。

B: 日本語の先生になりたいと思います。

A: そのために、どんなことをしてきましたか。

B: 日本語を勉強してきました。

A: これからも日本語を勉強していくつもりですか。

B: ええ、勉強していくつもりです。

IV. Pronoun の, the noun こと, and ことになる／ことにする

The particle の as in 大きいの (*large one*) and the word こと as in 仕事のこと (*thing about my job*) were introduced in *Nakama 1*. Here we will introduce the extended use of の and こと with clauses.

A. の as an indefinite pronoun

The pronoun の was introduced as an indefinite pronoun in Chapter 5 of *Nakama 1* as in 大きいの (*large one*). It can be used when the object it refers to is clear from the context.

このペンはちょっと小さいですね。もっと大きいのはありませんか。
This pen is a bit small. Is there a bigger one?

Strictly speaking, this の is not an indefinite pronoun. It is instead a particle connecting two nouns. The noun following の is omitted in this usage because it can be inferred from the context.

それは田中さんのプロジェクトですが、これは山田さんのプロジェクトです。
That is Ms. Tanaka's project but this is Mr. Yamada's.

However, the indefinite pronoun の does exist in Japanese. It occurs with a clause, and is translated as one, thing, or what (as in *what I want to do*).

私が先生に書いていただきたいのはすいせんじょうです。
What I want you to write is a letter of reference.

就職活動(しゅうしょくかつどう)で一番大切なのは自己(じこ)PR だ。
The most important thing in job hunting is self-promotion.

筆記(ひっき)試験に受かったのはトムだけだった。
The only person who passed the written exam was Tom.

面接(めんせつ)で聞かれたのはしぼう動機(どうき)と大学の専門(せんもん)についてだった。
What I was asked in the interview was the reason for my application and my specialization.

五年前サラリーマンだったのは中村(むら)先生です。
The person who was a salaried businessman five years ago is Professor Nakamura.

The pronoun の can be modified by nouns, adjectives, and verbs. Use な for the present affirmative form of both な-adjectives and nouns with the copula verb. Otherwise, use the plain form.

	い -adjective	な -adjectives	Noun+ copula verb	Verbs
	いい (*good*)	ひつようだ (*necessary*)	締切(しめきり)だ (*deadline*)	やとう (*to hire*)
Present affirmative	いいの	ひつようなの	締切(しめきり)なの	やとうの
Present negative	よくないの	ひつようじゃないの	締切(しめきり)じゃないの	やとわないの
Past affirmative	よかったの	ひつようだったの	締切(しめきり)だったの	やとったの
Past negative	よくなかったの	ひつようじゃなかったの	締切(しめきり)じゃなかったの	やとわなかったの

The particle の cannot be used by itself. It has to be preceded by an adjective, a verb, a phrase, or a clause, but not by demonstrative expressions such as この, その, あの, or どの.

きれいなの	*clean one*
きれいじゃないの	*the one that is not clean*
聞こえるの	*the one I hear / what I hear*
聞こえないの	*the one I can't hear / what I can't hear*
山田さんが昨日読んだの	*The one that Ms. Yamada read yesterday/What Ms. Yamada read yesterday*

The particle の can refer to either tangible or intangible things.

課長(かちょう)がえらんだのはこのおうぼ書類(しょるい)です。
What the section chief has selected is this application document.

課長(かちょう)がえらんだのは山田さんのアイデアです。
What the section chief has selected is Ms. Yamada's idea.

B. こと as a noun

The word こと is a noun that refers to an intangible thing and can be translated as *thing* or *matter.* Just like any other noun, こと is used in noun modifying clauses.

先生がおっしゃったことを覚えていますか。 *Do you remember what the teacher said?*

私が言わなかったことを言っていた。 *He was saying things that I did not say.*

社長がごぞんじないことは何もありません。 *There is nothing that the CEO does not know.*

こと can be modified by nouns, adjectives and verbs, and the formation is identical to の, except that the particle の is used to modify こと with a noun, as in 履歴書(りれきしょ)<u>の</u>こと.

大事なことは忘れません。

I don't forget important things.

石田さんはこの手続き(てつづ)のことをよく知っている。

Mr. Ishida knows a lot (of things) *about this procedure.*

来年就職(しゅうしょく)するために、今からしておかなければならないことは、どんなことでしょうか。

What kind of things should we do now to find employment next year?

先生がすいせんじょうに書いていたことは本当のことなんでしょうか。

Is what the professor wrote in the recommendation letter true?

Unlike の, which cannot stand alone, こと can be used by itself and can also co-occur with demonstrative words such as この, その, and あの.

ことが大きくなってしまうと、みんながこまる。 *If that matter gets blown up, it will be a big hassle for all of us.*

そのことは、だれにも言わないで下さい。 *Please do not tell anyone about that matter.*

The construction noun のこと is often translated as *about* ~ when it is used with verbs such as 話す, 知っている, 言う, and 読む.

山田さんは、その活動(かつどう)のことをよく知っていた。

Mr. Yamada knew about all about that activity.

広告(こうこく)の締切(しめきり)のことを話す。

I will talk about the deadline for the advertisement.

C. Expressing personal decisions using ～ことにする

The expression noun + にする, *to decide on* ～, to indicate the speaker's decision, is introduced in Chapter 9 of *Nakama 1.* You learned in Chapter 11 of *Nakama 1* that the adverbial form of the adjective + する, as in はやくする, indicates that the speaker has caused a change of state to occur. The plain present form of the verb +ことにする is related to these expressions, except that ～ことにする expresses the speaker's decision to do something. It follows a clause that ends with a plain present affirmative or a plain present negative form.

Plain present affirmative form of verbs	行くことにする
Plain present negative form of verb	行かないことにする

筆記試験を受けることにしました。

I have decided to take a written exam.

その会社に興味があるので、エントリーすることにした。

I am interested in the job, so I've decided to do an entry form.

返事をもらったので、説明会に行くことにした。

I received a response, so I've decided to go to the briefing session.

他の会社におうぼしないで、面接の結果を待つことにしました。

I've decided to wait for the results of the interview and not apply for jobs at other companies.

新聞の広告に出ていた仕事におうぼすることにしました。

I've decided to apply for a job that was advertised in the newspaper.

今晩課長とカラオケに行くことにしたんだけど、一緒に行かない？

We've decided to go out for karaoke with the section chief this evening; would you like to come with us?

The expression 〜ことにしている expresses a habit or routine activity that has evolved as a result of a personal decision. It is translated as *I have decided to do ~* or I *have made it a rule to do~*. It is similar to 〜ようにしている (Chapter 10), but ようにしている implies that the speaker is making an effort do something rather than that he or she has made a decision to something.

返事はすぐすることにしている。　*I make it a rule to reply promptly.*

返事はすぐするようにしている。　*I make an effort to reply promptly.*

D. Expressing something that has been decided or come about using 〜ことになる, *it has been decided that* 〜

While 〜ことにする expresses the speaker's own decision, 〜ことになる expresses the idea that something has been decided or has happened due to circumstances beyond the speaker's control. The use of する implies the existence of an actor responsible for the action of the verb, whereas なる describes an action where the actor is unknown or where a change of state has come about naturally. The clause preceding 〜ことになる must end with the plain present form of the verb.

今度東京に引っ越すことになりました。

It has been decided that I will move to Tokyo.

このプロジェクトについては、私が説明することになりました。

It has been decided that I will explain this project.

悪い結果を知らせることになった。

It's been decided that I will be the one to notify people of the bad results.

会議に山本先生をご招待することになりました。

It's been decided that we will invite Professor Yamamoto to the conference.

If the speaker cannot be involved in the decision-making process, ～ことになる must be used. But in some cases ～ことになる is used even though the decision was in fact made by the speaker. This use of ことになる is more humble and polite than ～ことにする.

新しい人をやとうことにしました。 *We've decided to hire a new person.*

新しい人をやとうことになりました。 *It's been decided that we will hire a new person.*

The phrase ～ことになっている indicates a decision was made at some point in the past and the result of the decision is still in effect. It is often used to express customs, regulations, rules, regularly scheduled events, and expectations.

アメリカでは二十一さい以上じゃないと、おさけを飲んではいけないことになっている。

It's been a rule that you cannot drink alcohol in the United States unless you are over 21 years old.

The expression ～ことになっている can also be used to avoid responsibility by obscuring who made the decision.

明日の九時にれんらくすることになっている。

It's been decided that I am to contact him/her at nine o'clock tomorrow.

話してみましょう

Activity 1 Read the statements and make questions that fit the answer using の.

Example: 山田さんは昨日手紙を書きました。

A: 手紙です。

山田さんが昨日書いたのは何ですか。

1. 鈴木さんは会社の説明会で自己しょうかいをさせられました。
   A: 自己しょうかいです。
2. 山田さんは日本語の研究に興味があります。
   A: 日本語の研究です。
3. スミスさんは面接の結果を待っています。
   A: 面接の結果です。
4. ジョンソンさんは履歴書を送らなければなりません。
   A: 履歴書です。
5. 鈴木さんは出張で東京に出かけました。
   A: 東京です。
6. 木村さんは自己 PR が上手じゃありません。
   A: 自己 PR です。

Activity 2 Work with a partner. Ask each other about things that you might often do on the following occasions, and complete the chart. Use casual speech.

Example: A: 友達によく話すことって、どんなこと?
B: そうだね、好きな人のことかな。

	パートナーの答え
友達に話します	
ブログに書きます	
新聞で読みます	
インターネットで見ます	
学校で聞きます	

Activity 3 The following offers and suggestions are made to you. Respond using ～ことにする.

Example: この車は7,000ドルの車ですが、1,000ドル安くしますから、買いませんか。
<u>この車を買うことにします。</u> or <u>この車は買わないことにします。</u>

1. 田中さんが日本に帰るそうですから、一緒(しょ)に見送りに行きませんか。
2. そんなに大変なら、がんばらなければいいんですよ。
3. しぼう動機(どうき)を説明してくれませんか。
4. 課長(かちょう)には相談(そうだん)しなくてもいいんじゃない?
5. 履歴書(りれきしょ)がひつようかどうかれんらくしてみたらどうですか。
6. ご飯を食べる時には新聞を読まない方がいいんじゃないですか。

Activity 4 The people at your workplace and your parents have made the following requests that you could not refuse, so you will be doing them favors. Express what's been decided using ～ことになる.

Example: 今度の休みに家に帰って来てもらいたいんだ。
<u>今度の休みに家に帰ることになりました。</u>

1. 明日からニューヨークに出張(しゅっちょう)してもらいたいんだが、いいね?
2. 来週までに今度のプロジェクトのじょうほうを集めてほしいんだが、いいね?
3. 明日締切(しめきり)だから、今日書類(しょるい)を作っておいてくれないか?
4. 国に帰って、お父さんの仕事を手伝ってほしいんだけど。

5. お母さんが病気だから、家に帰って、弟の世話をしてほしいんだ。
6. お金がないから、悪いけど、大学には行かないでほしい。
7. 田中さんの就職(しゅうしょく)祝いのプレゼントをえらんでほしいんだけど。
8. むかえに行く時間がないから地下鉄に乗ってきて。

Activity 5 Work with the class. Ask your classmates about their mottos, using 〜ことにしている.

Example: A: 〜さんはどんなことをモットー (*motto*) にしていますか。
B: そうですね。私は人の悪口は言わないことにしています。
それから、自分がされたくないことは人にしないことにしています。

名前	〜することにしている

Activity 6 Work in groups of four. Compare public rules and regulations in United States, Japan, and/or your home country using the given cues and 〜ことになっている. Then summarize some of the similarities and differences.

Example: 日本では男の人は十八さいにならないと結婚できません。
A: 日本では男の人は十八さいにならないと結婚できないことになっているようですね。
B: そうですか。女の人はどうですか。
A: 女の人は十六さいでも結婚できることになっていますよ。
B: そうですか。アメリカでは何さいで結婚できることになっていますか。

1. 日本では十八さいになれば、運転めんきょが取れます。
2. 日本では二十さいにならないと、おさけは飲んではいけません。
3. 日本では大人じゃなくてもおさけが買えます。
4. 日本では少しでもおさけを飲んだら、車を運転してはいけません。
5. 日本ではお金をはらう時、小切手(こぎって) (*check*) は使いません。
6. 日本の旅館は朝御飯を出します。
7. 日本では神社でおいのりをする時、手をたたきます。(たたく = *to clap*)
8. 日本では、はしからはしへ食べ物をわたしてはいけません。(わたす = *to pass*)

V. Expressing quantity-related emphasis using quantity expression + も

Quantity expressions such as 一度も and 何度も are used to either emphasize a large quantity or the lack of quantity, depending on the quantity preceding も. This chapter explains how the construction quantity expression + も works in sentences.

A. Expressing zero quantity or frequency, using 1 + counter + も ~negative

Expressions of quantity or frequency where the number one is followed by も and a negative ending indicate zero quantity or frequency and are translated as not even one/once.

山田さんは一度も車をぶつけたことがありません。
Mr. Yamada has never hit anything with his car. (lit.: not even once)

昨日のパーティには知り合いは一人も来なかった。
Not even a single acquaintance (of mine) *came to the party yesterday.*

中村(むら)先生はビールを一本もめし上がりませんでした。
Professor Nakamura did not drink any beer at all. (honorific)

今年はおうぼが一つもないですね。
There are no applicants this year.

B. Emphasizing large quantity or high frequency, using number/question word + counter + も～ affirmative

When も follows a quantity or frequency expression in an affirmative sentence, it emphasizes the speaker's feeling that the quantity or frequencies are abnormally large.

就職活動(しゅうしょくかつどう)のために二十回も会社説明会へ行った。
I went to TWENTY orientation sessions as part of my efforts to find a job.

トムはステーキを四まいも食べた。
Tom ate FOUR steaks.

その面接(めんせつ)は三時間もかかった。
The interview lasted THREE HOURS!

In the following example, the difference between 電話で二時間話した and 電話で二時間も話した is that, in the first sentence, the speaker does not think a two-hour telephone conversation is long, while in the second sentence, the speaker thinks two hours are very long.

大木：昨日何度も電話したんですが。
I called you MANY TIMES yesterday.

道子：ああ、ごめんなさい。知り合いから電話がかかってきて、二時間ぐらい話していたんです。
Oh, I'm sorry. I got a phone call from an acquaintance and talked to him for two hours.

大木：え、二時間も話してたんですか。
Really? You talked for TWO HOURS?

If a quantity or frequency expression with も contains a question word instead of a number, it means many, much or a lot of and is used to emphasize a large quantity or high frequency. The sentence must end with an affirmative verb form.

このプロジェクトについては何回も会議(かいぎ)をした。
We had meetings MANY TIMES regarding this project.

さとるには今まで何度もからかわれたから、おこってるんだ。
I've been teased by Satoru MANY TIMES before, so I am mad at him.

書類(しょるい)を作るため、何さつも本を読まなければならない。
I must read MANY BOOKS in order to compile the document.

話してみましょう

Activity 1 The following chart illustrates what Mr. Aoki and Mr. Chung did or did not do last week. Answer the questions about them, using quantity or frequency expressions and も .

Example: A: 青木さんは先週ご両親に電話をかけましたか。チョンさんはどうですか。

B: 青木さんは一度もかけませんでした。チョンさんは四回もかけました。

	青木	チョン
両親に電話をかける	０回	四回
テレビを見る	二十時間	０時間
本を読む	五さつ	０さつ
犬の散(さん)歩に行く	０回	十回
アルバイトをする	十回	二十回
ピアノをひく	０時間	０時間
部屋をそうじする	三度	一度
作文を書く	１ページ	１０ページ
大家さんに注(ちゅう)意される	六回	０回

1. 青木さんはテレビを見ましたか。チョンさんはどうですか。
2. チョンさんは本を読みましたか。青木さんはどうですか。
3. チョンさんは犬の散(さん)歩に行きましたか。青木さんはどうですか。
4. チョンさんはアルバイトをしましたか。青木さんはどうですか。
5. 青木さんはピアノをひきましたか。チョンさんはどうですか。
6. 青木さんは部屋をそうじしましたか。チョンさんはどうですか。
7. チョンさんは作文を書きましたか。青木さんはどうですか。
8. 青木さんは大家さんに注(ちゅう)意されましたか。

Activity 2 Work with the class. Ask your classmates about things that other people did many times that they found annoying.

Example: A: 〜さんはいやなことをたくさんされたことがありますか。

B: ええ、あります。小学校の時、同じクラスにいた男の子に何度もからかわれたことがあります。

Activity 3 Work with the class. Ask your classmates whether they have done the things listed. If they have, ask them how frequently. Find out who in the class has performed each of the actions most frequently.

Example: A: 日本に行ったことがありますか。

B: いいえ、一度もありません。

or

B: はい、あります。

A: 何度ぐらい行ったことがありますか。

B: 三度ぐらいあります。

A: 三度も行ったんですか。いいですね。

	名前	〜度／〜かい／〜か月／〜年, etc.
日本に行く		
日本に住んでいる		
何かぬすまれる		
面接(めんせつ)を受ける		
変な (*strange*) うわさをされる		
筆記(ひっき)試験におちる		
先生にしかられる		

聞く練習

面接(めんせつ)試験 A job interview

聞く前に

1. Work with a partner. Discuss and make at least five questions in Japanese that a potential employer might ask an applicant.
2. Politely answer the questions you created in Exercise A as though you were applying for a job.

聞いてみましょう

Listen to the three interviews between applicants and a representative of IACE Travel. Take notes about each applicant and complete the following table. Then rank them.

	1	2	3
名前			
おうぼした理由			
専攻(せんこう)			
英語			
コンピュータ			
外国に住む			

聞いた後で

Work with a group of four. Discuss your information and decide which person is the best candidate and why.

聞き上手話し上手

Responding to compliments and expressing politeness and modesty in formal situations

Compliments are often used to start a conversation. In the United States, compliments on clothing, hairstyles, or other visual features such as "you have a nice ring," express friendliness. In Japan, however, complimenting visual features as a means of breaking the ice is not as common as it is in the US. Close friends may compliment clothing if it is related to the topic of the conversation. The Japanese are more likely to compliment a person's skill or intelligence, especially in formal situations.

Compliment responses can be classified into three types: acceptance, denial, and avoidance. Studies in compliment responses show that English speakers tend to use the acceptance strategies more than Japanese and rarely use the denial strategy. Japanese speakers use the denial strategy more than English speakers, but they still use the avoidance strategy or the acceptance strategy more often than the denial strategy.

The avoidance strategy may be expressed in an explanation of why the speaker obtained the item being complimented (前からほしかったんで、買ったんです。 *I wanted it for a long time, so I bought it*), when he/she get it (前に買ったんですけど。 *I bought it a while ago*), or who gave it to him/her (父にもらったんです。) Another way to avoid responding to the compliments is to return the question (そうですか。), offer the item to the person who complimented it (あげましょうか。), or simply keeping silent or shifting the topic.

To accept the compliment, you may express your gratitude (ありがとうございます。), agreement (そうなんですよ。*That's right*), your happiness at receiving the compliment

(そういってもらえうると、うれしいです。 *I'm glad to hear you say so*) or return the same compliments to your coversational partner.

In formal situations the Japanese may use denial to respond to compliments. This is because stating something negative about yourself indicates that you are lowering your own social status and raising the listener's status, thereby showing respect and politeness. This type of denial is common for compliments directed to you personally or to your family members. Instead of saying "Thank you," you can express regret (すみません) or disagree by saying:

そんなことないですよ。／そんなことはありませんよ。	*No, that is not the case.*
そうでもありません。／そうでもございません。	*No, not really.*
まあまあです。	*I am just so-so./ It's just so-so.*

These expressions can be followed by a negative or positive statement. For example, when you say something in Japanese, you may be complimented immediately on your proficiency in Japanese, no matter how rudimentary it is. If you receive such a compliment, you can respond by saying まだまだです。(*I still have a lot to learn*).

青木：日本語がお上手ですね。
Your Japanese is very good.

山田：いいえ、まだまだです。
No, I still have a lot to learn.
or
ありがとうございます。でも、まだまだなんです。
Thank you very much. But I still have a lot to learn.

A. Write the appropriate responses to the following compliments.

1. 日本語がお上手ですね。
2. よく仕事が出来るんですね。
3. 〜さんの会社はとても立派(りっぱ)ですね。
4. 〜さんは頭がいいんですね。
5. いい車をお持ちですね。
6. テニスがお上手なんですね。

B. Listen to the dialogue. Assuming that you are Mr. Smith in the dialogue, respond to the compliment.

Example: You hear: A: はじめまして、スミスと申(もう)します。どうぞよろしくおねがいします。

B: 山本です。こちらこそ。スミスさんは日本語がお上手ですね。

You write: いいえ、まだまだです。

C. Work with a group of four. Three of you will be interviewers from Human Resources and one of you will be a job speaker. Decide on the type of company and the type of employees being sought. Read the job interview manners your instructor will supply you and role-play a job interview situation.

iLrn Self-tests

Example: A: 〜さん。

B: はい。（ノック、ノック）

A: どうぞお入り下さい。

B: 失礼します。

漢字

Electronic tools for reading and writing Japanese

In addition to electronic dictionaries (電子辞書 でんしじしょ) mentioned in the **kanji** section in Chapter 8, there is a wide range of electronic tools available to help you read Japanese text in general, including **kanji**.

Online help with reading Japanese text

Rikai.com is one of the most popular online tools available. It embeds a bilingual dictionary in any Web page so that it opens pop-up windows containing vocabulary information when you touch words with the mouse. Pop Jisyo is another site that works similarly to rikai.com.

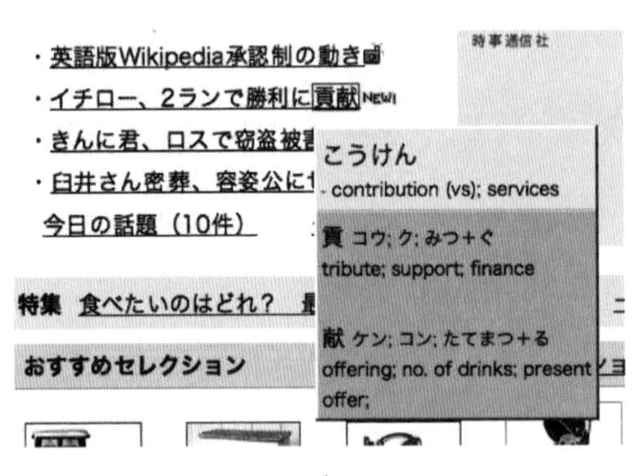

www.rikai.com

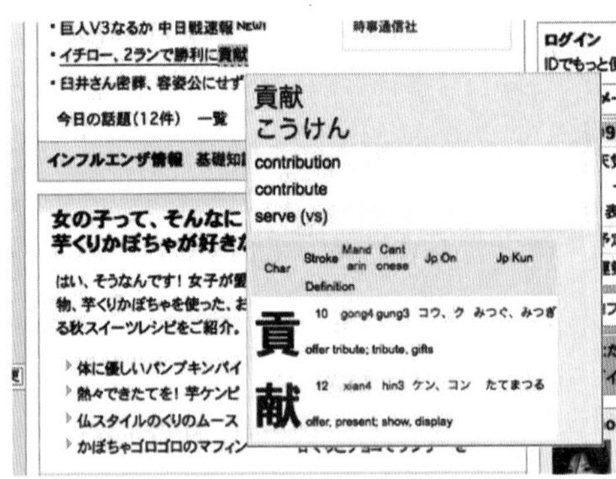

www.popjisyo.com

Reading Tutor (リーディングチュウ太) requires you to copy and paste Japanese text to process it; however, it provides more comprehensive information about vocabulary for the entire Japanese text.

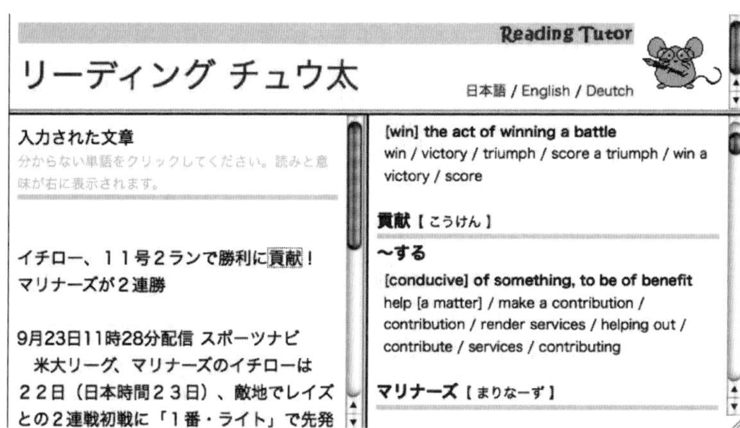

language.tiu.ac.jp

Goo 辞書 (dictionary.goo.ne.jp) and Yahoo! 辞書 (dic.yahoo.co.jp) are good examples of free on-line multiple dictionaries.

れじぶる N.C. by NICER (National Information Center for Educational Resources) converts any Japanese text according to a stated grade level of a Japanese primary school. You can control the number of **kanji** used in an authentic Japanese text with this tool. (www.nicer.go.jp/cgi-bin/legible/legibleNC/index.cgi)

Writing Japanese with a computer

With the wide-spread use of the Internet, electronic communication has become the main channel of information exchange, including e-mail and blogs. This, in turn, is changing the mode of writing in Japanese, and virtually all newer PCs can handle Japanese text without additional software. There are some steps you have to go through to enable Japanese characters for your computer. Once you enable Japanese support on your PC, you will type Japanese text through romanization. The computer will automatically convert romanization to **hiragana**, and then to **kanji**, **kanji** and **kana** combinations, or **katakana**. One thing you have to be careful about is that you cannot make spelling errors when you type. A series of **kana** that contains a spelling error will not be converted to the correct **kanji** or **kanji** compounds. For example, がくせい must be typed as *gakusei* to be converted to 学生. Another caution is that you may end up producing sentences that you may not be able to read because the conversion dictionary can convert words into **kanji** you do not know yet. We recommend you do not over-convert words into **kanji** so that the text you type reflects your current ability.

We recommend that you practice writing **kanji** by hand until you learn about 500 **kanji** because this will provide you with a good knowledge of the basic structure of **kanji** components. At the same time, however, you should not be hesitant to take advantage of available tools.

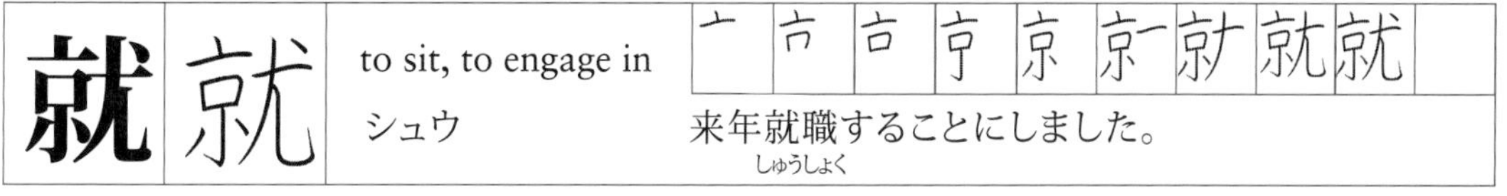

就 就
to sit, to engage in
シュウ
来年就職することにしました。
しゅうしょく

Flashcards

職	職	employment ショク	日本で就職(しゅうしょく)が決まりました。
相	相	each other, mutual あい　ソウ	先生に相談(そうだん)する。　相手(あいて)
談	談	to talk ダン	いつでも相談(そうだん)して下さい。
面	面	to begin, to start おもて　メン	明日仕事の面接(めんせつ)があります。
接	接	to come into contact セツ・セッ	面接(めんせつ)は九時からです。
記	記	chronicle キ	ここに名前を記入(きにゅう)して下さい。　日記(にっき)
給	給	to supply キュウ	この仕事は給料(きゅうりょう)が安いんですよ。
立	立	to stand た(つ)　リツ・リッ	立(た)って下さい。　立派(りっぱ)なホテル
派	派	group, party, school ハ・パ	立派(りっぱ)な病院ですね。
申	申	to say (humble) もう(す)　シン	田中と申(もう)します。　申込用紙(もうしこみようし)
有	有	to exist, to have あ(る)　ユウ	有名(ゆうめい)な先生です。　車が有(あ)ります。　有(あ)り難(がと)う

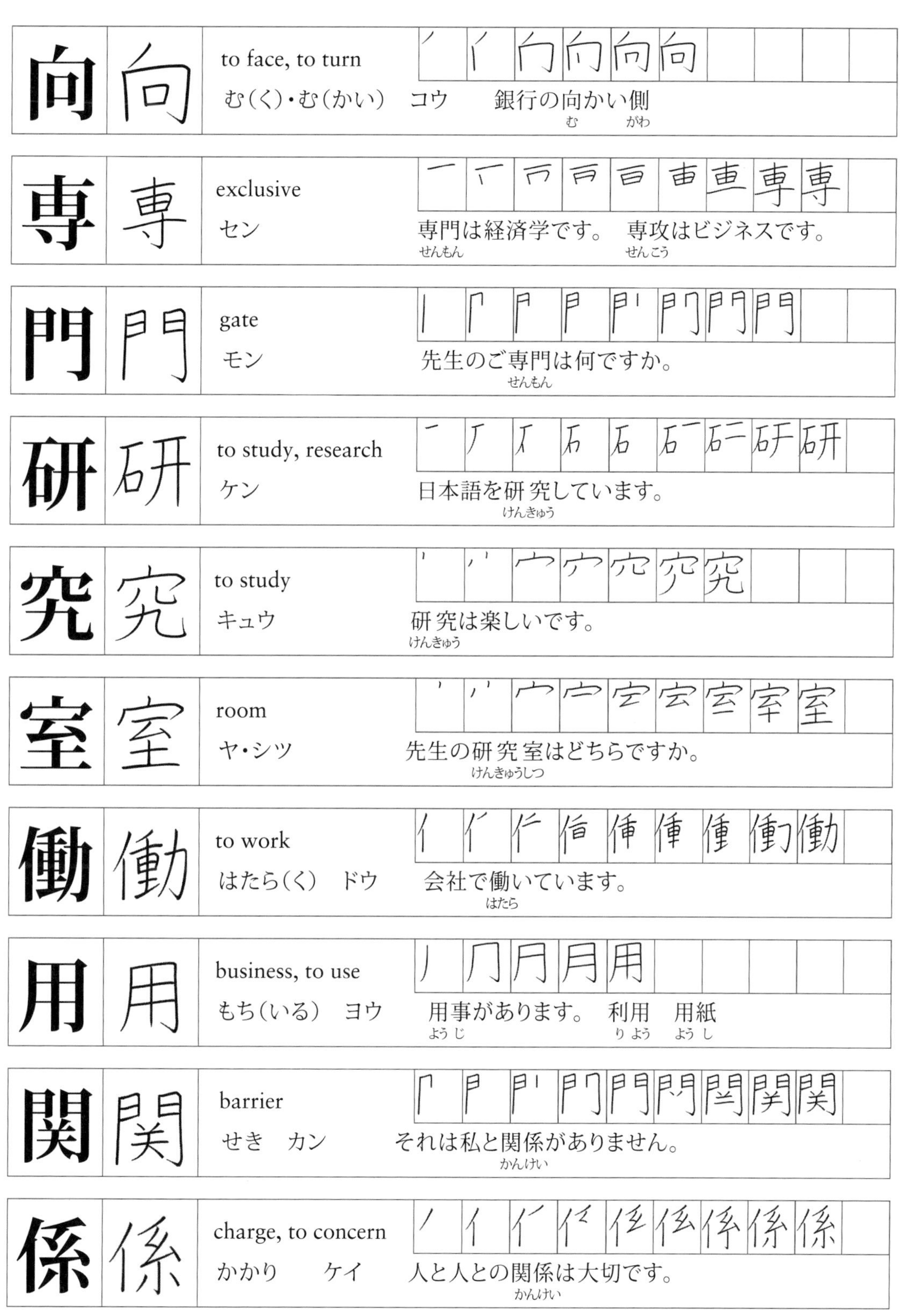

向	to face, to turn	む(く)・む(かい)　コウ	銀行の向(む)かい側(がわ)
専	exclusive	セン	専門(せんもん)は経済学です。　専攻(せんこう)はビジネスです。
門	gate	モン	先生のご専門(せんもん)は何ですか。
研	to study, research	ケン	日本語を研究(けんきゅう)しています。
究	to study	キュウ	研究(けんきゅう)は楽しいです。
室	room	ヤ・シツ	先生の研究室(けんきゅうしつ)はどちらですか。
働	to work	はたら(く)　ドウ	会社で働(はたら)いています。
用	business, to use	もち(いる)　ヨウ	用事(ようじ)があります。　利用(りよう)　用紙(ようし)
関	barrier	せき　カン	それは私と関係(かんけい)がありません。
係	charge, to concern	かかり　ケイ	人と人との関係(かんけい)は大切です。

新しい読み方

就職　相談　面接　記入　日記　給料　立派　立つ　申し込む　申込用紙　有る
有名　有り難う（ございます）　向かい側(がわ)　専門　専攻(こう)　研究室　働く　用事
関係　相手　広告(こく)

下の文を読んで下さい。

1. 先生、就職のことでご相談したいんですが。
2. 昨日は日本語の面接試験があったので遅くなりました。
3. 私の専攻はコンピュータ工学です。先生のご専門は何ですか。
4. この仕事は給料がとても安いので、あまり働きたくありません。
5. 山田先生の研究室はとても立派な部屋です。
6. トヨタの車の作り方は有名になりました。
7. お客さんに失礼なことを言ってはいけません。

読む練習

上手な読み方

仕事さがし **Job hunting**

読む前に

下の質問に答えて下さい。

1. 求人(きゅうじん)広告(こく) (*help-wanted ads*) にはどんなことが書いてあるか考えて下さい。
2. 求人(きゅうじん)広告(こく)にはどんな単語が使ってありますか。それを日本語では何といいますか。知らない言葉を先生に聞いて下さい。

読んでみましょう

A. 下はジャパントラベルという会社の求人(きゅうじん)広告(こく)です。知らない単語がたくさんありますが、どういう意味か考えながら、質問に答えて下さい。

ジャパントラベル

正社員・パート募集
・マーケティングアナリスト
・ツアーガイド
経験者、バイリンガル優遇(ゆうぐう)
詳細は山本まで
電話 (03) 3331-1234
ファックス (03) 3331-1235

1. ジャパントラベルは何の会社だと思いますか。
2. この会社は何が出来る人がほしいと思いますか。
3. この会社に就職したいと思う人は、だれに電話をしたらいいですか。

B. 下の二つの履歴(りれき)書はジャパントラベルに来たものです。一人は日本人で、もう一人はアメリカ人です。二人の履歴(りれき)書を見て、質問に答えて下さい。

1. 日本の履歴(りれき)書にあって、アメリカの履歴(りれき)書にないものがありますか。
2. アメリカの履歴(りれき)書にあって、日本の履歴(りれき)書にないものがありますか。
3. どんなことが日本の履歴(りれき)書にもアメリカの履歴(りれき)書にも書いてありますか。
4. この二人のどちらの方がジャパントラベルに就職できると思いますか。どうしてですか。

Jeff McGlone

Current Address	Permanent address
1-1-1 Nakano	316 Hamilton Street
Nakano-ku, Tokyo	Lafayette, Indiana 47906
phone: (03) 1234-5678	phone: (765) 123-4567

Education	
Bachelor of Arts in Japanese	
Purdue University	2005
Nanzan Exchange program	2003
Westside Senior High school	2001

Work Experience	
JET Japanese language program	2006–present
(worked as a JET assistant in Hiroshima)	

Certificates and Awards	
Japanese Proficiency Test (Level 2)	2007

履 歴 書

平成 11 年 7 月 3 日現在

ふりがな	さ とう かず ひろ
氏 名	佐藤 和広 (印)
昭和 49 年 4 月 10 日生（満 25 歳）	※ 男・女 (男 circled)

ふりがな とうきょうと おおたく ちゅうおう	電話
現住所 〒143-0024 東京都 大田区 中央 4-5-6	(03) 1234-5678
ふりがな	電話
連絡先 〒 （現住所以外に連絡を希望する場合のみ記入） 方	

年	月	学歴・職歴（各別にまとめて書く）
昭和55	4	大田区立大森第三小学校入学
〃 61	3	同校卒業
〃 61	4	大田区立大森第二中学校入学
平成 1	3	同校卒業
〃 1	4	東京都立富士高等学校入学
〃 4	3	同校卒業
〃 4	4	日本大学経済学部入学
〃 8	3	同校卒業
		職 歴
平成 8	4	JR東日本株式会社 入社
		賞 罰
		なし

記入上の注意 ①鉛筆以外の黒または青の筆記具で記入。 ②数字はアラビア数字で、文字はくずさず正確に書く
③※印のところは、該当するものを　で囲む。

年	月	学歴・職歴（各別にまとめて書く）

年	月	免許・資格
平成4	8	普通自動車免許
〃6	6	英語検定一級合格

志望の動機、特技、好きな学科など	通勤時間	
旅行・観光に関連した職種を希望	約　時間　分	
好きな学科　英語　スポーツ　スキー・テニス	扶養家族数（配偶者を除く）　人	
趣味　旅行	配偶者　※　有・無	配偶者の扶養義務　※　有・無

本人希望記入欄（特に給料・職種・勤務時間・勤務地・その他についての希望などがあれば記入）

特になし

保護者（本人が未成年者の場合のみ記入）		電話
ふりがな		
氏名	住所 〒	

古紙配合率100%の再生紙を使用しています。

日本法令　労務12　10.7改

C. 下はマグローンさんの履歴書を日本語で書いたものです。これを見ながら自分の履歴書(りれき)を日本語で書いてください。

履歴書　平成10年8月8日現在

ふりがな		男 女
氏名　マグローン ジェフ		印
明治 大正 (昭和) 平成　48年3月3日生 (満26才)	本籍　アメリカ合衆国 インディアナ州　都道府県	

ふりがな　とうきょうと なかのく なかの	電話 市外局番 (03)
現住所　東京都中野区中野1—1—1　方	1234-5678 (方呼出)
ふりがな	電話 0011 市外局番 (765)
連絡先 (現住所以外に連絡を希望する場合のみ記入) 316 Hamilton Street, Lafayette, Indiana 47906　方	555-1234 (方呼出)

年	月	職歴, 学歴 (格別にまとめて書く)
		学歴
昭和54	8	Hamilton Elementary School 入学
昭和60	6	同校卒業
昭和60	8	Hamilton Junior High School 入学
昭和62	6	同校卒業
昭和62	8	Westside Senior High School 入学
平成2	6	同校卒業
平成2	8	パデュー大学 入学
平成4	8	南山大学交換留学プログラム参加
平成5	6	同プログラム終了
平成7	6	パデュー大学 外国語学科　卒業
		職歴
平成7	8	JET日本語プログラム講師
		賞罰
		なし
		以上

平成 10 年 8 月 8 日現在

ふりがな 氏名 マグローン ジェフ	とうきょうと なかのく なかの 現住所 (〒 156) 東京都中野区中野 1－1－1	電話 市外局番 (03) 1234-5678 (方呼出)

特技	健康状態	特記事項
日本語	良好	
得意な学科	スポーツ	
日本語	ゴルフ	
趣味	希望の動機	
映画	日本語が使える仕事につきたい	通勤時間 分 利用交通機関 JR 私鉄 バス 徒歩

年	月	免許・資格
昭和62	6	運転免許取得
平成9	1	日本語検定試験２級取得

本人希望欄 (給料・職種・勤務地・その他)

	氏名	性別・間柄	年令	扶養義務	
家	マグローン ジェームス	父	55	有 (無)	大学教員
	マグローン ローラ	母	54	有 (無)	レストラン経営
				有 無	
族				有 無	
				有 無	

連絡先 (本人が未成年の場合は保護者) ふりがな 氏名 マグローン ジェフ	住所 (〒 156) 東京都中野区中野 1－1－1 方	電話 市外局番 (03) 1234-5678 (方呼出)

D. Write a letter to your professor/instructor to request a recommendation. Use the following templates.

Written requests

In general, this type of letter does not have to be long or does not have to be overly polite, but the proper honorific language should be used. You should give ample time for a writer to finish the letter. One month will usually be sufficient. Since e-mail has become a convenient and common mode of communication, sending a request letter by e-mail is not considered to be rude.

The basic structure of a request letter along with some common phrasings is as follows:

① Opening

- ごぶさたしておりますが、いかがおすごしですか。
  It's been a while since we met, how have you been?
- いつもお世話になっております。
  I thank you for your assistance. (This is a common phrase when you are in constant contact with the person.)

② Reason for the request

- 来年卒業するので、就職活動をしています。
  I have begun job hunting since I am graduating next year.
- 日本で働きたいと思っております。
  I want to work in Japan.

③ Request

- すいせんじょうを書いていただけないでしょうか。
  Would you mind writing a letter of recommendation?
- 先生にすいせんじょうを書いていただきたいのですが、おねがいできませんでしょうか。
  I would very much like you to write a letter of recommendation. May I ask you to write one? (polite)

④ Closing:

- お忙しいところ、申しわけありませんがよろしくおねがいいたします。
  I am sorry to bother you at a busy time, but please assist me.

Sample request letter for a recommendation

> 山田先生
>
> いつもお世話になっております。私は来年卒業する予定ですので、就職活動を始めました。専攻(こう)は日本語とアジア研究ですから、日本語を使える仕事がしたいと考えています。新聞にジャパントラベルという日本の旅行会社の求人(きゅうじん)広告(こく)がありましたので、おうぼしようと思っています。そこで、先生にすいせんじょうを書いていただきたいのですが、おねがいできませんでしょうか。おうぼのしめきりは 11 月 30 日です。お忙しいところ、申しわけありませんがよろしくおねがいいたします。
>
> ダニエル・ジョンソン

Students often forget to send a thank-you letter. You should inform the writer of the outcome of your application whether it is successful or not. The letter does not have to be long, but sending a letter is important and considered to be good manners. It ensures the continuation of your relationship with the writer so that you can feel more comfortable asking him/her to write another one if the occasion arises.

Thank-you letters

① Thanking

- この間は、お忙しいところすいせんじょうを書いてくださって、どうもありがとうございました。
  I thank you very much for writing a letter of recommendation for me at a time when you were so busy.

② Reporting the result

Successful case

- おかげさまで就職できました。
  Because of your support, I was able to get the job.

Unsuccessful case

- 残念ながら、私の力不足で、就職はできませんでした。

  Regrettably, due to my lack of ability, I was not able to get the job.

③ Closing:

- これからもよろしくおねがいいたします。

  I ask for your continued assistance.

Sample thank-you letter for a successful result

> 山田先生
>
> この間は、お忙しいところすいせんじょうを書いてくださって、どうもありがとうございました。おかげさまで、ジャパントラベルに就職できることになりました。会社の仕事は大変かもしれませんが、がんばろうと思っています。これからもよろしくおねがいいたします。本当にありがとうございました。
>
> ダニエル・ジョンソン

Sample thank-you letter for an unsuccessful result

> 山田先生
>
> この間は、お忙しいところすいせんじょうを書いてくださって、どうもありがとうございました。残念ながら、私の力が足りず、就職することはできませんでした。せっかく先生にすいせんじょうを書いていただいたのに、申しわけありません。またおねがいすることもあるかと思います。これからもよろしくおねがいいたします。
>
> ダニエル・ジョンソン

総合練習

新しい仕事

1. Work with a group of four. You are staff at a company and you need to hire someone, either for a full-time or a part-time position. Discuss what kind of company you work at, what position you wish to offer, and fill out the following chart. Then make a job ad and post it on the black board, along with a box or envelop to collect applications.

Example: A: どんな会社にしましょうか。

B: コンピュータの会社はどうですか。

C: おもしろそうですね。

D: わたしは、旅行会社はどうかと思うんですが。

A: それもよさそうですね。どうしましょうか。

会社について	
名前	
どんな会社か	
仕事について	
フルタイムかパートか	
どんな仕事か	
どんな人がほしいか	
休み	
ボーナス (*bonus*)	
給料	

2. Using the forms provided by your instructor, each person in the class should now prepare a resume, and make a few copies of it. Each person is looking for a job. Look at the ads on the blackboard, and apply for two jobs by placing your resume in the box provided by the companies. You are not allowed to apply for the job you have helped draft.
3. Go back to your original groups. Read the resumes and choose at least three candidates, and write a short message to invite them for an interview. Discuss with your group what questions need to be asked.
4. Interview the candidates. Take notes of each interview. After all interviews are done, go back to your company group and negotiate with each other to decide who will get the job offer. Report to your instructor who has been selected and why you have selected that person.

ロールプレイ

1. You are a secretary to the president of your company. He has several meetings today. Make a schedule and report to him using honorific forms.
2. You are talking with a consultant at an employment agency. Tell the person your educational background, other qualifications, and what kind of jobs you would like to do. Use polite expressions.
3. Your boss is assigned a project you are interested in, so you would like him/her to consider including you on the project team. Tell him/her why he/she should choose you. Use humble forms.

APPENDIX A

LIST OF PARTICLES

Particle	Meaning	Use	Text Reference
か	1. Question	ジョンさんはアメリカ人ですか。 *Are you an American, John?* 何時に寝ますか。 *What time do you go to bed?*	1-50
	2. Indirect question	どこでその人に会ったかおぼえていません。 *I don't remember where I met that person.* その人に会ったかどうかおぼえていません。 *I don't remember whether I met that person.*	2-186
が	1. Subject marker A subject is also marked by が in a noun-modifying clause or a subordinate clause with conjuntions such as とき, のに, ので, or から.	だれが来ますか。 *Who is coming?* 山田さんと中山さんが来ます。 *Yamada-san and Nakayama-san are coming.* 私が先週買った本はこれです。 *The book I bought last week is this one.*	1-103, 1-193, 1-447, 1-503
	2. Object with potential form When the verb is in the potential form, the direct object of the verb takes either が or を, except for できる, which takes only が.	にくが／を食べられます。 *I can eat meat.* テニスができます。 *I can play tennis.*	2-48
	3. but	こうちゃは好きですが、コーヒーはあまり好きじゃありません。 *I like black tea, but do not like coffee very much.*	1-272
から	from	日本語の授業は十時から十一時までです。 *The Japanese class is from 10 o'clock to 11 o'clock.*	1-190
しか	nothing/nobody/no~ but~ only ~ negative	ジョンは英語しか分かりません。 *John can only understand English.* これは日本でしか食べられません。 *You can't eat this anywhere but in Japan.*	2-373
だけ	only ~ affirmative	山田さんだけ（が）きました。 *Only Yamada-san came.* 山田さんにだけ話した。 *I told only Yamada-san.*	2-373

で	1. among ~	世界で一番高い山はヒマラヤです。 *The Himalayas are the highest mountains in the world.*	1-275
	2. at; in; on (Location of action)	図書館で勉強します。 *I study at the library.* 日本で日本語を勉強しました。 *I studied Japanese in Japan.*	1-101
	3. Means	バスで大学に行きます。 *I go to the university by bus.* 日本語で話して下さい。 *Please speak in Japanese.*	1-190
	4. Scope and limit	あと一週間で休みです。 *Vacation starts in a week.* そのみかんは五つで３００円です。 *Those oranges are 300 yen for five.*	2-230
と	1. and	ニューヨークとシカゴで仕事をしました。 *I worked in New York and Chicago.*	1-222
	2. Name or quote	私は山田と申します。 *I am Yamada.* 「タイタニック」という映画を見ました。 *I saw a movie called "Titanic."*	1-409, 2-289
に	1. to (Destination)	明日家に帰ります。 *I am going back home tomorrow?* 両親に手紙を書きました。 *I wrote a letter to my parents.*	1-100, 1-223
	2. Extent of action	一週間に一度映画を見ます。 *I watch a movie once a week.*	1-497
	3. at, in , on (Location of existence)	いすの上にねこがいます。 There is a cat on the chair. 山田さんはどこにいますか。 *Where is Yamada-san?*	1-142, 1-151
	4. Agent in a passive or causative sentence (the agent is the doer of an action.)	上司は山田さんに東京へ行かせた。 *My boss made Yamada-san go to Tokyo.* 私は先生にほめられました。 *I was praised by my teacher.*	2-360, 2-409
	5. by, from (Source with receiving verb)	私は姉にゆびわをもらいました。 *I received a ring from my sister.* 田中さんは山田さんに花をもらいました。 *Tanaka-san received a flower from Yamada-san.* 弟は父にコンピュータを買ってもらった。 *My brother got my father to buy him a computer.* 私は先生に本を貸していただいた。 *I had the teacher lend me the book.*	2-277, 2-406

	6. at, in, on (Time)	何時に起きますか。 *What time do you get up?* 日本語の授業は水曜日にあります。 *The Japanese class is held on Wednesday.*	1-106
	7. Purpose	本を読みに図書館に行きます。 *I go to the library to read books.*	1-224
ね	Seeking agreement	おすしはおいしいですね。 *Sushi is good, isn't it?*	1-95, 1-155
の	1. it is that ~ (casual speech) -- (This is a contracted form of ～のです. It is often used by female speakers.)	どうして食べないの。 *Why are you not eating?* おなかがいたいの。 *It is because my stomach hurts.*	1-311
	2. ~ing, that ~ (Nominalizer)	私は本を読むのが好きです。 *I like reading books.* 日本語で映画を見るのはおもしろいです。 *Watching movies in Japanese is interesting.*	1-268
	3. of, 's, in, from	山田さんは私の友達です。 *Yamada-san is my friend.* 山田さんはイリノイ大学の学生です。 *Yamada-san is a student of University of Illinois.* これは山田さんのペンです。あれは私の（ペン）です。 *This is Yamada's pen. That is mine (my pen).*	1-53
	4. one (Pronoun). This の is classfied as a pronoun, not as a particle.	私は黒いのが好きです。 *I like the black one.* 去年買ったのはあまりよくありませんでした。 *The one I bought last year was not very good.*	2-500
は	topic and contrast marker	きのうは何も食べませんでした。 *I did not eat anything yesterday.* (topic) 東京は人が多い。 *There are a lot of people in Tokyo.* (topic) 新聞をよく読みますが、雑誌はあまり読みません。 *I often read newspaper, but I don't read magazines very often.* (contrast)	1-46, 1-116, 1-271
まで	until	きのう二時まで勉強しました。 *I studied until two o'clock yesterday.*	1-190
までに	by (Time limit)	明日までに宿題をします。 *I will do the homework by tomorrow.*	2-157

も	1. also	山田さんも文学部の学生です。 *Yamada-san is also a student in the school of liberal arts.* ディズニーランドはフロリダにあります。東京にもあります。 *Disney Land is in Florida. It is also in Tokyo.*	1-61, 1-193
	2. both ~ and ~ (Lack of preference)	東京も京都もおもしろい所です。 Both Tokyo and Kyoto are interesting places.	1-278
	3. as many as ~, not even one ~ (Emphasis on quantity)	ジョンはステーキを三まいも食べられる。 *John can eat as many as three steaks.* 日本に一度も行ったことがありません。 *I have not been to Japan even once. (I have never been to Japan.)*	2-507
	4. any ~ (question word + でも), no ~ (question word + も)	私は何でも食べられます。 *I can eat anything.* 病気で今は何も食べられません。 *Due to my sickness, I can eat nothing.*	2-332
や	~ and ~ and so on (Inexhaustive listing)	山田さんや田中さんがゴルフをしている。 *Yamada-san and Tanaka-san and others are playing golf.*	1-264
よ	Giving information	これはおいしいですよ。 *This is good, you know.*	1-42, 1-155
より	than	大阪の方が京都より大きいです。 *Osaka is bigger than Kyoto.*	1-276
を	1. Direct object	山田さんは水をたくさん飲みます。 *Yamada-san drinks a lot of water.* 七時にごはんを食べます。 *I eat at seven.*	1-99
	2. out of ~ , from (Point of detachment)	新宿で電車をおります。 *I get off the train at Shinjuku.* 朝七時に家を出ます。 *I leave home at seven in the morning.*	2-42, 2-230
	3. in, on, across, through (Route)	私はこの道を通って、大学に行きます。 *I take this road to the university.* 公園を通ります。 *I go through the park.*	2-230

APPENDIX B

KANJI LIST

No.	Kanji	Ch.	Kun-reading	On-reading	Examples
1	大	1-4	おお(きい)	ダイ	大学、大きい、大学院、大学院生
2	学	1-4	まな(ぶ)	ガク、ガッ	学生、学校、学生、～学
3	校	1-4		コウ	学校、高校
4	先	1-4	さき	セン	先生、先週
5	生	1-4	なま、う(まれる)	セイ	学生、先生、一年生、留学生、生活
6	山	1-5	やま	サン、ザン	山川さん、富士山 、山の上
7	川	1-5	かわ、がわ	セン	小川さん、川中さん、ミシシッピー川
8	田	1-5	た、だ	デン	上田さん、田中さん
9	人	1-5	ひと	ジン、ニン	日本人
10	上	1-5	うえ、かみ	ジョウ	テーブルの上
11	中	1-5	なか	チュウ	へやの中 、中国
12	下	1-5	した、くだ(さい)	カ、ゲ	まどの下、いって下さい
13	小	1-5	ちい(さい)	ショウ	小さいへや
14	日	1-5	ひ、び	ニチ、ニ、ジツ、カ	日本、 昨日、今日、明日
15	本	1-5	もと	ホン、ボン、ポン	山本さんの本、日本
16	今	1-6	いま	コン	今、何時ですか。、今週、今日
17	私	1-6	わたし、わたくし	シ	私は日本人です。
18	月	1-6	つき	ゲツ、ガツ	月、月曜日
19	火	1-6	ひ	カ	火曜日
20	水	1-6	みず	スイ	水曜日
21	木	1-6	き	モク	木曜日
22	金	1-6	かね	キン	金曜日
23	土	1-6	つち	ト、ド	土曜日
24	曜	1-6		ヨウ	日曜日
25	何	1-6	なに、なん		何曜日、何ですか。何時ですか。
26	週	1-6		シュウ	今週の週末、先週
27	末	1-6	すえ	マツ	週末
28	休	1-6	やす(む)	キュウ	休みの日
29	時	1-7	とき	ジ	一時、二時半、五時間べんきょうします。その時
30	間	1-7	あいだ	カン	時間がありません。
31	分	1-7	わ(ける)・わ(かる)	フン、ブン、プン	二十分、分かりました。
32	半	1-7		ハン	毎日六時半におきます。
33	毎	1-7		マイ	毎週シカゴにいきます。毎日、毎月
34	年	1-7	とし	ネン	三年生、毎年
35	好	1-7	す(き)	コウ	テニスが好きです。
36	語	1-7	かた(る)	ゴ	日本語、フランス語ではなします。
37	高	1-7	たか(い)	コウ	古い高校、高い山
38	番	1-7		バン	やさいが一番好きです。

No.	Kanji	Ch.	Kun-reading	On-reading	Examples
39	方	1-7	かた	ホウ	サッカーの方がフットボールより好きです。
40	新	1-7	あたら(しい)	シン	新しいレストラン
41	古	1-7	ふる(い)	コ	カラオケで古いうたをうたいます。
42	安	1-7	やす(い)	アン	今日はやさいが安いです。
43	友	1-7	とも	ユウ	友達と買い物に行くのが好きです。
44	一	1-8	ひと(つ)	イチ	一つ、一本、いぬが一匹います。
45	二	1-8	ふた(つ)	ニ	りんごが二つあります。二さつ、二本
46	三	1-8	みっ(つ)	サン	けしゴムを三つ買いました。三本
47	四	1-8	よ・よん・よっ(つ)	シ	四つ、四時、ビールが四本あります。
48	五	1-8	いつ(つ)	ゴ	五つ、ベルトが五本あります。
49	六	1-8	むっ(つ)	ロク・ロッ	六つ、六時、えんぴつが六本あります。
50	七	1-8	なな(つ)	シチ	七時、七本、オレンジが七つあります。
51	八	1-8	やっ(つ)	ハチ・ハッ	八つ、八時、ペンが八本あります。
52	九	1-8	ここの(つ)	キュウ・ク	九つ、九時、バナナが九本あります。
53	十	1-8	とう	ジュウ・ジュッ	いすが十あります。十本、十時
54	百	1-8		ヒャク・ビャク・ピャク	二百、三百、六百
55	千	1-8		セン・ゼン	二千、三千、八千、千円
56	万	1-8		マン	一万円、百万円
57	円	1-8		エン	五十円、このセーターは7800円です。
58	店	1-8	みせ	テン	大きい店、店の人
59	行	1-9	い(く)	コウ	銀行、来年日本に行きます。
60	来	1-9	く(る)	ライ	いつアメリカに来ますか。来週は来ない
61	帰	1-9	かえ(る)	キ	たいてい七時にうちに帰ります。
62	食	1-9	た(べる)	ショク	あさごはんを食べてください。学食
63	飲	1-9	の(む)	イン	ビールを二本飲みました。
64	見	1-9	み(る)	ケン	えいがを見に行きませんか。
65	聞	1-9	き(く)	ブン	インターネットでラジオを聞く、新聞
66	読	1-9	よ(む)	ドク	本を読むのが好きです。
67	書	1-9	か(く)	ショ	てがみをあまり書きません。
68	話	1-9	はな(す)	ワ	電話、友達と日本語で話すのが好きです。
69	出	1-9	で(る)・で(かける)・だ(す)	シュッ	銀座に出かけます。
70	会	1-9	あ(う)	カイ	人と会って、カフェで話をします。
71	買	1-9	か(う)	バイ	買い物が好きです。
72	起	1-9	お(きる)	キ	毎朝六時に起きます。
73	寝	1-9	ね(る)	シン	十二時ごろ寝ます。
74	作	1-9	つく(る)	サク	ばんごはんはカレーを作りましょう。
75	入	1-9	はい(る)・い(れる)	ニュウ	はこに入れます。店に入ります。

No.	Kanji	Ch.	Kun-reading	On-reading	Examples
76	男	1-10	おとこ	ダン	女の人と男の子がいます。
77	女	1-10	おんな	ジョ	山本さんはぼうしをかぶった女の人です。
78	目	1-10	め	モク	目がわるいです。上から二番目です。
79	口	1-10	くち・ぐち	コウ	口が小さいです。川口
80	耳	1-10	みみ	ジ	私は耳があまりよくありません。
81	足	1-10	あし	ソク	ジョンはせが高くて、足がながいです。
82	手	1-10	て	シュ	手がきれいですね。テニスが上手です。
83	父	1-10	ちち・とう	フ	父のなまえはジョンです。お父さん
84	母	1-10	はは・かあ	ボ・モ	母のしごとは高校の先生です。お母さん
85	姉	1-10	あね・ねえ	シ	姉は私より三さい上です。お姉さん
86	兄	1-10	あに・にい	ケイ・キョウ	兄が一人います。お兄さん　兄弟
87	妹	1-10	いもうと	マイ	妹はいません。
88	弟	1-10	おとうと	ダイ	弟は四時にアルバイトにいきます。兄弟
89	家	1-10	いえ・うち	か	父は七時ごろ家に帰ります。
90	族	1-10		ゾク	私の家は四人家族です。
91	両	1-10		リョウ	両親はニューヨークにすんでいます。
92	親	1-10	おや	シン	両親はアメリカが好きです。親切な人
93	子	1-10	こ	シ	男の子が三人います。母のなまえは「よし子」です。
94	天	1-11		テン	明日の天気はいいでしょう。
95	気	1-11		キ	昨日は天気がよくありませんでした。
96	雨	1-11	あめ	ウ	雨がしずかにふっています。
97	雪	1-11	ゆき	セツ	明日は大雪です。
98	風	1-11	かぜ	フウ	風がつよいです。台風が来ます。
99	晴	1-11	は(れる)	セイ	ずっと晴れていて、雨がふりません。
100	温	1-11	あたた(かい)	オン	先週は気温が35度まで上がりました。
101	度	1-11		ド	おふろの温度は42度ぐらいです。
102	東	1-11	ひがし	トウ	まちの東の方にこうえんがあります。
103	西	1-11	にし	セイ	きょうとは東京の西にあります。
104	南	1-11	みなみ	ナン	南のうみはとてもきれいで温かいです。
105	北	1-11	きた	ホク	ほっかいどうは日本の北にあります。
106	寒	1-11	さむ(い)	カン	カナダのふゆは寒いです。
107	暑	1-11	あつ(い)	ショ	東京のなつはむし暑いです。
108	多	1-11	おお(い)	タ	シンガポールは雨が多いです。
109	少	1-11	すく(ない)・すこ(し)	ショウ	このまちは人が少ないです。
110	冷	1-11	つめ(たい)	レイ	暑いから冷たいものを飲みましょう。
111	春	1-12	はる	シュン	春は雨が多いです。
112	夏	1-12	なつ	カ	日本の夏は暑いです。
113	秋	1-12	あき	シュウ	秋の山はとてもきれいです。
114	冬	1-12	ふゆ	トウ	冬は寒いから、時々雪がふります。
115	朝	1-12	あさ	チョウ	日曜日の朝、おそくまで寝るのが好きです。
116	昼	1-12	ひる	チュウ	母が昼ごはんを作りました。
117	晩	1-12		バン	明日の晩ごはんは天ぷらです。

No.	Kanji	Ch.	Kun-reading	On-reading	Examples
118	午	1-12		ゴ	月曜日の午後、両親と家族が来ます。午前
119	前	1-12	まえ	ゼン	午前中にしゅくだいをします。中学の前、名前
120	後	1-12	あと・うし(ろ)・のち	ゴ	午後は暑かったです。一か月ぐらい後、つくえの後ろ
121	去	1-12	さ(る)	キョ	去年南アメリカに行きますた。
122	昨	1-12		サク	一昨年日本に行きました。昨日
123	供	1-12	とも・ども	キョウ	子供が二人います。
124	元	1-12	もと	ゲン	父は元気です。元気なお母さん
125	思	1-12	おも(う)	シ	昨日の朝は風がつよかったと思います。
126	明	1-12	あか(るい)	メイ	明るいへや、明日、明るい人
127	回	1-12	まわ(る)	カイ	私の弟は一か月に十回ぐらいラーメンを食べます。

No.	Kanji	Ch.	Kun-reading	On-reading	Examples
1	病	2-1	やま(い)	ビョウ	病気になる。病院に行く。
2	院	2-1		イン	入院する。大学院をそつぎょうする。
3	医	2-1		イ	医者になる。山田医院は大きい病院です。
4	者	2-1	もの	シャ	今日は歯医者に行きます。
5	体	2-1	からだ	タイ・テイ	体が大きい。体がうごかない。
6	歯	2-1	は	シ	歯が痛い。歯医者に行く。
7	変	2-1	か(わる)	ヘン	大変です。変な人がいます。
8	熱	2-1	あつ(い)	ネツ	熱がある。熱いコーヒー
9	薬	2-1	くすり	ヤク	これはいい薬です。
10	顔	2-1	かお	ガン	顔色がわるい。
11	色	2-1	いろ	ショク・シキ	顔の色がくろい。
12	指	2-1	ゆび	シ	指がながいですね。親指は *thumb* です。
13	切	2-1	き(る)	セツ	「あっ、痛い、指を切った。」
14	歩	2-1	ある(く)	ホ	家まで歩いて帰る。
15	走	2-1	はし(る)	ソウ	毎日１０キロ走っています。
16	勉	2-1	つと(める)	ベン	日本語を勉強する。
17	強	2-1	つよ(い)	キョウ	この薬は強いです。
18	忘	2-1	わす(れる)	ボウ	走って、ストレスを忘れます。
19	早	2-1	はや(い)	ソウ	朝早く起きる。
20	持	2-1	も(つ)	ジ	指を切ったので、かばんが持てません。
21	痛	2-1	いた(い)	ツウ	昨日走りすぎて、足が痛い。
22	頭	2-1	あたま	ズ	頭が痛いです。
23	海	2-2	うみ	カイ	海が好きです。海外旅行
24	外	2-2	そと	ガイ	家の外、外国人
25	国	2-2	くに	コク・ゴク	小さい国、中国
26	旅	2-2	たび	リョ	旅行が好きです。
27	館	2-2		カン	旅館、図書館、学生会館
28	予	2-2	あらかじ(め)	ヨ	予定があります。ホテルの予約。
29	定	2-2	さだ(める)	テイ	明日は病院に行く予定です。
30	約	2-2		ヤク	旅館を予約した。
31	計	2-2	はか(る)	ケイ	旅行の計画をたてる。高い時計ですね。
32	画	2-2	カク	ガ	来年の計画はまだありません。
33	荷	2-2		ニ・カ	大きい荷物を持って行く。
34	物	2-2	もの	ブツ・モツ	荷物、食べ物、飲み物
35	答	2-2	こた(える)	トウ	しつもんに答える。
36	知	2-2	し(る)	チ	名前を知っています。知らない人
37	泊	2-2	と(まる)	ハク・パク	二泊三日の旅行　ホテルに泊まる。
38	乗	2-2	の(る)	ジョウ	タクシーに乗る。
39	着	2-2	つ(く)・き(る)	チャク	日本に着く。シャツを着る。
40	名	2-2	な	メイ・ミョウ	お名前は何ですか。
41	空	2-2	そら	クウ	成田空港に行きます。空がきれいです。

No.	Kanji	Ch.	Kun-reading	On-reading	Examples
42	森	2-2	もり	シン	これは森田先生の荷物です。
43	林	2-2	はやし	リン	林さんは旅館に泊まりました。
44	言	2-3	い(う)・こと	ゲン・ゴン	もう一度言って下さい。
45	葉	2-3	は	ヨウ	韓国の言葉は日本語と違います。
46	漢	2-3		カン	中西さんは漢字がたくさん書けます。
47	字	2-3		ジ	漢字を読むのは大変です。
48	質	2-3		シツ・シチ・チ	旅行の計画について質問する。
49	問	2-3	と(う)・と(い)	モン	漢字の質問はありますか。
50	卒	2-3		ソツ	大学を来年の五月に卒業する予定です。
51	業	2-3	わざ	ギョウ・ゴウ	大学の卒業式、日本語の授業
52	授	2-3	さず(ける)	ジュ	授業を三つとっています。
53	仕	2-3	つか(える)	シ・ジ	新しい仕事を中国で始める。
54	事	2-3	こと	ジ	来年の仕事がいそがしい。
55	結	2-3	むす(ぶ)	ケツ・ケッ	来年、結婚する。
56	婚	2-3		コン	結婚式の予約をとりました。
57	式	2-3		シキ	友達の卒業式に行く。
58	社	2-3	やしろ	シャ	会社の社長の仕事は大変です。
59	同	2-3	おな(じ)	ドウ	同じ本を読んだ。高校の同窓会がある。
60	違	2-3	ちが(う)・ちが(い)	イ	この答えは間違っています。
61	留	2-3	と(める)・と(まる)	リュウ・ル	留学生センター
62	達	2-3	たち	タツ・ダチ	昨日、子供の時の友達と会った。
63	電	2-3		デン	携帯電話の番号を知りません。電気をつける。電車
64	英	2-3		エイ	会社の仕事は英語でしています。
65	客	2-3		キャク	お客さんがたくさん来ました。
66	郵	2-4		ユウ	この葉書に郵便番号を書いて下さい。
67	便	2-4	たよ(り)	ベン・ビン	郵便ポスト、宅配便、便利な
68	局	2-4		キョク	郵便局に行きます。NHKはテレビ局です。
69	銀	2-4		ギン	銀行に行きます。きれいな銀のネックレスですね。
70	送	2-4	おく(る)	ソウ・チ	メールを送る。送別会
71	紙	2-4	かみ	シ	手紙を書きます。コピー用紙を下さい。
72	住	2-4	す(む)	ジュウ	東京に住んでいます。住所が分かりません。
73	所	2-4	ところ	ショ	住んでいる所はどこですか。
74	引	2-4	ひ(く)	イン	銀行からお金を引き出す。
75	練	2-4	ね(る)	レン	会話の練習をする。
76	習	2-4	なら(う)	シュウ	テニスを練習する。
77	宿	2-4	やど	シュク	宿題を出すのを忘れてしまった。
78	題	2-4		ダイ	今晩、宿題をしなければなりませんか。
79	試	2-4	こころ(みる)・ため(す)	シ	日本の入学試験は二月にあります。
80	験	2-4		ケン	明日の日本語の会話試験は大変です。
81	受	2-4	うけ(る)	ジュ	試験を受ける。受験する。

No.	Kanji	Ch.	Kun-reading	On-reading	Examples
82	教	2-4	おし(える)	キョウ	天ぷらの作り方を教えて下さい。
83	文	2-4	ふみ	ブン・モン	「明日、作文と文法の試験があります。」
84	法	2-4		ホウ	この文法の使い方を教えて下さい。
85	意	2-4		イ	言葉の意味が分かりません。
86	味	2-4	あじ	ミ	この文の意味を説明して下さい。
87	石	2-4	いし	セキ	「石田」という漢字はやさしいです。
88	場	2-5	ば	ジョウ	駐車場、売り場、場所、会場
89	寺	2-5	てら	ジ	大きいお寺、東大寺、清水寺
90	橋	2-5	はし	キョウ	橋をわたります。橋本さん、大橋さん
91	町	2-5	まち	チョウ	大きい町に住んでいます。
92	映	2-5	うつ(る)・うつ(す)	エイ	映画、映画館
93	公	2-5	おおやけ	コウ	公園
94	園	2-5	その	エン	動物園じゃなくて遊園地に行きたい。
95	図	2-5	はか(る)	ズ・ト	図書館の近くの地図をみる。
96	地	2-5		チ・ジ	デパートの地下、地下鉄の地図
97	鉄	2-5		テツ	地下鉄
98	駅	2-5		エキ	地下鉄の駅、電車の駅
99	育	2-5	そだ(てる)・そだ(つ)	イク	体育館で遊ぶ。
100	道	2-5	みち	ドウ	道なり、横断歩道を歩く、道路
101	部	2-5		ブ・ヘ	部屋、全部で学部は十あります。
102	屋	2-5		ヤ・オク	駅のそばの本屋、私の部屋はきれいです。
103	車	2-5	くるま	シャ	車、自転車、電車、各駅停車
104	右	2-5	みぎ	ウ	道の右側、右手 、右足
105	左	2-5	ひだり	サ	駅の左側、左耳
106	近	2-5	ちか(い)	キン	大学の近く、最近、遊園地に近い
107	遠	2-5	とお(い)	エン	公園から遠い。
108	通	2-5	とお(る)	ツウ	小さい町を通って行きました。
109	飛	2-5	と(ぶ)	ヒ	飛行機で行きます。
110	犬	2-6	いぬ	ケン	家に犬がいます。かわいい子犬です。
111	花	2-6	はな	カ	母の日の花はカーネーションです。生け花
112	形	2-6	かたち	ケイ・ギョウ	日本人形
113	服	2-6		フク	洋服、紳士服、婦人服
114	辞	2-6	や(める)	ジ	お礼に辞書をあげました。
115	礼	2-6		レイ	お礼にと思いまして。
116	祝	2-6	いわ(う)	シュク	これはお祝いです。
117	誕	2-6		タン	誕生日のお祝い
118	自	2-6	みずか(ら)	ジ・シ	自分、自転車を運転する
119	転	2-6	ころ(がる)・ころ(ぶ)	テン	自転車に乗る。
120	運	2-6	はこ(ぶ)	ウン	毎日運動します。運転免許証
121	動	2-6	うご(く)	ドウ	手の運動、動物園、足が動かない
122	使	2-6	つか(う)	シ	大使館、気を使う。車を使う。

No.	Kanji	Ch.	Kun-reading	On-reading	Examples
123	写	2-6	うつ(す)	シャ	古い写真がたくさんあります。
124	真	2-6	ま	シン	写真、真っすぐ、真ん中
125	絵	2-6		エ・カイ	ピカソの絵を買いました。
126	雑	2-6		ザツ	これは日本の雑誌みたいですね。
127	誌	2-6		シ	この雑誌はおもしろいですよ。
128	音	2-6	おと	オン	日本の音楽
129	楽	2-6	たの(しむ)	ガク・ラク	音楽は楽しいです。
130	世	2-6		セ・セイ	犬の世話をします。
131	取	2-6	と(る)	シュ	日本語の授業を取りたいと思っています。
132	料	2-7		リョウ	日本料理をつくる。料理の材料、授業料
133	理	2-7		リ	フランス料理が好きです。無理です。
134	飯	2-7	めし	ハン	ご飯を食べる。炊飯器
135	野	2-7	の	ヤ	野球が好きです。野菜を食べます
136	菜	2-7		サイ	この野菜サラダはおいしいです。
137	魚	2-7	さかな	ギョ	魚をつる、魚料理
138	鳥	2-7	とり	チョウ	私は鳥肉を食べません。
139	肉	2-7	にく		肉を食べる。肉料理
140	止	2-7	と(める)・や(める)	シ	車を止める、タバコを止める
141	始	2-7	はじ(まる・める)	シ	始めに、学校が始まる。
142	終	2-7	お(わる)・お(える)	シュウ	宿題が終わる。
143	洗	2-7	あら(う)	セン	手を洗う。洗濯をする。
144	悪	2-7	わる(い)	アク	つごうが悪い。
145	黒	2-7	くろ(い)	コク	黒い犬がいます。黒板で書いて下さい。
146	白	2-7	しろ(い)	ハク	白いねこ、雪は白いです。
147	青	2-7	あお(い)	セイ	青い海、空が青い。
148	赤	2-7	あか(い)	セキ	赤いりんご
149	茶	2-7		チャ・サ	茶色いかばん、お茶を飲む。喫茶店
150	短	2-7	みじか(い)	タン	このズボンは短いです。
151	長	2-7	なが(い)	チョウ	長い、会社の社長
152	次	2-7	つぎ	ジ	次の問題をして下さい。
153	焼	2-7	や(く)	ショウ	火事で家が焼ける。
154	笑	2-8	わら(う)	ショウ	友達に笑われました。
155	泣	2-8	な(く)	キュウ	子供に泣かれて、困りました。
156	泳	2-8	およ(ぐ)	エイ	魚みたいに泳ぎます。
157	払	2-8	はら(う)	フツ	レストランでお金を払わなかった。
158	売	2-8	う(る)	バイ	ネットでギターを売りました。
159	落	2-8	お(ちる)・お(とす)	ラク	試験に落ちました。
160	助	2-8	たす(かる・ける)	ジョ	とても助かります。
161	考	2-8	かんが(える)	コウ	あの人のことしか考えていない。
162	決	2-8	き(める)・き(まる)	ケツ	日本に行くことに決めました。
163	待	2-8	ま(つ)	タイ	パーティに招待されました。待って下さい。

No.	Kanji	Ch.	Kun-reading	On-reading	Examples
164	遊	2-8	あそ(ぶ)	ユウ	友達と遊園地で遊びました。
165	呼	2-8	よ(ぶ)	コ	タクシーを呼んで下さい。
166	招	2-8	まね(く)	ショウ	食事に招待されました。
167	忙	2-8	いそが(しい)	ボウ	試験があるので、とても忙しい。
168	静	2-8	しず(か)	セイ	先生の家がある所はとても静かです。
169	暗	2-8	くら(い)	アン	暗いから気をつけて下さい。
170	点	2-8		テン	この間の試験の点は９０点でした。
171	夜	2-8	よる	ヤ	夜はさむくなりますよ。
172	心	2-8	こころ	シン	母の病気のことが心配です。
173	配	2-8	くば(る)	ハイ・バイ	心配しないで下さい。
174	困	2-8	こま(る)	コン	となりの人がうるさくて困っています。
175	経	2-8		ケイ・キョウ	日本の経済、経済学、経験
176	化	2-9	ば(ける)	カ	日本の文化、インド文化
177	治	2-9	おさ(める)・なお(す)	ジ・チ	病気を治す、政治
178	京	2-9		キョウ・ケイ	京都から東京へ行きます。
179	説	2-9		セツ	意味を説明して下さい。
180	調	2-9	しら(べる)	チョウ	図書館で調べる。
181	集	2-9	あつ(める・まる)	シュウ	九時に集まって下さい。
182	的	2-9	まと	テキ	日本的な建物
183	失	2-9	うしな(う)	シツ	失礼します。
184	々	2-9	N/A	N/A	人々、色々な国に行きました。、国々、時々
185	難	2-9	むずか(しい)	ナン	説明が難しかった。
186	不	2-9		フ	ここは不便です。
187	利	2-9		リ	電車を利用する。、便利
188	当	2-9	あ(たる)	トウ	本当ですか。
189	期	2-9		キ	秋学期と春学期、期末試験
190	和	2-9		ワ	和食、平和 (*peace*)、和風 (*Japanese style*)
191	重	2-9	おも(い)	ジュウ	重い荷物。
192	活	2-9		カツ	生活がくるしい。
193	弱	2-9	よわ(い)	ジャク	体が弱い。
194	界	2-9		カイ	世界で一番高い山、世界旅行
195	正	2-9	ただ(しい)	セイ・ショウ	正しい答えは何ですか。正座
196	由	2-9		ユウ	理由がわかりません。
197	付	2-9	つ(く)・つ(ける)	フ	会社の受付、病院の受付
198	全	2-10	まった(く)	ゼン	全然悪くありません。全部、安全
199	然	2-10		ゼン・ネン	病気が全然よくならない。
200	注	2-10	そそ(ぐ)	チョウ	ラーメンを注文する。注意
201	合	2-10	あ(う)	ゴウ	知り合いの赤ちゃん
202	覚	2-10	おぼ(える)・さ(める)	カク	名前を覚える。
203	歌	2-10	うた(う)	カ	歌を歌う。
204	句	2-10		ク	あまり文句を言わないで下さい。

No.	Kanji	Ch.	Kun-reading	On-reading	Examples
205	号	2-10		ゴウ	郵便番号を書いて下さい。
206	直	2-10	なお(す)	チョク	コンピュータを直せます。
207	残	2-10	の(ころ)・の(こす)	ザン	仕事が残っています。残念
208	貸	2-10	か(す)	タイ	本を貸して下さい。
209	借	2-10	か(りる)	シャク	辞書を借りてもいいですか。
210	返	2-10	かえ(す)	ヘン	借りた本を明日返します。
211	置	2-10	お(く)	チ	つくえの上に置いて下さい。
212	急	2-10	いそ(ぐ)	キュウ	急にくらくらなりました。急行、特急
213	広	2-10	ひろ(い)	コウ	広い家ですね。広い公園
214	最	2-10	もっと(も)	サイ	最近
215	声	2-10	こえ	セイ	大きい声で歌う。
216	開	2-10	ひら(く)・ あ(く・ける)	カイ	まどを開ける。
217	閉	2-10	し(める・まる)	ヘイ	ドアを閉める。
218	伝	2-10	つた(える)	デン	勉強を手伝う。
219	横	2-10	よこ	オウ	テーブルの横、横断歩道
220	就	2-11		シュウ	来年就職することにしました。
221	職	2-11		ショク	日本で就職が決まりました。
222	相	2-11	あい	ソウ	先生に相談する。相手
223	談	2-11		ダン	いつでも相談して下さい。
224	面	2-11	おもて	メン	明日仕事の面接があります。
225	接	2-11		セツ・セッ	面接は九時からです。
226	記	2-11		キ	ここに名前を記入して下さい。
227	給	2-11		キュウ	この仕事は給料が安いんですよ。
228	立	2-11	た(つ)	リツ・リッ	立って下さい。立派なホテル
229	派	2-11		ハ・パ	立派な病院ですね。
230	申	2-11	もう(す)	シン	田中と申します。申込用紙
231	有	2-11	あ(る)	ユウ	有名な先生です。車が有ります。有り難う
232	向	2-11	む(く)・む(かい)	コウ	銀行の向かい側
233	専	2-11		セン	専門は経済学です。専攻はビジネスです。
234	門	2-11		モン	先生のご専門は何ですか。
235	研	2-11		ケン	日本語を研究しています。
236	究	2-11		キュウ	研究は楽しいです。
237	室	2-11		ヤ・シツ	先生の研究室はどちらですか。
238	働	2-11	はたら(く)	ドウ	会社で働いています。
239	用	2-11	もち(いる)	ヨウ	用事があります。利用
240	関	2-11	せき	カン	それは私と関係がありません。
241	係	2-11	かかり	ケイ	人と人との関係は大切です。

JAPANESE-ENGLISH GLOSSARY

This glossary contains all Japanese words that appear in the vocbulary list of each chapter. They are listed according to *gojuuon-jun* (Japanese alphabetical order). Each entry follows this format: word written in kana, word written in kanji, part of speech, English translation, and chapter *number* where the word first appears. In general, notations are identical to the labels used in each chapter's vocabulary list.

adv.	adverb	*conj.*	conjunction	*q. word*	question word
い*-adj.*	い-adjective	*inter.*	interjection	*pref.*	prefix
な*-adj.*	な-adjective	*count.*	counter	*suf.*	suffix
う*-v.*	う-verb	*n.*	noun	*part.*	particle
る*-v.*	る-verb	*exp.*	expression	*cop. v.*	copula verb
irr. v.	irregular verb	*demo.*	demonstrative	*number*	number

A - あ

ATM *n.* automated teller machine 4

J R *n.* Japan Railway, pronounced ジェーアール. Formerly government-owned, now privatized, railway system 5

あいさつ (挨拶) *n.* greeting ～にあいさつ(を)する to greet ～ 9

あいだ (間) *n.* between 5

あいて (相手) *n.* interlocutor, the other party 10

あう (遭う・遇う) う*-v.* to encounter 8

あかちゃん (赤ちゃん) *n.* baby 10

あく (開く) う*-v.* (for something) to open 3

あける (開ける) る*-v.* to open (something) 1, 3

あげる (上げる) る*-v.* to raise (something) cf. あがる to rise 1

あげる る*-v.* to give (to a socially equal person) 6

あげる (揚げる) る*-v.* to deep-fry 7

あじ (味) *n.* flavor 7

あたためる (温める) る*-v.* to heat (something) up 7

あつまる (集まる) う*-v.* to get together, to gather 2

あつめる (集める) る*-v.* to collect (something/someone) 3

アドバイス *n.* advice アドバイスをする to advice 9

アニメ *n.* animation 9

あまりきをつかわないで下さい。(あまり気を使わないで下さい。) *exp.* Please don't put yourself out for me. 6

あやまる (謝る) う*-v.* to apologize 9

あらう (洗う) う*-v.* to wash 7

ありがとう。たすかります。(有り難う。助かります。) *exp.* Thank you. It helps me a lot. 4

アレルギー *n.* allergy 1

あんぜん(な) (安全[な]) な*-adj.* safe 8

い

いいえ、ちがいます(よ)。 *exp.* No, you have a wrong number (lit.: No, it's not correct.) 2

いいかげんにしてよ (いい加減にしてよ) *exp.* Give me a break. (female speech) 10

いいかげんにしろよ (いい加減にしろよ) *exp.* Give me a break. (male speech) 10

いき (息) *n.* breath 1

～いき (～行き) *suf.* bound for ～, とうきょういき (東京行き) bound for Tokyo, きょうといき (京都行き) bound for Kyoto 5

いけばな (生け花) *n.* flower arrangement 9

いじめ *n.* bullying いじめにあう be bullied 8

いじめる る*-v.* to bully 8

いしゃ (医者) *n.* doctor 1

イスラムきょう (イスラム教) *n.* Islam 9

いたい (痛い) い*-adj.* hurt, painful 1

いたす (致す) う*-v.* to do (humble) 11

いただく (頂く)　う -*v.* to eat, to drink (humble) 11
いただく (頂く)　う -*v.* to humbly receive 6
いためる (炒める)　る -*v.* to stir-fry (cooking) 7
いちご (苺)　*n.* strawberry 7
いのり (祈り)　*n.* prayer おいのりをする to pray 9
いみ (意味)　*n.* meaning 4
いらっしゃる　う -*v.* to go, to come, to return, to be (honorific) 11
いる (要る)　う -*v.* to need おかねがいる (お金が要る) to need money 4
いろいろおせわになりました。(色々お世話になりましした。)　*exp.* You've done a lot for me. 9
いろいろ (な) (色々 [な])　な -*adj.* various 1
〜いわい (祝い)　*suf.* congratulatory gift, けっこんいわい wedding gift, しゅうしよくいわい gift on getting a new job, そつぎょういわい graduation gift 6
インターネット　*n.* internet, can be abbreviated as ネット 9
インフルエンザ　*n.* flu, influenza 8

う

うかがう (伺う)　う -*v.* to visit, to ask (humble) 11
うける (受ける)　る -*v.* to receive, to get しけんをうける to take an exam. 4
うごかす (動かす)　う -*v.* to move (something) (transitive verb) 1
うごく (動く)　う -*v.* to move 1
うさぎ (兎)　*n.* rabbit 8
うすい (薄い)　い -*adj.* thin, あじがうすい not much flavor 7
うそ (嘘)　*n.* lie 8
うっそー　*exp.* No way! (very casual) 8
うまれる (生まれる)　る -*v.* (for someone/something) to be born 3
うる (売る)　う -*v.* to sell 8
うるさい　い -*adj.* noisy , shut up! (when used as a phrase by itself) 10
うわさ　*n.* rumor 8
うんてんめんきょしょう (運転免許証)　*n.* driver's license 4

え

えいがかん (映画館)　*n.* movie theater 5
ええ、ええ　*exp.* uh-huh (conversational response to show attention) 8
ええっと／すみません、それはちょっと（こまるんですが)。　*exp.* Well, that is a little bit (troublesome). 1
えさ (餌)　*n.* food (for animals, fish, etc.) 6
えび (海老)　*n.* shrimp えびだんご（海老団子）　shrimp dumpling 7
えらぶ (選ぶ)　う -*v.* to choose 6
エンジニア　*n.* engineer 3
エントリー　*n.* an entry process of requesting information from a company and expressing your interest エントリー•シート (a form required for the process) 11

お

おいでになる　う -*v.* to come in, to show up (honorific) 11
おいわい (お祝い)　*n.* congratulatory gift 6
おうだんほどう (横断歩道)　*n.* pedestrian crossing 5
おうぼ (応募)　*n.* application おうぼ（を）する to apply 11
おえる (終える)　る -*v.* to end (something) , to finish (something) 3
おお〜 (大〜)　*pref.* heavy, big 大雨 heavy rain, 大雪 heavy snow 大かじ big fire, 大じしん big earthquake 8
おおさじ (大さじ)　*n.* tablespoon 7
オーブン　*n.* oven 7
おおや (大家)　*n.* landlord, landlady 10
おかえし (お返し)　*n.* thank-you gift 6

おかげ（さま）で（お陰［様］で） *exp.* thanks to ～ 9
おかげさまで（お陰様で） *exp.* Because of your help (common phrase when thanking somebody for assistance) 11
おかし（お菓子） *n.* sweets, candy 6
おかね（お金） *n.* money 2
おきもの（置物） *n.* ornament or object placed in a house (alcove, cabinet, desk) such as a figurine, clock, piece of pottery or other art piece 6
おきる（起きる） る *-v.* to happen, to take place 8
おきをつかわせてしまいまして。（お気を使わせてしまいまして。） *exp.* I'm sorry to have caused you so much trouble. 6
おきをつかわないで下さい。（お気を使わないで下さい。） *exp.* Please don't concern yourself on my behalf. 6
おくりもの（贈り物） *n.* gift 6
おくる（送る） う *-v.* to send 4
おくれる（遅れる） う *-v.* to be late for ～ 10
おこす（起こす） う *-v.* to wake up (someone) 3
おこす（起こす） う *-v.* to cause (something) to happen 8
おこる（怒る） う *-v.* to get angry 10
おじいさん *n.* elderly man 6
おしえる（教える） る *-v.* to tell, to teach 4
おじぎ（お辞儀） *n.* bowing おじぎをする to bow 9
おじさん *n.* middle-aged man, someone else's uncle 6
おすきだとよろしいのですが。（お好きだとよろしいのですが。I) *exp.* I hope you like it. 6
おせいぼ（お歳暮） *n.* end-of-year gift exchange 6
おせわにっております（お世話になっております。） *exp.* I thank you for your assistance 11
おそう（襲う） う *-v.* to attack 8
おだいじに（お大事に） *exp.* Please take care of yourself. 1
おちゅうげん（お中元） *n.* mid-year gift exchange 6
おちる（落ちる） う *-v.* (for something) to fall 3
おちる（落ちる） る *-v.* to fall かみなりがおちる lightening strikes 8
おっしゃる う *-v.* to say (honorific) 11
おと（音） *n.* sound 10
おとす（落とす） う *-v.* to drop (something) 3
おとな（大人） *n.* adult 10
おどろく（驚く） う *-v.* to be surprised ~ におどろく to be surprised at/by ~ 8
おとをたてる（音を立てる） *exp.* to make noise 10
おなか（お腹） *n.* stomach 1
おなじ（同じ） な *-adj.* same A はBとおなじ A is the same as B.（な must be deleted before nouns, as in おなじ人）3
おばあさん *n.* elderly woman 6
おばさん *n.* middle-aged woman, someone else's aunt, also used when speaking to one's own aunt 6
おぼえる（覚える） る *-v.* to memorize おぼえている to remember, to recall 4
おみまい（お見舞い） *n.* sympathy gift 6
おみやげ（お土産） *n.* souvenir 2
おめでとうございます。 *exp.* congratulations 6
おめにかかる（お目にかかる） う *-v.* to meet (humble) 11
おめにかける（お目にかける） る *-v.* to show (humble) 11
おもい（重い） い *-adj.* heavy 9
おもちゃ *n.* toy 6
おやすみになる（お休みになる） う *-v.* to sleep (honorific) 11
おりる（降りる） る *-v.* to get off 5
おる う *-v.* to exist, to be (humble) 11
おれい（お礼） *n.* thank-you gift 6
おれいにとおもいまして。（お礼にと思いまして。） *exp.* I thought it would be a token of my appreciation. 6

おわる (終わる)　う -*v.* (for something) to end 3
おんせん (温泉)　*n.* hot spring 2

か

か　*part.* or, either or 3
カード　*n.* card 4
カーネーション　*n.* carnation 6
〜かい (〜会)　*suf.* party どうそうかい reunion そうべつかい farewell party たんじょうかい birthday party 3
かいがい (海外)　*n.* overseas, かいがいりょこう overseas travel 2
かいぎ (会議)　*n.* meeting, conference 11
がいこくじんとうろくしょう (外国人登録証)　*n.* alien registration card 4
かいさつ (ぐち) (改札 [口])　*n.* ticket gate 5
かいじょう (会場)　*n.* meeting venue 3
かいだん (階段)　*n.* stairs 5
ガイドブック　*n.* guidebook 2
かいわ (会話)　*n.* conversation 4
かう (飼う)　う -*v.* to raise, to keep (an animal) 6
かえす (返す)　う -*v.* to return (something to someone) 4
かえる (替える / 変える)　る -*v.* to change セクションをかえる (セクションを替える) to change a section 4
かおいろ (顔色)　*n.* facial tone 1
かかる　う -*v.* (for a telephone) to ring 3
かぎ (鍵)　*n.* key かぎをかける to lock 10
かくえきていしゃ (各駅停車)　*n.* local train (literally: a train that stops at every station) 5
かける (掛ける)　る -*v.* to hang, hook かぎをかける to lock 10
かける　る -*v.* to pour 7
かじ (火事)　*n.* fire (accident/disaster) 8
かす (貸す)　う -*v.* to rent out, to lend 4
かぜ (風邪)　*n.* a cold かぜをひく to catch a cold 1
ガソリンスタンド　*n.* gas station 5
〜かた (〜方)　*suf.* how to, way of 〜 ing 4
かたづける (片付ける)　る -*v.* to clean up, to organize 10
かちょう (課長)　*n.* section chief 11
かつどう (活動)　*n.* activity 11
カップ　*n.* cup, measuring cup 7
かど (角)　*n.* corner 5
かに (蟹)　*n.* crab 7
かのじょ (彼女)　*n.* girlfriend, she, her 8
かべ (壁)　*n.* wall 10
かみなり (雷)　*n.* lightening かみなりがおちる lightening strikes 8
かめ (亀)　*n.* turtle, tortoise 8
かゆい (痒い)　い -*adj.* itchy 1
からかう　う -*v.* to tease 10
からだ (体)　*n.* body 1
かりる (借りる)　る -*v.* to borrow 4
かれ (し) (彼 [氏])　*n.* boyfriend, he, him 8
〜がわ (〜側)　*suf.* side, こちらがわ this side, むかいがわ the other side, the opposite side, みぎがわ right-hand side, ひだりがわ left-hand side 5
かわる (変わる／替わる)　う -*v.* (for something) to change 3
かわる (変わる)　う -*v.* (for something) to change 8
かんがえる (考える)　る -*v.* to think (about something), to take (something) into consideration 3

かんこう (観光) *n.* sightseeing, かんこうする to go sightseeing, かんこうバス chartered bus for sightseeing, かんこうりょこう sightseeing trip 2
がんばる (頑張る) う *-v.* to try to do one's best, to hang on 3

き

きえる (消える) る *-v.* (for something) to go out, to go off 3
きがつかなくて。(気が付かなくて) *exp.* I didn't realize (that). 10
キス *n.* kiss キスをする to kiss 9
きたない (汚い) い *-adj.* dirty 10
きって (切手) *n.* postage stamp 4
きっぷ (切符) *n.* ticket 2
きぶん (気分) *n.* feeling きぶんがわるい to feel sick 1
きまる (決まる) う *-v.* (for something) to be decided 3
きめる (決める) う *-v.* to decide 2
きもち (気持ち) *n.* feeling きもちがわるい to feel nausea 1
きゃく (客) *n.* customer, かんこうきゃく tourist 2
キャベツ *n.* cabbage 7
キャンディ *n.* candy 6
きゅうこう (れっしゃ) (急行 [列車]) *n.* express train 5
ぎゅうにく (牛肉) *n.* beef 7
きゅうり *n.* cucumber 7
きょういく (教育) *n.* education 9
きょうみ (興味) *n.* interest ～にきょうみがある interested in 9
キリストきょう (キリスト教) *n.* Christianity 9
きる (切る) う *-v.* to cut 1
きをつける (気を付ける) *exp.* to be careful, to pay attention 10
きんじょ (近所) *n.* neighborhood, きんじょの人 neighbor, きんじょのおばさん a middle-aged woman in the neighborhood 6

く

くうこう (空港) *n.* airport 2
クジラ *n.* whale 8
くすり (薬) *n.* medicine, drug 1
くださる (下さる) う *-v.* to give (from a social superior to the speaker or in-group person) 6
～くち・ぐち (～口) *suf.* ～ entrance/exit, にしぐち west exit 5
くに (国) *n.* country 2
くび (首) *n.* neck 1
くま (熊) *n.* bear 8
グラム *n.* gram 7
クレジットカード *n.* credit card 2
くれる る *-v.* to give (to a socially equal or inferior in-group person) 6
くわえる (加える) る *-v.* to add (an ingredient) 7

け

けいかく (計画) *n.* plan 2
けいけん (経験) *n.* experience 経験する to have an experience 8
けいざい (経済) *n.* economy 9
げいじゅつ (芸術) *n.* (fine) art 9
けいたいでんわ (携帯電話) *n.* cellular phone, mobile phone; can be referred as just けいたい . けいたいメール , email on a phone. 2

けが (怪我) *n.* injury 1
けしき (景色) *n.* scenery けしきがいい nice scenery 2
けす (消す) う *-v.* to turn off, erase 3
けっか (結果) *n.* result, outcome 11
けれども *conj.* however 2
けんか (喧嘩) *n.* fight 8
けんきゅう (研究) *n.* research けんきゅう (を) する to do research 3
けんきゅうしゃ (研究者) *n.* researcher 3
けんこう (な) (健康) な *-adj.* healthy けんこうな人 healthy person (can be used as a noun; けんこうのため for the sake of one's health) 1

こ

こ (子) *n.* child こ is usually preceded by a modifier . としうえのこ (年上の子) older child いいこ (いい子) good child 10
こ～ (子～) *pref.* baby ～ こいぬ puppy, こねこ kitten 6
こい (濃い) い *-adj.* thick. あじがこい to have a strong flavor 7
こうこく (広告) *n.* advertisement 11
こうざ (口座) *n.* bank account 4
こうさてん (交差点) *n.* intersection 5
こうずい (洪水) *n.* flood 8
こうつう (交通) *n.* traffic こうつうじこ traffic accident 8
こうはい (後輩) *n.* one's junior at a school, university etc. 6
コーヒーカップ *n.* coffee cup, mug 6
コーンスターチ *n.* corn starch 7
こくない (国内) *n.* domestic こくないりょこう domestic travel 2
こころぼそい (心細い) い *-adj.* lonely, helpless 9
こさじ (小さじ) *n.* teaspoon 7
ござる う *-v.* to exist (polite verb for ある and いる) 11
こし (腰) *n.* lower back 1
こしょう *n.* pepper (spice) 7
こたえる (答える) る *-v.* to answer しつもんにこたえる to answer a question 2
こちらがわ (こちら側) *n.* this side 5
こづつみ (小包) *n.* parcel post 4
ことば (言葉) *n.* language, words, expressions 2
ことわる (断る) う *-v.* to refuse 9
ごぶさたしております (ご無沙汰しております) *exp.* I'm sorry to have been out of touch for so long. 11
こまる (困る) う *-v.* to be in trouble 8
ごみ / ゴミ *n.* trash, garbage (ごみ can be written in either hiragana or katakana.) 10
こむ (混む) う *-v.* to become crowded 5
こむぎこ (小麦粉) *n.* flour 7
(お) こめ ([お] 米) *n.* uncooked rice 7
ごめいわくおかけしてもうしわけありません (ご迷惑おかけして申しわけありません) *exp.* I'm sorry to cause you problems. 10
ごめん (なさい) (ご免 [なさい]) *exp.* I am sorry. (used only for apologies, more colloquial than すみません) 4
ごらんになる (ご覧になる) う *-v.* to look at (honorific) 11
こる (凝る) う *-v.* to have stiffness, かたがこる to have stiff shoulders 1
これからもどうぞよろしく (おねがいします) (これからもどうぞよろしく [お願いします]) *exp.* Please stay in touch (with me) in the future, too. 9
ころす (殺す) う *-v.* to kill, to murder 8
こわい (怖い) い *-adj.* frightening, scary 8
こわす (壊す) う *-v.* to destroy 8

さ

〜さ　*suf.* suffix to convert adjectives to nouns for measurement 大きさ (size) 高さ (height) 長さ (length) 重さ (weight) 6
さいがい (災害)　*n.* disaster, calamity 8
さいごに (最後に)　*conj.* lastly, at last, finally 7
さいふ (財布)　*n.* wallet, purse 3
ざいりょう (材料)　*n.* material, ingredient 7
サイン　*n.* signature サインをする to sign 4
さがす (探す／ 捜す)　う *-v.* to look for 〜 Use 捜す to look for something that has been lost. Otherwise, use 探す 2
さき (先)　*n.* beyond, further ahead 5
さくぶん (作文)　*n.* composition 4
(お) さけ ([お] 酒)　*n.* liquor, alcoholic beverage, Japanese rice wine 6
さげる (下げる)　る *-v.* to lower (something) cf. さがる to go down 1
さしあげる (差し上げる)　る *-v.* to give (to a socially superior out-group person) 6
さつじん (殺人)　*n.* murder 8
さとう (砂糖)　*n.* sugar 7
さどう (茶道)　*n.* tea ceremony 9
(お) さら (皿)　*n.* plate, dish 7
サラダオイル　*n.* vegetable oil (lit. salad oil) 7
さる (猿)　*n.* monkey 8
さわぐ (騒ぐ)　う *-v.* to make noise 10
ざんねんながらわたしのちからぶそくで (残念ながら私の力不足で)　*exp.* Regrettably, due to my lack of ability. . ., (unfortunately I was unable to . . .) 11

し

し (詩)　*n.* poetry 9
しあわせ (な) (幸せ [な])　な *-adj.* happy 10
しお (塩)　*n.* salt 7
しかたがない (仕方がない)　*exp.* There is nothing one can do about it, there is no use. 10
しかる　う *-v.* to scold 8
じかん (時間)　*n.* time 2
しき (式)　*n.* ceremony 3
〜しき (〜式)　*suf.* ceremony, そつぎょうしき graduation ceremony, にゅうがくしき entrance ceremony, けっこんしき wedding ceremony 3
しけん (試験)　*n.* examination 4
じこ (事故)　*n.* accident こうつうじこ traffic accident 8
じこ PR (自己 PR)　*n.* self-promotion 11
じこしょうかい (自己紹介)　*n.* self-introduction 11
じしん (地震)　*n.* earthquake 8
しっている (知っている)　る *-v.* to know; Use しらない to express do not know. しる means come to know, and is a う -verb. 2
じつは (実は)　*exp.* Actually, 4
しつれい (な) (失礼 [な])　な *-adj.* rude 9
しぬ (死ぬ)　う *-v.* to die 3
じぶん (自分)　*n.* self, oneself, I 3
しぼう (志望)　*n.* a wish, a desire, an ambition しぼうする to desire 11
しまる (閉まる)　う *-v.* (for something) to close 3
しめきり (締め切り)　*n.* deadline 11
しめる (閉める)　る *-v.* to close (something) 3
しゃかい (社会)　*n.* society 9
じゃがいも　*n.* potato 7
しやくしょ (市役所)　*n.* city hall 5
しゃちょう (社長)　*n.* company president 3

ジャム *n.* jam 7
じゆう (自由) *n.* freedom 3
じゆう (な) (自由 [な]) な *-adj.* free じゆうなせいかつ free lifestyle 3
しゅうかん (習慣) *n.* custom 9
しゅうきょう (宗教) *n.* religion 9
しゅうじ (習字) *n.* calligraphy 9
じゅうしょ (住所) *n.* address 4
しゅうしょく (就職) *n.* getting a job ～にしゅうしょくする to get a job at ～ 3
しゅうしょくかつどう (就職活動) *n.* job hunt; abbreviated as しゅうかつ (就活) in casual conversation 11
じゅぎょうりょう (授業料) *n.* tuition 4
しゅっちょう (出張) *vn.* business trip しゅっちょう (を) する to go on a business trip 11
じゅんび (準備) *n.* preparation, じゅんびする to prepare 2
～しょう (～証) *suf.* card (for identification) 学生証 (しょう) student ID 4
じょうし (上司) *n.* boss 6
しょうじき (な) (正直 [な]) な *-adj.* honest 10
しょうじょう (症状) *n.* symptom 1
しょうせつ (小説) *n.* novel 6
しょうたい (招待) *n.* invitation しょうたいする to invite 3
しょうたいじょう (招待状) *n.* invitation letter or card 3
じょうだんじゃない (わ) よ (冗談じゃない [わ] よ) *exp.* You've got to be kidding. 10
じょうほう (情報) *n.* information 11
しょうゆ (しょう油) *n.* soy sauce 7
しょうらい (将来) *n.* future 3
しょっき (食器) *n.* cooking dish 6
しょるい (書類) *n.* document 11
しらせる (知らせる) る *-v.* to notify 11
しらべる (調べる) る *-v.* to check, to investigate, to explore 2
しりあい (知り合い) *n.* acquaintance 10
しんごう (信号) *n.* traffic signal 5
しんじる (信じる) る *-v.* to believe 9
しんとう (神道) *n.* Shinto religion 9
しんぱい (心配) *n.* anxiety, anxious 心配する to be worried 8
(そんな) しんぱいしないでください。([そんな] 心配しないで下さい。) *exp.* Please do not worry about me. 6

す

す (酢) *n.* vinegar 7
スイーツ *n.* sweets 6
すいせんじょう (推薦状) *n.* letter of reference, recommendation 11
すいはんき (炊飯器) *n.* rice cooker 7
すう (吸う) う *-v.* to inhale たばこをすう to smoke 1
スーツケース *n.* suitcase 2
すぐ *adv.* immediately, right away 1
すぐ *adv.* soon, shortly 5
すこしずつ (少しずつ) *adv.* little by little 7
すてる (捨てる) る *-v.* to throw away, to discard 8
ストレス *n.* stress 1
スプーン *n.* spoon 7
すわる (座る) う *-v.* to sit down 9

せ

せいざ (正座) *n.* formal Japanese-style sitting position せいざをする to sit in formal Japanese style 9
せいじ (政治) *n.* politics 9

せかい (世界) *n.* world 9
せき (咳) *n.* cough 1
せっけん (石けん) *n.* soap 6
ぜったい (に) (絶対 [に]) *adv.* definitely 9
せつめい (説明) *n.* explanation せつめいする to explain 4
せつめいかい (説明会) *n.* a briefing session, an explanatory meeting 11
せなか (背中) *n.* back, upper back 1
せわになる (世話になる) *exp.* to be cared for or helped by somebody 6
〜せん (〜線) *suf.* Line (train line), やまのてせん the Yamanote Line, ちゅうおうせん the Chuo Line 5
せんぱい (先輩) *n.* one's senior at a school, university, etc. 6
せんもん (専門) *n.* field of specialty 11

そ

ぞう (象) *n.* elephant 8
そういってもらえうると、うれしいです (そう言ってもらえると、嬉しいです) *exp.* I'm glad that you said so. 11
そうだん (相談) *n.* consultation そうだんする (相談する) to consult with 10
そうでもありません／そうでもございません *exp.* No, not really. 11
そうなんですよ。 *exp.* That's right. 11
そうべつかい (送別会) *n.* farewell party 3
ソース *n.* sauce 7
そして *conj.* and, then 2
そつぎょう (卒業) *n.* graduation 〜をそつぎょうする to graduate from ~ 3
そのあいだ (に) (その間 [に]) *conj.* during that time 2
そのあと (で) (その後 [で]) *conj.* after that 2
そのとき (に) (その時 [に]) *conj.* at that time 2
そのまえ (に) (その前 [に]) *conj.* before that 2
それで *conj.* then, so 2
それで…そのあと、どうなったんですか。(それで…その後、どうなったんですか。) *exp.* Well then . . . what happened after that? 8
それはおきのどくでしたね (それはお気の毒でしたね) *exp.* I am sorry to hear that 8
そろそろしつれいします (そろそろ失礼します。) *exp.* I should be going 9
ぞんじておる (存じておる) う -*v.* to know (humble) 11
ぞんじる (存じる) る -*v.* to think (humble) 11
そんなことないですよ／そんなことはありませんよ *exp.* No, that is not the case. 11

た

ターミナル *n.* terminal 5
ダイエット *n.* diet 1
だいじ (な) (大事 [な]) な-*adj.* important 3
たいしかん (大使館) *n.* embassy 5
たいしたものじゃありませんから。(たいした物じゃありませんから。) *exp.* It is of little value. 6
たいせつ (な) (大切 [な]) な -*adj.* precious 6
タオル *n.* towel 6
だから *conj.* so 2
たく (炊く) う -*v.* to cook rice ごはんをたく to cook rice 7
タクシー *n.* taxi 5
たくはいびん (宅配便) *n.* parcel delivery service. Also called 宅急便 (たっきゅうびん), which is a registered trademark of one such company but is commonly used as a generic term. 4
だけど *conj.* but 2
だし *n.* broth 7
たす (足す) う -*v.* to add, to make up (for a deficit) 7

だす（出す） う *-v.* to take out, to prescribe, to submit, くすりをだす to prescribe medicine, しゅくだいをだす to submit homework 1
たすかります。（助かります） *exp.* That will be helpful. 4
たすける（助ける） る *-v.* to save, to help 9
たずねる（訪ねる） る *-v.* to visit 11
たたく う *-v.* to hit, to slap 10
たつまき（竜巻） *n.* tornado 8
たてる（建てる／立てる） る *-v.* to build, to establish, to make 建てる is for buildings. Otherwise, use 立てる 2
たてる（立てる） る *-v.* to make something (stand up), おとをたてる to make noise 10
たのみ（頼み） *n.* request 9
たばこ・タバコ（煙草） *n.* cigarette 1
だます（騙す） う *-v.* to deceive 8
たまねぎ（玉ねぎ） *n.* onion 7
たまらない い *-adj.* cannot stand, unbearable 10
だめ（な）（駄目［な］） な *-adj.* no good, impossible, hopeless, not useful, not acceptable 4
ためる（貯める） る *-v.* to save (money) 4
たんご（単語） *n.* vocabulary 4
たんじょうかい（誕生会） *n.* birthday party 3

ち

ちかい（近い） い *-adj.* close to, near, こうえんにちかい close to the park 5
ちがう（違う） う *-v.* to be different AとBはちがう（AとBは違う） A and B are different AはBとちがう （AはBと違う） A is different from B. 3
ちかてつ（地下鉄） *n.* subway 5
チケット *n.* ticket (for entertainment such as movies, theaters, and concerts) 6
ちず（地図） *n.* map 5
ちちのひ（父の日） *n.* Father's day 6
チップ *n.* tip, gratuity 9
ちゃわん（茶碗） *n.* rice bowl 7
ちゅうい（注意） *n.* attention, warning ちゅうい（を）する（注意［を］する） to warn, to call attention to 10
ちゅうしゃじょう（駐車場） *n.* parking lot 5
ちょっとおねがいがあるんですけど（ちょっとお願いがあるんですけど） *exp.* I have a small favor to ask. 4

つ

ツアー *n.* tour 2
つかう（使う） う *-v.* to use 2
つかれる（疲れる） る *-v.* to become tired つかれている be tired 1
つぎ（次） *n.* next 5
つきあい *n.* correspondence 9
つきあう う *-v.* to go out with, to keep company with , to have a steady relationship 9
つきあたり（突き当たり） *n.* the end of a street, T-intersection 5
つぎに（次に） *conj.* next 2
つく（着く） う *-v.* to arrive 2
つく（付く） う *-v.* (for something) to turn on 3
つける（付ける） る *-v.* to attach, to apply (medicine) 1
つける る *-v.* to turn on (a TV, a light etc.) 3
つける（漬ける・浸ける） る *-v.* to dip, to soak, to pickle 7
つける（付ける） る *-v.* to write (in a diary) にっきをつける（日記を付ける） to keep a diary 10
つづける（続ける） る *-v.* to continue (something) 3
つつむ（包む） う *-v.* to wrap 6
つまる（詰まる） う *-v.* to clog 1
～つめ（～つ目） *suf.* indicator for ordinal numbers, ひとつめ（一つ目） first 5

つもり *n.* intention 2
つれていく (連れて行く) う *-v.* to take (someone to somewhere) 4
つれてくる (連れてくる) ir-*v.* to bring (someone to somewhere) 4

て

で *part.* limit 5
DVD *n.* DVD 6
ていねい (な) (丁寧 [な]) な *-adj.* polite 9
〜てき (な) (〜的 [な]) *suf.* suffix that converts kanji compound nouns to な -adjectives でんとうてき traditional, せいじてき political, けいざいてき , economic, きょういくてき educational, しゃかいてき social, 文学てき literary, ぶんかてき cultural 9
てきとう (な) (適当 [な]) な *-adj.* appropriate 7
でぐち (出口) *n.* exit 5
でござる う *-v.* to be (polite form of です) 11
デジカメ *n.* digital camera デジタルカメラ 2
ですから *conj.* therefore, so 2
てつだう (手伝う) う *-v.* to assist, to help 4
てつづき (手続き) *n.* procedure 11
てまえ (手前) *n.* just before, just in front of 5
〜てもいいですか。 *exp.* May I do 〜?, Is it OK to do 〜 ? 1
でる (出る) る *-v.* to come out, せきがでる to cough, ねつがでる to run a fever 1
でる (出る) る *-v.* to leave うちをでる (家を出る) to leave home 2
でんき (電気) *n.* electricity, lamp 3
でんしゃ (電車) *n.* train 5
でんしレンジ (電子レンジ) *n.* microwave oven 7

と

〜という *exp.* 〜 called 5
というのは *conj.* it's because 2
どうき (動機) *n.* motive しぼうどうき (志望動機) one's motive for applying to a company, school, etc. 11
どうしたらいいですか。 *exp.* What should I do? 1
どうしましたか。／どうしたんですか。 *exp.* What's wrong? 1
どうそうかい (同窓会) *n.* reunion party 3
どうぶつ (動物) *n.* animal 6
どうもごちそうさま (でした)。(どうもご馳走様 [でした]) *exp.* Thank you very much for the meal/drinks. 9
どうりょう (同僚) *n.* co-worker, colleague 6
どうろ (道路) *n.* road, street 5
とおい (遠い) い *-adj.* far from, こうえんからとおい far away from the park 5
とおる (通る) う *-v.* to go through, to pass 5
とくに (特に) *adv.* especially, in particular 2
ところで *conj.* by the way 2
とし (年) *n.* year, age 年をとる to become old 年が上だ older 3
としうえ (年上) *n.* older 10
としした (年下) *n.* younger 10
とっきゅう (れっしゃ) (特急 [列車]) *n.* limited express train 5
とどく (届く) う *-v.* (for something) to arrive 4
とどける (届ける) る *-v.* to deliver, to send 4
とまる (泊まる) う *-v.* to stay (overnight) 2
とまる (止まる) う *-v.* (for someone or something) to stop [intransitive verb] 5
とめる (止める) る *-v.* to stop (something) [transitive verb] 1 5
とり (鳥) *n.* bird 8
とりにく (鳥肉) *n.* chicken meat 7

ドル *n.* dollar 4
ドレッシング *n.* salad dressing 7
どろぼう (泥棒) *n.* thief 8

な

ナイフ *n.* knife (silverware) 7
なおす (直す) う *-v.* to fix, to repair (something) 3
なおる (直る) う *-v.* (for something) to heal, to be fixed 3
なか (仲) *n.* relationship (among people) なかがいい to have a good relationship なかがわるい to have a bad relationship 10
なくなる (亡くなる) う *-v.* to pass away 3
なさる う *-v.* to do (honorific) 11
なべ (鍋) *n.* pot 7
ならう (習う) う *-v.* to learn (from a tutor etc.) 10

に

に *part.* from 〜にもらう to receive something from 〜 6
にげる (逃げる) る *-v.* to run away, to escape 8
〜について *exp.* about ~, そのりょこうについて about the trip 2
にっき (日記) *n.* diary にっきをつける to keep a diary 10
にもつ (荷物) *n.* one's belongings, luggage 2
にゅういんする (入院する) ir-*v.* to become hospitalized 1
にゅうがく (入学) *n.* entering a school 〜ににゅうがくする to enter ~ 3
にる (煮る) る *-v.* to boil, to stew 7
にんぎょう (人形) *n.* doll 6

ぬ

ぬいぐるみ *n.* stuffed animal 6
ぬぐ (ぬぐ) う *-v.* to take off (shoes, clothes) 3
ぬすむ (盗む) う *-v.* to steal 8

ね

ねぎ *n.* green onion 7
ねつ (熱) *n.* fever, temperature 1

の

のこす (残す) う *-v.* to leave (something) 3
のこる (残る) う *-v.* (for something) to be left, to remain 3
のせる (乗せる) る *-v.* to give a ride (to someone) 3
のど (咽) *n.* throat 1
のり (海苔) *n.* seaweed 7
のりかえる (乗り換える) る *-v.* to transfer, to change transportation 5
〜のをたのしみにしています (〜のを楽しみにしています) *exp.* to be looking forward to 〜 , お会い出来るのをたのしみにしています I am looking forward to seeing you. 5

は

は (歯) *n.* tooth 1
はい／ええ、かまいません。 *exp.* I don't mind. (=yes, please) 1
はい／ええ、どうぞ。 *exp.* Yes, please. 1
はい／ええ、もちろん。 *exp.* Yes, of course, sure. 1
はいく (俳句) *n.* Japanese poetry comprising lines of five, seven and five syllables. 9
はいけんする (拝見する) irr.*-v.* to look at (humble) 11

はがき (葉書) *n.* postcard 4
はかる (計る) う -*v.* to measure 1
はく (吐く) う -*v.* to exhale, to throw up 1
〜はく (〜泊) *suf.* counter for nights 〜はく〜日 ~ nights and ~ days 2
ハグ *n.* hug ハグをする to hug 9
はし (橋) *n.* bridge 5
はし (箸) *n.* chopstick(s) 7
はじまる (始まる) う -*v.* (for something) to begin 3
はじめてなんですが。 *exp.* This is my first time... 1
はじめる (始める) る -*v.* to begin (something) 3
ばしょ (場所) *n.* location 2
はしる (走る) う -*v.* to run 1
バスてい (バス停) *n.* bus stop 5
パスポート *n.* passport 2
パソコン *n.* personal computer, PC 6
バター *n.* butter 7
はたらく (働く) う -*v.* to work 1
はちうえ (鉢植え) *n.* potted plant, house plant 6
はっきり *adv.* clearly, explicitly 9
はっけん (発見) *n.* discovery 発見する to discover 8
はな (花) *n.* flower 6
はははのひ (母の日) *n.* Mother's Day 6
ハム *n.* ham 6
はやる (流行る) う -*v.* to spread, to gain popularity 8
ばら・バラ (薔薇) *n.* rose 6
はらう (払う) う -*v.* to pay 2
ハリケーン *n.* hurricane 8
バレンタインデー *n.* Valentine's Day 6
はんこ (判子) *n.* seal 4
はんざい (犯罪) *n.* crime 8
〜ばんせん (〜番線) *suf.* track *number*, さんばんせん Track 3 5

ひ

ひ (火) *n.* fire 7
ひ (日) *n.* day 10
ピアノ *n.* piano 10
ひえる (冷える) る -*v.* (for something) to cool down 3
ひがい (被害) *n.* damage, loss 8
ひがえり (日帰り) *n.* day trip 2
ひきだす (引き出す) う -*v.* to withdraw (money), to pull out 4
ひく う -*v.* to catch, かぜをひく catch a cold 1
ひく (弾く) う -*v.* to play (a stringed instrument) ピアノをひく（ピアノを弾く）to play the piano 10
ひくい (低い) い -*adj.* low 10
ひだり (左) *n.* left 5
ひっきしけん (筆記試験) *n.* a paper-and-pencil test 11
ひっこし (引っ越し) *n.* moving (one's residence) 10
ひっこす (引っ越す) う -*v.* to move residence 3
ひつよう（な）(必要 [な]) な -*adj.* necessary; similar to 〜がいる (to need) 11
ひどい い -*adj.* serious, extensive, severe (used in negative contexts such as injury or damage) 1, 8
ひやす (冷やす) う -*v.* to chill, to let (something) cool down 3
びょうき (病気) *n.* sickness 1

ひらく (開く)　う -*v.* to open こうざをひらく to open a bank account 4

ふ

ふうとう (封筒)　*n.* envelope 4
ふえる (増える)　る -*v.* to increase 8
フォーク　*n.* fork (silverware) 7
ぶか (部下)　*n.* junior employee, subordinate, one's man 6
ぶたにく (豚肉)　*n.* pork 7
ふつう (普通)　*n.* ordinary, regular 3
ふつうよきん (普通預金)　*n.* regular savings bank account 4
ふつう (れっしゃ) (普通 [列車])　*n.* local train, same as かくえきていしゃ (各駅停車) 5
ぶっきょう (仏教)　*n.* Buddhism 9
ぶつける　る -*v.* to hit, to crash into 8
ふね (船)　*n.* ship 2
ふべん (な) (不便 [な])　な -*adj.* inconvenient 8
ふむ (踏む)　う -*v.* to step on 8
フライパン　*n.* frying pan, skillet 7
フルーツ　*n.* fruit 6
ブログ　*n.* blog 9
プロジェクト　*n.* project 11
ぶんか (文化)　*n.* culture 9
ぶんぽう (文法)　*n.* grammar 4

へ

へえ、そうですか。　*exp.* Oh, I see 8
ペット　*n.* pet 6
へび (蛇)　*n.* snake 8
へん (辺)　*n.* area, このへん (この辺) this area 5
べんごし (弁護士)　*n.* lawyer 3
へんじ (返事)　*n.* response へんじ (を) する to respond 11
べんり (な) (便利 [な])　な -*adj.* convenient 2

ほ

ぼうえき (貿易)　*n.* trading ぼうえきがいしゃ trading company 3
ほうちょう (包丁)　*n.* kitchen knife, butcher knife 7
ボウル　*n.* mixing bowl 7
ほうれんそう (ほうれん草)　*n.* spinach 7
ボール　*n.* ball 6
ほか (他)　*n.* other ほかの人 other people, ほかの学生 other students 9
ポスト (ポスト)　*n.* public post 4
ほっといてくれよ　*exp.* Leave me alone. (male speech) 10
ほっといてよ　*exp.* Leave me alone. (female speech) 10
ほめる (誉める)　る -*v.* to praise 8
ほんとう (本当)　*n.* truth ほんとうに (本当に) indeed, really 10
ほんとにいいんですか。(本当にいいんですか。)　*exp.* Are you sure you're OK with it? 4
ほんのきもちですから。(ほんの気持ですから。)　*exp.* Just a token of my appreciatio*n.* 6
ほんのすこしですから。(ほんの少しですから)　*exp.* Just a little bit. . . 6

ま

まあまあです。　*exp.* so-so. 11
まいる (参る)　う -*v.* to go, to come (honorific) 11
まがる (曲がる)　う -*v.* (for someone or something) to turn [intransitive verb] 5

まさか。 *exp.* You're kidding 8
まじー *exp.* Are you serious? (very casual) 8
まずはじめに (まず始めに) *conj.* first (of all) 2
まぜる (混ぜる) る *-v.* to mix 7
まだ *adv.* still, yet 2
また *conj.* also 2
まだまだです。 *exp.* I still have a lot to learn. 11
まちがう (間違う) う *-v.* (for someone) to be mistaken; commonly used as まちがえている 3
まちがえる (間違える) る *-v.* to miss (something), to make a mistake 3
マッサージ *n.* massage 1
まっすぐ (真っ直ぐ) *adv.* straight 5
までに *part.* by 五時までにかえる I will come back by 5 o'clock 3
マヨネーズ *n.* mayonnaise 7
マンガ (漫画) *n.* comic, graphic novel 9

み

み (ん) な (皆) *n.* all, everyone みなさん everyone, "Ladies and Gentlemen" 9
みえる (見える) る *-v.* can see ～ (literally: something is visible) 5
みおくり (見送り) *n.* farewell 9
みおくる (見送る) う *-v.* to see someone off みおくりに行く to send someone off 9
みぎ (右) *n.* right 5
ミキサー *n.* (electric) mixer 7
みずうみ (湖) *n.* lake 2
みそ (味噌) *n.* soy bean paste 7
みち (道) *n.* road, street, way 5
みちなりに (道なりに) *exp.* following the road 5

む

むかいがわ (向かい側) *n.* the other side, the opposite side 5
むかえる (迎える) る *-v.* to welcome むかえに行く to go to pick someone up. 9
むす (蒸す) う *-v.* to steam 7
むだ (な) (無駄 [な]) な *-adj.* useless, futile, no good 8
むね (胸) *n.* chest, breast 1
むり (無理) *n.* overwork, overstrain むりをする overwork 1
むりをする (無理をする) *exp.* to overstrain, overwork 1

め

めいわく (迷惑) *n.* trouble めいわくをかける (迷惑をかける) to give (someone) problems 10
めいわく (な) (迷惑 [な]) な *-adj.* troublesome, annoying 10
～メートル *suf.* meters (distance measurement), 1 0 メートル ten meters 5
めしあがる (召し上がる) う *-v.* to eat, to drink (honorific) 11
めんせつ (面接) *n.* interview めんせつしけん an oral exam, interview 11

も

もう *adv.* already, yet, any more 2
もうしあげる (申し上げる) る *-v.* to say (humble) 11
もうしこむ (申し込む) う *-v.* to apply もうしこみようし application form 4
もうしわけありません (申し訳ありません) *exp.* I'm sorry. (polite and formal) 10
もうしわけございません (申し訳ございません) *exp.* I'm sorry. (extremely polite and formal) 10
もうす (申す) う *-v.* to say (humble) 11
もしもし *exp.* Hello (on the phone) 2
もつ (持つ) う *-v.* to hold, もっている to be holding, to own 2

もつ (持つ)　う -*v.* to hold, to own 3
もっていく (持って行く)　う -*v.* to take (something) 2
もってくる (持って来る)　ir-*v.* to bring (something) 4
もんく (文句)　*n.* complaint もんくをいう (文句を言う) to complain 10

や

～や (～屋)　*suf.* owner of ～ retail store さかなや fish market owner にくや butcher はなや 花屋 flower shop owner 本屋 bookstore owner 3
やく (焼く)　う -*v.* to bake, to fry, to grill 7
やくにたつ (役に立つ)　*exp.* useful 6
やける (焼ける)　る -*v.* to burn 8
やすむ (休む)　う -*v.* to rest 1
やとう (雇う)　う -*v.* to employ 11
やめる (止める)　る -*v.* to quit, to stop 3
やめろ　*exp.* Cut it out. (male speech) 10
やりがい (やり甲斐)　*n.* worth doing やりがいがある it is worth doing 11
やる　う -*v.* to give (to socially a inferior person, animal, etc.) 6
やる　う -*v.* to do 7

ゆ

(お) ゆ (お湯)　*n.* warm water, hot water 3
ゆうびんうけ (郵便受け)　*n.* mail box to receive mail 4
ゆうびんばんごう (郵便番号)　*n.* postal code 4
ゆか (床)　*n.* floor 9
ゆでる (茹でる)　る -*v.* to boil, to poach 7
ゆび (指)　*n.* finger 1
ゆるす (許す)　う -*v.* to forgive 10
ゆれる (揺れる)　る -*v.* to shake 8

よ

ようし (用紙)　*n.* form, paperwork 4
ようふく (洋服)　*n.* Western-style clothing 6
よきん (預金)　*n.* bank account よきんする to deposit money よきんがある to have money in the bank 4
よごす (汚す)　う -*v.* to make (something) dirty 3 8
よこになる　*exp.* to lie down 1
よごれる (汚れる)　る -*v.* (for something) to become dirty 3
よてい (予定)　*n.* schedule, plan 2
よなか (夜中)　*n.* late at night、the middle of the night 10
よぶ (呼ぶ)　う -*v.* to call, to invite 8
よやく (予約)　*n.* reservation きっぷのよやくをする・きっぷをよやくする to reserve a ticket 2
よる (寄る)　う -*v.* to drop by 5
よるおそくまで　*exp.* until late at night 1
よろこぶ (喜ぶ)　う -*v.* to be pleased 6
よろしい　い　-*adj.* good (polite) 11

ら

ライオン　*n.* lion 8
らくがき (落書き)　*n.* graffiti らくがきをする (落書きをする) write graffiti 10
らくご (落語)　*n.* rakugo, traditional storytelling performance 9

り

リボン　*n.* ribbon リボンをかける to put a ribbon on 6

りゆう (理由) *n.* reason 9
りゅうがく (留学) *n.* study abroad りゅうがく (を) する to study abroad 3
りょかん (旅館) *n.* Japanese-style inn 2
りれきしょ (履歴書) *n.* vita, resume 11

れ

レポート *n.* report, paper 4
れんしゅう (練習) *n.* practice 練習 (れんしゅう) する to practice 4
れんらく (連絡) *n.* contact ～にれんらくする to make contact with, to get in touch with 11

わ

ワイングラス *n.* wine glass 6
わかい (若い) い *-adj.* young; わかい is used to describe teenagers and young adults rather than small children. 3
わかす (沸かす) う *-v.* to bring (water, e.g. a bath) to a boil 3
わかれる (別れる) る *-v.* to leave, to break up 8
わく (沸く) う *-v.* (for water, e.g. a bath) to boil 3
わすれる (忘れる) る *-v.* to forget 1
わたる (渡る) う *-v.* to cross (a bridge, road, etc.) 5
わるい (悪い) い *-adj.* bad 1
わるくち (悪口) *n.* bad-mouthing, speaking ill of a person 8

を

を *part.* from じゅぎょうを休む be absent from a class 1
を *part.* place in which movement occurs 5
を *part.* out of ～ , from ～ 5 ～をください (～を下さい) *exp.* Please give me ～ , 8

ENGLISH-JAPANESE GLOSSARY

A

about ~, そのりょこうについて about the trip ～について *exp.*, 2
accident こうつうじこ traffic accident じこ (事故) *n.*, 8
acquaintance しりあい (知り合い) *n.*, 10
activity かつどう (活動) *n.*, 11
Actually, じつは (実は) *exp.*, 4
to add (an ingredient) くわえる (加える) る -*v.*, 7
to add, to make up (for a deficit) たす (足す) う -*v.*, 7
address じゅうしょ (住所) *n.*, 4
adult おとな (大人) *n.*, 10
advertisement こうこく (広告) *n.*, 11
advice アドバイス *n.*, 9 アドバイスをする to advise
after that そのあと (で) (その後で) *conj.*, 2
airport くうこう (空港) *n.*, 2
alien registration card がいこくじんとうろくしょう (外国人登録証) *n.*, 4
all, everyone みなさん everyone み (ん) な (皆) *n.*, 9
allergy アレルギー *n.*, 1
already, yet, any more もう *adv.*, 2
also また *conj.*, 2
and, then そして *conj.*, 2
animal どうぶつ (動物) *n.*, 6
animation アニメ *n.*, 9
annoying, troublesome めいわく (な) (迷惑 [な]) な -*adj.*, 10
to answer こたえる (答える) る -*v.*, 2 しつもんにこたえる to answer a question
anxiety, anxious しんぱい (心配) *n.*, 8 心配する to be worried
to apologize あやまる (謝る) う -*v.*, 9
application おうぼ (応募) おうぼ (を) する to apply *n.*, 11
application form もうしこみようし (申込用紙) *n.*, 4
to apply (medicine) つける (付ける) る -*v.*, 1
to apply (for a position) もうしこむ (申し込む) う -*v.*, 4 もうしこみようし application form
appropriate てきとう (な) (適当 [な]) な -*adj.*, 7
Are you serious? (very casual) まじー *exp.*, 8
Are you sure you're OK with it? ほんとにいいんですか。(本当にいいんですか。) *exp.*, 4
area, このへん (この辺) this area へん (辺) *n.*, 5
(for something) to arrive とどく (届く) う -*v.*, 4
to arrive つく (着く) う -*v.*, 2
art げいじゅつ (芸術) *n.*, 9
to assist, to help てつだう (手伝う) う -*v.*, 4
at that time そのとき (に) (その時 [に]) *conj.*, 2
at the end of a street, T-intersection つきあたり (突き当たり) *n.*, 5
to attach, to apply (medicine) つける (付ける) る -*v.*, 1
to attack おそう (襲う) う -*v.*, 8
attention, warning ちゅうい (注意) *n.*, 10 ちゅうい (を) する (注意 [を] する) to warn, to call attention to
automatic teller machine ATM *n.*, 4

B

baby あかちゃん (赤ちゃん) *n.*, 10
baby こ～ (子～) *pref.*, 6 ～ こいぬ puppy, こねこ kitten
back, upper back せなか (背中) *n.*, 1
bad わるい (悪い) い -*adj.*, 1

bad-mouthing, speaking ill of a person わるくち (悪口) *n.*, 8
to bake, to fry, to grill やく (焼く) う *-v.*, 7
ball ボール *n.*, 6
bank account こうざ (口座) *n.*, 4
bank account よきん (預金) *n.*, 4 よきんする to deposit money よきんがある to have money in the bank
to be (polite version of です) でござる う *-v.*, 11
(for water, e.g. a bath) to boil わく (沸く) う *-v.*, 3
(for someone/something) to be born うまれる (生まれる) る *-v.*, 3
to be cared for or helped by somebody せわになる (世話になる) *exp.*, 6
(for something) to be decided きまる (決まる) う *-v.*, 3
to be different ちがう (違う) う *-v.*, 3 A と B はちがう (A と B は違う) A and B are different A はBとちがう (A は B と違う) A is different from B.
to be in trouble こまる (困る) う *-v.*, 8
to be late for ～ おくれる (遅れる) う *-v.*, 10
(for something) to be left, to remain のこる (残る) う *-v.*, 3
to be looking forward to ～のをたのしみにしています (～のを楽しみにしています) *exp.*, 5 ～ , お会い出来るのをたのしみにしています I am looking forward to seeing you.
(for someone) to be mistaken; commonly used as まちがえている まちがう (間違う) う *-v.*, 3
to be pleased よろこぶ (喜ぶ) う -v., 6
to be surprised ~ におどろく to be surprised at ~ おどろく (驚く) う *-v.*, 8
to be, to exist (humble) おる う *-v.*, 11
bear くま (熊) *n.*, 8
Because of your help (common phrase when thanking somebody for assistance) おかげさまで (お陰様で) *exp.*, 11
to become careful, to pay attention きをつける (気を付ける) *exp.*, 10
to become crowded こむ (混む) う *-v.*, 5
(for something) to become dirty よごれる (汚れる) る *-v.*, 3
to be hospitalized にゅういんする (入院する) ir-*v.*, 1
to become tired つかれる (疲れる) る *-v.*, 1 つかれている be tired
beef ぎゅうにく (牛肉) *n.*, 7
before that そのまえ (に) (その前に) *conj.*, 2
(for something) to begin はじまる (始まる) う *-v.*, 3
to begin (something) はじめる (始める) る *-v.*, 3
to believe しんじる (信じる) る *-v.*, 9
between あいだ (間) *n.*, 5
beyond, further ahead さき (先) *n.*, 5
bird とり (鳥) *n.*, 8
birthday party たんじょうかい (誕生会) *n.*, 3
blog ブログ *n.*, 9
body からだ (体) *n.*, 1
to boil, to stew にる (煮る) る *-v.*, 7
to boil, to poach ゆでる (茹でる) る *-v.*, 7
to borrow かりる (借りる) る *-v.*, 4
boss じょうし (上司) *n.*, 6
bound for ～いき (～行き) *suf.*, 5 ～ , とうきょういき (東京行き) bound for Tokyo, きょうといき (京都行き) bound for Kyoto
bowing おじぎ (お辞儀) *n.*, 9 おじぎをする to bow
boyfriend, he, him かれ (し) (彼 [氏]) *n.*, 8
to break up, to leave わかれる (別れる) る *-v.*, 8
breast, chest むね (胸) *n.*, 1
breath いき (息) *n.*, 1
bridge はし (橋) *n.*, 5
briefing session, explanatory meeting せつめいかい (説明会) *n.*, 11

to bring (someone) つれてくる (連れてくる) ir-*v.*, 4
to bring (something) もってくる (持って来る) ir-*v.*, 4
to boil (water, e.g. in a bath) わかす (沸かす) う -*v.*, 3
broth だし *n.*, 7
Buddhism ぶっきょう (仏教) *n.*, 9
to build たてる (建てる／立てる) る -*v.*, 2, to establish, to make Use 建てる for structures. Otherwise, use 立てる
to bully いじめる る -*v.*, 8
bullying いじめ *n.*, 8 いじめにあう be bullied
to burn やける (焼ける) る -*v.*, 8
bus stop バスてい (バス停) *n.*, 5
business trip しゅっちょう (出張) *n.*, 11 しゅっちょう（を）する to go on a business trip
but だけど *conj.*, 2
butter バター *n.*, 7
by までに *part.*, 3 五時までにかえる I will be back by 5 o'clock
by the way ところで *conj.*, 2

C

cabbage キャベツ *n.*, 7
～ called ～という *exp.*, 5
calligraphy しゅうじ (習字) *n.*, 9
can see ～ (literally: something is visible) みえる (見える) る -*v.*, 5
candy キャンディ *n.*, 6
cannot stand, unbearable たまらない い -*adj.*, 10
card カード *n.*, 4
card (for identification) ～しょう (～証) *suf.*, 4 学生証（しょう） student identification
carnation カーネーション *n.*, 6
to catch ひく う -*v.*, 1, かぜをひく catch a cold
to cause (something) to happen おこす (起こす) う -*v.*, 8
cellular phone, mobile phone けいたいでんわ (携帯電話) *n.*, 2 It can be referred just as けいたい . けいたいメール , email on a phone.
ceremony しき (式) *n.*, 3 けっこんしき wedding ceremony そつぎょうしき graduation ceremony
ceremony (type of) ～しき (～式) *suf.*, 3, そつぎょうしき graduation ceremony, にゅうがくしき entrance ceremony, けっこんしき wedding ceremony
(for something) to change かわる (変わる／替わる) う -*v.*, 3
to change (something) かえる (替える / 変える) る -*v.*, 4, セクションをかえる (セクションを替える) to change the section one is in
to check, to investigate, to explore しらべる (調べる) る -*v.*, 2
chest, breast むね (胸) *n.*, 1
chicken meat とりにく (鳥肉) *n.*, 7
child こ (子) *n.*, 10 こ is usually preceded by a modifier . としうえのこ（年上の子） older child いいこ（いい子） good child
to chill, to let (something) cool down ひやす (冷やす) う -*v.*, 3
to choose えらぶ (選ぶ) う -*v.*, 6
chopstick(s) はし (箸) *n.*, 7
Christianity キリストきょう (キリスト教) *n.*, 9
cigarette たばこ・タバコ (煙草) *n.*, 1
city hall しやくしょ (市役所) *n.*, 5
to clean up, to organize かたづける (片付ける) る -*v.*, 10
to clog つまる (詰まる) う -*v.*, 1
(for something) to close しまる (閉まる) う -*v.*, 3
to close (something) しめる (閉める) る -*v.*, 3
close to, near ちかい (近い) い -*adj.*, 5, こうえんにちかい close to the park

co-worker, colleague　どうりょう (同僚) *n.*, 6
coffee cup, mug　コーヒーカップ *n.*, 6
cold　かぜ (風邪) *n.*, 1, かぜをひく to catch a cold
to collect (something/someone)　あつめる (集める) る *-v.*, 3
to come in, to show up (honorific)　おいでになる う *-v.*, 11
to come out　でる (出る) る *-v.*, 1, せきがでる to cough, ねつがでる to run a fever
comic, graphic novel　マンガ (漫画) *n.*, 9
company president　しゃちょう (社長) *n.*, 3
complaint　もんく (文句) *n.*, 10, もんくをいう (文句を言う) to complain
composition　さくぶん (作文) *n.*, 4
conference, meeting　かいぎ (会議) *n.*, 11
Congratulations!　おめでとうございます。 *exp.*, 6
congratulatory gift　おいわい (お祝い) *n.*, 6
congratulatory gift (for ～)　～いわい (祝い) *suf.*, 6, けっこんいわい wedding gift, しゅうしよくいわい gift for getting a new job, そつぎょういわい graduation gift
consultation　そうだん (相談) *n.*, 10, そうだんする (相談する) to consult with
contact　れんらく (連絡) *n.*, 11, ～にれんらくする to make contact with , to get in touch with
to continue (something)　つづける (続ける) る *-v.*, 3
convenient　べんり (な) (便利 [な]) な *-adj.*, 2
conversation　かいわ (会話) *n.*, 4
to cook rice　たく (炊く) う *-v.*, 7, ごはんをたく to cook rice
(for something) to cool down　ひえる (冷える) る *-v.*, 3
corn starch　コーンスターチ *n.*, 7
corner　かど (角) *n.*, 5
correspondence　つきあい *n.*, 9
cough　せき (咳) *n.*, 1
country　くに (国) *n.*, 2
crab　かに (蟹) *n.*, 7
credit card　クレジットカード *n.*, 2
crime　はんざい (犯罪) *n.*, 8
to cross (bridge, road, etc.)　わたる (渡る) う *-v.*, 5
cucumber　きゅうり *n.*, 7
culture　ぶんか (文化) *n.*, 9
cup, measuring cup　カップ *n.*, 7
curriculum vitae, résumé　りれきしょ (履歴書) n., 11
custom　しゅうかん (習慣) *n.*, 9
customer　きゃく (客) *n.*, 2, かんこうきゃく tourist
to cut　きる (切る) う *-v.*, 1
Cut it out. (male speech)　やめろ *exp.*, 10

D

damage, loss　ひがい (被害) *n.*, 8
day　ひ (日) *n.*, 10
day trip　ひがえり (日帰り) *n.*, 2
deadline　しめきり (締め切り) *n.*, 11
to deceive　だます (騙す) う *-v.*, 8
to decide　きめる (決める) う *-v.*, 2
to deep-fry　あげる (揚げる) る *-v.*, 7
definitely　ぜったい (に) (絶対 [に]) *adv.*, 9
to deliver, to send　とどける (届ける) る *-v.*, 4
to destroy　こわす (壊す) う *-v.*, 8
diary　にっき (日記) *n.*, 10, にっきをつける to keep a diary

to die　しぬ (死ぬ) う *-v.*, 3
diet　ダイエット *n.*, 1
digital camera　デジタルカメラ　デジカメ *n.*, 2
to dip, to soak, to pickle　つける (漬ける・浸ける) る *-v.*, 7
dirty　きたない (汚い) い *-adj.*, 10
disaster, calamity　さいがい (災害) *n.*, 8
to discard, to throw away　すてる (捨てる) る *-v.*, 8
discovery　はっけん (発見) *n.*, 8 発見する to discover
dish　しょっき (食器) *n.*, 6
to do　やる う *-v.*, 7
to do (honorific)　なさる う *-v.*, 11
to do (humble)　いたす (致す) う *-v.*, 11
doctor　いしゃ (医者) *n.*, 1
document　しょるい (書類) *n.*, 11
doll　にんぎょう (人形) *n.*, 6
dollar　ドル *n.*, 4
domestic　こくない (国内) *n.*, 2 こくないりょこう domestic travel
driver's license　うんてんめんきょしょう (運転免許証) *n.*, 4
to drop (something)　おとす (落とす) う *-v.*, 3
to drop by　よる (寄る) う *-v.*, 5
drug　くすり (薬) *n.*, 1
during that time　そのあいだ (その間) *conj.*, 2
DVD　DVD *n.*, 6

E

earthquake　じしん (地震) *n.*, 8
to eat, to drink (honorific)　めしあがる (召し上がる) う *-v.*, 11
to eat, to drink (humble)　いただく (頂く) う *-v.*, 11
economy　けいざい (経済) *n.*, 9
education　きょういく (教育) *n.*, 9
elderly man　おじいさん *n.*, 6
elderly woman　おばあさん *n.*, 6
electricity, lamp　でんき (電気) *n.*, 3
elephant　ぞう (象) *n.*, 8
embassy　たいしかん (大使館) *n.*, 5
to employ　やとう (雇う) う *-v.*, 11
to encounter　あう (遭う・遇う) う *-v.*, 8
(for something) to end　おわる (終わる) う *-v.*, 3
to end (something) , to finish (something)　おえる (終える) る *-v.*, 3
end-of-year gift exchange　おせいぼ (お歳暮) *n.*, 6
engineer　エンジニア *n.*, 3
entering a school　～ にゅうがく (入学) *n.*, 3
～ entrance/exit　～くち・ぐち (～口) *suf.*, 5, にしぐち west entrance/exit
an entry process of requesting information from a company and expressing your interest　エントリー *n.*, 11, エントリー・シート (a form required for the entry.)
envelope　ふうとう (封筒) *n.*, 4
especially, in particular　とくに (特に) *adv.*, 2
everyone　み(ん)な (皆) *n.*, 9, みなさん everyone, all
examination　しけん (試験) *n.*, 4
to exhale, to throw up　はく (吐く) う *-v.*, 1
to exist (polite verb for ある and いる)　ござる う *-v.*, 11
to exist, to be (humble)　おる う *-v.*, 11

exit　でぐち（出口）*n.*, 5
experience　けいけん（経験）*n.*, 8 経験する to have an experience
explanation　せつめい（説明）*n.*, 4 せつめいする to explain
explicitly　はっきり *adv.*, 9
express train　きゅうこう（れっしゃ）（急行［列車］）*n.*, 5

F

facial tone　かおいろ（顔色）*n.*, 1
(for something) to fall　おちる（落ちる）う -*v.*, 3
to fall　おちる（落ちる）る -*v.*, 8 かみなりがおちる lightening strikes
far (from)　とおい（遠い）い -*adj.*, 5, こうえんからとおい far away from the park
farewell　みおくり（見送り）*n.*, 9
farewell party　そうべつかい（送別会）*n.*, 3
Father's Day　ちちのひ（父の日）*n.*, 6
feeling　きぶん（気分）*n.*, 1 きぶんがわるい to feel sick
feeling　きもち（気持ち）*n.*, 1 きもちがわるい to feel nausea
fever, temperature　ねつ（熱）*n.*, 1
field of specialty　せんもん（専門）*n.*, 11
fight　けんか（喧嘩）*n.*, 8
finger　ゆび（指）*n.*, 1
to finish (something), to end (something)　おえる（終える）る -*v.*, 3
fire　ひ（火）*n.*, 7
fire (accident/disaster)　かじ（火事）*n.*, 8
first (of all)　まずはじめに（まず始めに）*conj.*, 2
to fix, to repair (something)　なおす（直す）う -*v.*, 3
flavor　あじ（味）n., 7
flood　こうずい（洪水）*n.*, 8
floor　ゆか（床）*n.*, 9
flour　こむぎこ（小麦粉）*n.*, 7
flower　はな（花）*n.*, 6
flower arranging　いけばな（生け花）*n.*, 9
flu, influenza　インフルエンザ *n.*, 8
following the road　みちなりに（道なりに）*exp.*, 5
food (for animals, fish)　えさ（餌）*n.*, 6
to forget　わすれる（忘れる）る -*v.*, 1
to forgive　ゆるす（許す）う -*v.*, 10
fork　フォーク *n.*, 7
form (paperwork)　ようし（用紙）*n.*, 4
formal Japanese-style sitting posture　せいざ（正座）*n.*, 9 せいざをする to sit in a formal Japanese style
free　じゆう（な）（自由［な］）な -*adj.*, 3 じゆうなせいかつ free lifestyle
freedom　じゆう（自由）*n.*, 3
frightening, scary　こわい（怖い）い -*adj.*, 8
from　に *part.*, 6 〜にもらう to receive something from 〜
from　を *part.*, 1 じゅぎょうを休む be absent from a class
fruit　フルーツ *n.*, 6
frying pan, skillet　フライパン *n.*, 7
future　しょうらい（将来）*n.*, 3

G

garbage, trash　ごみ／ゴミ *n.*, 10（ごみ can be written in either **hiragana** or in **katakana**)
gas station　ガソリンスタンド *n.*, 5
to gather, to get together　あつまる（集まる）う -*v.*, 2
to get angry　おこる（怒る）う -*v.*, 10

to get off (a bus, etc.)　おりる (降りる) る *-v.*, 5
to get together, to gather　あつまる (集まる) う *-v.*, 2
getting a job　しゅうしょく (就職) *n.*, 3, ～にしゅうしょくする to get a job at ～
gift　おくりもの (贈り物) *n.*, 6
girlfriend, she, her　かのじょ (彼女) *n.*, 8
to give (from a social superior to me or a member of my in-group)　くださる (下さる) う *-v.*, 6
to give (from not-me to a socially equal or inferior in-group person)　くれる る *-v.*, 6
to give (to a socially equal person)　あげる る *-v.*, 6
to give (to a socially superior out-group person)　さしあげる (差し上げる) る *-v.*, 6
to give (to a socially inferior person, animal, etc.)　やる う *-v.*, 6
to give a ride (to someone)　のせる (乗せる) る *-v.*, 3
Give me a break. (female speech)　いいかげんにしてよ (いい加減にしてよ) *exp.*, 10
Give me a break. (male speech)　いいかげんにしろよ (いい加減にしろよ) *exp.*, 10
to go out with, to keep company with, to have a steady relationship　つきあう う *-v.*, 9
(for something) to go out, to go off, to disappear　きえる (消える) る *-v.*, 3
to go through, to pass　とおる (通る) う *-v.*, 5
to go, to come (honorific)　まいる (参る) う *-v.*, 11
to go, to come, to return, to be (honorific)　いらっしゃる う *-v.*, 11
good (polite)　よろしい い *-adj.*, 11
graduation　そつぎょう (卒業) *n.*, 3, ～をそつぎょうする to graduate from ~
graffiti　らくがき (落書き) *n.*, 10 らくがきをする (落書きをする) write graffiti
gram　グラム *n.*, 7
grammar　ぶんぽう (文法) *n.*, 4
green onion　ねぎ *n.*, 7
greeting　あいさつ (挨拶) *n.*, 9 ～にあいさつ (を) する to greet ～
to grill, to bake, to fry　やく (焼く) う *-v.*, 7
guidebook　ガイドブック *n.*, 2

H

haiku (a Japanese poetic form comprising lines of five, seven, and five syllables)　はいく (俳句) n., 9
ham　ハム *n.*, 6
to hang on, to try to do one's best　がんばる (頑張る) う *-v.*, 3
to hang, hook　かける (掛ける) る *-v.*, 10 かぎをかける to lock
to happen, to take place　おきる (起きる) る *-v.*, 8
happy　しあわせ (な)　(幸せ [な]) な *-adj.*, 10
to have stiffness　こる (凝る) う *-v.*, 1, かたがこる to have stiff shoulders
(for something) to heal, to be fixed　なおる (直る) う *-v.*, 3
healthy　けんこう (な) (健康) な *-adj.*, 1 けんこうな人 healthy person (can be used as a noun: けんこうのため for the sake of health)
to heat up　あたためる (温める) る *-v.*, 7
heavy　おもい (重い) い *-adj.*, 9
heavy, big　おお～ (大～) *pref.*, 8 大雨 heavy rain, 大雪 heavy snow 大かじ big fire, 大じしん big earthquake
Hello (on the phone)　もしもし *exp.*, 2
to help, to assist　てつだう (手伝う) う *-v.*, 4
to help, to save　たすける (助ける) る *-v.*, 9
to hit, to crash into　ぶつける る *-v.*, 8
to hit, to slap　たたく う *-v.*, 10
to hold, to own　もつ (持つ) う *-v.*, 3
to hold　もつ (持つ) う *-v.*, 2, もっている to be holding, to own
honest　しょうじき (な)　(正直 [な]) な *-adj.*, 10
hot spring　おんせん (温泉) *n.*, 2
hot water, warm water　(お) ゆ (お湯) *n.*, 3

how to, way of ～ ing　～かた（～方）*suf.*, 4
however　けれども *conj.*, 2
hug　ハグ *n.*, 9 ハグをする to hug
hurricane　ハリケーン *n.*, 8
hurt, painful　いたい（痛い）い *-adj.*, 1

I

I am sorry to hear that.　それはおきのどくでしたね（それはお気の毒でしたね）*exp.*, 8
I am sorry. (used only for apology, more colloquial than すみません)　ごめん（なさい）（ご免 [なさい]）*exp.*, 4
I did not realize that.　きがつかなくて。（気が付かなくて）*exp.*, 10
I don't mind. (=Yes, please.)　はい／ええ、かまいません。*exp.*, 1
I have a small favor to ask....　ちょっとおねがいがあるんですけど（ちょっとお願いがあるんですけど）*exp.*, 4
I hope you like it.　おすきだとよろしいのですが。（お好きだとよろしいのですが。I）*exp.*, 6
I should be going.　そろそろしつれいします（そろそろ失礼します。）*exp.*, 9
I still have a lot to learn.　まだまだです。*exp.*, 11
I thought it would be a token of my appreciation.　おれいにとおもいまして。（お礼にと思いまして。）*exp.*, 6
I'm sorry. (polite and formal)　もうしわけありません（申し訳ありません）*exp.*, 10
I'm sorry. (very polite and formal)　もうしわけございません（申し訳ございません）*exp.*, 10
I'm sorry to cause you problems.　ごめいわくおかけしてもうしわけありません（ご迷惑おかけして申しわけありません）*exp.*, 10
I'm sorry to have caused you so much trouble.　おきをつかわせてしまいまして。（お気を使わせてしまいまして。）*exp.*, 6
I'm sorry to have stayed out of touch for so long.　ごぶさたしております（ご無沙汰しております）*exp.*, 11
I've received a lot of hospitality.　いろいろおせわになりました。（色々お世話になりましした。）*exp.*, 9
I'm glad that you said so.　そういってもらえうると、うれしいです（そう言ってもらえると、嬉しいです）*exp.*, 11
immediately, right away　すぐ *adv.*, 1
important　だいじ（な）（大事 [な]）な *-adj.*, 3
inconvenient　ふべん（な）（不便 [な]）な *-adj.*, 8
(for something) to increase　ふえる（増える）る *-v.*, 8
information　じょうほう（情報）*n.*, 11
ingredient, material　ざいりょう（材料）*n.*, 7
to inhale, to suck, to slurp　すう（吸う）う *-v.*, 1 たばこをすう to smoke
injury　けが（怪我）*n.*, 1
inn (Japanese style)　りょかん（旅館）*n.*, 2
intention　つもり *n.*, 2
interest　きょうみ（興味）*n.*, 9 ～にきょうみがある interested in
interlocutor, the other party　あいて（相手）*n.*, 10
internet　インターネット *n.*, 9, can be abbreviated as ネット
intersection　こうさてん（交差点）*n.*, 5
interview　めんせつ（面接）*n.*, 11 めんせつしけん an oral exam, interview
invitation　しょうたい（招待）*n.*, 3 しょうたいする to invite
invitation letter or card　しょうたいじょう（招待状）n., 3
to invite　よぶ（呼ぶ）う *-v.*, 8
Islam　イスラムきょう（イスラム教）*n.*, 9
It is of little value.　たいしたものじゃありませんから。（たいした物じゃありませんから。）*exp.*, 6
it's because　というのは *conj.*, 2
itchy　かゆい（痒い）い *-adj.*, 1

J

jam　ジャム *n.*, 7
Japan Railway　J R *n.*, 5, pronounced as ジェーアール. A formerly government-owned, now privatized, railway system
Japanese-style inn　りょかん（旅館）*n.*, 2
job hunt　しゅうしょくかつどう（就職活動）*n.*, 11 abbreviated as しゅうかつ（就活）in casual conversation

Judaism　ユダヤきょう (ユダヤ教) n., 9
junior employee, subordinate, one's man　ぶか (部下) *n.*, 6
Just a little bit. . .　ほんのすこしですから。(ほんの少しですから) *exp.*, 6
Just a token of my appreciation.　ほんのきもちですから。(ほんの気持ですから。) *exp.*, 6
just in front of　てまえ (手前) *n.*, 5

K

key　かぎ (鍵) *n.*, 10 かぎをかける to lock
to kill, to murder　ころす (殺す) う -*v.*, 8
kiss　キス *n.*, 9 キスをする to kiss
kitchen knife, butcher's knife　ほうちょう (包丁) *n.*, 7
knife　ナイフ *n.*, 7
to know (humble)　ぞんじておる (存じておる) う -*v.*, 11
to know　しっている (知っている) る -*v.*, 2 Use しらない to express *do not know*. しる means *come to know*, and is an う -verb.
to know (humble)　ぞんじる (存じる) る -*v.*, 11

L

lake　みずうみ (湖) *n.*, 2
landlord, landlady　おおや (大家) *n.*, 10
language, words, expressions　ことば (言葉) *n.*, 2
lastly, at last, finally　さいごに (最後に) *conj.*, 7
late at night、the middle of the night　よなか (夜中) *n.*, 10
lawyer　べんごし (弁護士) *n.*, 3
to learn (with a tutor/from somebody)　ならう (習う) う -*v.*, 10
to leave (something)　のこす (残す) う -*v.*, 3
Leave me alone. (female speech)　ほっといてよ *exp.*, 10
Leave me alone. (male speech)　ほっといてくれよ *exp.*, 10
to leave　でる (出る) る -*v.*, 2 うちをでる (家を出る) to leave home
to leave, to break up　わかれる (別れる) る -*v.*, 8
left (side, direction)　ひだり (左) *n.*, 5
letter of reference, recommendation　すいせんじょう (推薦状) *n.*, 11
lie　うそ (嘘) *n.*, 8
to lie down　よこになる *exp.*, 1
lightning　かみなり (雷) *n.*, 8 かみなりがおちる lightning strikes
limit　で *part.*, 5
limited express train　とっきゅう (れっしゃ) (特急 [列車]) *n.*, 5
Line (train line)　～せん (～線) *suf.*, 5, やまのてせん the Yamanote Line, ちゅうおうせん the Chuo Line
lion　ライオン *n.*, 8
liquor, alcoholic beverage, Japanese rice wine　(お) さけ (お酒) *n.*, 6
little by little　すこしずつ (少しずつ) adv., 7
local train (literally, a train that stops at every station)　かくえきていしゃ (各駅停車) *n.*, 5
local train　ふつう (れっしゃ) (普通 [列車]) *n.*, 5, same as かくえきていしゃ (各駅停車)
location　ばしょ (場所) *n.*, 2
lonely, helpless　こころぼそい (心細い) い -*adj.*, 9
to look at (honorific)　ごらんになる (ご覧になる) う -*v.*, 11
to look at (humble)　はいけんする (拝見する) irr.-*v.*, 11
to look for ～　さがす (探す／ 捜す) う -*v.*, 2 Use 捜す to look for something that has been lost. Otherwise, use 探す
low　ひくい (低い) い -*adj.*, 10
to lower (something) c.f. さがる to go down　さげる (下げる) る -*v.*, 1
lower back　こし (腰) *n.*, 1
luggage　にもつ (荷物) *n.*, 2

M

mailbox (for receiving mail) ゆうびんうけ (郵便受け) *n.*, 4
to make (something) dirty よごす (汚す) う *-v.*, 3
to make a mistake, to miss (something) まちがえる (間違える) る *-v.*, 3
to make noise おとをたてる (音を立てる) *exp.*, 10
to make noise, to fuss さわぐ (騒ぐ) う *-v.*, 10
to make something dirty よごす (汚す) う *-v.*, 8
to make something stand up たてる (立てる) る *-v.*, 10, おとをたてる to make noise
map ちず (地図) *n.*, 5
massage マッサージ *n.*, 1
material, ingredient ざいりょう (材料) *n.*, 7
May I ～?, Is it OK to ～? ～てもいいですか。 *exp.*, 1
mayonnaise マヨネーズ *n.*, 7
meaning いみ (意味) *n.*, 4
to measure はかる (計る) う *-v.*, 1
medicine, drug くすり (薬) *n.*, 1
to meet (humble) おめにかかる (お目にかかる) う *-v.*, 11
meeting, conference かいぎ (会議) *n.*, 11
to memorize おぼえる (覚える) る *-v.*, 4 おぼえている to remember, to recall
meter (measure of distance) ～メートル *suf.*, 5, １０メートル ten meters
microwave oven でんしレンジ (電子レンジ) *n.*, 7
mid-year gift exchange おちゅうげん (お中元) *n.*, 6
middle-aged man, someone else's uncle, also used when addressing one's own uncle おじさん *n.*, 6
middle-aged woman, someone else's aunt, also used when addressing one's own aunt おばさん *n.*, 6
to miss (something), to make a mistake まちがえる (間違える) る *-v.*, 3
to mix まぜる (混ぜる) る *-v.*, 7
(electric) mixer ミキサー *n.*, 7
mixing bowl ボウル *n.*, 7
money おかね (お金) *n.*, 2
monkey さる (猿) *n.*, 8
Mother's Day ははのひ (母の日) *n.*, 6
motive どうき (動機) *n.*, 11 しぼうどうき（志望動機）one's motive for applying to a company, school, etc.
to move うごく (動く) う *-v.*, 1
to move (something) (transitive verb) うごかす (動かす) う *-v.*, 1
to move (residence) ひっこす (引っ越す) う *-v.*, 10
movie theater えいがかん (映画館) *n.*, 5
moving (one's residence) ひっこし (引っ越し) *n.*, 10
murder さつじん (殺人) *n.*, 8

N

near, close to ちかい (近い) い *-adj.*, 5 こうえんにちかい close to the park
necessary ひつよう（な）(必要 [な]) な *-adj.*, 11, similar to ～がいる (to need)
neck くび (首) *n.*, 1
to need いる (要る) う *-v.*, 4 おかねがいる (お金が要る) to need money
neighborhood きんじょ (近所) *n.*, 6, きんじょの人 neighbor, きんじょのおばさん a middle-aged woman in the neighborhood
next つぎ (次) *n.*, 5
next つぎに (次に) *conj.*, 2
～ nights (of a stay) ～はく (～泊) *suf.*, 2 ～はく～日 nights and days
no good, impossible, hopeless, not useful, not acceptable だめ（な）(駄目 [な]) な *-adj.*, 4
No way! (very casual) うっそー *exp.*, 8
No, not really. そうでもありません／そうでもございません *exp.*, 11

No, that is not the case.　そんなことないですよ／そんなことはありませんよ *exp.*, 11
No, you have the wrong number (lit.: No, it's not correct.)　いいえ、ちがいます（よ）。 *exp.*, 2
noisy, shut up! (when used as a phrase by itself)　うるさい い *-adj.*, 10
to notify　しらせる (知らせる) る *-v.*, 11
novel　しょうせつ (小説) *n.*, 6

O

Oh, I see.　へえ、そうですか。 *exp.*, 8
older　としうえ (年上) *n.*, 10
one's belongings, luggage　にもつ (荷物) *n.*, 2
one's junior at a school, university, etc.　こうはい (後輩) *n.*, 6
one's senior at a school, university, etc.　せんぱい (先輩) *n.*, 6
onion　たまねぎ (玉ねぎ) *n.*, 7
(for something) to open　あく (開く) う *-v.*,
to open (something)　あける (開ける) る *-v.*, 3
to open　ひらく (開く) う *-v.*, 4 こうざをひらく to open an account
or, either or　か *part.*, 3
ordinal numbers　〜つめ (〜つ目) *suf.*, 5, ひとつめ (一つ目) first
ordinary, regular　ふつう (普通) *n.*, 3
to organize, to clean up　かたづける (片付ける) る *-v.*, 10
ornaments placed in an alcove or on a desk, cabinet, etc., e.g. figurines, clocks, pottery, or other art pieces　おきもの (置物) *n.*, 6
other　ほか (他) *n.*, 9 ほかの人 other people, ほかの学生 other students
out of 〜 , from 〜　を *part.*, 5
oven　オーブン *n.*, 7
overseas　かいがい (海外) *n.*, 2, かいがいりょこう overseas travel
to overstrain, overwork　むりをする (無理をする) *exp.*, 1
overwork, overstrain　むり (無理) *n.*, 1 むりをする to overwork
to own, to hold　もつ (持つ) う *-v.*, 3
owner of 〜 (retail store)　〜や (〜屋) *suf.*, 3 さかなや fish market owner にくや butcher はなや 花屋 flower shop owner 本屋 bookstore owner

P

painful　いたい (痛い) い *-adj.*, 1
a paper-and-pencil (written) test　ひっきしけん (筆記試験) *n.*, 11
parcel delivery service　たくはいびん (宅配便) *n.*, 4. Also called 宅急便 (たっきゅうびん), which is a registered trademark of one of the companies but is commonly used as a generic term
parcel post　こづつみ (小包) *n.*, 4
parking lot　ちゅうしゃじょう (駐車場) *n.*, 5
party　〜かい (〜会) *suf.*, 3 どうそうかい reunion そうべつかい farewell party たんじょうかい birthday party
to pass away　なくなる (亡くなる) う *-v.*, 3
passport　パスポート *n.*, 2
to pay　はらう (払う) う *-v.*, 2
to pay attention, to be careful　きをつける (気を付ける) *exp.*, 10
pedestrian crossing　おうだんほどう (横断歩道) *n.*, 5
pepper　こしょう *n.*, 7
personal computer　パソコン *n.*, 6
pet　ペット *n.*, 6
piano　ピアノ *n.*, 10
place in which movement occurs　を *part.*, 5
place of meeting　かいじょう (会場) *n.*, 3
plan　けいかく (計画) *n.*, 2
plan, schedule　よてい (予定) *n.*, 2

plate, dish　(お)さら(皿) *n.*, 7
to play (a stringed instrument)　ひく(弾く)う *-v.*, 10 ピアノをひく(ピアノを弾く) to play the piano
Please do not worry about me.　(そんな)しんぱいしないでください。([そんな]心配しないで下さい。) *exp.*, 6
Please don't concern yourself on my behalf.　おきをつかわないで下さい。(お気を使わないで下さい。) *exp.*, 6
Please don't put yourself out for me.　あまりきをつかわないで下さい。(あまり気を使わないで下さい。) *exp.*, 6
Please stay in touch (with me) in the future, too.　これからもどうぞよろしく(おねがいします)(これからもどうぞよろしく[お願いします]) *exp.*, 9
Please take care of yourself.　おだいじに(お大事に) *exp.*, 1
poetry　し(詩) *n.*, 9
polite　ていねい(な)(丁寧[な]) な *-adj.*, 9
politics　せいじ(政治) *n.*, 9
pork　ぶたにく(豚肉) *n.*, 7
postage stamp　きって(切手) *n.*, 4
postal code　ゆうびんばんごう(郵便番号) *n.*, 4
postcard　はがき(葉書) *n.*, 4
pot　なべ(鍋) *n.*, 7
potato　じゃがいも *n.*, 7
potted plant, house plant　はちうえ(鉢植え) *n.*, 6
to pour　かける る *-v.*, 7
practice　れんしゅう(練習) *n.*, 4 練習(れんしゅう)する to practice
to praise　ほめる(誉める)る *-v.*, 8
prayer　いのり(祈り) *n.*, 9 おいのりをする to pray
precious　たいせつ(な)(大切[な]) な *-adj.*, 6
preparation　じゅんび(準備) *n.*, 2, じゅんびする to prepare
to prescribe, to submit　だす(出す)う *-v.*, 1, くすりをだす to prescribe medicine, しゅくだいをだす to submit homework
procedure　てつづき(手続き) *n.*, 11
project　プロジェクト *n.*, 11
public post (mail)　ポスト(ポスト) *n.*, 4
purse, wallet　さいふ(財布) *n.*, 3

Q

to quit, to stop　やめる(止める)る *-v.*, 3

R

rabbit　うさぎ(兎) *n.*, 8
to raise (something)　あげる(上げる)る *-v.*, 1, see also あがる to rise
to raise, to keep (an animal)　かう(飼う)う *-v.*, 6
rakugo (traditional storytelling performance)　らくご(落語) *n.*, 9
reason　りゆう(理由) *n.*, 9
to receive (humble)　いただく(頂く／戴く)う *-v.*, 6
to receive, to get　うける(受ける)る *-v.*, 4 しけんをうける to take an exam
recommendation, letter of reference　すいせんじょう(推薦状) *n.*, 11
to refuse　ことわる(断る)う *-v.*, 9
Regrettably, due to the lack of my ability . . . , (unfortunately I was unable to . . .)　ざんねんながらわたしのちからぶそくで(残念ながら私の力不足で) *exp.*, 11
regular savings bank account　ふつうよきん(普通預金) *n.*, 4
relationship (among people)　なか(仲) *n.*, 10 なかがいい to have a good relationship なかがわるい to have a bad relationship
religion　しゅうきょう(宗教) *n.*, 9
to remain, (for something) to be left　のこる(残る)う *-v.*, 3
to rent out, to lend　かす(貸す)う *-v.*, 4
to repair (something), to fix　なおす(直す)う *-v.*, 3

report, paper　レポート *n.*, 4
request　たのみ (頼み) *n.*, 9
research　けんきゅう (研究) *n.*, 3 けんきゅう (を) する to do research
researcher　けんきゅうしゃ (研究者) *n.*, 3
reservation　よやく (予約) *n.*, 2 きっぷのよやくをする・きっぷをよやくする to reserve a ticket
response　へんじ (返事) *vn.*, 11 へんじ (を) する to respond
to rest　やすむ (休む) う *-v.*, 1
result, outcome　けっか (結果) *n.*, 11
résumé, curriculum vitae　りれきしょ (履歴書) *n.*, 11
retail store, owner of ～　～や (～屋) *suf.*, 3 さかなや fish-market owner にくや butcher はなや flower-shop owner 本屋 bookstore owner
to return (something to someone)　かえす (返す) う *-v.*, 4
reunion party　どうそうかい (同窓会) *n.*, 3
ribbon　リボン *n.*, 6 リボンをかける to put a ribbon
(uncooked) rice　（お）こめ (お米) *n.*, 7
rice bowl　ちゃわん (茶碗) *n.*, 7
rice cooker　すいはんき (炊飯器) *n.*, 7
right (side, direction)　みぎ (右) *n.*, 5
right away　すぐ *adv.*, 1
(for a telephone) to ring　かかる う *-v.*, 3
road, street　どうろ (道路) *n.*, 5
road, street, way　みち (道) *n.*, 5
rose　ばら・バラ (薔薇) *n.*, 6
rude　しつれい（な）(失礼 [な]) な *-adj.*, 9
rumor　うわさ *n.*, 8
to run　はしる (走る) う *-v.*, 1
to run away, to escape　にげる (逃げる) る *-v.*, 8

S

safe　あんぜん（な）(安全 [な]) な *-adj.*, 8
salad dressing　ドレッシング *n.*, 7
salt　しお (塩) *n.*, 7
same　おなじ (同じ) な *-adj.*, 3, A と B はおなじ A and B are the same, A は B とおなじ A is the same as B. (な is not used before nouns, as in おなじ人)
sauce　ソース *n.*, 7
to save (money)　ためる (貯める) る *-v.*, 4
to save, to help　たすける (助ける) る *-v.*, 9
to say (humble)　もうす (申す) う *-v.*, 11
to say (honorific)　おっしゃる う *-v.*, 11
to say (humble)　もうしあげる (申し上げる) る *-v.*, 11
scenery　けしき (景色) *n.*, 2 けしきがいい nice scenery
schedule, plan　よてい (予定) *n.*, 2
to scold　しかる う *-v.*, 8
seal　はんこ (判子) *n.*, 4
seaweed　のり (海苔) *n.*, 7
section chief　かちょう (課長) *n.*, 11
to see someone off　みおくる (見送る) う *-v.*, 9 みおくりに行く to see someone off
self-introduction　じこしょうかい (自己紹介) *n.*, 11
self-promotion　じこ PR(自己 PR) *n.*, 11
self, oneself, I　じぶん (自分) *n.*, 3
to sell　うる (売る) う *-v.*, 8
to send　おくる (送る) う *-v.*, 4

serious, severe　ひどい い *-adj.*, 8
serious (injury)　ひどい い *-adj.*, 1
to shake (intransitive)　ゆれる (揺れる) る *-v.*, 8
Shinto (religion)　しんとう (神道) *n.*, 9
ship　ふね (船) *n.*, 2
to show (humble)　おめにかける (お目にかける) る *-v.*, 11
shrimp　えび (海老) *n.*, 7 えびだんご（海老団子） shrimp dumpling
sickness　びょうき (病気) *n.*, 1
side　〜がわ (〜側) *suf.*, 5, こちらがわ this side, むかいがわ the other side, the opposite side, みぎがわ right-hand side, ひだりがわ left-hand side
sightseeing　かんこう (観光) *n.*, 2, かんこうする to go sightseeing, かんこうバス chartered bus for sightseeing, かんこうりょう sightseeing trip
signature　サイン *n.*, 4 サインをする to sign
to sit down　すわる (座る) う *-v.*, 9
to sleep (honorific)　おやすみになる (お休みになる) う *-v.*, 11
snake　へび (蛇) *n.*, 8
so　だから *conj.*, 2
so-so.　まあまあです。 *exp.*, 11
soap　せっけん (石けん) *n.*, 6
society　しゃかい (社会) *n.*, 9
soon, shortly　すぐ *adv.*, 5
sound　おと (音) *n.*, 10
souvenir　おみやげ (お土産) *n.*, 2
soybean paste　みそ (味噌) *n.*, 7
soy sauce　しょうゆ (しょう油) *n.*, 7
spinach　ほうれんそう (ほうれん草) *n.*, 7
spoon　スプーン *n.*, 7
to spread, to gain popularity　はやる (流行る) う *-v.*, 8
stairs　かいだん (階段) *n.*, 5
to stay　とまる (泊まる) う *-v.*, 2
to steal　ぬすむ (盗む) う *-v.*, 8
to steam　むす (蒸す) う *-v.*, 7
to step on　ふむ (踏む) う *-v.*, 8
still, yet　まだ *adv.*, 2
to stir-fry　いためる (炒める) る *-v.*, 7
stomach　おなか (お腹) *n.*, 1
to stop (something)　とめる (止める) る *-v.*, 1
to stop (something) [transitive verb]　とめる (止める) る *-v.*, 5
(for someone or something) to stop [intransitive verb]　とまる (止まる) う *-v.*, 5
to stop, to quit　やめる (止める) る *-v.*, 3
straight　まっすぐ (真っ直ぐ) *adv.*, 5
strawberry　いちご (苺) *n.*, 7
street, road　どうろ (道路) *n.*, 5
street, way, road　みち (道) *n.*, 5
stress　ストレス *n.*, 1
study abroad　りゅうがく (留学) *n.*, 3 りゅうがく (を) する to study abroad
stuffed animal　ぬいぐるみ *n.*, 6
to submit　だす (出す) う *-v.*, 1, しゅくだいをだす to submit homework
subway　ちかてつ (地下鉄) *n.*, 5
suffix that converts **kanji** compound nouns to な -adjectives　〜てき（な）(〜的 [な]) *suf.*, 9, でんとうてき traditional, せいじてき political, けいざいてき , economic, きょういくてき educational, しゃかいてき social, 文学てき literary, ぶんかてき cultural

suffix that converts adjectives to nouns of measurement　～さ *suf.*, 6, 大きさ (size), 高さ (height), 長さ (length), 重さ (weight)
sugar　さとう (砂糖) *n.*, 7
suitcase　スーツケース *n.*, 2
sweets, candy　スイーツ *n.*, 6
sweets, candy　おかし (お菓子) *n.*, 6
sympathy gift　おみまい (お見舞い) *n.*, 6
symptom　しょうじょう (症状) *n.*, 1

T

tablespoon　おおさじ (大さじ) *n.*, 7
to take (someone somewhere)　つれていく (連れて行く) う *-v.*, 4
to take off (shoes, clothes)　ぬぐ (ぬぐ) う *-v.*, 3
to take out, to prescribe, to submit　だす (出す) う *-v.*, 1, くすりをだす to prescribe medicine, しゅくだいをだす to submit homework
to take, to bring (something somewhere)　もっていく (持って行く) う *-v.*, 2
taxi　タクシー *n.*, 5
tea ceremony　さどう (茶道) *n.*, 9
to teach, to tell　おしえる (教える) る *-v.*, 4
to tease　からかう う *-v.*, 10
teaspoon　こさじ (小さじ) *n.*, 7
to tell, to teach　おしえる (教える) る *-v.*, 4
terminal　ターミナル *n.*, 5
Thank you very much for the meal/drinks.　どうもごちそうさま（でした）。(どうもご馳走様 [でした]) *exp.*, 9
Thank you. It helps me a lot.　ありがとう。たすかります。(有り難う。助かります。) *exp.*, 4
thank-you gift　おかえし (お返し) *n.*, 6
thank-you (gift)　おれい (お礼) *n.*, 6
thanks to ～　おかげ（さま）で (お陰（様）で) *exp.*, 9
That will be helpful.　たすかります。(助かります) *exp.*, 4
That's right.　そうなんですよ。 *exp.*, 11
the other side, the opposite side　むかいがわ (向かい側) *n.*, 5
then, so　それで *conj.*, 2
There is nothing one can do about it; there is no use.　しかたがない (仕方がない) *exp.*, 10
therefore, so　ですから *conj.*, 2
thick　こい (濃い) い *-adj.*, 7. あじがこい to have a strong taste
thief　どろぼう (泥棒) *n.*, 8
thin, weak　うすい (薄い) い *-adj.*, 7, あじがうすい not to have much taste
to think intellectually, to take (something) into consideration　かんがえる (考える) る *-v.*, 3
This is my first time...　はじめてなんですが。 *exp.*, 1
this side　こちらがわ (こちら側) *n.*, 5
throat　のど (咽) *n.*, 1
to throw away, to discard　すてる (捨てる) る *-v.*, 8
to throw up　はく (吐く) う *-v.*, 1
ticket (for trains, etc.)　きっぷ (切符) *n.*, 2
ticket (for entertainment such as movies, theaters, and concerts)　チケット *n.*, 6
ticket gate　かいさつ（ぐち）(改札 [口]) *n.*, 5
time　じかん (時間) *n.*, 2
tip, gratuity　チップ *n.*, 9
tooth　は (歯) *n.*, 1
tornado　たつまき (竜巻) *n.*, 8
tour　ツアー *n.*, 2
towel　タオル *n.*, 6

toy おもちゃ *n.*, 6
track number 〜ばんせん (〜番線) *suf.*, 5, さんばんせん Track 3
trading ぼうえき (貿易) *n.*, 3 ぼうえきがいしゃ trading company
traffic こうつう (交通) *n.*, 8 こうつうじこ traffic accident
traffic signal しんごう (信号) *n.*, 5
train でんしゃ (電車) *n.*, 5
to transfer, to change transportation のりかえる (乗り換える) る *-v.*, 5
trash, garbage ごみ / ゴミ *n.*, 10 (ごみ can be written in either **hiragana** or in **katakana**)
trouble めいわく (迷惑) *n.*, 10 めいわくをかける (迷惑をかける) to give (someone) problems
troublesome, annoying めいわく (な)(迷惑 (な)) な *-adj.*, 10
truth ほんとう (本当) *n.*, 10 ほんとうに (本当に) indeed, really
to try to do one's best, to hang on がんばる (頑張る) う *-v.*, 3
tuition じゅぎょうりょう (授業料) *n.*, 4
(for someone or something) to turn [intransitive verb] まがる (曲がる) う *-v.*, 5
to turn off けす (消す) う *-v.*, 3
(for something) to turn on つく (付く) う *-v.*, 3
to turn on (a TV, a light etc.) つける る *-v.*, 3
turtle, tortoise かめ (亀) *n.*, 8

U

uh-huh ええ、ええ *exp.*, 8
unbearable, cannot stand たまらない い *-adj.*, 10
someone else's uncle, middle-aged man おじさん *n.*, 6
until late at night よるおそくまで *exp.*, 1
to use つかう (使う) う *-v.*, 2
useful やくにたつ (役に立つ) *exp.*, 6
useless, futile, no good むだ (な) (無駄 [な]) な *-adj.*, 8

V

Valentine's Day バレンタインデー *n.*, 6
various いろいろ (な) (色々 [な]) な *-adj.*, 1
vegetable oil (lit.: salad oil) サラダオイル *n.*, 7
vinegar す (酢) *n.*, 7
to visit たずねる (訪ねる) る *-v.*, 11
to visit, to ask (humble) うかがう (伺う) う *-v.*, 11
vocabulary たんご (単語) *n.*, 4

W

to wake (someone) up おこす (起こす) う *-v.*, 3
wall かべ (壁) *n.*, 10
wallet, purse さいふ (財布) *n.*, 3
warm water, hot water (お) ゆ (お湯) *n.*, 3
warning, attention ちゅうい (注意) *n.*, 10, ちゅうい (を) する (注意 [を] する) to warn, to call attention to
to wash あらう (洗う) う *-v.*, 7
way, road, street みち (道) *n.*, 5
to welcome むかえる (迎える) る *-v.*, 9, むかえに行く to go to pick someone up
Well then . . . what happened after that? それで…そのあと、どうなったんですか。(それで…その後、どうなったんですか。) *exp.*, 8
Well, that is a little bit (troublesome). ええっと／すみません、それはちょっと (こまるんですが)。 *exp.*, 1
western-style clothing ようふく (洋服) *n.*, 6
whale クジラ *n.*, 8
What should I do? どうしたらいいですか。 *exp.*, 1
What's wrong? どうしましたか。／どうしたんですか。 *exp.*, 1

wine glass　ワイングラス *n.*, 6
wish, desire, ambition　しぼう (志望) *n.*, 11 しぼうする to desire
to withdraw (money), to pull out　ひきだす (引き出す) う *-v.*, 4
words, expressions, language　ことば (言葉) *n.*, 2
to work　はたらく (働く) う *-v.*, 1
world　せかい (世界) *n.*, 9
worth doing　やりがい (やり甲斐) *n.*, 11 やりがいがある it is worth doing
to wrap　つつむ (包む) う *-v.*, 6
to write (a diary)　つける (付ける) る *-v.*, 10 にっきをつける（日記を付ける）to write a diary
year, age　とし (年) *n.*, 3 年をとる to become old 年が上だ older

Y

Yes, of course, sure.　はい／ええ、もちろん。 *exp.*, 1
Yes, please.　はい／ええ、どうぞ。 *exp.*, 1
yet, still　まだ *adv.*, 2
You've got to be kidding.　じょうだんじゃない (わ) よ (冗談じゃないよ) *exp.*, 10; わ is feminine speech
You're kidding!　まさか。 *exp.*, 8
young　わかい (若い) い *-adj.*, 3; わかい is used to describe teenagers and young adults rather than small children.
younger　としした (年下) *n.*, 10

INDEX

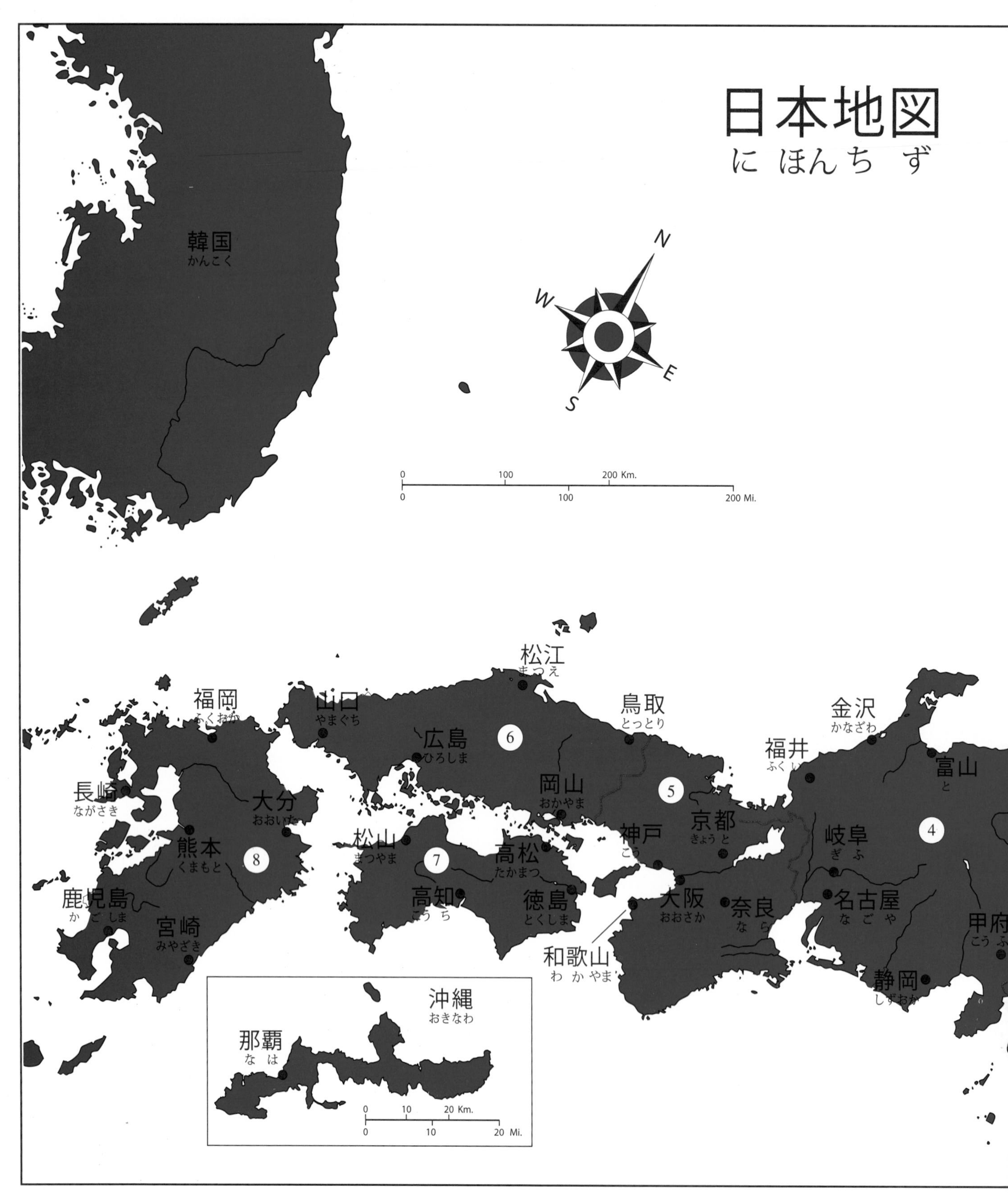
日本地図
にほんちず
韓国
かんこく
N
W
E
S
0
100
200 Km.
0
100
200 Mi.
松江
まつえ
山口
やまぐち
福岡
広島
ひろしま
6
鳥取
とっとり
金沢
かなざわ
福井
富山
長崎
ながさき
大分
岡山
おかやま
5
京都
きょうと
熊本
くまもと
8
松山
まつやま
7
高松
たかまつ
神戸
岐阜
ぎふ
4
鹿児島
かごしま
高知
こうち
徳島
とくしま
大阪
おおさか
奈良
なら
名古屋
なごや
甲府
宮崎
みやざき
和歌山
わかやま
静岡
沖縄
おきなわ
那覇
なは
0
10
20 Km.
0
10
20 Mi.

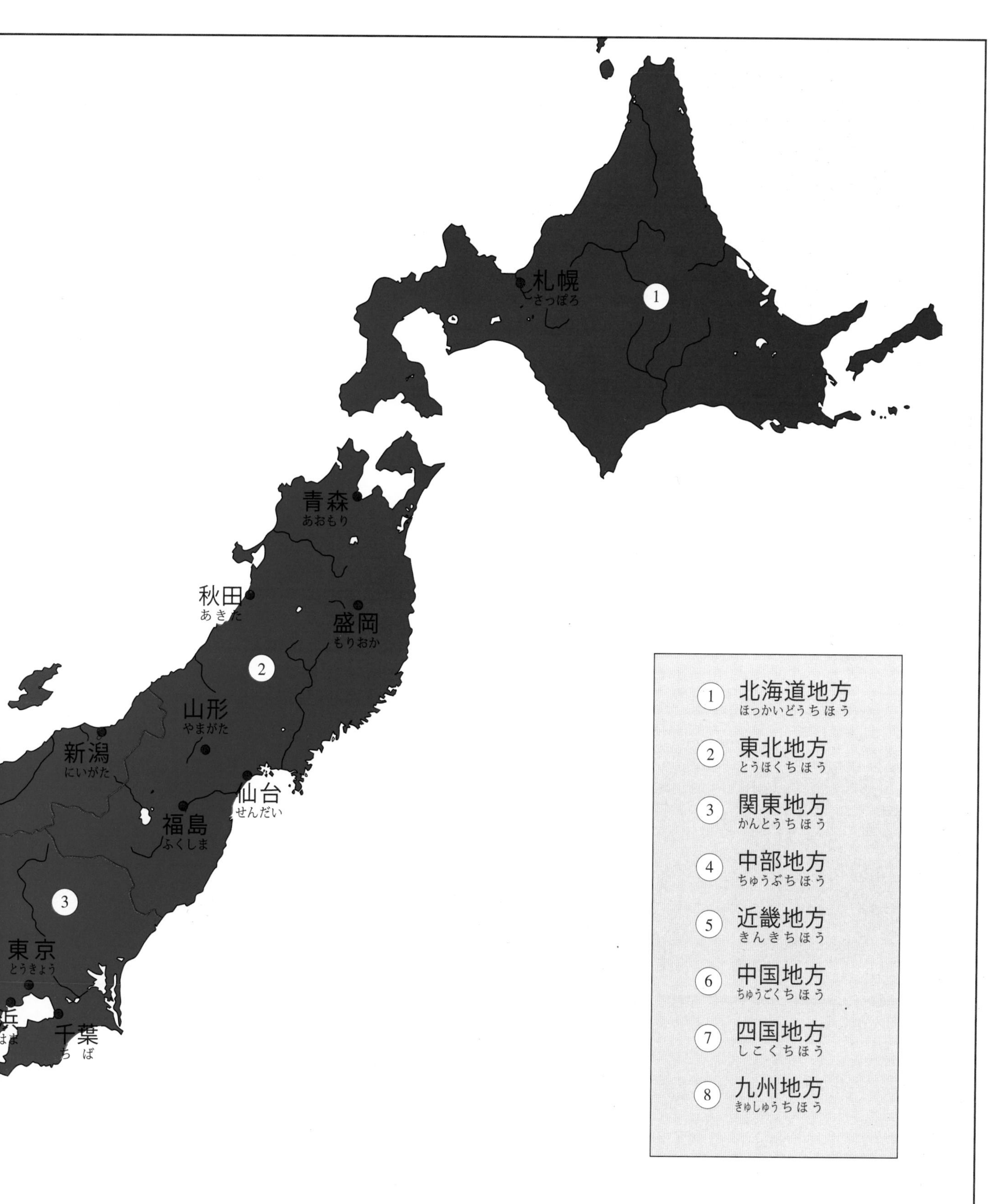

札幌
さっぽろ
1
青森
あおもり
秋田
あきた
盛岡
もりおか
2
山形
やまがた
新潟
にいがた
仙台
せんだい
福島
ふくしま
3
東京
とうきょう
浜
千葉
ちば
1 北海道地方
ほっかいどうちほう
2 東北地方
とうほくちほう
3 関東地方
かんとうちほう
4 中部地方
ちゅうぶちほう
5 近畿地方
きんきちほう
6 中国地方
ちゅうごくちほう
7 四国地方
しこくちほう
8 九州地方
きゅしゅうちほう